The Ladd Family: A Genealogical And Biographical Memoir

Warren Ladd

In the interest of creating a more extensive selection of rare historical book reprints, we have chosen to reproduce this title even though it may possibly have occasional imperfections such as missing and blurred pages, missing text, poor pictures, markings, dark backgrounds and other reproduction issues beyond our control. Because this work is culturally important, we have made it available as a part of our commitment to protecting, preserving and promoting the world's literature. Thank you for your understanding.

THE
LADD FAMILY.

A GENEALOGICAL AND BIOGRAPHICAL

MEMOIR

OF THE DESCENDANTS OF

DANIEL LADD, OF HAVERHILL, MASS.,

JOSEPH LADD, OF PORTSMOUTH, R. I.,

JOHN LADD, OF BURLINGTON, N. J.,

JOHN LADD, OF CHARLES CITY CO., VA.

COMPILED BY

WARREN LADD (No. 1506,)

OF NEW BEDFORD.

PRINTED FOR THE AUTHOR
BY
EDMUND ANTHONY & SONS, NEW BEDFORD, MASS.
1890.

INTRODUCTION.

In this progressive age,—this age of investigation and research,—when everything of the past, present, and the future, is challenged; when knowledge of the minutest atom is studied by the microscope, and with the telescope the broad arch of heaven is closely scanned for new constellations, and perhaps for a new sun with its revolving planets, one need not make any apology for a desire to learn something of his ancestors,—where they lived, their moral character, their social position, their business qualities, and the influence they exerted on their time and generation and upon their descendants. We are all more or less under hereditary influences, and it will be wise for us all to learn their strength and character, in order to combat the evil and cultivate the good.

My father, during the latter part of his life, made a genealogical record of his immediate ancestors. At his death that record came to me, and some eight years since I commenced to extend and enlarge it; in fact, to look up the genealogy of the Ladd family. But I was not then aware how much time, labor, and life's energies it would require. My intention, at first, was to compile a simple genealogical record of the family, but I had not proceeded far with the work before it became evident that to make the book interesting it should contain traditions, scraps of history, and biographical sketches. This change in the scope of the work necessitated much additional labor.

The record is made mostly of the descendants of Daniel Ladd, who took the "oath of Supremacy and Allegiance to pass to New England in the Mary and John of London, Robert Sayres, master, March 24, 1633," and who settled first at Ipswich, next at Salisbury, and then went to Haverhill with Rev. John Ward and eleven others, and was one of the original settlers of that town.

We also have the names of quite a number of Ladds, who without any doubt are descendants of Daniel, but we regret to say that there is a "*link*" connecting them with him which we have not been able to find.

We have quite a number of the descendants of Joseph Ladd, who we feel confident was a younger brother of Daniel Ladd, and who came over at the same time he did. We also have a record of some of the descendants of John Ladd, who arrived at Burlington, N. J., in 1678. Then we have a John Ladd, who was in Virginia in 1673, and descendants of William and Amos Ladd, of Virginia, who are supposed to have been sons of John of 1673. We shall give a brief record of the Ladds of England, though the ancestors of Daniel Ladd in England have not been traced.

We find the name spelled De Lade, Le Lade, Lad, Lade, Ladde, and Ladd. There is a tradition that the first Ladds came to England from France with William the Conqueror, and settled at Deal, Kent county.

We take great pleasure in stating that all, with very few exceptions, bearing the name of Ladd, or connected therewith, of whom we have solicited information, have kindly and promptly sent us all the facts in regard to themselves and their ancestors of which they were possessed. We would be glad to mention them all by name, but space will not permit. We will therefore only mention the names of a few of those who have rendered special aid and assistance : Alexander H. Ladd, of Portsmouth, N. H. ; Charles H. Ladd, of Washington, D. C. ; Francis Ladd Cutter, of New York ; Matthew J. Harvey, of Epping, N. H. ; Miss Maria S. Ladd, of North Hero, Vt. ; Nathaniel W. Ladd and David M. Ladd, of Boston ; Miss Elizabeth M. Ladd, of Benson, Vt. ; William Dudley Ladd, of Concord, N. H. ; George W. Ladd, of Bangor, Me. ; Mrs. Ellen C. Conklin and Miss Mariana C. Ladd, of Brooklyn, N. Y. ; Gardner P. Ladd, of Groveland ; Lewis A. Ladd and Dyer S. Smith, of Deerfield, N. H. ; and Joshua Ladd Howell, Philadelphia, Pa.

This record has been compiled with great care, and extra effort has been made to have it correct; and yet we are aware that in it many errors may be found, but we trust there will be none which will mar its interest or impair its value.

One great trouble in obtaining correct results has been the

large repetition of christian names, which in some cases became badly mixed; and it required a great deal of time and patience to unravel them.

ABBREVIATIONS.—Bo., born; ma., married; dau., daughter; d., died. When towns are mentioned, but not the State, it means Mass.; *thus*, John Ladd, Haverhill, — John Ladd, Haverhill, N. H.

LADDS OF ENGLAND.

While no special effort has been made by me, or by any one to my knowledge, to trace in England the ancestors of Daniel Ladd, who came from London in the Mary and John in 1633, a brief record of some of the Ladds of England may be not only interesting, but may, at some future time, be useful as a reference to any one who desires a more extensive knowledge of the character and genealogical record of those who bear the name of Ladd.

We learn from Edward Wilds Ladd, of London, that his ancestry, the "first Lads, came to England with William the Conqueror from France.—settled at Deal, Kent county, where a portion of land was granted them, eight miles from Dover,—Downes,—name spelled Lad, Lade, Ladd; his remote ancestors were seafaring people, Goverment pilots at Margate."

This looks reasonable when we remember that William the Conqueror first landed in England at Peuencey in the southeast part of Sussex co., moved his army to Hastings, which he fortified, and where the great "battle of Hastings," in which he won the right and title to the Crown of England, was fought. Dover, Deal, and Margate, in Kent co., are not far from Hastings, in Sussex, and it seems natural that many of William's followers should settle in Sussex and Kent counties. Elsewhere we find that "not many generations after the Norman Conquest the name of De Lad appears among the owners of land in the County of Kent, and ever since that day descendants of that family, spelling their name variously, according to the changes of time and circumstances, De Lad, Le Lad, Lad, Ladde, and Ladd, have held land in that and adjoining counties.

"Hastead, in his History of Kent, says the family is one of good antiquity in this county, in several parts of which they were possessed of land which still bears their name.

"In Snodland, near Rochester, and in Acris, there is an estate called Lad's, which had owners of that name in King Edward's first reign, and at Eleham * * there is one called 'Ladwood,' which is elsewhere spoken of as a Manor. * * * Boswick, now called Boyke, is a Manor in the south part of the parish, which in very ancient times was the residence of the Lads, who in several evidences are written De Lad. He also alludes to other lands that were owned by them.

"In the History of Hampshire, one William Ladd is mentioned as a juryman in 1294 in the reign of Edward I. In the History of Surry it is said that in 1325 King Edward II. bought the Manor of Henle from Walter De Henley, of which he granted the custody to Walter, Bishop of Exeter, but the next year revoked the grant and transferred it to Walter Lad. This Manor contains 1344 acres, and yields a net revenue for the year of £17 11s. 10d. From 1713 to 1722 John Ladd represented Southwark, in Surry, in Parliament, and was created a Baronet in 1740."

[From Burke's History of the Landed Gentry of England, Scotland, and Ireland, for 1853, page 685.]

LADE OF BOUGHTON HOUSE.

John Pryce Lade, Esq., of Boughton House, Co. Kent, is a magistrate of that county, and Major in the East Kent Regiment of Militia.

LINEAGE.

John Ladd, senior, of Eleham, Co. Kent, dying in 1476, left a son John Ladd of Eleham, who d. in 1527, having had by Alice his wife, with other issue, three sons: 1, Stephen, father of Thomas Ladd, of Otling; 2, John, father of Nicholas Ladd, of Wooton, whose eldest son Nicholas, of Swingfield, Co. Kent, gent., d. in 1669, leaving a son, Nicholas of Swingfield, buried at Hythe in 1699; and 3d, Thomas Ladd, of Barham, whose son, Thomas Ladd of Barham, ma. Elizabeth, sister and heir of Thomas Mumbra, of Sutton, near Dover, and d. in 1602, aged 76, leaving, with daughters, a son Vincent Ladd, of Barham, who ma. in 1575 Agnes, dau. of Vincent Denne, Esq., of Denne Hill, and d. in 1625, having had with other issue Robert, of whom presently; and Thomas of Barham, gent., who ma. 1614 Margaret, dau. of William Denwood, and d. 1662, leaving, with other issue, two sons: 1, Vincent, bo. in 1615, father, by Elizabeth Knowles, his wife, of an elder son, Thomas, who ma. and had issue, and 2d, Thomas of Warbleton, Co. Sussex, father of Sir John Lade, M. P., created a Baronet in 1730. (See Burke's Extinct Baronetage.) Mr. Vincent Lad's eldest son, by Agnes, his wife, Robert Lade, Esq., of Barham, Recorder of Canterbury in 1663, ma. in July, 1619, Mary, dau. of William Lovelace, of the Friary of Canterbury, and d. in 1666, leaving, with younger issue, a son, Lancolet Lade, Esq., barrister at law, who d. in. 1687, leaving, by Elizabeth Barrett, his wife, with other issue, two sons, Vincent, of whom presently, and Philip. of Barham, gent., who ma. Catharine Nethersole, and had numerous issue. The former, Vincent Lade of Archbishop's Palace, and afterwards of Burgate, ma. Ann, dau. of Kite, Esq. of Hoad House, in Bleane, and by her, who d. in 1720, left, at his decease in 1730, with other issue, who d. unm., two sons: John, the elder, bo. in 1695, ma. in 1723 Mary, dau. of William Frend, gent., of Wingham, and d. in 1766, leaving two dau. Ann ma. Isaac Ismay, of London, merchant, and Sarah ma. Charles Topping, of London. The younger son, Michael Lade, Esq., bo. in 1698, ma. 1st, in 1723, Eliza Evel, by whom he had two dau. who d. young. He ma. 2d, in Oct., 1730, Elizabeth Dodd, of Haverhill, widow, and by her was father (with a dau. Elizabeth, ma. to Benjamin Brown,) of two sons. Michael, the younger, barrister in law, ma. Sophia, relict of James, 6th Baron Cranstown. The elder John Lade, Esq., of Boughton, bo. 18 April, 1734, ma. 12 June, 1757, Hester, dau. of Hills Hobday, of Faversham, and had (with one dau., Hester, ma. to Will Stacy Coast, of Chartham Deanery,) three sons: John Hobday, of whom presently, William of Jesus Coll., Camb., and Charles, an officer in the army. The eldest, John Hobday Lade, of Boughton, an officer in the army, ma. 2 Jan., 1791, Eliza, dau. of Evers, Esq., and niece of Sir John Powell Pryce, Bart. of Newton Hall, Co. Montgomery, and by her had (with a dau. Marie, ma. to Wastee Brisco, Esq., of Bohemie, Co. Sussex,) a son, the present John Pryce Lade, Esq., of Boughton House.

Arms.—Arg. a fesse, wavey, between three escallops, sa. Crest.—A leopard's head, ppr. Seat.—Boughton House, near Faversham, Kent.

In "Nooks and Corners of English Life," by John Timbs, page 155, there is an expense account of Queen Isabella in 1358. Among many items charged is one of the 12th Sept. After the Queen's death a payment of twenty shillings is made to William Ladde of Shene, (Richmond,) on account of the burning of his house by accident while the Queen was staying at Shene.

[Westminster Abbey Register, page 412. Burials.]

1770, May 8. Miss Maria Ladd,[10] aged 11 years, 5 months; in West Cloister. 10—Daughter, and evidently only Child of Nicholas Lade, one of the Abbey Choir. She died, according to the Funeral Book, 4th May. Her father died at Windsor, 9th July, 1783, and was described in the Journals of the day as "Mr. Nicholas Ladd, Senior, gentleman of the H. Ms. Chapel Royal, at St. James, a member of St. Peter's Westminster, father of the Choir of H. M. Chapel of St. George in Windsor Castle, and a member of the Collegiate Chapel of Eton." He was a sworn gentleman of the Chapel Royal, 15 Aug., 1743. His will (signed Nicholas Lade) as of Windsor Castle, Gent., dated 2 June, 1783, was proved 18 Sept. following by his relict Frances. He directed to be buried, if he died in London, in the Abbey Cloister, near his daughter and her grandmother. (See her burial as Mrs. Mary Smith, 17 Sept., 1773.) He bequeathed his real estate to his wife absolutely, and also the interest of £450 for her life, after which the principal was to go to Hannah Lade, widow of his deceased brother Charles Lade, her three daughters, Frances Ann, and Hannah Lade, and his niece Daloe. If his nephew, Charles Lade, who was at Madras when last heard from, should return to England, he was to have his musical instruments.

ADDITIONS AND CORRECTIONS.

Page 14. For Charles Runalet, read Charles Rundlet.

Page 16. Add, David Ladd removed from Haverhill to Norwich, Conn., and settled at what was then called "West Farms," now Franklin, Conn.

Page 34. For Farman, read Farnam.

Page 57. To Jonathan Ladd, add ma. Elizabeth Patterson.

Page 58. For Uriah Ladd (242), read (342.)

Page 74. For Martha H. Richardson, read Martha H. Buchanan.

Page 184. For David Lang, read Daniel Lang.

Page 218. For Catharine Harvey, read Catharine Haverly.

Page 240. For William W. Ladd (2438), read (2238.)

Page 352. Index; Eliphalet Ladd, for page 77, read 79.

---

53) John Ladd, of Windham, Conn., (son of David,[49]) ma. Lucy Wales.

Children.

919. Denison, bo. June 16, 1793; ma. Sophia Edgerton, Jan. 25, 1826.
920. William, bo. May 22, 1795; ma. Roxana Hisington.
921. Caroline, bo. May 5, 1797; ma. Asa Johnson. Children: [1]Lucy; [2]Sophronia.
922. Shubael, bo. July 25, 1799; ma. Polly Bailey.
923. Charlotte, bo. March 10, 1802; ma. James Browne. Children: [1]Mary; [2]Henry; [3]James; [4]David; [5]John; [6]Jane.
924. Lucy, bo. July 6, 1804: ma. Walter Olmstead.
925. John, bo. Feb. 23, 1807; ma. Frances Stevens. No children.
926. David, bo. Oct. 22, 1810; ma. Jane Risley. No children.
927. George, bo. Feb. 23, 1813; ma. Julia Burleigh.
928. Harry, bone June 22, 1815; ma. Augusta Ladd.
929. Sophronia, bo. Oct. 15, 1818; ma. Martin Tipple. Children: [1]Josephine; [2]George; [3]Alice; [4]Elida.

(4919) Denison Ladd, (son of John,[153]) ma. Sophia Edgerton, Jan. 25, 1826.

Children.

4930. Ambrose E., bo. June 2, 1827; ma. Harriet Cook.
4931. Eunice E., bo. Aug. 11, 1829; not married.
4932. Julia, bo. Feb. 15, 1831; not married.
4933. John W., bo. Nov. 31, 1832; ma. Mary A. Bard.
4934. Lucy J., bo. Oct. 26, 1835; ma. Nathaniel K. Wood, April 18, 1860. Children: [1]John D., bo. Dec. 8, 1861; [2]Clara, bo. May 16, 1866; [3]Charles, bo. Dec. 8, 1868; [4]Mary, bo. Aug. 9, 1870.

(4920) William Ladd, of Hastings, N. Y., (son of John,[153]) ma. Roxana Hisington.

Children.

4935. Horace, bo. Nov. 1, 1820; ma. Clarinda Moore, March 1, 1849.
4936. Cordelia, bo. Jan. 26, 1826; ma. Hiram Eggleston, Jan. 1, 1849.
4937. William, bo. March 27, 1831; d. aged 4 years and 7 months.
4938. Joseph, bo. June 17, 1833; ma. Marcia Sperry, March, 1861.
4939. Charles, bo. April 4, 1836; ma. Catharine Clute, Oct. 3, 1859.

(4922) Shubael Ladd, of Oneida Co., N. Y., (son of John,[153]) ma. Polly Bailey; ma. 2d, Ann Bleans.

Children.

4940. Mary, bo. ——.
4941. Shubael, bo. ——.
4942. Ellen, bo. ——.

Child by second wife.

4943. Ina, bo. ——.

(4925) John Ladd, of Brooklyn, Mich., (son of John,[153]) ma. Frances Stevens; ma. 2d, Dolly Lewis; ma. 3d, ——.

Children.

4944. Sarah, bo. ——.
4945. Edward, bo. ——.

Children by second wife.

4946. Randolph, bo. ——.
4947. Frederick, bo. ——.

Children by third wife.

4948. Sumner, bo. ——.
4949. Effie, bo. ——.

(4927) George Ladd, of Michigan, (son of John,[153]) ma. Julia Burleigh.

Children.

4950. Herbert, bo. ——.
4951. Harry, bo. ——.

4928) Harry Ladd, of California, (son of John,[153]) ma. Augusta Ladd in Michigan, where he lived several years, but after the death of his wife he removed to California.

Child.

4952. Estella, bo. ——.

4930) Ambrose Ladd, (son of Denison,[4919]) ma. Harriet Cook.

Children.

4953. Warren C., bo. ——.
4954. Hattie, bo. ——.
4955. Ella, bo. ——.
4956. Mary, bo. ——.

4933) John W. Ladd, of Mexico, N. Y., (son of Denison,[4919]) ma. Mary A. Bard. She d. June 2, 1886, and he ma. 2d, Mary E. Martin.

Child by first wife.

4957. Edith, bo. Sept. 10, 1866.

4935) Horace Ladd, of Hastings, N. Y., (son of William,[4920]) ma. Clarinda Moore, March 1, 1849. She d. Sept. 5, 1880, and he ma. 2d, Mrs. Eunice Giles, March 7, 1881.

Children.

4958. William, bo. ——.
4959. Amos, bo. ——.
4960. Byron, bo. ——.

939) Charles Ladd, of Hastings, N. Y., (son of William,[4920]) ma. Catharine Clute, Oct. 3, 1859.

Children.

4961. Edward, bo. Sept. 13, 1863; ma. Ina Melvin, Oct. 30, 1888.
4962. Effie, bo. March 13, 1870.

234) John Wanton Ladd, of Wyandotte, Kansas, (son of Job,[4183]) was born in Warwick, R. I., Aug. 10, 1793. He ma. Lydia S. Brown, Sept. 10, 1812, and lived at Warwick, R. I., until 1817, when he removed to Worthing, Ohio. In 1851 he removed to Wyandotte, Kansas, now Kansas City, where he died Sept. 25, 1865. His widow died March 3, 1869.

Children.

1963. Sarah Potter, bo. Sept. 9, 1813; ma. Claudius Prevost, May 1, 1880.
1964. Anna Haven, bo. Aug. 14, 1815; d. Oct. 17, 1885.

4965. Lydia Brown, bo. May 18, 1817; ma. Mathew R. Walker, Sept. 3, 1840. She d. April 29, 1884.
4966. Mary Ann, bo. July 1, 1819; ma. Joel Walker, May 9, 1844. She d. Feb. 18, 1866.
4967. Job Dexter, bo. July 13, 1821; ma. Eliza J. Campbell, April 18, 1849.
4968. John Wanton, bo. Aug. 27, 1823; ma. Mary S. Campbell, Oct. 31, 1847.
4969. Elizabeth Warner, bo. Dec. 14, 1825.
4970. Artless Jane, bo. Feb. 5, 1831; ma. Lawrence P. Brown, Oct. 24, 1854.
4971. Celia Alverson, bo. Oct. 3, 1832; d. Dec. 4, 1854.

(4967) Job Dexter Ladd, of Lewis Centre, Ohio, (son of John Wanton,[4234]) ma. Eliza J. Campbell, April 18, 1849.

Children.

4972. Mary Annetta, bo. Feb. 13, 1852; ma. Frank H. Whitehead, Oct. 16, 1878.
4973. Frances Jane, bo. May 18, 1854; ma. Milton S. Thompson, Sept. 9, 1854.

DANIEL LADD.

(1) Daniel Ladd took the Oath of Supremacy and Allegiance to pass to New England in the Mary and John of London, Robert Sayres, master, 24th of March, 1633-4.

The first record we find of Daniel Ladd, after his arrival in New England, was at Ipswich, where "the 5th of February, 1637, there was granted Daniel Ladd six acres of land." On this land he built a dwelling-house, which eleven years later he sold to Henry Kingsbury, as we find by the following deed:

This present writing witnesseth that Daniel Ladd, of Haverhill, in the County of Norfolk, husbandman, for and in consideracon of ten pounds to him in hand paid, have bargayned and sould and by these presents doth confirm that his bargayne and sale unto Henry Kingsbury, of Ipswich, in the County of Essex, husbandman, all that his house wherin the said Henry now dwelleth; situate and being in Ipswich, aforesaid, in the street called High street, having the orchard and garden of William Payne on the Northwest, a lane towards the Southeast; one end abutting on the said street; butting at the other end on the land of Thomas Safford. To have and to hold the said house with the land about it, and all the apprtences and privelidges thereto belonging; unto the aforesaid Henry Kingsbury and his heirs for ever.

In witness whereof I have hereunto set my hand and seal, 31 of March, 1648.   ℘ the mark of Daniel Ladd.
Sealed and Delivered in the presence
of SAMUEL SYMONDS.
  JAMES CHEWTE.

We next find him at Salisbury, where, Oct. 29, 1639, "According to ye first division of ye town of Salisbury there was granted unto Daniel Ladd one acre, more or less, for a house lot, lying between the house lot of John Ayer and Robert Fitts; also there was granted him four acres, more or less, for a planting lott, lying between the planting lotts of John Clough and Willie Allen, butting upon the highway leading to the mill and the great swamp, lying towards the ferrie."

Also there was granted him two acres, more or less, of meadow, lying between the lotts of Anthony Sadler, &c.

1640, 7th 9 mo. Att a Gen. Meeting of ye ffreemen there was granted unto Daniel Ladd two acres meadow, more or less, lying to the eastward of the Elder's meadow towards Hampton.

Y^e 20th of 12 mo., 1642, at a general meeting of ye ffreemen, it was ordered y^t ye 22 lotts granted on the east side of Merrimack and Pauwaus River shall be to these persons that have drawn lotts for y^m. Daniel Ladd's lot No. 21. All ye lands granted to these (22) persons above named to be layed out at ye West end of ye second range of lotts on the West of ye Pauwaus River and to be contained betwen y^t and ye great pond on ye West. 15th of y^e 11th mo., 1643. At a generall meeting of the ffreemen there was granted unto John Ayer, Daniel Ladd, John Clough, John Dickson, two acres of meadow, each of them, lying upon the north-east side of y^e little River, over ag^s. Mr. Dow's and Mr. Munday's Meddow.

Y^e 12th of April, 1654. These p_rsents wittnes y_t I, Daniel Ladd of Haverhill, in y^e County of Norfolk, have bargained and sold unto Vallentine Rowell of y^e same County in Salisbury, four acres of planting land n^{tt} comonage belonging thereto att Salisbury old towne, bounded by John Clough on y^e south west, and Willis Allen on y^e North East and Swamp at ye lower end and ye highway at ye upper end, for and in consideracon of a valuable consideracon Allready pay'd wch four acres of planting land more or less and comonage ye aforesaid partee or grantee is to have and to hold to him, his heirs, executors and assigns forever. In witness whereof I have hereunto sett my hand: DANIEL LADD. his T marke.
In ye prsence of RICH: LITTLEHALE, ROGER LANCKTON.

This bill of Sale was acknowledged by Daniel Ladd to be his act and deed in ye Court held att Salisbury, ye 11th of ye 2^d m^o., 1654.

L me THO: BRADBURY, rec'd.

Daniel Ladd removed from Salisbury to Haverhill, and was one of the original settlers of that town.

Chase, in his history of Haverhill, says: "The first company of settlers in the wild woods of Pentucket (Haverhill) was as follows: William White, Samuel Gile, James Davis, Henry Palmer, John Robinson, Christopher Hussey, John Williams, Richard Littlehale, Abraham Tyler, Daniel Ladd, Joseph Merrie, Job Clement."

Land granted Daniel Ladd, as per Town Records:

Six acres of accommodation, Four acres to his house lot, more or less; Robert Clements bounding on the East, and Henry Savage on the West; Five acres in the plain, William White on the East and John Williams on the North.

Nine acres up the great river, Thomas Ayer on the East, and George Brown on the West, Four acres of meadow in the east meadow, more or less, Joseph Peasly on the south and George Brown on the north. One acre and a half of meadow in the pond meadow; James Davis, Sen., on the south, and Robert Clement, Jun., on the north; one acre of meadow at Hawkes' meadow; John Davis on the south, and Thomas Whittier on the north. All these parcels are so much as is expressed, more or less.

It was acknowledged by John Robinson at a town meeting on the 16th of April, '49, that Daniel Ladd had bought six acres of accommodations of him, which the town granted him.

Daniel Ladd's 2d Division, containing twenty-seven (27) acres of upland be it more or less, with sixteen acres of ox common, and a half, bounded by George Corley and John Hutchins on the west; by a black oak, and a white oak, a red oak and a walnut on the south, by a walnut and a white oak on the east, by two white oaks and an ash on the north; Three (3) acres of meadow lying on Spiket River, bounded by Thomas Davis on the South and Robert Clement on North; and one spot of meadow at Primrose swamp, and another spot at the East meadow, at the head of the meadow that was John Davis's adjoining his own.

For the land that was taken off Daniel Ladd's 3d division we added a piece on the north side of the highway round the meadow that was Goodman Hale's, bounded by the highway and Merrie's creek.

3d Division of meadow containing 5 acres, be it more or less, bounded by John Page on the south, a pine on the east, his own upland on the west and upland on the north of the said meadow, lying in Mistake meddow.

Daniel Ladd, Sen., Laid out to Goodman Ladd sixty acres of third division land lying upon Mistake meadow, bounded as followeth, viz.: A swamp by Samuel Gile east, and a black oak west, and a white oak south, and a white oak south-east. This parcel, according to the bounds mentioned being returned under the hands of George Brown and James Davis, Jun., as lot layers and by them allowed to be entered and recorded, was accordingly done, July 29, 1673.

We whose names are here subscribed, namely, James Davis and Robert Swan, Lot layers, having laid out a parcel of land of three score acres unto Daniel Ladd, Sen., which was addition to his third Division and cut off by the line, and it appearing that we were mistaken in the measure, the land wanting measure, having visited the land again; have now settled the bounds as followeth:—

Beginning at a great marked pine tree in a swamp, which is the north corner bounds of a parcel of land laid out formerly to John Ayer, and from thence to a black oak northward, upon the north-side of a pine swamp, and so eastwardly, or north-east to a pine tree marked, standing upon a knoll, to the northward of a hill called John Ayer's Darby-hill, on the north-east side of a small brook, and from thence southward to a marked pine tree on the south, or toward the south-east side of the aforesaid Darby-hill, which is the north-east corner bound of John Ayer's land, and so upon John Ayer's line to the first mentioned bound tree, which land was laid out by us, James Davis and Robert Swan. This parcel coming under the hands of James Davis, Jun., and Robert Swan as lot layers and being allowed to be recorded under the hands of James Davis, Jun., and Robert Clement, April 4, 1678. Was according to the said return entered upon record April the 4th 1678.

Upon April the 16th 1691 this which followeth was presented to me to be recorded, viz.:

Dated in Haverhill the 21st, 1688.

Daniel Ladd, Sen., having the better part of his third division of meadow at Mistake taken off by the line, and so by that means is content to lay down all his meadow there and to take it up other where. We whose names are underwritten being lot layers appointed for that end have laid out instead thereof three parcels of meadow and meadow bottoms, as followeth to the said Ladd, viz.:

One piece of meadow by the north-east corner of an oak-hill, which hill is about two miles north-eastwardly from the upper bridge at Spicket river.

The bounds of the meadow are, a white oak marked at the lower end eastward, and so round southwardly and westwardly by upland to another white oak marked, and so cross the brook to another white oak marked, and so eastwardly by upland and across the brook to the first named. The second is a rubbidgy piece of meddow bottom about a hundred rods eastwardly of the first, bounded by a pine on the north side, and so round by the upland running westwardly and so by the upland eastwardly to another pine tree marked, and so on to the first named.

The third is a little piece of pretty good meadow, about a half a mile eastward of the second, being bounded in all parts by the upland; with a convenient way to all the said pieces of meadow from said Spicket meadow or bridge.

Laid out by us, JAMES DAVIS, ROBERT SWAN.

Underwritten,—Allowed to be recorded by us. JAMES DAVIS, ROBERT CLEMENT.

As an addition to the return of the three pieces mentioned and entered April 10, 1691. This that follows was underwritten:—Know that whereas, the above writing does express that I, Daniel Ladd, Sen.;

is content to lay down my interest in my meadow at Mistake and to take it up otherwhere; I do hereby declare that on the consideration of the above expressed three parcels of meadow being allowed of record and confirmed to me, I do renounce all my right and interest in that and in every part of that meadow at Mistake before named.

As witness my hand this 9th day of April 1691.

Witness.   DANIEL LADD, SEN., and a mark.
JOSIAH GAGE.
EZEKIEL LADD'S mark /.

Daniel Ladd Sen.'s 4th division of upland.

The forty third lot in the fourth division with the additions, is laid out to Daniel Ladd, containing one hundred and eighty acres, more or less,—bounded with a white oak marked C. L., thence north ninety poles to a white oak marked L. W., thence west three hundred thirty-two poles to an ash marked L. W. standing at the east end of Mr. Ward's 4th division lot, thence south ninety poles to a black oak marked C. L., thence east three hundred thirty-two poles to the bounds first mentioned; reserving what meadow there may be laid out in it, and what meadow is unlaid out in said lot, exceeding two acres in a piece with a highway to them, having also made allowance for an highway twelve rods wide across the west end of the lot. This lot adjoins on the north side of the 42 lot, laid out to the commoners. This being returned and subscribed by Richard Hassen and James Ayer as lot layers, for the *fourth* division, was accordingly entered June the thirteenth day 1718.

This fourth lot was laid out by the town in 1659, but it would seem that Daniel Ladd's lot in this division was not entered until 1718.

Chase, in his History of Haverhill, page 62, says: "Daniel Ladd doubtless found farming quite a different thing from what most farmers of the present day find it. His house lot was in the village; his planting ground in two places,—a part of it 'in the plain,' from one to two miles east of the village, and the other part 'up the great river,' at least as far, on the west of the village,—while his meadow lands were in seven lots, and as many distinct meadows. East meadow was in the easterly part of the town, three miles from his home lot, while Spicket meadow was at least eight miles in the opposite direction. Pond meadow was two miles north-east; Hawkes' meadow some three miles west; Primrose swamp two miles north-west; and Mistake meadow somewhere in the westerly part of the town.

"When we reflect that in those days 'highways' were at best

but primitive cart paths through the woods, with stumps still standing, hills ungraded, and streams unbridged, and that the land was new, rough, and worked only by great labor, we may have a faint idea of some of the hardships of our first settlers. Had they not been men of iron nerve, tireless muscle, and indomitable energy and perseverance, our now beautiful town, with its unsurpassed mosaic of cultivated fields, green hills, smiling lakes, its majestic river, and murmuring streams, would still be a waste and howling wilderness, the home of wild beasts, and the hunting ground of the miserable aborigines."

In 1646 Daniel Ladd was taxed forty pounds (£40.)

At a town meeting, June 12, 1651, it was ordered that Hugh Sherratt, Theophilus Satchwell, Bart Heath, James Fiske, and *Daniel Ladd*, "Shall view the upland that is fit to plough, by the last of March or the tenth of April next, and that they bring in their intelligence to the town by that time."

In 1659, "*Daniel Ladd* and Theophilus Shatwell, having received liberty from the town, erected a saw-mill on Spiggot (Spicket) River. It was built within the present limits of Salem, N. H., and was the first one erected upon that stream. The proprietors were required to pay the town *five pounds* per annum for the privilege."

In 1668, Daniel Ladd was one of the selectmen of Haverhill.

In 1683, Daniel Ladd voted against building a new meeting-house "upon the lot where the old meeting-house stands."

He was a very energetic and enterprising man, and held many positions of trust and responsibility. The records indicate that he was an extensive farmer, and that he dealt quite largely in land.

In 1675, Daniel Ladd, Peter Ayer, and Thomas Whittier, were appointed to designate what houses should be garrisoned.

From Registry of Deeds, Old Norfolk:

Daniel Ladd, Sen., and his wife Ann of Haverhill, sold George Brown of same place, five acres of planting land in the lower playne, be it more or less, bounded by land holden by William White, on ye east and at ye north-east corner wth a white oak markt, and at ye same side at ye River wth a stake, and on ye west side by land holden by John Williams, Sen., and wth a stake at ye north-west wth a stake, for and consideration of ye full sum of five and twenty pounds all ready paid, to have and to hold, &c. Signed by these marks, viz.: T his mark,) her mark. March 6, 1661. 1 : 208.

Daniel Ladd, Sen., of Haverhill, husbandman, sold to Ens. William Russell of Salisbury, about three acres of meadow in Haverhill, at Hogg Hill meadow, adjoining some meadow then owned by said W. Russell, a brook running through it, south-west corner of it runneth by a small strip up into a swamp, and is surrounded by ye upland, which is ye bounds of said meadow. His mark here is F. Dec. 8, 1669. 2 : 236.

Daniel Ladd, Sen., of Haverhill, and wife Ann, sold to John Johnson, of Haverhill, blacksmith, the house and land, about four acres, that was formerly John Robinson's, in Haverhill, bounded on the eastward and westward side by land then in possession of said Johnson, and on north end by said Johnson and on ye south end by ye highway, next unto and lying upon the great River of Merremack. Ladd reserving the eastward end of the dwelling and the loose boards that are in the inside of the west end of ye same, and ye roof plates and boards of ye barne, and the small nurserie of trees in ye garden, and about twenty apple trees, and one plumb tree in the orchard, and the summer crop, and Johnson to take possession of the house in March following. Dated July 17, 1669. Ack. July 20, 1669. His T mark. 2 : 372.

Daniel Ladd, Sen., of Haverhill, sold to Thomas Hale, Jr., of Newbury, three score acres of land in Haverhill which was laid out to him April 4, 1678, for the third division :—bounded, beginning at a great markt pine tree in a swamp, which is ye north corner bounds of a parcel of land layed out formerly to John Ayer, and from thence to a black oak northward upon ye north side of a pine swamp and so easterly, or north-east, to a pine tree marked, standing upon a knowle to ye northward of an hill called John Ayer, his Darby hill, on the north-east side of a small brook, and from thence southward to a marked pine tree, on ye south or towards ye south-east side of ye aforesaid Darby Hill, which is ye north-east corner bound of John Ayer, and so upon John Ayer, his land to ye first mentioned bound tree. Signed by Daniel L̦ Ladd, Sen., and Ann) Ladd, April 5, 1678. 3: 136.

He sold, for and in consideration of three pounds and a flitch of bacon, to Nathaniel Merrill of Newbury, an acre of meadow land in Haverhill, bounded with ye land of Michaell Emerson, on ye north-east, and ye land of Peter Ayer on ye south-east, and staked out with stakes at ye four corners, with all and singular ye profits and appurtenances thereunto belonging. April 19, 1678. 3 : 190. No wife's name mentioned in this deed.

Ipswich Series :

Daniel Ladd, Sen., and wife Ann of Haverhill, on ye north of Merrimack in New England, sold John Whittier of the same place, four acres in East Meadow, bounded on ye westward end by a river called yᵉ East Meadow river on yᵉ northward side by an old stake standing in an alder bush, from thence running eastward to an old stake standing in yᵉ meadow near to a swamp, and so to yᵉ upland, running upon yᵉ line with the other, &c., it having been peaceably possessed above thirty years. March 27, 1682, when they acknowledged the same. 5: 528.

Salem Series:

Daniel Ladd, Sen., of Haverhill, gave to his son Daniel Ladd, Jr., a parcel of swamp on Hawkes' meadow way which was granted to him on an ox common right, about six acres, " bounded on yᵉ south-east by a walnut markt upon yᵉ common, and thence to a white oak on yᵉ N. E., and a maple at yᵉ N. W., joining on my other land, and so to Hawkes' meadow way to a red oak, and so by said way to yᵉ first walnut tree," together with a piece of meadow in Haverhill, at Providence meadow, being one acre as it is accounted, " bounded by Nathaniel Elethrop on yᵉ south and a brooke and upland on the other part and one commonage. To have," &c. March 23, 1691. Acknowledged by him and wife Ann, March 25, 1692. 10: 181.

Daniel Ladd, Sen., of Haverhill, " in consideration of marriage consummated between Onesiphorus Marsh, Jr., of Haverhill, and my daughter, Sarah Ladd, in way of portion which I give with my daughter, gave to him four acres lying near my barne, bounded as followeth: at yᵉ south corner by an alder, at yᵉ east corner by an hornbeam, at yᵉ north corner by a walnut, at yᵉ west corner by a white oak, all marked, also one commonage in yᵉ said town. To have," &c. May 14, 1692. 12: 179.

Daniel Ladd, Sen., and wife Ann, of Haverhill, gives to his dutiful son Samuel one half of his 3d division, lying at or near yᵉ west meadow in yᵉ said town, to be laid out at yᵉ end of it, yt is near or adjoining unto yᵉ land yt was George Corliss, yᵉ which said Samuel hath built upon. To have and to hold, &c. His mark at this time [. July 10, 1682. Ackᵈ. Sept. 18, 1682.

Samuel Ladd and his wife Martha. Son and daughter of George Corliss, of Haverhill, received a deed of gift from him of a piece of land beginning at a marked white oak at yᵉ south-east corner by Spicket way and so westerly by yᵉ said way about 30 rods to a stake, and so northerly on a straight line to a walnut tree marked, near to Merrie's pond, so-called, and from thence to yᵉ eastward to a black oak marked, yᵉ said pond being yᵉ bounds on yᵉ north end, and from thence on a straight line southeasterly to a white oak first mentioned, and also one commonage in yᵉ said town, according to town orders. June 13, 1682.

Daniel Ladd, Sen., of Haverhill, husbandman, sold to Josiah Gage, of Haverhill, his son-in-law, three pieces of meadow. One piece was by yᵉ north-east corner of an oak hill, which hill is about two miles northwesterly from the upper bridge at Spicket river, one piece near the first, and the third piece about a ¼ mile from the first mentioned. Also a privilege in ye cow common in Haverhill. April 10, 1691. Ack^d. by him and wife Ann, March 8, 1692.

Daniel Ladd, Sen., of Haverhill, "did long since, about five or six years, or thereabouts, bargain and sell to my son Samuel Ladd, for a young beast, which he then paid me to my full satisfaction, and therefore do hereby sell and confirm to him, my said son Samuel, one acre of meadow in ye West Meadow in Haverhill aforesaid. Lying between Tho. Eaton's on ye west side, and John Johnson's on ye east side, and ye upland on both ends.

Signed by mark of Daniel (F) and Ann (☉). April 28, 1693.

Daniel Ladd left a will dated Jan. 30, 1692. It is now, 1887, on file in the Probate Office at Salem, Mass., but it is so badly defaced that a true copy of it cannot be made. We gather from what remains that his widow should be "honourably maintained as long as she remained his widow; that his children should have his estate divided equally among them, counting in the value of what he had given by deed to some of them; that my son-in-law, Josiah Gage, in particular, should have meet recompence for ye time I have been at his house, and ye trouble I have already put him unto." Signed Daniel / Ladd. O.

From documents filed with the will it is evident, for some reason, that the will was not probated; that it was set aside, and his estate settled by an administrator. His son, Daniel Ladd, was appointed administrator, Jan. 9, 1694, and gave bonds for £150.

Josiah Gage, of Haverhill, petitions the Judge of Probate that Daniel Ladd, administrator of the estate of his father, Daniel Ladd. deceased, be cited to appear before his Honor. "A writ of settlement of said estate made and owned by the said Daniel Ladd, deceased, and before his son Daniel, in the presence of witnesses, was committed to Col. Saltonstall, and is now in his hands, and that I may have liberty and opportunity to speak to the same. In so doing it will much oblige your humble petitioner." Signed, Josiah Gage. March 27, 1695.

Gage was notified, June 27, 1695, to appear before the judge on Monday, July 1, 1695.

An agreement between Gage and others, sworn to by the witnesses of the same, before Nathaniel Saltonstall, July 1, 1695:

Josiah Gage, in persuance and for the fulfillment of an obligation made the 11 of this instant, went this 12 day of the same month and made a division of the home land of Daniel Ladd, Sen., deceased, which is as followeth:—For that part at the east end, bounded by a little walnut tree, near the gape that is by the Spicket way, against the house, and from thence on a straight line to a stake by a rock, near an apple tree, and from thence on a straight line to a red oak near the Hawkes' meadow way, by a little swamp sid, and on the same range to said way; and the middle part is bounded, on all parts upon the above named, on the east and on the west by Spicket way, by a clump of willow bushes within the fence, from thence on a straight line to a red oak tree near the Hawkes' meadow way, and on the same range unto said way, which tree stands near a stone brig, near the corner of John Ayer's, his fence; and the third division or lot is bounded on the north by the upper Spicket way, on the east by the above said second division, on the south by Hawk's meadow way and land of Nathaniel Ladd, and on the west by land of Samuel Hutchins and land of John Corliss: be it here understood that Daniel Ladd doth hereby renounce all right and interest in all and every part of this whole home land, by virtue of his former deed given to him by his father, and do hereby covenant to and with Josiah Gage and Caleb Richardson to deliver to them the said deed in a short time. The parties concerned have made their choice of the above said divisions of land as foloeth: Daniel Ladd having his first choyce, choses this most eastern division, and Caleb Richardson having his next choyce, or choyce next, choses the most western part: and the middle part is hereby seated upon Josiah Gage, as his part in the said home land, and in witness of all above written act, persons conserned, here set their hands this 12 day April, 1694.

Witnesses—JOHN JOHNSON, SEN.,   DANIEL ^{His} LADD,
               TIMOTHY JOHNSON.   mark.
                                         JOSIAH GAGE,
                                         CALEB RICHARDSON.

Inventory of Daniel Ladd, Sen.'s, estate, made by David Hazelton, William Sterlin, Robert Hastins, Stephen Coffin, and John Hazelton, July 9, 1695:

Homestead, with dwelling-house and orchard,	£68
A parcel of out lands, adjoining Merrie's creek,	13
Meadow at Providence, commonly so called,	7

The apprizers say the following are several parcels of lands which we are informed by the administrator were given by the deceased to the children:

To Daniel Ladd, six acres, or thereabout, at	£6
Nathaniel Ladd, eight acres, or thereabout, at	8
Onesiphorus Marsh, four acres, or thereabout, at	4
Samuel Ladd, a parcel of land adjoining Merrie's creek, at	13

Daniel Ladd, a parcel of meadow and one commonadge, at	4.10
Nathaniel Smith, deceased, a parcel of meadow at Primrose swamp,	2
Josiah Gage, one commonadge,	1.10
Onesiphorus Marsh, Jr., one commonadge,	1.10

(1) Daniel Ladd married Ann ——, but we have been unable to find her maiden surname, where she lived, or the date of their marriage. He d. at Haverhill, July 27, 1693. His wife Ann d. Feb. 9, 1694.

Children.

2. Elizabeth, bo. Nov. 1, 1640, in Salisbury; ma. Nathaniel Smith, May 14, 1663.
3. Daniel, bo. July 26, 1642, in Salisbury; ma. Lydia Singletery, Nov. 4, 1668; no children. He was Representative from Haverhill in 1693 and 1694.
4. Lydia, bo. April 8, 1645, in Salisbury; ma. Josiah Gage.
5. Mary, bo. Feb. 14, 1646, in Haverhill; ma. Caleb Richardson, of Newbury, July 31, 1682. Her children: [1]Mary, bo. Jan. 12, 1684; [2]Ruth, bo. March 1, 1686.
6. Samuel, bo. Nov. 1, 1649, in Haverhill; ma. Martha Corliss.
7. Nathaniel, bo. March 10, 1651, in Haverhill; ma. Elizabeth Gilman.
8. Ezekiel, bo. Sept. 16, 1654, in Haverhill; ma. Mary Folsom.
9. Sarah, bo. Nov. 4, 1657, in Haverhill; ma. Onesiphorus Marsh, Jr., Dec. 12, 1685.

A descendant of the emigrant Daniel Ladd writes:

"Horace Walpole, when speaking of the times of Charles the 2d, said 'that there were no Englishmen then left in England, for that all men worthy the name had gone to America;' and though this is the language of hyperbole, there was enough of truth in it to give it point; and Lord Brougham said that 'New England was founded by men of whom Old England was not worthy.' It has been wisely as well as beautifully said[*] that 'God sifted a whole nation that He might send choice grain over into this wilderness.' Of this grain was 'that Daniel Ladd' from whom we are descended. He came here in the prime of his youth, and for sixty years thereafter labored, trusting in God and fearing nothing, — neither labor, nor cold, nor privation, nor savage enemies, so that he might help to build up, on these rough shores, a better England than he had left behind.

[*] By the Rev. Mr. Stoughton, in his Election Sermon, Memorial History of Boston, vol. 1, p. 148.

And wisely his work, and the work of those who were like him, do follow them.

"That Daniel Ladd was accounted a man of good social position, when that was a matter of no small consequence, though all were practically nearly on the same level in point of fortune, we have every reason to believe. He held at one time the rank of 'Lieutenant,' and his son Nathaniel, who came to Exeter, married there the daughter of Hon. John Gilman, one of the Council for the Government of Province, Speaker of the House of Assembly in 1697, and the leading man, both for wealth and influence, in the Province out of Portsmouth, and the founder of a family which, down to this day, has been one of the most distinguished in the Province and State. Other marriages, in this and the next generation, bear witness to the respectability and social consideration of the Ladd family."

(6) Samuel Ladd, of Haverhill, (son of Daniel,[1]) ma. Martha Corliss, dau. of George Corliss, Dec. 1st, 1674. He lived in the West Parish, and his house stood on the spot where the West Parish church now (1889) stands. Chase, in his History of Haverhill, says: "Feb. 22d, 1698, this Samuel Ladd, with his son Daniel, and Jonathan Haynes, with his son Joseph, who lived in the western part of the town, had started that morning with their teams, consisting of a yoke of oxen and a horse each, to bring home some hay which had been cut and stacked the preceding summer in their meadow in the extreme western part of the town. While they were slowly returning, little dreaming of present danger, they suddenly found themselves between two files of Indians, who had concealed themselves in the bushes on each side of their path. There were seven of them on each side, with guns presented and cocked, and the fathers seeing that it was impossible to escape begged for 'quarter.' To this the Indians replied 'boon quarter, boon quarter!' (good quarter.) Young Ladd, who did not relish the idea of being quietly taken prisoner, told his father that he would mount the horse and endeavor to escape. But the old man forbade him to make the attempt, telling him it was better to risk remaining a prisoner. He cut his father's horse loose, however, and giving him the lash the horse started off at full speed, and though repeatedly fired at by the Indians, succeeded in reaching home, and

was the means of giving an immediate and general alarm. Two of the Indians then stepped behind the fathers and dealt them a heavy blow upon the head. Mr. Haynes, who was quite aged, instantly fell, but Ladd did not. Another of the savages then stepped before the latter and raised his hatchet as if to strike. Ladd closed his eyes, expecting the blow would fall, but it came not, and when he again opened his eyes he saw the Indian laughing and mocking at his fears. Another immediately stepped behind him and felled him at a blow. The Indians, on being asked why they killed the old men, said they killed Haynes because 'he was so old he no go with us,' meaning that he was too aged and infirm to travel; and that they killed Ladd, who was a fierce, stern looking man, because 'he so sour.' They started for Penacook, where they arrived with the two boys."

Children.

10. Daniel, bo. Nov. 19, 1676; ma. Susannah Hartshorn, Nov. 17, 1701.
11. Lydia, bo. Sept. 25, 1679; d. May 22, 1684.
12. Samuel, bo. May 22, 1682; ma. Hannah Hartshorn, Sept. 26, 1705. No children.
13. Nathaniel, bo. Sept., 9 1684; ma. Abigail Bodwell.
14. Ezekiel, bo. Feb. 14, 1686; ma. Jemima Foster, of Boxford. He lived in Boxford. No children.
15. David, bo. April 13, 1689; ma. Hephziba Hazen.
16. Jonathan, bo. April 13, 1689; ma. Susannah Kingsbury.
17. Abigail, bo. Sept. 29, 1691; ma. Samuel Roberts.
18. John, bo. June 22, 1694; ma. Mary Merrill.
19. Joseph, bo. May 16, 1697; d. June 9, 1697.

(7) Nathaniel Ladd, of Haverhill, (son of Daniel[1] and Ann Ladd,) was born in Haverhill, March 10th, 1651. When a young man he removed to Exeter, N. H. He ma. July 12th, 1678, Elizabeth, daughter of Hon. John Gilman, of Exeter, N. H., who in 1679 " was appointed by the Crown one of the Council for the government of the Province of New Hampshire under Pres. John Cutts and Gov. Cranfield, and was later a delegate to the Assembly and Speaker of the House, and was the founder of a family which for 200 years has been among the most distinguished in the annals of the Province and the State."

Nathaniel Ladd thus became, by his marriage, a member of the leading family of that part of New Hampshire. He was implicated in Gove's rebellion against Gov. Canfield, was arrested, and on Dec. 6th, 1683, "was examined before Barefoot, a judge of the special court for the trial of Gove and his associates, for treason, and entered into recognizance, with William and Charles Hilton as his sureties, in £100 for his good behavior and for his appearance at court when called for to answer to the charge of treason." We find no evidence that his case was ever called for trial.

In the summer of 1690 an expedition was fitted out in Massachusetts, with a contingent from New Hampshire, to protect the more eastern settlements, in which Nathaniel Ladd was one of the volunteers from Exeter, N. H. On the 22d of September the party landed at Maquoit, near Cape Elizabeth, and soon fell into an ambush, and in the fight which ensued were compelled to retreat to their vessels. These being aground, the Indians made a bold effort to take them, but after a hard fight they were repulsed, with a loss to the English of eight killed and twenty-four wounded. Of the last was Nathaniel Ladd, who died of his wounds at Exeter, N. H., Aug. 11th, 1691.

Children.

20. Nathaniel, bo. April 6, 1697; ma. Catharine Gilman.
21. Elizabeth, bo. Jan. 6, 1680; ma. John Glidden. Children: [1]Nathaniel, [2]John, [3]Elizabeth, [4]Hannah, [5]Anna.
22. Mary, bo. Dec. 28, 1682; ma. Jacob Gilman. Children: [1]Daniel, [2]John, [3]Elizabeth, [4]Jacob, [5]Mary, [6]Abigail, [7]Moody, [8]Stevens.
23. Lydia, bo. Dec. 27, 1684; ma. Charles Runalet. Children; [1]Nathaniel, [2]Charles, [3]Lydia, [4]Catharine, [5]Anna, [6]Mary.
24. Daniel, bo. March 18, 1686; ma. Mehitable Philbrook, April 19, 1712.
25. John, bo. July 6, 1689; ma. Elizabeth Sanborn, April 14, 1714.
26. Ann, bo. Dec. 25, 1691; ma. Jonathan Folsom. Children: [1]Gen. Nathaniel, [2]Col. Samuel.

(8) Ezekiel Ladd, (son of Daniel,1) was born in Haverhill, Sept. 16, 1654; ma. Nov. 30, 1687, Mary, dau. of Samuel Folsom, of Exeter, N. H. He removed from Haverhill to Exeter, N. H. In 1697, while living in Exeter, he sold to Simeon Wainwright land in Haverhill which he inherited from his father. In 1707 he was one of the petitioners to the Legislature for a new charter. In 1718 he was in Stratham, N. H., and purchased a pew in the meeting-house. His wife died in Stratham, N. H., July 3, 1741.

Children born in Haverhill.

27. Lydia, bo. Feb. 18, 1688.
28. Mary, bo. Jan. 17, 1690.
29. ——, bo. May 6, 1693. No name given on the record of Haverhill.
30. Nathaniel, bo. Nov. 12, 1695.

(10) Daniel Ladd, of Haverhill, (son of Samuel,[6]) ma. Susannah Hartshorn, of Rowley, Nov. 17, 1701. At the time his father was killed by the Indians, he was captured by them. Chase, in his History of Haverhill, gives an account of his capture, from which we make the following synopsis: "Samuel Ladd was killed by the Indians at Haverhill, Feb. 22, 1698, and his son Daniel taken prisoner and carried to Penacook, N. H. Soon after reaching Penacook young Ladd made an attempt to escape. He left the wigwam when all were asleep, and had gone but a short distance when it occurred to him that a hatchet might be needed. He returned, and entered the wigwam where a squaw was sick. She noticed him, gave an alarm, awakened the other Indians, and he was recaptured. His hands were bound and he was laid upon his back, with one foot fastened to a tree. In this condition he was kept fourteen days. As soon as he was bound his face was gashed, powder was inserted into the wounds, and remained there until it became so indented in his flesh that it was impossible to remove it. The dark spots never left his face, and he was often referred to by his descendants as the *marked man*. Some years after his capture he escaped and returned to Haverhill." He d. June 15, 1751. His wife d. June 22, 1750.

Children.

31. Mary, bo. Aug. 6, 1702.
32. Susannah, bo. May 10, 1704.
33. Samuel, bo. April 20, 1709; ma. Hannah Hartshorn.
34. Daniel, bo. Nov. 15, 1710; ma. Mehitable Roberts.
35. Ruth, bo. May 11, 1712; ma. James Haseltine.
36. John, bo. Feb. 21, 1717.

(13) Nathaniel Ladd, of Haverhill, (son of Samuel,[6]) ma. Abigail Bodwell, dau. of Henry and Bethia (Emery) Bodwell, of Methuen. He removed to Norwich "West Farms," now Franklin, Conn., and from there to Coventry, Conn., where he died, June 11, 1757. His wife died Aug. 7, 1798. At Franklin he was of considerable prominence in civil and ecclesiastical affairs,

having served as selectman in 1721, and having been chosen to important offices in the society.

Children.

37. Timothy, bo. Feb. 12, 1710; ma. Esther Parker, June 17, 1734.
38. Sarah, bo. Jan. 6, 1712; ma. Jonathan Porter, of Coventry, Conn., June 20, 1734.
39. Nathaniel, bo. Jan. 30, 1714; ma. Elizabeth Rust, Nov. 16, 1738.
40. Henry, bo. Jan. 30, 1716; ma. Abigail Lilly, Sept. 8, 1740.
41. Abigail, bo. March 20, 1719; ma. Samuel Lilly, May 14, 1741. Children: ¹Emma, bo. Aug. 20, 1742; ²Abigail, bo. June 28, 1744; ³Hannah, bo. Jan. 5, 1747.
42. Phebe, bo. Feb. 25, 1723.
43. Samuel, bo. Sept. 14, 1727; ma. Ann Woodward, Oct. 18, 1750.

(15)   David Ladd, of Haverhill, (son of Samuel,[6]) ma. Hepzibah Hazen, of Rowley, Oct. 1, 1716. She died March 20, 1728. He ma. 2d, Mary Waters, of Colchester, Conn., March 20, 1729.

Children.

44. Azubah, bo. Nov. 13, 1717; ma. Daniel Allen, Oct. 6, 1741.
45. Hepzibah, bo. July 12, 1719; ma. Alexander Gaylord, Feb. 9, 1743.
46. Bethsheba, bo. July 6, 1721.
47. Jeremiah, bo. Oct. 8, 1723; ma. Jerusha Sabin, Nov. 21, 1748.
48. Hannah, bo. Oct. 1725; ma. Seth Allen, Nov. 9, 1749.
49. David, bo. Dec. 10, 1727; ma. Mary Walbridge.

Children by second wife.

50. Samuel, bo. June 7, 1730; ma. Hannah Hyde, Jan. 15, 1757.
51. Ezekiel, bo. Aug. 6, 1731; ma. Ruth Hyde, Jan. 1, 1759.
52. Joseph, bo. April 20, 1733; ma. Silence Hyde, Jan. 16, 1763.
53. Daniel, bo. Jan. 8, 1735; ma. Hannah Boynton.
54. Abigail, bo. March 20, 1738; ma. Joseph Sampson, of Haverhill.
55. Abner, bo. May 11, 1740; ma. Abigail Perkins, Jan. 26, 1764.

(16)   Jonathan Ladd, (son of Samuel,[6]) was born in Haverhill, April 13, 1689; ma. Susannah Kingsbury, of Norwich, Conn., Dec. 28, 1713. He settled in Norwich, Conn. He purchased of Nathaniel Wallis, of Windham, Conn., deed dated Feb. 11, 1720, a farm in Tolland, Conn., and moved on to it soon after.

Children.

56. Ezekiel, bo. Jan. 31, 1715; ma. Hannah Bigelow.
57. Elizabeth, bo. March 14, 1716.
58. Jonathan, bo. March 5, 1718; ma. Ann Taylor.
59. Mary, bo. Feb. 6, 1720; ma. Jonathan Grant.
60. Susannah, bo. Feb. 17, 1722; ma. Phineas Trask.

61. Ephraim, bo. Jan. 30, 1725; d. Dec. 13, 1726.
62. Abigail, bo. March 26, 1728.
63. Zurvia, bo. March 30, 1730; ma. Joel Nash.
64. Jesse, bo. April 10, 1732; ma. Rachel Taylor.
65. Susannah, bo. March 29, 1734; d. Dec. 24, 1736.

(18) John Ladd, of Haverhill, (son of Samuel.[6]) He ma. Mary, dau. of Nathaniel and Sarah (Woodman) Merrill, of Haverhill, Oct. 17, 1717. He was one of the selectmen in 1747 and 1748.

Children.

66. John, bo. Feb. 14, 1718.
67. Timothy, bo. Nov. 1, 1719; ma. Lydia Marble.
68. Lydia, bo. Dec. 8, 1721; ma. John Carleton.
69. Nathaniel, bo. April 5, 1724; ma. Abigail Bodwell.
70. Abigail, bo. July 12, 1726; ma. Josiah Gage.
71. Mary, bo. Oct. 21, 1728; ma. Joseph Butler, bo. in Woburn, Dec. 1, 1713. He removed to Pelham, N. H., where he owned a large farm, afterwards known as Butler's Mills. His wife Mary (Ladd) Butler was "considered one of the finest women of her day, and was greatly beloved by all who knew her." The general remark at her death was: " What a good Christian woman she has always been." Their children: [1]Mary, bo. Dec. 15, 1755, ma. Timothy Ladd (220) ; [2]Jesse, bo. Dec. 15, 1757, ma. Molly Greely, 2d Mehitable Daly; [3]Thaddeus, bo. Nov. 15, 1759, ma. Miss Beetle, of Salem; [4]Hannah, bo. Jan. 26, 1761, ma. George Tolland; [5]Phebe, bo. Aug. 27, 1763; [6]Elijah, bo. April 13, 1765; [7]James, bo. Nov. 2, 1767; [8]William, bo. April 2, 1769; [9]Abigail, bo. May 11, 1771.
72. Rebecca, bo. Jan. 3, 1731; ma. Evan Jones.
73. Martha, bo. Jan. 24, 1733: d. Dec. 22, 1735.
74. William, bo. Jan. 24, 1738; ma. Hannah Ayer.

(20) Nathaniel Ladd, of Exeter, N. H., (son of Nathaniel,[7]) ma. Catharine Gilman, dau. of Edward Gilman, of Exeter, N. H. She died, and he ma. 2d, Rachel Rawlins, who d. at Stratham, N. H., July, 22, 1717, without issue. He ma. 3d, Mrs. Mercy Hilton, widow of Dudley Hilton, and dau. of Kingsley Hall, of Exeter, N. H. May, 1742, he gave a part of his brick house in Exeter to his son Elias, and in 1747 he sold his farm in Stratham, N. H., on which he lately lived, to his son Paul. He was a millwright and a dealer in land. Lived first in Exeter, then in Stratham, and then in Exeter. The brick house he built in Exeter is now (1888) owned by John Perry, M. D.

Children.

75. Nathaniel, bo. ——: ma. Ann Hilton, dau. of Dudley Hilton.
76. Daniel, bo. ——; ma. Alice ——.
77. Edward, bo. June 22, 1707; ma. Catharine Thing.
78. Elias, bo. ——; ma. Ann Gilman.
79. Josiah, bo. May 29, 1713; ma. Sarah Morse.

Children by third wife.

80. Paul, bo. March 6, 1719; ma. Martha Folsom.
81. Love, bo. March 6, 1719.
82. Dudley, bo. ——. Lost at sea.
83. Mercy, bo. ——.

(24)   Capt. Daniel Ladd, of Kingston, N. H., (son of Nathaniel,[7]) ma. Mehitable Philbrook, of Kingston, N. H., April 29, 1712. She d. Jan. 23, 1779. "He lived for fifty years or more in the same vicinity, Exeter, Brentwood, and Kingston, N. H., the lines of the towns moving if he did not. In 1766 he lived in Haverhill, but in 1769 was in Brentwood again."

Children.

84. Mehitable, bo. June 30, 1713; ma. Samuel Colcord, Nov. 28, 1732.
85. Elizabeth, bo. Feb. 11, 1716; ma. John Nay, Dec. 21, 1731.
86. Anna, bo. June 25, 1718.
87. Hannah, bo. April 17, 1720; ma. Samuel Huntoon, May 6, 1742.
88. Mary, bo. Jan. 3, 1722; ma. Samuel Dudley, April 24, 1740.
89. Daniel, bo. Jan. 25, 1725; ma. Joannah Dudley.
90. Stephen, bo. Aug. 30, 1728; ma. Abigail Webster.
91. Joannah, bo. July 27, 1735; ma. Josiah Huntoon, Dec. 11, 1755.
92. John, bo. Oct. 24, 1737; ma. Mary Moody.

(25)   John Ladd, of Kingston, N. H., (son of Nathaniel,[7]) ma. Elizabeth Sanborn, of Kingston, N. H., April 11, 1714.

Children.

93. Love, bo. March 25, 1716; d. June 19, 1720.
94. Benjamin, bo. April 25, 1718; ma. Mary French.
95. John, bo. May 7, 1720; ma. Alice Thing.
96. Nathaniel, bo. June 17, 1722; ma. Sarah Clifford.
97. Jonathan, bo. Aug. 25, 1724; not ma.; went as a physician in the Louisburg Expedition.
98. Trueworthy, bo. May 21, 1726; ma. Lydia Harriman.
99. Love, bo. Feb. 1, 1728.
100. Dorothy, bo. Nov. 22, 1730; ma. Benjamin Sanborn.

(33) Samuel Ladd, of Haverhill, (son of Daniel.[10]) He removed to Norwich, Conn., now Franklin, Conn.; ma. Hannah Hartshorn, Dec. 29, 1730. His wife died June 21, 1779. He ma. 2d, Dorcas Haskins, March 29, 1781.

Children by first wife.

101. Samuel, bo. Feb. 8, 1732, in Haverhill.
102. Hannah, bo. Nov. 11, 1734, in Haverhill.
103. John, bo. Sept. 19, 1737, in Norwich, Conn.
104. Susannah, bo. May 31, 1741; d. June 30, 1750.
105. Daniel, bo. Nov. 11, 1752; ma. Rachel Haskins, April 2, 1774.
106. Sarah, bo. June 5, 1755.

(34) Daniel Ladd, of Haverhill, (son of Daniel,[10]) ma. Sept. 20, 1733, Mehitable Roberts.

Children.

107. Susannah, bo. July 7, 1734; ma. Stephen Webster.
108. Asa, bo. March 10, 1736; ma. Sarah Merrill.
109. Ezekiel, bo. April 10, 1738; ma. Ruth Hutchins.
110. Daniel, bo. April 21, 1740; ma. Dorothy Foot.
111. Mehitable, bo. Feb. 11, 1742; ma. Samuel Cross.
112. Samuel, bo. Nov. 9, 1744; ma. Martha Hubbert.
113. John, bo. April 17, 1746; ma. Hannah Eastman.
114. David, bo. July 8, 1748; ma. ——.
115. Abigail, bo. July 27, 1750.
116. James, bo. April 10, 1752; ma. Hannah Lock, Dec. 3, 1772.
117. Ruth, bo. Oct. 10, 1757; d. June 4, 1764.
118. Jonathan, bo. Dec. 10, 1760; ma. Sarah Lock.

(37) Timothy Ladd, of Coventry, Conn., (son of Nathaniel,[13]) ma. Esther Parker, Jan. 17, 1734.

Children.

119. Anna, bo. Oct. 31, 1734; ma. Jonathan Delano, Oct. 8, 1754. Their children: [1]Jabez, bo. July 1, 1755; [2]Jonathan, bo. Aug. 10, 1757; [3]Anna, bo. Aug. 11, 1759; [4]Philip, bo. June 13, 1761; [5]Esther, bo. Aug. 13, 1764; [6]Zebulon, bo. Feb. 19, 1767; [7]Chlorinda, bo. June 10, 1769; [8]Margarette, bo. 1773; [9]Hibbard, bo. Aug. 26, 1776.
120. Rachel, bo. May 8, 1736.
121. Timothy, bo. July 3, 1738; ma. Rachel Spencer, May 7, 1761.
122. Phineas, bo. Jan. 8, 1741; ma. Hulda Curtis, March 31, 1808?
123. Zebulon, bo. May 22, 1743.
124. Nathaniel, bo. July 15, 1745.

(39) Nathaniel Ladd, of Coventry, Conn., (son of Nathaniel,[13]) ma. Elizabeth Rust, Nov. 16, 1738. He d. Dec. 19, 1744.

Children.

125. Phebe, bo. Jan. 3, 1741.
126. Irene, bo. March 20, 1744.

(40)   Henry Ladd, of Coventry, Conn., (son of Nathaniel,[13]) ma. Abigail Siley, Sept. 8, 1740. He d. April 6, 1768.

Children.

127. Jerusha, bo. June 20, 1741; d. Oct. 8, 1741.
128. Henry, bo. Jan. 25, 1742; ma. Abiel Richardson, June 26, 1766.
129. Nathaniel, bo. Jan. 7, 1749; ma. Rachel Tilden, March 11, 1773.
130. Abigail, bo. Oct. 5. 1752; d. March 5, 1768.
131. Amasa, bo. Oct. 18, 1762; ma. Betsey Cox.

(43)   Samuel Ladd, of Coventry, Conn., (son of Nathaniel,[13]) ma. Ann Woodward, Oct. 18, 1750. He d. Feb. 16, 1816. His wife d. Feb. 16, 1808.

Children.

132. Nathaniel, bo. Oct. 4, 1751; ma. Abigail Scripture.
133. Samuel, bo. July 6, 1753; ma. Elizabeth Redington.
134. Dorcas, bo. Oct. 19, 1756; ma. Josiah Babcock.
135. Ashbel, bo. Jan. 15, 1759; ma. Irene Babcock, April 4, 1782.
136. Oliver, bo. Oct. 1, 1760; ma. Mary Babcock, Dec. 19, 1782.
137. Anna, bo. Nov. 17, 1762; ma. John Lovejoy.
138. Frederick, bo. Oct. 9, 1764; ma. Fanny Hodges, Nov. 10, 1788.
139. Phebe, bo. June 15, 1767; ma. Roswell Pryor.
140. Rogers, bo. ——; ma. Sally Pryor.

(47)   Jeremiah Ladd, of Franklin, Conn., (son of David,[15]) ma. Jerusha Sabin, Nov. 21, 1748.

Children.

141. John, bo. April 12, 1749; ma. Welthea Perkins.
142. Ann, bo. Sept. 5, 1751.
143. Esther, bo. March 27, 1753.
144. Cyrus, bo. Dec. 30, 1755; ma. Amy Allen.
145. Sarah, bo. May 16, 1758.
146. Benijah, bo. Nov. 16, 1760; ma. Deborah Grant, of Stonington.
147. Welthea, bo. Feb. 19, 1763; ma. Daniel Foster, Feb. 12, 1803. Their children: [1]Fidelia Welthea, who ma. Augustus Hyde; [2]Lafayette S. "He served with distinction in the war of the Revolution, taking part in the battles of White Plains, Stillwater, and Saratoga. She was connected by lineage with some of the principal colonial families of Eastern Connecticut, and was a woman of great energy and shrewdness, of more than common intellectual ability, and highly gifted in conversational powers." She d. Feb. 11, 1851. Their son,

Lafayette Sabin Foster, was born Nov. 22, 1806. "His education was begun in the common schools of his native town. At the age of sixteen he entered upon his preparation for college, under the tuition of the Rev. Abel Flint, D. D., of Hartford, with whom he studied for nine months. In 1824 he completed his preparatory studies with the Rev. Cornelius B. Everest, of Windham, and in Feb. 1825, he entered Brown University at Providence, R. 1., where he graduated in September, 1828, with the highest honors of his class. He studied law in the office of Judge Calvin Goddard, at Norwich, Conn., and was admitted to the bar of New London County at the November term of the court in 1831. In the Spring of 1839 he was chosen one of the representatives of the town of Norwich in the General Assembly of the State. This honor was repeated in the years of 1840, 1846, 1847, 1848, and 1854. In 1847 he was elected Speaker of the House, and was re-elected in 1848. In 1854 he was chosen Speaker for the third time, and on the 19th of May, 1854, he was elected a Senator of the United States, and on the 8th of June the same year he resigned his office of Speaker and his seat in the House. On the 10th of May, 1860, Mr. Foster was returned to the Senate for a second term of six years. On the 6th of March, 1865, Mr. Foster, who had been often called to the chair, and was the favorite presiding officer, was chosen President *pro tem* of the Senate. Upon the assassination of President Lincoln, some six weeks afterwards, he became acting Vice-President of the United States. This position he held for nearly two years, until the close of his senatorial term. Mr. Foster cherished a peculiar, tender affection for his mother, and his care of her and his only sister throughout their lives was unceasing. It is said by those who knew both Mr. Foster and his mother intimately, that he strongly resembled her in some of his intellectual traits." He married, Oct. 2, 1837, Joanna Boylston, daughter of Hon. James Lanman, of Norwich, Conn. He died Sept. 19, 1880. We are indebted for the above facts in regard to Mr. Foster to a very able and elaborate "Memorial Sketch" of him, written by W. H. W. Campbell, and printed by Rand & Avery in Boston, in 1881.

(49) David Ladd, of Franklin, Conn., (son of David,[15]) ma. Mary Walbridge, of Norwich, Conn., May 16, 1752, who d. June 12, 1761. He ma. 2d, Oct. 28, 1765, Eunice Guild, who d. March 23, 1796. He d. April 28, 1796.

Children.

148. Eunice, bo. Feb. 22, 1753; d. Jan. 7, 1754.
149. William, bo. Sept. 27, 1754; d. Oct. 5, 1776.
150. Roger, bo. Aug. 6, 1757.
151. Eunice, bo. July 3, 1759.
152. Temperance, bo. May 14, 1761.

Children by second wife.

153. John, bo. Oct. 15, 1767.
154. Charlotte, bo. Oct. 16, 1769; ma. Elijah Blackman. She d. March 25, 1796.
155. Hazen, bo. July 31, 1771; ma. Rhoda Smith.
156. Whiting, bo. Dec. 30, 1773.
157. Caroline, bo. Feb. 15, 1775.
158. Charles, bo. April 30, 1780; ma. Lydia Wales.

(50) Samuel Ladd, of Franklin, Conn., (son of David,[15]) ma. Hannah, dau. of Jacob Hyde, Jan. 15, 1757. She d. Feb. 11, 1775.

Children.

159. David, bo. Oct. 23, 1757; ma. Eunice Sabin, June 4, 1783.
160. Elizabeth, bo. March 28, 1760; not married.
161. Jacob, bo. March 17, 1762; d. unmarried, July, 1823.
162. Hannah, bo. Aug. 7, 1764; ma. Aaron Bailey.
163. Samuel C., bo. Oct. 17, 1768; ma. Abigail Ladd (193.)

(51) Ezekiel Ladd, of Franklin, Conn., (son of David,[15]) ma. Ruth, dau. of Jacob Hyde, Jan. 18, 1759. He d. July 21, 1802.

Children.

164. Andrew, bo. Oct. 29, 1759; ma. Hannah Sanford.
165. Philena, bo. Sept. 6, 1761; d. unmarried, Jan. 20, 1815.
166. Abby, bo. Oct. 6, 1763; ma. James Armstrong.
167. Mary, bo. March 9, 1767; had three children.
168. Elijah, bo. Sept. 12, 1769; d. unmarried, Aug. 24, 1786.
169. Elizabeth, bo. March 4, 1772; ma. Daniel Ladd (221.)
170. Darius, bo. Sept. 4, 1774; ma. Polly Fink.
171. Jabez, bo. April 4, 1777; ma. Phebe Farnham; no children.
172. Ruth, bo. Dec. 8, 1779; ma. Daniel Ladd (221.)
173. Ruby, bo. April 25, 1782; ma. Festus Ladd (194.)

(52) Joseph Ladd, of Franklin, Conn., (son of David,[15]) ma. Silence, dau. of Jacob Hyde, Jan. 6, 1763. He d. Feb. 25, 1815, and his wife d. May 8, 1793.

Children.

174. Asher, bo. May 19, 1764; not married.
175. Esther, bo. May 30, 1766; not married.
176. Phebe, bo. Aug. 9, 1770; not married.
177. Albert, bo. March 12, 1777; ma. Betsey Liffingwall.
178. Dudley, bo. Feb. 14, 1780; d. unmarried, Oct. 20, 1851.
179. Nancy, bo. April 5, 1784.

(53) Daniel Ladd, of Franklin, Conn., (son of David,[15]) ma. Hannah Boynton, Oct. 24, 1760, who d. March 8, 1764. He ma. 2d, June 12, 1765, Rebecca Armstrong, who d. He ma. 3d, Elizabeth Cady, Jan. 7, 1773. He d. Feb. 1823, aged 87 yrs.

Children.
180. Aphia, bo. Feb. 12, 1762; ma. Levi Crandell, Jan. 27, 1791.

Children by second wife.
181. Hannah, bo. June 22, 1766; ma. Rev. Amaziah Fillmore. Children: [1]Daniel, [2]Jehiel, [3]Mahala, [4]Almira.
182. Asael, bo. Dec. 22, 1767; ma. Rebecca Armstrong; no children.

Children by third wife.
183. James, bo. Aug. 8, 1774; ma. Esther Brown.
184. Elizabeth, bo. Nov. 26, 1777; ma. Elijah Green. Children: [1]William, [2]Hart.
185. Anna, bo. June 17, 1782; ma. 1st, Stone, 2d, Austin, 3d, Blodgett.
186. Rebecca, bo. Sept. 14, 1784; ma. Levi Andrews.
187. Zacheus, bo. Aug. 6, 1786; d. Oct. 6, 1799.
188. Samuel C., bo. March, 1789; ma. Celinda Otis, Nov. 30, 1809.

(55) Abner Ladd, of Franklin, Conn., (son of David,[15]) ma. Abigail Perkins, Jan. 26, 1764.

Children.
189. Lydia, bo. May 8, 1765; d. Jan. 10, 1768.
190. Jedediah Perkins, bo. Feb. 16, 1767; ma. Rebecca Hazen.
191. Abner, bo. April 16, 1769; ma. Sally Cook.
192. Erastus, bo. June 27, 1771; ma. Sarah Hazen.
193. Abigail, bo. Sept. 19, 1773; ma. Samuel Ladd (163.)
194. Festus, bo. Feb. 25, 1776; ma. Ruby Ladd (173.)
195. Rebecca, bo. Jan. 26, 1779; ma. Eleazer Ager.
196. Anna, bo. June 2, 1783.
197. George Washington, bo. June 2, 1783; ma. Lucy Augusta Mott, April 2, 1832.
198. Wealthy, bo. Aug. 15, 1787; ma. Stephen Prentice, June 1, 1810.

(56) Ezekiel Ladd, of Tolland, Conn., (son of Jonathan,[16]) ma. Hannah Bigelow, Nov. 3, 1740.

Children.
199. Lucy, bo. May 1, 1741.
200. Samuel, bo. June 7, 1742; ma. Margaret Chapman.
201. Ruth, bo. Jan. 12, 1744; d. Sept. 3, 1766.
202. Hannah, bo. Sept. 6, 1745.
203. Daniel, bo. April 9, 1747.
204. Ephraim, bo. May 11, 1749; ma. Lois Chapman, July 14, 1774.

205. Elizabeth, bo. April 28, 1751.
206. Elisha, bo. March 7, 1753.
207. Ezekiel, bo. May 1, 1755; ma. Sibel Loomas, March 6, 1777.
208. David, bo. July 27, 1757.
209. Lydia, bo. July 3, 1761.
210. Eunice, bo. March 13, 1764; d. in infancy.

(58) Jonathan Ladd, of Tolland, Conn., (son of Jonathan,[16]) ma. Anna Taylor, June 27, 1751. He d. Aug. 27, 1810, and his wife d. Aug. 19, 1803.

Children.

211. Anna, bo. Aug. 27, 1752; d. young.
212. Eliab, bo. April 21, 1754; ma. Susalla Lothrop. He d. Dec. 15, 1800.
213. Ahijah, bo. Feb. 27, 1756; ma. Huldah Fuller.
214. John, bo. April 3, 1758; ma. Esther Wood, Dec. 11, 1785.
215. Sarah, bo. April 27, 1760; ma. Jacob Benton.
216. Jonathan, bo. June 15, 1762; d. Aug. 21, 1762.
217. Anna, bo. June 15, 1762; ma. Noah Davis, of Stafford, Conn.
218. Jonathan, bo. March 20, 1764; ma. Sept. 26, 1799, Lydia Johnson, of Ashford, Conn.
219. Ruth, bo. March 30, 1767; ma. Samuel Darby, of Tolland, Conn.

(64) Jesse Ladd, of Tolland, Conn., (son of Jonathan,[16]) ma. Rachel Taylor.

Children.

220. Jesse, bo. March 5, ——; ma. Ruby Brewster.
221. Daniel, bo. March 5, 1772; ma. Elizabeth Ladd (169.)
222. Chloe, b. ——; ma. —— Cook.
223. Eunice, b. ——; ma. —— Johnson.
224. William, b. ——; ma. ——.
225. Elias, bo. ——; ma. Betsey Percival.

(67) Timothy Ladd, of Haverhill, (son of John,[18]) ma. Lydia Marble, Nov. 13, 1740. After the birth of two children he removed to Plaistow, N. H., and then to Salem, N. H. He was a justice of the peace, a surveyor, and during the Revolutionary war was engaged in purchasing beeves for the army. There is a tradition that he ma. for his second wife a widow Page, who was a dau. of Hannah Dustan.

Children.

226. Martha, bo. Dec. 3, 1742; ma. David Currier.
227. John, bo. Aug. 20, 1745.
228. Dillie, bo. Feb. 23, 1747; ma. David Clement, 1767.
229. Lydia, bo. Feb. 24, 1749.

230. Timothy, bo. July 3, 1752; ma. Molly Butler, of Woburn.
231. Eliphalet, bo. Feb. 19, 1755; ma. Mary Park.

(69) Nathaniel Ladd, of Haverhill, (son of John,[18]) ma. Abigail Bodwell, June 16, 1748, dau. of Daniel Bodwell, of Methuen, who d. March 5, 1771. He ma. 2d, May 21, 1772, Mary Harvey. He d. March 10, 1773.

Children.

232. John, bo. Dec. 4, 1748; d. unmarried at Methuen, Dec. 23, 1833.
233. Bodwell, bo. Dec. 12, 1750; ma. Martha Lewis.
234. Heman, bo. Feb. 26, 1753; d. unmarried at West Indies, 1775.
235. Nathaniel, bo. Oct. 22, 1755; ma. Sarah Noyes.
236. Thadeus, bo. Jan. 5, 1758; ma. Hannah Dow.
237. Abigail, bo. June 28, 1760; ma. Joshua Sargent, Nov. 9, 1780.
238. Achsah, bo. Aug. 7, 1762; ma. James Messer, of Methuen, Oct. 21, 1783.
239. Caleb, bo. May 29, 1765; ma. Betsey Taplin.
240. Ruth Ingalls, bo. Sept. 4, 1768; ma. Elisha Richardson, Aug. 23, 1787.

Children by second wife.

241. Timothy, bo. March 10, 1773; ma. Martha McCleary, March 1, 1803.

(74) William Ladd, of Haverhill, (son of John,[18]) ma. Hannah, dau. of Dr. William Ayer, of Haverhill, Dec. 7, 1758. He removed to Wrentham, then to Dunbarton, N. H., and from there to Hopkinton, N. H., where he died. He was a farmer.

Children.

242. Abigail, bo. Jan. 7, 1760; not married.
243. William, bo. Dec. 4, 1761; d. July 4, 1762.
244. Mary, bo. April 26, 1763; ma. Ladd Hazeltine, 2d wife.
245. Hannah, bo. April 11, 1765; ma. Ladd Hazeltine, 1st wife, 1783.
246. Lydia, bo. Dec. 29, 1766.
247. William, bo. Dec. 4, 1768; not married.
248. John, bo. Nov. 3, 1770; d. young.
249. John, bo. ——; not married.
250. Mehitable, bo. 1776; ma. John Tucker, June 16, 1811.
251. Susan, bo. April 9, 1778; ma. Bimsley Perkins, Dec. 13, 1804. Children: [1]Louisa A. P., bo. March 1, 1808, ma. Joseph Stanwood, Nov. 11, 1829. She d. at Hopkinton, N. H., April 29, 1890. Children: [1]Henry Perkins, bo. July 13, 1832; [2]Frederick Williams, bo. Dec. 16, 1836; [3]Susan Ladd, bo. Dec. 25, 1838, ma. Reginald Heber Chase, of Cambridge, May 31, 1859. Children: [1]Joseph Stanwood, bo. March 12, 1860; [2]Lerin Joynes, bo. Feb. 6, 1862; [3]Philander, bo. April 29, 1867, d. Oct. 6, 1873. Mr. Chase died Jan. 11, 1885, at Chestnut Hill, Philadelphia, Pa., and his three children were born there. [4]Helen

Hamilton, bo. March 27, 1839, ma. Rev. Edward F. Putnam, July 18, 1849; [b]Louisa Ayer Perkins, bo. April 10, 1843, not ma. in 1888.

(75) Nathaniel Ladd, of Exeter, N. H., and Stratham, N. H., (son of Nathaniel,[20]) ma. Ann, dau. of Dudley Hilton, and granddaughter of Hon. Kinsley Hall.

Children.

252. Nathaniel, bo. ——; ma. Mrs. Rebecca (Emery) Smith, May 28, 1755, widow of Capt. Daniel Smith. Mr. Ladd did not have any children. He was a large dealer in real estate. He died in 1776. "He left a will, but named no executor in it. Administration (with the will annexed) was granted, June 28, 1776, to Dudley Ladd, of Haverhill, in the Province of Mass. Bay, who was named as the residuary legatee therein. He bequeathed the freedom to a negro man and woman, 'Scipeo' and 'Bess,' and their two children, 'Patta' and 'Dinah,' a yoke of oxen to the man, a feather bed, a cow and six chairs, to his wife's granddaughter Margarett Smith, and to his wife Rebecca one third part of his personal estate not before herein disposed of, and to his brother Dudley Ladd, of Haverhill, all the rest and residue of his estate, real and personal." The inventory amounted to £349.14.4, not including the negroes, who were exempt from valuation at that time.
253. Dudley, bo. ——; ma. Alice Hurley, Dec. 15, 1748.

(76) Daniel Ladd, of Epping, N. H., (son of Nathaniel,[20]) ma. Alice ——.

Children.

254. Daniel, bo. Aug. 21, 1742; ma. Judith Lyford.
255. Nathaniel, bo. March 9, 1745; ma. Mary Ames.
256. Jeremiah, bo. ——; ma. Tamison Sias.

(77) Edward Ladd, of Belmont, N. H., (son of Nathaniel,[20]) ma. Catharine, dau. of Samuel and Abigail (Gilman) Thing. He d. July 5, 1787. His wife d. Feb. 10, 1773.

Children.

257. Abigail, bo. Dec. 7, 1734; d. 1747.
258. Edward, bo. April 13, 1736; ma. Hannah ——.
259. Thing, bo. July 5, 1738.
260. Nathaniel, bo. Dec. 25, 1740.
261. Samuel, bo. Feb. 21, 1744; ma. Abigail Flanders.
262. John, bo. Sept. 19, 1746; d. April 11, 1770.
263. Abigail, bo. July 21, 1749; d. April 19, 1754.

(78) Elias Ladd, of Exeter, N. H., (son of Nathaniel,[20]) ma. Ann, dau. of Capt. John Gilman, Jr., Nov. 27, 1740. His will was dated April 20, 1790; proved March 13, 1801.

Children.

264. Elias, bo. ——; ma. Nancy Thompson.
265. Dorothy, bo. ——; ma. Jacob Smith.
266. Abigail, bo. ——; ma. Bradbury Richardson.
267. Ann, bo. Sept. 30, 1744; ma. —— Winslow.
268. John, bo. May 26, 1750; ma. Judith Smith.
269. Elizabeth, bo. Dec. 20. 1754; ma. Benjamin Gilman, April 21, 1774.
   Her children: [1]Benjamin, [2]Nathaniel, [3]Betty, [4]Judith.
270. Love, bo. ——; ma. —— Kimball.

(79) Josiah Ladd, (son of Nathaniel,[20]) ma. Jan. 8, 1738, Sarah, dau. of Philip Morse, of Newburyport, who was born July 23, 1710, and who died Nov. 8, 1780. He d. at Exeter, N. H., Nov. 8, 1785. He was a millwright and carpenter, was for many years deacon of the First Congregational Church, at Exeter, N. H., and was much esteemed for his practical good sense and for his upright and blameless life.

Children.

271. Simeon, bo. May 18, 1742; ma. Ruth Ayer.
272. Eliphalet, bo. May 30, 1744; ma. Abigail Hill, May 14, 1772.
273. Molly, bo. April 5, 1748; ma. Josiah Kimball.
274. Sarah, bo. July 22, 1750; ma. —— Sanborn.

(80) Paul Ladd, (son of Nathaniel[20] and Mercy (Hilton) Ladd,) was born in Exeter, N. H., March 6th, 1719. He ma. Martha, dau. of Nathaniel Folsom, of Exeter, 1747. He d. Feb., 1783. His wife died July 17, 1804. He settled in Stratham, N. H., on a farm deeded to him by his father, Nathaniel Ladd, March 28, 1747. He had lived in Stratham but a few years before he sold his farm there and removed to Epping, N. H., where he bought a farm on the road leading from Epping Corner (that now is) to Nottingham Square, where he built a log house near a spring, where the road run at that time. The place has since been known as the Drake farm, and is a part of the Nottingham town farm. At or near the commencement of the French and Indian war of 1754, being afraid, as tradition says, of hostile Indians, he bought a farm on Red Oak Hill, in Epping, N. H., (not far from his other place, but in a more thickly settled neighborhood) of Edward Dearborn, of Stratham, N. H. The

deed is dated 1755. He was a well-to-do farmer, whose education was as good as could be obtained at that time in the common town schools. He was a man of sound and discriminating judgment, and was often consulted by his neighbors and townspeople in times of difficulties, trials and trouble. In religion he was a disciple of Whitefield, at that time called " New Lights," and declined to pay to the Congregationalist a minister's tax, which caused some trouble.

Children.

275. Paul, bo. Feb. 26, 1749; not married.
276. Dudley, bo. Feb. 26, 1749; ma. Lydia Haines.
277. Lois, bo. April 22, 1751; ma. John Folsom. She d. March, 1816.
278. Martha, bo. Oct., 1752; d. 1756.
279. Mercy, bo. March, 1755; d. at Epping, 1763.
280. Simeon, bo. Jan. 15, 1757; ma. Lizzie Hines.
281. Martha, bo. March, 1758; ma. Steven Smith. Children: [1]Benjamin, bo. Aug. 17, 1783, ma. Lydia Ladd (676); [2]Emma, bo. July 6, 1785, ma. John Smith; [3]Josiah, bo. 1787, ma. Susan Tucker; [4]Greenleaf, bo. 1790, d. young; [5]Jonathan, b. 1792, d. young; [6]Steven, bo. July 13, 1796, ma. Nancy Staples; [7]Susannah, bo. Feb. 26, 1799, ma. Aaron Rollins.
282. Nathaniel, bo. Jan. 15, 1760; ma. Polly Smith.
283. Josiah, bo. Nov., 1762; ma. Polly Gale.
284. Susannah, bo. Oct. 26, 1768; not ma.; d. Oct. 21, 1849.

(89) Daniel Ladd, (son of Daniel,[24]) was born in Kingston, N. H., Jan. 25, 1725. He ma. Joannah, dau. of Judge James Dudley, about 1748. She died, and he ma. for his 2d wife Susannah Dow, of Brentwood, N. H. She died, and he ma. for his 3d wife Ruth Bradley, of Brentwood, N. H. He was a soldier in the army that captured Louisburg; was taken prisoner in an assault made on the fort, May 26, 1745, carried to France, was exchanged, returned home and settled at Deerfield, N. H. He was a blacksmith and a manufacturer of iron; had a large shop, and a trip-hammer that was operated by water; employed a large number of men, who were engaged in digging ore and converting it into iron. He was a very active and enterprising business man; was one of the selectmen in 1767 and 1775. He made the first survey of the town of Unity, N. H. He died April, 1809.

Children.

285. Daniel, bo. about 1749. Killed by a falling tree.
286. James, bo. about 1751; ma. Margarett Glidden, Feb. 9, 1775.
287. Nathaniel, bo. May 12, 1753; ma. Sally Marshall.

Children by second wife.

288. Peter, bo. about 1756; ma. Abigail Martin, of Deerfield.
289. Joses, bo. about 1758; ma. Rachel Fifield, Oct. 16, 1784.
290. Joannah, bo. about 1760; ma. Theodore Marston, Dec. 25, 1785, of Mt. Vernon, Me.
291. Samuel, bo. about 1762; ma. Dolly Brown.
292. Susannah, bo. about 1764; ma. Benjamin Bartlett, Dec. 29, 1786, of Kingston, N. H. Children: [1]Benjamin O., bo. Jan. 15, 1788; [2]Peter, bo. May 13, 1789.
293. Jedediah, bo. about 1767; ma. Nancy Brown.
294. Jeremiah, bo. about 1769; not ma. Lost at sea.
295. Mehitable, bo. about 1771; ma. Eleazer Robbins, of Mt. Vernon, Me.
296. Polly, bo. about 1773; ma. Sawyer Brown. Lived in Maine.
297. Miriam, bo. about 1775; ma. 1st, —— Proctor, 2d, Nathaniel Ladd (323.)

(90) Stephen Ladd, of Brentwood, N. H., (son of Daniel,[24]) ma. Abigail Webster. She d. and he m. 2d Bethia Sweet.

Children.

298. Mehitable, bo. Dec. 6, 1755.
299. Thomas, bo. Sept. 9, 1757.
300. Abigail, bo. April 4, 1759; ma. Stephen Gordon.
301. Stephen, bo. Feb. 1, 1761; ma. Betsey Bean.
302. Phebe, bo. Nov. 24, 1763; d. Dec., 1809.
303. Samuel, bo. April 7, 1765; ma. Comfort Dow.

Children by second wife.

304. Joannah, bo. Feb. 7, 1768; ma. William Gordon, March 27, 1788.
305. Elizabeth, bo. May 7, 1770; ma. Zebidee Thing, Feb. 9, 1795.
306. Huldah, bo. Feb. 11, 1772; ma. Stephen Leavitt.
307. Nancy, bo. Jan. 6, 1774; not ma.; d. Dec. 3, 1844.
308. Hannah, bo. Dec. 6, 1775; not ma.; d. Jan. 21, 1851.
309. Judith, bo. ——; ma. Enoch Gordon.
310. John, bo. May 29, 1779; ma. Lydia Sanborn.

(92) John Ladd, (son of Daniel,[24]) was born in Kingston, N. H., Oct. 24, 1737; ma. Mary Moody, of Brentwood, N. H. He was one of the original settlers of the town of Unity, N. H. He d. March 15, 1784. She d. Nov. 25, 1815, aged 75 years. I find upon the town records of Unity: "At a meeting of the Proprietors of the Township of Unity, holden at Kingston, N.

H., July 3, 1769, on Article 5th it was voted, 'That we give thirty acres of land to John Ladd's wife, as a gratis for her, she being the first woman that moved into the town.'" At the first town meeting ever held in the town of Unity, Dec. 15th, 1773, John Ladd was chosen moderator, and chairman of the board of selectmen. He was a farmer, and had the best orchard in town; was prominent in town affairs, and a highly respected citizen. He died March 15, 1784, leaving a widow and nine children, seven girls and two boys, whom his widow, who was a very active, intelligent woman, " brought up, married them off, and fitted them out nicely."

Children.

311. Elizabeth, bo. 1762; ma. Capt. John Glidden. She d. March 1, 1838.
312. Sarah, bo. ——; ma. Jacob Smith, of Claremont, N. H.
313. John, bo. Feb. 2, 1768; ma. Sarah Hibbard.
314. Mehitable, bo. 1770; ma. Henry Perkins, of Unity, N. H., April 1, 1790.
315. Mary, bo. 1772; ma. James Lawrence; 2d, Cyrus Field. She d. 1851. Her children by Field: [1]Forbes, bo. Feb. 10, 1812; [2]Josiah, bo. Aug. 27, 1815.
316. Hannah, bo. Aug. 5, 1775; ma. —— Harrington, June 3, 1804. Their children: [1]Marchia, bo. March 25, 1805, d. Aug. 9, 1844; [2]Warren, bo. March 3, 1807; [3]Mary Ladd, bo. July 10, 1809; [4]Anna, bo. March 21, 1811; [5]Luther, bo. Feb. 19, 1813; [6]Leonard Clark, bo. July 2, 1816; [7]Diantha Hannah, bo. April 6, 1818; [8]David Alonzo, bo. March 26, 1821.
317. Joanna, bo. 1777; ma. Jabez Perkins, of Unity, N. H. She d. July 23, 1850.
318. Josiah, bo. Nov. 14, 1779; ma. Anna Chappell, Nov. 26, 1801.
319. Anna, bo. ——; ma. —— Palmer.

(94) Benjamin Ladd, of Kingston, N. H., (son of John,[25]) ma. Mary French, of Salisbury, Sept. 11, 1741.

Child.

320. Mary, bo. Sept. 20, 1760; ma. James Prince, of Lee, N. H., April 6, 1780.

(96) Nathaniel Ladd, of Kingston, N. H., (son of John,[25]) ma. Sarah Clifford, Aug. 12, 1741. After the birth of his children, he, with his family, removed to Alexandria, N. H.

Children.

321. Jeremiah, bo. Oct. 3, 1742; ma. Priscilla Sanborn.
322. Nathaniel, bo. Sept. 28, 1744; ma. ——.
323. Love, bo. Sept. 27, 1746; ma. Timothy Simons.

324. Isaac, bo. June 2, 1749; ma. Dolly Blaisdell.
325. John, bo. Sept. 26, 1751; ma. ——.
326. Benjamin, bo. Sept. 25, 1753; ma. Deborah Allen.
327. Elizabeth, bo. Jan. 6, 1756; ma. Jacob Draper, of Plymouth, N. H.
328. Sarah, bo. Dec. 13, 1757; ma. Samuel Thompson, of Deerfield, June 12, 1777.

(98) Capt. Trueworthy Ladd, (son of John,[25]) was born in Kingston, N. H., May 1, 1726. He ma. Lydia Harriman, Nov. 1, 1750. He died at Goffstown, N. H., April 26, 1778. His widow died April 8, 1819. In 1755 he was clerk of Capt. Alcock's company, Peter Gilman's regiment. In 1756 he was lieutenant in Capt. Winslow's company. In 1757 he was lieutenant in a company in Col. Meserve's regiment, and captain of a company in Col. John Hart's regiment, Canada service, in 1758. He was surveyor of highways in Goffstown, N. H., 1771 and 1772, and his son Jonathan held the same office in 1780. We copy the following patriotic letter from him from the Provincial Records of New Hampshire, vol. 7, p. 472.

GOFFSTOWN, N. H., May 13, 1775.

To the Honorable Congress sitting at Exeter:

GENTLEMEN,—After my regards to your Honours, with freedom, whereas it is thought there will be a number of soldiers called for out of this Province, for the assistance and defence of North America, for our privileges and liberties, I would inform your Honours that if occasion should call for a number, I am ready to serve your Honours in the Government and my country, for the defence of our privilege, and the enjoyment of liberty in America.

If your Honours should call for me, I am ready to serve my country with all the freedom and assistance that I am capable of, as I think it is the duty of all well-wishers to liberty and the North America.

Wishing success to liberty, so I subscribe myself your well-wisher and humble servant,

TRUEWORTHY LADD.

His services thus generously offered were accepted, as we find his name on the muster roll of Capt. Samuel McConnell's company, Col. Moor's regiment, which was raised to reinforce the army at New York, July 26, 1776.

Children.

329. Jonathan, bo. Aug. 7, 1751.
330. Mehitable, bo. Jan. 26, 1753; ma. —— Heath.
331. John, bo. Jan. 6, 1755; ma. Jerusha Lovejoy, June 6, 1775.

332. Betsey, bo. Sept. 3, 1756; ma. Aaron Noyes.
333. Lydia, bo. Jan. 4, 1759; ma. Jonathan Eaton.
334. Love, bo. Jan. 29, 1761; ma. Joel Emery. Children: [1]Lydia, bo. April 21, 1779; [2]James, bo. Jan. 26, 1781; [3]John, bo. Sept. 19, 1785; [4]Joel, bo. Oct. 10, 1787; [5]Betsey, bo. Nov. 13, 1789; [6]Mary, bo. Oct. 10, 1795; [7]Jonathan, bo. Dec. 11, 1797; [8]Seava, bo. Jan. 15, 1801; [9]Ira.
335. Keziah, bo. Feb. 13, 1763; ma. Moses Hacket.
336. Lois, bo. Jan. 4, 1767; ma. David Morgan, July 29, 1788. She d. in Bow, N. H., Dec. 6, 1835. Children: [1]Trueworthy Ladd, bo. July 4, 1789; [2]David, bo. March 9, 1792; [3]Jeremiah, bo. Sept. 8, 1796; [4]Lois, bo. April 6, 1798; [5]Jesse, bo. Sept. 11, 1800; [6]Ira, bo. Dec. 3, 1805; [7]Lucinda, bo. Aug. 14, 1809.
337. Lucy, bo. 1769; ma. Stephen Clement, June 26, 1778.

(105) Daniel Ladd, of Norwich, Conn., (son of Samuel,[33]) ma. Rachel Haskins, April 2d, 1774.

Children.

338. Lydia, bo. Oct. 7, 1778.
339. Hannah, bo. Oct. 16, 1781.
340. Daniel, bo. Jan. 9, 1784; ma. Abigail Crossman, April 14, 1808.
341. Enoch, bo. Nov. 14, 1785; ma. Mary Wilbur, March 2, 1814.
342. Uriah, bo. April 12, 1791; ma. Zurvia Chapman, Nov. 10, 1816.
343. Rachel, bo. Aug. 20, 1794.
344. Clarissa, bo. April 3, 1797.

(108) Asa Ladd, of Haverhill, (son of Daniel,[34]) ma. Sarah Merrill, of Haverhill, Dec. 28, 1757. He. ma. for his 2d wife Hannah Clough.

Children.

345. Sarah, bo. Sept. 24, 1758; ma. —— Clough.
346. Asa, bo. Jan. 9, 1762; ma. Martha Chase, Sept. 14, 1784.

Children by second wife.

347. Richard, bo. April 14, 1766; ma. Bettie Woodman.
348. Dustan, bo. July 1, 1768.
349. Dudley, bo. Jan. 30, 1771.
350. Merrill, bo. Jan. 12, 1773.
351. Dilley, bo. Nov. 19, 1775.

(109) Hon. Ezekiel Ladd, of Haverhill, (son of Daniel,[34]) removed to Haverhill, N. H.; ma. in 1760, Ruth Hutchins. Powers' History of Coos County, N. H., pages 53 and 60, says: "Ezekiel Ladd, of Haverhill, Mass., was one of the early settlers of Haverhill, N. H. He became one of the principal men of the

place, and occupied the most responsible positions. The wife of Mr. Ladd had seen and tasted some of the refinements of life, and in after years she often related her extreme mortification on the first Sabbath she attended meeting at her new home. She had been recently married, and thinking she must appear as well as her neighbors, she put on her wedding silk, with muffled cuffs extending from the shoulder to the elbow, and there made fast by brilliant buttons. She wore silk hose and florid shoes. Her husband also appeared in his best, and they took their seats early in the sanctuary. But, as she said, 'they went alone, sat alone, and returned alone,' for it was not possible for her to get near enough to any of the women to hold conversation with them. They were actually afraid of her, and kept a safe distance lest they should spoil her dress. The next Sabbath she appeared in a clean check-linen dress, with other articles in accordance, and found no difficulty in making the acquaintance of her neighbors, who proved to be social and warmhearted friends. Mr. Ladd afterwards became widely known as 'Judge Ladd,' and was highly respected and beloved."

The History of Haverhill, N. H., by Rev. J. Q. Bittinger, page 65, says Mr. Ladd "was one of the earliest tavern-keepers in the town, was also engaged in tannery business, and was a man of prominence in the settlement. He served as selectman for a number of years, and was also treasurer of the town and one of the judges of the Court of Sessions."

He died July 12, 1818. His wife died July 8, 1817.

Children.

352. Abiah, bo. Jan. 21, 1761; ma. Joshua Young.
353. Joseph, bo. Dec. 15, 1764; ma. Sarah Ring.
354. Molly, bo. Feb. 14, 1766; ma. Jacob Bailey, of Newbury, Vt.
355. Ezekiel, bo. May 18, 1768; ma. Elizabeth Swan, 1796.
356. Hannah, bo. May 3, 1772; ma. John Bailey, of Newbury, Vt.
357. Abigail, bo. May 27, 1774; ma. Jacob Williams.
358. Moody, bo. Dec. 15, 1777; ma. Olive Williams.
359. James, bo. July 6, 1782; ma. Lucy Sellors.

(110) Daniel Ladd, of Haverhill, N. H., (son of Daniel,[34]) ma. Dorothy Foot.

Children.

360. Elizabeth, bo. July 27, 1762; ma. James Cochrane, June 1, 1784.
Children: [1]Vashti, bo. Dec. 1, 1786; [2]John, bo. June 10, 1787; [3]Rob-

ert, bo. March 9, 1789; ⁴Betsey, bo. Feb. 9, 1790; ⁵James, bo. Nov. 19, 1792.
361. Jesse, bo. Sept. 14, 1764; ma. Thankful Holmstead; d. 1804.
362. Ruth, bo. Aug. 17, 1766; d. 1802.
363. Sampson, bo. Feb. 28, 1770; d. 1804.
364. Daniel, bo. Sept. 10, 1773; ma. Lydia Dow, Oct. 8, 1801.
365. Joshua, bo. Sept. 13, 1775; ma. Sarah Merrill.
366. John, bo. June 21, 1779; ma. Euseba Henry.

(112) Samuel Ladd, of Haverhill, N. H., (son of Daniel,³⁴) ma. Martha Hubbert, June, 1769. He kept a public house in Haverhill, N. H., in 1791. His will was proved Sept. 13, 1815. His wife Martha died, and he ma. for his 2d wife Mrs. Cynthia (Hastings) Arnold, Dec. 16, 1794, widow of Dr. Jonathan Arnold, of St. Johnsbury, Vt.

Children.

367. William, bo. March 8, 1770; ma. Abigail Spaulding.
368. Ruth, bo. June 18, 1771; ma. Dr. Martin Phelps. She d. April, 1804.
369. Anna, bo. Oct. 30, 1772; d. March 11, 1777.
370. Laben, bo. Feb. 27, 1775; d. March 21, 1777.
371. Samuel, bo. April 6, 1778; d. May 11, 1778.

Children by second wife.

372. Cynthia A., bo. May 11, 1796; ma. Jeremiah Farman. Children: ¹Anne Watson, bo. Oct. 13, 1824, ma. Theron Howard, Dec. 1, 1864; ²Samuel Ladd, bo. Sept. 12, 1829, ma. Alma Case, Sept. 12, 1858; ³Cynthia Hastings, bo. Sept. 13, 1831, ma. Carlos Fulton, May, 1866; ⁴Mariam Eliza, bo. June 10, 1836, d. March 26, 1841; ⁵Eleanor Louisa, bo. March 10, 1841, ma. Leonard Cady, April, 1879.
373. Jonathan A., bo. April 24, 1798; ma. Mary Burbeck.
374. Samuel, bo. Aug. 25, 1800; ma. Mary Ward.
375. Martha, bo. Aug. 25, 1800; ma. Rev. B. F. Kimball, Jan. 10. 1826; 2d, Philip Goss, Nov. 16, 1829.
376. Elizabeth, bo. Aug. 15, 1802; ma. Charles Swan, Aug., 1825.
377. Horace Hall, bo. June 4, 1807; ma. Amanda Jutau, Jan. 16, 1833.

(113) John Ladd, of Haverhill, N. H., (son of Daniel,³⁴) ma. Hannah Eastman.

Children.

378. Daniel, bo. Oct. 26, 1777; ma. Elizabeth Huse.
379. Asher, bo. ——;* ma. Wealthy Wright, Sept. 13, 1813.
380. John, bo. ——;* ma. Miriam Owen, Oct. 5, 1809.
381. Avis, bo. ——; ma. William Knights, Jan. 24, 1815.
382. Irene, bo. ——; ma. David Wright, June 21, 1815.
383. Rebecca, bo. ——;* ma. Jacob Dudley, Dec. 19, 1820.

* Baptized at Haverhill, N. H., May 22, 1791.

384. Ruth, bo. ——;* ma. Abel Bridgman, of Hanover, N. H. Children: [1]Emeline M., b. Dec. 20, 1815; [2]John Ladd, bo. Nov. 26, 1817; [3]Eliza A., bo. Sept. 24, 1826; [4]George W., bo. July 28, 1833. Mr. John L. Bridgman, from the age of 17 until he was 37, was in the employ of the Boston & Lowell Railroad Co.; for ten years had charge of the freight house; the remainder of the time was in the general ticket clerk's office; left the road in 1852. Since that time he has devoted himself to his farm of five hundred and twenty-five acres; has on it 62 head of Jersey cows and heifers, part of which are registered and are very valuable. He is a Director and Vice-President of the Dartmouth National Bank, one of the Trustees of the Savings Bank, and for fourteen years chairman of the board, and for some years sheriff of the county.

385. Mehitable, bo. ——.
386. Moses, bo. ——; ma. Sarah Luevey.
387. Susannah, bo. ——.
388. Hannah, bo. ——;* ma. —— Tyler.
389. Burroughs, bo. ——.

(114) David Ladd, of Haverhill, N. H., (son of Daniel,[34]) ma. ——.

Children.

390. Stephen, bo. ——.
391. Betsey, bo. ——.
392. Abiah, bo. ——.
393. Lydia, bo. ——; ma. Jacob Benham, Jr., March 11, 1809.
394. Polly, bo. ——; ma. William Willey, July 29, 1806.
395. Ruth, bo. ——.
396. Nancy, bo. ——.
397. David, bo. ——.
398. Docia, bo. ——; ma. Ward Buel, Dec. 5, 1811.

(116) James Ladd, of Haverhill, N. H., (son of Daniel,[34]) ma. Hannah Lock, of Haverhill, N. H., Dec. 3, 1772. He died at Piermont, N. H., Dec. 5, 1836. His widow died Nov. 7, 1841.

Children.

399. Tryphena, bo. June 23, 1774; ma. —— Goodwin; 2d, David Heath.
400. Phebe, bo. Feb. 24, 1776; ma. William Kelsey.
401. Abigail, bo. Dec. 3, 1778; ma. William Tarleton, March 5, 1800.
402. Susannah, bo. Feb. 1, 1780; ma. Simeon Olmstead, Sept. 3, 1805.
403. Théodora, bo. Dec. 19, 1782; ma. Amos Tarleton.
404. James, bo. April 6, 1784; not married.
405. Timothy, bo. Sept. 18, 1786; ma. Ester Pillsbury.
406. Ethan Smith, bo. May 31, 1791; ma. Roxana Davis.
407. Samuel, bo. Aug. 25, 1793; ma. Mary Dudley Melvin.

* Baptized at Haverhill, N. H., May 22, 1791.

408. Hannah, bo. Jan. 27, 1796; not married.
409. Roxanna, bo. June 12, 1800; ma. Benjamin Martin.

(118) Jonathan Ladd, of Haverhill, N. H., (son of Daniel,[34]) ma. Sarah, dau. of Elisha Lock. He died March 11, 1833.

Children.

410. Theodocia, bo. Feb. 15, 1786; ma. —— Smith.
411. Elisha Lock, bo. June 14, 1787; ma. Asenath Batchelder, Jan. 1, 1822.
412. Ruth, bo. July 4, 1789; ma. John Boise, July 6, 1849.
413. Isaac, bo. July 6, 1792; ma. Nancy Riggs.
414. William Wallace, bo. Nov. 25, 1794.
415. James, bo. Feb. 12, 1797.
416. Tryphina, bo. March 11, 1803.

(128) Dr. Henry Ladd, of Coventry, Conn., (son of Henry,[40]) ma. Abiel Richardson, June 26, 1766. He died Aug. 9, 1778. She died in 1814.

Children.

417. Jerusha, bo. Feb. 15, 1767; d. Aug. 11, 1767.
418. Henry, bo. Aug. 18, 1768; ma. Lavina Hawkins.
419. Herman, bo. Feb. 6, 1770; ma. Mary Morse.
420. Jerusha, bo. April 11, 1772; d. Feb. 2, 1776.
421. Perry Green, bo. Jan. 1, 1774; ma. Dolly Whitney, Aug. 30, 1797. No children.
422. Corrin, bo. June 8, 1775; d. Dec. 10, 1777.
423. Hiram, bo. Oct. 16, 1776; d. Sept. 20, 1800.
424. Benoni, bo. July 24, 1778; ma. Roana Ransom.

(129) Nathaniel Ladd, of Chittenden, Vt., (son of Henry,[40]) ma. Rachel Tilden, of Tolland, Conn., March 11, 1773. His wife died May 6, 1829. He died Jan. 12, 1832.

Children.

425. Nathaniel, bo. Jan. 16, 1774; d. young.
426. Lois, bo. Feb. 7, 1776; ma. —— Edminister. She d. Feb. 21, 1835.
427. Jason, bo. April 7, 1778; ma. Betsey Fuller. He d. in Rutland, Vt., 1828.
428. Anson, bo. April 20, 1780; ma. Harriet Baird.
429. Roger, bo. March 31, 1782; ma. Sarah Henderson.
430. Submit, bo. May 9, 1784; not ma.; d. 1847.
431. Rachel, bo. Dec. 4, 1786; ma. Elisha Drury, of Pittsford, Vt.
432. Clara, bo. April 10, 1790; ma. Needham Drury.
433. Polly, bo. April 17, 1792; ma. Joseph Langley.
434. Nathaniel, bo. May 29, 1794; ma. Charlotte Stoughtenburg.

(132)   Nathaniel Ladd, (son of Samuel,[43]) was born in Coventry, Conn., Oct. 4, 1757; ma. Abigail, dau. of Simeon and Ann (Slafter) Scripture; settled at Woodstock, Conn., and was deacon of the Congregational Church there. From there he removed to Woodstock, Vt., where he purchased a large tract of wild land, built on it a log-house, commenced at once clearing it up, and lived on it as a farmer until he died, Oct. 31, 1837.

Children.

435. Nancy, bo. Oct. 15, 1774; d. June 6, 1776.
436. Abigail, bo. July 3, 1776; ma. —— Thomas.
437. Levina, bo. July 27, 1780; ma. Richard Smith, of Montgomery. N. Y.
438. Nathaniel, bo. June 17, 1782; ma. Patience Simmons.
439. Ephraim, bo. Oct. 23, 1784; ma. Thankful Simmons.
440. Mason, bo. March 23, 1788; ma. Susan Dutton, Jan. 22, 1815.
441. Parthena, bo. Feb. 12, 1790; ma. Charles Smith, of Le Roy, N. Y.
442. Betsey, bo. Oct. 6, 1793; ma. Henry King, March 7, 1816, of Montgomery, N. Y.
443. Nancy, bo. June 12, 1798; ma. Moses Thatcher, Sept. 24, 1820, of Benson, Vt.

(133)   Samuel Ladd, of Coventry, Conn., (son of Samuel,[43]) ma. Elizabeth Reddington, May 18, 1775. He removed to Sharon, Vt.

Children.

444. Anson, bo. March 2, 1776; ma. Ruth Moulton.
445. Wealthy, bo. March 14, 1778; ma. Daniel Parks. March. 1800. Children: [1]Hannah, [2]Eliza. [3]Ann, [4]Susan, [5]Wealthy, [6]Charles.
446. Anna, bo. ——; ma. Cary Bingham; 2d, Elias Curtis, of Royalton, Vt. Children: [1]Abigail, [2]Cary, [3]Elizabeth, [4]Wealthy.
447. Samuel, bo. Aug. 15, 1783; ma. Esther H. Turner, Jan. 11, 1808.
448. Betsey, bo. ——; ma. Hovey Hutchinson.
449. John Reddington, bo. 1749; ma. Sarah Kingsbury, Jan. 20, 1817.

(135)   Ashbel Ladd, of Sharon, Vt., (son of Samuel,[43]) ma. Irene Babcock, April 4, 1781. He died 1851.

Children.

450. Ashbel, bo. Oct. 4, 1782; ma. Phebe Howe.
451. Phebe, bo. June 5, 1784; ma. Isaac Blake.
452. Philander, bo. Dec. 1, 1786; d. young.
453. Lucinda, bo. Aug. 23, 1788; ma. William Baldwin.
454. Ralph, bo. March 20, 1790; ma. Persis Robinson, Dec. 21, 1815.
455. Alfred, bo. Sept. 24, 1793; ma. Samantha Ives.

(136)   Oliver Ladd, of Stafford, Vt., (son of Samuel,[43]) ma. Mary Babcock, April 4, 1782. He died Jan. 28, 1833.

Children.

456. Polly, bo. April 4, 1785; ma. Dr. Eleazer Baldwin, Nov. 1803.
457. Alpheus, bo. Aug. 4, 1787; ma. Betsey Carpenter, Aug. 29, 1809.
458. Clarissa, bo. Jan. 13, 1792; ma. Joseph Sanborn; 2d, Joseph Parker.
459. Marilla, bo. Feb. 25, 1794; ma. Abraham Brewster, Jan. 25, 1834.
460. Sally, bo. April 4, 1797; ma. Lyman Brockway; 2d, Calvin Davis.

(138)   Frederick Ladd, of Sharon, Vt., (son of Samuel,[43]) ma. Fanny Hodges, of Pomfret, Conn., Nov. 10, 1788. He died June 8, 1851. She died Aug. 7, 1858.

Children.

461. Frederick, bo. Sept. 26, 1789; ma. Anna Chandler.
462. Charlotte, bo. Sept. 17, 1791; ma. William Pixley, March 10, 1824.
463. Alfred, bo. Nov. 14, 1793; ma. Sarah Straton, March 20, 1824.
464. Roxanna, bo. Sept. 11, 1796; ma. Ira Morse, Nov. 12, 1817.
465. Orrin, bo. May 9, 1799; d. Feb. 12, 1800.

(140)   Roger Ladd, of Strafford, Vt., (son of Samuel,[43]) ma. Sally Pryor.

Children.

466. Henrietta, bo. ——; ma. Pliny Day.
467. Elvira, bo. ——; ma. David Lane.
468. Sally, bo. 1801; d. May 20, 1882.
469. Laura, b. ——; ma. Horace Dary.
470. Maria, b. ——; d. Aug. 7, 1817.

(141)   John Ladd, of Franklin, Conn., (son of Jeremiah,[47]) ma. Weltha Perkins, March 11, 1772.

Children.

471. Malinda, bo. Nov. 9, 1772.
472. Rowena, bo. Dec. 14, 1774.
473. Jerusha, bo. Dec. 13, 1776.
474. John, bo. ——; ma. Lydia Abel.

(144)   Cyrus Ladd, of Franklin, Conn., (son of Jeremiah,[47]) ma. Mary Allen, Dec. 5, 1781.

Children.

475. George Wylles, bo. Nov. 27, 1782.
476. Sally Allen, bo. June 19, 1784.

(146) Benijah Ladd, of Franklin, Conn., (son of Jeremiah,[47]) ma. —— Grant, of Stonington, Conn.

Children.

477. Beaufort, bo. Sept. 18, 1798, in Franklin, Conn., and graduated at Amherst College, class of 1824. He ma. May, 1833, Almira, dau. of Richard Holmes, of Sangerfield, N. Y. She died Sept. 24, 1833. He ma. 2d, Nov. 29, 1839, Mary E., dau. of Diodate Lord, of Ogden, N. Y. She died March 24, 1848. He ma. 3d, May, 1848, Mrs. Clarissa H. (Williams) Wood, dau. of Rev. William Williams, of Red Creek, N. Y. No children.
478. Grant, bo. July 2, 1801; ma. Elizabeth R. Baker.
479. Esther, bo. ——; ma. —— Chapin.
480. Emily, bo. ——; ma. Ephraim Halstead.
481. Augustus, bo. ——; ma. Jane Armstrong.
482. Jane, bo. ——; ma. John Edgar.
483. Cornelia, bo. ——; ma. Charles Copeland.

(155) Hazen Ladd, of Franklin, Conn., (son of David,[49]) ma. Rhoda Smith, April 8, 1792. He died April 21, 1834.

Children.

484. Anna, bo. Oct. 7, 1793; not married.
485. Harriet, bo. Dec. 9, 1794; not married.
486. Marvin, bo. April 4, 1796; ma. Betsey Smith.
487. Eunice, bo. July 6, 1797; ma. Jabez Smith.
488. Clarissa, bo. April 1, 1799; not married.
489. Calvin, bo. Aug. 16, 1800; ma. Lois Hazen.
490. Septa, bo. Dec. 6, 1801; ma. Patta Ladd.
491. Israel S., bo. Jan. 4, 1804; ma. Luranda Ladd.
492. Almira K., bo. Aug. 18, 1805; ma. —— Bellows.
493. Pelatia Armstrong, bo. Jan. 9, 1807; not married.
494. Betsey Griswold, bo. Jan. 29, 1809; not married.
495. Charles, bo. Oct. 16, 1811; d. May 12, 1812.
496. Adeline, bo. April 27, 1812; not married.

(158) Charles Ladd, of Franklin, Conn., (son of David,[49]) ma. Lydia Wales, May 4, 1802, of Windham, Conn.

Children.

497. Henry Wales, bo. Oct. 4, 1803.
498. Elisha Abbie, bo. June 26, 1806.

(159) David Ladd, of Franklin, Conn., (son of Samuel,[50]) ma. Eunice Sabin, June 4, 1783. He died April 6, 1849. She died **Feb. 24, 1808.**

Children.

499. Rufus, bo. July 21, 1784.
500. Russell, bo. June 3, 1787; ma. Ruth Armstrong, June 19. 1817.
501. Asa, bo. ——; ma. Nancy Peck.
502. Marvin, bo. ——; d. in infancy.
503. Sophia, bo. ——; ma. William Frazier.

(163) Samuel C. Ladd, of Franklin, Conn., (son of Samuel,[50]) ma. Abigail Ladd (193,) dau. of Abner (55.)

Children.

504. Jedediah Perkins, bo. Aug. 1796; ma. Eliza Brewster, March 16, 1820.
505. Hannah, b. ——; ma. John Hazen.
506. Alvira, b. ——; d. young.
507. Caroline, b. ——; d. young.

(164) Andrew Ladd, of Grand Isle, Vt., (son of Ezekiel,[51]) ma. Hannah Sanford, April 17, 1788.

Children.

508. Ulysses, bo. Nov. 8, 1791; ma. Electa Hazen.
509. Almira, bo. Jan. 20, 1795; ma. Stephen Pierce, of Grand Isle, Vt.
510. Lewis, bo. April 28, 1797; ma. Maria Hyde, Feb. 28, 1842.
511. Jabez, bo. Nov. 8, 1799; ma. Martha Wright, Jan. 27, 1838.
512. Alverado, bo. June 7, 1802; ma. Margaret Flemming.

(170) Darius Ladd, of Franklin, Conn., (son of Ezekiel,[51]) ma. Polly Fink, of Stonington, Conn., June 11, 1797. He died May 19, 1833.

Children.

513. Noyes, bo. April 17, 1798; ma. Harriet E. Williams.
514. Curtis, bo. Oct. 6, 1799; not married.
515. Minerva, bo. July 17, 1802; ma. Ezra Bailey, of Groton, Conn.
516. Sophronia, bo. Oct. 27, 1804; ma. Elias Potter, of Kingston.
517. Eunice, bo. Dec. 23, 1806; d. Dec. 14, 1813.
518. Luther Manning, bo. Nov. 8, 1808; ma. Wealthy B. Eames.
519. Ezekiel Hyde, bo. Dec. 10, 1811; ma. Ruth A. Scott.
520. Margaret Fink, bo. Aug. 10, 1813; ma. Lucius Scott.
521. Ruth Kingsbury, bo. Feb. 11, 1817; ma. Eli Hazen, April 2, 1837. Children: [1]Charles E., bo. July 22, 1838; [2]Ruth I., bo. Sept. 24, 1840; [3]Dwight B., bo. Sept. 4, 1842; [4]Marcus M., bo. Nov. 30, 1848; [5]Curtis L., bo. March 26, 1852.

(177) Albert Ladd, of Franklin, Conn., (son of Joseph,[52]) ma. Betsey Liffingwell, Nov. 13, 1803. He died Nov. 9, 1814.

Children.

522. Elizabeth L. Hyde, bo. May 8, 1805; not married.
523. Joseph Dudley, bo. Aug. 25, 1811; ma. Mrs. —— Green.

(183) James Ladd, of Franklin, Conn., (son of Daniel,[53]) ma. Esther Brown.

Child.

524. James, bo. ——.

(188) Samuel Cady Ladd, of Franklin, Conn., (son of Daniel,[53]) ma. Nov. 30, 1809, Celinda, dau. of James Otis, of Stonington, Conn. He was a farmer; lived and died on the farm on which he was born, and which came to him from his father and grandfather. He was a sergeant in a military company stationed at New London, Conn., in the war of 1812.

Children.

525. Celinda Angeline, bo. Feb. 28, 1811; ma. Daniel Fillmore Abel, May 17, 1829.
526. Alonzo, bo. June 9, 1812; not married.
527. Frances Emblen, bo. July 25, 1814; ma. Gordon S. Fenner; 2d, W. P. Scott.
528. Esther Brown, bo. June 27, 1815; ma. Amos E. Closson.
529. Mary Ann, bo. Oct. 26, 1817; ma. Newel Wyllys.
530. Austin, bo. Jan. 30, 1820; ma. Electa Noble.
531. Charlotte Ayer, bo. Nov. 23, 1821; ma. Obed McLean.
532. Merrimett, bo. Sept. 2, 1823; not married; d. Oct. 4, 1843.
533. Lydia Ann, bo. Jan. 17, 1826; ma. James D. Charleton.
534. James Ephraim, bo. Oct. 17, 1828; ma. Henrietta Esther Carpenter, Dec. 24, 1854.
535. Electa Jane, bo. Nov. 27, 1830; ma. James Lamb; 2d, Lynde Huntington.

(200) Samuel Ladd, of Tolland, Conn., (son of Ezekiel,[56]) ma. Margaret, dau. of Capt. Samuel Chapman, April 28, 1768. He died May 18, 1814. His wife died Feb. 4, 1813.

Children.

536. Ruth, bo. Jan. 18, 1769.
537. Samuel, bo. May 11, 1770.
538. Margaret, bo. Oct. 8, 1772.
539. Mary, bo. Nov. 28, 1775.
540. Wareham, bo. April 23, 1778; ma. Abigail Fellows, Nov. 30, 1815.
541. Jacob, bo. Dec. 14, 1781; ma. Rebecca Charter.

(204) Ephraim Ladd, (son of Ezekiel,[56]) was born in Tolland, Conn., May 11, 1749. He ma. July 14, 1774, Lois Chapman. After the birth of his children in Tolland, Conn., Feb. 3, 1800, he emigrated to Pennsylvania and took up land near New Albany, Bradford county, and settled on it. He brought his family with him on two ox-sleds and one two-horse team. He was a resolute, energetic, and pushing man, and he soon had a cleared farm and a comfortable home for himself and family.

Children.

542. Nancy, bo. Aug. 5, 1776; d. Dec. 5, 1820.
543. Roxanna, bo. Dec. 23, 1777; d. June 21, 1797.
544. Horatio, bo. Jan. 21, 1780; ma. Asenath Ives, Jan. 30, 1800.
545. Charles Warren, bo. Sept. 5, 1781; ma. Philinda Alden, Nov. 22, 1818.
546. Almira, bo. Feb. 22, 1784; ma. D. R. Smith.
547. John Chapman, bo. Nov. 16, 1785; not married; d. May 5, 1804.
548. Lydia, bo. Oct. 31, 1787; ma. David Holcomb. She d. Oct. 8, 1865.
549. Milton, bo. Oct. 28, 1789; d. Feb. 19, 1790.
550. Willis, bo. Aug. 3, 1791; d. Nov. 13, 1791.
551. Electa, bo. June 5, 1793; ma. Daniel Stone. She d. Sept. 22, 1832.
552. Lois, bo. Oct. 29, 1795; ma. Augustus Pierce. She d. Aug. 24, 1872.
553. Ephraim, bo. Sept. 19, 1797; ma. Susan Irish. He d. in Kentucky, Nov. 3, 1867.

(212) Eliab Ladd, of Tolland, Conn., (son of Jonathan, Jr.,[56] and grandson of Jonathan,[16]) was born April 21, 1754, on the Ladd homestead in the north-west part of Tolland, Conn. He ma. Susalla, dau. of John Lathrop, Jr., Jan. 14, 1779, with whom he lived till his death, Dec. 15, 1800. His widow ma. Jesse Meacham, Sen., and died Sept. 27, 1827.

In the distribution of his father's farm, Mr. Ladd's share was seventy acres. He bought a brother's share of seventy acres, and built himself a home which his sons inherited in 1801. He was a large, strong man, and weighed more than two hundred pounds. He was a man of energy and skill as a farmer, fertile in resources, and untiring in industry. In addition to his farm he owned and ran a saw-mill, and in rolling logs and handling lumber laid the foundation of difficulties, resulting in death a comparatively young man.

Tradition says he was a noted wrestler, and as a competitor it was difficult to match him; and from his great strength he was known as "Armstrong." When on a town-meeting day two men in their quarrel came to a fight, and friends were vainly endeavoring to separate them, he stepped between them saying, "Let me handle these men;" and taking one by the collar with each hand, he placed them at arm's length on each side. The men at once sprang to strike him. Taking advantage of their motions, he brought their heads together like two fighting rams. Placing them at arm's length again, he said: "Careful, gentlemen; the next time your heads come together your noses will bleed." This ended the fight.

Walking from meeting, one very cold Sunday, a neighbor in his company was overcome with the cold and sat down to sleep. He refused to go any further, and wanted to rest for a while and then proceed to his home. He was freezing to death without knowing it. Mr. Ladd cut some walnut rods and whipped him into motion, hurrying him home in double quick time. The next day the neighbor called and thanked him for his severity, declaring that he had saved his life.

Children.

554. Joseph, bo. Oct. 22, 1779; d. April 3, 1780.
555. Luther, bo. Dec. 20, 1780; d. Sept. 23, 1781.
556. Ariel, bo. Feb. 9, 1783; ma. Mary Winchel, Oct. 11, 1811.
557. Stephen, bo. Nov. 8, 1784; ma. Hannah Kingsbury, Aug. 24, 1811.
558. Lura, bo. Oct. 30, 1786; d. May 22, 1816.
559. Roxy, bo. Sept. 8, 1788; d. Dec. 24, 1788.
560. Roxy, bo. Jan. 29, 1790; d. April 9, 1790.
561. Presinda, bo. Sept. 9, 1791; ma. Azariah Benton, May 23, 1851.

(213) Ahijah Ladd, of Tolland, Conn., (son of Jonathan,[56]) ma. Huldah Fuller, of Hebron, Conn., Feb. 21, 1785. He died April 15, 1826. His widow died Nov. 20, 1834.

Children.

562. Lois, bo. Nov. 18, 1785; d. May 25, 1787.
563. Ahijah, bo. Aug. 15, 1788; ma. Almy Cobb.
564. Levi, bo. Dec. 20, 1790; ma. Lois Davis.
565. Joel, bo. March 8, 1793; ma. Roxy Darba. No children.
566. Ezra, bo. Feb. 23, 1795; d. Feb. 4, 1810.
567. Alvan, bo. May 17, 1797; ma. Nabby Fuller.
568. Huldah, bo. Sept. 26, 1799; not married; d. July 13, 1868.
569. Daniel, bo. Jan. 28, 1804; d. Feb. 9, 1807.

(214) John Ladd, of Tolland, Conn., (son of Jonathan,[58]) ma. Esther Wood, Dec. 11, 1783.

Children.

570. Esther, bo. Sept. 14, 1784; ma. Samuel Stebbens.
571. Luther, bo. May 10, 1786.
572. Eunice, bo. June 26, 1788; ma. Morgan Brooks.
573. John, bo. Oct. 22, 1790; ma. Sarah Smith.
574. Laura, bo. Aug. 20, 1792; ma. Alfred Ely, of West Springfield.
575. Nathan, bo. May 26, 1795; ma. Hannah Webster.
576. Marcia, bo. May 9, 1797; ma. Daniel Benton, of Tolland, Conn.
577. Eliab, bo. Oct. 11, 1799; not married; d. Aug. 31, 1824.
578. Lathrop, bo. Nov. 6, 1801; ma. Hannah Parsons.
579. Lois, bo. June 18, 1805; ma. Jacob Benton, Oct. 4, 1830.

(220) Jesse Ladd, Jr., (son of Jesse,[64]) was bo. in Tolland, Conn., March 5, 17—; ma. Ruby, dau. of Wadsworth and Jerusha (Newcomb) Brewster, of Chatham, Conn., a lineal descendant of Elder William Brewster, who came over in the Mayflower, 1620, through his son Love. In 1812 he removed to Madison, Ohio, where he died Aug. 15, 1827.

Children.

580. Ruby Bliss, bo. July 18, 1800; ma. Edward Bissell, Feb. 7, ——.
581. Flavia Brewster, bo. March 13, 1802; ma. Cushing Cunningham, Jan. 15, 1824.
582. Grata Taylor, bo. Sept. 25, 1804; ma. Dr. A. Merriam, Dec. 27, 1821.
583. Marcia Almira, bo. Sept. 3, 1807; ma. Dr. Edward Plympton.
584. Silas Trumball, bo. Jan. 29, 1810; ma. Elizabeth Williams, March 3, 1841.

(221) Daniel Ladd, of Manlius, N. Y., (son of Jesse,[64]) ma. Elizabeth Ladd (169,) Jan. 5, 1802. She d. March 20, 1808. He ma. 2d, Ruth Ladd (172,) July 10, 1809. She d. July 5, 1872. He d. April 19, 1861.

Children.

585. Jabez S., bo. Oct. 4, 1802; not married; d. Feb. 23, 1828.
586. William Marshall, bo. April 2, 1804; ma. Julia Ann Hobbie.
587. Aurelia Hyde, bo. Jan. 1, 1806; not ma.; d. at Eaton, N. Y., 1848.
588. Ruth Kingsbury, bo. Jan. 10, 1808; ma. Elijah Scott, of Green, N.Y., Oct. 5, 1840.

Children by second wife.

589. Orson, bo. April 21, 1810; ma. Dorothy Stearnes, Oct. 24, 1843.
590. Roswill H., bo. Aug. 26, 1812; ma. Rebecca Chamberlain, Aug. 1843.
591. Elizabeth, bo. July 2, 1814; ma. Josiah Peck, May 21, 1834. She d. Feb. 11, 1877. Children: [1]Ellen A., bo. April 25, 1835, d. Nov. 3, 1842; [2]Barton P., bo. April 18, 1837, d. June 3, 1842; [3]Mary A., bo. Aug. 20, 1839, ma. James R. Clark, Sept. 4, 1841; [4]Eugene, bo. April

9, 1842, ma. Charles E. Wills, April 1. 1868; ⁵Lewis J., bo. June 9, 1844, d. Sept. 30, 1865; ⁶Samuel W., bo. Sept. 20, 1846, d. June 29, 1848; ⁷Henry C., bo. Aug. 1, 1850, ma. Carrie Copple, April 14, 1880; ⁸Hannah B., bo. Oct. 29, 1853.

592. Betsey P., bo. Sept. 17, 1816; not married.
593. Jesse T., bo. March 16, 1819; ma. Harriet M. Morse.
594. Lathrop W., bo. Aug. 24, 1823; ma. Sarah Hardsborough, 1851.

(253) Dudley Ladd, of Haverhill, (son of Nathaniel,[75]) ma. Alice Hurley, of Haverhill, Dec. 15, 1748. He died March 6, 1811. His widow died Dec. 25, 1811.

Children.

595. Ann, bo. Nov. 20, 1749; ma. Davidson Dudley.
596. Ruth, bo. May 17, 1751.
597. Sarah, bo. Oct. 1, 1752; d. young.
598. Alice, bo. June 27, 1754.
599. Nathaniel, bo. June 22, 1756.
600. Dudley, bo. July 8, 1758; ma. Bethia Hutchins.
601. Sarah, bo. May 31, 1760.
602. Olive, bo. April 19, 1762; ma. Samuel Greenleaf.
603. Elizabeth, bo. Oct. 20, 1764; d. March 14, 1814.

(254) Daniel Ladd, of Louden, N. H., (son of Daniel,[76]) ma. Judith Lyford. He died Aug. 28, 1801.

Children.

604. Mary, bo. May 17, 1766; m. Dr. Weir.
605. Olive, bo. June 16, 1769; ma. —— Balch.
606. Judith, bo. Nov. 5, 1771; ma. William Moulton, of Stanstead, Canada.
607. John, bo. May 19, 1774; ma. Lydia Sanborn.
608. Elsa, bo. Jan. 29, 1777; ma. John Rollins, of Gilmanton, N. H.
609. Susan, bo. May 19, 1779; ma. Levi French, of Louden, N. H.
610. Gideon, bo. Feb. 23, 1782; ma. Polly Osgood.
611. James, bo. July 29, 1784; d. April 29, 1786.

(255) Nathaniel Ladd, (son of Daniel,[76]) was born in Epping, N. H., 1745, in the easterly part of the town, near Lampry river; ma. Mary Ames, of Canterbury, N. H. He built in Epping, on the North River road, a handsome house upon an attractive estate, which was occupied by himself and his descendants for nearly a century. He was a man of cultivated tastes, and published some essays on moral and economical subjects. He died July, 1798. His widow died in 1829. [See History of Rockingham County, N. H.]

Children.

612. James, bo. Aug. 9, 1769; ma. Elizabeth Gould.
613. Daniel, bo. ——; ma. Elizabeth Goodwin.
614. Nathaniel, bo. ——; ma. Dolly Smith.
615. Mary, bo. ——; ma. Elisha Sanborn, of Louden, N. H. Children: ¹Eliza, ²Nathaniel, ³James.
616. John, bo. Jan. 28, 1782; ma. Profinda Robinson, July 2, 1806.

(256) Jeremiah Ladd, of Lee, N. H., (son of Daniel,[76]) ma. Tamison Sias. Was a farmer. Will proved Nov. 21, 1806.

Children.

617. Daniel, bo. July 13, 1781; ma. Grace Powell.
618. Alice, bo. ——; ma. Thomas Ford.

(258) Edward Ladd, of Andover, N. H., (son of Edward,[77]) ma. Hannah ——.

Children.

619. Thing, bo. Jan 27, 1762; ma. Elizabeth Jimson.
620. John, bo. ——; ma. Sally ——.
621. Joseph, bo. Jan. 30, 1763; ma. Polly Thing.
622. Caleb, bo. ——.
623. Edward, Jr., bo. ——; ma. Miriam Avery, Dec. 19, 1809.
624. Polly, bo. ——.
625. Nathaniel, bo. ——; ma. Nabby ——.
626. Philip, bo. ——.

(261) Col. Samuel Ladd, of Belmont, N. H., (son of Edward,[77]) ma. Abigail Flanders, Nov. 10, 1768. He died April 9, 1801. His widow died June 8, 1803.

Children.

627. Samuel, bo. Dec. 4, 1769; ma. Polly Davis.
628. John, bo. March 25, 1771; ma. Mehitable Gale.
629. Edward, bo. March 22, 1773; ma. Hannah Hoit.
630. Isaac, bo. Feb. 6, 1775; ma. Lois Woodman.
631. Abigail, bo. Jan. 1, 1777; ma. Stephen Perley. She d. Oct. 3, 1798.
632. Jonathan, bo. Jan. 21, 1779; ma. Rachel Prescott, Feb. 17, 1808.
633. Dudley, bo. Dec. 23, 1780; ma. Abigail Plummer.
634. Mehitable, bo. April 5, 1783; ma. Stephen Perley.
635. Thomas, bo. May 26, 1785; ma. Eunice Lyford.

(271) Simeon Ladd, of Exeter, N. H., (son of Josiah,[79]) ma. Ruth Ayer, of Haverhill, March 13, 1764. She d. Nov. 14, 1784. He ma. 2d, Aphia, dau. of Benjamin and Aphia (Hobert) Phillips, June 12, 1785. She d. Oct. 24, 1788. He ma. 3d, Deb-

orah, dau. of Theophilus Gilman, Jan. 31, 1789. She d. Dec. 18, 1834. He was for many years High Sheriff of Rockingham County. He d. Dec. 17, 1811.

Children by first wife.

636. Hannah, bo. April 11, 1765; ma. —— Gordon.
637. Josiah, bo. July 12, 1767; not married; d. Feb. 4. 1797.
638. Eliphalet, bo. Aug. 16, 1769; ma. Elizabeth Bragg.
639. Nathaniel, bo. Nov. 17, 1771; d. Aug. 23, 1773.
640. Molly, bo. Sept. 28, 1774; not married; d. in Exeter, N. H.
641. Nathaniel, bo. Sept, 5, 1779; d. Sept. 7, 1779.

Children by third wife.

642. Rufus, bo. Aug. 21, 1791; d. Oct. 2, 1792.
643. Charles, bo. June 5, 1794; ma. Abigail Hilton.

(272) Col. Eliphalet Ladd, (son of Josiah,[79]) ma. May 14, 1772, Abigail, dau. of Elisha and Mary (Plaisted) Hill, of South Berwick. Me. She d. (as the widow of Rev. Joseph Buckminster D. D.) Sept. 17, 1838, aged 88 years 8 months. At the early age of twenty-three, in 1767, he was captain and part owner of a brig in trade to the West Indies. Later he was a merchant and ship-builder at Exeter, N. H., where he rapidly accumulated property. During the Revolutionary war he was interested in several privateers and letters of marque, and having a reputation for great force of character and sound judgment, was often consulted by the Committee of Safety, and by leading members of the Legislature. He was aid on the staff of Gov. John Taylor Gilman during his whole fourteen years of consecutive service as Governor of New Hampshire, whence came his title of "Colonel," by which he was always afterwards known. He removed to Portsmouth. N. H., in May, 1792, and interested himself mainly in the welfare of that then growing and prosperous town. He was a strong Federalist in politics, and represented the town for several years in the State Legislature. He enjoyed a high credit in England, by the aid of which his business and commerce were largely extended and very profitable; but he suffered severely from the French spoliations prior to 1800, and also by the great fire by which the town was desolated in December, 1802. But at the time of his death, which occurred Feb. 24, 1806, at the age of 61, he was one of the wealthiest of the many wealthy merchants of Portsmouth. He was a Christian by profession, "upright towards God and

48

downright towards man," and won the respect and good will of all men.

Children.

644. Sarah, bo. July 6, 1774; ma. Rev. William T. Rowland, June 10, 1793. She d. Oct. 12, 1798.
645. Elizabeth, bo. Aug. 12, 1776; ma. Samuel Chauncy. She d. Nov. 17, 1821. Had one son: Dr. Charles W. Chauncy.
646. William, bo. May 10, 1778; ma. Sophia Ann Stodolph. No children. He was educated at the public schools, prepared for college at Phillips Academy in his native town, and entered Harvard University, Cambridge, at the age of fifteen. At college he was distinguished for his high flow and buoyancy of spirit, for his fondness for social enjoyment, and by the kindliness of his disposition. These traits of character made him beloved by his comrades, and did not interfere with a full average attention to his studies. He had an honorable appointment in his class when he graduated. His father had in the meantime removed from Exeter, N. H., to Portsmouth, N. H., and was extensively engaged in commerce. When William came home one of his father's ships was lying at the wharf ready for sea. He applied for permission to go in her as a passenger, and his father, that his son might see something of the world before he entered upon the active duties of life, gave his consent. He embarked, but in a short time his situation as passenger, without employment, became irksome to him; he cut off the skirt of his coat to make, as he said, "a sailor's jacket extempore," and though living as an officer, performed the duties of a seaman. In a second voyage he went as mate of the ship; in the next took command as master, and became one of the most successful of his father's captains. He soon became part owner, and for several years sailed ships belonging to himself and brother. He continued in commercial business until the war of 1812 drove him from the ocean. He then retired to Minot, Me., where his family owned a large tract of land. He purchased the whole of it, built a large house, and began the business of farming and wool-growing with his accustomed energy. Soon he had a flock of six hundred blooded stock, and continued his interest in farming and wool-growing until his death. His wife was an English lady from London, who with her parents had made the passage to this country with him. She survived him many years. It was not until after his retirement to Minot, Me., that his mind received a strong religious impression, and he was awakened to an interest in the spiritual world. His conscience became excited and his character changed. He was President of the American Peace Society, and was called the "Apostle of Peace." He died suddenly at Portsmouth, N. H., April 9, 1841, the very evening he arrived there to join his family, after his long and toilsome journey in the State of New York, in which he had exhausted his whole strength

in his labor of love. He willed all of his property to the cause of Peace, all to be expended within ten years, except enough to give his wife a moderate income, which also reverted to the American Peace Society at the death of his widow. For a more extended biography of Mr. Ladd and his untiring efforts in the cause of Peace, we refer our readers to an able article in the Democratic Review of 1842, vol. 10, pp. 211-223, from which the above facts were obtained.

647. Henry, bo. May 1, 1780; ma. Hannah Hurd.
648. Charlotte, bo. April 9, 1782; ma. John Langdon, son of Hon. Woodbury Langdon, Sept. 22, 1808. Children: [1]Charlotte, [2]Elizabeth, [3]Caroline, [4]John, [5]Harriet, [6]Sophia, [7]Mary, [8]Sarah.
649. Alexander, bo. May 9, 1784; ma. Maria Tufton Haven.
650. Caroline, bo. May 4, 1786; d. March 10, 1803.
651. Sophia, bo. May 12, 1788; ma. Hon. John P. Lord, of South Berwick, Me., 1830. Children: [1]Rev. John, ma. Mary Porter; [2]William, ma. Percis Kendall; [3]Caroline, ma. Mr. Bacon; [4]Rev. Charles; [5]Buckminster; [6]Harriet, ma. Samuel G. Thorne; [7]Susan, ma. Rev. Mr. Mussey; [8]Samuel Perkins, ma. —— Colgate.
652. Eliphalet, bo. April 25, 1791; ma. Mary L. Hurd. No children. He d. April 24, 1821.
653. Harriet, bo. Aug. 27, 1793; d. July 31, 1800.

(264)   Elias Ladd, of Sandwich, N. H., (son of Elias,[78]) ma. Nancy Thompson, of Sandwich, N. H., Sept. 20, 1770.

Children.

654. John, bo. May 29, 1772; ma. Dolly Colby, March 5, 1799.
655. Elias, bo. Jan. 17, 1774; ma. Dorcas Moore.
656. Polly, bo. Jan. 24, 1776; ma. Jesse Atwood.
657. Josiah, bo. Feb. 5, 1778; ma. Miriam Webster.
658. Nancy, bo. May 8, 1780; ma. Josiah Ladd (666,) Dec. 18, 1800.
659. James, bo. Jan. 30, 1784; ma. Hannah Harriman, Feb. 7, 1806.
660. Betsey, bo. May 9, 1786; ma. Enoch Blake.
661. Samuel, bo. Dec. 1, 1788; not married.
662. Stephen, bo. July 9, 1791; d. April 9, 1793.
663. Nabby, bo. April 9, 1793; d. July 30, 1795.
664. Stephen, bo. Feb. 11, 1796; d. Dec. 26, 1800.

(268)   John Ladd, of St. Johnsbury, Vt., (son of Elias,[78]) ma. Judith Smith.

Children.

665. Josiah, bo. May 25, 1777; ma. Nancy Ladd (658.)
666. Judith, bo. April 6, 1779; ma. Otis Lathrope Hidden. Children: [1]David, bo. July 17, 1800; [2]Joel, bo. Sept. 4, 1802; [3]Polly, d. young; [4]Hubbard, bo. Oct. 25, 1806; [5]James, bo. June 14, 1808; [6]Nancy, bo. 1810; [7]John, bo. 1812; [8]Charles, bo. 1814; [9]Otis, bo. 1816.
667. Jonathan, bo. Feb. 18, 1782; ma. Electa Ferguson.

668. John, bo. May 25, 1784; ma. Patty Umphstead.
669. Eliphalet, bo. Nov. 3, 1786; not married.
670. Dudley, bo. Oct. 23, 1788; ma. Sarah Humphrey.
671. Samuel, bo. Sept. 4, 1791; ma. Hope Allen.
672. Abigail, bo. Oct. 1793; ma. Daniel Katherns; 2d, Mr. Richardson.

(276) Dudley Ladd, of Deerfield, N. H., (son of Paul,[80]) ma. Lydia, dau. of Daniel Haines. He was a deputy sheriff for Rockingham Co. for twenty years, and was a school teacher for quite a number of years. He died July 3, 1818.

Children.

673. John Folsom, bo. April 19, 1775; ma. Dorothy Smith.
674. Mercy, bo. 1783; not married; d. Aug. 1852.
675. Lydia, bo. April 14, 1785; ma. Benjamin Smith, of Epping, N. H. Children: [1]Dudley, bo. Nov. 12, 1804; [2]Stephen, bo. Dec. 2, 1806; [3]Mercia, bo. Dec. 22, 1810; [4]Lydia L., bo. July 9, 1814; [5]Benjamin, bo. July 3, 1818; [6]Mary Jane, bo. Sept. 23, 1822; [7]John Folsom, bo. April 20, 1824. Stephen Smith (2) ma. Mary Robinson, Dec. 3, 1840. Children: [1]Dyer S., bo. March 18, 1849, who ma. Aureanna J. Ladd (2557.)

(280) Simeon Ladd, (son of Paul,[80]) was born in Epping, N. H., Jan. 15, 1757; was a farmer; ma. Lizza Hines, of Nottingham, N. H., where he lived for a time, and removed from there to Winthrop, Me.

Children.

676. Mehitable, bo. ——; ma. Samuel Harvey, Aug. 17, 1795.
677. Thomas, bo. ——; ma. Dorcas Lowell.
678. Mercy, bo. ——; ma. Ansel Blossom.
679. Simeon, Jr., bo. Feb. 23, 1780; ma. Mercy Folsom.
680. Paul, bo. ——; ma. Rebecca Billington. No children. He was killed in 1824, at Winthrop, Me., by the falling of a church frame.
681. Mary, bo. ——; ma. Cyrus Jones.
682. Elizabeth, bo. ——; not married.

(282) Nathaniel Ladd, of Epping, N. H., (son of Paul,[80]) ma. Polly, dau. of Benjamin Smith, 1782. He was educated in the public schools, and was for many years deputy sheriff of Rockingham Co., N. H. In 1800 he removed to Stanstead, Canada, where he died in 1821. His widow died in 1844.

Children.

683. Lois Folsom, bo. June 6, 1786; ma. James Harvey, son of Jonathan and Susan (Hedlock) Harvey, of Nottingham, N. H. Children: [1]Dudley L. Harvey, bo. Aug. 11, 1811; ma. Mary, dau. of Jonathan

and Sarah (Dearborn) Swain. He was educated at the common schools, learned the trade of a cooper, but left it for lumbering, farming, and nursery growing. He began life poor, but is now in good financial circumstances, being the owner of more than three hundred acres of good farming land. Was commissioned as captain in the New Hampshire State militia in 1836, and served as such four years; was appointed justice of the peace in 1846, and served four years; held the office of selectman, and was for three years chairman of the board; was a trustee of the Epping Savings Bank; and for six years was a director in the Rockingham Fire Insurance Co. He has all the requisites of a model farmer, and ranks with the leading agriculturists of that section of New Hampshire. He has kept his eyes and ears open to all sources of information in his favorite field, and has become well and favorably known to a very large circle by his thirty years of contributions to the Boston Cultivator, Germantown Telegraph, and other agricultural journals. (See History of Rockingham Co.) His children: [1]Mary A., bo. Oct. 31, 1845; [2]Jonathan S., bo. Dec. 13, 1850.

[2]Nathaniel G. Harvey, bo. April 1, 1813; ma. 1st, Louisa Lydia Watson Ladd (2407); had no children by her. She died May 27, 1848. He ma. 2d, Helen Hartwich, Nov. 30, 1852. He was educated at the district schools, at the academy at Hampton, N. H., and at the academy at Hopkinton, N. H. Commenced keeping school at the age of 16; taught many years in the district where he resided and in other districts in the town, also in the towns of Nottingham, Deerfield, Brentwood, and other towns in New Hampshire. Was appointed superintendent school committee of Epping, N. H., when quite young. He removed from Epping, N. H., to Beaver Dam, Wis., where he was principal of the high school for twenty years, and was chosen superintendent of public instruction of the city; was interested in real estate; left teaching on account of deafness; sold his property, removed to Chicago, thence to Washington, Ill., where he purchased a farm on which he lived many years; was burnt out, built again, then sold out and bought a farm at Long Pine, Neb., where he now (1888) resides.

[3]Matthew J. Harvey was born October 14, 1821; was educated at the district school, but at the age of 13 he left school to help his father on the farm, and his education after that time was derived from his love of books and his studious habit of reading all the histories, biographies, scientific and political works which at that time came within his reach. He is a farmer, and resides at Red Oak Hill, Epping, N. H., on the farm which he inherited from his father, but has since, by purchase, added to it many acres. He was a Representative from Epping to the New Hampshire Legislature in 1855–6; was a member of the committee on military affairs, and was its secretary. He drew up and presented to the House a series of resolutions on the "Foreign Policy of the National Administration," which

were referred to a special committee of which he was chairman. Since 1847 he has written quite extensively for several papers, including the Boston Cultivator, in which there appeared a number of poems from his pen, viz.: the "Ice Ship," the "Rescue," the "Prophet's Valley," "Natural Music," "October," "Indian Summer," and others. He has also written letters to the Rural American, Boston Post, Journal of Agriculture, and was for twenty years a correspondent of the New England Farmer, and lately of the Manchester Union. He ma. June 1. 1856, Susan F., dau. of Peltiah and Susannah Thompson, of Lee, N. H., who was educated at the academy in Durham, N. H., and at the Mt. Holyoke Female Seminary at South Hadley. His children: [1]Abby E., bo. Aug. 14, 1857, ma. Ulysses S. Osgood, July 14, 1884; [2]James B., bo. Dec. 3, 1858, ma. H. Alice Whitman, Jan. 24, 1883; [3]Joseph T., bo. March 11, 1861, d. Oct. 8, 1862; [4]Fanny M., bo. Oct. 26, 1863, ma. Edward A. Adams, Jan. 11, 1885; [5]Nathaniel, bo. Aug. 8, 1865; [6]John M., bo. Sept. 28, 1868; [7]Matthew, bo. March 6, 1870.

684. Polly, bo. ——; ma. Robert Rowe.
685. Samuel G., bo. 1790; ma. Martha Fox.

(283) Josiah Ladd, of Gilmanton, N. H., (son of Paul,[80]) ma. Mary Gale.

Children.

686. Dudley F., bo. Dec. 23, 1794; ma. Polly Mason. March 18, 1817.
687. Rhoda, bo. Oct. 20, 1796; ma. Ebenezer Varney.
688. Effel, bo. March 22, 1800; d. young.
3707. *Hannah, bo. May 20, 1802; ma. Franklin Forrest.
3708. Josiah, bo. Feb. 12, 1804; d. Aug. 25, 1804.
3709. Henry, bo. July 9, 1805.
3710. Josiah, bo. Feb. 26, 1808; ma. ——.
3711. John, bo. Jan. 21, 1813; ma. Lydia Ann Pervier.
3712. Hazen, bo. Oct. 15, 1815. Lost at sea about 1853.

* Received after the others were entered, hence the break in the number.

(286) James Ladd, of Unity, N. H., (son of Daniel,[89]) ma. Margaret Glidden, Feb. 9, 1775.

Children.

689. Jeremiah, bo. ——; ma. Nancy Rowe.
690. Noah, bo. Oct. 16, 1778; ma. Lucy Bartlett, Sept. 2, 1804.
691. Charles Ira, bo. ——; ma. Peggy Hutoon, Feb. 24, 1811.
692. Mehitable, bo. ——.
693. Abigail, bo. ——.
694. Hannah, bo. ——.
695. ——, bo. ——; ma. —— Gale.

(287) Nathaniel Ladd, of Unity, N. H., (son of Daniel,[89]) ma. Sally Marshall. He d. June 8, 1824. His widow d. April 13, 1834.

Children.

696. Betsey, bo. Nov. 27, 1775; ma. John Thurston, son of Moses and Elizabeth (Clifford) Thurston.
697. Daniel, bo. Oct. 13, 1777; ma. Elizabeth Smith.
698. Moses, bo. March 6, 1779; ma. Lorenda Robinson.
699. Dudley, bo. Aug. 28, 1780; ma. Louisa Perry.
700. Susannah, bo. Aug. 22, 1782; ma. Simeon B. Chase. Children: [1]Daniel, bo. May 17, 1810; [2]Nathaniel L., bo. Oct. 30, 1813; [3]Phebe G., bo. March 15, 1812; [4]Hannah L., bo. Aug. 19, 1815; [5]Amos, bo. Feb. 18, 1818; [6]Joseph, bo. May 1, 1821; [7]Mary, bo. May 1, 1821; [8]Sally, bo. Feb. 22, 1823; [9]Simeon B., bo. Feb. 5, 1829.
701. Lucretia, bo. May 1, 1784; ma. Samuel Daniels. Children: [1]Sylvester, bo. Oct. 10, 1812; [2]Betsey, bo. Oct. 14, 1814; [3]Zarina, bo. May 31, 1816; [4]Almira, bo. April 14, 1818; [5]Louisa S., bo. Dec. 8, 1819; [6]Sylvanus, bo. July 14, 1822; [7]Abigail, bo. May 4, 1824; [8]Lorenda, bo. May 14, 1827.
702. Nathaniel, bo. June 18, 1786; ma. Abigail Weed.
703. Aaron, bo. Nov. 1, 1790; ma. Nancy Buck.
704. John, bo. March 31, 1793; ma. Sally Weed.

(288)   Peter Ladd, of Deerfield, N. H., (son of Daniel,[89]) ma. Abigail Martin. He moved to Mt. Vernon, Me.

Children.

705. John, bo. ——; ma. Nancy Woodcock, March 21, 1806.
706. Betsey, bo. ——; ma. Jonathan ——.
707. Susan, bo. ——; ma. James Smiley.

(289)   Joses Ladd, bo. in Deerfield, N. H., (son of Daniel,[89]) removed to Mt. Vernon, Me.; ma. Rachel Fifield, Oct. 16, 1784. His wife died Oct. 9, 1850.

Children.

708. Joseph, bo. Jan. 14, 1786; ma. Sarah Hamlin.
709. Betsey, bo. June 23, 1789; ma. James Smith.
710. Polly, bo. July 13, 1790; ma. Daniel Towle, Feb. 6, 1808.
711. Rhoda, bo. April 3, 1792; ma. Samuel Sprague.
712. Daniel, bo. Aug. 27, 1793; ma. Rachel Richards.
713. Jesse Eaton, bo. Oct. 10, 1795; ma. Sophronia Worthley, Sept. 11, 1823.
714. Asenath, bo. Dec. 13, 1799; ma. Elijah Howland.
715. Lucinda, bo. Dec. 3, 1801; ma. Thomas Nickerson, March, 1819.
716. Stephen, bo. Nov. 27, 1804; ma. Melinda French, 1828.
717. Joannah, bo. Nov. 27, 1804; ma. Joseph French, Dec. 6, 1823.
718. Susannah, bo. Aug. 22, 1807; ma. Edward French, Oct. 8, 1826.

(291) Samuel Ladd, of Deerfield, N. H., (son of Daniel,[89]) ma. Dolly, dau. of John Brown, of Deerfield, N. H. He d. April, 1794.

Children.

719. Lois, bo. Feb. 14, 1790; ma. Daniel Ring, March 21, 1817.
720. Samuel, bo. 1791.
721. Timothy, bo. Feb. 11, 1792; ma. Mary Lane, of Hampton, N. H.
722. Mehitable, bo. ——.

(293) Jedediah Ladd, of Deerfield, N. H., (son of Daniel,[89]) ma. Nancy, dau. of John Brown, March 20, 1794. She died April 16, 1815. He ma. for his 2d wife Judith Burleigh. No issue by her.

Children.

723. Polly, bo. Dec. 20, 1794; ma. Benjamin O. Bartlett, of Epsom, N. H., June 4, 1817.
724. Daniel, bo. March 4, 1796; ma. Martha Clemmens, May 4, 1820.
725. John, bo. July 31, 1797; ma. Mary Beane, June 19, 1824.
726. Nancy, bo. Dec. 20, 1799; ma. William Robinson, Nov. 27, 1826, of Epsom, N. H. Children: [1]Horace, bo. Sept. 12, 1827; [2]Franklin, bo. April 23, 1827; [3]Susan, bo. May 20, 1833; [4]Thomas, bo. Sept. 28, 1836.
727. Melinda, bo. Sept. 5, 1802; ma. Andrew Ladd (1375,) April 9, 1827.
728. Ruth, bo. May 11, 1806; ma. Thomas Robinson, Oct. 9, 1829.
729. Stephen F., bo. July 22, 1809; ma. Susan Bruce, of Claremont, N. H.
730. Susan, bo. 1813; d. at the age of 20 months.

(301) Stephen Ladd, of Brentwood, N. H., (son of Stephen,[90]) ma. Betsey Beane. He died Nov. 2, 1837.

Children.

731. Levi, bo. July 18, 1798; ma. Arvilla Beane, Nov. 12, 1848. No children.
732. Stephen, bo. April 26, 1800; ma. Dorothy Morrill. No children.

(303) Samuel Ladd, of Brentwood and Melvin Village, N. H., (son of Stephen,[90]) ma. Comfort Dow, of New Hampton, N. H. He died Jan. 17, 1817, and his widow died Feb. 6, 1842.

Children.

733. Ruth, bo. Sept. 21, 1794; ma. Eben C. Gordon, 1818. She d. 1884.
734. Abigail, bo. Oct. 10, 1796; ma. Daniel Morrison, 1816. She d. 1854.
735. Stephen, bo. July 4, 1798; ma. Amanda Austin, 1821.
736. Nancy, bo. 1800; ma. Eben Morrison, 1827. She d. Aug. 1844.
737. Samuel, bo. Dec. 12, 1803; ma. Nancy Young.

738. Lewis, bo. June, 1806; d. Nov. 8, 1865.
739. Jonathan, bo. May, 1808; ma. Susan Young.
740. Levi D., bo. March 10, 1811; ma. Hannah Young.
741. Gordon, bo. Aug. 3, 1813; ma. Dolly Young, Dec. 27, 1840.

(310) John Ladd, of Brentwood, N. H., (son of Stephen,[90]) ma. Lydia Sanborn. She died May 6, 1813. He ma. 2d, Susan Sanborn.

Children.

742. Phebe, bo. Sept. 19, 1806; not married; d. Nov. 20, 1862.
743. Huldah, bo. May 8, 1808; ma. George Waldren. Nov. 30, 1842.
744. Sarah, bo. April 20, 1810; ma. Jeremiah Fletcher.
745. John, Jr., bo. Sept. 20, 1812; ma. Betsey L. Marston, Dec. 26, 1841.

Child by second wife.

746. Samuel, bo. July 6, 1817; ma. Hannah Clement, Feb. 18, 1843. No children. He indulged a hope in Christ while teaching in Plaistow, N. H., in 1837; was baptized by Rev. Benjamin Wheeler. He was ordained as pastor of the Baptist Church of South Hampton, N. H., June 1, 1842, but resigned the following October on account of ill health. He was again pastor of the same church in 1850. He preached in Lyman, Me., Ottawa and Fremont, Ill. He died at his father's, in Brentwood, N. H., in 1854.

(313) John Ladd, of Unity, N. H., (son of John,[92]) ma. Sarah Hibbard. He died Dec. 1843.

Children.

747. John H., bo. Oct. 3, 1798; ma. Anna McCready.
748. Hiram, bo. Aug. 19, 1800; ma. Aurelia Palmer.
749. Enoch H., bo. Oct. 6, 1801; ma. Lucy L. Plumb.
750. Joseph, bo. Oct. 28, 1803; ma. Eliza Johnson.
751. Mary M., bo. Jan. 20, 1806; ma. Rev. Benjamin D. Brewster, June 8, 1835.
752. Ruth B., bo. Feb. 19, 1808; ma. Rev. Jacob French; 2d, Benjamin Bowls, of Lisbon, N. H.

(318) Josiah Ladd, of Unity, N. H., (son of John,[92]) ma. Anna Chappell, of Lancaster, N. H., Nov. 26, 1801. He died Dec. 30, 1829. His widow died Sept. 18, 1857.

Children.

753. Daniel, bo. Jan. 22, 1804; ma. Charlotte H. Ketchell.
754. Crawford, bo. Nov. 8, 1805; ma. Jane Byington, 1841.
755. Hannah, bo. March 4, 1808; ma. John Thurber, Sept. 6, 1826.
756. Mehitable, bo. Sept. 7, 1810; d. Dec. 24, 1824.
757. Josiah, bo. Aug. 7, 1813; d. March, 1814.

758. Stephen, bo. Sept. 17, 1815; ma. Mrs. Harriet A. Smith.
759. Josiah, bo. Jan. 26, 1818; ma. Sarah Swasey.
760. Ann M., bo. April 21, 1821; ma. Dr. Abel W. Brown.
761. John, bo. Sept. 15, 1824; ma. Sarah Hathaway, Sept. 1849.

(321)   Jeremiah Ladd, of Alexandria, N. H., (son of Nathaniel,[96]) ma. Priscilla Sanborn. She died, and he ma. for his 2d wife, Meribah Simons, July 24, 1791.

Children.

762. Peter, bo. ——; ma. Rhoda Quimby, May 27, 1789.
763. Elizabeth, bo. ——; ma. Nathaniel Heath.

Children by second wife.

764. Abigail, bo. ——; ma. Jeremiah Phillips.
765. Samuel, bo. ——; not married.
766. Aaron, bo. ——; not married.
767. Moses, bo. ——; not married.
768. John, bo. March 21, 1804; ma. Fanny Collins, June, 1828.
769. Jane, bo. ——; ma. Joseph Smith.
770. Sarah, bo. ——; ma. William Parsons.
771. Susan, bo. ——; ma. Edwin Dodge.
772. William, bo. ——; not married.

(322)   Nathaniel Ladd, of Mt. Vernon, Me., (son of Nathaniel,[96]) ma. ——, who died. He ma. 2d, Mrs. Miriam (Ladd) Proctor, dau. of Daniel Ladd (89,) of Deerfield, N. H.

Children.

773. Timothy, bo. ——; ma. Jane Coy.
774. John, bo. 1777; ma. Lydia French, Sept. 9, 1809. No children.
775. Moses, bo. 1778; ma. Nancy Roberts, Dec. 17, 1803.
776. Sally, bo. ——; ma. Joshua Wells.
777. Hannah, bo. ——; ma. Timothy White.
778. Jonathan, bo. 1784; d. April 7, 1803.
779. Polly, bo. ——; ma. Moses Batchellor.
780. Dorothy, bo. ——; ma. Daniel Carr.
781. Nancy, bo. ——; ma. Rev. Thomas Doloff.
782. Betsey, bo. ——; ma. —— Young; 2d, David Watson.

Child by second wife.

783. Nathaniel, bo. Feb. 12, 1816; ma. Drusilla Elliot.

(324)   Isaac Ladd, of Alexandria, N. H., (son of Nathaniel,[96]) ma. Dolly Blaisdell. He was a cooper in Sandown, N. H., in 1770. In 1775 he bought of his father, in that town, fourteen acres of land.

Children.

784. Hannah, bo. ——; ma. —— Somers.
785. Sally, bo. July 1, 1776; ma. Josiah Sanborn.
786. Jonathan, bo. June 21, 1777; ma. Hannah Ball.
787. William, bo. ——; ma. Hannah Pike, of Hebron, N. H.
788. Peter, bo. ——; not married.
789. Martha, bo. ——; ma. Daniel Bailey.
790. Isaac, Jr., bo. July 14, 1784; ma. Huldah Heath.
791. Nathan, bo. ——; ma. Sally Kemp.
792. Dolly, bo. ——; ma. David Morse.
793. John, bo. ——; ma. Mary C. Huse, of Sandown, N. H.

(326) Benjamin Ladd, of Deerfield, N. H., (son of Nathaniel,[96]) ma. Deborah, dau. of Jude Allen, of Deerfield, N. H. She d., and he ma. for 2d wife ——.

Children.

794. Deborah, bo. 1777; ma. Joseph Fisk, Aug. 17, 1799.
795. Benjamin, Jr., bo. 1779; ma. Betsey Blaisdell. He d. 1810.
796. Salome, bo. 1781; ma. Benjamin Seavey, Aug. 1, 1802.
797. Eleazer, bo. March 26, 1783; ma. Betsey Rollins, Nov. 15, 1802.
798. Sally, bo. 1785; ma. David Rollins, of Gilmanton, N. H.

Children by second wife.

799. Lavinna, bo. ——; ma. Charles Higgins, of Searsport, Me.
800. Benjamin, bo. Nov. 29, 1814; ma. Joannah Field, Nov. 17, 1840.
801. Hannah, bo. ——; ma. Royal Higgins.

(329) Jonathan Ladd, (son of Trueworthy,[98]) was born in Kingston, N. H., Aug. 7, 1751. He settled in Antrim, N. H., about 1785; lived there nearly ten years, and then removed to Tunbridge, Vt. He ma. ——.

Child.

802. Robert, bo. ——; ma. Olive Chapman, June 5, 1800.

(331) John Ladd, of Pembroke, N. H., (son of Trueworthy,[98]) ma. Jerusha, dau. of Caleb and Mehitable Lovejoy, June 6, 1775. He died June 8, 1835.

Child.

803. Mehitable, bo. March 9, 1776; ma. Benjamin Fowler, Jan. 15, 1795, son of Simonds and Hannah (Weeks) Fowler, of New Market, N. H. Children: [1]Jerusha, bo. June 24, 1795, ma. Chandler Hutchinson; [2]Esther, bo. March 16, 1797, ma. William Abbott, Jr.; [3]Mehitable, bo. May 27, 1798, not ma.; [4]Benjamin, bo. March 17, 1800, ma. Hannah Campbell; [5]John Ladd, bo. Aug. 1, 1801, ma. Lavinia Abbott; [6]Samuel, bo. Sept. 30, 1803, not ma., d. Dec. 1878; [7]Polly, bo. July

7, 1805, d. July 28, 1805; [8]David, bo. April 5, 1807, d. May 9, 1807; [9]Asa, bo. Feb. 23, 1811, ma. Mary D. C. Knox; [10]Clarissa, bo. Feb. 21, 1815, d. May 16, 1815; [11]Trueworthy Ladd, bo. Dec. 21, 1816, ma. Catharine Sargent.

(340) Daniel Ladd, of Courtlandville, N. Y., (son of Daniel,[105]) ma. Abigail Crossman, April 14, 1808. He d. Sept. 21, 1868.

Children.

804. Celia Carsey, bo. Nov. 1, 1809; ma. Lyman Anise, June 21, 1830.
805. Clarissa, bo. July 19, 1811; ma. Horace Baker, July 14, 1831.
806. Benjamin Franklin, bo. March 2, 1814; ma. Susan Smith, Sept. 23, 1835.
807. William, bo. Jan. 23, 1816; ma. Sally Willis, Jan. 2, 1842.
808. Sullivan, bo. Oct. 6, 1819; ma. Mary Trowbridge, Dec. 22, 1851.
809. Leander, bo. Dec. 11, 1823; ma. Mary F. Brown, Nov. 15, 1850.

(341) Enoch Ladd, of Franklin, Conn., (son of Daniel,[105]) ma. Mary Wilbur, March 2, 1814.

Children.

810. Eliza Ann, bo. Dec. 20, 1814.
811. Enoch Haskins, bo. May 13, 1816; ma. Mary S. Griswold, Dec. 26, 1841.
812. Daniel Valson, bo. April 30, 1818; ma. Jane Matilda Griswold.

(242) Uriah Ladd, of Franklin, Conn., (son of Daniel,[105]) ma. Zurvia Chapman, dau. of John Chapman, Nov. 10, 1816.

Children.

813. Uriah, bo. Sept. 8, 1819; ma. Catharine Burdick, April 5, 1848.
814. Benjamin, bo. Sept. 13, 1827.

(346) Asa Ladd, of Enosburg, Vt., (son of Asa,[108]) ma. Martha Chase, Sept. 14, 1784. He died June 1, 1851, and his wife died June 11, 1820.

Children.

815. Alpheus, bo. May 8, 1785; ma. Jane French.
816. Ruth, bo. Oct. 26, 1786; ma. Samuel Smith, Nov. 1, 1807.
817. Asa, bo. Sept. 17, 1788; ma. Louisa Hopkins, Dec. 3, 1812.
818. Sarah, bo. Feb. 22, 1791; ma. James Mathews, Sept. 23, 1823.
819. Rebecca, bo. July 14, 1793; ma. Ira Forsyth, Dec. 1, 1814.
820. Avery S., bo. Nov. 26, 1796; ma. Lucy Cole, Feb. 13, 1820.
821. Abigail, bo. Feb. 5, 1799; ma. Rev. Raymond Austin, Oct. 2, 1817.
822. Edna, bo. Dec. 12, 1803; ma. Anson Fassett, March 16, 1826.
823. David M., bo. Feb. 20, 1806; ma. Harriet Hinman, April 9, 1829.
824. Martha, bo. July 11, 1808; ma. Asa Darwin, March 16, 1842.

(347) Richard Ladd, of Hopkinton, N. H., (son of Asa,[108]) ma. Bettie Woodman, of Newburyport, Dec. 9, 1790. He was divorced, and she ma. Benjamin Fellows, of Hopkinton, N. H., June 28, 1803.

Child.

825. Timothy, bo. June 30, 1791; ma. Deidamia Swallow, Aug. 26, 1819.

(353) Joseph Ladd, of Haverhill, N. H., (son of Ezekiel,[109]) ma. Sarah Ring, of Newburyport. He was educated at the public schools, and was a merchant at Haverhill, N. H., many years. He held the office of town clerk in 1799, 1800, 1803, 1805, and 1806. He d. Dec. 21, 1836. His widow d. March 8, 1851.

Children.

826. Pamelia, bo. June 27, 1786; d. Nov. 18, 1832; not married.
827. Lavinia, bo. Sept. 18, 1787; ma. John Buxton. She d. Aug. 20, 1855. Children: [1]Harriet B., bo. 1816; [2]Charlotte, bo. 1819; [3]Mary T., bo. 1821; [4]Sarah L., bo. 1823; [5]Lavinia L., bo. 1825; [6]Henry M., bo. 1827.
828. Joseph, bo. May 20, 1789; not married; d. Nov. 6, 1840.
829. Otis Freeman, bo. Feb. 23, 1791; ma. Caroline R. Heath.
830. Persis, bo. Jan. 11, 1793; ma. Dea. Daniel Thompson. He was a blacksmith, and lived many years in Francestown, N. H.
831. Lewis, bo. Aug. 13, 1794; ma. Catharine Colburn.
832. Sally, bo. June 27, 1796; d. Jan. 25, 1810.
833. Amasa Scott, bo. March 17, 1799; ma. Mary Ann Childs, Oct. 31, 1818.
834. William Hutchins, bo. July 4, 1801; d. at Valparaiso, S. A., Dec. 1824.
835. Louisa B., bo. Aug. 4, 1803; ma. Warren Ives. She died Feb. 1871.
836. Peabody Webster, bo. Aug. 15, 1805; ma. Elizabeth Lowell Johnson.
837. Calvin P., bo. Aug. 1809; ma. Mary Parson Harmon, Sept. 1, 1830.
838. Charlotte, bo. Aug. 18, 1814; d. March 14, 1815.

(355) Ezekiel Ladd, of Haverhill, N. H., (son of Ezekiel,[109]) ma. Elizabeth Swan, 1796. He was moderator in 1822, 1824, 1826, 1827, and 1830, was selectman 1810–11, treasurer 1810–11, and representative in 1815.

Children.

839. Austin, bo. May 22, 1798; ma. Miriam Farman.
840. Isaac, bo. May 22, 1800; d. July 10, 1802.
841. Hiram, bo. June 12, ——; ma. Eliza Crouch, Dec. 16, 1830.
842. George W., bo. May 9, 1805; d. at New Orleans, Sept. 20, 1847.
843. Horatio Nelson, bo. Nov. 11, 1807; not married.
844. Caroline, bo. Feb. 9, 1809; not married.
845. Eliza, bo. June 10, 1810; not married; d. Nov. 15, 1867.
846. Harriet, bo. July 31, 1813; ma. Hiram Tracy, of Burlington, Vt.

(358) Moody Ladd, of Haverhill, N. H., (son of Ezekiel,[109]) ma. Olive Williams.

Children.
847. Julia, bo. May 5, 1805; not married; d. Nov. 3, 1877.
848. Harvey Williams, bo. Nov. 24, 1810; not married; d. Aug. 30, 1839.
849. Franklin Hutchins, bo. Nov. 24, 1810; not married; d. Oct. 5, 1842.
850. Oliver Williams, bo. March 9, 1815; d. Aug. 8, 1865.
851. Martha, bo. Dec. 24, 1817; ma. Thomas Anderson. Children: [1]Ellen, [2]Frank, [3]Carrie J., [4]Mary, [5]Albert.
852. Emily, bo. Oct. 21, 1820; ma. J. C. Gile, Sept. 5, 1850. Children: [1]Mary Emma, [2]Willie H.
853. John Quincy Adams, bo. April 25, 1828; ma. Elizabeth Brown, of Hartford, Conn., 1850.

(359) James Ladd, bo. in Haverhill, N. H., July 6, 1782, (son of Ezekiel,[109]) ma. Lucy Sellors, Oct. 29, 1807. When twenty years old he went to Portsmouth, N. H., where he was in business for several years; was in the Custom House for twenty years. He removed to Boston and from there to Salisbury. He died Sept. 20, 1873. His wife died June 14, 1865.

Children.
854. James Leander Sellors, bo. July 23, 1808; ma. Henrietta B. Anthony.
855. Sophia Adala, bo. May 11, 1810; ma. Andrew W. Bell, Jr.
856. Lucy Amanda, bo. Nov. 19, 1811; ma. James M. Story. She d. March 8, 1876.
857. Charles Edwin, bo. Feb. 4, 1815; d. June 20, 1846.
858. Frances Matilda, bo. Dec. 28, 1816; not married.
859. Cecelia E., bo. May 22, 1819; d. Aug. 10, 1820.
860. Cecelia E., bo. Jan. 18, 1821.
861. Ruth Marie, bo. Nov. 25, 1823; ma. Silas Frost.

(361) Jesse Ladd, of Salem, N. H., (son of Daniel,[110]) ma. Thankful Holmestead, Sept. 7, 1788. He removed to Northern New York. He died Oct. 12, 1804, at Elizabethtown, N. Y.

Children.
862. Dorothy, bo. Aug. 19, 1789.
863. Ann, bo. May 5, 1791; ma. —— Hartshorn, of Boston. She d. June 1, 1827.
864. Betsey, bo. March 30, 1793; ma. Elijah Alvord, June 7, 1824. She d. Sept. 9, 1876.
865. John, bo. Jan. 2, 1796; d. Aug. 7, 1796.
866. Jesse, bo. Aug. 3, 1797; ma. Roby Wilbur, of Little Compton, R. I., March 10, 1822.
867. James, bo. May 16, 1799; ma. Charity Willey, Jan. 16, 1825.

868. Nancy, bo. Feb. 25, 1801; ma. Philip Brien, Dec. 25, 1855.
869. Lois, bo. March 3, 1803; ma. William Bush, 1834. She d. July, 1838.

(364) Daniel Ladd, of Plymouth, N. H., (son of Daniel,[110]) ma. Lydia Dow, of Plymouth, N. H., Oct. 8, 1801.

Children.

870. George W., bo. ——; ma. Catharine ——.
871. Bela Orlando, bo. 1805; ma. Elizabeth Robertson, Dec. 1, 1831.
872. William H., bo. Feb. 12, 1807; ma. Hannah B. Goodrich.
873. Charles, bo. ——.

(365) Joshua Ladd, of Salem, N. H., (son of Daniel,[110]) ma. Sally Merrill, Sept. 1, 1803.

Children.

874. Sampson, bo. Dec. 18, 1804; ma. Elmira Jones.
875. Isabel, bo. Feb. 7, 1806; ma. Darius Morse. She died 1837.
876. Dorothy, bo. Aug. 25, 1808; ma. John R. Jones, 1833.
877. Esther M., bo. May 15, 1810; ma. William B. Heath, 1832.
878. Perley M., bo. March 2, 1812; ma. Hannah Reidhead, Dec. 1839.
879. Emeline S., bo. March 1, 1816; not married; d. 1840.
880. Hannah D., bo. Jan. 23, 1818; ma. G. S. Phippen, of Melrose.

(366) John Ladd, of Boston, (son of Daniel,[110]) ma. Eusebia Henry, of Lunenburgh, Vt., Sept. 1, 1805.

Children.

881. John, Jr., bo. April 2, 1806; not married.
882. Mary Jane, bo. Sept. 23, 1809; not married.
883. Daniel Gorham, bo. Sept. 12, 1811; ma. Betsey Jane Trumbull.
884. Elizabeth Ann, bo. Jan. 7, 1815; ma. Samuel H. Brown.
885. Eleanor Dean, bo. Sept. 9, 1819; ma. James F. Sargent.
886. George Henry, bo. Dec. 13, 1821; ma. Sarah Darling. No children.
887. Caroline Matilda, bo. Feb. 28, 1825; ma. James W. Peck. Children: [1]James Benjamin, [2]George Walter.

(367) William Ladd, of Haverhill, N. H., (son of Samuel,[112]) ma. Abigail Spaulding. His will was proved May 30, 1823.

Children.

888. Elvira M., bo. June 12, 1799; ma. Horace Spaulding, June 25, 1825.
889. Abigail Maria, bo. April 11, 1805.
890. Martha Phillips, bo. June 17, 1807.
891. Mary Ann, bo. May 27, 1809.
892. Azel Parkhurst, bo. Sept. 5, 1811; ma. Louisa M. Burrill.
893. Cynthia Hastings, bo. Aug. 3, 1815.
894. William, bo. ——.

895. Laben, bo. ——.
896. Levi Spaulding, bo. ——.

(373) Jonathan Ladd, of Haverhill, N. H., (son of Samuel,[112]) ma. Mary Burbeck. He died Nov. 9, 1878.

Children.

897. Hastings A., bo. July 15, 1823; ma. Rebecca B. Haven.
898. Martha. bo. ——; ma. H. B. Sherman.
899. Mary, bo. ——.
900. Charles L., bo. ——.
901. Cynthia Hastings, bo. 1830; ma. Henry Carr.
902. Eliza Swan, bo. May 28, 1832; ma. —— Chapman.

(374) Samuel Ladd, of Haverhill, N. H., (son of Samuel,[112]) ma. Mary Ward, of Haverhill, N. H., Oct. 18, 1822. He d. April 2, 1841. His widow d. May 8, 1872.

Children.

903. Mariana, bo. July 3, 1829; ma. W. A. Lincoln.
904. Henry B., bo. Aug. 15, 1834; ma. Eliza Lather; 2d, Eliza Graham. No children.
905. Mary Isabel, bo. Aug. 12, 1838; ma. William Hyde. Children: [1]James B., bo. 1864; [2]Martha B., bo. 1865; [3]William; [4]Lula May; [5]Isabella.

(377) Horace Hall Ladd, of Haverhill, N. H., (son of Samuel,[112]) ma. Amenda Jutua, of Boston, Jan. 16, 1833. He died in New York, March 12, 1866.

Children.

906. Mary Frances, bo. July 10, 1834, in Boston; d. in Lyndon, Vt., July 19, 1867.
907. Horace Hall, bo. Sept. 14, 1837; d. in New York, April 22, 1838.

(378) Daniel Ladd, of Newburyport, (son of John,[113]) ma. Elizabeth Huse, of Newburyport, dau. of Samuel Huse. He died July 12, 1846.

Children.

908. William Huse, bo. June 22, 1811; ma. Sally Lane, 1843; 2d, Mrs. Harriet (Colby) Brown.
909. Elizabeth, bo. July 12, 1813; ma. Joseph Janvrien, Dec. 25, 1833.
910. Joseph, bo. April 30, 1815; ma. Louis Aguste Marie Soldan, June 2, 1844.
911. Mary Ann, bo. March 8, 1818; ma. John M. Boyson, Oct. 25, 1844.

(386) Moses Ladd (son of John,[113]) was born in Haverhill, N. H. From there he went to Mt. Desert, Me., where he ma. Sarah Luvey about 1801. After his marriage he returned and settled in Newbury, Vt., (across the river from Haverhill, N. H.,) where four of his children were born. He enlisted as a soldier in the war of 1812, and died at Plattsburgh, N. Y., of canker-rash. Soon after his death, in 1812, his widow, with her children, returned to her father's house at Mt. Desert, Me., where Sarah, their youngest child, was born.

Children.

912. Daniel, bo. Nov. 11, 1803; ma. Elizabeth R. Gott. Dec. 23, 1824.
913. Susan, bo. Aug. 1805; ma. Hiram Candage.
914. Irene Lorilla, bo. March 11, 1807; ma. Jonathan Stanley, 1827. Children: [1]Thomas Hanley, ma. Abigail Spaulding. [2]Hannah, bo. Oct. 9, 1829, ma. Albion Moore, Dec. 25, 1881. [3]Sarah L., bo. Sept. 26, 1831, ma. Nathaniel N. Tucker, Sept. 29, 1857, and had children: [1]Horace D., bo. Feb. 15, 1859, d. June 25, 1860; [2]Lena S., bo. Feb. 20, 1866; [3]Edward P., bo. Oct. 29, 1868; [4]George, bo. April 25, 1870, d. July, 1872. [4]Lucinda, bo. Sept. 12, 1833, ma. John Stanley, Jan. 1, 1856. [5]Mary E., bo. Feb. 1, 1835. [6]Elizabeth, bo. Dec. 21, 1837, d. Sept. 1848. [7]Hiram, bo. May 1, 1842, d. Aug. 3, 1848. [8]Margaret, bo. June 8, 1840, ma. —— Fernal, and d. Aug. 30, 1867. [9]Gilman, bo. Sept. 20, 1844, d. June 18, 1861. [10]Abigail, bo. March 18, 1847, d. Sept. 29, 1848.
915. Hiram, bo. May 28, 1809; ma. Jane Rowen, of Liverpool, Eng. No children.
916. Sarah, bo. Jan. 20, 1813; ma. Josiah Closson.

(405) Timothy Ladd, of Piermont, N. H., (son of James,[116]) ma. Esther Pillsbury.

Child.

917. Emeline, bo. May 11, 1822; ma. John Hartwell, Dec. 11, 1847.

(406) Ethan Smith Ladd, of Haverhill, N. H., (son of James,[116]) ma. Roxanna Davis. He was a soldier in the war of 1812. He died Dec. 24, 1879. His wife died Nov. 3, 1879.

Children.

918. Eliza Ann, bo. Sept. 1821; ma. James H. Harriman.
919. Catharine, bo. 1825; ma. H. M. Dunbar.
920. Horace, bo. ——; not married.
921. Charles, bo. ——; not married.

(407) Samuel Ladd, of Waltham, (son of James,[116]) ma. Mary Dudley, dau. of Ethan and Elizabeth Melvin, Nov. 21, 1822. He died June 27, 1882. His wife died Jan. 26, 1875.

Children.

922. Mary Hannah, bo. April 19, 1825; ma. George Barry, Oct. 31, 1849.
923. Samuel James, bo. March 9, 1830.
924. Adeline, bo. June 13, 1834; d. Feb. 23, 1851.

(411) Elisha Locke Ladd, of Atlanta, Ga., (son of Jonathan,[118]) ma. Asanath Batchelder. He died April 28, 1845. His widow died Sept. 17, 1863.

Children.

925. Daniel B., bo. July 19, 1822; ma. Lucinda E. Wiley, April 30, 1846. No children.
926. Roxana, bo. Jan. 17, 1825; d. Dec. 13, 1832.
927. Phebe B., bo. Feb. 22, 1827; d. Jan. 13, 1833.
928. Stephen B., bo. March 23, 1829; d. Jan. 23, 1833.
929. Alonzo Chace, bo. Jan. 30, 1832; ma. Mary E. Ladd, Oct. 27, 1858.

(413) Isaac Ladd, of Warren, Trumbull Co., Ohio, (son of Jonathan,[118]) ma. Nancy Riggs. He died Oct. 15, 1849.

Children.

930. William, bo. 1820; d. 1821.
931. Henry R., bo. Oct. 13, 1822.
932. Martha, bo. June, 1824.
933. Isaac, bo. 1826.

(418) Henry Ladd, of Chazy, N. Y., (son of Dr. Henry,[128]) ma. Lavina Hawkins, Jan. 1789.

Children.

934. Nabby, bo. Oct. 10, 1789; not married; d. Jan. 8, 1864.
935. James, bo. March 22, 1791; ma. Melissa Chipman.
936. Lemuel, bo. March 26, 1793; ma. Hannah Andrews.
937. Allura, bo. Aug. 9, 1795; ma. Rev. Phineas Doane. She d. Aug. 22, 1852.
938. Benoni, bo. July 27, 1797; d. July 10, 1801.
939. Jonathan R., bo. Nov. 28, 1799; ma. Elizabeth Thomas.
940. Henry, bo. ——; d. young.
941. Henry, bo. Oct. 16, 1802; ma. Zervia Sherman, Nov. 1833.
942. Dolly, bo. March 7, 1805; ma. Douglas Adams.
943. Hiram, bo. Oct. 2, 1807; ma. Adeline M. Dickerson, Nov. 3, 1833.
944. George E. M. J. F., bo. Oct. 27, 1809; ma. Elizabeth Bell, Nov. 13, 1831.

(419) Herman Ladd, of Avon, N. Y., (son of Dr. Henry,[128]) ma. Mary Morse.

Children.

945. Warren, bo. 1790; ma. Alda Whimple.
946. Martha, bo. 1801; ma. Ira M. Daniels.
947. Fanny, bo. 1804; ma. William Pierson.
948. Marie, bo. Aug. 17, 1809; ma. Robert F. Stage.

(424) Benoni Ladd, of Benson, Vt., (son of Dr. Henry,[128]) ma. Roanna Ransom, May 28, 1806. She died Jan. 29, 1813. He ma. for his 2d wife Abigail Nash, Sept. 6, 1813.

Children.

949. Abial Richardson, bo. April 13, 1807; ma. Ann Elizabeth Farnsworth, April 28, 1833.
950. Perre Green, bo. Oct. 11, 1809; ma. Tryphena Moore.
951. Irena Wells, bo. Jan. 9, 1811; ma. Horace Slosson.
952. Roanna Ransom, bo. Jan. 22, 1813; ma. Walt Merrill. Children: ¹Burke, ²Herbert, ³Henry, ⁴Harriet.

Children by second wife.

953. Woodward N., bo. June 28, 1817.
954. George C., bo. Sept. 6, 1821; d. Feb. 28, 1822.
955. Lafayette, bo. June 17, 1824; d. April 24, 1825.
956. Harriet K., bo. Feb. 4, 1826; d. March 3, 1844.

(429) Roger Ladd, of Rutland, Vt., (son of Nathaniel,[129]) ma. Sarah Henderson, 1807, of Salem, N. Y. He d. Nov. 28, 1859.

Children, all born in Chittenden, Vt.

957. Laura, bo. Nov. 20, 1808; ma. Dr. Thomas Manly, March 21, 1831.
958. Sophronia, bo. Dec. 7, 1809; ma. Lucius V. Brice, Jan. 1, 1840. She d. April 24, 1882.
959. Almond D., bo. April 1, 1811; ma. Anna M. Poorler, Feb. 22, 1846. No children. He d. April 23, 1877.
960. Amasa, bo. Feb. 7, 1813; d. April 27, 1813.
961. Spencer, bo. Feb. 11, 1814; ma. Lucy E. Hudson, March 1, 1840.
962. Green, bo. April 5, 1816; d. Aug. 26, 1816.
963. Phebe, bo. April 5, 1816; d. Aug. 24, 1822.
964. Naomi, bo. June 7, 1818; ma. Lucius W. Wright, Feb. 5, 1837.
965. Helen Diana, bo. April 28, 1820; not married; d. March 5, 1877.
966. Charles Green, bo. June 22, 1822; ma. Ermina Williams.

(434) Nathaniel Ladd, of Flint, Mich., (son of Nathaniel,[129]) ma. Charlotte Stoughtenburg, of Toronto, Canada.

Child.

967. Pauline, bo. ——.

(438) Nathaniel Ladd, of Woodstock, Vt., (son of Nathaniel,[132]) ma. Patience Simmons. She d. Dec. 8, 1819. He ma. 2d, Lydia Lord; was divorced from her, and ma. 3d, Sally Gilbert, Sept. 17, 1826. She d. April 12, 1856. He d. Aug. 25, 1844.

Children.

968. Hope S., bo. Aug. 23, 1812; ma. Amasa Paine.
969. Franklin, bo. March 12, 1815; not married. Lived at Woodstock, Vt.
970. Thankful S., bo. May 25, 1817; ma. Edward Edgerton, of Hyde Park, Vt.

Children by third wife.

971. Marshall Conant, bo. June 29, 1828; ma. Phebe Doggett.
972. Charles Nathaniel, bo. Sept. 9, 1833; not married; d. Nov. 8, 1859.

(439) Ephraim Ladd, of Wolcott, Vt., (son of Nathaniel,[132]) ma. Thankful Simmons.

Children.

973. William C., bo. July 5, 1816; ma. Mary Aiken, 1841.
974. Philura, bo. 1822; ma. Marcus Peck, Dec. 18, 1853.

(440) Mason Ladd, (son of Nathaniel,[132]) was born in Woodstock, Vt., March 23, 1788. He ma. Susan Dutton, of Woodstock, Vt., dau. of Capt. David and Elizabeth (Damon) Dutton, June 22, 1815. She was born April 7, 1793, and died Jan. 25, 1867. He was a successful farmer; lived on the old homestead, and died there June 14, 1871. They celebrated their golden wedding June 22, 1865.

Children.

975. David D., bo. Aug. 7, 1816; ma. Marian Pink, Jan. 1841. No children.
976. Edwin O., bo. Dec. 13, 1817; ma. Sarah A. Crandall, Feb. 27, 1845.
977. Elizabeth D., bo. Oct. 18, 1819; ma. M. R. Allen Savage, of Stowe, Vt.
978. Susan M., bo. Aug. 6, 1821; d. Aug. 7, 1840.
979. Abigail S., bo. Aug. 19, 1823; ma. Harper I. Savage, Jan. 4, 1843.
980. Mary S., bo. Nov. 6, 1825; ma. L. Henry Dismore, July 20, 1851.
981. Harriet F., bo. Jan. 29, 1833; ma. Franklin B. Rice, Sept. 2, 1863.
982. Mason W., bo. Jan. 9, 1839; ma. Caroline Walker, Nov. 26, 1861.

(444) Anson Ladd, of Tunbridge, Vt., (son of Samuel,[133]) ma. Ruth Moulton, of Tunbridge, Vt.

Children.

983. Ruth, bo. ——.
984. Anson, bo. ——.
985. Sarah, bo. ——.
986. Darwin, bo. ——.

(447) Samuel Ladd, of Tunbridge, Vt., (son of Samuel,[133]) went from Tunbridge Vt., to Farmington, Me.; ma. Esther H., dau. of Reuben and Lucy (Everett) Turner, of Farmington, Me., Jan. 11, 1809. He taught school many years, and was a farmer. He died in Temple, Me. His wife Esther died Feb. 28, 1839. He ma. 2d, Phebe Bacon, of Byron, Me., in 1840.

Children.

987. Electa, bo. Nov. 22, 1810; ma. Hiram Wyman, July 2, 1834, of Auburn, Me. Children: [1]Hannibal G., bo. July 2, 1835, ma. Lewis Pulsifer, Nov. 1864; [2]Esther E., bo. Feb. 19, 1838, ma. William Sturtevant, 1857; [3]George P., bo. March 27, 1840, ma. Maria Jones, 1860; [4]Pliney Ladd, bo. April 25, 1843, ma. Sarah Howard, 1873; [5]Mary S., bo. May 23, 1847, ma. Joseph Robinson, 1870; [6]Julia F., bo. April 13, 1853.
988. Oliver Hazard Perry, bo. July 6, 1814; ma. Emily Keene.
989. Lucy Ann, bo. Aug. 15, 1816; ma. Charles Palmer. He d. Jan. 20, 1861. Children: [1]Jane H., bo. May 11, 1841. [2]Charles W., bo. May 17, 1843. He enlisted in the 28th Maine Reg., Co. B, served his time, re-enlisted in the 2d Maine Cavalry, and died in the hospital at New Orleans, Aug. 6, 1864. [3]Nancy A., bo. Feb. 24, 1845. [4]Rose M., bo. Dec. 17, 1848.
990. Caroline, bo. April 30, 1818; ma. David S. Masterman. Children: [1]Phebe Maria, bo. July 3, 1843; [2]Esther Jane, bo. April 7, 1845; [3]Clara Ann, bo. May 5, 1848; [4]Eliza Evelyn, bo. Nov. 15, 1854.
991. Pliny Day, bo. June 20, 1822; ma. Sophia Keene; 2d, Sarah Halley.
992. Laura, bo. March 30, 1824; ma. William Coombs. Children: [1]Esther, bo. Oct. 28, 1845; [2]Emma, bo. Dec. 12, 1847; [3]Hattie, bo. April 2, 1851; [4]William P., bo. Nov. 27, 1860.
993. Porter, bo. Feb. 1826; ma. Lizzie Perkins.
994. Marcia, bo. July 15, 1830; ma. Levi Hersey.
995. Hiram, bo. Sept. 27, 1832; ma. Eva Bass.
996. Charlotte, bo. Oct. 17, 1835; ma. Enoch Harlow.

Children by second wife.

997. Lucia A., bo. Jan. 1841; ma. Hollis Harlow.
998. Samuel, bo. 1843; not married; d. 1868.
999. Frank, bo. ——.
1000. Milo, bo. ——.
1001. Charles, bo. ——.

(449) John Reddington Ladd, of Tunbridge, Vt., (son of Samuel,[133]) ma. Sarah Kingsbury, Jan. 20, 1817.

Children.

1002. Ruth R., bo. Aug. 5, 1817; not married; d. in South America.
1003. William R., bo. Oct. 7, 1818; not married; d. at Royalton, Vt., 1840.

1004. Isaac Watts, bo. Jan. 1, 1820; not married; d. in South America.
1005. Lydia H., bo. 1821; not married; d. at Royalton, Vt., 1843.
1006. Elizabeth R., bo. 1823; d. in Lowell, 1844.
1007. Sarah, bo. ——.
1008. Anson, bo. ——.

(454) Ralph Ladd, of Sharon, Vt., (son of Ashbel,[135]) was a farmer, and lived on the homestead of his father. He ma. Dec. 21, 1815, Persis, dau. of Daniel and Betsey (Buell) Robinson, of Strafford, Vt. She d. April 19, 1883. He d. Sept. 3, 1877.

Children.

1009. Chester B., bo. May 14, 1820; ma. Charlotte Brown.
1010. Ephraim, bo. July 4. 1822; d. 1825.
1011. Semantha, bo. Aug. 22, 1825; ma. Pelatiah T. Abbott, 1852.

(455) Alfred Ladd, of George, Vt., (son of Ashbel,[135]) ma. Samantha Ives, March 28, 1819. She was born in Wallingford, Conn., Dec. 1, 1800.

Children.

1012. Charles J., bo. Dec. 12, 1819; ma. Elma C. Willis, Oct. 14, 1853.
1013. Ephraim Lewis, bo. July 22, 1823; ma. Fannie Ann Leonard, March 26, 1848.
1014. Louisa Ann, bo. Jan. 20, 1826; d. Sept. 7, 1844.
1015. Cordelia W., bo. April 7, 1833; ma. Chas. A. Hotchkiss, Aug. 10, 1859.

(457) Alpheus Ladd, of Stafford, Vt., (son of Oliver,[136]) ma. Mary Babcock, April 4, 1782. He died Jan. 28, 1833.

Children.

1016. Polly, bo. April 4, 1785; ma. Dr. Eleazer Baldwin, Nov. 1803.
1017. Alpheus, bo. Aug. 4, 1787; ma. Betsey Carpenter, Aug. 29, 1809.
1018. Clarrissa, bo. Jan. 13, 1792; ma. Joseph Sanborn; 2d, Joseph Parker.
1019. Marilla, bo. Feb. 25, 1794; ma. Abraham Brewster, Jan. 25, 1834.
1020. Sally, bo. April 4, 1797; ma. Lyman Brockway; 2d, Calvin Davis.

(461) Frederick Ladd, Jr., of Sharon, Vt., (son of Frederick,[138]) ma. Ann Chandler, of Strafford, Vt., March 12, 1817. He d. Dec. 3, 1879. His wife d. May 6, 1863.

Children.

1021. Orrin C., bo. May 13, 1818; ma. Harriet H. Brown.
1022. Angelina, bo. April 4, 1820; ma. Walter S. Benson.
1023. Lucy Maria, bo. March 22, 1822.
1024. Arzo A., bo. Aug. 15, 1824; d. July 8, 1827.
1025. Chandler, bo. March 18, 1827; ma. Caroline P. Day.

1026. Martha E., bo. March 26, 1829; ma. Harvey Dodge.
1027. Mary A., bo. Nov. 6, 1831; ma. David S. Wilcox.

(478) Grant Ladd, of Amherst, N. Y., (son of Benijah,[146]) ma. Elizabeth R. Baker, Jan. 13, 1828. She died, and he ma. for his 2d wife Lydia Brewster, Oct. 16, 1833.

Children.

1028. Emily, bo. July 16, 1830; ma. James S. Tompkins, Oct. 27, 1859.
1029. Elizabeth, bo. Oct. 7, 1832; ma. Augustus Westfall, Oct. 14, 1857.

Children by second wife.

1030. Lydia Eliza, bo. July 22, 1835; ma. James Hitchcock, May 4, 1871. Had one son: James Ladd, bo. Nov. 14, 1876.
1031. Eleanor M., bo. Sept. 22, 1837.
1032. Lenora Anna, bo. Dec. 6, 1840; ma. Augustus Bissell, June 6, 1877. Children: [1]Eleanor G., bo. Feb. 28, 1879; [2]Harry B., bo. July 13, 1880; [3]Harry H., bo. Jan. 25, 1882; [4]Albert Ladd, bo. Mar. 17, 1884.
1033. Henry Clay, bo. Feb. 18, 1845; ma. Ella Clark, Feb. 16, 1881. No children.

(489) Calvin Ladd, of Franklin, Conn., (son of Hazen,[155]) ma. Lois Hazen, of Franklin, Conn., May 13, 1824.

Children.

1034. Henry Merrill, bo. Feb. 13, 1825; ma. Elizabeth Loomis.
1035. Simeon Hyde, bo. ——; not married.
1036. Rebecca Burgess, bo. Dec. 16, 1832.
1037. Lois Ann Elizabeth, bo. March 6, 1837; ma. —— Atchson.

(490) Septa Ladd, of Franklin, Conn., (son of Hazen,[155]) ma. Patta Amanda Ladd, (1625,) May 22, 1825.

Children.

1038. Sarah Ann, bo. June 8, 1826; ma. Frank Burdick.
1039. Jane Marie, bo. May 11, 1829; d. Sept. 23, 1831.
1040. Septa George, bo. Sept. 20, 1831; not married.
1041. Thomas Jefferson, bo. July 12, 1833; ma. Mary Sweet, Aug. 26, 1853.
1042. Jane Helen, bo. July 21, 1836; ma. Rufus Spaulding Ladd (1640.)
1043. Edwin, bo. Jan. 7, 1839; not married.
1044. Edward, bo. Jan. 7, 1839; ma. Rhoda Littlebridge.
1045. William Lewis, bo. Jan. 21, 1841; ma. Jennie R. Graham, July 10, 1861.
1046. Rhoda Adeline, bo. July 9, 1846; ma. Edward Douglass.
1047. Charles H., bo. July 31, 1848; ma. Rebecca A. Steer.

(491) Israel S. Ladd, of Franklin, Conn., (son of Hazen,[155]) ma. Lurena Ladd, (1623,) dau. of Abner, (55,) Jan. 21, 1828.

Children.

1048. Abner, bo. Feb. 27. 1829; not married.
1049. Marvin, bo. May 2, 1831.
1050. Andrew Jackson, bo. June 18, 1833.
1051. James Smith, bo. July 6, 1835.
1052. John Edwin, bo. Oct. 30, 1837.
1053. Ann Maria, bo. Dec. 8, 1840.

(500)　Dr. Russell Ladd, of Franklin, Conn., (son of David,[159]) ma. Ruth, dau. of James and Abigail (Ladd) Armstrong, Jan. 19, 1817. He removed to Vanburen, N. Y.

Children.

1054. Jacob, bo. Jan. 20, 1818.
1055. James A., bo. May 8, 1820; ma. Margaret Paull, May 8, 1845.
1056. Sophia, bo. Oct. 10, 1824.
1057. Fanny, bo. Oct. 28, 1829.

(501)　Asa Ladd, of Franklin, Conn., (son of David,[159]) ma. Nancy Peck, March 11, 1816.

Children.

1058. Rufus Marvin, bo. Aug. 21, 1818; ma. Mary E. Morgan.
1059. Sophia Ann, bo. Nov. 9, 1821.
1060. Mary Ann Lathrop, bo. April 11, 1824.
1061. Eunice Peck, bo. June 11, 1829.
1062. Sarah Huntington, bo. Aug. 7, 1834.

(504)　Jedediah Perkins Ladd, (son of Samuel,[163]) ma. Elizabeth Brewster, March 16, 1820.

Children.

1063. Louisa Eliza, bo. Feb. 23, 1821; ma. George W. Frink.
1064. Samuel Jedediah P., bo. Sept. 9, 1822; ma. Philena B. Hazen.

(508)　Ulysses Ladd, of Backmanton, N. Y., (son of Andrew,[164]) ma. Electa, dau. of Thomas Hazen, of Franklin, Conn.

Children.

1065. Henry, bo. Jan. 9, 1830; ma. Lucy Richards, Feb. 18, 1849.
1066. Addison, bo. Feb. 27, 1832; ma. Aurilla Moors. No children.
1067. Eliza, bo. July 27, 1834; not married; d. March, 1854.
1068. Charles, bo. Aug. 7, 1836; not married; d. March, 1863.
1069. Hannah, bo. Jan. 1, 1839; ma. Patrick Hunt.
1070. Noah, bo. Sept. 14. 1846; ma. Seba Parsons, Sept. 13, 1880.

(510) Lewis Ladd, of Grand Isle, Vt., (son of Andrew,[164]) ma. Maria Hyde, Feb. 28, 1842.

Children.

1071. Margaret, bo. Dec. 5, 1842; ma. Winan Gordon.
1072. Alfred, bo. Feb. 28, 1848; not married.

(511) Hon. Jabez Ladd, of Grand Isle, Vt., (son of Andrew,[164]) was a farmer, and for a long time a prominent citizen. He represented the town in the Legislature in 1841-2, was one of the selectmen eight years, constable six years, justice of the peace twelve years, judge of probate in 1844-47, and assistant judge of the county court in 1853 and 1867. He ma. Martha Wright, Dec. 27, 1838.

Children.

1073. Hannah E., bo. April 19, 1845; ma. George W. Winch, Nov. 10, 1875.
1074. Herbert W., bo. Sept. 3, 1846; ma. Helen Lovelace.

(512) Alvarado Ladd, of Grand Isle, Vt., (son of Andrew,[164]) ma. Mary Flemming.

Children.

1075. Malvina, bo. April 22, 1851.
1076. Margaret A., bo. ——.

(513) Noyes Ladd, of Franklin, Conn., (son of Darius,[170]) ma. Hannah E. Williams.

Children.

1077. Noyes, Jr., bo. March 21, 1822; ma. —— Williams.
1078. Zurvia Williams, bo. Oct. 22, 1823; d. Aug. 1826.
1079. Elizabeth, bo. ——; ma. John A. Ralston.
1080. William Stanton, bo. ——; d. May 12, 1843.
1081. Curtis, bo. ——; d. 1850.
1082. Cyrus F., bo. ——. Drowned in North River, May 17, 1849, on the way to Illinois.
1083. Darius, bo. ——. Drowned May 17, 1849, in North River, on the way to Illinois.
1084. Nathan Stanton, bo. ——. Drowned May 17, 1849, in North River, on the way to Illinois.
1085. Elias W., bo. ——. Drowned May 17, 1849, in North River, on the way to Illinois.

(519) Dr. Ezekiel Hyde Ladd, (son of Darius,[170]) ma. Ruth Scott, Jan. 1, 1837.

Children.

1086. Ellen Holmes, bo. Sept. 9, 1837.
1087. Sarah Jane, bo. Oct. 1, 1841.
1088. Anna Maria, bo. Oct. 9, 1843.
1089. Marietta, bo. Sept. 20, 1845.

(530) Austin Ladd, of Franklin, Conn., (son of Samuel C.,[188]) was a farmer, and lived on the old homestead bought by his great-grandfather. He ma. March 8, 1846, Electa Noble, of Wellington, Conn.

Child.

1090. Noble Austin, bo. Sept. 1, 1848.

(534) James Ephraim Ladd, (son of Samuel Cady[188] and Celenda (Otis) Ladd,) was born Oct. 17, 1828, in Franklin, Conn. He was educated at the public schools in Franklin, and lived at home until 1847, when he went to Worcester to work, where he remained until the Spring of 1848, when he went to South Glastonbury, Conn., where he engaged in a cotton mill weave room for his brother-in-law, Newel Wylls. He remained there until the Spring of 1850, when he went to Bristol, Conn., where he learned the clock-maker's trade, after which he contracted to make parts of clock movements, at which business he was engaged about twenty years, during which time he employed a good many young men, to whom he taught the art of making the several parts of a clock movement. In 1873 he was employed by a manufacturing company in Bristol, Conn., to take charge of the manufacture and sale of turbine water wheels and other machinery. He continued in the service of this company, as secretary and treasurer, for twelve years. While engaged with them he had the management of a patent law suit that was carried up to the United States Court, where it was decided in his favor. In 1885 he engaged with another manufacturing company as salesman, which business he is now engaged in. He ma. Dec. 24, 1854, Henrietta Esther, dau. of William B. and Henrietta (Ives) Carpenter, of Bristol, Conn.

Children.

1091. Henrietta Ives, bo. April 11, 1856; d. Jan. 8, 1865.
1092. Wyllys Carpenter, bo. July 6, 1858. He was educated at the public schools in Bristol, Conn., and graduated at its High school and at the Hartford, Conn., Business College. For fourteen years he was employed as book-keeper, and is now a salesman for a manufactur-

ing corporation in Bristol, Conn. He ma. Oct. 8, 1890, Edith, dau. of Wallace and Eliza Barnes, of Bristol, Conn.
1093. Herbert Ives, bo. Oct. 27, 1866. He graduated at the Hartford, Conn., public High school, and entered the employ of the Waterbury Manufacturing Company as book-keeper in 1887.

(673) John Folsom Ladd, of Deerfield, N. H., (son of Dudley,[276]) ma. Dorothy, dau. of Samuel and Rachel (Brown) Smith, Dec. 13, 1798. He d. May 27, 1817. His widow d. Aug. 13, 1852.

Children.

1094. David. bo. April, 1799; d. young.
1095. Lois, bo. Feb. 13, 1801; ma. Mark Wadleigh.
1096. David, bo. July 7, 1802; ma. Harriet Hoit, Sept. 7, 1826.
1097. Pulonia, bo. Feb. 9, 1804; ma. Cyrus Mann, of Pembroke, N. H.
1098. Dudley, bo. Feb. 11, 1806; ma. Mahala Haines, Aug. 8, 1839. No children.
1099. Lydia, bo. Oct. 9, 1808; ma. John Dunham.
1100. John F., bo. Aug. 10, 1810; ma. Mary M. Rollins.
1101. Lucy, bo. March 22, 1812; not married; d. Oct. 1885.
1102. Sally, bo. March 22, 1814; ma. Luther Fuller; 2d, Andrew Ladd (2870.)
1103. Harriet, bo. March 22, 1816; ma. William Treadwell, of Lowell.

(677) Thomas Ladd (son of Simeon[280]) was born in Nottingham, N. H.; removed to Winthrop, Me., and from there to Orrington, Me. He ma. Dorcas Lowell.

Children.

1104. Lois, bo. Feb. 15, 1819; not married.
1105. Simeon, bo. ——; ma. and had two children.
1106. Thomas, bo. Feb. 5, 1824; ma. Eliza Lowell.
1107. Dianna. bo. ——; ma. George Lowell. Children: [1]Dean, [2]Eliza, [3]Lois Ann, [4]Richard, [5]Frederick, [6]Thomas.
1108. Sarah, bo. ——; ma. 1st, —— Pike; 2d, Thomas Huter. Children by 1st husband: [1]Hiram, [2]Sarah, [3]Mary.

(685) Samuel G. Ladd, of Stanstead, Canada, (son of Nathaniel,[283]) ma. Martha Fox.

Children.

1109. Orzo A., bo. Aug. 8, 1818; ma. Susan Fox.
1110. Amantha, bo. July 12, 1821; ma. Stephen A. White.
1111. Amanda, bo. July 5, 1823; d. July, 1827.
1112. Martha, bo. Aug. 17, 1826; ma. Alonzo Caswell.
1113. Uriah G., bo. Feb. 12, 1829; ma. Eleanor Mason.
1114. Samuel G., bo. March 27, 1831; ma. Eliza Bigelow.
1115. Mary S., bo. April 27, 1833; ma. Roswell Blanchard.
1116. Carleton, bo. Aug. 28, 1835.
1117. Pamelia, bo. May 4, 1839; ma. Orzo Bartlett.

(686) Dudley F. Ladd, of Sanberton, N. H., (son of Josiah,[263]) ma. Polly Mason, March 18, 1817. He died March 19, 1847.

Children.

1118. Mary J., bo. May 18, 1818; ma. Gilman R. Morrison, Dec. 26, 1843.
1119. Lorenzo S., bo. Aug. 19, 1824; ma. Martha H. Richardson, May 8, 1854.
1120. Josiah M., bo. March 15, 1829; ma. Lydia A. Jesseman, Aug. 7, 1853.
1121. Amoretta, bo. May 13, 1836; ma. Samuel B. Burnham, June 3, 1852.
1122. John W., bo. June 1, 1838; ma. Louisa Rock, July 24, 1864.
1123. Plummer B., bo. July 3, 1844; ma. Luella Whitney, July 21, 1868.

(689) Jeremiah Ladd, of Unity, N. H., (son of James,[286]) ma. Nancy Rowe.

Children.

1124. Mary, bo. ——; ma. Alvin Reed.
1125. Jeremiah W., bo. March 7, 1828; ma. Clarie N. Robie, July 15, 1856.
1126. Nancy, bo. ——; ma. Wilbur W. Ireland. She d. Feb. 1811.
1127. Joannah, bo. ——; not married; d. 1854.
1128. Noah, bo. Nov. 7, 1835; ma. Sarah D. Hall, July 4, 1856.

(690) Noah Ladd, of Unity, N. H., (son of James,[286]) ma. Sally Bartlett, Sept. 2, 1804. She died Feb. 14, 1864. He died Jan. 31, 1861.

Children.

1129. Lorinda, bo. July 26, 1805; d. Nov. 5, 1809.
1130. Caroline, bo. March 14, 1807; ma. John Sleeper, Nov. 29, 1827. Children: [1]Gilbert C., bo. March 1, 1829, ma. Emily Bartlett; [2]Melinda S., bo. May 27, 1831, ma. William Jillson; [3]Harriet, bo. March 1, 1839, ma. Charles Pervis, March 5, 1857.
1131. Lorinda, bo. May 23, 1810; ma. Wilson Bartlett, Feb. 25, 1830. She d. Jan. 4, 1843.
1132. Washington T., bo. July 4, 1812; d. April 20, 1820.
1133. Adeline, bo. Jan. 25, 1815; ma. Stephen Glidden.
1134. James Monroe, bo. June 1, 1818; ma. Sarah Graves, March 23, 1842.
1135. Harriet, bo. April 12, 1820; ma. Alvin Rounda, Feb. 28, 1842. Children: [1]Flora Gertrude, bo. Jan. 16, 1851, d. young; [2]Flora Gertrude, bo. May 30, 1855; [3]Carrie Belle, bo. March 5, 1859.
1136. Washington T., bo. Nov. 10, 1822; ma. Frances Neal, May 22, 1849. She d. March 31, 1862.
1137. Noah Jefferson, bo. Sept. 14, 1825; d. June 1, 1850.
1138. Wallace Wingate, bo. April 22, 1829; ma. Ann Jones, March 9, 1853.

(691) Charles Ira Ladd, of Unity, N. H., (son of James,[286]) ma. Peggy Huntoon, Feb. 24, 1811.

Children.

1139. Samantha, bo. ——.
1140. Oscar, bo. ——.

(697) Daniel Ladd, of Unity, N. H., (son of Nathaniel,[287]) ma. Eliza Smith, Feb. 19, 1803. He died Feb. 22, 1856.

Children.

1141. Jacob S., bo. May 17, 1804; ma. Polly Nichols, Dec. 3, 1827.
1142. Aurin, bo. Aug. 11, 1805; ma. Louisa Walling, Aug. 10, 1831.
1143. Louisa, bo. Oct. 4, 1807; d. April 22, 1811.
1144. Mary S., bo. Jan. 12, 1814; ma. Leonard Fisher, March 18, 1852. She died Jan. 8, 1880.
1145. Elizabeth, bo. Sept 9, 1822.

(698) Rev. Moses Ladd, of Unity, N. H., (son of Nathaniel,[287]) ma. Lorenda Robinson.

Children.

1146. Sally, bo. May 1, 1807; ma. William Webster.
1147. Betsey, bo. Oct. 28, 1809; ma. Verman Webster.
1148. Lorenzo Dow, bo. Oct. 23, 1813; ma. Laura Dunnel.
1149. Philander, J., bo. Sept. 20, 1816; ma. Ruth W. Adams.

(699) Dudley Ladd, of Unity, N. H., (son of Nathaniel,[287]) ma. Louisa Perry, dau. of Thomas Perry. He died Jan. 29, 1859. His widow died Feb. 20, 1865.

Children.

1150. William M., bo. Sept. 19, 1813; ma. Adelphia C. Parkhurst.
1151. Dudley P., bo. Oct. 20, 1814; not married; d. March 16, 1839.
1152. Luther, bo. March 17, 1816; d. Jan. 14, 1817, aged 10 months.

(702) Nathaniel Ladd, of Claremont, N. H., (son of Nathaniel,[287]) ma. Abigail Weed, Dec. 31, 1818. He died Aug. 1859.

Children.

1153. Susan, bo. Oct. 14, 1819; died young.
1154. Abigail, bo. Jan. 24, 1822.
1155. Susan, bo. Sept. 1827.
1156. Betsey F., bo. Sept. 25, 1829.

(703) Aaron Ladd, (son of Nathaniel,[287]) was born in Unity, N. H., Nov. 1, 1790. When about 20 years old he went to Middlesex, Vt., where he continued to reside. He taught school winters for a few years, and then commenced business as a shoemaker, in which he continued as long as he was able to work. He was

postmaster for a number of years, and for about forty years held the office of justice of the peace, during which time he presided at nearly all the justice courts held in the town. He took great interest in schools, and was school committee for several years at different times. He was an adjutant in the State militia for a long time. He. ma. Nancy Buck. She died, and he ma. 2d, Sally McElroy.

Children.

1157. Almon A., bo. Dec. 13, 1817; ma. Emeline White.
1158. Horatio H., bo. July 3, 1820; ma. Mary Jane Currier.
1159. Nancy E., bo. March 5, 1822; ma. Frank A. Brown, Sept. 19, 1818.
1160. Vernon A., bo. March 15, 1824; ma. Rose Holden.
1161. Norman N., bo. June 15, 1828; ma. Isabella Holt. No children.

Children by second wife.

1162. Marion M., bo. June 6, 1834; ma. Dr. W. A. Webster, Aug. 9, 1858. He died Feb. 7, 1887.
1163. Daniel P., bo. March 3, 1838; ma. Mary Shattuck.
1164. Dudley P., bo. Oct. 29, 1839; ma. Judith C. Boody.
1165. Leonard E., bo. Jan. 24, 1844; ma. Ida May, dau. of John Q. Brown, Dec. 27, 1882.

(704) John Ladd, (son of Nathaniel,[287]) removed from Unity, N. H., to Newport, N. H. He ma. Sally F. Weed, Jan. 1, 1820.

Children.

1166. Lucretia, bo. March 1, 1821; ma. Rev. Charles E. Rogers, June 22, 1858. Child: ¹Angis, bo. Dec. 25, 1859, d. Sept. 14, 1862.
1167. Joseph W., bo. March 10, 1824; ma. Marietta Howlet, May 6, 1851.
1168. Nathaniel Marshall, bo. March 17, 1826; ma. Emily Brooks.
1169. Wilbur Aaron, bo. May 7, 1828; ma. Caroline Ellen Kent, Dec. 18, 1854. No children.

(706) John Ladd, of Sidney, Me., (son of Peter,[288]) ma. Nancy Woodcock, March 25, 1806.

Children.

1170. Nancy E., bo. June 28, 1807; ma. Hosea Blaisdell.
1171. Lurenda, bo. Nov. 26, 1810; ma. Horace Blaisdell.
1172. Charles M., bo. Oct. 4, ——; d. in infancy.
1173. Comfort M., bo. April 10, 1815; ma. Harriet Patterson. No children.
1174. Welcome M., bo. March 3, 1824; ma. Elizabeth A. Ellis, Sept. 11, 1848.

(708) Joseph Ladd, (son of Joses,[289]) was born in Deerfield, N. H., Jan. 14, 1786. He removed with his father, soon after the Revolution, from Deerfield, N. H., to Mt. Vernon, Me. He

left his father at Mt. Vernon and went to Augusta, Me., where he completed his education with Rev. Payson Stone, an Orthodox clergyman, intending to become a minister, but changed his mind and engaged in business as a merchant, adding mills and shipping interests as the country improved. He did large manufacturing for the times, in sawing lumber, in carding and dressing cloth, in grinding grain, and in farming. He built and owned a line of packets, which ran from Maine to the St. Marks River, Florida. In 1832 he was interested in an extensive mercantile business, having a branch in Florida, where he died of yellow fever in 1835, just as he was ready to return to his home in Augusta, Me. He was a stockholder in the first woolen factory that was operated in Maine. He married June 30, 1811, Sarah, dau. of Theophilus Hamlin, of Augusta, Me.

Children.

1175. Joseph Edwin, bo. April 20, 1812; ma. Sarah E. Potter, Dec. 8, 1836.
1176. Theophilus H., bo. Nov. 30, 1813; d. Sept. 31, 1834.
1177. Franklin Bacon, bo. Sept. 10, 1815; ma. Sarah Ann Van Norden.
1178. Daniel, bo. March 21, 1817; ma. Elizabeth Overstreet.
1179. George Washington, bo. Sept. 28, 1818; ma. Marcia C. P. Ingraham.
1180. James Madison, bo. Feb. 23, 1820; d. at Norfolk, Va., Nov. 26, 1847.
1181. Mary Hamlin, bo. Sept. 5, 1821; ma. William C. Hollis.
1182. Alfred W., bo. Sept. 5, 1823; ma. Fannie W. Walker.
1183. Hannah, bo. Aug. 3, 1825; d. in Augusta, Me., 1838.
1184. Sarah R., bo. Aug. 3, 1828; ma. H. W. Fuller, of Bangor, Me.

(712) Daniel Ladd (son of Joses,[289]) was born in Mt. Vernon, Me., Aug. 27, 1793; ma. Rachel Richards, Jan. 22, 1817. He left home before the war of 1812; was a sailor; after the war began he was taken prisoner, and was confined in Dartmoor prison, in England, a long time. After his release he came home, and as a slight reward for his sufferings while in prison, was employed in the navy yard at Brooklyn, N. Y., as superintendent of one the blacksmith shops, he having learned the trade when a young man, and continued there until his death.

Children.

1185. Henry Edwin, bo. May 22, 1818; d. July 22, 1819.
1186. Mary Louise, bo. July 20, 1820; ma. George Bennett.
1187. Rachel, bo. June 8, 1824; ma. George H. O'Neal.
1188. Rosanna A., bo. Feb. 16, 1827; ma. James Henry Brown.
1189. Margaretta A., bo. Sept. 30, 1829; ma. John Coope, Aug. 3, 1849.
1190. Jane A., bo. June 30, 1832; d. 1833.

1191. Daniel, bo. Dec. 23, 1833; ma. Sarah Jane Ferguson.
1192. George Franklin, bo. 1839; ma. Mary Warren. No children.

(713) Jesse Eaton Ladd, (son of Joses[289] and Rachel (Fifield) Ladd,) was born in Mt. Vernon, Me., Oct. 10. 1795. He ma. Sophronia Worthley, Sept. 11, 1823. He was educated in the common schools, and at Farmington Academy. He taught school several years in his younger days. After his marriage he worked at blacksmithing and stone-cutting, and followed these trades as long as he lived, except for a short time he was engaged in carding wool and dressing cloth. While living in the town of Phillips, Me., he was captain of a military company for several years. He always took great pride in his office, and as he was a fine looking man and quite proud, he would have the best uniform on the muster-field. He removed from Phillips, Me., to Gardiner, Me., where he died March 5, 1883.

Children.

1193. Diana W., bo. July 11, 1824; ma. Charles P. Craig, Feb. 20, 1842.
1194. Louisa, bo. Oct. 25, 1825; ma. Parsons Witham, May 25, 1851.
1195. George W., bo. Sept. 7, 1827; ma. Sarah White, May 3, 1855.
1196. Joseph E., bo. Aug. 6, 1829; ma. Elmeda Huntoon, Aug. 16, 1854.
1197. Sarah J., bo. June 4, 1831; ma. Lyman Morse, March 4, 1852.
1198. Marcia M., bo. Aug. 6, 1833; ma. Marcellus Springer, Oct. 4, 1860.
1199. Ammi S., bo. June 17, 1835; ma. Lydia F. Golder, July 10, 1861.
1200. Vesta A., bo. July 6, 1837; d. Jan. 6, 1838.
1201. Vesta A., bo. Feb. 22, 1840; ma. Samuel P. Ridley, Aug. 14, 1868.
1202. Emma W., bo. July 5, 1842; ma. Edward Webb, June, 1870.

(716) Stephen Ladd, of Mt. Vernon, Me., (son of Joses,[289]) ma. Melinda French. He d. Jan. 1, 1871. His wife d. July 6, 1864.

Children.

1203. ——, bo. June 20, 1828; d. July 31, 1828.
1204. Daniel, bo. April 9, 1830.
1205. James, bo. Aug. 19, 1832; d. at Baton Rouge, La., March 7, 1863.
1206. Abel, bo. Jan. 16, 1835; ma. Eunice A. ——.
1207. Joannah, bo. June 4, 1838; ma. Jesse Jacobs.
1208. Joseph, bo. Dec. 20, 1840.
1209. Alfred, bo. May 6, 1843; d. in Andersonville Prison, Sept. 30, 1864.
1210. Susannah, bo. Jan. 17, 1846.
1211. John W., bo. Aug. 19, 1848; ma. Elvira A. ——.

(721) Timothy Ladd, of Piermont, N. H., (son of Samuel,[291]) ma. Mary Lane, of Hampton, N. H. He died Sept. 18, 1873.

Children.

1212. Jeremiah T., bo. May 2, 1819; ma. Abbie Bartlett. No children.
1213. Lucy A., bo. Aug. 7, 1822; ma. Amos B. Rodiman.
1214. Enoch G., bo. July 23, 1824; ma. Mary J. W. Emerson, Sept. 29, 1850. No children.
1215. Mary, bo. June 30, 1832; ma. John W. Palmer.
1216. Timothy D., bo. March 13, 1834; ma. Julia Barton. No children.
1217. Andrew S., bo. July 1, 1836; ma. Betsey C. Doty, Feb. 22, 1860. No children.

(724) Dea. Daniel Ladd, of Deerfield, N. H., (son of Jedediah,[298]) ma. Martha Clemmens, of Boston, May 4, 1820. She d. April 23, 1880. He d. March 2, 1839.

Children.

1218. Susan A., bo. April 4, 1821; ma. Samuel Whittier, Jr., May 3, 1840.
1219. Lewis A., bo. April 21, 1823; ma. Sarah Ann Lang, Oct. 4, 1846.
1220. Daniel B., bo. Jan 6, 1826; ma. Rebecca E. Dearborn, Nov. 25, 1847.
1221. Martha A., bo. Feb. 25, 1828; ma. Isaiah S. Lang, of Candia, N. H., Sept. 12, 1848.
1222. William D., bo. June 4, 1830; ma. Lucinda Lang, June 10, 1851.
1223. Julia B., bo. Dec. 21, 1835; d. Dec. 12, 1837.
1224. George H., bo. Jan. 22, 1839; ma. Amanda M. Alger, Dec. 4, 1858.

(725) John Ladd, of Deerfield, N. H., (son of Jedediah,[298]) ma. Mary Beane, of Candia, N. H., June 19, 1854.

Children.

1225. A daughter, bo. Oct. 29, 1828; d. Nov. 1, 1828.
1226. John Warren, bo. Feb. 23, 1830; ma. Deborah Beane, Nov. 1, 1854.
1227. Enoch Place, bo. Aug. 25, 1832; ma. Hannah M. Rand.
1228. David Beane, bo. Oct. 14, 1834; ma. Lezza S. Beane, Nov. 29, 1860.
1229. Abraham G., bo. Sept. 14, 1836; ma. Nellie Lock, Oct. 24, 1877.
1230. Loren Dudley, bo. Dec. 23, 1838; ma. Anna L. Thompson, June 26, 1867.
1231. Mary J., bo. Nov. 1, 1842; d. May 1, 1845.

(729) Stephen F. Ladd, of Deerfield, N. H., (son of Jedediah,[298]) ma. Susan P., dau. of Joseph Bruce, of Clairmont, N. H., Oct. 20, 1834.

Children.

1232. George W., bo. Dec. 30, 1835; not married.
1233. Sarah M., bo. Aug. 29, 1837; not married.
1234. Mary Ann, bo. Aug. 12, 1839; ma. George T. Hunting, Feb. 14, 1865.
1235. Alfred, bo. Jan. 24, 1841; not married.
1236. Edward A., bo. April 28, 1843; ma. Almira B. Brown, April 2, 1868.
1237. Lewis, bo. Nov. 23, 1845; not married.

1238. Frank P., bo. June 10, 1847; ma. Sarah E. Akerman, April 2, 1868.
1239. Charles P., bo. Nov. 16, 1850; ma. Catharine I. Cary, July 10, 1871.
1240. Herbert B., bo. March 20, 1853; not married in 1888.
1241. Emma L., bo. Feb. 3, 1860.

(735) Stephen Ladd, of Hartford, N. Y., (son of Samuel,[303]) ma. Amanda Austin, 1821. He died July 21, 1878. His widow died Aug. 8, 1882.

Children.

1242. James H., bo. Feb. 1825; ma. Maggie Brown, 1854.
1243. Mary A., bo. Jan. 1, 1827; d. March 2, 1843.
1244. Sarah E., bo. Sept. 14, 1829; ma. Joel M. Kenyon, Feb. 22, 1865.
1245. Maria, bo. Dec. 30, 1832; d. Feb. 18, 1845.
1246. Maggie C., bo. Jan. 14, 1834.
1247. Stephen S., bo. March 7, 1837; d. March 31, 1862.
1248. William H., bo. July 10, 1841; ma. Angie Taylor, 1875.
1249. Noah B., bo. June 10, 1849.

(737) Samuel Ladd, (son of Samuel,[303]) was born in New Hampton, N. H., Dec. 12, 1803, where he lived a life common to most farmers' boys of his time until he was 13 years of age, when his father died, leaving quite a large family of children, and on him, at this tender age, guided by his mother's counsels, fell the burden of care. In 1818 they removed to Tuftonborough, N. H., where he purchased a tract of land on the easterly side and adjoining Lake Winnipiseogee, then covered with wood, on which he erected buildings. June 24, 1830, he ma. Nancy, dau. of John and Hannah (Ham) Young. Success followed industry and good judgment, and more land was added to his farm, and an island in the lake was purchased, a new house built, additions made to his barn to accommodate the increasing herds, until 1860, when he sold out and purchased a large estate in Moultonborough, N. H., where he is now (1888) living at the age of 84 years, in the enjoyment of good health, resting in a firm belief that he shall soon see his Savior, and be joined to those who have gone on before. His wife Nancy died Sept. 1, 1840. He married for his second wife Mary Moulton.

Children.

1250. John A., bo. Sept. 1, 1832; ma. Mary Ann Clark, March 5, 1862. She d. Dec. 12, 1889. No children.
1251. Levi, bo. May 20, 1834; ma. Elizabeth Appleton.
1252. Lyman S., bo. Jan. 25, 1836. "He was in Hamilton, C. W., when President Lincoln issued his call for 600,000 men. He came over to

81

Worcester and enlisted in the 36th Regiment of Volunteers, but his strength was not equal to a soldier's life. His health began to fail soon after leaving Washington, D. C., and he became a victim of the convalescent camp, and was discharged when just ready to die with consumption. He reached home Jan. 27, and died Feb. 9, 1863."

Children by second wife.

1253. Nancy, bo. June 12, 1842; ma. Samuel L. Victory.
1254. Eliza E., bo. June 21, 1844.
1255. Sarah, bo. Feb. 9, 1846; d. June 10, 1868.
1256. Matilda, bo. April 8, 1848; ma. Charles Severence.
1257. Mary, bo. April 19, 1850; ma. Benjamin F. Counce.
1258. Martha Abby, bo. May 31, 1853; ma. Warren Vittum.

(739) Jonathan Ladd, of Tuftonborough, N. H., (son of Samuel,[303]) ma. Susan Young, Feb. 1, 1839.

Children.

1259. Samuel E., bo. April 22, 1840; d. Sept. 22, 1840.
1260. Nancy M., bo. April 4, 1842; ma. Francis Kierman.
1261. Susie M., bo. Aug. 16, 1845; ma. Jesse F. Hiscock.
1262. Amanda M. bo. June 6, 1848; ma. Elisha Woodworth, May 23, 1867.
1263. Ruth M., bo. Oct. 1, 1849; ma. Thomas E. Lang.

(740) Levi D. Ladd, of Melvin Village, N. H., (son of Samuel,[303]) ma. Hannah Young.

Children.

1264. Lois, bo. ——.
1265. Martha A., bo. ——.
1266. Jane, bo. ——; ma. —— Jenell, of Stratham, N. H.

(741) Gordon Ladd, of Melvin Village, N. H., (son of Samuel,[303]) ma. Dolly Young, Dec. 27, 1840. She died May 8, 1854, and he ma. 2d, Eliza Moulton, Nov. 30, 1854.

Children.

1267. Levi Woodbury, bo. July 11, 1843; ma. Mrs. Maranda (Miles) Hunting, 1866.
1268. Lydia, bo. March 7, 1848; d. Dec. 20, 1882.
1269. Frank H., bo. Sept. 27, 1853.

Children by second wife.

1270. George M., bo. Oct. 2, 1855; ma. Juliet Bickford.
1271. Harvey A., bo. Oct. 23, 1857.
1272. Clarabell, bo. Aug. 15, 1859; ma. Marshall D. Richardson, Aug. 26, 1877.

(747) John Hibbard Ladd, of Maywood, Ill., (son of John,[313]) was born in Unity, N. H., Oct. 3, 1798. He ma. Anna McCready. He d. June 18, 1888. We copy the following obituary of Mr. Ladd from the Inter-Ocean, of Chicago, Ill. :

"John Hibbard Ladd, born at Unity, N. H., 1798, died at his home, No. 1450 Michigan avenue, Monday, June 18. His strong and well-balanced mind, his interest and influence in the affairs of men, and his full, rounded and peaceful life, gave significance to the phrase—"A ripe old age." Leaving New England in 1818, he came to New Lisbon, Ohio, at the time considered the Far West of America. The following year he married Anna McCready, who journeyed with him, a true and devoted companion, for more than fifty years of his eventful life. Many years of his early manhood were spent in Kingwood, Va., interested in the improvement and development of the country. From Virginia he came north, where for more than a quarter of a century he held the office of Justice of the Peace in the village of Lima, Ind. He was ever and always a friend of the poor, and the champion of the wronged and oppressed. He was contemporanous with, and the personal friend of, William Lloyd Garrison, Gerret Smith, and the Lovejoys. John Hibbard Ladd was an uncompromising total abstinence man from youth to the last day he lived, and was ever the enthusiastic advocate of an unconditional prohibition of the liquor traffic. The sunset of his long and useful life was spent here in Chicago with his grandchildren, La Ome and Jennie Ladd, and his daughter, Mrs. J. S. Lewis, of No. 1450 Michigan avenue."

Children.

1273. Hiram, bo. ——; ma. Melinda Mansfield, Sept. 8, 1848.
1274. Clara, bo. ——; ma. Samuel Gibson. Children: [1]Mary, [2]Annie, [3]William, [4]Charles.
1275. Rhoda, bo. ——; ma. Waldron Pollock. Children: [1]Narcissus, [2]John.
1276. Rebecca, bo. ——; ma. George W. Baker. Child: George W., who was a soldier in the Union army and died in the service.
1277. Chester, bo. ——; ma. Charlotte M. Ball.
1278. Jennie Sarah, bo. ——; ma. Charles Sanford; 2d, Edwin E. Lewis.
1279. Erastus Enoch, bo. ——; not married.
1280. John, bo. ——; d. in infancy.

(748) Hiram Ladd, (son of John,[313]) was born in Unity, N. H., Aug. 19, 1800. He ma. Aurelia Palmer, at Castleton, Vt. He was a man of unaffected piety and unimpeachable integrity. He removed from Unity to Dalton, N. H., in 1827; was one of the pioneers, and settled on a farm about half a mile from the village of Whitefield, N. H., and built a large house in which he lived. He remained there until about 1836, when he moved

to the western part of the town, on the Connecticut river, and embarked in trade in a country store with Benjamin Fay. The business did not prove a success, and he returned about 1839 to a farm adjoining the one on which he first settled, where he remained, living the life of a farmer, until about 1873, when he went to Wattsburg, Erie County, Pa., to reside with his eldest son. In 1877 he fell from a fence, and received injuries from which he soon after died. He was a good and true man, kind and courteous to all, and one from whom neighbors often sought advice under trying and difficult circumstances. He was a justice of the peace, and held several town offices.

Children.

1281 Hannibal E., bo. June 26, 1828; ma. Martha A. Sammons, Sept. 19, 1856.
1282. William S., bo. Sept. 5, 1830; ma. Maria Barnes Fletcher, July 5, 1860.
1283. Mary, bo. April 20, 1833; ma. Prof. George N. Abbott, of Newbury, Vt., May, 1853.
1284. Lucy, bo. Oct. 23, 1834; ma. George W. Stratton, May, 1862.
1285. Kate, bo. Oct. 1, 1838; ma. William Barry Smith, April 30, 1867.

(749) Rev. Enoch H. Ladd, of Unity, N. H., (son of John,[318]) ma. Lucy L. Plumb.

Children.

1286. Mary Ann, bo. Jan. 1832.
1287. Sarah J., bo. Oct. 1833; ma. Daniel Davis, of Manchester, N. H.
1288. Rhoda J., bo. June 1, 1835.
1289. Ellen R., bo. June 1, 1838.
1290. Enoch, bo. ——; d. aged 2 years.

(750) Joseph Ladd, of Bristol, N. H., (son of John,[318]) ma. Eliza Johnson, of Nahant, May 11, 1833. He was a manufacturer of woolen cloth; removed to North Andover, then to Derry, N. H., where he died Oct. 10, 1870.

Children.

1291. A son, bo. Feb. 27, 1834; d. at birth.
1292. Joseph Johnson, bo. April 27, 1835; ma. Lucy A. Dunham, Oct. 1861.
1293. Mary Elizabeth, bo. Nov. 17, 1836; ma. Rev. J. C. Smith, June 5, 1867.
1294. Charles Hibbard, bo. Nov. 19, 1843; ma. Elizabeth Dorsett. She died in 1873, and he ma. for his 2d wife Elizabeth Firman, 1876.
1295. Sarah Ella, bo. May 20, 1838; d. July 24, 1839.
1296. Pamelia Johnson, bo. June 13, 1845.

(753)   Rev. Daniel Ladd, of Middlebury, Vt.. (son of Josiah,[318]) ma. Charlotte H. Kitchell, June 9. 1836. We copy the following sketch of Mr. Ladd from Rev. H. D. Kitchell, D. D.'s genealogy of the Kitchell family:

"Rev. Daniel Ladd, bo. Jan. 22, 1804, graduated at Middlebury, Vt.. College in 1832. and at Andover Theological Seminary in 1836. He ma. June 9, 1836, Charlotte H. Kitchell. They sailed for the Mediterranean in the service of the A. B. C. F. M., and began their missionary labor at Lamka, in the island of Cypress, where after a few years the Greek Mission was generally discontinued, and they were transferred to the American Mission, and labored many years in that connection at Brovsa, Smyrna, and Constantinople. After thirty years of missionary work they returned to this country and resided at Middlebury, Vt., where he died suddenly of heart disease, Oct. 11, 1872. He was a man of Godly sincerity. a scholar, a faithful missionary, and eminently a student of the scriptures."

Children.

1297. Daniel, bo. April 15, 1839; d. May 18, 1839.
1298. Henry R., bo. April 11. 1841; d. April 28, 1842.
1299. Caroline K., bo. Oct. 14, 1843; ma. Prof. George N. Webber.
1300. Charlotte H., bo. Oct. 14, 1843; d. Feb. 16, 1846.
1301. Henry Martyn, bo. Nov. 10, 1849; ma. Sadie E. Harvey, June 16, 1875.

(754)   Crawford Ladd, of Litchfield, Conn., (son of Josiah,[318]) ma. Jane Byington, 1841.

Child.

1302. Charles, bo. 1843.

(759)   Josiah Ladd, of North Livermore, Me., (son of Josiah,[318]) ma. Sarah Swasey, of Burke, Vt., Jan. 1846. She died April, 1849. He ma. for his 2d wife, Oct. 31, 1850, Betsey Fuller, of Livermore, Me.

Child.

1303. Philip S., bo. March 10, 1849.

Child by second wife.

1304. Sarah Elizabeth, bo. Dec. 30, 1852; d. July 18, 1855.

(761)   Dr. John Ladd, of North Livermore, Me., (son of Josiah,[318]) studied medicine with Dr. Abel Brown, of Burke, Vt., attended a course of medical lectures at Woodstock, Vt., then went to Canton, Me., and studied with Dr. Benjamin Swasey, and took his diploma at Brunswick, Me. He ma. Sarah Hathaway, Sept.

3, 1850. She died March 10, 1860. He ma. for his 2d wife Ann E. Moulton, Nov. 29, 1861.

Child by first wife.

1305. Edmund P., bo. Sept. 6, 1852.

(762) Peter Ladd, of Bristol, N. H., (son of Jeremiah,[321]) ma. Rhoda Quimby, May 27, 1789. He died Jan. 19, 1818. He was town clerk of Alexandria, N. H., 1804–5, and was representative in 1806.

Children.

1306. Nancy, bo. Nov. 22, 1790; ma. Samuel Fay.
1307. Lydia, bo. Nov. 2, 1791; ma. Peter Fellows. She d. Aug. 3, 1828.
1308. Priscilla, bo. July 14, 1793; not married.
1309. Polly, bo. July 4, 1795; ma. John Simonds.
1310. Betsey Sleeper, bo. July 9, 1797; not married; d. May 12, 1889.
1311. Peter, Jr., bo. May 21, 1799; d. Sept. 9, 1800.
1312. David Chandler, bo. Aug. 6, 1801; ma. Judith Atwood, Aug. 1, 1823.
1313. Ruth, bo. Dec. 13, 1803; ma. Eben Corliss, of Concord, N. H.
1314. Jeremiah Quimby, bo. July 25, 1805; ma. Abigail Collins.

(768) John Ladd, of Alexandria, N. H., (son of Jeremiah,[321]) ma. Fannie Collins, June, 1828. She died Feb. 1851. He ma. 2d Sarah Fellows Collins, June 26, 1852.

Children by first wife.

1315. George Lovering, bo. Aug. 29, 1829; d. Feb. 1, 1830.
1316. Mahala Williams, bo. Dec. 7, 1830; ma. Jeremiah Dow, Oct. 21, 1858.
1317. Emily Jane, bo. Sept. 28, 1832; ma. Dugal H. Barr.
1318. Esther Ann, bo. Nov. 20, 1834; ma. Dr. John Pray, 1868.
1319. Tirza Harvey, bo. Aug. 29, 1836; ma. Walter Simonds, 1858.
1320. Sylvester Sleeper, bo. July 25, 1838; d. Dec. 9, 1839.
1321. Charles Wesley, bo. Nov. 1839; d. Aug. 1842.
1322. Mary Augusta, bo. May 12, 1841; ma. Edwin Judkins, June 6, 1864.
1323. Luther Crawford, bo. Dec. 22, 1843. He was living in Lowell at the breaking out of the Rebellion, enlisted in Co. D, 6th Regt. Mass. Vols., and was killed while marching through Baltimore, Md., April 19, 1861.
1324. Ellen Frances, bo. Oct. 2, 1850; ma. William H. Stevens, June 26, 1852.

(773) Timothy Ladd, of Mercer, Winthrop, and Vienna, Me., (son of Nathaniel,[322]) ma. Jane Cary.

Children.

1325. Reuben, bo. March 12, 1792; ma. Nancy Hayden.
1326. Benjamin, bo. Oct. 1, 1794; ma. Louisa Trask.
1327. Moses, bo. Oct. 28, 1795; ma. Phebe Taylor, 1817.

1328. Daniel, bo. May 10, 1799; ma. Abigail French.
1329. Asa, bo. Feb. 25, 1801; ma. Nancy Sanborn, June 18, 1823.
1330. William, bo. Jan. 15, 1803; ma. Mary A. Grant.
1331. Nancy, bo. Oct. 7, 1804; ma. James Gilman.
1332. Timothy, bo. Nov. 21, 1806; ma. Mary Woodman.
1333. Jane, bo. Sept. 1808; ma. William Edes.
1334. Sarah, bo. Aug. 22, 1810; ma. Moses Carr. Children: [1]Albion, bo. July 30, 1832; [2]Franklin, bo. July 26, 1834; [3]Hiram, bo. Feb. 4, 1838; [4]Sarah Jane, bo. Oct. 26, 1839; [5]Calvin, bo. Aug. 10, 1846; [6]Helen, bo. Jan. 4, 1851.
1335. John, bo. 1812; ma. Mary Follet.
1336. Ansel, bo. 1814; ma. Mehitable Meader.
1337. Warren, bo. 1818; ma. Eleanor Meader.

(775) Moses Ladd, of Mt. Vernon, Me., (son of Nathaniel,[322]) ma. Nancy Roberts, Dec. 12, 1803. He died June 1, 1840.

Children.

1338. Asenath, bo. Dec. 12, 1804; ma. Gilbert Taggart.
1339. Reuben, bo. Oct. 6, 1815; ma. Christianna Gould.

(783) Nathaniel Ladd, of Abbott, Me., (son of Nathaniel,[322]) ma. Drucilla Elliott. She d. and he ma. 2d, Martha Roberts.

Children.

1340. Betsey, bo. March 1, 1845; ma. —— Paine; 2d, —— Coverly.
1341. Mary, bo. Jan. 1847; ma. A. P. Hardy.
1342. Nathaniel, bo. Oct. 3, 1848; ma. Anna L. Sears.
1343. Nellie, bo. Jan. 4, 1851; ma. L. W. Greenleaf.
1344. Clara, bo. May 22, 1853; ma. J. L. Gott.
1345. Sarah, bo. July 26, 1858; ma. L. F. Brown.
1346. Eva, bo. Jan. 6, 1861; ma. F. H. Roberts.

(786) Jonathan Ladd, of Alexandria, N. H., (son of Isaac,[324]) ma. Hannah Ball, of Hebron, N. H., June 15, 1802, who d. March 15, 1822. He ma. 2d, Tetratia Berry, Dec. 29, 1822.

Children.

1347. Lucy, bo. March 3, 1803; ma. Josiah Ingalls, of Alexandria, N. H., Oct. 18, 1832.
1348. Lizzie, bo. Jan. 18, 1806; d. March 25, 1820.
1349. Cyrus, bo. March 6, 1807; ma. Rectina Bow, May 21, 1837.
1350. Bridget B., bo. Feb. 1, 1813; ma. Seth Cass, of Alexandria, N. H.
1351. Hannah B., bo. Oct. 1, 1816; ma. J. L. Kenniston, of Manchester, N. H.

(787) William Ladd, of Hebron, N. H., (son of Isaac,[324]) ma. Hannah Pike.

Children.

1352. Sarah, bo. ——; ma. George Page, of East Cambridge.
1353. Wesley, bo. ——; ma. Caroline Colburn, of Hebron, N. H.
1354. Betsey, bo. ——; ma. 1st, Archibel Thomas; 2d, Luther Colby.
1355. Catherine, bo. ——; ma. Moses Sawyer, of Alexandria, N. H.
1356. Charlotte, bo. ——; ma. —— Doloff.

(790) Isaac Ladd, of Alexandria, N. H., (son of Isaac,[324]) ma. Huldah Heath. He died Sept. 22, 1866. His widow died March 17, 1877.

Children.

1357. Angelina S., bo. July 24, 1818; ma. Calvin Hill, Aug. 6, 1848.
1358. Jonathan, bo. Sept. 26, 1819; ma. Eunice Stickney, Jan. 18, 1848.
1359. Eliza, bo. April 25, 1821; ma. Thomas Mead; 2d, Edward Longmaid.
1360. Emeline H., bo. Nov. 22, 1822; ma. William Russell, of Bellows Falls, Vt.
1361. Caroline, bo. Dec. 23, 1824; ma. Lewis P. Moody, Dec. 20, 1842.
1362. Sampson B., bo. Sept. 12, 1826; d. Feb. 19, 1827.
1363. Amos Brewster, bo. Jan. 4, 1828; d. Jan. 18, 1844.
1364. George Sullivan, bo. April 2, 1830; not married; d. March 29, 1862.
1365. Amanda M., bo. Aug. 22, 1832; not married.
1366. William M., bo. July 7, 1834.
1367. Sarah Jenney, bo. Dec. 19, 1836; not married.

(791) Nathan Ladd, of Hebron, N. H., (son of Isaac,[324]) ma. Sally Kempt, of Francistown, N. H.

Children.

1368. Lucy, bo. ——; ma. Nathaniel Whitefield.
1369. Artemas, bo. ——; ma. Susan H. Keyser.

(793) John Ladd, of Alexandria, N. H., (son of Isaac,[324]) ma. Mary C. Huse, of Sandown, N. H.

Children.

1370. Wallace, bo. ——.
1371. Harriet Amenda, bo. ——.
1372. Moses, bo. ——.

(795) Benjamin Ladd, of Bridgewater, N. H., (son of Benjamin,[326]) ma. Betsey Blaisdell. She died in 1843. He was drowned at Alexandria, N. H., 1810.

Children.

1373. Asenath, bo. ——; ma. —— Williams.
1374. Lavinia, bo. ——.
1375. Deborah, bo. ——.
1376. Salome, bo. ——; ma. —— Simons.

(797)   Eleazer Ladd, of Deerfield, N. H., (son of Benjamin,[326]) ma. Betsey, dau. of Aaron Rollins, Nov. 15, 1802. She died Sept. 15, 1854. He ma. for his 2d wife Mrs. Betsey (Cram) Robinson. He died May 5, 1857.

Children.

1377. Andrew, bo. May 4, 1806; ma. Melinda Ladd, (728,) April 9, 1827.
1378. Eliza, bo. April 22, 1810; ma. Paul S. Gile, April 18, 1830.
1379. Sarah Dearborn, bo. March 7, 1814; ma. Benjamin J. Prescott. Children: [1]Celesta, bo. May 25, 1842; ma. John Pingree. [2]Otis, bo. Nov. 15, 1844. [3]Heman, bo. Aug. 30, 1846; he enlisted in Co. E, 1st New Hampshire Regt. Heavy Artillery, Sept. 5, 1864, and died Feb. 1867. [4]Alvan, bo. Aug. 11, 1848. [5]Nahum, bo. Aug. 30, 1850. [6]Laura, bo. March 8, 1852; ma. Byron F. Curtis, Nov. 19, 1878. [7]Abbie M. bo. Feb. 7, 1854; ma. March 26, 1871, Nathaniel P. Richardson, of Cambridge.
1380. Benjamin, bo. Nov. 12, 1817; drowned at West Newbury, July 30, 1837.
1381. Caroline, bo. April 3, 1819; ma. William Hewes, April 26, 1848.
1382. William Perry, bo. May 21, 1821; ma. Mary Ann Brown.
1383. George W., bo. Jan. 17, 1823; ma. Mary A. Elliott, Jan. 27, 1848.
1384. Mary Jane, bo. Dec. 5, 1827; ma. —— Swan. Children: [1]Josiah, bo. March 4, 1847; [2]Mary Jane, bo. July 20, 1850. She ma. 2d, Andrew J. Gilson, Nov. 1851, and had children: [3]Freeman P., bo. Aug. 19, 1853; [4]Wilbur, bo. July 25, 1859; [5]Henry, bo. July 30, 1861; [6]Charles, bo. May 23, 1863.
1385. Lavinia, bo. March 17, 1829; ma. Samuel Weeks; 2d, John Stevens.

(800)   Benjamin Ladd, of Searsmont, Me., (son of Benjamin,[326]) ma. Joannah Field, Nov. 17, 1840.

Children.

1386. Hervey Willard, bo. Nov. 26, 1841; ma. Olive Mackie, Nov. 7, 1865.
1387. Mary E., bo. Sept. 4, 1843; ma. Edward Barker, Dec. 22, 1867.
1388. Annette F., bo. July 23, 1846; ma. Sands Hunt, Sept. 3, 1871.
1389. Augustus, bo. July 7, 1848.
1390. Nancy E., bo. March 20, 1851; ma. Lewis Fowles, July 13, 1873.
1391. Charles F., bo. April 7, 1856; ma. Addie Ranger, July 3, 1876.
1392. Lizzie G., bo. June 19, 1859.
1393. George B., bo. Dec. 20, 1861.

(233) Bodwell Ladd, of Mohawk, N. Y., (son of Nathaniel,[69]) ma. Martha Lewis, of Mohawk, N. Y. She died Oct. 22, 1812. He died at Theresa, N. Y., Oct. 15, 1829. He was a member of a company commanded by Major Samuel Bodwell, of Methuen, at the battles of Lexington and Concord, and was in the battle of Bunker Hill.

Children.

1395. Mary, bo. Oct. 19, 1799; ma. Valentine Turpening.
1396. Bodwell, bo. Sept. 4, 1801; ma. Deborah Salisbury.
1397. Achsah, bo. May 3, 1805; ma. Dr. Ichabod Thompson.
1398. Harriet, bo. Jan. 11, 1809; ma. Daniel Lock.

(235) Nathaniel Ladd, (son of Nathaniel[69] and Abigail Bodwell Ladd) was born in Methuen, Oct. 22, 1755; ma. Sarah, dau. of Thomas and Ann (Follensbee) Noyes, at Haverhill, June 27, 1782. He lived in Haverhill.

Thomas Noyes was the son of Joseph and Hannah (Wadleigh) Noyes, grandson of Col. Thomas and Martha (Pierce) Noyes, great-grandson of Rev. James and Sarah (Brown) Noyes. Rev. James Noyes took the oath of Allegiance and Supremacy to pass to New England in the Mary and John, March 24, 1633. His wife was the daughter of Mr. Joseph Brown, of Southampton, England. He was born in 1608, in Chaulderton, County Wiltshire, England, and was the son of the Rev. William Noyes, who married a sister of the celebrated Rev. Robert Parker, of whom the Rev. Cotton Mather wrote, in Magnalia Christi Americana, page 433: "It may without any ungrateful comparisons be asserted, that one of the *greatest scholars* in the English nation was that renowned ROBERT PARKER, who was driven out of the nation for his *non-conformity* to its unhappy ceremonies in the worship of God."

We quote from the same work, page 440: "The Rev. James Noyes was a man of singular qualifications, in piety excelling, an implacable enemy to all heresies and schism, and a most able warrior against the same. He was of reaching and ready apprehension, a large invention, a most profound judgment, a rare and tenacious and comprehensive memory, fixed and unmovable in his grounded conceptions; sure in words and speech, without rashness; gentle and mild in all expressions, without all passion or provoking language. He was resolute for the truth, and in defence thereof had no respect to any person. He was courageous in dangers, and still was apt to believe the best, and made fair weather in a storm. He was much honoured and esteemed in the country, and his death was much bewailed. I think he may be reckoned among the greatest worthies of this age."

Mr. Ladd was a blacksmith, and carried on the business at East Haverhill, Rocks village. He was a Justice of the Peace, and held Justice Court for the trial of such civil and criminal cases as were at that time within the jurisdiction of a justice court. I have the record book of the cases tried, and notice that he was neither severe in his judgments or extravagant in his charges. I copy from the records one civil and one criminal case:

"Nov. 24, 1821. At a Justice Court holden before me, Nathaniel Ladd, Esq., one of the Justices of the Peace for the County of Essex, at my dwelling-house in Haverhill, in said County, on the 24th day of November, at ten of the clock in the forenoon, Greenleaf Woodman, of Haverhill, plaintiff, vs. Paul Bailey, of Newbury, defendant, in a plea of the case, for that the said Bailey was indebted to the plaintiff, as he says, seventeen dollars, as is set forth in the writ, to the damage of the said Woodman, as he saith, the sum of twenty dollars; the parties appear, the plaintiff enters his action, and the defendant comes and defends, and saith that he doth not owe the plaintiff, as is set forth in the writ, and therefore puts himself on trial and the plaintiff likewise. Whereupon the case is fully heard, and after a full hearing it appears to me that the defendant doth owe the plaintiff the sum of twelve dollars and fifty cents; it is therefore considered by me, the said Justice, that Greenleaf Woodman recover against the said Paul Bailey the sum of twelve dollars and fifty cents debt or damage, and cost of suit taxed at two dollars and fifty-one cents.

	2.51
Debt,	12.50
	15.01 "

"Haverhill, July 16, 1835. On complaint of Timothy Kinnerson, Ephraim Orne, and Timothy Flanders, Rhoda Willcomb was apprehended and brought before me, Nathaniel Ladd, one of the Justices for the keeping of the peace: after hearing the evidence and examining the case, it was adjudged by me, the said Justice, that she was guilty of the charge made against her in said complaint, and that she be sent to the County House in Ipswich, in said County of Essex, and there confined to labor for the term of three months.

NATHANIEL LADD, Justice of the Peace."

Bill of costs in Miss Willcomb's case:

"Complaint and warrant,	$1.00
Four witness, travel one mile each,	.32
Attendance one day each,	1.32
Entry,	.75
Trial,	.50
Officer's attendance one day,	.30
Two subpenas,	.20
For filing papers, making up judgment and recording the same,	1.00
Officer's fees for serving writ,	.50
Stephen Hall for keeping prisoner,	.50 = $6.39 "

He was a soldier in the Revolutionary War. The following record, written by himself, of his service in the army, was found among his papers after his death:

"The first time that I was out in the service, I enlisted for three months as a private soldier, on the last of December, 1775, in a company commanded by Capt. Timothy Johnson, of Haverhill; marched to Winter Hill in Charlestown; joined the army on Jan. 1st, 1776; was there when the British army left Boston, went into Boston with General Washington, and served my time out, which expired the first of April; was discharged and returned.

"The second time I was out was in the year 1777; enlisted the last of July of that year in a company commanded by Capt. Samuel Johnson, of Andover; marched the first of August for New York; joined the army at Stillwater; was wounded in the battle on the 7th of October, by a musket ball in my left hip; was carried to the hospital in Albany; remained there until I had so far recovered as to be able to ride, when I returned home, and was under the care of Dr. Benjamin Kittridge for four weeks after my return. In consequence of the wound I received, I am now receiving a pension of eight dollars per month.

"The third time I was out in the service of my country, I enlisted in a company commanded by Capt. Timothy Johnson, of Haverhill, the last of July, 1778, and marched on the first of August for Rhode Island; joined the army commanded by Gen. Sullivan. When the French fleet left the harbor of Newport we were obliged to retreat and leave the island. We stayed our time out; did duty in Providence and vicinity; were discharged and sent home; were out two months this time.

"The fourth and last time I was out in the service of my country was in the year 1779. I enlisted as a private soldier in a company commanded by Capt. Timothy Johnson, of Haverhill, the last of July in that year, for three months. We marched the first of August through Connecticut into New York; marched through New Haven,

East Haven, Fairfield, Norfolk, Green Farms, Horseneck, and Rye. Our regiment did duty in that part of the State of New York until the time of enlistment expired. I was not with the regiment but a small part of the time. The drummer belonging to our company was taken sick, sent to Stamford, Ct., and I was sent with him to take care of him, which I did until he died, which was about the time the term of our enlistment expired, when we were discharged and returned home. From the time I enlisted until I arrived home was four months."

Mr. Ladd, when 71 years old, attended the celebration at Newburyport, July 4, 1826, and offered at the dinner the following sentiment: " May the surviving officers and soldiers of the revolutionary army ever hold in grateful remembrance the hospitality of the citizens of Newburyport towards us who fought and bled to gain the independence which we are assembled this day to celebrate." He was kind and generous in his family, a good neighbor, and a highly respected citizen. His wife Sarah died, and he ma. for his 2d wife Miriam Pressey, 1826. He died Feb. 16, 1837.

Children.

1399. Betsey, bo. Sept. 21, 1784; ma. Benjamin Chase, Feb. 2, 1802. Children: [1]Mary Jane, bo. Nov. 23, 1803, ma. Ebenezer Fullington; [2]Eliza, bo. June 9, 1810, ma. —— Hall; [3]John, bo. March 27, 1812; [4]Eustice, bo. Sept. 23, 1823. She d. Feb. 21, 1841.
1400. Nathaniel, bo. Sept. 17, 1786; ma. Sally Ingersoll.
1401. Sally, bo. Jan. 20, 1789; ma. William Poor. Children: [1]William B., bo. May 3, 1808; [2]Frederick L., bo. Dec. 7, 1817.
1402. John, bo. Sept. 27, 1791; ma. Sophia Jaques.
1403. Abigail, bo. Oct. 11, 1794; ma. Moses George, May 4, 1818. She d. Aug. 1868; he d. Feb. 10, 1851. Children: [1]Abbie W., bo. May 23, 1819, ma. Daniel T. Goss; [2]Elizabeth A., bo. Sept. 4, 1821, ma. William W. Colby; [3]Marette Theresa, bo. May 22, 1823, d. Nov. 20, 1840; [4]Amos E., bo. Aug. 22, 1825, d. Aug. 16, 1829; [5]Wallace T., bo. March 1, 1827, ma. Sarah F. Kinison, Oct. 3, 1851; [6]Gideon B., bo. Sept. 9, 1829, ma. Sophia Ann Ross, Dec. 18, 1856, and d. June 5, 1888; [7]Nathan C., bo. Sept. 7, 1831; [8]Eliza H., bo. Oct. 3, 1835, ma. Niles T. Stickney, Feb. 17, 1859; [9]Mary J. F., bo. Jan. 1, 1834, ma. Daniel S. Balch, Aug. 20, 1861; [10]Willard Kingman, bo. April 17, 1839, d. Feb. 15, 1870.
1404. Frederick P., bo. Jan. 21, 1797; ma. Maria Thayer.
1405. Heman, bo. Nov. 3, 1798; ma. Hannah Gilman.
1406. Ann, bo. Nov. 4, 1800; ma. Thomas Chase, of West Newbury. Child: Thomas P., bo. June 9, 1833. She died June, 1889.
1407. George Washington, bo. June 9, 1803; d. March 29, 1830; not ma.

1408. Rufus King, bo. June 9, 1803; ma. Emily Pollard.
1409. Emery, bo. June 9, 1805; ma. Louisa C. Knowlton.

(236) Thaddeus Ladd, (son of Nathaniel,[69]) ma. Hannah Dow, of Hopkinton, N. H., where several of his children were born. He removed from there to Telford, Vt., where he died.

Children.

1410. Heman, bo. Feb. 2, 1783; d. in infancy.
1411. Nabby, bo. Nov. 9, 1785; ma. Sylvanus Baldwin.
1412. Polly, bo. March 17, 1787; ma. Humphrey Currier.
1413. Hannah, bo. May 31, 1789; ma. James Abbott.
1414. Achsah, bo. May 23, 1791; ma. James Crocker.
1415. Sally, bo. March 17, 1793; ma. Lyman Smith. Children: [1]Mary, [2]Azuba, [3]Frances.
1416. Lucretia, bo. May 12, 1795; ma. Royal Jackman, and had one child: Lyman Jackman.
1417. Nancy, bo. June 10, 1797; ma. John Hammond.
1418. Welcome D., bo. Oct. 1, 1799; ma. Nabby Hammond.
1419. Jedediah P. B., bo. March 2, 1802; ma. Eliza Baldwin.
1420. Sophronia, bo. April 24, 1804.
1421. Richmond, bo. Aug. 2, 1806; d. in infancy.
1422. Louisa, bo. March 22, 1809; ma. George W. Benton, Nov. 22, 1836. Children: [1]George W., bo. Feb. 15, 1838; [2]Reuben C., bo. March 27, 1840; [3]Ada L., bo. July 18, 1844; [4]Helen L., bo. March 15, 1847; [5]Henrietta E., bo. Jan. 2, 1849; [6]Solon L., bo. Sept. 27, 1853; [7]Mary C., bo. Nov. 12, 1851.

(239) Caleb Ladd, of Corinth, Vt., (son of Nathaniel,[69]) ma. Betsey Taplin, Dec. 4, 1794. He died Aug. 18, 1807. His widow died 1850, aged 73.

Children.

1423. John, bo. Feb. 12, 1795.
1424. Bodwell, bo. April 2, 1797; ma. Hannah Sawyer, March 7, 1822.
1425. Sally, bo. April 21, 1800; ma. Jonathan Roble.
1426. Caleb, bo. May 4, 1802; ma. Mary Ann Watson.

(241) Timothy Ladd, (son of Nathaniel,[69] and Mary (Harvey) Ladd,) was born in Methuen, March 22, 1773. He ma. March 1, 1803, Martha, dau. of Thomas and Sarah (Montgomery) Mc Cleary, of Salem, N. Y. When he was sixteen years old he went to Newburyport and learned the trade of "house joiner" of a Mr. Kimball. When he left Mr. Kimball he went to Salem, N. Y., where he worked at his trade until after his marriage, when he removed to Hopkinton, N. H., where he went into the business of house building with his brother John, under the firm

name of "Timothy and John Ladd," and remained there until the death of his mother, who lived with him, in 1815. In the winter of 1816 he and his brother John sold out their Hopkinton property, and he removed to Salem, N. Y., where he remained about two years, when he sold out and purchased a large farm in Hebron, a town adjoining Salem. From there he removed to Rupert, Vt.; remained there about two years, and then removed to Castleton, Vt.; from there to Utica, N. Y., where he resided until the Fall of 1831, when he removed to Dearborn, Mich., where he died in the Fall of 1854, and where his widow died in 1856.

Children.

1427. Nathaniel, bo. Dec. 20, 1803; ma. Margaret Hilton, April 3, 1831.
1428. Thomas McCleary, bo. March 4, 1807; ma. Perly Ann Mead, Aug. 12, 1832.
1429. Timothy Harvey, bo. June 2, 1809; d. 1854.
1430. David Montgomery, bo. Feb. 25, 1813; ma. Martha Ann Hartwell, Nov. 30, 1840.
1431. Sarah Maria, bo. May 4, 1816; d. Feb. 21, 1817.
1432. John Sanford, bo. Sept. 8, 1818; d. 1841.
1433. Martha Eliza, bo. Dec. 16, 1823.

(806) Benjamin Franklin Ladd, of Groton, N. Y., (son of Daniel,[340]) ma. Susan Smith, of Groton, N. Y., Sept. 23, 1835.

Children.

1434. Catharine, bo. June, 1836; ma. Wallace Backus, June 30, 1855.
1435. Sophia, bo. Jan. 30, 1838; ma. George Ingalls, July 3, 1865.
1436. Louisa, bo. Jan. 9, 1842; ma. Henry Parker, April 18, 1873.

(807) William Ladd, of Groton, N. Y., (son of Daniel,[340]) ma. Sally Willis, Jan. 2, 1842.

Children.

1437. Sullivan, bo. June 12, 1844.
1438. Charles, bo. July 10, 1846; ma. Mary Hathaway, Feb. 5, 1867.
1439. George, bo. Aug. 8, 1850.
1440. Willie, bo. Sept. 9, 1857.

(808) Sullivan Ladd, of Groton, N. Y., (son of Daniel,[340]) ma. Mary E. Trowbridge, Dec. 22, 1853.

Child.

1441. Arnold Daniel, bo. March 19, 1855.

(809) Leander Ladd, of Groton, N. Y., (son of Daniel,[340]) ma. Mary F. Brown, Nov. 15, 1850.

Child.

1443. Carrie Bell, bo. March 22, 1862; ma. Dana G. Ingalls, Nov. 7, 1877.

(813) Uriah Ladd, of Lebanon, Vt., (son of Uriah,[342]) ma. Catharine Burdick, of Newport, R. I., April 5, 1848.

Child.

1444. John H., bo. Oct. 20, 1849.

(817) Asa Ladd, of Enosburgh Falls, Vt., (son of Asa,[346]) ma. Louisa Hopkins, Dec. 3, 1812. He died June 8, 1848.

Children.

1445. Avery S., bo. July 7, 1814; d. Aug. 1840; not married.
1446. Philander, bo. Sept. 20, 1816; ma. Susan Thompson, March 17, 1840.
1447. Henry, bo. July 21, 1818; ma. Celia Leavins, Dec. 20, 1854.
1448. Ebenezer B., bo. Aug. 20, 1820; ma. Rosetta McAlster, March 1, 1861.
1449. Hiram, bo. July 29, 1823; ma. Lovina A. Libby, March 2, 1854. No children.
1450. Sarah T., bo. Feb. 11, 1825; ma. Robert Armstrong, June 12, 1859.
1451. Jackson Ami, bo. Aug. 1, 1828; ma. Anna M. Allen, Dec. 23, 1860.
1452. Auretta H., bo. July 19, 1830; not married.
1453. Martha C., bo. July 28, 1832; ma. J. Hyde, Feb. 28, 1852.
1454. Althea L., bo. Aug. 19, 1835; ma. John Whitney, March 8, 1853.
1455. Samantha, bo. June 29, 1839; ma. J. M. Whitcomb, March 13, 1867.

(820) Avery S. Ladd, of Morrisville, Vt., (son of Asa,[348]) ma. Sally Cole, Feb. 13, 1820. He lived at Hyde Park, Johnson, Morristown, and Enosburgh, Vt. He died Jan. 3, 1839. His widow died Sept. 16, 1861.

Children.

1456. Eliza, bo. Nov. 25, 1820; ma. Seth Stephens, June 14, 1871.
1457. Alphonso, bo. March 3, 1822; ma. Mary Braley, Oct. 22, 1846.
1458. Martha J., bo. Oct 6, 1824; ma. Ira Ober.
1459. Rebecca A., bo. March 9, 1826; ma. Loa Jones.
1460. John A., bo. Oct. 13, 1828; ma. Martha Byam, Aug. 21, 1848.
1461. Alden, bo. Feb. 19, 1830; ma. Sarah M. Edwards; 2d, Mary E. Prentice.
1462. Mary R., bo. Nov. 2, 1831; ma. Henry Cole, Jan. 7, 1865.
1463. Cordelia, bo. Aug. 12, 1834; ma. Daniel E. Smith, June 8, 1858.
1464. George W., bo. Aug. 17, 1836; ma. Sarah E. Leach, Sept. 10, 1856; 2d, Emma C. Cary, Nov. 8, 1869.
1465. Carlos, bo. Sept. 27, 1839; d. Oct. 13, 1860.

(823) Rev. David Morrill Ladd, (son of Asa,[346] and Martha (Chace) Ladd,) was born in Haverhill, N. H., Feb. 20, 1806. He ma. Harriet Hinman, dau. of Clark and Olive (Huntington) Hinman, of Berkshire, Vt., April 9, 1829. When a boy he was sent, in the Summer, to the common school, and in the Winter two terms to the academy, in Haverhill, N. H. When he was but ten years old his father and family removed to Enosburgh, Vt., then a new county, with no school near them, and his chances for obtaining a good education were small; but he had an earnest desire for knowledge, and while working upon his father's farm he spent what leisure time he could obtain in studying, and was aided by his mother, and after her death in 1820 by an elder sister, who was a teacher of a school in a town near by. When he was seventeen years old he made a profession of religion, and was baptized and received as a member of the Free Will Baptist Church at Enosburgh, Vt. At this time it was his intention to devote his life to religious work, but at the earnest request of his father that he would take charge of the farm and stay with him the remainder of his life, he decided to gratify his father's desire. After the death of his father in 1851, he felt it to be his duty to carry out a long cherished purpose to prepare for the ministry, and commenced to study for that purpose. He was ordained at Enosburgh, Vt., by Elder Moses Dudley and Mark Atwood. He preached two years in Canada, and the rest of his active life was a minister at Enosburgh, Vt., where he is now (1888) living at the ripe old age of 82.

Children.

1466. Mary G., bo. Feb. 23, 1830; ma. M. D. Kendall. She d. Aug. 1, 1857.
1467. Emory O., bo. May 15, 1833; ma. N. E. Baker, Feb. 3, 1858.

(825) Timothy Ladd, of Whitehall, Ill., (son of Richard,[347]) ma. Deidamia Swallow,˙ Aug. 26, 1819. He died Nov. 11, 1858. His widow died May 15, 1862.

Children.

1468. Frederick, bo. June 15, 1820; d. Sept. 22, 1821.
1469. Julia, bo. Nov. 4, 1821; d. Aug. 9, 1823.
1470. Olivia, bo. Sept. 26, 1823; ma. Hiram Ellis, Dec. 28, 1842. She d. May 18, 1855.
1471. Luthera, bo. Nov. 26, 1825; ma. George Smith. Dec. 9, 1846.
1472. Lora Ann, bo. March 4, 1828; ma. Smith Post, June 4, 1848.

1473. Augustus, bo. March 3, 1830; d. July 12, 1832.
1474. Augusta, bo. March 3, 1830; ma. Edward A. Giller, March 1, 1849.
1475. Nahum, bo. July 6, 1833; d. Jan. 23, 1837.
1476. Edwin, bo. July 29, 1834; d. Sept. 15, 1835.
1477. Chester, bo. Nov. 23, 1836; d. Jan. 29, 1837.
1478. Timothy Fellows, bo. March 5, 1838; ma. Sallie A. Avery, Dec. 15, 1860.
1479. Henry Harrison, bo. March 16, 1840; d. Sept. 27, 1842.
1480. Sophronia, bo. Sept. 11, 1841; d. Aug. 18, 1848.

(230) Timothy Ladd, of Dunbarton, N. H., (son of Timothy,[67]) ma. Molly, dau. of Joseph and Mary (Ladd[71]) Butler. He died March 15, 1808.

Children.

1481. Polly, bo. Jan. 13, 1777; ma. Eliphalet Jones. She d. 1836.
1482. Heman, bo. Nov. 24, 1878; ma. Mary Messer.
1483. Rachel, bo. June 9, 1780; ma. John Allison, of Peterboro', N. H. She d. 1824.
1484. John, bo. Aug. 9, 1783; d. 1816.
1485. Hannah, bo. May 17, 1787; ma. Jonathan Colby, 2d. She died 1855. Children: [1]John L., bo. May 16, 1820; [2]Martha Mary, bo. March 28, 1822; [3]Harriet Jane, bo. June 9, 1824; [4]Sarah Ann, bo. Dec. 30, 1826; [5]Lucy Peasly, bo. June 25, 1829.
1486. James, bo. March 1, 1789.
1487. William, bo. July 13, 1791; d. June 13, 1817.
1488. Timothy, bo. 1793; d. Feb. 1795.
1489. Fanny, bo. May 7, 1795; d. April 17, 1811.
1490. Sally, bo. June 7, 1797; d. Jan. 21, 1816.

(231) Eliphalet Ladd, of Windham, N. H., (son of Timothy,[67]) ma. Mary, dau. of Joseph Park, of Windham, N. H., May 13, 1778. He removed to Salem, N. H., where he lived four years; from there to Meredith, N. H., in 1806, where he died April 27, 1827. His wife died Nov. 6, 1824.

Children.

1491. Alice, bo. March 2, 1797; ma. John B. Swasey. Children: [1]George B.; [2]Jane B.; [3]Mary Park, ma. J. Chapman; [4]Cassandria, ma. Eben Stevens; [5]Asenath, d. young.
1492. Joseph Park, bo. July 22, 1781; ma. Mehitable Towne.
1493. Timothy, bo. Feb. 19, 1783; not married. His lower limbs withered in early childhood, and he never walked, but he was a brilliant scholar, especially in mathematics, and was for many years a famous teacher in Meredith, N. H., and for fourteen years a teacher in Pennsylvania.
1494. Lydia, bo. Dec. 19, 1784; ma. Benjamin Swasey in 1809. She d. 1875. Children: [1]Laura, bo. Dec. 4, 1809, ma. John J. Sanborn, of Balti-

more, Md., in 1836; [2]Darius, bo. Feb. 11, 1811, ma. Sylvia Davis, of Chicopee; [3]Alice J., bo. March, 1812, ma. Jonathan F. George, of Pelham, N. H.; [4]Emily, bo. Aug. 28, 1813; [5]Edwin. bo. May 15, 1815, ma. Mary Tarbel, of Lyndeboro', N. H.; [6]Alexis, bo. Dec. 1816, ma. Emily Torry, of Chicopee; [7]Mary Park, bo. Aug. 1818, ma. Henry Moore, of Marlboro'; [8]Lydia, bo. July 7, 1820, ma. Clark H. Obear, of New Ipswich, N. H., 1848, who d. April, 1888; [9]Benjamin, bo. Jan. 31, 1822, ma. Emily Marshall, of Chicopee; [10]Eliza, bo. May 20, 1824.

1495. Alexander Park, bo. Aug. 16, 1786; ma. Charlotte Hackett.
1496. Darius, bo. July 12, 1788; ma. Emily Augusta Prescott, Mar. 31, 1831.
1497. Mary Jane, bo. Dec. 22, 1789; ma. William Salmond, of Belfast, Me.
1498. Asenath, bo. Dec. 23, 1791; d. 1792.
1499. Asenath, bo. June 3, 1793; ma. James P. Bowman, of Belfast, Me.

(1396)   Bodwell Ladd, of Oneida, N. Y., (son of Bodwell,[233]) ma. Deborah Salisbury, May 12, 1823. She d. June 18, 1867. He d. at St. Lawrence, N. Y., Sept. 1, 1880.

Children.

1500. Martha, bo. May 30, 1824; ma. Calvin Weeks, Dec. 17, 1843.
1501. Edward, bo. May 16, 1828; not married.
1502. Louisa, bo. Dec. 29, 1830; ma. James Phillips, Dec. 29, 1851.
1503. Mason B., bo. March 29, 1834; ma. Adeline D. Ingerson, Sept. 5, 1865.
1504. Alexander P., bo. Sept. 17, 1837; ma. Octavia F. Tuttle, Oct. 23, 1862.

(1400)   Nathaniel Ladd, (son of Nathaniel[235] and Sarah (Noyes) Ladd,) was born in East Haverhill in what is now the Parsonage house, Sept. 17, 1786. He ma. July 14, 1811, Sarah, dau. of Col. Zebulon and Ruth (Moody) Ingersoll. Col. Ingersoll was born in Gloucester, Sept. 1757; was a soldier in the Revolutionary war, and at the close of the war settled in East Haverhill; was a merchant, a ship-builder, and an active and energetic business man. His line runs back: Zebulon,[6] Medifer,[5] David,[4] Samuel,[3] George,[2] Richard,[1] who came from Bedfordshire, England, in 1629, and settled in Salem. Ruth Moody was the dau. of Benjamin and Ann (Bradstreet) Moody, granddaughter of Dr. Humphrey and Sarah (Pierce) Bradstreet, great-granddaughter of Moses and Elizabeth (Harris) Bradstreet, and great-great-granddaughter of Humphrey and Bridget Bradstreet, who came from Ipswich, England, in the Elizabeth, Williams master, April, 1634, and settled in Ipswich, where he had land granted him, May 6, 1635. He was a Representative from Ipswich in 1635; was a member of the church in Rowley, at which place he died in the Summer of 1655, and where he was buried. Mr. Ladd, after his marriage, settled in East Bradford, now Groveland; was town clerk of Bradford one year, and one of the selectmen and assessors two years; was chairman of the board of selectmen of Groveland twelve years, treasurer of the Congregational Society twenty-four years, clerk of the said society forty-six years, and deacon of the Congregational Church thirty-four years; was secretary and treasurer of the Groveland Mutual Fire Insurance Company about twenty years. In 1840 he took the United States census in the towns of Boxford, Georgetown, and Rowley; was a justice of the peace from 1840 to 1875; did quite an extensive probate business, settled estates, wrote wills and deeds, and acted as guardian for minors and others who for any cause were not considered capable of managing their own affairs, and was a land surveyor. He was appointed postmaster of Groveland in 1850, and held the office ten years. He was an early friend of temperance, and a member of the first temperance society that was organized in Haverhill. An anti-slavery society was formed in East Bradford in 1837, and he was elected its secretary, and held that position several years. In politics he was a Whig and acted with that party, but being strongly opposed to secret societies he in 1832 voted for William Wirt, the anti-masonic candidate for President, and on the breaking up of the anti-masonic party in 1836, he cast his first Democratic vote for Martin Van Buren for President. He acted with the Democratic party until the breaking out of the war of the Rebellion, when he was a war Democrat, and as chairman of the board of selectmen he did all in his power to aid the general government to crush the rebellion and wipe out the Southern Confederacy. He was a man of sterling integrity, and always and under all circumstances, and at all times, was faithful and honest to his convictions of what he believed to be just and right. He was a kind and generous father, a good neighbor, a patriotic citizen, and an earnest Christian man, who was highly appreciated and respected by all with whom he came in contact. He died May 9, 1878. His wife died Aug. 10, 1870.

Children.

1505. Ellen Bradstreet, (name changed from Ruth,) bo. April 15, 1812; was a teacher in Bradford Academy. She d. Jan. 10, 1846. Her pastor, the Rev. Gardner B. Perry, D. D., preached a memorial sermon, from which we make the following extracts:

"The teachers of the seminary had lost an able assistant; the pupils an accomplished teacher, a disinterested guardian and friend. Education, religion,—whatever could be promoted by secret prayer or by humble, zealous and enterprising Christian example,—had sustained a loss. But the works of the dead would live after her, and the living might be incited both by her death and by her life, more perfectly to fulfill the precept. 'NOT SLOTHFUL IN BUSINESS; FERVENT IN SPIRIT; SERVING THE LORD.' * * * Her private correspondence was especially worthy of remark. Her personal friendships were fountains of pleasure to herself and her friends, which she ever wished to keep full and flowing. When she had formed a pleasant and valuable acquaintance, she could not allow it to be interrupted by separation. She cultivated it still by frequent writing, and so endeavored to keep the spring perennial. Instead of the adage, 'Out of sight out of mind,' which she abhorred, she seemed to have adopted the more generous sentiment. 'The want of sight made tolerable by correspondence.' The strength and heartiness of her friendship might be abundantly illustrated. To a friend who once said to her, 'I know not how I shall ever repay you for your kindness,' she replied, 'Love for love, you know, is the motto; we will speak of no other compensation.' In a letter to the same friend she writes: 'Is it not a delightful thought that if *ever* we get to heaven we cannot *there* love our friends *too much?* I thought tonight, as we were tearing ourselves away from the home where I had spent so many happy hours, that in heaven the assembly ne'er breaks up.' The following lines from a hymn of hers, written for a social occasion, are a true reflection of her heart:

'Brightly around our circle shines
The light of friends united,
We bless the tie of kindred minds,
The smile of hearts love lighted.'

"If Miss Ladd's letters were full of friendship, they were not merely *sentimental*. She wrote to impart consolation to the afflicted, instruction to the inquiring, and incentives to thought and duty to the careless. Her writings for the periodical press, which were numerous, were, some of them, so much esteemed by different judges, as to be copied from print to print, in this country and in Europe, and in some instances to be translated into other languages. And what she did, and what she became, was not to be attributed to any extraordinary circumstances, or any extraordinary powers. But few were present, of her age, who had not possessed as ample opportunities and as competent endowments as she, and who with the same persistence and ardency of pursuit, in the same Christian spirit, might not have equalled her in all her attainments. * * * When I first became acquainted with Miss Ladd she was three years old (thirty years ago.) I was visiting at her father's house; a comparative stranger among this people at that time. I was sitting at an open window, which was overrun with vines. On these were hanging many flowers. I may have seen this little girl before, among other children, but had never before distinguished her in particular. She had gathered a bunch of these flowers, and bringing them to me she said, modestly, ' I have picked these flowers for *you*, sir, and I hope you will take them and be *pleased* with them.' This was a very pleasant gift; it was pleasantly presented, and if I was to select an emblem of what her *life* has ever since been to me, and I believe to others, it would be THAT GIFT OF THE BUNCH OF FLOWERS."

1506. Warren, bo. July 21, 1813; ma. Lucy Washburn Kingman.
1507. Gardner Perry, bo. Oct. 23, 1814; ma. Lois Batchellor.
1508. John Ingersoll, bo. Feb. 22, 1816; ma. Mary Ann Greenough.
1509. Angelina, bo. Jan. 6, 1818; not married; d. Sept. 15, 1869.
1510. Rebecca Davis, bo. July 20, 1822; not married; d. Dec. 22, 1844.
1511. Rufus George, bo. April 3, 1825; not married; d. Nov. 20, 1844.

(1402) Major John Ladd, (son of Nathaniel[235] and Sarah (Noyes) Ladd,) was born in East Haverhill, Sept. 27, 1791. He ma. Sophia, dau. of Richard and Molly (Edwards) Jaques, Aug. 25, 1814. At the age of 14 he went to sea, sailing from Newburyport; rose to be mate, and assisted in bringing into this country the first Merino sheep, from Cadiz, Spain, for Consul Jarvis. He made several voyages across the Atlantic, sailing to various ports of England, Portugal, and Spain, up the Mediterranean, and several voyages to our southern ports. After seven years passed as a sailor he relinquished sea life in 1812, coming home from London, after war was declared, on a license from the English government. He then apprenticed himself to Richard Jaques, of West Newbury, to learn the comb-making business, and married his second daughter, as above. Settling at East Haverhill, where he resided most of his life, with short exceptions at Haverhill and Newburyport, he carried on the manufacture of combs for some years, then varied his employment with running a packet boat on the Merrimac River, transporting freight from Haverhill to Newburyport and *vice versa*, which occupation he followed for some ten years. Afterwards he was employed as a pilot on a steamer running between Haverhill and Newburyport. He also learned the art of making shoes, and was a natural mechanic in wood work. He was also prominent as a fisherman, in "the Spring season" catching fish in the Merrimac with nets, he owning one of the best fishing grounds on the river. Taking deep interest in local military affairs, he rose through the various grades to colonel of a militia regiment, but declined the honor and retired from the service. Having acted for several years as major, he was well known by that title. Mr. Ladd was always alive to the public interest, being a prominent member of the Baptist Church at East Haverhill, and an active worker for good public schools and temperance. Until the last years of his life he voted and acted with the Democratic party, but left it about 1850. He died Nov. 13, 1852. His widow died ——.

Children.

1512. Sarah P., bo. Dec. 17, 1817; ma. Greenleaf Clark, Oct. 1835. Children: [1]Judson G., bo. Jan. 1837; [2]Isabella T., bo. Sept. 1839, d. Dec. 1842; [3]Irvin K., bo. March 1, 1842; [4]Leverett C., bo. May 22, 1842; [5]Emily, bo. June 3, 1847; [6]Annie L., bo. Sept. 11, 1848; [7]Warren, bo. Dec. 31, 1854.

1513. Sophia B., bo. Sept. 20, 1819; ma. William Reed, May 14, 1842. Children: [1]William, bo. Dec. 1, 1842, editor and proprietor of the Taunton Gazette; [2]Sophia, bo. Jan. 14, 1844; [3]Maria, bo. Aug. 17, 1845; [4]Milton, bo. Oct. 1, 1848, is a prominent lawyer at Fall River, and has been mayor of that city; [5]Waldo, bo. June 2, 1850.

1514. John W., bo. Jan. 7, 1822; ma. Sarah B. Evans.
1515. Nathaniel, bo. Jan. 10, 1824; d. 1825.
1516. Nathaniel, bo. Nov. 29, 1825; d. Sept. 3, 1835.
1517. Byron G., bo. Jan. 6, 1828; ma. Merinda Alexander.
1518. George W., bo. June 15, 1830; ma. Rebecca Morse.
1519. Judson W., bo. June 8, 1832; d. 1833.
1520. Elizabeth C., bo. May 31, 1834; ma. Horace Morse, May 31, 1853. Children: [1]Horace H., bo. Dec. 12, 1854, d. 1856; [2]Nellie A., bo. April 30, 1856, d. 1862; [3]Frank B., bo. Jan. 6, 1858; [4]Leslie, bo. Jan. 8, 1860; [5]George H., bo. Jan. 28, 1862, d. 1864; [6]Gertrude, bo. Jan. 27, 1865; [7]Mabel, bo. May 23, 1869.
1521. Emily A., bo. Jan. 8, 1836; d. 1839.
1522. Maria A., bo. Sept. 9, 1839; d. 1842.

(1404) Frederick P. Ladd, of Brookline, (son of Nathaniel,[235]) ma. Marie Thayer, Dec. 4, 1821. She d. Feb. 1, 1840. He ma. 2d, Susan Forbes Jones, June, 1844. She d. Dec. 9, 1867. He d. Jan. 26, 1865. He was a commission merchant; did business in Boston; was engaged mostly in the Nova Scotia trade; was a very enterprising and successful business man.

Children.

1523. George F., bo. Oct. 16, 1823; d. 1838.
1524. Byron Parker, bo. Aug. 13, 1825; ma. Mary E. Davis.
1525. William A., bo. Dec. 2, 1828; not married; d. Sept. 1853.
1526. Maria Elizabeth, bo. March 29, 1830; not married; d. July 28, 1861.
1527. Helen Cecilia, bo. Dec. 23, 1833; ma. St. Clair Jones, of Weymouth, N. S., Oct. 10, 1855. Children: [1]Herbert Ladd, bo. Jan. 9, 1858; [2]Ernest Ladd, bo. Sept. 7, 1859; [3]Annie Maria, bo. April 26, 1861; [4]Howard Parker, bo. Sept. 7, 1863; [5]Sydney St. Clair, bo. March 5, 1866; [6]Harrison, bo. April 4, 1867; [7]Helen Augusta, bo. Feb. 3, 1869; [8]Cereno Percy, bo. May 29, 1870; [9]Grace L., bo. Oct. 5, 1871; [10]Josephine Moody, bo. June 19, 1874; [11]Frederick William, bo. Nov. 4, 1875.
1528. Josephine I., bo. Nov. 29, 1835; ma. Dr. Henry C. Moody, June 9, 1866.

Child by second wife.

1529. Frances Susan, bo. May 16, 1845; d. Aug. 4, 1855.

(1405) Heman Ladd, of Exeter N. H., (son of Nathaniel,[285]) ma. Hannah, dau. of Samuel and Martha Gilman, of Exeter, N. H., May 14, 1823. He was a student at Bradford Academy, (Mass.) 1813, and early developed a taste for literary pursuits. While still quite a young man he became the successful editor and publisher of "The Northern Chronicler," a prominent journal of those times, published in Newburyport, Mass. A few years later he was induced to visit the West with a view to settling there, but a malignant fever cut short a career full of ambitious hopes and aspirations. He died June 23, 1835.

Children.

1530. Samuel Gilman, bo. Sept. 7, 1825; not married.
1531. Martha, bo. May 5, 1824; ma. William Hedrick, Oct. 17, 1848.
1532. Augusta, bo. March 14, 1827; ma. Henry P. Sweetland, May 5, 1858; 2d. J. M. Hutchins, Sept. 13, 1880.

(1408) Rufus King Ladd, of Boston, (son of Nathaniel,[285]) ma. Emily, dau. of Gardner Pollard, of Lancaster, Oct. 6, 1836. He died March 22, 1862. His wife died Oct. 24, 1850.

Children.

1533. Vivian, bo. Oct. 15, 1837; d. young.
1534. May Gertrude, bo. March 28, 1839; not married.
1535. Lucy Blanche, bo. July 23, 1841; not married.
1536. George Vivian, bo. Feb. 3, 1844; ma. Charlotte Hines.
1537. Grace, bo. Oct. 3, 1846; d. Aug. 24, 1848.
1538. Ella, bo. Dec. 9, 1848; d. Sept. 1849.

(1409) Emery Ladd, of Brattleborough, Vt., (son of Nathaniel,[235]) ma. Louisa C., dau. of Nathaniel and Elizabeth Knowlton, Feb. 11. 1828. He d. Jan. 19, 1849. His wife d. Feb. 7, 1844.

Children.

1539. George D., bo. Nov. 26, 1829; not married; d. Feb. 21, 1878.
1540. William Rufus. bo. April 9, 1831; not married; d. April 9, 1855.
1541. Louisa, bo. Dec. 1, 1834; d. May 25, 1836.
1542. Edward N., bo. Aug. 5, 1836; ma. Nellie R. Reynolds, April 2, 1861.
1543. Constantine F. Volny, bo. April 19, 1838; ma. Ida M. Loomis, Oct. 9, 1868.
1544. Louisa M., bo. March 25, 1840; ma. Byron G. Ladd, (1511) June, 1887. His second wife.
1545. Mary M., bo. April 25, 1842; ma. George M. Colt, April 2, 1858.
1546. Sarah E., bo. June 30, 1844; ma. George W. Pierce, July 16, 1864.

(1418) Welcome D. Ladd, of Thetford, Vt., (son of Thaddeus,[236]) ma. Hannah Hammond, June, 1823. He was town treasurer for nearly twenty years, and held other town offices; settled, as administrator, a great many estates, having been engaged in this business more or less for forty years; was an intelligent and thrifty farmer. He died Jan. 1881.

Children.

1547. Solon, bo. Sept. 1824; ma. Maria Heaton, 1853. No children.
1548. George A., bo. Oct. 1828; ma. Louisa Porter, 1853.

(1419) Jedediah P. B. Ladd, of Worcester, Vt., (son of Thaddeus,[236]) ma. Eliza Baldwin. He died Sept. 9, 1844.

Children.

1549. Thaddeus B., bo. Aug. 9, 1826; ma. Harriet N. Russell.
1550. Asa B., bo. Dec. 24, 1828; d. Jan. 10, 1831.
1551. Marcia Eliza, bo. April 9, 1834; ma. Charles C. Abbott.
1552. Marcell Louisa, bo. May 10, 1840; ma. Dr. J. E. Macomber, June 12, 1858.

(1430) David Montgomery Ladd, of Milford, Mich., (son of Timothy,[241]) was born in Hopkinton, N. H., Feb. 25, 1813. He ma. Martha Ann, dau. of Samuel and Abigail (Davis) Hartwell, of Boylston, Nov. 30, 1840. While she was quite young her parents removed to Perrinton, N. Y. Her parents dying when she was about nine years old, she was adopted by Dr. Daniel Ames and wife, of Pennfield, N. Y., who removed to Milford, Mich., March, 1839. She d. Sept. 15, 1881. From 1831 to 1836 Mr.

Ladd was employed most of the time in collecting subscriptions for newspapers, which led him into almost every town and city in central and northern New York; was subsequently clerk in a dry goods house; then clerk in a general store in Northfield, Mich. In the Spring of 1837 he went to Milford, Mich., and was a clerk there until the Spring of 1838, when the great commercial panic caused such a stagnation of business that few clerks were required. Having saved some money in previous years, in the Fall of 1838 he commenced in a small way a general merchandise business, and continued in it until 1876, when he turned it over to his son, Frank M. Ladd, and retired from active business to enjoy the fruits of his labor.

Children.

1553. Sanford B., bo. Sept. 11, 1844; ma. Clara M. Fuller, June 12, 1870.
1554. Frank M., bo. April 4, 1847; ma. Lizzie M. Webb, Sept. 28, 1881.

(1423) John Ladd, (son of Caleb,[239]) was bo. in Corinth, Vt., Feb. 12, 1795. He went to New York State, and tradition says went to Warren, Mich. He ma. ——.

Children.

1555. Wyman, bo. ——.
1556. Zama, bo. ——.
1557. Adain, bo. ——.

(1424) Bodwell Ladd, of Corinth, Vt., (son of Caleb,[239]) ma. Hannah Sawyer, March 17, 1822. He d. April 5, 1867. His widow d. June 2, 1877. He was a farmer, and held the office of lister for several years.

Children.

1558. Thomas Sawyer, bo. Jan. 19, 1823; ma. Lydia M. Martin, Nov. 1851.
1559. Emily, bo. June 19, 1826; d. Jan. 17, 1832.
1560. Caleb, bo. April 24, 1832; ma. Susan L. Towle, Dec. 2, 1861.
1561. Emily Louisa, bo. Sept. 17, 1835; ma. John A. Hodges, Jan. 28, 1870.
1562. Charles Bodwell, bo. Feb. 9, 1845; ma. Sarah Merrill Sawyer, Oct. 29, 1866.

(1426) Caleb Ladd (son of Caleb,[239]) was born in Corinth, Vt., May 4, 1802. At the age of 21 he went to Boston and worked at stone-laying; was toll-keeper on the Mill Dam twelve years, when he hired to Frederick Tudor, late Tudor & Co., as agent in the ice business at Calcutta, where he remained for about thirty years, and during the last part having an interest in the company. He left their employ in 1864 and came to Watertown in 1866, where he lived until his death in 1876. He ma. Mary Ann Watson, Dec. 1838. She died May 5, 1873.

Children.

1563. Mary Ann, bo. Dec. 9, 1839; ma. Nathaniel Sherborn, June 6. 1861. Children: [1]Eveline Mary, [2]Caleb Charles, [3]William Whipple, [4]Mabel Estella Catherine, [5]Ephel Madoline, [6]Nathaniel Archibald, [7]Gertrude Amelia.
1564. Sarah, bo. Sept. 30, 1841; d. in Calcutta, Nov. 28, 1859.
1565. Caleb Bodwell, bo. Sept. 29, 1843; d. Oct. 8, 1845, in Calcutta.
1566. Joseph Hartwell, bo. Aug. 14, 1845; ma. Amelia Allen Eldridge, Oct. 5, 1875.
1567. Julia Elizabeth, bo. Nov. 13, 1847; ma. William Penn Bigelow, June 1, 1865. Child: William Ford.
1568. Emma Harriet, bo. March 12, 1850; ma. William Russell, Sept. 4, 1869. Child: William Ladd, bo. Oct. 22, 1870.
1569. Emily Abigail, bo. May 1, 1852; ma. Frank A. Brown, June 16, 1874. Children: [1]Lucy Ladd, [2]Frank Howard.
1570. Thomas Henry, bo. Dec. 27, 1856.
1571. Helen Louisa, bo. Dec. 27, 1858; ma. Harry E. Dadmun, Aug. 22, 1877. Child: Guy Ladd, bo. Sept. 5, 1878.

(600) Dudley Ladd, of Concord, N. H., (son of Dudley,[253]) ma. Bethia Hutchins, of Harvard, March 13, 1783, dau. of Col. Gordon and Dolly (Stone) Hutchins. In 1777 he was a volunteer to reinforce the northern army. He died Dec. 23, 1841. His wife died Jan. 29, 1835.

Children.

1572. Samuel Greenleaf, bo. April 14, 1784; ma. Caroline D. Vinal.
1573. John, bo. Aug. 9, 1786; ma. Abigail Prowse.
1574. Dudley, bo. Aug. 19, 1789; ma. Charlotte Eastman.
1575. Nathaniel Green, bo. Sept. 25, 1791; ma. Ann Morrow.
1576. William Manley, bo. Feb. 9, 1794; ma. Betsey Collins.

(638) Eliphalet Ladd, of Dover, N. H., (son of Simeon,[271]) ma. Elizabeth, dau. of Samuel Bragg. We copy the following sketch of him from the History of Rockingham and Strafford Counties, N. H., p. 837: " Eliphalet Ladd came to Dover from Massachusetts about the year 1790. Was the pioneer in newspaper printing in Strafford County. His paper, which was entitled ' The Political and Sentimental Repository, or Strafford Register,' was started July 15, 1790. The title, after a few months, was abbreviated to ' The Political Repository and Straf-

ford Record,' and as such published until Jan. 19, 1792, when the printing office was destroyed by fire. Mr. Ladd either saved enough of his material or immediately purchased a new outfit and started another paper, which he called 'The Phœnix,' so named, doubtless, from the fact that it sprang from the ashes of its predecessor. This he continued to publish until Aug. 29, 1795, when he sold the establishment to his brother-in-law, Samuel Bragg, Jr., who had served his apprenticeship in the office." Chase, in his History of Haverhill, says: "The first newspaper published in Haverhill was the 'Guardian of Freedom,' published by Eliphalet Ladd and S. Bragg. The first number was issued Sept. 6, 1793. On May 10, 1794, Eliphalet Ladd assumed the sole proprietorship of the paper, and on the 29th of the same month he sold out to Samuel Aiken." He died Sept. 12, 1802.

Children.

1577. Samuel Bragg, bo. Feb. 11, 1793; ma. Larissa D. Mattock.
1578. Abby, bo. ——; ma. Jesse Varney.
1579. Eliza, bo. ——; not married.
1580. William, bo. ——; not married.

(643) Charles Ladd, of Everett, (son of Simeon,[271]) ma. Abigail Hilton, of New Market, N. H., May 20, 1822. She died Jan. 6, 1832. He ma. 2d, Mrs. Mary Ann (Burrill) Cummings. He died Oct. 25, 1879.

Children by first wife.

1581. Charles Edward, bo. May 28, 1826; not married; d. April 9, 1884.
1582. George G., bo. June 15, 1831; ma. Martha Josephine Nichols, Oct. 9, 1860.

(647) Henry Ladd, of Portsmouth, N. H., (son of Eliphalet[272] and Abigail (Hill) Ladd,) was born in Exeter, N. H., April 30, 1780. Was educated at Phillips Exeter Academy. His father removed to Portsmouth, N. H., in 1792, where Henry joined him on leaving school, and received his business education in his counting-room. At the age of 21 his father gave him an interest in one of his vessels and sent him as supercargo to Europe, to make his own business acquaintances and connections. In person Mr. Ladd was a trifle over six feet in height, with an erect carriage, light wavy hair, large blue eyes, clear complexion, and a calm, dignified and intelligent expression, which at

once won for him respect and confidence. In England his striking appearance and bearing earned for him the sobriquet of "Prince Harry." On his return to this country he established himself in business as a shipping merchant, and soon after the death of his father in 1806, (who had left an estate, of which Henry was executor, that was said to be the largest in New Hampshire up to that date,) he united his business with his brother Alexander, under the firm name of Henry and Alexander Ladd. They successfully conducted their business through the trying times of the embargo and the war of 1812-15, to their separation in 1832, when his brother retired to take charge of the estate of his father-in-law, the Hon. Nathaniel A. Haven. Mr. Henry Ladd was for many years a director and the last president of the New Hampshire Bank, the charter for which for 50 years his father had obtained from the New Hampshire Legislature. This was the first bank chartered by the State. Having wound up the affairs of the bank, he was unanimously elected president of the Portsmouth Savings Bank, vacated by the death of the Hon. N. A. Haven, who had been the president from its organization. While engaged in these responsible positions, he was frequently urged by his townsmen to represent them and to take office, which he steadily and firmly declined. In his political views he was a pronounced Federalist of the Washington and Hamilton school, as were also all of the members of his father's and mother's large families, who have continued for four generations, without exception, Federalists, Whigs, and Republicans. In his religious views Mr. Ladd clung to the faith of his fathers, and was a prominent member of the First Congregational Society of Portsmouth, and a constant attendant on the preaching of the Rev. Joseph Buckminster and the Rev. Israel Putnam. In 1808 he married Hannah Hurd, daughter of Joseph Hurd, Esq., a wealthy merchant of Charlestown, Mass. She died May 27, 1873. He died in 1842 without an enemy in the world, universally beloved, respected and lamented, and leaving to his widow his three surviving sons and four daughters, the heritage of his good name and an ample fortune.

Children.

1583. Henry Hurd, bo. May 10, 1810; ma. Elizabeth M. Long, Jan. 23, 1839. No children.

1584. Hannah Hurd, bo. Aug. 27, 1811; ma. Ralph Cross Cutter, Sept. 16, 1835, son of Jacob and Miriam (Cross) Cutter, at Portsmouth, N. H. Extracts from the History of the Cutter Family: " Passing three years at Exeter Academy, Mr. Cutter fitted for college, but abandoning that plan went to the island of Hayti as a clerk to a merchant, an intimate friend of his father. At the early age of twenty years he commenced business there on his own responsibility, and for several years was largely engaged in importing American produce and exporting the produce of the island. * * * * He contributed a series of papers to the Knickerbocker Magazine of 1841, under the caption, ' Notes of Life in Hayti.' He was a member of the last board of selectmen of the town of Portsmouth, also of the same board under the new city government, and chairman of the High school committee. The New York Tribune of July 21, 1884, said: ' Ralph C. Cutter died on Saturday at his home, 182 Warren street, Brooklyn, at the age of 74. He was born in Portsmouth, N. H., in 1810. About twenty years ago he came to this city and began the coal business, in which he remained until a few years ago. He was an enthusiastic collector of rare engravings, of which he formed a valuable collection of 25,000, and spent much time in arranging and cataloguing.' " He died suddenly of apoplexy, leaving a widow and two sons. His issue: 1, Ralph Ladd, bo. Oct. 11, 1839, at Portsmouth, N. H.; ma. April 3, 1867, Laura Maria, dau. of Wyllys and Lucy (Camp) Eliot, of Guilford, Conn., and a lineal descendant of John Eliot, the far-famed Indian Apostle; resides in Brooklyn, N. Y.; issue: [1]Laura Eliot, bo. June 17, 1868; [2]Ralph Eliot, bo. Jan. 4, 1870, d. April 26, 1876; [3]Miriam Eliot, bo. Jan. 5, 1874, d. Feb. 19, 1874; [4]Eliot, bo. May 10, 1877; [5]Anna Ladd, bo. April 18, 1878; [6]Guilford Eliot, bo. Dec. 6, 1882, d. Dec. 10, 1882. 2, Henry Ladd, bo. June 27, 1849. 3, Annie Josephine, bo. Sept. 6, 1844; d. March 14, 1858. 4, Charles William, bo. July 16, 1846; d. Aug. 16, 1846. 5, Charles Jacob, bo. Sept. 27, 1848; d. Aug. 26, 1849. 6, Francis Ladd, bo. Aug. 10, 1851.

1585. Caroline Lucy, bo. Oct. 7, 1813; d. June 3, 1876.
1586. Frances Ruth, bo. July 31, 1815.
1587. Mary Josephine, bo. March 18, 1817; d. May 15, 1818.
1588. Joseph Hurd, bo. Feb. 22, 1820; ma. Mary Wales.
1589. Eliphalet, bo. Jan. 5, 1822; ma. Augusta Niles.
1590. Eleanor Mary, bo. March 12, 1824; ma. Rev. William S. Smith, Oct. 1853. Children: [1]Ella Belle, bo. Sept. 28, 1854; [2]Henry Ladd, bo. Feb. 22, 1858; [3]Mary, bo. Sept. 6, 1861; [4]Fanny Easterbrooks, bo. June 26, 1863.

(649) Alexander Ladd, of Portsmouth, N. H., (son of Eliphalet,[272]) was bo. at Exeter, N. H., May 9, 1784, and married, Dec. 29, 1807, Maria Tufton Haven, dau. of Hon. Nathaniel Appleton

and Mary Tufton (Moffatt) Haven, and granddaughter of Col. John Tufton Mason, who in 1745 sold the title to New Hampshire to the Masonian Proprietors. Mr. Ladd was a merchant and ship-owner, in partnership with his brother Henry, who was president of the New Hampshire bank from 1823 to 1842. He was himself a director in the branch bank of the United States from the time of its establishment in Portsmouth in 1816 until it was closed in 1837, and its president from 1832. He was active in town affairs, and served for several years in the State Legislature. He was the principal proprietor of the Portsmouth and Concord Railroad in 1842, and gave liberally of his time and means to all measures designed to raise the intellectual and moral tone, or to restore the declining business prosperity of Portsmouth, and for many other worthy purposes. He filled many places of trust and responsibility, and lived hospitably and generously. He died June 24, 1855, and Mrs. Ladd died at Washington, D. C., Sept. 2, 1861.

Children.

1591. Haven, bo. June 3, 1809. He graduated at Dartmouth, class of 1829, and died in Philadelphia, Pa., Sept. 22, 1829.
1592. Alexander Hamilton, bo. July 10, 1810; d. Sept. 7, 1812.
1593. Charles Haven, bo. March 4, 1812; ma. Susan Lowell Fowle, Nov. 5, 1839.
1594. Charlotte Haven, bo. Sept. 29, 1813; ma. Hon. Samuel Elliot Cowes, May 29, 1833. Children: [1]Hannah Ladd, bo. July 10, 1834, d. Feb. 2, 1836; [2]Meana Tufton, bo. March 26, 1837, d. Nov. 6, 1839; [3]Dr. Elliott, U. S. A., bo. Sept. 9, 1842; [4]Lewis Dwight, bo. May 3, 1845; [5]Grace Darling, bo. Sept. 4, 1847, ma. Charles Albert Page, Oct. 1877.
1595. Alexander Hamilton, bo. July 27, 1815; ma. Elizabeth W. Jones.
1596. Mary T. Haven, bo. Oct. 29, 1816; not married; d. June 2, 1841.
1597. Caroline Sarah, bo. May 27, 1818; ma. John Lord Hayes, May 27, 1839. Children: [1]Alexander Ladd, bo Sept. 20, 1841; [2]William Allen, bo. June 29, 1843; [3]Maria Tufton Ladd, bo. Feb. 28, 1846; [4]Susan Lord, bo. April 8, 1847; [5]Caroline, bo. Feb. 20, 1854.
1598. Elizabeth Chauncy, bo. Nov. 29, 1819; d. Sept. 9, 1820.
1599. Maria Tufton, bo. March 1821; d. July 21, 1835.
1600. Emily Appleton, bo. March 5, 1823; d. June 12, 1826.
1601. John Tufton Mason, bo. Jan. 8, 1826; d. April 8, 1827.
1602. Adeline Haven, bo. July 16, 1828; d. Jan. 19, 1836.
1603. Sophia Catharine, bo. May 26, 1831; d. Feb. 23, 1836.

(815) Alpheus Ladd, of Enosburgh Falls, Vt., (son of Asa,[847]) ma. Jane French, of Haverhill, N. H., March 11, 1811. He died Sept. 3, 1832.

Children.

1604. Sarah, bo. Dec. 10, 1811; ma. Daniel Jones, Jan. 13, 1852.
1605. Anna, bo. July 4, 1813; ma. F. P. Leach, June 16, 1852.
1606. Jane, bo. Aug. 9, 1815; ma. Robert Barber, Jan. 1, 1839.
1607. Anson S., bo. April 5, 1817; ma. Louisa M. Griswold, Jan. 1, 1840.
1608. Hazen B., bo. Sept. 23, 1818; ma. Hepilonea Woodworth, Jan. 1, 1849.
1609. Adeline, bo. Nov. 2, 1824; ma. Arthur W. Woodworth, Nov. 15, 1848.
1610. Rosina S., bo. Dec. 28, 1830; not married.

(190) Jedediah Perkins Ladd (son of Abner[55]) was bo. in Franklin, Conn., Feb. 16, 1767; ma. Rebecca, dau. of Joseph Hazen. He removed from Franklin, Conn., to North Hero, Vt., about 1787. "The first store in North Hero was built in 1809 by Jedediah P. Ladd, who was the first postmaster, and built the only hotel ever erected in town, in 1803. For twenty years it was used for judicial purposes, and was provided with a court-room and jail. Mr. Ladd occupied the building forty-two years, during which time it had served as court-house, church, and tavern. It was burnt down in 1857. Mr. Ladd, who had served as representative, sheriff, register of probate, and judge of the county court, died June 2, 1845."—*History of New England, vol. 2, p. 308.* His widow died Sept. 20, 1847.

Children.

1611. Laura, bo. 1787; ma. Thomas Stoddard. She d. 1847.
1612. Lydia, bo. 1789; ma. Albert Doty. She d. 1876.
1613. Sumner, bo. 1791; ma. Phebe Ames. He d. June 30, 1812.
1614. Ralph, bo. 1793; not married; d. Aug. 23, 1814.
1615. Abigail, bo. 1797; ma. Paul Torry, 1822. She d. 1868.
1616. Abner, bo. Jan. 6, 1800; ma. Susan Whitney, May 24, 1824.
1617. Maria, bo. 1803; not married; d. 1827.
1618. Welthea, bo. 1805; ma. Augustus Knights, 1822. She d. 1862.
1619. Sally, bo. 1806; ma. Merrill Ladd (1632.)

(191) Abner Ladd (son of Abner[55]) ma. Sally Cook, of Franklin, Conn., Aug. 25, 1793.

Children.

1620. Nancy, bo. Feb. 24, 1794.
1621. Gordon, bo. April 11, 1796; ma. Polly Robinson.
1622. Maria, bo. Aug. 21, 1799.
1623. Lurinda, bo. Feb. 25, 1802; ma. Israel S. Ladd (491.)
1624. George, bo. Feb. 27, 1804; not married.
1625. Patta Amenda, bo. Aug. 15, 1806; ma. Septa Ladd (490.)
1626. Jane Adeline, bo. Jan. 6, 1809; ma. Owen Stead.
1627. William Lewis, bo. Oct. 16, 1811; ma. Abigail Robinson.

(192) Erastus Ladd, of Franklin, Conn., (son of Abner,[55]) ma. Sarah Hazen, Jan. 12, 1792. He died April 10, 1813. His widow died Nov. 11, 1842.

Children.

1628. William, bo. July 17, 1792; ma. Malissa Peck, Oct. 3, 1816.
1629. Fredus, bo. May 15, 1794; ma. Lucy Peck.
1630. Harriet, bo. Aug. 21, 1796; ma. Robert Stanton.
1631. Bradley, bo. Dec. 1798; d. Feb. 7, 1801.
1632. Merrill, bo. July 27, 1803; ma. Sally Ladd (1619.)
1633. Sally, bo. Aug. 19, 1805; d. July 8, 18—.
1634. Erastus Perkins, bo. April 29, 1808; ma. Betsey Ladd (1640.)
1635. Sally, bo. Oct. 1, 1811; ma. Charles Perry.

(194) Festus Ladd, of Franklin, Conn., (son of Abner,[55]) ma. Ruby Ladd,[173] of Franklin, Conn., Oct. 10, 1801.

Children.

1636. Asa Spaulding, bo. April 18, 1802; ma. Harriet Cary, July 4, 1825.
1637. Lura, bo. Jan. 7, 1805; d. June 27, 1838.
1638. Austin, bo. April 8, 1807; d. Jan. 27, 1808.
1639. Eliza, bo. April 4, 1809.
1640. Betsey, bo. Dec. 11, 1811; ma. Erastus Perkins Ladd (1634.)
1641. Jabez H., bo. Nov. 9, 1814; d. Nov. 15, 1814.
1642. William, bo. Feb. 4, 1816; ma. Lucretia Waldo.
1643. Laura, bo. Jan. 7, 1819.
1644. Charlotte, bo. Sept. 20, 1821; d. April 5, 1843.
1645. Rufus Spaulding, bo. Aug. 1824; ma. Jane Helen Ladd (1044.)
1646. Lydia S., bo. March 7, 1828.

(1627) William Lewis Ladd (son of Abner[191]) ma. Abigail Robinson, of Franklin, Conn. He died June 6, 1880.

Children.

1647. Sarah Emma, bo. June 5, 1838.
1648. George Lewis, bo. Dec. 25, 1844.

(167) Buel Ladd, of Norwich, Conn., (son of Mary,[167] grandson of Ezekiel,[51]) ma. Clarissa Peck, Nov. 17, 1816. He ma. 2d, Almira Fillmore. He died July 4, 1879.

Children.

1649. Jabez Buel, bo. Sept. 20, 1817; ma. Jane Hyde.
1650. Mary Clarissa, bo. Dec. 18, 1819; ma. John N. Cutler.
1651. Chester Hyde, bo. Dec. 29, 1821; not married.
1652. Seba Ayer, bo. Jan. 26, 1824; ma. Anson F. Deane.
1653. Harriet Aurelia, bo. April 15, 1826; ma. Edmund W. Deane.
1654. William H. Webb, bo. June 11, 1828; ma. Mary E. Grant.

1655. Angelina A., bo. Jan. 12, 1830; ma. Elijah Leach.
1656. Julia Emily, bo. Jan. 11, 1832; ma. James C. Griswold.
1657. Electa E., bo. Jan. 12, 1834; ma. Gideon H. Abel.
1658. Leonard Wesley, bo. Sept. 19, 1836; ma. Mary Hough.
1659. DeWitt Clinton Lathrop, bo. Oct. 28, 1839; ma. Alvira D. Long.

(627) Samuel Ladd, of Gilmanton, N. H., (son of Col. Samuel,[261]) ma. Polly Davis. He died April 12, 1836.

Children.

1660. Mehitable, bo. ——; not married.
1661. Betsey, bo. ——; ma. James Boyd.
1662. Samuel, bo. ——; ma. Sarah Gale. No children.
1663. Nathaniel, bo. ——; not married.
1664. Charles, bo. ——; ma. Dorothy Willey.
1665. George W., bo. ——; ma. Susan Mason.
1666. Joseph, bo. ——; ma. Hannah Hill.
1667. Abigail, bo. ——; ma. John Smith.
1668. Jonathan, bo. ——; ma. Hannah Ladd.
1669. Gilman, bo. ——; not married.

(628) John Ladd, of Sanbornton, N. H., (son of Samuel,[261]) ma. Mehitable Gale, of Gilmanton, N. H., June 16, 1793. He died June 12, 1860.

Children.

1670. Abigail, bo. July 10, 1794; ma. Joseph Kezer.
1671. John, Jr., bo. Dec. 13, 1796; ma. Nancy Badger.
1672. Susan, bo. Oct. 8, 1798; ma. Moses Taylor.
1673. Dudley, bo. Oct. 9, 1800; d. March 24, 1827.
1674. Stephen G., bo. Feb. 6, 1803; not married; d. March 26, 1826.
1675. Gould Dimond, bo. Feb. 11, 1805; ma. Betsey Chase.
1676. Mary, bo. April 5, 1807; ma. Henry M. Pearson.
1677. Eliza L., bo. Aug. 22, 1809; ma. Barnett H. Ladd (1682.)
1678. Daniel, bo. Oct. 18, 1811.
1679. Eunice, bo. Oct. 18, 1813; ma. John A. Lawrence, Feb. 2, 1831.

(629) Edward Ladd, of Belmont, N. H., (son of Col. Samuel,[261]) ma. Hannah Hoyt, July 3, 1798. He died July 14, 1820. His widow died March 10, 1856.

Children.

1680. Nancy, bo. Nov. 15, 1799; ma. Jonathan Taylor. She d. Mar. 4, 1839.
1681. Harriet, bo. March 16, 1803; ma. Daniel Sanborn.
1682. Barnett H., bo. July 9, 1807; ma. Eliza Ladd (1677.)
1683. Langdon, bo. July 5, 1811; ma. Sylvania Colby.

(630) Isaac Ladd, of Belmont, N. H., (son of Col. Samuel,[261]) ma. Lois Woodman. He died July 30, 1881. His wife died March 28, 1828.

Children.

1684. Henry. bo. July 11, 1802; d. Oct. 26, 1802.
1685. Charlotte, bo. Sept. 9, 1803; ma. George L. Mead, of Laconia, N. H.
1686. Charles, bo. May 24, 1805; d. Sept. 17, 1831.
1687. Isaac, Jr., bo. Feb. 1, 1807.
1688. George S., bo. June 13, 1808.
1689. Harriet, bo. Aug. 6, 1810; d. May 7, 1877.
1690. John W., bo. Feb. 5, 1813.
1691. Mary J., bo. Dec. 30, 1815.

(632) Jonathan Ladd, of Laconia, N. H., (son of Col. Samuel,[261]) ma. Rachel, dau. of Col. Dudley and Martha (Swain) Prescott, Feb. 17, 1808, who died 1815. He ma. 2d, Betsey Lawrence, April 17, 1816. He died March 16, 1826.

Children.

1692. Susan Augusta, bo. Feb. 16, 1810; ma. Andrew Watkins, Dec. 1, 1835.
1693. Lucian A., bo. March 11, 1812; d. Dec. 29, 1812.

Children by second wife.

1694. Lucian A., bo. Aug. 18, 1821; ma. Mary Jane Smith, July 31, 1843.
1695. Olive Jane, bo. June 7, 1824.

(633) Dudley Ladd, of Belmont, N. H., (son of Col. Samuel,[261]) ma. Abigail, dau. of David Plummer, of Newbury.

Children.

1696. Hannah P., bo. April 29, 1812; ma. Ebenezer S. Lawrence.
1697. David Plummer, bo. Nov. 13, 1816; ma. Julia A. Hoyt.

(635) Thomas Ladd, of Belmont, N. H., (son of Col. Samuel,[261]) ma. Eunice Lyford, Dec. 11, 1806.

Children.

1698. John Lyford, bo. Sept. 27, 1807; ma. L. Jane Eager.
1699. Drusilla, bo. Dec. 12, 1808; ma. Jeremiah Jaques. She d. Oct. 11, 1866.
1700. Ransom S , bo. May 12, 1811; ma. Rhoda Gove. No children.

(573) John Ladd, of Chester, (son of John,[214]) ma. Sarah Smith, of New Haven, Conn.

Children.

1701. Sarah R., bo. Nov. 2, 1820; ma. Samuel M. Converse, Jan. 19, 1848.
1702. Laura W., bo. Nov. 15, 1823; ma. Horace Converse, Nov. 14, 1847.
1703. Eliab, bo. Feb. 6, 1825; ma. Augusta Weeks, 1853.

1704. Samuel S., bo. April 18, 1826; ma. Cynthia Boynton, 1856.
1705. Harlow, bo. March 29, 1828; ma. Sarah E. Packard, Jan. 26, 1871.
1706. Harriet S., bo. Nov. 3, 1829; ma. Dexter Hunter, June, 1847.
1707. Susan O., bo. Nov. 26, 1832; ma. George Bennett, April 10, 1855.
1708. Mary, bo. Sept. 25, 1834; ma. Eli W. Bartlett.
1709. Alfred E., bo. Jan. 17, 1837; ma. Nancy Sanderson.
1710. Helen, bo. Jan. 1, 1839; ma. Oliver Ames, Sept. 1857.
1711. Marcia Ann, bo. Oct. 6, 1840; ma. Charles Morey, 1859.

(578)   Lathrop Ladd, of Haydenville, (son of John,[214]) ma. Hannah Parsons, of Hinsdale.

Children.

1712. Warren, bo. ——.
1713. Mary, bo. ——; ma. Obed Ames.
1714. Jeanette, bo. ——; not married.
1715. Esther, bo. ——; ma. Richard Atwood.

(1703)   Eliab Ladd, of Haydenville, (son of John,[573]) ma. Augusta Weeks, 1853.

Child.

1716. Alice, bo. ——.

(1704)   Samuel S. Ladd, of Bristol, Conn., (son of John,[573]) ma. Cynthia Boynton, July 25, 1852. She died July 28, 1856. He ma 2d, Marietta Barrett, of Burlington, Conn., June 19, 18—.

Children by second wife.

1717. Ida S., bo. March 2, 1861; ma. Charles Locey, Dec. 15, 1886.
1718. Sylvester, bo. June 18, 1865.

(1705)   Harlow Ladd, of Northampton, (son of John,[573]) ma. Sarah E. Packard, Jan. 26, 1871.

Children.

1719. Eva M., bo. Dec. 3, 1872.
1720. George Harlow, bo. Oct. 12, 1876.

(584)   Silas Trumball Ladd, of Painsville, Ohio, (son of Jesse,[320]) ma. Elizabeth Williams, March 3, 1841. He moved to Madison, Ohio, in 1812; went as a boy into business in Painsville, Ohio; went to Hudson, Ohio, in 1842; was treasurer of Western Reserve College until 1850; removed to Painsville, Ohio, and continued in business there until his death, Dec. 1879. He was deacon of the Congregational Church a great many years.

Children.

1721. George T., bo. Jan. 19, 1842; ma. Cornelia A. Tollman, Dec. 8, 1869.
1722. Mary E., bo. Jan. 2, 1844; ma. Prof. James A. Towle, Nov. 30, 1868.
1723. Martha B., bo. June. 1846; ma. L. O. Brastow.
1724. Laura W., bo. Feb. 1849.
1725. Clara B., bo. April 15, 1851; ma. Charles O. Higgins.

(586)   Dr. William Marshall Ladd (son of Daniel[221]) was born April 2, 1804, near Eaton, Madison Co., N. Y. "Up to the time of his early manhood his life was occupied in acquiring the rudiments of an education, such as were afforded by the schools of his neighborhood, and assisting his father in the work of the mill and farm. He early developed studious habits, scholarly attainments, and the desire for a position, — something better than the ordinary result of his surroundings would appear to promise. At the early age of 20 he was appointed teacher of public schools, which vocation was followed some two or three years, when, under the patronage of the eminent Dr. Merriman, a kinsman, he entered the Hudson (Ohio) College, to prepare himself for the study of medicine, which profession he subsequently took up, graduating with high honors in 1830, and settling to establish his practice at Fitchville, Huron County, Ohio, then practically a wilderness, but a locality rapidly filling up with some of the best pioneer blood of New York and New England. Here, in the year 1832, he married Julia Ann Hobbie, daughter of Hon. Ebenezer Hobbie, of Cayuga County, N. Y., formerly of Greenwich, Conn., and where his children were born. Rising rapidly to the front rank of his profession, his practice soon covered a field in extent that appears impossible to cover by practitioners of the present day. All night rides through almost trackless forests, to reach the bedside of the suffering pioneer, was but an incident in the early practice of this backwoods physician. Endowed with brilliant talent adapted to his profession, a physique moulded in lines that apparently defied hardships, and a sense of duty unswerving in his convictions, all tended to give him a most honorable place in the affections of that people, who, as the country improved, urged upon him positions of honor and preferment. So wedded was he to his profession but little outside of it was congenial to his tastes. His lectures on medical science covered a wide field, and were eagerly sought and lis-

tened to by the then rising generation of aspirants for medical honors, several of whom were constantly pursuing their studies under his mentorship, and obtaining information in the school of his extended practice. Among these may be found physicians occupying the highest places in the profession. The hardships endured planted the seed of disease the most vigorous constitution could not withstand. At the early age of 49 he passed away, giving up his practice but a few days prior to his demise, dying in his chair. A devoted husband, a loving father, a Christian gentleman. 'Twas such as he that blazed the way, and made the Great West possible." He died April 29, 1853. His widow died March 12, 1875.

Children.

1726. Mary J., bo. Oct. 25, 1833; ma. Lyman Fay, of New London, Ohio, Aug. 24, 1853.
1727. William M., bo. July 7, 1837; ma. Mrs. Frances (Jones) Stephens, July 7, 1884.
1728. Emma Louisa, bo. March 10, 1839; ma. C. K. Smith, Nov. 12, 1868. Children: [1]Emma L., bo. April 15, 1871; [2]Celeste, bo. April 12, 1872; [3]Fred. Fay, bo. Aug. 15, 1875.
1729. Georgianna E., bo. June 18, 1841; ma. W. M. Eccles, July 29, 1875.

(589) Orson Ladd, of Eaton, N. Y., (son of Daniel,[221]) ma. Dorothy Stevens, Oct. 24, 1843.

Children.

1730. Elizabeth Irene, bo. Feb. 2, 1845; ma. Henry W. Wilcox, Oct. 4, 1864.
1731. Simeon, bo. March 9, 1849.
1732. Daniel, bo. Dec. 4, 1854; ma. Anna M. Frink, March 7, 1877. No children.

(590) Roswell Ladd, of Melone, N. Y., (son of Daniel,[221]) ma. Rebecca Chamberlain, of Erlain, N. Y.

Children.

1733. Daniel, bo. Oct. 1, 1845.
1734. Frederick, bo. Jan. 10, 1848.
1735. George, bo. Jan. 1850.
1736. Ella, bo. 1854.

(593) Jesse T. Ladd, of Eaton, N. Y., (son of Daniel,[221]) ma. Harriet M.. dau. of Abner Morse, of Nelson, N. Y., Sept. 28, 1852. He died Oct. 20, 1865.

Children.
1737. Orrilla Aletta, bo. Jan. 18, 1854.
1738. Mattie, bo. Sept. 10, 1859; d. Oct. 26, 1862.
1739. Minnie B., bo. July 20, 1863.

(540) Wareham Ladd, of Vernon, Conn., (son of Samuel,[200]) ma. Abigail Fellows, Nov. 30, 1815.

Children.
1740. Ira Fellows, bo. Nov. 9, 1816.
1741. Eliza Ann, bo. Nov. 29, 1817; ma. Emilus Sharpe, April 23, 1844.
1742. William Rice, bo. Nov. 6, 1818; ma. Elizabeth E. Tryon, May 1, 1855.
1743. Laura Adeline, bo. Dec. 14, 1819; ma. Gilbert Lane, April 27, 1844.
1744. Samuel Chapman, bo. Dec. 23, 1820; ma. Mary E. McDowell, Nov. 28, 1852.
1745. Abigail Sophia, bo. May 14, 1823; ma. George Tryon, Aug. 23, 1846.
1746. Amarel Calista, bo. Nov. 28, 1826.
1747. Charles Augustus, bo. March 26, 1830; ma. Amaria Fuller, Aug. 23, 1853.

(541) Jacob Ladd, of Tolland, Conn., (son of Samuel,[200]) ma. Rebecca Charter, Nov. 26, 1812. He died March 29, 1856. His widow died Dec. 21, 1868.

Children.
1748. Caroline, bo. Aug. 8, 1813; ma. Orson A. Richardson, 1835.
1749. Horace W., bo. July 11, 1815; ma. Charlotte Bates, 1834.
1750. Samuel W., bo. April 28, 1817; ma. Margaret Davis, 1837.
1751. Frederick R., bo. Sept. 10, 1819; ma. Roxey Clapp, 1850.
1752. Almira, bo. April 19, 1823; ma. Joseph Butler, 1847.
1753. Calista, bo. Dec. 13, 1826; ma. Roger Vose, 1852.
1754. Edwin W., bo. Feb. 18, 1829; ma. Mary L. Baily, 1855.
1755. Theodore A., bo. April 11, 1836; not married.

(607) John Ladd, of Louden, N. H., (son of Daniel,[254]) ma. Feb. 17, 1800, Lydia, dau. of John Sanborn. He died 1818.

Children.
1756. Ruth, bo. Feb. 22, 1801; d. Aug. 8, 1803.
1757. Daniel, bo. Sept. 29, 1802; ma. Abigail Martin.
1758. Ruth, bo. July 4, 1804; ma. John Blake.
1759. Louisa, bo. June 8, 1806; ma. True Perkins.

(610) Gideon Ladd, of Louden, N. H., (son of Daniel,[254]) ma. Sept. 7, 1808, Polly Osgood. He died Feb. 2, 1848. His widow died Nov. 6, 1870.

Children.

1760. Rosina, bo. Nov. 6, 1809; ma. D. E. Smith, of Gilmanton, N. H.
1761. Seldon Osgood, bo. Oct. 1811.
1762. James Gilman, bo. Feb. 24, 1813; d. July 13, 1813.
1763. Olive Maria, bo. June 15, 1815; ma. J. B. Marston, of Gilmanton, N. H.
1764. Albert Warren, bo. April 2, 1816; ma. Mary M. Wallace.
1765. Seneca Augustus, bo. April 29, 1819; ma. Susan Tilton.
1766. Newell Corser, bo. May 6, 1821; ma. Sarah Smith.
1767. Philander M., bo. March 4, 1823; d. March 30, 1843.
1768. Parish Badger, bo. July 1, 1825; ma. ——.
1769. Joseph Warren, bo. Sept. 30, 1827; d. Oct. 27, 1833.
1770. Benjamin F., bo. June 8, 1829; d. July 7, 1846.
1771. Charles Joseph, bo. Dec. 12, 1831; ma. Eliza Lang.

(612) James Ladd, of Epping, N. H., (son of Nathaniel,[255]) ma. Elizabeth Gould, of Henniker, N. H.

Children.

1772. Mary A., bo. ——; ma. Franklin B. Ingraham.
1773. James A., bo. ——; not married.
1774. Nathaniel Gould, bo. July 13, 1798; ma. Abigail Kelly Mead.
1775. Betsey Gould, bo. ——; ma. Walter Stuart Abbott.
1776. Zoroaster, bo. April 24, 1800; ma. Eleanor Starkweather, Jan. 1, 1827.
1777. Seneca, bo. ——; ma. Mehitable Gardner.
1778. Ira Wadleigh, bo. ——.
1779. Eudotia, bo. ——.
1780. Sophronia S., bo. ——; ma. Moses S. Abbott.
1781. William Pearson, bo. ——.
1782. Susan Lauretta, bo. ——; ma. John Rogers.

(613) Daniel Ladd, of Stewartstown, N. H., (son of Nathaniel,[255]) ma. Elizabeth Goodwin.

Children.

1783. Harriet, bo. ——; ma. Washington Chandler.
1784. David, bo. ——; ma. Betsey Ingalls; 2d, Hulda Owen.
1785. Mary, bo. April 12, 1814; ma. Stephen Morrison, Sept. 1832.
1786. Samuel, bo. ——; not married.

(614) Nathaniel Ladd, of Concord, N. H., (son of Nathaniel,[255]) was born in Epping, N. H.; ma. Dolly Smith. He settled at Concord, N. H., and carried on there quite an extensive tanning business for several years, but became financially embarrassed, and to escape the then existing law of imprisonment for debt was obliged to leave the country. He went to Trinidad, a port of Spain, where he built up another tanning business, and died there in 1820.

Children.

1787. Nathaniel, bo. ——; ma. Mrs. Mary (Gordon) Folsom.
1788. Dolly, bo. ——; ma. Winthrop Hilton.
1789. Daniel Watson, bo. May 21, 1798; ma. Rebecca Plummer, 1820.

(616)   Dr. John Ladd, of Epping, N. H., (son of Nathaniel,[255]) was born in Epping, N. H., Jan. 28, 1782. "He was a student of Phillips Academy, Andover, when the death of his father occurred, which interrupted the course of his classical studies, which he had intended to pursue in preparation for entering the medical profession. By teaching school he obtained the means of accomplishing his purpose, and commenced the study of medicine with the eminent Dr. Lyman Spaulding, president of the College of Surgeons of New York University, western district, from which school he received his degree. He was commissioner upon the medical staff of the Eleventh Regiment, United States Infantry, in the war of 1812. From 1806 to 1829 he was a resident of Lee, N. H., in the county of Strafford, where he was elected to various responsible offices. He was an active member of the Jeffersonian Republican party, and was invited to deliver occasional public addresses. He wrote with facility in prose and verse, and was a frequent contributor to the newspapers of the day. His range of information was extensive, especially in history, philosophy, and theology. His opinions were broad, liberal and hospitable to all forms of faith. At his house clergymen of all classes always found a cordial welcome, and it is worthy of note that there, for nearly thirty years, with only incidental interruptions, a regular conference meeting was held every week, which the friends of various denominations in the neighborhood were accustomed to attend." He ma. Profinda Robinson, July 2, 1806, who was born in New Market, N. H., Nov. 24, 1798. He died at Epping, N. H., Aug. 23, 1845. His widow died Aug. 18, 1885. (See History of Rockingham Co., N. H.)

Children.

1790. Caroline Profinda, bo. May 16, 1807; ma. Benjamin Watson, of Lowell, Sept. 13, 1833. She d. ——.
1791. John Savillian, bo. July 2, 1809; ma. Adealia Babson.
1792. Mary Augusta, bo. Nov. 24, 1816; ma. Benjamin P. Brown, May 4, 1840. Children: ¹Lucy Caroline, bo. Feb. 13, 1841; ²Frances Adilea, bo. July 19, 1842. Mr. Brown d. at Lowell, March 5, 1843. She ma. 2d, Benjamin Watson, of Lowell, Oct. 6, 1844, whose first wife was

her sister, (1795) by whom she had: [1]Caroline Profinda, bo. Dec. 19, 1845; [2]Frances Ella Augusta, bo. April 26, 1849; [3]Clarence Benjamin, bo. Aug. 21, 1852, d. Oct. 8, 1853; [4]Effie Claribel, bo. Aug. 21, 1852.

(617) Daniel Ladd, of Lee, N. H., (son of Jeremiah,[256]) ma. Grace Rowell, of Nottingham, N. H. He removed from Lee to Garland, Me., June, 1820, and bought a farm there. He died Feb. 29, 1867. His widow died May 21, 1869.

Children.

1793. Betsey, bo. Oct. 25, 1802; ma. Enoch Rollins, 1820.
1794. Jeremiah, bo. Oct. 2, 1804; ma. Philanda L. Reed.
1795. Rice R., bo. Nov. 12, 1806; ma. Sarah Holt, 1838. He d. Sept. 21, 1842.
1796. Daniel, bo. Jan. 19, 1808. Was drowned in Lee, July 29, 1821.
1797. Israel, bo. April 26, 1810; ma. Isabel Keyes, April 10, 1834.
1798. Abram, bo. March 14, 1812; not married; d. Oct. 20, 1884.
1799. Alice Jane, bo. Aug. 18, 1813; ma. John K. Haskell, 1836.

(654) John Ladd, of Sutton, Vt., (son of Elias,[264]) ma. Dolly Colby, March 5, 1799.

Children.

1800. Thomas Colby, bo. Feb. 27, 1800; ma. Lucy Walker, 1827.
1801. Ira, bo. May 26, 1802; ma. Eliza Gallaher, 1831.
1802. Samuel, bo. Nov. 21, 1803; ma. Sally Jones, 1826.
1803. Louisa, bo. May 3, 1806; ma. Chauncy Holman, 1840. Child: Sylvester J.
1804. John, bo. June 17, 1808; ma. Abigail Beckwith, 1833.
1805. James S., bo. Aug. 23, 1811; ma. C. Ann Barber, Jan. 26, 1841. No children. He was hopefully converted in the Spring of 1833; was baptized into the fellowship of the Baptist Church of LeRoy, N.Y., March, 1834. Entered Middlebury Academy, N. Y., 1834; entered the Freshman Class of Madison University, April, 1837; graduated June 10, 1840. Was ordained as a Baptist minister in the Autumn of 1840, and continued to preach until April, 1880, when loss of sight in one eye forbade further public labor. He baptized over eight hundred converts.
1806. Eliphalet, bo. Sept. 4, 1818.
1807. Alonzo, bo. Nov. 3, 1822.
1808. Lorenzo, bo. Nov. 3, 1822.

(655) Elias Ladd, of Holderness, N. H., (son of Elias,[264]) ma. Dorcas Moore, of Kittery, Me.

Children.

1809. Abigail, bo. Oct. 22, 1796; ma. Samuel Curry, of Holderness, N. H.
1810. William, bo. Aug. 3, 1798; ma. Polly Sturtevant.

1811. Charlotte, bo. March 21, 1800; d. Dec. 1, 1800.
1812. Asa, bo. July 3, 1802; ma. Betsey Carter.
1813. Charlotte, bo. Sept. 20, 1804; d. Sept. 13, 1806.
1814. Polly, bo. May 29, 1807; ma. Jesse Smith, May 26, 1830.
1815. Jesse, bo. Feb. 23, 1811; ma. Arthusa Marston.
1816. Samuel, bo. July 22, 1814; d. Sept. 15, 1818.
1817. Newell, bo. July 22, 1818; d. Oct. 15, 1825.

(657) Josiah Ladd, of Moultonborough, N. H., (son of Elias,[264]) ma. Miriam Webster, Oct. 26, 1800. He died at Lyndon, Vt.

Children.

1818. Stephen, bo. March 8, 1801; ma. Sally Adams.
1819. Jonathan, bo. Oct. 15, 1802; ma. Mercy Glines, Oct. 20, 1821.
1820. Asa, bo. Dec. 6, 1804; ma. Mercy Quimby.
1821. Smith, bo. May 2, 1806.
1822. Abigail, bo. Feb. 4, 1808; ma. Thomas Blakely.
1823. Daniel, bo. Feb. 9, 1810.
1824. Elbridge, bo. July 17, 1812; ma. Hannah Kane.
1825. John, bo. March 9, 1814; not married.
1826. Rhoda, bo. April 14, 1817; ma. Greenleaf Prescott, March 13, 1835.
1827. Moses, bo. Sept. 1819; ma. Adeline Sawyer.
1828. Charles, bo. Sept. 30, 1822; ma. Sarah Quimby.

(659) James Ladd, of Clinton, Me., (son of Elias,[264]) ma. Hannah Harriman, July 7, 1806. He died at North Marlborough, Me.

Children.

1829. Calvin B., bo. March 4, 1807; ma. Elizabeth Atwood.
1830. Asenath T., bo. Oct. 9, 1808; ma. Joseph Snow, Nov. 1829.
1831. Lorinda B., bo. Oct. 3, 1810; ma. Thomas Brown, Jr., Oct. 1, 1835.
1832. Philona, bo. Nov. 14, 1812; d. May 10, 1824.
1833. Newell H., bo. Feb. 16, 1815; ma. Lorinda W. Brown, Jan. 11, 1842.
1834. Mary E., bo. Jan. 11, 1819; ma. James Harriman, Oct. 24, 1841.
1835. James, bo. March 4, 1821; d. July 4, 1825.
1836. Hannah M., bo. Nov. 19, 1823; d. Aug. 7, 1833.
1837. Betsey A., bo. Feb. 21, 1826; ma. John Hutchinson, Oct. 8, 1844.
1838. Maria E., bo. April 10, 1829; ma. Wesley Owen, Feb. 4, 1854.

(679) Simeon Ladd, Jr., of Redfield, Me., (son of Simeon,[280]) ma. Mercy, dau. of Nathaniel Folsom, of Mt. Vernon, Me. She d. Sept. 1, 1820, and he ma. 2d, Lydia Sanborn.

Children.

1839. Gorham, bo. July 22, 1809; ma. Charlotte Whittier.
1840. Paul, bo. Dec. 25, 1810; ma. Hannah Whittier.
1841. Warren, bo. Jan. 21, 1812; ma. Lydia Wellman.
1842. Harvey, bo. Jan. 21, 1814; ma. Laura Ann Packard.
1843. Hiram, bo. March 1, 1816; ma. Julia Ann Dexter.

Children by second wife.

1844. Cyrus A., bo. Nov. 3, 1822; ma. Louisa Crane.
1845. Mercy Ann, bo. Jan. 11, 1825; d. 1826.
1846. Mercy Ann, bo. Feb. 28, 1828; ma. Hiram Wellman.
1847. Mary Elizabeth, bo. July 28, 1833; ma. Lyman Trask.

(1482) Heman Ladd, of Dunbarton, N. H., (son of Timothy,[230]) ma. Mary Messer, Dec. 1, 1808. She died March 13, 1864.

Children.

1848. Achsah Messer. bo. Aug. 9, 1809.
1849. James, bo. July 21, 1811.
1850. Mary Butler, bo. Nov. 21, 1813.
1851. John Messer, bo. Sept. 13, 1816; d. Nov. 23, 1820.
1852. Abigail Bodwell, bo. Jan. 19, 1819; ma. W. W. Richardson.
1853. Milton G., bo. Sept. 5, 1821; d. July 15, 1848.

(1492) Joseph Park Ladd, of Belfast, Me., (son of Eliphalet,[231]) ma. Mehitable C. Towne, July 26, 1808. He died Feb. 4, 1830. His widow died Sept. 25, 1862, in Chicago.

Children.

1854. Almatia M., bo. Aug. 9, 1809; ma. George W. Russ, Sept. 22, 1834.
1855. Aurelia F , bo. Feb. 11, 1811; ma. John A. Rollins, Oct. 23, 1835.
1856. Aurelius F., bo. Nov. 24, 1813; ma. Lydia Washburn, Oct. 17, 1841.
1857. Attilus Alexis, bo. Dec. 6, 1815; ma. Jane C. Russ, Feb. 2, 1840.
1858. Acelia A. S., bo. Oct. 17, 1817; ma. Edson H. Tafts, Sept. 23, 1872.
1859. Arnaldo W. P., bo. May 26, 1819; ma. Mary Reynolds, May 24, 1846.
1860. Alphonso S., bo. Aug. 19, 1821; ma. Mary Grady, 1851.
1861. Aticus R., bo. Sept. 5, 1827; ma. Louisa B. Beck, Oct. 15, 1870.

(1495) Alexander Park Ladd, of Meredith, N. H., (son of Eliphalet,[231]) ma. Charlotte Hacket, of Holderness, N. H., March, 1814.

Children.

1862. Mary Taylor, bo. Dec. 22, 1814; ma. William Ladd; 2d, Pingree Cummings; 3d, Ira Davis.
1863. John Orr Monroe, bo. Sept. 10, 1816; ma. Nancy Coombs; 2d, Ruth Abbott. No children.
1864. Timothy Boyd, bo. April 14, 1820; ma. Susan Emerson, 1851.
1865. Joseph Park, bo. May 22, 1822; ma. Charlotte Virgin, Oct. 12, 1851. No children.
1866. Eugene Hackett, bo. Nov. 22, 1834; ma. Josephine Fournival. No children.

(1496)　Darius Ladd, of Boston, (son of Eliphalet,[331]) ma. Emily Brewster, dau. of Jonathan and Betsey (Richards) Brewster, March 31, 1831.

Children.

1867. Harrison, bo. ——; d. young.
1868. Emily Julia, bo. ——; ma. Thomas R. Wharton.
1869. Ellen, bo. ——.

(745)　John Ladd, of Brentwood, N. H., (son of John,[310]) ma. Betsey L. Marston, Dec. 26, 1841. She died Feb. 15, 1862. He ma. 2d, Mrs. Mary Wales, Aug. 28, 1862. She died at Amesbury, Sept. 24, 1883.

Children.

1870. George O., bo. Feb. 15, 1843; ma. Betsey Britton.
1871. John Abbott, bo. 1844; d. March 30, 1868.
1872. Sarah Elizabeth, bo. March 31, 1847; d. May 18, 1865.
1873. Ella Amanda, bo. Aug. 28, 1852.

(619)　Thing Ladd, of Salisbury, N. H., (son of Edward,[258]) removed to Cabot, Vt., and from there to Peacham, Vt., where he died. He ma. Elizabeth Jimson.

Children.

1874. Sally, bo. in Salisbury, N. H.; ma. John Randlet.
1875. Hannah, bo. in Salisbury, N. H.; ma. Abel Webster. Children: ¹Julia, ²Mary Ann.
1876. Moses, bo. in Salisbury, N. H., June 27, 1791; ma. Hannah Carr.
1877. Samuel, bo. in Salisbury, N. H.; d. at Peacham, Vt., 1811.
1878. Nancy, bo. in Salisbury, N. H.; ma. Joel Weeks.
1879. Martha, bo. in Salisbury, N. H.; ma. Ephraim Goodnough.
1880. John, bo. in Salisbury, N. H.; ma. Nabby Williams.
1881. Shaw, bo. in Salisbury, N. H.; ma. Dorcas Norris.
1882. Edward, bo. in Salisbury, N. H.; ma. Sophia Gookin.
1883. Betsey, bo. in Salisbury, N. H.; not married.
1884. Joseph, bo. in Salisbury, N. H., Jan. 27, 1800; ma. Betsey Hunt, Dec. 5, 1821.
1885. Polly, bo. in Cabot, Vt.; ma. Aaron Potter.
1886. Louisa, bo. in Cabot, Vt.; ma. Justus Hunt.
1887. Hollis, bo. in Cabot, Vt.; ma. Elvira Taylor.

(620)　John Ladd, of Tunbridge, Vt., (son of Edward,[258]) ma. Sally Clough.

Children.

1888. James, bo. July 20, 1796.
1889. Deborah, bo. Nov. 5, 1797; ma. ——.

1890. Hannah, bo. July 17, 1799; ma. Benjamin Severns. Children: First four d. young; [5]Hannah E., bo. 1823, ma. Charles West, and died Dec. 24, 1888; [6]George, bo. Sept. 23, 1831, ma. Josephine Clough; [7]Lizzie, bo. Sept. 25, 1832, ma. S. B. Horton, May 27, 1856; [8]Roxanna, bo. Nov. 29, 1834, ma James J. Green, who died, and she ma. 2d, Warren A. Himes.
1891. John Shaw, bo. Feb. 3, 1801; ma. Mary Chamberlain.
1892. Elijah Shaw, bo. 1802; ma. Phila West. June 6, 1828.
1893. Tyler. bo. ——; ma. Alfa Rand.
1894. Isaac, bo. Nov. 8, 1809; ma. Mary ——.
1895. Enoch, bo. Nov. 10, 1811; d. about 1833.
1896. Roxanna, bo. Oct. 1814; ma. Charles Newton. Children: [1]Charles Isaac, [2]Norman, [3]Truman, [4]Roxanna, [5]Diana, [6]George, [7]Rix, [8]Fanny.

(621) Joseph Ladd, of Andover, N. H., (son of Edward,[258]) ma. Polly Thing. He removed, in 1838, to Peoria, Peoria County, Ill. He died at Lancaster, Ill., Sept. 24, 1852.

Children.

1897. Joseph, bo. Feb. 23, 1801; d. June 24, 1802.
1898. Anna, bo. Dec. 4, 1802; ma. Amos Sargent, 1827.
1899. Hannah, bo. Dec. 2, 1804; d. March 5, 1805.
1900. William, bo. Sept. 13, 1807; ma. Mary Taylor Ladd (1862,) Dec. 1, 1850. No children.
1901. Deborah, bo. Oct. 30, 1812; ma. Hiram Daniels.
1902. Joseph, Jr., bo. July 16, 1814; ma. Oraline A. Barnes.

(623) Edward Ladd, of Andover, N. H., (son of Edward,[258]) ma. Miriam Avery, Dec. 19, 1809.

Child.

1903. Solomon, bo. Oct. 13, 1814; ma. Mary E. Caverly, Sept. 16, 1847.

(625) Nathaniel S. Ladd, of Andover, N. H., (son of Edward,[258]) ma. Nabby ——. She died, and he ma. 2d. Deborah ——. He removed to Stafford, Vt., and died at Worcester, Vt., Jan. 26, 1849.

Children.

1904. Hannah, bo. Feb. 21, 1808, in Andover, N. H.
1905. Mark, bo. Dec. 22, 1809, in Strafford, Vt.; d. June 13, 1811.

Children by second wife.

1906. Polly, bo. March 19, 1812.
1907. Mark P., bo. ——; ma. Lois Bruce.

(544) Horatio Ladd (son of Ephraim,[204]) was born in Tolland, Ct., Jan. 21, 1780; was a farmer, removed to and lived in New Albany, Pa. He ma. Asenath Ives, Jan. 30, 1800. She was by nature well fitted for pioneer life; was ambitious, brave, capable, healthy, with strong powers of endurance. In 1814 she made a trip to Connecticut, three hundred miles, alone, and on horseback. He d. Jan. 12, 1850. His widow d. Aug. 28, 1854.

Children.

1908. Clarissa, bo. Oct. 4, 1800; ma. Elisha Harris; 2d, Joseph Marshall.
1909. Moses Ashley, bo. July 3, 1803; ma. Susanna Lawrence.
1910. Eliza, bo. June 20, 1805; ma. William Lawrence. She d. Apr. 27, 1847.
1911. Lucinda, bo. Sept. 7, 1807; d. Jan. 14, 1814.
1912. Olivia, bo. May 25, 1810; ma. Jason Horton. She d. Sept. 12, 1847.
1913. Arumah, bo. June 16, 1812; d. July 20, 1814.
1914. Lucinda, bo. Nov. 12, 1814; ma. James Martin. She d. Oct. 26, 1840.
1915. Asenath Selinda, bo. April 13, 1817; ma. Dr. David C. Codding.
1916. Arumah, bo. March 14, 1820; ma. Laura Bunce.

(545) Charles Warner Ladd, of New Albany, Pa., (son of Ephraim,[204]) was bo. in Tolland, Conn., Sept. 5, 1781. Removed from there with his father's family, in the Winter of 1800, to New Albany, Bradford Co., Pa. He was a man of good address and fair education; his occupation was that of a farmer. He ma. Nov. 26, 1818, Philinda, dau. of Timothy Alden, of New Albany, Pa. He died Sept. 15, 1832.

Children.

1917. Amelia Lois, bo. Oct. 10, 1819; ma. Oliver Lathrop, April 21, 1842.
1918. Charles Kingsbury, bo. Jan. 21, 1822; ma. Rose Spaulding Dec. 4, 1852.
1919. Sophronia, bo. April 21, 1823; d. when about 20 years old.
1920. Myron Alden, bo. Jan. 5, 1825; d. aged 5 years.
1921. Jared Woodruff, bo. April 3, 1829; d. about 1843.

(556) Ariel Ladd, of Tolland, Conn., (son of Eliab,[212]) was born in Tolland, Conn., Feb. 9, 1783; ma. Mary Winchell, dau. of Oliver and Charity Winchell, of Turkey Hills, Windsor, Conn., Oct. 11, 1811. He died June 3, 1868, aged 85 years. His wife died Oct. 30, 1874, aged 87 years and 6 months. Mr. Ladd passed most of his life in his native town. His education was limited to that afforded by the common school of his day. After leaving his father's home he worked for a time at shipbuilding, and had considerable experience in house-carpentering. He was deputy sheriff and county jailor, and keeper of

the county house, a hotel or tavern owned by the county in connection with the jail, for several years. He was a member of the General Assembly of Connecticut in 1840, and served as a justice of the peace by appointment of the General Assembly from 1838 to 1840, and from 1842 to 1850. He was a director of the Tolland County Bank, located at Tolland, and for nearly thirty years was president of the Tolland County Mutual Fire Insurance Company, which last office he held at the time of his death. About the year 1830 he bought a small farm of thirty acres of land in Tolland, and a few years later a saw-mill, and farming and sawing and dressing lumber were his principal occupations during most of the years thereafter of his active life. His dwelling was near the centre of the village, and was a plain, square house of two stories, with a large chimney built of stone passing through the centre and out at the ridge of the roof, after the manner of many of the country houses of sixty years ago. He was a regular attendant upon the services of the Congregational Church, and his house was the convenient resort of the farmers and their wives from the outlying districts, who gathered there between the morning and afternoon sermons almost every Sunday, to talk over the news of the week and eat the luncheon they had brought from their several homes for their noon repast. On these occasions the luncheon was supplemented by a generous supply of apples and a large "mug" of the best New England cider that Mr. Ladd's cellar afforded. In stature he was about five feet nine inches in height, broad shouldered, erect, compactly built, and of full habit. As a neighbor he was hospitable, kind, and always obliging, pleasant and social in his intercourse, upright in his dealings, and sincere in his friendships. He seemed somewhat stern and cold to those who did not know him well; but he had a large sympathy, which led him to aid others from his limited means, and by the indorsement of notes he brought to himself great discomfort, embarrassment, and ultimate loss. He was reserved in his manner, and a man of few words; modest almost to bashfulness, and seldom took part in the discussion of matters in the annual town or other public meetings. He was a man of strong common sense and sound judgment. As a magistrate he was uniformly fair and just, and presided with a quiet dignity in the trial of all causes that came before him. He had a keen sense of humor, and enjoyed the witty but harmless attack and sharp repartee that often enlivens the conversation of intelligent country farmers. It is related of him that on one occasion a man notorious for his untruthfulness was brought before him, charged with some slight misdemeanor. The magistrate, in a distinct voice, read the charge, and then asked the prisoner, "What say you, sir, to this charge; are you guilty or not guilty?" The prisoner answered, much to the surprise of every one present, "Guilty, sir!" The magistrate responded, with a merry twinkle in his eye, "Under ordinary circumstances, sir. I should be unwilling to take your word without corroborating testimony to support it, but in this particular instance I am willing to believe you;" and then imposed the lawful penalty. He was a member of the Masonic fraternity for more than fifty years, and his funeral was attended by a delegation of the brotherhood from a neighboring town.

Children.

1922. Randolph E., bo. July 6, 1812; ma. Charlotte Pease; d. Aug. 5, 1874.
1923. Mary J., bo. Nov. 11, 1814; d. July 7, 1816.
1924. Lucius E., bo. June 17, 1817; ma. Della Van Horne, Nov. 24, 1842.
1925. William R., bo. Aug. 10, 1819; d. July 17, 1824.
1926. Charles R., bo. April 9, 1822; ma. Mrs. Ella M. Weaver, April 3, 1886.
1927. Mary J., bo. Jan. 17, 1825; ma. Benjamin Lathrop, of Tolland, Conn. She d. Jan. 1889.
1928. Ariel, bo. Sept. 2, 1827; ma. Caroline M. Gates.
1929. William F., bo. Dec. 30, 1830; d. in infancy.

(557) Stephen Ladd, of Tolland, Conn., (son of Eliab,[212]) ma. Hannah, dau. of Jabez Kingsbury, of Tolland, Conn., Aug. 29, 1811. She died Sept. 7, 1829, and he ma. 2d, Mrs. Susan (Sessions) Bradley, March 31, 1830. He was an enterprising farmer, and lived on the old homestead of his ancestors.

Children.

1930. Otis K., bo. Oct. 13, 1816; ma. Hannah Warner, May 30, 1869.
1931. Anna Calesta, bo. May 16, 1818; ma. Giles Meacham.
1932. Sally, bo. July 17, 1820; ma. Chauncy Hibbard. She died ——.
1933. Sabrina Talcot, bo. Aug. 4, 1822; ma. Gilbert Stacy. She d. May 20, 1869.
1934. John Mosely, bo. Oct. 17, 1824; ma. Rebecca Kennedy.
1935. Samuel William, bo. Sept. 6, 1826; ma. Amanda Shulter.
1936. Mary Amelia, bo. Nov. 4, 1828; ma. Chauncy Hibbard.

Children by second wife.

1937. Julia, bo. Feb. 4, 1831; ma. Edwin McLean.
1938. Elizabeth, bo. Nov. 9, 1833; d. Sept. 14, 1850.

(563) Dr. Ahijah Ladd, of Tolland, Conn., (son of Ahijah,[213]) was born in Tolland, Conn., Aug. 15, 1788. He ma. Almy Cobb, Jan. 20, 1818. We copy the following sketch of Dr. Ladd from Waldo's History of Franklin, Conn., page 126: "He studied medicine with Dr. Judah Bliss, and was licensed to practice in 1813. He always had respectable practice; in one or two branches he was decidedly superior; was reasonable in his charges, and very indulgent to his customers. He maintained a respectable position in society, and was a very useful man. He exercised a most wholesome influence in the circle in which he moved; always on the side of good order and strict morality; discountenancing all improprieties and immoral conduct; possessing all the qualities that characterize the good neighbor; and without exhibiting any disposition to complain or wrangle when others were more successful than himself. Conservative in all his actions and words of thought, he seldom, if ever, took ultra grounds on any subject, and avoided all angry and unprofitable disputations. With a kind heart and honest purpose, seeking to do right himself rather than to compel others to act according to his views, and contrary to their own, he secured many friends, and was generally esteemed."

Children.

1939. William Cobb, bo. Mar. 26, 1820; ma. Harriet E. Johnson, May 4, 1845.
1940. Charles A., bo. March 10, 1822; ma. Achsah Chapin, March 26, 1848. No children.
1941. Theodore Stearns, bo. Sept. 4, 1826; ma. Delia Abbott. He d. April 6, 1886. No children.

(564) Levi Ladd, of Tolland, Conn., (son of Ahijah,[213]) ma. Lois Davis. She died, and he ma. 2d, Nancy Upham, June 22, 1831, who died Nov. 22, 1843.

Children.

1942. Lucinda, bo. Feb. 6, 1814; ma. Edward Harner.
1943. Lucina, bo. Dec. 13, 1815; ma. Absolem Stockwell.
1944. Lois Davis, bo. Sept. 29, 1817; d. March 16, 1831.
1945. Noah D., bo. Feb. 29, 1820; ma. Nancy Johnson.
1946. Philip Levi, bo. Nov. 20, 1821; d. Oct. 19, 1822.
1947. Roxa Almy, bo. June 27, 1823; ma. Isaac Faskett. She d. Nov. 9, 1865.
1948. Joel Levi, bo. June 27, 1827; ma. Achsah Parsons.

Children by second wife.

1949. Ann Eliza, bo. Sept. 2, 1832; ma. George Lyman.
1950. Henry Otis, bo. Jan. 20, 1836; d. July 30, 1850.
1951. George Perley, bo. Aug. 28, 1838; ma. Rebecca E. Barnes.

(1588) Joseph Hurd Ladd, of Brooklyn, N. Y., (son of Henry,[647]) ma. Mary, dau. of S. R. B. Wales, of Bellows Falls, Vt., Oct. 28, 1846.

Children.

1952. Mary Josephine, bo. Aug. 26, 1847; ma. Edward Fowler, Dec. 5, 1866.
1953. Harry, bo. Feb. 3, 1849; d. Aug. 23, 1849.
1954. Florence Wales, bo. Dec. 3, 1850; d. Nov. 8, 1851.
1955. Charles Wales, bo. Aug. 7, 1852.
1956. Caroline Lucy, bo. Feb. 14, 1854; ma. Peter Gilsey, June 18, 1874.
1957. Eveline Hurd, bo. Sept. 2, 1864; ma. John Gilsey.

(1589) Eliphalet Ladd. of New York City, (son of Henry,[647]) ma. Augusta Niles, Oct. 6, 1846. She died March 16, 1860, and he ma. 2d, Mary E., dau. of William H. Barnes, Sept. 18, 1862. He was for a number of years a prominent merchant in New York City. He removed to Windsor, Conn., 1853, and died there Oct. 29, 1885, of locomotive ataxie, a disease from which he suffered for twenty years.

Children.

1958. Christine, bo. Dec. 1, 1847; ma. Fabian Franklin, Aug. 24, 1882, of Baltimore, Md. He was Associate Professor of Mathematics in Johns Hopkins University. She graduated at Vassar College 1869; taught scientific subjects at various advanced schools for several years; made a number of contributions to mathematical journals, and was called to a fellowship at Johns Hopkins University in 1879, (being the only woman upon whom this honor has ever been conferred); held this fellowship three years, during which she made contributions to the American Journal of Mathematics, and wrote a paper on the "Algebra of Logic," which was published in "Studies in Logic by Members of the Johns Hopkins University;" has since contributed original memoirs and reviews to the American Journal of Psychology, Mind (London), the Nation, and Science. In 1887 Vassar College conferred upon her the degree of LL. D., a distinction not hitherto granted to any other of its graduates.
1959. Henry, bo. June 12, 1850; ma. Bessie Hoxie, April 12, 1855.
1960. Jane Augusta, bo. Oct. 31, 1854; ma. Alfred Edward McCordia, July 3, 1889.

Children by second wife.

1961. Katharine, bo. April 28, 1865.
1962. George B., bo. July 2, 1867; d. Jan. 7, 1881.

(1592) Charles Haven Ladd, of Portsmouth, N. H., (son of Alexander,[649]) "was born at Portsmouth, N. H., March 4, 1812, and when 13 years old was sent to the then famous Round Hill school at Northampton, under the charge of Mr. Joseph G. Cogswell, afterwards the first librarian of the Astor Library at New York, and Mr. George Bancroft, the historian, and a numerous corps of assistants. Here he remained three years, enjoying exceptional opportunities for acquiring the rudiments of a good education. Within a year after leaving school he entered the counting-room of Henry and Alexander Ladd, where he remained until he was of age. He then spent a Winter at the South, mostly at Charleston and Savannah, returning via New Orleans, Cincinnati, and Niagara, and reaching home in July. Two or three years later he and his brother, Mr. Alexander H. Ladd, formed together the mercantile house of C. H. & A. H. Ladd, which continued until he left Portsmouth in 1863. In the year 1851, at a time when the expenditures at the Portsmouth navy yard were unusually large, the accounts of the then navy agent became involved, and the officer sent from Washington to investigate them suggested to him to apply for the office. This he did, and though he had never taken any active part in politics, and used little or no influence, a commission as navy agent was sent to him, and he filled the place for about eighteen months. On the coming in of the Pierce administration a Democrat was of course appointed in his place. In 1863 he left Portsmouth, N. H., to take part in a large iron and steel manufacturing company in the vicinity of New York, and lived in the city and at Elizabeth, N. J., for the next fifteen years. Since then he has been in no active business, and has resided the greater part of the time at Washington, D. C. He has always been a lover of books, and still more of nature, and was for many years a keen sportsman. Perhaps it is partly owing to these tastes that he is now, in his seventy-seventh year, still in vigorous health. On the 5th of Nov. 1839, he ma. at Alexandria, Va., Susan Lowell, dau. of William Fowle, Esq., a merchant of that place, and for several years the president of the Bank of the Old Dominion."

Children.

1963. William Fowle, bo. Aug. 21, 1845; ma. Caroline Willis, June 12, 1877.

1964. Esther Dashill, bo. April 11, 1847; ma. William W. Johnston, April 11, 1871.

(1595) Alexander Hamilton Ladd, of Portsmouth, N. H., (son of Alexander,[649]) was born in Portsmouth, N. H., July 27, 1815; ma. June 11, 1840, Elizabeth N., dau. of William Jones, Esq., of Portsmouth, N. H., who was born Nov. 29, 1818, and died Sept. 21, 1865. He was sent to Phillips Academy at Exeter in 1827, and from there entered Dartmouth College, in the class of 1835. Preferring an active business life to studying for a profession, he prepared for it by a course of training in the counting-room of his late brother-in-law, Samuel E. Cowes, and the late Gov. J. Goodwin, and in 1838 formed a partnership with his brother, Charles H. Ladd, and with him established a manufactory of sperm oil, mainly to supply the large cotton mills of the vicinity. On the opening of railroads, some years later, this ceased to be profitable, and was given up. In the meantime he had taken an active part in getting up the Portsmouth Steam Factory for the extensive manufacture of lawns, of which he was a director. In 1842 he joined in an enterprise for the production of pig iron. which, though very successful at first, was, in common with all the iron industries of the country, ruined by the tariff of 1846. He then accepted the position as agent for several of the largest cotton mills in New England, for the purchase of cotton for them at Galveston, Texas, in which he spent the cooler months of the year until 1857, when his brother relieved him until 1859. After the war he resumed the work for ten years, and the house, in the hands of his nephew, is still, forty years after its establishment, one of the largest cotton buying houses in Texas. About the year 1875 he withdrew from all active business, finding sufficient to interest him in the growing families of his children, in the care of his superb garden with its many thousands of choice tulips and other flowers, and the duties of hospitality. With these to fill his thoughts he has entered upon a vigorous old age, which all who know him pray may be long continued.

Children.

1965. Mary Tufton Haven, bo. March 13, 1841; ma. Lieut. Charles Follen Blake, Mar. 1, 1868. He d. Feb. 20, 1879, at West Platte, Nebraska. Children: [1]Edith, bo. Dec. 31, 1868; [2]Charles Chandler, bo. Oct. 31, 1872; [3]Eleanor, bo. Feb. 26, 1875; [4]Agnes, bo. Feb. 12, 1878.
1966. Anna Perry, bo. April 3, 1842; ma. Major John Langdon Ward, Oct. 25, 1871. Children: [1]A son, bo. 1872, d. early; [2]Alexander Ladd,

bo. Jan. 21, 1874; ³Miles, bo. Jan. 3, 1878, d. Feb. 12, 1881; ⁴Twins, bo. Dec. 2, 1880, only one of whom, Eshere, lived.

1967. William Jones, bo. Feb. 4, 1844; ma. Annie Russell Watson, June 21, 1869.

1968. Elizabeth Hamilton, bo. June 25, 1845; ma. Charles Eben Wentworth, son of Mark H. and Susan (Jones) Wentworth, Sept. 30, 1867. Children: ¹Alice bo. Oct. 1, 1870, d. March 1, 1873; ²Stanford, bo. Aug. 5, 1872; ³Elizabeth, bo. Dec. 16, 1875; ⁴Mark, bo. April 5, 1879, at Cambridge.

1969. Maria Haven, bo. April 1, 1848; ma. Manning Emery, son of Hon. James W. and Martha (Bell) Emery, Aug. 3, 1875. Children: ¹Eliphalet, bo. June 7, 1876; ²Manning, bo. Aug. 5, 1879; ³Ruth, bo. June 7, 1880.

1970. Alexander, bo. July 22, 1853; d. Dec. 9, 1873.

1971. Charles Albert, bo. June 26, 1857; d. Jan. 13, 1863.

1972. Horace Appleton, bo. Feb. 20, 1859.

(1572) Gen. Samuel Greenleaf Ladd, born in Concord, N. H., April 14, 1784, (son of Dudley,⁶⁰⁰) settled very early in life at Hallowell, Me., where he married, Oct. 3, 1815, Caroline D. Vinal, formerly of Boston. In this town he was engaged in the hardware business, and reared a family of eleven children. He became interested in military affairs, and was made captain of a company of Maine militia during the war of 1812–14, in which he engaged a short time in the field. He subsequently held the office of adjutant-general of the State of Maine for several terms. Gen. Ladd moved to Farmington, Me., in 1840, living there for about ten years, and afterwards at Auburn and Brunswick. Me. He moved to Kingston, Penn., in 1856, where he died in April, 1863, at the age of 79 years.

Children.

1573. Mary Caroline, bo. Aug. 21, 1816; ma. Horatio W. Fairbanks, June 12, 1839. Children: ¹Ellen Ladd, bo. Dec. 15, 1844, ma. Frank S. Abbott, M. D., and d. March 2, 1872; ²Carrie, bo. Aug. 26, 1850, ma. Benjamin R. Tubbs, of Kingston, Pa.

1574. Samuel G., bo. April 13, 1818; not married.

1575. Francis Dudley, bo. May 20, 1820; ma. Caroline Rose, June 16, 1846.

1576. Ellen S., bo. Feb. 19, 1822; ma. Rev. Henry H. Welles, of Kingston. Pa., Oct. 12. 1849. Children: ¹Henry H., bo. Jan. 21, 1861; ²Theodore L., bo. Nov. 2, 1862; ³Charlotte E., bo. April 28, 1864.

1577. Julia M., bo. Aug. 16, 1824; ma. Lewis H. Titcomb, of Boston.

1578. Theodore, bo. Nov. 20, 1826; not married. Lived in Bradford, Pa.

1579. Anna Louisa, bo. Nov. 15, 1829; ma. Col. J. S. Fillebrown.

1580. Martha Augusta, bo. Sept. 1, 1831; ma. Erastus F. Dana, of Rutland, Vt.

1981. Charlotte S., bo. Jan. 8, 1834; ma. Major Robert H. Rose, of Minn.
1982. Henry W., bo. March 20, 1836; d. Jan. 22, 1848.
1983. Horatio O., bo. Aug. 31, 1839; ma. Harriett Abbott.

(1573) John Ladd, of Hallowell, Me., (son of Dudley,[600]) ma. Abigail Prowse, April 4, 1817. He sailed for South America as supercargo, and died there about 1820.

Children.

1984. William, bo. ——; ma. Lucretia Goodale.
1985. Elizabeth, bo. Jan. 31, 1809; ma. Aaron A. Palmer, March 8, 1838. Children: [1]Abbie L., bo. Jan. 24, 1839; [2]Lucretia Jane, bo. March 24, 1840; [3]John W., bo. Oct. 18, 1841; [4]Heber Chace, bo. March 26, 1843; [5]George Bullard, bo. Jan. 6, 1846; [6]Clara Ladd Hutchins, bo. Oct. 4, 1847; [7]Charlotte Elizabeth, bo. Sept. 4, 1868; [8]Charles Gilman, bo. Feb. 4, 1852.
1986. John, Jr., bo. Jan. 9, 1820; ma. Sarah Jane Nourse, Aug. 31, 1837.

(1574) Dudley Ladd, of Franklin, N. H., (son of Dudley,[600]) ma. Charlotte, dau. of Ebenezer Eastman, of Salisbury, N. H., May 21, 1823. She died June 30, 1826, and he ma. 2d, Amanda Palmer, Dec. 22, 1837. He died March 20, 1875. His life was an exceedingly quiet and uneventful one. He was a merchant, engaged in the hardware trade. In the latter part of his life he retired from active business, and found pleasure and enjoyment in looking after his farm.

Child.

1987. Charlotte, bo. ——; ma. Edward H. Barrett, of Franklin, N. H., Oct. 28, 1845. Children: [1]Frank E., bo. July 24, 1847; [2]Walter S., bo. Aug. 24, 1849; [3]Herbert E., bo. Jan. 31, 1852; [4]Carrie M., bo. Jan. 17, 1855, at Utica, Minn., said to be the first white girl born in that town; [5]Willie J., bo. Sept. 4, 1858; [6]George H., bo. Aug. 18, 1861, d. March 5, 1862; [7]Rollo F., bo. March 3, 1864; [8]George A. P., bo. Feb. 23, 1869.

Children by second wife.

1988. Ellen Frances, bo. Nov. 6, 1838; ma. June 15, 1863, Daniel F. Murphy. Child: Herman Dudley, bo. Aug. 25, 1867.
1989. Harriet Louisa, bo. Nov. 11, 1840.
1990. Julia Amanda, bo. Oct. 21, 1842; ma. Aug. 21, 1861, George Baker. Children: [1]John Ladd, bo. Oct. 12, 1862; [2]Lillian M., bo. Oct. 20, 1865, d. Dec. 11, 1868; [3]Alice Hutchins, bo. Aug. 17, 1872; [4]Charles Dudley, bo, June 7, 1877, d. June 8, 1877.
1991. Maria Fletcher, bo. July 4, 1844.
1992. Charles Dudley, bo. Aug. 13, 1847.

(1575) Nathaniel Green Ladd, of New York City, (son of Dudley,[600]) ma. Ann, dau. of William and Eleanor (Lewis) Morrow, May 14, 1817. He left home when a boy and for a time followed the sea, but becoming tired of a seafaring life he went, when quite young, to New York, where he found employment, and was for over thirty years in service at the Custom House. But a few years before his death his health failed and he gave up his position, and rested from active duties until he died, Dec. 27, 1863. He was a fond and loving husband and father, and a faithful and steadfast friend; was thoroughly honest, true, and good, and was highly respected by all with whom he came in contact, either on business or pleasure. His widow d. Oct. 16, 1866.

Children.

1993. Ann Bethia, bo. Oct. 5, 1818; ma. Edward Luff, April 4, 1841. She d. Jan. 28, 1864.
1994. Lucinda Parsons, bo. Jan. 17, 1821; ma. Daniel Patterson, Sept. 9, 1852.
1995. Eleanor Lewis, bo. March 23, 1823; ma. Austin A. Hall, July 1, 1846.
1996. William Dudley, bo. April 14, 1825; ma. Mary Ann Emerson, Nov. 1847.
1997. Mary Jane, bo. March 13, 1828; ma. M. D. Lafette Sharkey, Oct. 15, 1845.
1998. Margarette, bo. Sept. 15. 1830; d. Aug. 28, 1848.
1999. Charles George, bo. June 3, 1833; ma. Anna M. Sullivan, June 14, 1866.
2000. Sarah Lockwood, bo. June 3, 1833; ma. Wm. L. Corwin, Oct. 1, 1855.
2001. Nathaniel, bo. Nov. 3, 1836; ma. Mary Jane Irwin, Jan. 4, 1876.
2002. Julia Hutchins, bo. Sept. 7, 1839.

(1576) William Manley Ladd, of Lynn, (son of Dudley,[600]) was bo. in Concord, N. H., Feb. 9, 1794; ma. Betsey, dau. of Zaccheus and Theodate (Farrington) Collins, of Lynn, Nov. 22, 1822. He learned the trade of book-binder, and after his marriage lived for a few years in Augusta, Me. His health failed, and he was obliged to give up business for more than a year, and went back to Concord, N. H. When health returned he established himself at Meredith Bridge, now Laconia, N. H., in a store where he kept drugs, teas, coffee, sugar and molasses, and also books, such as were then used in the district schools and the academy of the town, being the first store in town which kept books for sale. *In 1844 he removed to Lynn and started in business as a druggist, and was so well skilled in the art of preparing drugs, and had so good a knowledge of their medicinal qualities that many families, when unwell, depended upon his advice, instead of calling a regular physician. He gave up business in 1871, and died March 17, 1883, in Lynn, honored and respected by all who knew him.

Children.

2003. William Henry, bo. Dec. 29, 1824; ma. Jane Pearson.
2004. Ann Elizabeth, bo. Dec. 29, 1829; not married.

(1839)   Gorham Ladd, of Readfield, Me., (son of Simeon,[679]) ma. Charlotte Whittier, Oct. 12, 1834. He died March 6, 1868.

Children.

2005. Lucinda Whittier, bo. May 21, 1835; ma. J. H. Richardson, July 3, 1883.
2006. Amanda Rosamond, bo. Dec. 29, 1836; not married.
2007. Lydia Ann, bo. July 24, 1839; ma. Gustavus Smith, Nov. 14, 1863. She d. March 23, 1879. Children: [1]Eva C., [2]Harry Chester, [3]Walter Gorham, [4]Annie Estelle.
2008. Mary Octavia, bo. Jan. 7, 1841; not married.
2009. Orrin Gorham, bo. March 28, 1842; not married; d. June 22, 1877.
2010. John Almon, bo. June 12, 1843; not married; d. 1883.
2011. Charlotte Maria, bo. Jan. 22, 1847; ma. Geo. P. Lowell, Nov. 10, 1872.

(1840)   Paul Ladd, of Readfield, Me., (son of Simeon,[679]) ma. Hannah Whittier, Jan. 21, 1834. He died at Mt. Vernon, Me., Jan. 19, 1872.

Children.

2012. Hiram, bo. Oct. 10, 1835; ma. Carrie Wiggin, Dec. 15, 1863.
2013. Horace A., bo. Nov. 23, 1837; not married; d. Sept. 17, 1867.
2014. Mary Ann, bo. June 23, 1839; ma. Henry Stone, July 21, 1858.
2015. Martha Jane, bo. Feb. 7, 1841; ma. Martin Beane, Aug. 8, 1862.
2016. Eveline, bo. Aug. 23, 1847; d. Oct. 5, 1867.

(1841)   Warren Ladd, of North Wayne, Me., (son of Simeon,[679]) ma. Lydia Wellman, Nov. 9, 1842. She died March 9, 1849, and he ma. 2d, Mrs. Emeline Pratt, April 28, 1866.

Children.

2017. Warren Dudley, bo. Sept. 25, 1843; ma. Betsey Williams, Mar. 15, 1872.
2018. Cyrus Augustus, bo. Aug. 2, 1846; ma. Kate Smith, Oct. 31, 1875.
2019. Emily Elizabeth, bo. Oct. 24, 1848; ma. Daniel Luce, Aug. 30, 1868.
2020. Sarah Norton, bo. Oct. 24, 1848; d. Aug. 8, 1867.

Child by second wife.

2021. Ora Angie, bo. March 19, 1867.

(1842)   Harvey Ladd, of Winthrop, Me., (son of Simeon,[679]) ma. Laura Ann Packard, Sept. 30, 1839.

Children.

2022. Harriet Ellen, bo. April 21, 1841; ma. —— Arnold.
2023. Laura Frances, bo. April 21, 1843; ma. Lewis Luce, Dec. 24, 1874. She d. Jan. 7, 1846, and he ma. 2d, Rebecca Holmes, Mar. 10, 1847. No children by 2d wife.

(1843) Hiram Ladd, of Winthrop, Me., (son of Simeon,[679]) ma. Julia Ann, dau. of Freeman and Abigail Dexter, June 13, 1847.

Child.

2024. Mattie, bo. April 13, 1851; ma. Charles B. Stanton, Feb. 1, 1870, of Monmouth, Me.

(1844) Cyrus A. Ladd, of Readville, Me., (son of Simeon,[679]) ma. Louisa Cram, Feb. 27, 1862. He is a farmer.

Children.

2025. Lydia E., bo. May 18, 1863.
2026. Frank A., bo. June 12, 1864.
2027. Mary J., bo. June 7, 1870.

(839) Austin Ladd, of Haverhill, N. H., (son of Ezekiel,[355]) ma. Miriam Farnam, Nov. 29, 1821.

Children.

2028. Chester F., bo. Feb. 23, 1823; ma. Lucy B., dau. of Alexander Strong, May 24, 1849.
2029. Helen Louisa, bo. Dec. 7, 1825; ma. Dr. William S. Carpenter, Oct. 1, 1845.
2030. Harriet, bo. July 1, 1833; ma. William B. Stevens, Sept. 17, 1856.

(854) James Leander Sellers Ladd, of Portsmouth, N. H., (son of James,[359]) ma. Henrietta B. Hathaway.

Children.

2031. John Anthony, bo. ——.
2032. Lucy, bo. ——.

(866) Jesse Ladd, of Little Compton, R. I., (son of Jesse,[361] (ma. Roby Wilbur, of Little Compton, R. I., March 16, 1846.

Child.

2033. Lydia, bo. ——; ma. Lorenzo D. Smith, July 16, 1846.

(867) James Ladd, of Menasha, Wis., (son of Jesse,[361]) ma. Charity, dau. of Darius and Mary (Pulsifer) Willey, at Compton, N. H., Jan. 16, 1825. She died Dec. 10, 1865, and he ma. 2d, Theresa M., dau. of Chauncy and Helen Kellogg.

Children.

2034. Adeline, bo. Dec. 1, 1826; ma. Dwight D. Donaldson, June 1, 1849.
2035. Christopher, bo. July 14, 1829; ma. Mrs. Roxanna (Thombs) Fargo. No children.
2036. James William, bo. May 5, 1838; ma. Mary Elizabeth Jackson.
2037. George H., bo. July 22, 1842; ma. Ellen Maria Bidwell.

(871) Bela Orlander Ladd, of Boston, (son of Daniel,[364]) ma. Elizabeth Robertson, Dec. 31, 1831.

Children.

2038. Richard Fletcher, bo. Nov. 4, 1832; ma. Esther E. Barney, Dec. 19, 1854.
2039. Henry, bo. ——; d. young.
2040. George F., bo. ——.

(872) William H. Ladd, of Boston, (son of Daniel,[364]) was born in Plymouth, N. H., Feb. 12, 1807. He was educated at the public schools, and learned the carriage-maker's trade at Haverhill; went to Boston in 1836, and kept a good eating-house in Lindall street. About 1851 he became one of the owners of the "Daily Bee," which afterwards became the "Daily Atlas." About 1870 he was appointed agent at the Roxbury station on the Boston & Providence Railroad, and subsequently of the Chickering station, where he remained until he died, Nov. 10, 1886. He ma. Dec. 29, 1831, Hannah B. Goodrich, of Haverhill.

Children.

2041. George V. B., bo. Nov. 13, 1833; ma. Margarette Butler.
2042. Bela Dow, bo. Feb. 24, 1835; ma. Susan M. Harrison, Dec. 29, 1855.
2043. Elizabeth D., bo. Feb. 4, 1846; ma. F. A. Hastings, Jan. 15, 1872.
2044. Hannah B., bo. Sept. 17, 1866.

(874) Sampson Ladd, of Haverhill, (son of Joshua,[365]) ma. Elmira Jones, Sept. 1840.

Children.

2045. Edward, bo. 1841; d. in infancy.
2046. Ellen, bo. 1841; not married.
2047. Emma, bo. 1844; ma. Joseph Femsey.
2048. Walter S., bo. 1856; ma. Mattie Davis.

(878) Perley M. Ladd, of Minneapolis, Minn., (son of Joshua,[365]) was born in Salem, N. H., March 2, 1812; was educated at the public schools; ma. Dec. 1839, Hannah L. Reedhead, in Boston; was a farmer in Salem, N. H., until 1857, when he re-

moved to Haverhill, where he followed the trade of carpenter until the Spring of 1866, when he removed to Minneapolis, Minn., where he now (1888) resides.

Children.

2049. Isabel, bo. June, 1841; d. 1844.
2050. Henry E., bo. Dec. 1847, in Salem, N. H.; was educated in the public schools. In 1866 he went with his father to Minneapolis, Minn. He ma. Nov. 22, 1874, Annie M., dau. of R. H. and Nancy Hager, of Union, Knox Co., Me. He has been engaged in several kinds of business, and in each was successful, having never made a failure. He is now (1888) in Minneapolis, Minn., where for the past eight years he has been doing a large " real estate and loan collection " business. His business motto is, " Do unto others as you would wish others in like circumstances should do unto you;" or, in other words, he believes it his duty to deal as honestly and fairly with others as he wants others to deal honestly and fairly with him.

(883) Daniel Gorham Ladd (son of John[366]) ma. Betsey Jane Trumball, of Stoughton.

Children.

2051. Lizzie Henry, bo. March 17, 1853; ma. Hazen Johnson.
2052. Ella Louise, bo. Aug. 7, 1855; ma. Albert Norcross.
2053. Edward Everett, bo. April 26, 1858; ma. Henrietta Towle.

(892) Dr. Azel Parkhurst Ladd, of Shullsburg, Wis., (son of William,[367]) ma. Louisa M. Burrill, 1845. He taught school in New Bedford and at Westport, and studied medicine with Dr. Lyman Bartlett, of New Bedford.

Children.

2054. Andrew Robeson, bo. Sept. 8, 1846; ma. Eugene Levere, Oct. 22, 1877.
2055. Frank W., bo. June 12, 1848; ma. Wina Bailey, 1871.
2056. George R., bo. July 24, 1850; ma. Mary E. Skews, 1870.
2057. William P., bo. July 1, 1852; ma. Clara Cathren, 1882.

(897) Hasting A. Ladd, of Boston, (son of Jonathan,[373]) was born at Haverhill, N. H., July 15, 1823. He is engaged in the plumbing and gas fitting business at Boston. He ma. Rebecca B. Haven, Jan. 4, 1846.

Children.

2058. Henrietta H., bo. July 26, 1848; ma. Henry F. Knowles.
2059. Charles H., bo. May 17, 1851; ma. Mary Regan.
2060. Albert W., bo. Oct. 23, 1853; ma. Lilian Walker.
2061. Edwin H., bo. July 28, 1856; d. 1867.

(665) Josiah Ladd, of St. Johnsburgh, Vt., (son of John,[268]) ma. Nancy Ladd,[659] Dec. 18, 1800. He died Oct. 13, 1845. His widow died Nov. 8, 1864.

Children.

2062. Alvaro, bo. June 5, 1801; ma. Nancy Shotwell, 1830.
2063. Loram, bo. March 8, 1803; ma. Elizabeth Ridley, Nov. 29, 1834.
2064. Lemuel, bo. March 10, 1805; not married; d. June 2, 1831.
2065. Orrin, bo. March 16, 1807; ma. Lucinda Young, May 9, 1825.
2066. Phila, bo. July, 1809; ma. Asa Grondyke.
2067. Abigail, bo. Jan. 1811; d. 1814.

(667) Jonathan Ladd, of Sandusky, Ohio, (son of John,[268]) ma. Electa Ferguson. He died at Sandusky, Ohio.

Children.

2068. Polly, bo. ——; not married; d. about 1825.
2069. Leafie, bo. ——; ma. —— Carver.

(668) John Ladd (son of John[268]) ma. Patta Umpstead.

Children.

2070. Selina, bo. ——; ma. Renzo Meigs; 2d, —— Quimby.
2071. Cynthia, bo. ——; ma. Luther Morrill.
2072. Mandora, bo. ——; ma. Alonzo Rowell Hall, Feb. 1833.

(670) Dudley Ladd, of Delaware, Upper Canada, (son of John,[268]) ma. Sarah Humphrey. He died Oct. 1, 1847. He went from St. Johnsburg, Vt., to Sutton, Vt., and in 1835 removed to Delaware, Upper Canada.

Children.

2073. Lorenzo, bo. June 26, 1812; d. March 12, 1815.
2074. John, bo. June 1, 1814; d. March 6, 1815.
2075. Alanson, bo. Feb. 19, 1816; ma. Charlotte Decker, July 15, 1852.
2076. Sarah, bo. March 10, 1818; ma. Peter Lawson, Sept. 29, 1842. Children: [1]George D., bo. Oct. 4, 1843; [2]Frank R., bo. Jan. 23, 1849; [3]Peter, bo. June 17, 1852.
2077. Calvin, bo. April 6, 1821; ma. Lydia F. Lawson, Sept. 28, 1843.

(671) Samuel Ladd, of Marshall, Mich., (son of John,[268]) was born in St. Johnsbury, Vt., Sept. 4, 1791; ma. Hopey Allen, of Otsego, N. Y., Oct. 10, 1814. She was born at Otsego, N. Y., Oct. 20, 1795. He lived at Laurens, N. Y., and subsequently at Honeoye Falls, N. Y.; from there he went to Canada about 1830, and engaged in trade and warehousing; and about 1840

he settled upon his farm at Marshall, Mich., where he died April 8, 1866.

Children.

2078. Erastus D., bo. Sept. 10, 1815; ma. Julia Shockley.
2079. Horace Comstock, bo. March 20, 1817; ma. Ann Sarah O'Donoghue, Sept. 26, 1840.
2080. George H., bo. Jan. 30, 1823; d. young.
2081. George Solon, bo. Sept. 30, 1830; d. young.
2082. John Allen, bo. May 3, 1836; ma. Mary Ellen Mott, Nov. 4, 1854.

(1506)   Warren Ladd, of New Bedford, (son of Nathaniel[1400] and Sarah (Ingersoll) Ladd,) was born at East Bradford, (now Groveland,) July 21, 1813. We copy the following sketch of Mr. Ladd from the History of Bristol County, Mass., compiled under the supervision of D. Hamilton Hurd, and published by J. W. Lewis & Co., Philadelphia, 1883, page 155:

"Warren Ladd was educated in the public schools and at Merrimac Academy. Coming to New Bedford in July, 1840, he entered the employ of the New Bedford & Taunton Railroad Company as clerk in the freight office; was soon promoted to freight agent, and then to general agent at New Bedford. In 1862 he was appointed superintendent of the road, which position he held until 1877. His connection with this road continued from its opening, in 1840, to its consolidation with the Boston, Clinton & Fitchburg, a period of about thirty-seven years. This long term of service is the highest possible compliment to his integrity, ability, and faithfulness. Though actively engaged in arduous and responsible duties, he found time for intellectual culture, and by a judicious course of reading acquired a general knowledge of scientific, mechanical and economical subjects. He took a deep interest in municipal affairs, and gave his influence and active effort to the promotion of every measure which in his judgment promised to increase the growth and prosperity of the city. For this reason he was repeatedly called to the service of the city: for five years as member of the Common Council, and one year as its president; for five terms a member of the Board of Aldermen; for several years one of the School Committee, and a trustee of the Free Public Library. Of the latter he may rightly be called the father. At the laying of the corner-stone of the present library building, Mayor Howland, in his address referring to the origin of the library, said: 'On the

8th of the seventh month (July) of the same year, (1851.) Warren Ladd, a member of the common council from Ward One, introduced an order into that branch of the city government " for the raising of a committee to consider the expediency of establishing in this city a Free Public Library." This order was adopted in the common council, but was non-concurred in by the board of aldermen. This is believed to be the first order ever introduced into any representative body for the establishment of such an institution, and to this gentleman must, and does, belong the honor of having taken the initiatory step toward the establishment of a library for the public by the people themselves.'

" Mr. Ladd was an early and persistent advocate of the introduction of water, and one of three commissioners under whose direction the water-works were built. As showing the breadth of his views and his terseness in stating them, we quote from a report (written by him) of a committee which had the matter under consideration: 'Your committee are fully of the opinion that the introduction of an ample supply of pure water into the city is an imperative necessity, and one which should not be much longer delayed. It is a part of wise statesmanship to look at the future, to anticipate its wants, and guard against its casualties. Cities, like men, flourish and prosper only by their own exertions, and it becomes those whom the people have placed in power to be equal to the present emergency. We have the interest and the honor of the city in our hands. We know its wants and necessities, and can comprehend the crisis in our affairs. Shall we grasp and control the crisis, turn it with a steady hand to our interest and prosperity, or allow it silently and timidly to pass by and float beyond our reach? Shall we legislate only for to-day, and shrink from looking the great future in the face; or shall we, knowing the necessity and perceiving the remedy, fearlessly perform our duty?' He was upon the committee to which was referred the question of introducing gas; was an earnest advocate of the construction of common sewers, and introduced into the common council the first order for the appointment of a committee to consider the expediency of purchasing a steam fire engine. The enlargement and improvement of the city common was in a great measure due to his influence and exertion. In the late civil war he was a member of the Committee on Enlistments, and took an active part, as its records show, in every effort made by the city to aid the national government in putting down the rebellion. He has been connected as director with several corporations, and is now president of the New Bedford & Fairhaven Street Railway Co., and a trustee of the Five Cents Savings Bank. For thirty years he has held the commission of justice of the peace. Naturally conservative, Mr. Ladd has none of that blind reverence of the past which prevents one from keeping abreast with the spirit of the age, and adopting any new devices and improvements that genius and enterprise may invent and discover. In politics, originally an ardent Whig, he early became an equally earnest and active Republican; has been chairman of the Republican City Committee, and in 1876 was Presidential Elector from the First Congressional District. He has written largely for the press; was for many years the New Bedford correspondent of the Haverhill Gazette over the signature of 'Warren,' and has contributed many able articles to the New Bedford papers over the *nom de plume* of 'Julius.' He is a member of the New England Historic Genealogical Society, the Webster Historical Society, and the Bristol County Historical Society."

He ma. Nov. 22, 1842, Lucy Washburn, dau. of Hon. Abel and Betsey (Manly) Kingman, of North Bridgewater, now Brockton.

We copy the following sketch of Mr. Kingman from the History of North Bridgewater, page 562: "Mr. Kingman occupied a conspicuous place in the administration of the municipal government. Few men lived longer or led a more active and enterprising life. We find his name on nearly every page of the old town of Bridgewater, previous to its division, after he became of age. He was selectman of that town at the time of the incorporation of the town of North Bridgewater, and was active in that movement. For a number of years he represented the town in the Legislature of Massachusetts, and for two years occupied a seat in the State Senate from Plymouth County; was a justice of the peace for a long time, also a captain in the militia, besides other public offices. He possessed a strong, clear, discriminating mind; a man of sound judgment, indomitable energy, and a steadiness of purpose before which every object thrown in his path vanished; a firm, consistent member of the church of Christ; of warm and generous temperament, fair and upright in all his dealings, kind and affectionate to all, and where best known was the most honored and respected, and was one of the most useful and valued citizens of the town."

Children.

2083. Herbert Warren, bo. Oct. 15, 1843; ma. Emma F. Burrows, May 25, 1870.
2084. Sarah Ella, bo. Sept. 1, 1845; ma. Charles S. Davis, of South Dartmouth, July 9, 1874. Children: [1]Florence Ladd, bo. June 9, 1875; [2]Susan Ella, bo. June 24, 1880, d. Aug. 3, 1881; [3]Warren Ladd, bo. Jan. 11, 1883.
2085. Florence Kingman, bo. Oct. 1, 1846; ma. Charles Ariel Munger, May 25, 1882, of New York.
2086. Anna Winthrop, bo. Sept. 23, 1850; ma. Rufus Roscoe Drummond, Sept. 21, 1876, of Bath, Me. Children: [1]Herbert Ladd, bo. June 24, 1883; [2]Edith, bo. Oct. 18, 1886; [3]Roscoe, bo. Jan. 18, 1889.
2087. George Milton, bo. Oct. 3, 1852; ma. Mrs. Lydia (Springer) Durfee, May 3, 1888.

(1507) Gardner Perry Ladd, of Groveland, (son of Nathaniel,[1400]) was born in East Bradford, now Groveland, Oct. 23, 1814; ma. Nov. 10, 1836, Lois Hardy, dau. of George H. A. and Martha G. (Perley) Batchellor. He was educated in the common schools and at the Merrimac Academy; was a member from Groveland of the Constitutional Convention in 1853; was treasurer and tax collector of Groveland for sixteen consecutive years, and holds the office now (1888); was chairman of the board of selectmen six years, and an assessor for the same time; is a member of the Congregational Society, and has held the office of assessor and treasurer for more than twelve years; is one of the trustees of the Groveland Savings Bank, and a director in the Groveland Mutual Insurance Company. He is an ardent and earnest Republican, honest and fair in all his dealings, and is highly respected.

Children.

2088. Jeremiah Benjamin Perley, bo. March 28, 1838; ma. Ann G. George.
2089. Nathaniel E., bo. June 16, 1840; ma. Isabel S. Parker.
2090. Rufus George, bo. Dec. 31, 1844; d. Aug. 1848.
2091. Martha G., bo. May 7, 1849; ma. George E. Dawkins, Nov. 26, 1874. Child: George.

(1508) John Ingersoll Ladd, of Groveland, (son of Nathaniel,[1400]) was born in East Bradford, now Groveland, Feb. 22, 1816; ma. Nov. 2, 1837, Mary Ann, dau. of Bailey and Betsey (Parker)

Greenough. He was educated at the common schools and at Merrimac Academy. Oct. 1878, he removed to West Boxford, where he now lives on a small farm. When in Groveland he was engaged most of the time in manufacturing shoes; in 1851-2 he was inspector-general of leather; was constable in 1851-2, and town treasurer in 1854; county commissioner in 1856-8; trial justice for five years, commencing in 1859. His wife Mary Ann died Feb. 8, 1870. He ma. 2d, Mrs. Larissa C. (Tyler) Hovey, Nov. 3, 1875, dau. of Phineas Parker and Sarah (Day) Tyler, of West Boxford.

Children.

2092. George W., bo. Aug. 16, 1842; d. Oct. 1, 1842.
2093. Clara E., bo. Sept. 12, 1844; not married; d. March 17, 1889.
2094. Ellen R., bo. Jan. 22, 1846; d. Aug. 22, 1846.
2095. Edward L., bo. Feb. 8, 1848; d. Aug. 28, 1848.
2096. William B., bo. June 10, 1858; ma. Gertrude G. Phelps.

(1514) John W. Ladd, of Haverhill, (son of John,[1402]) was born in Newburyport, Jan. 7, 1822; was educated at the public schools at Newburyport, and at the academy in Haverhill. Soon after leaving school he worked in his father's comb factory, and afterwards learned the shoemaker's trade. He was toll-keeper at the bridge over the river at East Haverhill for a number of years, and was postmaster there during the administration of Pierce and Buchanan. For the last fifteen years of his life he lived in Haverhill, working at his trade of shoe cutting. He died March 28, 1880, from the effects of a cancer on his face, which had caused him terrible suffering for several years, which he bore with remarkable bravery and patience. He ma. Sarah C., dau. of John and Abigail (Smith) Evans, 1845. She died in 1862. He ma. 2d, Eliza D., dau. of Simeon and Eliza Wardell, of Andover, Jan. 1872.

Children.

2097. Frances Abbie, bo. June 21, 1845; ma. Andrew J. Fullerton, Feb. 1865.
2098. Mary S., bo. March 30, 1848; ma. Stephen W. Hall; 2d, Charles Niles.
2099. John E., bo. Oct. 17, 1849.
2100. Sally P., bo. Aug. 11, 1851; ma. Charles Barnes.
2101. Lizzie Inez, bo. 1854; d. young.
2102. Eliza E., bo. July 27, 1858; ma. Joseph Faunce.

Child by second wife.

2103. Fred H., bo. Aug. 31, 1878.

(1518) George W. Ladd, of Haverhill, (son of John,[1402]) was born at East Haverhill, June 15, 1830; was educated at the public schools; ma. Rebecca W., dau. of Horace T. and Charlotte (White) Morse, Nov. 27, 1851. She died Dec. 21, 1854, and he ma. 2d, April 6, 1856, Eliza A., dau. of John J. and Nancy (Dickey) Priest. He lived in Farmington, Iowa, where he kept a retail shoe store; in Lowell, where he kept a fancy goods store; and is now (1888) living in Bradford, and is in the furniture business in Haverhill. He has been surveyor, a member of the board of health, on the board of selectmen, and was treasurer for ten years of the Bradford Farmers and Mechanics Institute. He is a director in the Haverhill Cooperative Bank, and has been for the past nine years; is a member of the I. O. of O. F., and has been treasurer and held various other offices in the order.

Child.

2104. Lynn B., bo. Aug. 5, 1852; ma. Laura A. Graham, Feb. 6, 1872.

Children by second wife.

2105. Josephine M., bo. Dec. 3, 1860; ma. R. A. Wood, of Brentwood, N. H., Dec. 8, 1881; 2d, George W. Christie.
2106. Edgar L., bo. May 8, 1863; d. Aug. 24, 1864.
2107. George Edgar, bo. July 23, 1864; ma. Mary Oceana Hammond, May 24, 1889.
2108. Jennie B., bo. Sept. 29, 1865.

(1517) Byron G. Ladd, of Bradford, (son of John,[1402]) ma. Mirinda Alexander, dau. of Robert and Mary (Dickey) Alexander, Dec. 7, 1865. She died July 31, 1876. He ma. 2d, Louisa M. Ladd,[1586] June 15, 1887.

Children.

2109. Anne Sophia, bo. Feb. 19, 1867; d. Sept. 21, 1877.
2110. Louisa M., bo. May 14, 1871; d. Aug. 9, 1871.

(1524) Byron Parker Ladd, of Yarmouth, N. S., (son of Frederick,[1404]) was born in Boston, Aug. 13, 1825; he ma. Mary E., dau. of Hubbard and Azuba Davis, of Yarmouth, N. S., Jan. 27, 1853. She was educated at Westport, N. S. He is now (1888) doing a mercantile business at Yarmouth, where he has resided for the last eighteen years.

Children.

2111. Helen Cecelia, bo. May 20, 1854; d. June 17, 1854.
2112. Frances Susan, bo. Oct. 18, 1855.
2113. Frederick Arthur, bo. Dec. 11, 1858; ma. Grace F. Brown, May 20, 1886.
2114. Mary Byron, bo. Nov. 6, 1861; ma. Charles Pratt.
2115. Frank Irwin, bo. Nov. 30, 1864; d. June 6, 1873.

(1536) George Vivian Ladd, of Haverhill, (son of Rufus King,[1408]) ma. Cora Susan, dau. of —— Blackwood, at North Pembroke, Me., Sept. 14, 1866. She died July 29, 1867, and he ma. 2d, Charlotte, dau. of Benjamin and Amelia Hines, of Boston, Jan. 9, 1869.

Children by second wife.

2116. Daisy Maud, bo. April 21, 1870.
2117. Augustus Clark, bo. Dec. 29, 1872; d. Aug. 2, 1873.
2118. Lilian, bo. Nov. 13, 1874; d. Nov. 19, 1880.
2119. Eva Poor, bo. Jan. 1, 1883.

(1428) Thomas McCleary Ladd (son of Timothy[241]) ma. Percy Ann Mead, Aug. 12, 1832.

Children.

2120. Sarah Smith, bo. 1833; d. 1833.
2121. Martha Wells, bo. May 28, 1835.
2122. Amos Mead, bo. March 18, 1837. He was an officer in the 2d Michigan Infantry, and was killed at Gettysburg, Va., July 2, 1863.
2123. Adeline Bridgman, bo. Oct. 16, 1838.
2124. Sarah McCleary, bo. Jan. 10, 1841.
2125. Elizabeth Chipman, bo. Dec. 17, 1842.
2126. Ann Electa, bo. July 13, 1846.

(1503) Mason B. Ladd, of Oneida, N. Y., (son of Bodwell,[1396]) ma. Adeline D. Ingerson, Sept. 5, 1865.

Children.

2127. Maud, bo. ——.
2128. Mary B., bo. ——.
2129. Greeley, bo. ——.
2130. Ida, bo. ——.

(1504) Alexander P. Ladd, of Clayton, N. Y., (son of Bodwell,[1396]) ma. Octavia F. Tuttle, Oct. 23, 1862.

Children.

2131. Nelson, bo. Sept. 8, 1864; d. Feb. 4, 1865.
2132. Minnie M., bo. Nov. 13, 1865; d. Sept. 4, 1866.
2133. Bodwell, bo. April 5, 1867.

2134. Alexander L., bo. Sept. 8, 1869.
2135. Florence M., bo. May 21, 1871.
2136. Mertle A., bo. May 4, 1873.
2137. Larry H., bo. March 25, 1875.
2138. Fred H., bo. March 6, 1877.
2139. Joy L., bo. July 30, 1879.
2140. Mollie A., bo. May 20, 1881.
2141. Laura L., bo. Feb. 15, 1883.
2142. Edith, bo. Jan. 29, 1885.
2143. Ethel, bo. Jan. 29, 1885.

(1548) George A. Ladd, of Thetford, Vt., (son of Welcome D.,[1418]) ma. Louisa Porter.

Children.

2144. Martha Louisa, bo. Oct. 1856.
2145. Eugene Frederick, bo. Sept. 1859.
2146. Willie Porter, bo. Oct. 1861.
2147. Arline Estel, bo. Dec. 1875.

(1549) Dr. Thaddeus Ladd, of Worcester, Vt., (son of Jedediah P. B.,[1419]) ma. Harriet N. Russell, Dec. 5, 1850.

Children.

2148. Emeline E., bo. July 6, 1852.
2149. Ellen Eliza, bo. July 21, 1854.

(1566) Joseph Hartwell Ladd, of South Framingham, (son of Caleb,[1426]) was born in Calcutta, East India, Aug. 14, 1845; ma. Oct. 5, 1875, Amelia Allen, dau. of Henry and Amelia W. H. Eldridge, of Fairhaven. He was brought to this country when but two years old; returned to Calcutta, then came back when nine years of age, and lived with an aunt at Orange, Vt., except when at school and college, until 1866, when his father returned from Calcutta and settled at Watertown. He fitted for college at Barre, Vt., graduated at Dartmouth College in 1867, and at Harvard Law School in 1871, and was admitted to the Suffolk bar the same year. He practiced at Watertown one year, spent about four years farming, then went to Holliston, where he remained from Aug. 1876, to June, 1885, when he returned to Watertown. Besides the practice of law, he has held the position of clerk of the First District Court of South Middlesex, sitting at South Framingham, since Aug. 30, 1880.

Children.

2150. Caleb Henry, bo. Nov. 8, 1877.
2151. Joseph Hartwell, bo. March 19, 1883.
2152. Olive Pauline, bo. Jan. 30, 1885.

(1558) Thomas Sawyer Ladd, of Corinth, Vt., (son of Bodwell,[1424]) ma. Lydia M., dau. of William and Huldah (Kendall) Martin, Dec. 4, 1851. He was a farmer, held the office of lister two years, and was selectman five years. Lydia, his wife, died July 22, 1862, and he ma. 2d, Caroline M. Andrews, April, 1863, who died Feb. 27, 1873. He ma. 3d, Elizabeth Waterman, Aug. 1873.

Children.

2153. Ida May, bo. June 15, 1854; ma. Warren Crafts, Jan. 19, 1882.
2154. William Bodwell, bo. Dec. 28, 1856; ma. Addella M. Hillery, March 22, 1880.
2155. Ann Sawyer, bo. July 20, 1859.

(1560) Caleb Ladd, of Corinth, Vt., (son of Bodwell,[1424]) ma. Susan L. Towle, dau. of Jonathan and Lorena Towle, Dec. 2, 1861. He was a farmer. He died July 22, 1873.

Child.

2156. Charles Herbert, bo. Aug. 24, 1862.

(1562) Charles Bodwell Ladd, of Corinth, Vt., (son of Bodwell,[1424]) ma. Sarah Merrill, dau. of Jonathan and Kate (Collins) Sawyer, Oct. 27, 1866. He died April 15, 1882.

Children.

2157. Charles Allen, bo. Sept. 13, 1867.
2158. Jennie E., bo. March 9, 1870; d. March 17, 1873.
2159. Ernest Howard, bo. Aug. 10, 1878.

(1757) Daniel Ladd, of Louden, N. H., (son of John,[607]) ma. Abigail, dau. of Nathaniel and Mary (Blake) Martin, Oct. 26, 1826. He died June 17, 1881.

Children.

2160. Mary, bo. Sept. 27, 1827; ma. Stephen Ambrose Brown. Child: Mary Ashton.
2161. John Martin, bo. July 29, 1829; ma. Kate Hanrahan.
2162. Daniel Tilton, bo. Nov. 13, 1834; ma. Ruth Jane, dau. of Daniel Sanborn.
2163. Abbie, bo. May 20, 1836; d. May 18, 1838.
2164. Abbie F., bo. July 11, 1840; ma. Abial H. Clough.

(1764)   Albert Warren Ladd (son of Gideon[610] and Polly (Osgood) Ladd) was born in Louden, N. H., April 2, 1816. He ma. Feb. 28, 1842, Mary M., dau. of William Wallace, of Henniker, N. H. The following sketch of the life of Mr. Ladd we copy from the Folsom Genealogy, by John A. Folsom, pages 27–28 :

" We propose to write a few lines upon the man, his life and his accomplishments, and we do it with augmented pleasure as he is a *fixed* Bostonian, living among us and contributing largely to the spirit of enterprise in our city and the well-being of the community. We refer to Albert W. Ladd, Esq., of the firm of A. W. Ladd & Co., pianoforte manufacturers, Boston. He is an excellent example of what indomitable perseverance and invincible energy, joined to a truly New England character and high purpose, will accomplish. * * *   He left home at the age of 17 to learn a trade with a relative in the town of Raymond. At the age of 21 he commenced business for himself in a neighboring town. But feeling the necessity of a more thorough education, he soon after concluded to devote himself to the completion of the same, at the Gilmanton Academy, previous to following his inclination for seeking a more extensive field for future operations. In the Fall of 1838 he came to Boston, a stranger in a strange place, and immediately set about obtaining a situation suited to his taste and ambition. The pianoforte business being then comparatively new in this country, he determined to engage in that, and accordingly soon obtained employment in one of the oldest and most respectable establishments. He soon rose to the direction of the most important trust, and was at one time offered a partnership in the firm, which he declined. In 1848, just ten years from the time he came to Boston, Mr. Ladd entered upon his new and hazardous enterprise, with but a limited capital, the savings of his own hard toil. But having two good hands, a courageous heart, a master genius, and firm with a lofty purpose, he determined to leave his *mark*. It was at this time that he effected negotiations with Chief Justice Shaw for the erection of a massive and beautiful granite building, for a manufactory and salesrooms of pianofortes. The building was completed in the Fall of 1848, and he immediately took possession of it. * * *   In a few years it became necessary to enlarge the premises, in order to extend his rapidly growing business. The adjoining estate was built up and added to the premises, making one of the finest and most extensive establishments in the great metropolis of New England."

The following brief announcement appeared in Dwight's Journal of Music, Aug. 2, 1856: " A. W. Ladd, Esq., of Boston, Mass., was officially notified by the last mail from Europe that he had been admitted as a brother member of the Grand Imperial Society of Pianoforte Makers of Paris, as a distinctive mark of honor." He died Jan. 6, 1864.

Children.

2165. Charles Albert, bo. Jan. 15, 1843; d. Aug. 23, 1860.
2166. Marietta, bo. Sept. 9, 1845; ma. Charles E. Murphy, Dec. 4, 1882.
2167. George Wallace, bo. March 29, 1848; d. in New York, Jan. 15, 1882.
2168. Ella Martha, bo. Dec. 2, 1850.
2169. Albert Wallace, bo. Oct. 14, 1862.

(1765) Senaca Augustus Ladd, of Meredith, N. H., (son of Gideon,[610]) was born in Louden, N. H., April 29, 1819. He ma. Susan Tilton, March 21, 1840. She died Aug. 14, 1850, and he ma. 2d, Catharine S., dau. of William Wallace, June 1, 1852. We copy the following sketch of him from the Genealogy of the Folsom Family, by John A. Folsom, page 29 :

"At the age of 13 years he went to Raymond to learn the carriage, sleigh, and painting business. He served a time of four years at this business, when at the age of 17 he went to Meredith, N. H., and worked some two years at his trade, and at the age of 19 he went to Boston and worked as journeyman one year at the pianoforte business with Timothy Gilbert, the second piano manufactory established in the United States. From here he returned to Meredith, in July, 1839, at the age of 20 years. Here he purchased mills and at once erected a large carriage manufactory, and carried on that business until April, 1850, at which time his mills and carriage factory, with all their contents, were totally destroyed by fire. He at once leased the cotton factory in Meredith village, which was then lying idle, and cleared the building from the old cotton machinery and put in new machines for the manufacture of pianos and melodeons. This business he carried on in both Meredith and Boston for about eighteen years, or until Nov. 1868, when he and others procured the charter from the legislature and established the Meredith Village Savings Bank, of which he was elected its first treasurer and secretary, which office he has held to the present time; and during all this time, for the last forty years, he has spent some three hours out of each day in the study of geology, mineralogy, and nature, and in his office may be seen one of the best private collections in the State. He has ever possessed good health and enjoyed life by laboring more hours than any person in town, and never meeting with the slightest business failure in his life."

Children.

2170. Fannie C., bo. Aug. 26, 1841; ma. D. Wadsworth Coe, July 1, 1878.
2171. Charles F., bo. May 28, 1847; d. April 21, 1851.

Children by second wife.

2172. Virginia B., bo. Sept. 7, 1861.

(1766) Newell Corson Ladd, of Concord, N. H., (son of Gideon,[610]) ma. Sarah, dau. of Robert Smith. He died Sept. 22, 1877. His wife died Feb. 21, 1863.

Children.

2173. Florence M., bo. Aug. 13, 1843; ma. Frederick Boardman, May, 1882.
2174. Austin S., bo. April 12, 1845; ma. Fannie Blake, 1875.
2175. Addie R., bo. Sept. 6, 1850.
2176. Wendell Phillips, bo. Nov. 21, 1852.
2177. Jennie B., bo. April 20, 1855.
2178. Waldo E., bo. Dec. 30, 1858.
2179. Minnie E., bo. Dec. 30, 1858.
2180. Charles P., bo. Dec. 17, 1860.

(1768) Parish Badger Ladd, of San Francisco, Cal., (son of Gideon,[610]) ma. ——.

Children.

2181. Frank, bo. ——.
2182. Willie, bo. ——.

(1771) Charles Joseph Ladd, of San Francisco, Cal., (son of Gideon,[610]) ma. Eliza Long.

Child.

2183. Mary, bo. May 28, 1861.

(1774) Dr. Nathaniel Gould Ladd, of Malden, (son of James,[612]) was born in Chelsea, Vt., July 13, 1798. "He commenced the study of medicine with Dr. John Ladd,[617] of Lee, N. H.; afterwards read with Dr. Thomas Sargent, of Chester, Vt.; attended medical lectures at Hanover, N. H., and graduated at that institution in 1825. He commenced practice at Morgan, Vt., where he remained nine years; removed to Meredith village, N. H., in March, 1832, and remained there until 1835, when he came to Sanbornton Bridge, (Northfield one year,) and was here actively engaged in his profession until about 1864, when he removed to Malden. He ma. in Derby, Vt., Dec. 29, 1825, Abigail Mead, of Meredith, N. H." The above sketch of Dr. Ladd is from Runnel's History of Sanbornton, N. H.

Children.

2184. William Sargent, bo. Oct. 10, 1826; ma. Caroline A. Elliot.
2185. Helen Marr, bo. Jan. 1, 1829; ma. Geo. C. Kendall, of New Orleans, La.
2186. Smith Mead, bo. Jan. 4, 1831; d. Feb. 21, 1851.
2187. John Wesley, bo. Nov. 29, 1832; ma. Sarah Loring.
2188. Mary Fletcher, bo. Sept. 21, 1834; ma. James Steel, of Portland, Ore.
2189. Joseph Marshall, bo. July 15, 1838; not married; d. March 4, 1862.
2190. Gustavus Rush, bo. June 16, 1840; d. March 6, 1841.
2191. Abbie Josephine, bo. Dec. 18, 1842; ma. Edward Otta Schnägerl, of Paris, France.
2192. Stephen Olin, bo. Sept. 6, 1845; d. Aug. 25, 1847.

(1776) Zoroaster Ladd, of Plainfield, Vt., (son of James,[612]) ma. Eleanor Stearkweather, Jan. 1, 1827, who was born in Vernon, Vt., 1808.

Children.

2193. Hiram E., bo. May 13, 1828; ma. Emma Peck.
2194. Adeline A., bo. March 13, 1830; ma. Morrill Jenkins, April 24, 1858.
2195. Loren Gilbert, bo. Jan. 29, 1832; ma. Victor Baldwin, Dec. 18, 1860.
2196. Charles W., bo. March 20, 1834; ma. Caroline P. Allard, Sept. 17, 1854.
2197. Mary M., bo. Jan. 1, 1836; ma. Silas Jenkins, Oct. 20, 1858. She died April 2, 1861.
2198. Wesley Johnson, bo. Dec. 7, 1840; ma. Emeline Whittiker, Oct. 11, 1860.
2199. Emily E., bo. Oct. 7, 1842; ma. Myrick Pierce, Dec. 3, 1881.
2200. Senaca, bo. April 27, 1845; ma. Mary Varnum.
2201. Sarah O., bo. Sept. 4, 1847; d. April 4, 1849.
2202. Ira Marshall, bo. June 16, 1853; ma. Mary J. Winslow, April 21, 1881.

(1777) Senaca Ladd, of Danville, Vt., (son of James,[612]) ma. Matilda Gardner, May 7, 1823. She died in 1825, and he ma. 2d, Pamelia Easterbrooks, April 3, 1827. She died Aug. 26, 1846, and he ma. 3d, Mrs. Mary S. Dana, 1848. He died Oct. 16, 1868.

Child.

2203. Lacy M., bo. June 4, 1825.

Children by second wife.

2204. Gilbert, bo. Oct. 14, 1828; d. Jan. 25, 1850.
2205. John S., bo. April 24, 1830; ma. Mary Caroline Swan.
2206. George Senaca, bo. May 28, 1831; ma. Abby Bourland, May 28, 1856.
2207. Loretta D., bo. April 13, 1835.
2208. Ira Walter, bo. Feb. 26, 1837; ma. Emily Jane Sutherland, Mar. 7, 1858.
2209. Adelaide Amelia, bo. Dec. 3, 1840.

Children by third wife.

2210. Charles, bo. Sept. 3, 1849.
2211. Harvey E., bo. Sept. 29, 1855.

(1784) David Ladd, of Stewartstown, N. H., (son of Daniel,[613]) ma. Betsey Ingalls. She died, and he ma. 2d, Hulda Owen.

Child.

2212. Daniel, bo. ——.

Child by second wife.

2213. Nelson, bo. ——.

(1787) Rev. Nathaniel Ladd, of Epping, N. H., (son of Nathaniel,[614]) ma. Mrs. Mary (Gordon) Folsom. He d. Dec. 7, 1875.

Children.

2214. Louisa Lydia Watson, bo. July 5, 1816; ma. Nathaniel G. Harvey, Dec. 23, 1837.
2215. Mary J. Ames, bo. May 27, 1818; ma. Lyman Eastman.
2216. Olivia Ellis Kittridge, bo. June 24, 1822; ma. John Norris, of Exeter, N. H.
2217. Daniel Watson, bo. Feb. 24, 1825; ma. Lucy Ann Dustan.

(1789) Daniel Watson Ladd, of Epping, N. H., (son of Nathaniel,[614]) ma. Rebecca, dau. of Samuel Plumer, 1820. We copy the following sketch of him from the History of Rockingham County, N. H.:

"When only six weeks old he was adopted by his aunt, Lydia Watson, and his uncle, Daniel Watson, (his parents having passed away at that time,) by whom he was treated with the utmost tenderness. His advantages for education were limited to the public schools and private instructions by Rev. Mr. Holt, pastor of the Congregational Church at Epping. He was a fine scholar, and diligently improved his opportunities. His rapid progress, literary tastes and affable deportment made him a favorite with his fellow students and teachers. During his active life, amid the many duties arising from various departments of business, he ever found time to gratify his taste for reading. He commenced business with Daniel Watson, then a merchant at Epping Corners, N. H., and assisted him in keeping a public hotel at the Watson mansion, supervising his large landed estate in Epping and elsewhere, and at his death succeeded to his property. Mr. Ladd was pre-eminently a business man. In connection with the management of his large landed estate, he was for many years a director of the Rockingham Farmers' Mutual Insurance Company. In legal matters many preferred his counsel to that of professional lawyers, and such was the confidence reposed in the soundness of his judgment and his ability that his services were always in demand, and much of his time was given to probate business, referee trials, justice cases, and as pension agent, in which latter business he was very successful, seldom losing a case."

He died April 4, 1874.

Children.

218. Daniel Watson, bo. Aug. 9, 1821; ma. Dorothy Thing.
219. Sarah P., bo. Dec. 27, 1822; d. Feb. 24, 1854.
220. Samuel P., bo. Feb. 24, 1825; d. April 18, 1826.
221. Lydia Watson, bo. Jan. 28, 1827; not married.
222. Samuel Plumer, bo. Feb. 29, 1829; ma. Sarah J. Dodge.

(1791) Judge John Savilian Ladd, of Cambridge, (son of John,[616]) ma. Adelia Babson, of Rockport, 1841. She d. June 6, 1842, and he ma. 2d, Mary Ann, dau. of Samuel and Mary (Hill) Butler, Sept. 5, 1847. He graduated at Dartmouth College in 1835. After graduation he taught school, and studied law at Mt. Holly, N. J., and at Lowell. In 1839 he began to practice law at East Cambridge, and took an active part in town and municipal affairs, (Cambridge was incorporated as a city in 1846,) serving as a member of the common council and of the school committee. He was also a representative from Cambridge to the General Court, and was one of its delegates to the Constitutional Convention of 1853. In 1854, when the Cambridge Police Court was established, he was appointed its standing justice, and held this position until July, 1882, when the court was abolished. Prior to his appointment to judicial office he engaged in active political work, and was for a time chairman of the Whig county committee. Upon the dissolution of the Whig party he became a strong Republican.

Child.

2223. Charlotte Adelia, bo. May 30, 1842; d. Sept. 17, 1847.

Children by second wife.

2224. Babson S., bo. Sept. 6, 1848; ma. Ella Cora Brooks.
2225. Mary Adelia, bo. Feb. 21, 1850; d. Sept. 17, 1851.
2226. Story Butler, bo. Dec. 27, 1851; ma. Eliza Brigham Paine.
2227. Allston Channing, bo. June 20, 1854; ma. Harriet Amelia Hedenberg.
2228. John Franklin, bo. Nov. 30, 1856.

(1876) Moses Ladd, of Waterford, Vt., (son of Thing,[619]) was born in Salisbury, N. H., June 27, 1791. He ma. Hannah Carr, Oct. 15, 1812. She died March 1, 1890. He removed from Salisbury, N. H., to Waterford, Vt., Oct. 15, 1813. He was a carpenter and farmer. He died Feb. 6, 1879.

Children.

2229. Roxanna, bo. Nov. 3, 1814; ma. Jonathan Adams, Feb. 14, 1833.
2230. Sarah, bo. July 12, 1816; ma. Cyrus Hill, Dec. 29, 1838.
2231. Mary, bo. Oct. 12, 1818; not married; d. Jan. 24, 1855.
2232. Willard, bo. Aug. 21, 1820; ma. Lucinda Ireland, Sept. 6, 1846.
2233. John, bo. June 27, 1823; ma. Rebecca Powers, March 2, 1848.
2234. Orange S., bo. May 17, 1825; ma. Ann Eliza Parker, March 25, 1852.
2235. Alonzo, bo. July 11, 1827; ma. Miranda Brown, March 25, 1851.
2236. Jane, bo. May 30, 1829; ma. Francis Richardson, May 13, 1847.
2237. Milo E., bo. July 24, 1833; not married; d. Dec. 26, 1854.
2238. William W., bo. May 30, 1835; ma. Almanda Gilbert, Jan. 1, 1862.

(1880) John Ladd, of Peacham, Vt., (son of Thing,[619]) ma. Nabby Williams, Jan. 11, 1819. She died Feb. 7, 1822, and he ma. 2d, Sarah Summers, Oct. 28, 1823.

Children.

2239. Henry W., bo. Nov. 1, 1820; d. April 5, 1821.
2240. Abigail, bo. Jan. 27, 1822; d. Sept. 17, 1822.

Children by second wife.

2241. George W., bo. Aug. 2, 1824.
2242. Amy, bo. ——.
2243. Horace, bo. ——.

(1881) Shaw Ladd, of Danville, Vt., (son of Thing,[619]) ma. Dorcas Norris.

Children.

2244. Hannah, bo. ——.
2245. Zenas, bo. ——.
2246. Alvira, bo. ——.
2247. Lucy, bo. ——.

(1882) Edward Ladd, of Danville, Vt., (son of Thing,[619]) ma. Sophia Gookin, Nov. 22, 1826. She died July 5, 1849, and he ma. 2d, Lucella Clark, 1850. He died Nov. 8, 1877.

Children.

248. Edward Fenton, bo. Sept. 6, 1827; ma. Martha Beckwith, Dec. 5, 1854. No children.
249. Sophia, bo. Sept. 9, 1829; ma. Charles Harvey.
250. Leonard Worcester, bo. July 31, 1831; ma. Lewellen Clapp.
251. George Dana, bo. June 16, 1833; ma. Marion Laird.
252. Abigail Susan, bo. May 25, 1835; d. Sept. 25, 1835.
253. Arminda Carpenter, bo. March 9, 1837; ma. Ethel Benedict, of Wellington, Ohio.
254. Abigail, bo. May 20, 1839; d. Nov. 18, 1841.
255. Mary Harvey, bo. Aug. 26, 1841; not married.
256. William Brainard, bo. Feb. 2, 1844; ma. Mrs. Lewellen (Clapp) Ladd. No children.
257. Flora, bo. May 8, 1846; ma. Edward F. Webster.

Children by second wife.

258. Marilla Hortence, bo. May 7, 1855; ma. George C. Sanborn.
259. Georgiana, bo. Sept. 26, 1858; d. April 15, 1870.

(1884) Joseph Ladd, of Danville, Vt., (son of Thing,[619]) ma. Betsey Hunt, Dec. 5, 1821.

Children.

260. Clark H., bo. Dec. 9, 1823; ma. Susan C. Mason.
261. Emeline, bo. July 14, 1825; ma. John Cotes; 2d, Calvin Cotes.
262. Luther, bo. April 16, 1828; ma. Martha Ewell.
263. Charles Daniel, bo. April 22, 1843; ma. Maggie McKelsey.
264. Abbie Jane, bo. July 16, 1846; d. March 1, 1866.

(1887) Hollis Ladd, of Peacham, Vt., (son of Thing,[619]) ma. Elvira Taylor, Dec. 31, 1828.

Children.

265. Samantha, bo. June 24, 1830; d. Feb. 27, 1833.
266. Jasper, bo. Oct. 28, 1833; d. May 12, 1849.
267. Helen, bo. Oct. 4, 1836; d. March 11, 1854.
268. Nelson, bo. March 27, 1844; ma. Mary A. Marston, Dec. 5, 1871.
269. Mary, bo. Jan. 22, 1849; ma. Ambrose Parsons.

902) Joseph Ladd, Jr., of Lancaster, Ill., (son of Joseph,[621]) ma. Caroline A. Barnes, Nov. 7, 1841. He died Sept. 22, 1865. He held the office of justice of the peace, was supervisor of schools, treasurer of Timber Township, and for two years was treasurer of Peoria County.

Children.
2270. Henry T., bo. April 7, 1843; d. March 17, 1848.
2271. Martha A., bo. Nov. 5, 1845; ma. Samuel Glasford; 2d, Elzey Chamberlain.
2272. Rollin, bo. March 22, 1849; not married.
2273. Florence, bo. July 10, 1851; ma. Joseph Chellew.
2274. Electa, bo. June 6, 1853; ma. George W. Hess.
2275. Austin P., bo. June 3, 1855; not married.
2276. Oscar P., bo. June 3, 1855; d. April 23, 1857.
2277. Caroline M., bo. May 1, 1857; ma. Joel T. Matheny.

(1903) Solomon H. Ladd, of Lowell, (son of Edward,[628]) ma. Mary E., dau. of Joseph Gage Caverly, of Oxford, N. H., Sept. 16, 1847.

Children.
2278. Aaron, bo. July 28, 1849.
2279. Frank S., bo. Dec. 11, 1853.

(829) Otis Freeman Ladd, of Haverhill, N. H., (son of Joseph,[353]) ma. Caroline R. Heath, 1828. He died April 11, 1834.

Children.
2280. Arthur S., bo. July 2, 1830; ma. Ruth Ann Nettleton, 1870.
2281. Charlotte, bo. March 18, 1832.

(831) Lewis Ladd, of Essex, N. Y., (son of Joseph,[353]) ma. Catharine Colburn. She died, and he ma. 2d, Mrs. Emeline (Faxon) Platt, widow of Alfred G. Platt, Jan. 15, 1842.

Children.
2282. Lewis, Jr., bo. ——.
2283. Louisa, bo. ——.

Child by second wife.
2284. Harriet Luella, bo. Mar. 30, 1847; ma. Ransom S. Moore, Aug. 27, 1870.

(833) Amasa Scott Ladd, of Arcada, N. Y., (son of Joseph,[353]) was born in Haverhill, N. H., March 17, 1799. He ma. at New Bedford, Oct. 31, 1818, Mary Ann Childs. She died at Hartford, Conn., March 6, 1828, and he ma. 2d, Aug. 30, 1829, Martha B. Dwight. She died May 2, 1863, and he ma. 3d, Mary Robbins, Feb. 2, 1868. He removed from Hartford, Ct., to Barnett, Vt., about 1830. In 1840 he removed to Utica, N. Y., where he resided about two years, when he removed to Hume, Alleghany Co., N. Y., where he lived about fifteen years, and held the office of postmaster four years; moved from there

to Belfast, N. Y., where he resided until his wife's death. While in Belfast he held the office of coroner for six years, and was an overseer of the poor for several years. He removed to Franklinville, N. Y., in 1867. His business was that of furniture and undertaker, and while in Franklinville he continued in that business twelve years, when failing eyesight compelled him to retire from active work. On the death of his third wife, Jan. 27, 1882, he removed to Arcada, N. Y., residing with his son, William C. Ladd, until his death, Feb. 23, 1886. He was buried in Franklinville with Masonic honors.

Children.

2285. William Curtis, bo. Feb. 29, 1820; ma. Caroline Matilda Towne, 1850.
2286. James Madison, bo. Aug. 21, 1821; ma. Mary Ann Balcom.

Child by second wife.

2287. Henry Clay, bo. Sept. 30, 1830; ma. Welthy Amelia Whally, Sept. 29, 1852.

(836)   Hon. Peabody Webster Ladd, of Newbury, Vt., (son of Joseph,[353]) was born in Haverhill, N. H., Aug. 15, 1805, and was educated at the public schools. He ma. Aug. 30, 1827, Elizabeth Lowell, dau. of John and Abiab (Eaton) Johnson, of Newbury, Vt., and granddaughter of Col. Thomas and Elizabeth (Lowell) Johnson, and cousin of Hon. James Russell Lowell. She died May 8, 1880. He was a man of clear head and sound judgment, and held decided opinions upon all matters of town, state and national interest, as well as upon mechanical, economic, moral and scientific questions, which he never hesitated to express, without regard to what others might think or say; he was a positive man, and as a rule it is the positive men who succeed in whatever they undertake. He was superintendent of a Sunday-school for fifteen years; was chorister of the church choir for a long time; held the office of justice of the peace; and was judge of the county court. He is now (1889) living at the age of 84, in the enjoyment of good health, with a step as elastic as most men have at the age of 70, and his mind seems as clear and bright as ever.

Children.

2288. John Johnson, bo. May 11, 1828; ma. Sophia Stevens, Dec. 1, 1853.
2289. Mary Elizabeth, bo. Dec. 21, 1830; ma. David Childs, Sept. 27, 1855.
2290. Ezra, bo. Oct. 24, 1832; d. Oct. 29, 1856.

2291. Hallam, bo. Aug. 17, 1834; d. Feb. 4, 1842.
2292. Harriet Luella, bo. July 3, 1842; d. June 19, 1861.

(837) Calvin P. Ladd, of Dorchester, (son of Joseph,[353]) was born in Haverhill, N. H., Aug. 1809. He was educated at the public schools and the Haverhill Academy. He learned of Gookin & Herbert the trade of wooling machine manufacturer and the iron foundry business. He carried on the business for himself for some time, but sold out and entered the employ of E. & F. Fairbanks, scale manufacturers at St. Johnsbury, Vt., where he had charge of three of their shops. He remained with them three years, made some improvement in the movement of levers, obtained a patent for the same, and commenced the manufacture of scales under his patent under the firm name of Ladd & Jameson, at Irasburg, Vt.; sold out his business at Irasburg and removed to Montreal, Canada, and entered the employ of Hedge & Boomer as superintendent of their establishment for the manufacture of tools, stoves, machinery, etc.; continued with them for nine years and then bought them out, and carried on the business for himself for ten years. He was often employed as an expert in cases relating to machinery. While at Montreal he was appointed by the city of Montreal one of three commissioners to the great Hyde Park Exhibition in London, England, in 1851. He has the diploma and medal for services, signed by Prince Albert. On the 22d of February, 1861, his foundry and machine shops were destroyed by fire, and he sold out what property remained and returned to the States. He accepted a position in the chief engineer's office at the Brooklyn navy yard and remained there two years, then he superintended the Essex Felt Mill, New Jersey, for William Bloodgood, and remained with him and at his brother's factory in Brooklyn six years. He was a Royal Arch Mason and a member S. W. in Grand Lodge. He ma. Sept. 30, 1830, Mary Payson Harman, dau. of Hon. Daniel W. Harman. She died Sept. 27, 1861, and he ma. 2d, Charlotte F. Welsh, Nov. 10, 1864. He died Nov. 12, 1889.

Children.

2293. Ellen Maria, bo. Sept. 9, 1831; d. Aug. 22, 1835, at St. Johnsbury, Vt.
2294. Jane Fairbanks, bo. July 1, 1835; d. March 11, 1840, at Montreal, Ca.
2295. Elizabeth, bo. May 28, 1840; ma. John Bulwer, April 28, 1862. Children: [1]Mary E., bo. March 9, 1863; [2]John Edwin, bo. Oct. 25, 1865;

³Ida, bo. June 26, 1867; ⁴James, bo. Jan. 25, 1870; ⁵Ella, bo. July 3, 1872; ⁶Eva Florence, bo. April 7, 1874, d. July 16, 1874; ⁷Gertrude Maud, bo. April 7, 1874, d. July 14, 1874.

2296. Sarah Ring, bo. Aug. 29, 1843; d. Aug. 30, 1845, at Montreal, Ca.
2297. Victoria R., bo. May 24, 1845; ma. Thomas Alexander, Nov. 10, 1873.
2298. Harriet W., bo. Dec. 8, 1847; d. Oct. 18, 1848, at Montreal, Ca.
2299. Albert H., bo. June 24, 1850; d. April 7, 1869.
2300. Lucretia Ella, bo. Oct. 24, 1853; ma. Franklin Foster, Sept. 10, 1879.
Children: ¹Charles H., bo. Dec. 7, 1880; ²Victoria Hattie, bo. Sept. 1882.

Child by second wife.

2301. Lillian Maud, bo. Oct. 17, 1875; d. March 15, 1888, at Dorchester.

(1553) Sanford B. Ladd, of Kansas City, Mo., (son of David M.,¹⁴³⁰) was born in Milford, Mich., Sept. 11, 1844. He was educated in the public schools at Milford, Mich., and at Ann Arbor, and entered the University of Michigan at Ann Arbor in the Fall of 1861, and graduated in June, 1865. He studied law in Detroit with Hon. George V. N. Lothrop, late minister to Russia; was admitted to practice by the Supreme Court of Michigan, at Lansing, Sept. 1867. He went to Kansas City, Mo., in Dec. 1867, and formed a law partnership with John C. Gage, in April, 1869, as Gage & Ladd. He is now (Nov. 1888) a member of the law firm of Gage, Ladd & Small, which has been in existence since 1881. He ma. July 12, 1870, Clara M. Fuller. Has no children.

(1554) Frank M. Ladd, of Milford, Mich., (son of David M.,¹⁴³⁰) ma. Sophia M. Webb, Sept. 28, 1847. He was educated at the public schools at Milford and at Ypsilanti, Mich. When about 15 years old he entered his father's store as clerk, where he remained until 1876, when his father turned over the business to him, and he is now (1888) engaged in the general merchandise business, as his father was before him.

Children.

2302. Sanford B., bo. Dec. 1877.
2303. David Hartwell, bo. Sept. 2, 1881.

(912) Daniel Ladd, of Mt. Desert, Me., (son of Moses,³⁸⁶) ma. Eliza Gott, Dec. 23, 1824. She died Dec. 21, 1830, and he ma. 2d. Deborah Gott. She died, and he ma. 3d, Priscilla D. Richards, May 5, 1834. He died Sept. 29, 1834.

Children.

2304. Daniel, bo. Nov. 24, 1825; ma. Martha Southard, Dec. 5, 1852.
2305. Eliza Ann, bo. Jan. 6, 1828; ma. Samuel Newell Emery, March 18, 1847. Children: ¹Ernest, bo. May 1, 1849, ma. Sarah M. Clement, of Mt. Desert, Me., Dec. 30, 1875; ²Osmond, bo. Nov. 1, 1856, ma. Mina F. Harper, Nov. 6, 1886; ³Julian, bo. Feb. 21, 1859, ma. Addie J. Higgins, Dec. 21, 1888, and had one child, Malcom Carleton, bo. April 20, 1890; ⁴Lillian, bo. Feb. 21, 1859.
2306. Rufus Bailey, bo. May 9, 1830; ma. Hannah C. Stanley, Nov. 28, 1852.

(929) Alonzo Chace Ladd, of Atlanta, Ga., (son of Elisha Locke,[411]) ma. Mary C. Ladd, dau. of H. H. Ladd, of Galena, Ill., Oct. 27, 1858. She died at Rising Sun, Ind., Jan. 12, 1865, and he ma. 2d, Louisa G. Steubner, March 4, 1868.

Child.

2307. Hattie Melissa, bo. Oct. 2, 1861; ma. A. L. Delkin, Jan. 10, 1885.

Children by second wife.

2308. Freddie Elisha, bo. Dec. 20, 1868.
2309. Nora Asenath, bo. April 11, 1870; d. Sept. 14, 1870.

(935) James Ladd, of Chazy, N. Y., (son of Henry,[418]) ma. Melissa Chipman, of Waltham, Vt. He died Aug. 4, 1829.

Children.

2310. George, bo. ——.
2311. William, bo. ——; ma. Julia Martin.
2312. Charlotte, bo. ——; ma. John Hutchinson.
2313. James, bo. ——.

(936) Lemuel Ladd, of Chazy, N. Y., (son of Henry,[418]) ma. Hannah Adams, Sept. 1816. She died March 3, 1847. He died March 4, 1863.

Children.

2314. Almira, bo. July 19, 1817; ma. Amasa Brown, Dec. 31, 1840. Children: ¹Abbie E., bo. Aug. 3, 1846; ²Augusta E., bo. Feb. 27, 1849; ³William L., bo. June 13, 1854; ⁴Lemuel A., bo. July 12, 1856.
2315. William, bo. Oct. 23, 1821; ma. Mrs. Ellen Foley, Jan. 1867.
2316. Lorina, bo. Feb. 2, 1827; ma. John F. Niles.

(939) Jonathan R. Ladd, of Chazy, N. Y., (son of Henry,[418]) ma. Elizabeth Thomas. She d. July 18, 1864. He d. July 22, 1875.

Children.

2317. Whitney W., bo. July 31, 1823; ma. Mary Stone, April 6, 1855.
2318. Henry, bo. May 3, 1826; ma. Sarah Stone, Sept. 1857.

2319. Charlotte, bo. June 4, 1829; ma. McDonough McGregor, Mar. 20, 1849.
2320. Hiram, bo. March 4, 1833; ma. Electa Cooper, March 8, 1855.

(941) Henry Ladd, of Chazy, N. Y., (son of Henry,[418]) ma. Zurvia Sherman, Dec. 4, 1833.

Children.

2321. Maria Z., bo. Dec. 5, 1835; ma. Amasa Scott, April, 1857.
2322. Betsey, bo. Nov. 19, 1837; d. July 8, 1838.
2323. Helen M., bo. Nov. 28, 1838; d. Jan. 7, 1839.
2324. Alfred, bo. Nov. 16, 1840; not married; d. 1887.
2325. Edwin S., bo. April 26, 1843; ma. Laura Vaughn, April 22, 1876.
2326. Oscar DeW., bo. March 11, 1847; ma. Fanny Stott, Oct. 5, 1870.
2327. Lucy A., bo. Jan. 7, 1849; ma. Jay H. Farnsworth, March 30, 1870.
2328. Charles H., bo. Jan. 20, 1852; ma. Jenny June, Feb. 15, 1882.

(943) Hiram Ladd, of Chazy, N. Y., (son of Henry, [418]) ma. Adeline M. Dickerson, Nov. 3, 1833. She died Jan. 25, 1878.

Children.

2329. Abzina, bo. Dec. 28, 1834; not married.
2330. Lorina, bo. Sept. 20, 1836; ma. James Ostrander, March 12, 1856.
2331. Jane, bo. March 9, 1839; ma. H. J. Hinman, Sept. 29, 1860. She died May 14, 1880.
2332. Wilbur J., bo. Jan. 8, 1841; d. in 1887. Denio
2333. Marietta, bo. Dec. 21, 1842; ma. Albert P. Davis, Sept. 29, 1869.
2334. Henrietta, bo. Feb. 23, 1852; ma. Henry J. Hinman, Oct. 29, 1881.
2335. Ida, bo. Nov. 16, 1855; ma. Seymour Pike, March 1, 1884.

(944) George E. M. J. Florin Ladd, of Chazy, N. Y., (son of Henry,[418]) ma. Elizabeth Bell, of Grand Isle, Vt., Nov. 13, 1831.

Children.

2336. Henry Hazen Morris, bo. Feb. 14, 1835; ma. Harriet C. Denman, Jan. 8, 1869.
2337. Marion Allura Elizabeth, bo. Sept. 1, 1842; ma. Flavius Cisco, Nov. 3, 1864.
2338. Malvin Ransom, bo. Dec. 12, 1844; not married in 1887.
2339. John Milton, bo. May 12, 1847; ma. Mary M. Denman, Feb. 8, 1871.
2340. Martin Luther, bo. March 23, 1851.
2341. Martha Flavilla, bo. Dec. 15, 1854.

(945) Warren Ladd, of Avon, N. Y., (son of Herman,[419]) ma. Alda Whimple,

Children.

2342. Herman, bo. 1826; d. at the age of 15 years.
2343. Mary, bo. ——; not married.

2344. Martha, bo. ——; ma. John Humphrey.
2345. Adda, bo. ——; ma. William Humphrey.
2346. Charles, bo. 1834; not married; d. 1860.
2347. Warren, bo. ——; ma. Miss —— Johnson.

(949) Abial Richardson Ladd, of Poultney, Vt., (son of Benoni,[424]) ma. Elizabeth Farnsworth, April 28, 1833. She died April 27, 1878. He died Jan. 13, 1885.

Children.

2348. William Harmon, bo. July 17, 1834; d. Sept. 1, 1840.
2349. Mary Jane, bo. May 1, 1836; ma. Rockwell P. Walker, Mar. 31, 1863.
2350. Helen M., bo. Aug. 3, 1842; d. April 10, 1843.
2351. Margaret E., bo. Sept. 3, 1844; ma. Daniel F. Southworth, March 28, 1864. Children: [1]D. Frank, bo. Dec. 28, 1864; [2]Fred. L., bo. Feb. 28, 1867; [3]Ben. F. and [4]Ray E., bo. March 26, 1873.
2352. Benjamin F., bo. Sept. 11, 1847; d. April 2, 1849.
2353. Abial I. R., bo. May 22, 1852; d. May 22, 1864.

(950) Perre Green Ladd, of Benson, Vt., (son of Benoni,[424]) was born in Chazy, Clinton Co., N. Y., Oct. 11, 1809; ma. Dec. 22, 1829, Thryphena E., dau. of Daniel and Elizabeth (North) Moore. He was educated in the public schools; was a farmer in Clinton Co., N. Y., until 1838, when he removed to Benson, Vt., and continued farming until the Fall of 1846, when he bought the hotel property at Benson Landing, Vt., of Joel Gibbs, built a steamboat wharf and a store, entered into mercantile business, and formed a partnership with R. W. Converse, under the firm name of Ladd & Converse. In 1848 a post-office was established there, and Mr. Ladd was appointed postmaster, which office he held until 1867. In Feb. 1867, the hotel and nearly all its contents were burned, and soon after he sold his Benson Landing property and removed to De Kalb, Ill., bought a farm of 160 acres, and went to farming again; remained there until Jan. 1870, when he rented his Illinois farm and returned to Benson Landing, Vt., and rented the store he built and went into mercantile business again, with his son Kendall as partner, under the firm name of P. G. Ladd & Son, and continued in the business until he died, July 8, 1873. His widow died Dec. 26, 1889.

Children.

2354. Cornelia E., bo. Oct. 8, 1830; ma. Perum W. Converse, Mar. 30, 1848.
2355. Charlotte E., bo. Sept. 5, 1832; ma. Alexander Anderson, Mar. 27, 1856.

2356. Nelson G., bo. July 27, 1834; ma. Mary Ransom, Nov. 22, 1859.
2357. Mary M., bo. Aug. 24, 1836; ma. Rev. James L. Slason, May 25, 1881.
2358. Martha M., bo. July 12, 1838; ma. Allen L. Hall, Sept. 10, 1861.
2359. Elizabeth M., bo. Aug. 20, 1840.
2360. Kendall G., bo. Aug. 31, 1843; ma. Elizabeth Lowry, Nov. 10, 1869.
2361. Henry P., bo. June 24, 1847; d. June 27, 1847.
2362. Adelia J., bo. Oct. 9, 1850; ma. Rockwell P. Walker, Nov. 13, 1882.

(966) Charles Green Ladd, of Akron, Ohio, (son of Roger,[429]) ma. Ermina, dau. of Paul and Hannah Williams, July 13, 1845. He graduated at Western Reserve College and studied law with his brother-in-law, Lucius V. Bierce. He was mayor of Akron and judge of the court. He died at Akron, July 30, 1852. His widow died Oct. 3, 1868.

Children.

2363. Walter C., bo. June 21, 1846; ma. Ginevra T. Oviatt, Dec. 23, 1869.
2364. Lizzie Helen, bo. Nov. 21, 1848; ma. Martin L. Keller, Sept. 29, 1869. He d. June 6, 1874, and she ma. 2d, Gen. A. C. Voris, Feb. 21, 1882, of Akron, Ohio.
2365. Emma E., bo. Feb. 22, 1857; ma. Albert S. McNeil, July 10, 1873. He d. July 8, 1885. Child: Grace E., bo. June 23, 1880.

(971) Marshall Conant Ladd, of Bellows Falls, Vt., (son of Nathaniel,[438]) ma. Phebe Daggett, Feb. 19, 1855.

Children.

2366. Charles Wallace, bo. May 22, 1856.
2367. Willie Clayton, bo. Sept. 7, 1858; d. July 16, 1864.
2368. Jennie Alice, bo. Oct. 27, 1863; d. July 2, 1874.
2369. Hattie May, bo. Oct. 9, 1867.

(976) Edwin O. Ladd, of Milwaukee, Wis., (son of Mason,[440]) was born in Woodstock, Vt., Dec. 13, 1817; ma. Feb. 27, 1845, Sarah A., dau. of Thomas and Serepta (Smith) Crandall, of West Hartford, Vt. He acquired a common school education, and then entered the Castleton Seminary of Vermont, with the intention of pursuing a college course, but owing to sickness and trouble with his eyes he was compelled to abandon his long-cherished desire, and returned to his farm at Woodstock, Vt., where he lived until the Fall of 1856, when he removed with his family to Milwaukee, Wis., where he now (1888) resides. His business for the past twenty years has been life and fire insurance.

Children.

2370. Edwin Horace, bo. Sept. 21, 1848; ma. Jennie M. Atwater.
2371. George Dutton, bo. Oct. 7, 1850; ma. Annett A. Dutcher, Nov. 10, 1885.
2372. A son, bo. Feb. 26, 1854; not named; d. March 6, 1854.
2373. Frank M., bo. March 24, 1862.
2374. Hattie A., bo. May 9, 1864.
2375. Henry A., bo. May 9, 1864.

(982) Mason W. Ladd, of Woodstock, Vt., (son of Mason,[440]) was born in Woodstock, Vt., Jan. 9, 1839. He was educated at the public schools; was a farmer; lived on the farm which descended to him from his father and grandfather. He is a deacon of the Congregational Church, and is a highly respected and honored citizen. He ma. Nov. 26, 1861, Caroline, dau. of Seth and Lucia Walker. She died July 6, 1887.

Children.

2376. Lucia S., bo. Sept. 30, 1862.
2377. George E., bo. April 27, 1865.
2378. Alice M., bo. June 30, 1868.
2379. Charlotte M., bo. Oct. 15, 1873.

(988) Oliver Hazzard Perry Ladd, of Yarmouthville, Me., (son of Samuel,[447]) ma. Emily Keen, Oct. 30, 1843.

Children.

2380. Alonzo, bo. April 2, 1848; d. Oct. 30, 1852.
2381. Alonzo P., bo. Dec. 22, 1852; ma. Ada F. Lunt, Oct. 25, 1877.
2382. Isabel, bo. May 28, 1859; ma. Sumner B. Shorey, April 25, 1877.

(991) Pliny Day Ladd, of Boston, (son of Samuel,[447]) ma. Sophia Keene, Dec. 6, 1853. She died Dec. 22, 1854, and he ma. 2d, Sarah W. Haley, Nov. 25, 1858.

Child by first wife.

2383. Frank, bo. Sept. 14, 1854; d. June 6, 1865.

(993) Porter Ladd, of Weld, Me., (son of Samuel,[447]) ma. Lizzie Perkins, 1847.

Children.

2384. Jennie P., bo. June 22, 1848; d. Sept. 1854.
2385. David M., bo. April 12, 1852; d. Sept. 1854.
2386. William D., bo. Dec. 18, 1856; ma. Hattie M. Chandler, May 13, 1876.
2387. Flora A., bo. Sept. 22, 1859; d. Jan. 2, 1875.
2388. Pliny D., bo. Dec. 20, 1863.

2389. Nellie M., bo. Jan. 3, 1866.
2390. Wallace P., bo. Jan. 1, 1868.

(995) Hiram Ladd, of Weld, Me., (son of Samuel,[447]) ma. Eva Bass. He died in 1882.

Children.

2391. Charles P., bo. 1863; d. May, 1869.
2392. Hattie, bo. ——.
2393. Nettie, bo. ——.
2394. Mabel, bo. ——.
2395. Eddie, bo. ——.

(1009) Chester B. Ladd, of Strafford, Vt., (son of Ralph,[454]) was born in Sharon, Vt., May 14, 1820; was educated in the public schools. He lived in Manchester, N. H., four years; lived in Sharon, Vt.; has held several offices of trust and responsibility, and is a mechanic and farmer. He ma. June 9, 1844, Charlotte, dau. of Abraham and Naoma (Aldrich) Brown. She died Feb. 28, 1873, and he ma. 2d, Joannah E., dau. of Pliny and Henrietta[467] (Ladd) Day, May 23, 1875. She died Feb. 8, 1884, and he ma. 3d, April 26, 1886, Emily O., dau. of Lewis and Mary E. (Hamel) Dastous, of the Province of Quebec, a highly educated and accomplished woman.

Children by first wife.

2396. Mary A., bo. April 24, 1845; ma. Albert R. Preston, Nov. 27, 1866.
2397. Martha J., bo. April 21, 1848; ma. Charles E. Drown, Feb. 17, 1878.
2398. Pamelia A., bo. April 1, 1852.
2399. Harvey B., bo. Dec. 2, 1863.

(1012) Charles J. Ladd, of Milton, Vt., (son of Alfred,[455]) was born in Milton, Vt., Dec. 12, 1819; was educated in the public schools and at the academy in Georgia, Vt. He ma. Oct. 14, 1853, Elma C. Willis. She died Feb. 28, 1857, and he ma. 2d, Feb. 11, 1858, Ophelia C. Huse, of Lowell. He lived four years in Dundee, Mich., a short time in the State of New York, and in St. Albans, Vt., Georgia, Vt., and Milton, Vt., where he now resides. For the past twenty-two years he has been engaged in general merchandise business. He was representative from Milton in 1868–69, and a senator from Chittenden County in 1874–75.

Children.

2400. Ida C., bo. Aug. 29, 1854; ma. George W. Woodward, March 6, 1878.
2401. Elma Louise, bo. Feb. 8, 1857; ma. Orville W. Brown, July 11, 1879.

Children by second wife.
2402. Charles Alfred, bo. Nov. 12, 1863.
2403. Anna M., bo. Sept. 3, 1871.

(1013) Ephraim Lewis Ladd, of Georgia, Vt., (son of Alfred,[455]) was born in Milton, Vt., July 22, 1823; was educated in the public schools. He ma. March 26, 1848, Fannie Ann, dau. of Benjamin and Lucy (Chandler) Leonard. He removed in 1853 to Howard, Winnebago County, Ill., and remained there until 1863, when he returned and settled in Georgia, Vt. He has held the office of lister and selectman in Georgia, and is a justice of the peace.

Children.
2404. Oscar B., bo. Nov. 9, 1849; ma. Arvesta H. Lawton, Oct. 8, 1876.
2405. Carrie B., bo. Feb. 22, 1851; ma. Nathan N. Post.
2406. Hattie L., bo. May 20, 1855; ma. Fred. W. Bliss, Sept. 30, 1884.

(1025) Chandler Ladd, of Sharon, Vt., (son of Frederick,[461]) ma. Caroline P. Day, June 24, 1857.

Children.
2407. Fannie E., bo. Aug. 8, 1858.
2408. Elmer F., bo. May 20, 1861.
2409. Frederick D., bo. June 24, 1863.
2410. George A., bo. July 28, 1866.
2411. Alfred D., bo. July 16, 1870.
2412. Homer, bo. Feb. 20, 1874.

(1041) Thomas Jefferson Ladd, of Sprague, Conn., (son of Septa,[490]) ma. Mary Sweet, Aug. 26, 1853.

Children.
2413. Ellen Amanda, bo. May 16, 1854; d. Aug. 14, 1856.
2414. Harlow Thomas, bo. July 19, 1857; ma. Ida Clone, Aug. 27, 1885.
2415. Herbert Charles, bo. Nov. 29, 1860.
2416. George Septa, bo. Nov. 6, 1863.
2417. Everett Samuel, bo. Sept. 29, 1865.

(1044) Edward Ladd, of Sprague, Conn., (son of Septa,[490]) ma. Rhoda Lillibridge, Jan. 2, 1861.

Children.
2418. Nellie A., bo. Dec. 5, 1863; ma. Mark L. Greenleaf, Sept. 2, 1884.
2419. Eddie F., bo. Feb. 25, 1866.

(1045) William Lewis Ladd, of Wareham Point, Conn., (son of Septa,[490]) ma. Jennie R. Graham, July 10, 1861.

Children.

2420. Elmer L., bo. Dec. 19, 1862.
2421. Jennie E., bo. July 15, 1864.

(1047) Charles H. Ladd, of Sprague, Conn., (son of Septa,[490]) ma. Rebecca A. Steer, Jan. 24, 1869.

Children.

2422. Lydia A., bo. Feb. 3, 1870.
2423. Charles G., bo. Aug. 31, 1873; d. June 11, 1875.
2424. Carrie H., bo. Aug. 15, 1881.

(1064) Samuel Jedediah P. Ladd, of Plainfield, Conn., (son of Jedediah P.,[504]) ma. Philena B. Hazen, 1845.

Children.

2425. Philena Josephine, bo. Feb. 27, 1846; ma. Lovell R. Smith, Oct. 1866.
2426. Samuel Pierpont, bo. Dec. 5, 1847; ma. Sarah H. Meacham, June 7, 1869.
2427. Arthur Clinton, bo. Jan. 30, 1855; ma. Ida Browning, March, 1880.

(1065) Henry Ladd, of Blackmanton, N. Y., (son of Ulysses,[508]) ma. Lucy Richards, Feb. 4, 1849.

Children.

2428. Jedediah, bo. July 16, 1850; ma. Seba Johnson, June 29, 1876.
2429. Mary A., bo. 1853; d. 1861.
2430. Sanford H., bo. May 11, 1861; ma. Elizabeth Parsons, May 14, 1878.

(1070) Noah Ladd, of Beekhampton, N. Y., (son of Ulysses,[508]) ma. Seba Parsons, Sept. 3, 1880.

Child.

2431. Gracie H., bo. 1882.

(1074) Herbert W. Ladd (son of Jabez[511]) ma. Helen Loveland, Nov. 17, 1870.

Children.

2432. Arthur Jabez, bo. Nov. 11, 1872.
2433. Ida, bo. Oct. 7, 1875.
2434. Harry, bo. May 11, 1878.

1616) Abner Ladd, of North Hero, Vt., (son of Jedediah Perkins,[190]) was born in North Hero, Vt., Jan. 6, 1800. He was educated in the schools of Georgia and St. Albans, Vt. He ma. March 21, 1824, Susan, dau. of Dr. Samuel Whitney, of

Isle La Motte, Vt. He always lived in North Hero, with the exception of a few months which he spent in Mayfield, Ohio. He was town clerk, a representative in the legislature at Montpelier, and held various other town offices. He owned a large farm and managed it. He had a legal head, and was often employed in lawsuits; was a gifted man, but had poor health. He died March 16, 1867, highly respected by all who had the pleasure of his acquaintance.

Children.

2435. Helen M., bo. March 5, 1825; ma. Jerome Warner, 1857.
2436. Jedediah P., bo. Sept. 28, 1828; ma. Mary Hazen, Aug. 31, 1849.
2437. Maria S., bo. Dec. 11, 1830.
2438. Henry C., bo. April 30, 1833; ma. Nancy Moore.
2439. Linda S., bo. Sept. 8, 1835; d. June 6, 1860.
2440. Sumner, bo. May 11, 1838; ma. Roberta Moore.
2441. J. Gertrude, bo. March 7, 1842.

(2436) Jedediah P. Ladd, of Alburgh, Vt., (son of Abner,[1616]) was born in North Hero, Vt., Sept. 28, 1828; ma. Aug. 7, 1848, Mary, dau. of Jabez and Sophronia (Peters) Hazen. He was educated at the public schools and at several different academies. He resided at North Hero, Vt., until 1863, when he removed to Alburgh, Vt. In North Hero he held the office of justice of the peace, town clerk, superintendent of schools, and county sheriff. Since residing in Alburgh he has been superintendent of recruiting service for Grand Isle County, deputy collector of customs, captain of a Provincial militia company for the protection of the frontier during the war, captain of Co. A, 1st Reg. Vt. Militia, and colonel of the same regiment, representative to the General Assembly four years, State senator two years, and for two years State auditor. He is a lawyer by profession, and in politics an earnest and active Republican.

Children.

2442. Florence, bo. Nov. 11, 1850; ma. A. D. Whitney, 1869.
2443. Eva, bo. June 8, 1853; ma. Henry Smith, 1874.
2444. Winnie, bo. May 23, 1862.
2445. Allie, bo. May 23, 1862.
2446. Henry C., bo. Dec. 6, 1864.
2447. Jed. P., bo. Nov. 6, 1868.

(2438) Henry C. Ladd, of North Hero, Vt., (son of Abner,[1616]) ma. Oct. 26, 1861, Nancy, dau. of Augustus Moore, of North Hero.

She died Aug. 26, 1866, and he ma. 2d, Louisa, dau. of John Eddy, of Alburgh, Vt., Aug. 5, 1874. He has lived in Mayfield, Ohio, in Wisconsin, and in Iowa. He is now a farmer, and resides in North Hero, Vt., where he has been town clerk, auditor, and has held other town offices, and he has also held the office of deputy sheriff for Grand Isle County.

Child.

2448. Henry A., bo. Nov. 9, 1877.

(2440) Sumner Ladd, of Minneapolis, Minn., (son of Abner,[1616]) was born in Mayfield, Ohio, May 11, 1838. He ma. March 25, 1874, Roberta R., dau. of Col. Edward L. Moore. In the year 1859 he entered the University of Vermont, at Burlington, and there graduated in 1863 with what is called "highest honors," and being among what is termed the "first third" in scholarship. He commenced studying law in 1864 with Hon. Daniel Roberts, of Burlington, Vt., one of the ablest lawyers in the State; attended the Law School at Albany, N. Y., in 1865, and in August, 1865, was admitted to the bar in Grand Isle County, Vt., and the same Fall was elected on the Republican ticket State attorney for Grand Isle County. He went West in the Summer of 1866, and located at St. Peters, Minn., in the practice of law, and at once took a leading position in his profession, practicing with great success, especially in the Supreme Court. He was elected without opposition to the legislature (lower house) of Minnesota for the session of 1878, and was made chairman of the ways and means committee, and was one of the leading members of the judiciary committee. In 1882 he removed to Minneapolis, and is now in law practice there. In December, 1882, he delivered an address in Minneapolis before the sanitary council of the State, entitled the "Reign of Law," which attracted much attention, and which was published in full in the "Annual Report of the State Board of Health." For the past four years he has held the professorship of medical jurisprudence in the medical college at Minneapolis, called the "College of Physicians and Surgeons." His wife d. March 8, 1885.

Children.

2449. Sumner M., bo. March 13, 1875.
2450. Edwin W., bo. Dec. 27, 1881.

(1096)   David Ladd, of Deerfield, N. H., (son of John F.,[673]) ma. Hannah Hoyt, of Deerfield, Sept. 7, 1826.

Children.

2451. Mary E., bo. Nov. 2, 1827; not married.
2452. Wyman H., bo. June 30, 1831; not married.
2453. Susan H., bo. Aug. 9, 1842; ma. Daniel P. Haines, July 13, 1867.

(1100)   John F. Ladd, of Deerfield, N. H., (son of John F.,[673]) ma. Mary M., dau. of Ebenezer and Betsey Rollins.

Children.

2454. Mahala, bo. Jan. 24, 1839; not married.
2455. Alpheus, bo. Jan. 18, 1845; ma. Melissa Langley.
2456. George M., bo. March 14, 1848; ma. Ann A. Batchelder, Nov. 25, 1868.
2457. Mary A., bo. June 20, 1854; ma. John M. Hill.

(1106)   Thomas Ladd, of Bucksport, Me., (son of Thomas,[677]) ma. Eliza Lowell, Jan. 1, 1849.

Children.

2458. Simeon, bo. Oct. 9, 1849; ma. Alice M. Eaton, Oct. 28, 1879.
2459. Mary, bo. Oct. 16, 1851; ma. Merritt Smith, March 15, 1882.
2460. Thomas, bo. Aug. 23, 1853; d. young.
2461. Rosabell, bo. Sept. 25, 1855; d. young.
2462. Isabel, bo. Sept. 25, 1855; ma. James Fullom, March 14, 1882.

(1109)   Ozro A. Ladd, of Joliet, Ill., (son of Samuel G.,[685]) ma. Laura Fox, of Barnstown, P. Q., Can.

Child.

2463. Ellen, bo. ——; ma. —— Lyford.

(1113)   Uriah G. Ladd, of Stanstead, Can., (son of Samuel G.,[685]) ma. Eleanor Mason, March 24, 1853. He d. Aug. 30, 1882.

Children.

2464. Ella P., bo. June 15, 1854; d. Aug. 2, 1854.
2465. Emma F., bo. Aug. 15, 1855; ma. Hiram Young.
2466. George C., bo. Sept. 26, 1857.
2467. William D., bo. July 28, 1859; ma. Lillie Damon, March 2, 1881.
2468. Charles U., bo. Feb. 3, 1863; ma. Ella Chamberlin, March 26, 1883.
2469. Belia E., bo. April 23, 1865; ma. Abba Hane, Nov. 1882.
2470. Frederick H., bo. Oct. 3, 1870.

(1114) Samuel G. Ladd, of Lowell, (son of Samuel G.,[685]) ma. Eliza A. Bigelow.

Child.

2471. Henrietta L., bo. April 8, 1855.

(1119) Lorenzo S. Ladd, of Bethlehem, N. H., (son of Dudley F.,[686]) ma. Martha H. Buchanan, May 8, 1854. She d. Feb. 26, 1858, and he ma. 2d, Jane Buchanan, Dec. 2, 1858.

Children.

2472. Eva M., bo. Sept. 8, 1855; d. March 24, 1865.
2473. Harry B., bo. May 8, 1857.

Children by second wife.

2474. Lovie A., bo. July 4, 1860.
2475. Frank J., bo. Aug. 29, 1871.

(1120) Josiah M. Ladd, of Littleton, N. H., (son of Dudley F.,[686]) ma. Lydia A. Jesseman, July 7, 1853, of Franconia, N. H.

Children.

2476. Ella M., bo. Sept. 11, 1855; ma. William N. Waterman, Nov. 10, 1875.
2477. Alice M., bo. Nov. 6, 1857; ma. Henry A. Eaton, Oct. 25, 1881.
2478. Ida E., bo. June 16, 1860.
2479. Anna W., bo. Dec. 26, 1864.

(1122) John W. Ladd, of Montpelier, Vt., (son of Dudley F.,[686]) ma. Louisa Rock, of Northfield, N. H., July 14, 1864. He d. Dec. 3, 1870.

Children.

2480. Hattie L., bo. Nov. 18, 1865.
2481. Mary Alice, bo. Dec. 3, 1866; d. Jan. 3, 1871.
2482. Emma J. bo. April 13, 1869; d. Dec. 3, 1870.

(1123) Plummer B. Ladd, of Bethlehem, N. H., (son of Dudley F.,[686]) ma. Luella K., dau. of Augustus G. and Louisa M. Whitney, July 21, 1868.

Children.

2483. Mabel L., bo. May 2, 1870; d. Sept. 26, 1870.
2484. John Sidney, bo. Sept. 22, 1874.

(1125) Jeremiah W. Ladd, of Newport, N. H., (son of Jeremiah,[689]) ma. Clarie N. Robie, July 15, 1856.

Children.

2485. Frank B., bo. June 17, 1857.
2486. George B., bo. Dec. 15, 1858; drowned Nov. 14, 1876.
2487. Lora B., bo. Dec. 3, 1861.
2488. Nellie M., bo. June 10, 1864; d. July 14, 1881.
2489. Fred. W., bo. July 26, 1867.
2490. Ernest J., bo. June 25, 1875.
2491. Georgia D., bo. Aug. 14. 1880.

(1128) Noah Ladd, of Biddeford, Me., (son of Jeremiah,[689]) ma. Sarah D. Hall, of Gorham, N. H., July 4, 1856.

Children.

2492. Jessie Maria, bo. April 12, 1857.
2493. Fannie Hall, bo. Aug. 7, 1859.
2494. Eugene Belknap, bo. March 9, 1862.
2495. Walter Gorham, bo. Sept. 11, 1863.
2496. Annie Lincoln, bo. July 24, 1865.
2497. Alice Helena, bo. May 16, 1868.
2498. Mary Catheen, bo. Feb. 28, 1871.
2499. Grace Margaret, bo. Sept. 26, 1872.
2500. Willie Webster, bo. April 10, 1875.
2501. Edwin Carleton, bo. Aug. 27, 1877; d. Oct. 4, 1877.
2502. Harry Winter, bo. March 10, 1882.

(1141) Jacob S. Ladd, of Middlesex, Vt., (son of Daniel,[697]) ma. Polly Nichols, Dec. 3, 1829. He died April 5, 1868. His widow died Sept. 4, 1887. He was a farmer; was selectman in 1855, and representative in 1861–62.

Children.

2504. Ezra, bo. Dec. 31, 1832; ma. Martha Stevens, March 21, 1858.
2505. Harriet M., bo. July 4, 1834; not married.
2506. Orrissa L., bo May 4, 1836; ma. Issahar R. Dunsmore, Dec. 25, 1856.
2507. Mary S., bo. Oct. 22, 1839; ma. Newell Bliss, Oct. 24, 1858.
2508. Elizabeth B., bo. Jan. 4, 1844; d. Aug. 24, 1865.
2509. George Henry, bo. Sept. 22, 1847; ma. Emogene L. Leland, Oct. 25, 1868.

(1142) Aurin Ladd, of Plainfield, Vt., (son of Daniel,[697]) ma. Louisa Walling, Aug. 10, 1831. He died Nov. 19, 1861. His wife died May 18, 1860.

Children.

2510. Jacob P., bo. April 23, 1832; ma. Melissa I. Perkins, Jan. 20, 1863.
2511. Matilda E., bo. July 6, 1833; ma. Ambrose J. Batchelder, Aug. 25, 1863.
2512. Margaret L., bo. Jan. 1836; d. April 10, 1850.

(1150) Dr. William M. Ladd, of Claremont, N. H., (son of Dudley,[699]) ma. Adelphia C. Parkhurst, 1845, dau. of William and Abigail (Holbrook) Parkhurst. He died June 29, 1885. His wife died Dec. 11, 1879. We copy the following "Obituary" from a Claremont, N. H., paper:

"On Tuesday last, at 2.30 P. M., Dr. William M. Ladd, for forty years a leading physician and druggist of this town, passed quietly away. Although he had been in feeble health for some time, since leaving his business, three weeks prior to his death, he had made considerable improvement, and hopes were entertained that he might be about again, but on Monday a change was noticed, and the following morning it was plain that the end was near. Dr. Ladd was born in Unity, N. H., in the year 1813; graduated at Meriden, N. H., and studied medicine with his uncle, Dr. Charles Perry, at Rutland, Vt. After graduating at Vermont School of Medicine, he practiced at Townsend, Vt. For the following nine or ten years he led an active professional life. He moved to Claremont, N. H., and practiced for three years, when, his health failing, he was obliged to leave a lucrative practice. He at once opened a drug store in the building north of the Sullivan House. There he remained until the building of Brown's wooden block. The last store in the west end was fitted up for him, and here he has remained, doing a large business for nearly thirty years. During all these years he has held many important offices, being postmaster for nine years under Pierce and Buchanan. In those days it was customary to appoint a commissioner of schools for each county, and this position Dr. Ladd held for a number of years in Sullivan County, afterwards being superintendent of schools in Claremont. He also held the office of county commissioner. He was always a great lover of music, and was undoubtedly the best informed musician in this part of the State. The ease with which he could read the most difficult composition at sight was remarkable. He was a leading churchman, and for many years led the singing in the Episcopal Church, and was a teacher of music in all the public schools."

Child.

213. Minnie Adelphia Louise, bo. Nov. 18, 1847; ma. Clarence Monroe Leet, April 19, 1876. Children: [1]Bestina Adelphia, bo. Nov. 30, 1878; [2]Roscoe Ladd, bo. Sept. 10, 1880, d. April 5, 1881; [3]Jeffries Wilhelmina, bo. April 3, 1882; [4]Asa Parkhurst, bo. Jan. 28, 1888.

(1157)   Almon A. Ladd, of Middlesex, Vt., (son of Aaron,[708]) ma. Emeline White, March 11, 1841.

Child.

2514. Durant E., bo. Jan. 31, 1842; ma. Mary Jane Austin, Jan. 2, 1868. No children.

(1158)   Horatio H. Ladd, of Manchester, N. H., (son of Aaron,[708]) ma. Mary Jane Currier. He died Nov. 9, 1881. He was engaged in the jewelry business; was a member of the New Hampshire Legislature, and held various city offices.

Children.

2515. William Oscar, bo. April, 1844; ma. Ada M. Currier.
2516. Frank, bo. 1846; d. young.
2517. Ida May, bo. 1850; ma. A. Frank Morse.
2518. Fred Lee, bo. Feb. 29, 1852.
2519. Henry H., bo. Aug. 1854; ma. Susan Robinson.

(1160)   Vernon A. Ladd, of Worcester, (son of Aaron,[708]) was born in Middlesex, Vt., March 15, 1824. He went to Worcester when quite young, and resided there until his death, Nov. 19, 1881. He was engaged most of the time in the grocery business. He was a representative to the General Court, member of the common council, clerk of the board of overseers of the poor, and held other city offices. He ma. Rose Holden, of Mt. Holly, Vt.

Child.

2520. Carrie, bo. June, 1858.

(1163)   Daniel P. Ladd, of Philadelphia, Pa., (son of Aaron,[708]) was born in Middlesex, Vt., March 3, 1838. In 1861 he enlisted in the 1st New Hampshire Battery; was taken prisoner at the battle of Bull Run, Aug. 29, 1862; was paroled on the 30th, and reached the Union lines at Point of Rocks, Maryland, the next Wednesday. From there he was sent to a parole camp at Cumberland, Md., from there to Columbus, Ohio, and from there returned home, which he reached on the last of October. He remained at home a short time, when he joined his regiment just before the battle of Fredericksburg. Owing to some informality in his papers, he did not take part in the battle, but was in most of the engagements of the Army of the Potomac from that time until his term of service expired, Oct. 1864. He is now

(1888) in the employ of Hirsh & Bro., of Philadelphia, Pa., as a travelling salesman. He ma. Mary E. Shattuck, Dec. 22, 1871, dau. of Norman and Mary Asenath (Brown) Shattuck.

Children.

521. Blanche Emma, bo. Nov. 22, 1872; d. Dec. 15, 1872.
522. Florence E., bo. Aug. 31, 1874.

(1164) Dudley P. Ladd, of Wellington, (son of Aaron,[703]) was born in Middlesex, Vt., Oct. 29, 1839. He attended the district school until 1853, when he went to Manchester, N. H., to live with his sister, Mrs. F. A. Brown, where he attended the grammar and high schools for two years; was then employed in the daguerreotype and photograph rooms of his brother-in-law, Frank A. Brown, where he remained until 1861, when he enlisted in the 1st N. H. Battery and served until 1864, when his time expired and he was discharged. He was taken prisoner at the battle of Bull Run, Aug. 29, 1862, was paroled the next day, and reached our lines at Point of Rocks, Maryland, the next Wednesday. From there he was sent to the parole camp at Cumberland, Md., and from there to Columbus, Ohio, and from there returned home by the last of October; remained at home a few weeks, and then rejoined his company just before the battle of Fredericksburg, but did not take part in that battle, owing to some informality of his exchange papers; but he was in most of the engagements of the Army of the Potomac from that time until the expiration of his term of service in 1864. After leaving the army he was employed most of the time, until 1866, in the store of his sister-in-law, Mrs. E. C. Ladd, at Philadelphia, Pa., then entered the employment, as travelling agent, of Hirsh & Bro., manufacturers of umbrellas and parasols, and has been in their employ ever since. He ma. Dec. 11, 1867, Judith C., dau. of Aaron and Charlotte Boody, of Manchester, N. H., and removed to Bedford, where he resided until Oct. 1887, when he removed to Wellington, where he now (1888) resides.

Children.

523. Frank Brown, bo. Sept. 6, 1869.
524. Roy B., bo. Jan. 13, 1883.

(1167) Joseph W. Ladd, of Newport, N. H., (son of John,[704]) ma. Marietta Hewlet, May 6, 1851. He died Feb. 11, 1875.

Child.

2525. Carrie Ella, bo. July 2, 1860; ma. Albert Hitchcock, Dec. 25, 1880.

(1168) Nathaniel Marshall Ladd, of Newport, N. H., (son of John,[704]) ma. Emily Brooks. She died Jan. 10, 1855, without issue, and he ma. 2d, Mrs. Tryphena Webster (Mooers) Pratt, Feb. 17, 1856.

Child by second wife.

2526. Nathaniel Mooers, bo. Jan. 9, 1858.

(1175) Joseph Edwin Ladd, of Augusta, Me., (son of Joseph,[708]) ma. Sarah E. Potter, Dec. 8, 1836. He was a druggist and apothecary. He died Aug. 21, 1853, in Florida, while there on a visit.

Children.

2527. Caroline E., bo. Nov. 11, 1837.
2528. Ann Maria, bo. Aug. 22, 1839; d. Sept. 4, 1840.
2529. Edwin, bo. April 3, 1841; d. Sept. 9, 1872.
2530. Ann Potter, bo. Sept. 27, 1845.
2531. Theophilus, bo. Jan. 26, 1848.
2532. Charles Potter, bo. Feb. 17, 1849; ma. Lizzie Davis.
2533. Arthur, bo. Aug. 18, 1850.

(1177) Franklin Bacon Ladd, of Brooklyn, N. Y., (son of Joseph,[708]) ma. Sarah Ann Van Norden, Nov. 8, 1850.

Children.

2534. Jeremiah Francis, bo. Dec. 5, 1851.
2535. Julia Butler, bo. Dec. 30, 1855.

(1178) Daniel Ladd (son of Joseph[708] and Sarah (Hamlin) Ladd) was born in Augusta, Me., March 21, 1817. He ma. Elizabeth Overstreet, at Newport, Fla., April, 1850. When but 16 years old he went to Florida and entered his father's counting-room as clerk, and soon after took charge of his business. After his father's death in 1835 he continued his father's Florida business, and soon became a leading merchant of Middle Florida. He was extensively engaged in the lumbering business, and was the owner of several steam saw-mills and a large iron foundry and machine shop. He was the owner of two steamers, which he employed on the St. Marks River, and was a member of the

Florida Convention when the State seceded from the Union. The war of the rebellion nearly ruined his business, and when peace came he found himself in much reduced circumstances, but with his usual energy, pluck, and New England push, he worked hard to recover his property and restore his lost fortune, but his health failed, and he passed from the trials, troubles, and perplexities of the present, to the peaceful rest of a bright and beautiful hereafter, at Newport, Florida, Oct. 20, 1872. We copy the following just tribute to his memory from the "Floridan," of Tallahassee, Florida:

"It is with sincere sorrow that we record the death of this good and true man. For several days he had been suffering with a complication of diseases, his system seeming generally to give way, and on the morning of the 20th instant, at his home in Newport, he quietly breathed his last. Few names were more intimately associated with the mercantile interests of Middle Florida, and a large portion of Southern Georgia, before the war than his, and in everything connected with the welfare and prosperity of the people of Wakulla County, in this State, it was the foremost. For many long years his name has been a household word in all this section of country, and has ever carried with it the idea of everything that was public spirited, self-sacrificing and generous. Indeed, we doubt whether a more generous heart, one more susceptible to all the kindlier emotions of our better nature, ever beat within the breast of man. He was, beyond question, one of the very best men we ever knew, his deeds of charity towards the poor, the distressed and unfortunate, being numberless. Notwithstanding the loss of nearly everything by the late war, and his own hard struggle to keep himself in business even on a small scale, he seemed to forget his own adverse fortune, and was never satisfied unless helping somebody else along,—always ready to share the last crumb of bread with any who asked. In Daniel Ladd we have one of the brightest examples of pure and disinterested friendship and genuine love for his fellow-man that we will ever have presented to us in this too often cold and selfish world.

'He had a tear for pity and a hand
Open as day for melting charity.'

"We close this brief notice with sad hearts, trusting that at no distant day another pen will do fuller justice to the memory of one whose departure from among us has occasioned such general and heartfelt sorrow."

Children.

2536. George, bo. Jan. 17, 1851.
2537. Ella, bo. Feb. 25, 1855; d. 1856.
2538. Joseph Milton, bo. April 3, 1857.

(1179) Hon. George Washington Ladd, of Bangor, Me., (son of Joseph[708] and Sarah (Hamlin) Ladd,) was born in Augusta, Me., Sept. 28, 1828. He ma. Marcia C. P., dau. of Rev. J. H. Ingraham, Oct. 9, 1839. She was a granddaughter of Hon. Daniel Corey, and a niece of Hon. Ruel Williams, U. S. senator from 1837 to 1842. We find in P. C. Headley's "Public Men of To-day," page 461, a biography of Mr. Ladd, from which we make the following synopsis:

"His father, imbued with the New England idea of the value of education, furnished him all the facilities at his command by private instruction, in connection with that of the public schools. He was sent to the seminary at Kent's Hill, Me., and was afterwards fitted for college by Rev. J. H. Ingraham, a distinguished scholar and divine. Business affairs obliged young Ladd to suspend the pursuit of his studies, and he engaged himself as an apothecary's clerk in his native town. The six years passed in this establishment, at the capital of the State, afforded him excellent opportunities, not only for mental growth, in a general way, but for making the acquaintance of prominent men, and becoming familiar with public topics. His capacity for business was early developed, and at the age of 18 he was intrusted with the entire management of an extensive drug and apothecary establishment. Two years later he removed to the city of Bangor, prosecuting the same business there for fifteen years with marked success. Hon. Luther Severance, his uncle, the able editor of the Kennebunk Journal for a quarter of a century, rendered valuable assistance to him in his business life. Mr. Ladd was one of the pioneers of railroad building in Maine, to which he gave much attention. His speeches and printed articles on this subject attracted much notice, and were widely circulated. In politics he commenced as a Whig, and was a great admirer of Henry Clay. He was a member of the Whig State Committee for several years. After the disbanding of the Whig organization in 1856, he took but little interest in politics until 1860, when he became one of the leading members of the Constitutional Union party, then represented by Bell and Everett, and in 1864 he supported Gen. McClellan for President, and rendered the Democratic party efficient service in the campaign. In 1868 he was nominated by the Democrats of the Fourth District, who were then in a small minority, as a candidate for Congress, and was defeated. In 1878 he was again nominated by both the Democratic and Greenback conventions and was elected, and in 1880 he was re-elected. While in Congress he was chairman of the Committee on Expenditures in the Post Office Department, and also a member of the committee on Banking and Currency. Mr. Ladd has business capacity, and forty years of business life in Bangor have been marked by the closest application. Ambitious to obtain wealth, he sought it through the legitimate means of labor and forecast, rather than by doubtful expedients resorted to by the speculator and adventurer. His personal integrity was never questioned. He is an extensive reader, particularly of history, and has devoted much time and thought to subjects of finance and political economy generally. As a public speaker he is fluent, self-possessed, bold in attack, and quick at repartee. His devotion to his public duties, his uniform courtesy and fidelity to the interest of his constituents render him deservedly popular, and his friends indulge the hope that many years of public life and usefulness are yet reserved for him."

Children.

239. Abbie Coney, bo. Sept. 16, 1847.
240. Sarah Josephine, bo. Oct. 14, 1853.
241. William Hamilton, bo. Aug. 12, 1855; d. Jan. 28, 1856.

(1182) Alfred William Ladd, of New York City, (son of Joseph,[708]) was born in Augusta, Me., Sept. 5, 1823. He ma. June 1, 1848, Fannie, dau. of Dr. William A. Walker, of Boston. Was divorced from her in 1884. He was educated in the public schools, and graduated at the high school in Augusta, Me., in 1842, and soon after went into business for himself at Boston. He was at the South as prisoner during the war, and made to serve in the rebel army after being arrested for treason. He escaped with much difficulty and finally reached Washington, D. C., where he was treated with great consideration, and was offered a government appointment. He finally accepted a position and served on Gen. McClellan's staff in 1862. He is now (1888) in the railway supply business, dealer in locomotives, cars, and all kinds of railway material. He ma. 2d, Alice, dau. of the late H. O. Southworth, of Rome, N. Y.

Child by first wife.

2542. Bessie W., bo. Nov. 1, 1854.

(1191) Daniel Ladd, of Brooklyn, N. Y., (son of Daniel,[712]) ma. Sarah Jane Ferguson.

Child.

2543. Laura Virginia Cooper, bo. May 24, 1850.

(1195) George W. Ladd, of Augusta, Me., (son of Jesse Eaton,[713]) ma. Sarah A., dau. of George T. and Betsey White, May 3, 1855.

Children.

2544. Cora B., bo. June 19, 1856; ma. David H. Gilley. Children: 'Joseph W., ²George W., twins, bo. Aug. 29, 1877.
2545. Winfield Scott, bo. ——.

(1196) Joseph E. Ladd, of Gardiner, Me., (son of Jesse Eaton,[713]) was bo. in Phillips, Me., Aug. 16, 1829; ma. Elmeda, dau. of Enoch and Loraine Huntoon, of Meader, Me., Aug. 16, 1854. He was educated at the common and high school at Phillips, Me. He worked at stone-cutting, farming, carding, and cloth dressing, until he was 20 years old. In 1850 he went to serve an apprenticeship at the millwright trade; served three years and then went into the business for himself, and has continued in it up to the present date (1888.) He removed, March, 1855, to Gardiner, Me., where he is now living. He served several years in each branch of the city government, and in March, 1881, was elected mayor of the city. He was a candidate for mayor the next year, and was defeated on account of his radical temperance principles, but was again elected mayor in 1886. He held the office of master of a Masonic lodge for five years. He has always been identified with the temperance reform movement, and has held many important offices in various temperance organizations. In 1886 he was the Democratic candidate for representative to Congress, but was on the wrong side to be elected in that Republican district.

Children.

2546. Ida May, bo. Oct. 16, 1855; ma. Samuel H. Stevens, Nov. 1874.
2547. Edward Parsons, bo. June 29, 1867.
2548. Elizabeth Elmeader, bo. Sept. 27, 1869.

1199) Rev. Ammi S. Ladd, (son of Jesse E.[713] and Sophronia (Worthley) Ladd,) was born in Phillips, Me., June 17, 1835. He ma. Lydia F. Golder, of Augusta, Me., July 10, 1861. She died March 1, 1880, and he ma. 2d, Marion D. Meriweather, of Portland, Me., Nov. 30, 1881. She died in March, 1885, and he ma. 3d, Helen A. Osgood, of Bangor, Me., May 15, 1886. He was educated in the public schools and by private instruction. He joined the Maine Methodist Conference, April, 1860, and was licensed to preach April, 1860. He has been assigned to and preached in the following named towns in Maine: Wilton, Strong, Kent's Hill, Readfield, Waterville, Biddeford, (two pastorates.) Bath, (two pastorates,) Portland, Lewiston, Bangor, and is now (1887) in Auburn. He is a trustee in the Maine Wesleyan Seminary and Female College at Kent's Hill, Readfield, Me.; received the degree of A. M. from the Colby University in July, 1869; was a member from the Maine Conference to the General Cenference at Baltimore in 1876, and was at the head of the Maine delegation at the General Conference at Cincinnati in 1880. For several years he served as assistant secretary of the Maine Conference, and was once elected secretary but declined to serve.' He is an earnest and effective speaker, and has often been called upon to lecture in various towns on temperance and other kindred subjects. He has been chosen several times to represent Maine in International Sunday-School Conventions.

Children.

2549. Lizzie A., by 1st wife, bo. Sept. 17, 1862; d. Oct. 18, 1867.
2550. Lydia G., by 2d wife, bo. Oct. 22, 1882.
2551. John M., by 2d wife, bo. March 17, 1885; d. April 14, 1885.
2552. Marion E., by 3d wife, bo. Aug. 13, 1887; d. the same day.

206) Abel Ladd, of Mt. Vernon, Me., (son of Stephen,[716]) ma. Eunice A. ——.

Child.

2553. Abby, bo. July 11, 1864.

(1219)   Lewis Augustus Ladd, of Deerfield, N. H., (son of Dea. Daniel,[724]) was born in Deerfield, N. H., April 21, 1823, in the house where his father and grandfather were born, and which was built by his great-grandfather, Daniel Ladd, Esq.[89] The house is now (1888) occupied by Loren D. Ladd. He ma. Oct. 4, 1846, Sarah Ann, dau. of David and Sally (Sanborn) Lang, of Candia, N. H. He was educated at the public schools; is a farmer; has held the office of justice of the peace for over thirty years; has been agent for the Rockingham Farmers' Mutual Fire Insurance Company for more than twenty years.

Children.

2554. Edward A., bo. July 28, 1847; d. Dec. 6, 1847.
2555. Edward A., bo. Oct. 1, 1848; d. April 23, 1849.
2556. Martha A., bo. April 10, 1850; ma. Charles H. Davis, April 1, 1879, of Northwood, N. H. Children: [1]Sarah L., bo. April 29, 1881; [2]Lucinda L., bo. April 7, 1885.
2557. Aureannah J., bo. May 6, 1854; ma. Dyer S. Smith, son of Steven and Mary (Robinson) Smith, July 4, 1874. Children: [1]Edward A., bo. April 1, 1872; [2]Mercie Velma, bo. Feb. 7, 1878; [3]Archia B., bo. March 22, 1880; [4]Walter Stevens, bo. Oct. 18, 1882; [5]Ezra T., bo. Aug. 25, 1885; [6]Chellis V., bo. March 18, 1887.
2558. Ella S., bo. March 30, 1858; ma. Milton LeRoy James, son of Jeremiah and Elizabeth (Lane) James, Aug. 18, 1877. Children: [1]Lewis L., bo. June 14, 1878; [2]Genevia M., bo. May 1, 1887.
2559. Alice S., bo. April 30, 1868.

(1220)   Daniel B. Ladd, of Deerfield, N. H., (son of Daniel,[724]) ma. Rebecca E. Dearborn, Nov. 25, 1847. She died June 17, 1851, and he ma. 2d, Miriam S. Jones, Nov. 25, 1853.

Child.

2560. Julia A., bo. May 5, 1851; ma. Moses Day, Aug. 9, 1871.

Children by second wife.

2561. Arthur D., bo. March 21, 1855; ma. Edna E. Bigelow, Dec. 16, 1876.
2562. John S., bo. Oct. 7, 1856; ma. Belle M. Bagley, Oct. 20, 1881.
2563. Lewis A., bo. May 11, 1858.
2564. George H., bo. Dec. 14, 1862.
2565. Lydia A., bo. Sept. 18, 1865.
2566. Alvah J., bo. June 5, 1872.

(1222)   William D. Ladd, of Deerfield, N. H., (son of Daniel,[724]) ma. Lucinda, dau. of Daniel and Sarah (Sanborn) Lang, of Candia, N. H., June 10, 1851. In 1858 he removed to Candia, where he opened a general merchandise store; was selectman in 1864-65, and chairman of the board. In 1866 he was chosen a representative to the legislature from Candia. In 1867 he removed to Raymond Centre, where he continued in the general merchandise business, and in 1872 he was town treasurer and chairman of the board of selectmen. In 1877 he removed to Manchester, N. H., where in 1882 he was keeping a large boarding-house.

Children.

2567. Charles W., bo. April 14, 1854; d. Jan. 1, 1874.
2568. Cora A., bo. Jan. 13, 1856; ma. George W. Bailey, of Manchester, N. H., Nov. 1874. She died June 18, 1876, leaving one child, Cora E., who was born June 10, 1876, and died Sept. 1, 1877.
2569. Mary J., bo. June 9, 1858; ma. William F. Elliott, of Manchester, N. H., June 4, 1878. Child: William, bo. Nov. 15, 1878, d. July 3, 1879.

(1224) George H. Ladd, of Deerfield, N. H., (son of Daniel,[724]) ma. Amanda M., dau. of David and Sarah (Morse) Alger, Dec. 4, 1858. She was born in Canton, Sept. 9, 1834. He lived a few years in Methuen. He enlisted in Co. G, 22d Reg. Infantry, Sept. 16, 1861, and was killed at Malvern Hill, Va., July 1, '62.

Child.

2570. George Henry, bo. ——.

(1226) John Warren Ladd, of Raymond, N. H., (son of John,[725]) ma. Deborah, dau. of Dea. James Beane, of Deerfield, N. H., Nov. 1, 1854.

Children.

2571. J. Earle, bo. May 22, 1862.
2572. Harris B., bo. April 20, 1864.
2573. Grace D., bo. April 1, 1872.

(1227) Rev. Enoch Place Ladd, of Deerfield, N. H., (son of John,[725]) ma. Hannah M., dau. of Edmund Rand, Aug. 18, 1864. He taught school at Salisbury in 1859; studied divinity at Andover, and graduated in 1862; was a Free Will Baptist minister at Limerick, Me., where he died July 14, 1874.

Child.

2574. Eugene J., bo. Aug. 2, 1865.

(1228) David Beane Ladd, of Deerfield, N. H., (son of John,[725]) ma. Lizzie S., dau. of James Beane, Nov. 29, 1860. He was an enterprising and wealthy farmer.

Children.
2575. Everett, bo. March 15, 1862.
2576. Eveline M., bo. Sept. 29, 1865.
2577. Willis, bo. Oct. 12, 1870; d. July 18, 1872.
2578. Florence F., bo. June 7, 1878.

(1229) Abraham G. Ladd, of Raymond, N. H., (son of John,[725]) ma. Nellie Lock, Oct. 24, 1877. He was a representative from Deerfield in 1868 and 1870; removed to Raymond, and is in the lumber business.

Child.
*2579. Barron H., bo. Oct. 22, 1879.

(1230) Loren Dudley Ladd, of Deerfield, N. H., (son of John,[725]) ma. Anna L. Thompson, June 26, 1867. He is a carriage-maker.

Children.
2580. Arthur G., bo. April 25, 1868.
2581. Edith A., bo. April 11, 1871.
2582. John L., bo. July 2, 1875.
2583. Gordon B., bo. March 30, 1878.

(1236) Edward A. Ladd, of Deerfield, N. H., (son of Stephen,[729]) ma. Almira B., dau. of John W. Brown, Nov. 4, 1866.

Children.
2584. Edward B., bo. Aug. 4, 1869.
2585. Walter A., bo. April 10, 1872.

(1238) Frank P. Ladd, of Milwaukee, Wis., (son of Stephen,[729]) ma. Sarah E., dau. of James Akerman, April 2, 1868.

Children.
2586. Frederick A., bo. April 15, 1869.
2587. George W., bo. June 14, 1871.

(1239) Charles P. Ladd, of East Somerville, (son of Stephen,[729]) ma. Catherine T. Cary, July 10, 1871.

Children.
2588. Emma L., bo. June 3, 1872, in Milwaukee, Wis.
2589. Charles P., bo. Dec. 5, 1874, in Charlestown.
2590. Nellie B., bo. Aug. 19, 1875, in East Somerville.

(1242) James H. Ladd, of Hartford, N. Y., (son of Stephen,[785]) ma. Maggie Brown, 1854.

Children.

2591. Stephen A., bo. Dec. 1860; d. Feb. 1886.
2592. James H., bo. Dec. 1865.
2593. Frank, bo. Feb. 1867.

(1248) William H. Ladd (son of Stephen [785]) ma. Angie Taylor, 1875.

Children.

2594. Willie, bo. Dec. 8, 1874.
2595. Mary, bo. Oct. 6, 1877.

(1251) Levi Ladd, of Needham, (son of Samuel,[787]) was born in Tuftonboro, N. H., May 20, 1834. He was educated at the public schools. In 1853 he left home and went to Boston, and obtained employment in a wholesale store, where he remained about eight years, when sickness, brought on by indoor confinement, made it necessary for him to take a vacation, which he did at his New Hampshire home. Recovering in a few months, he returned to Boston and accepted a situation in a wholesale house as travelling agent; remained with the firm until 1865, when he became interested in the manufacture of rubber goods, in which he continued, and was very successful, until 1876, when his health failed him again, and he was obliged to discontinue and close up his business. In 1870 he removed from Cambridge to Needham, on the Charles river, where he purchased a farm, and where he now resides. By working on his farm for two years he regained his health. About 1872 he purchased an interest in a Vermont corporation and removed the manufactory to Needham, since which time he has been actively engaged in business. He is president and trustee of Odd Fellows' Hall Association, a director in the Needham Savings Bank, director in the Eagle Rubber Co., treasurer of the Colby Wringer Co., is, and has been for the past seven years, treasurer of the town of Needham, and is a member of the Norfolk Masonic Lodge of Needham. He ma. June 1, 1859, Elizabeth, dau. of Dr. John and Elizabeth M. Appleton, of Cambridge. Dr. Appleton was a graduate of the Boston Medical College, practiced until 1855, then devoted his time to literary pursuits until his death in 1869.

Children.

2596. Elizabeth Appleton, bo. Feb. 26, 1860.
2597. Georganla Young, bo. April 24, 1865; d. March 9, 1879.
2598. Alice Welling, bo. Dec. 24, 1869.
2599. Samuel Appleton, bo. Nov. 15, 1872.
2600. Martha Eleanor, bo. Jan. 12, 1875.
2601. John Lyman, bo. Aug. 24, 1879.

(1270) George M. Ladd, of Melvin Village, N. H., (son of Gordon,[741]) ma. Juliette Bickford, of Tamworth, N. H., Nov. 22, 1881.

Children.

2602. Myron D., bo. Nov. 24, 1882.
2603. Betha, bo. April 3, 1885.
2604. Agnes M., bo. July 1, 1886.

(1277) Chester Ladd (son of John Hubbard[747]) ma. Charlotte M. Ball.

Children.

2605. Jennie, bo. ——.
2606. Laome, bo. ——.

(1282) Hon. William S. Ladd, of Lancaster, N. H., (son of Hiram,[748]) was born in Dalton, Coos Co., N. H., Sept. 5, 1830. He ma. at Lancaster, N. H., July 5, 1860, Mira Barnes, dau. of Hiram A. and Persia (Hunkins) Fletcher. She was born Feb. 29, 1836. He has lived in Dalton, Colebrook, and Lancaster, N. H., where he now resides. He fitted for college at Tilton, N. H., at the N. H. Conference Seminary, and graduated at Dartmouth College in the class of 1855; then taught school at South Danvers (now Peabody,) then in Beverly; then studied law in the office of Alfred A. Abbott, then district attorney of Essex County, until the Spring of 1858, when he returned home on account of the illness of his mother, which continued for several months and terminated in her death. He then entered the law office of Burns & Fletcher, at Lancaster, N. H., where he remained until the April term of court, 1859, when he was admitted to the bar of Coos County, N. H. In June of that year he went to Colebrook, N. H., and opened a law office, and remained there until Sept. 1867, when he removed to Lancaster, N. H., and entered into partnership with Ossian Ray, under the firm name of Ray & Ladd, where they did a large business, as extensive, probably, as any lawyers in the State.

After remaining with Mr. Ray three years, he was appointed judge of the Supreme Judicial Court, Oct. 1870. On reorganizing the courts in 1874 he was appointed to the bench upon the Supreme Court of Judicature, which was the law court, and consisted of three members, Edmund Cushing, C. J., William S. Ladd, and Isaac W. Smith. In 1876 the courts were again reorganized, and then Mr. Ladd's judicial labor ended. There have been occasions since when he could have gone back to the bench, but economical reasons forbade it. Since 1876 he has been practicing law, mainly in the courts of New Hampshire. He is reporter of the decisions of the Supreme Court, and has held that office four years. He is president of the Siwoogauoch Guarantee Savings Bank of Lancaster, and a director in the Lancaster National Bank ; was a member of the legislature from Lancaster in 1883 ; is one of the trustees of the Holderness School for Boys ; has been vice-president of the Alumni of Dartmouth College, and of the American Bar Association, &c. In June, 1887, his *alma mater*, Dartmouth College, conferred upon him the degree of LL. D.

Children.

2607. Fletcher, bo. Dec. 21, 1862. He graduated at Dartmouth College in 1884; was in the Cambridge Law School in 1885; and in 1887 he was attending German lectures on the law in Heidelberg University.
2608. Edward Everett, bo. Jan. 15, 1865; d. Oct. 18, 1870.
2609. William Palmer, bo. May 13, 1870.
2610. Roger B., bo. Nov. 8, 1872.
2611. Mary Everett, bo. Dec. 24, 1878.

(1301) Rev. Henry M. Ladd, D. D., (son of Rev. Daniel,[753]) was born Nov. 10, 1849, at Broosa, Turkey in Asia. His father was an honored missionary of the American Board. His early life was spent largely in the cities of Smyrna and Constantinople. In the former place he resided fifteen years, with a break of two years and a half when he was about seven years of age, which time was spent in visiting this country. From Constantinople, whither the family had moved, he came to this country when he was 17 years of age, in the Summer of 1867. He spent one year at Middlebury, Vt., in preparation for college, and in the Fall of 1868 entered Middlebury College, of which his uncle, H. D. Kitchel, was president. He led his class through the whole course of four years, and graduated with the highest honors as valedictorian in 1872. In the Fall of the same year he entered the Theological Department of the Yale University, from which he graduated in 1875, having in his course taken the highest prize then offered in the University. June 16, 1875, he married Sarah Elizabeth Harvey, at Danbury, Conn., and the next week he received a unanimous call to the First Congregational Church of Walton, N. Y., one of the most influential churches in the interior of the State, which he accepted. In July of the same year he delivered the Master's oration at Middlebury College, and received the degree of Master of Arts. Three years later he was called back to deliver the poem before the Alumni Association. In 1880 he was elected to the position of foreign superintendent of the American Missionary Association, and in February, 1881, he accepted the office, resigned his charge, greatly to the regret of his church and the entire community, and ultimately removing his family to Danbury, Conn., he started upon a tour of inspection to the West Coast of Africa. Here his fitness for the work and ability to endure the trying climate being demonstrated, he returned after four months' absence and received a commission to explore more thoroughly the upper waters of the Nile and its tributaries in Central Africa, with a view to the establishment of missions in the Upper Nile basin. Accompanied by his family physician, he started in the Fall of 1881, organized the expedition in London and Cairo, and at the head of a company of about twenty-five men pushed his way up the Nile and across the great Atmoor Desert to Khartoum, and thence some six hundred miles into the heart of Africa, up the Sobat River and beyond it, till he was stopped by the insurrection under Mohammed Achmet the "False Prophet," by whom he was twice waylaid and nearly lost his life. He finally escaped after nine months of hazardous exploration, and made his way back to Alexandria. On his return to this country he was recognized as an authority on the vexed questions relating to the Soudan, and his services as lecturer were in constant demand. The Association about this time transferred all its foreign work to another society, and the Arthington Mission, which he had intended to plant and conduct, had to be given up on account of the unsettled state of the country. In view of his high attainments and remarkable record in connection with this work, his *alma mater* conferred upon him the degree of D. D. in 1882, although then only in his 32d year. In the Spring of 1883, when it was known that he was to leave the service of the A. M. A., he received three calls,—one to the church in Stratford, Conn., one to a secretaryship in New York city, and one to the Euclid Avenue Congregational Church in Cleveland, O. He accepted the last, and entered upon his duties May 1, 1883. His record there up to the present time has been characterized by his brother ministers in the same field as "a magnificent one." He found the church divided and disintegrating. He found new churches, at the rate of one a year for five years, springing up around him, within a half mile, and threatening to draw off his members. But he soon rallied the people, united them, persuaded them to tear down their old building and put up a new one, and now with the finest church buildings in the city entirely paid for, with a membership among the largest in the State, with benevolent contributions larger than ever before, without a cent of debt upon the society, and with numerous accessions at every communion, he is doing a work large enough and grand enough for any man.

Children.

2612. Mary Kitchell, bo. May 26, 1876.
2613. Charlotte Edith, bo. Nov. 25, 1877.
2614. Clarence Harvey, bo. June 2, 1879.
2615. Henry Martyn, bo. July 21, 1880.

(1312) David Chandler Ladd, of Bristol, N. H., (son of Peter,[762]) ma. Judith Atwood, Aug. 1, 1823. He was a farmer, and learned the trade of hewing ship timber. He d. June 17, 1839.

Children.

2616. James M., bo. May 24, 1824; d. June 17, 1839.
2617. Gustavus Bartlett, bo. June 29, 1829; d. May 12, 1854.
2618. Rhoda F., bo. Aug. 2, 1831; ma. Elisha Whittier, June 26, 1849. She died Sept. 24, 1852.
2619. David Newell, bo. March 17, 1834; ma. Sarah B. Pool, April 1, 1857.
2620. Melisse Jane, bo. Aug. 7, 1836; ma. Elisha Whittier, April 24, 1853.
2621. Leroy Sunderland, bo. Dec. 7, 1839; killed in front of Richmond, 1865.

(1313) Jeremiah Quimby Ladd, of Alexandria, N. H., (son of Peter,[763]) ma. Abigail Collins.

Children.

2622. Nathaniel William, bo. July 29, 1828; d. Aug. 5, 1843.
2623. Julia Ann, bo. Nov. 11, 1829; ma. Hiram Tilton, Nov. 27, 1843.
2624. Porlina Sargent, bo. Oct. 1, 1831; ma. Jas. N. Truax, 1847, of Lowell.
2625. Angeline Slade, bo. Feb. 16, 1833; d. Sept. 10, 1834.
2626. Rebecca, bo. Sept. 8, 1835; d. 1835.
2627. Isabel Slade, bo. Aug. 12, 1836; d. May 8, 1837.

(1326) Benjamin Ladd, of Mercer, Me., (son of Timothy,[773]) ma. Louisa Trask. She died, and he ma. 2d, Betsey Philbrook.

Children.

2628. Benjamin, bo. 1814; ma. Mary Weaver. No children.
2629. Julia, bo. 1818; ma. George Smith.
2630. Dearborn, bo. 1820; ma. Laura Hoyt.
2631. Eliza, bo. 1822; ma. Herbert Stone.
2632. William, bo. 1825; ma. Sarah E. Copp, Nov. 22, 1846. No children.
2633. Perley M. bo. Jan. 12, 1828; ma. Caroline McAlvain.

Children by second wife.

2634. Mary Ann, bo. 1832; ma. Enoch White.
2635. James Henry, bo. 1836; ma. Abigail Ladd (2880.)
2636. Caroline, bo. Dec. 1, 1839; ma. William Wait, July 20, 1857. Children: [1]Frank A., bo. March 31, 1859, ma. Ella L. Capron, Dec. 25, 1882; [2]Mattie F., bo. Jan. 24, 1861, ma. Alton Randall, July 27, 1880; [3]Mary E., bo. May 2, 1863, ma. Warren L. Pierce, Dec. 9, 1881; [4]Willie W., bo. Jan. 5, 1865; [5]Grace M., bo. Feb. 3, 1869; [6]Fred H., bo. May 22, 1872; [7]Cora E., bo. July 27, 1878.
2637. Charles, bo. 1841; ma. Irene Perkins.
2638. Albert, bo. 1844; ma. Lizzie French.
2639. Etta, bo. 1847; ma. Fred Pressey.
2640. Helen F., bo. 1849; ma. Rodney H. Wyman, Dec. 1, 1871.
2641. Frank, bo. 1859; ma. Lura Nason.

(1327) Moses Ladd (son of Timothy[773]) ma. Phebe Taylor.

Children.

2642. Rachel E., bo. 1818; d. 1838.
2643. Luther, bo. 1820; ma. Eliza J. Cheney, 1842.
2644. Betsey J., bo. 1822; ma. Thomas J. Rogers, 1836.
2645. Elvira D., bo. 1824; d. 1842.
2646. William, bo. April 24, 1827; ma. Sabra Luce, Jan. 1, 1849.
2647. Mark Taylor, bo. 1829; ma. Caroline M. Hildrith, 1852.
2648. Louisa R., bo. Aug. 9, 1831; ma. George D. Gale, 1851.
2649. Martha A., bo. 1834.
2650. Moses, bo. Nov. 29, 1837; ma. Mary Rollins, 1868. No children.
2651. Rachel E., bo. May 25, 1839; ma. A. D. Carter.

(1328) Daniel Ladd, of Vienna, Me., (son of Timothy,[773]) ma. Abigail, dau. of John French, 1818.

Children.

2652. Melvina, bo. Dec. 6, 1819; ma. Henry Thomas.
2653. Thomas D., bo. Sept. 4, 1821; ma. Sarah Pressey.
2654. Guilford S., bo. May 29, 1831; ma. Francis M. Gilman.
2655. Reuben E., bo. July 5, 1833; ma. Annie Eldred.
2656. Emeline, bo. Aug. 5, 1835; ma. Joseph R. Gilbert.
2657. Livinia, bo. June 3, 1837; ma. Henry L. Whitney.
2658. Moses, bo. Oct. 4, 1839; d. young.
2659. Laura, bo. May 12, 1841; d. young.

(1329) Asa Ladd, of Meredith, N. H., (son of Timothy,[773]) ma. Nancy Sanborn, of Meredith, N. H., June 18, 1823.

Children.

2660. Elizabeth, bo. Aug. 13, 1824; not married; d. June 28, 1878.
2661. Jonathan, bo. Aug. 8, 1826; ma. Anna Harris, of Boston.
2662. Mary Jane, bo. Sept. 25, 1828; not married.
2663. Annette, bo. Dec. 10, 1830.
2664. George W., bo. Aug. 17, 1833; ma. Rose Evans, Dec. 12, 1867. No children.
2665. Asa, Jr., bo. Oct. 10, 1835; not married; d. July, 1862.
2666. Louisa B., bo. Oct. 30, 1838; ma. Alonzo Benton.
2667. Sophronia J., bo. March 11, 1841; ma. Charles C. Pickney.

(1330) William Ladd, of Boston, (son of Timothy,[773]) ma. Mary A. Grant, April 5, 1827.

Children.

2668. George W., bo. ——.
2669. Eliza Ann, bo. ——.
2670. Lyman, bo. ——.
2671. Elizabeth, bo. ——.
2672. William Warren, bo. ——.
2673. Elvira, bo. ——.

(1331) Thomas H. Ladd, of Abbott, Me., (son of Nancy,[1331]) was brought up by his uncle, Ansel Ladd.[1336] He ma. Ann M. Dyer, dau. of James Dyer, of Hallowell, Me., Nov. 18, 1848.

Children.

2674. Victory, bo. Sept. 8, 1850; ma. Frank Weymouth.
2675. Frank J., bo. Jan. 11, 1852; not married; d. 1884.
2676. Hiram C., bo. July 6, 1853; not married; d. 1884.
2677. Wallace S., bo. May 15, 1855; ma. Eva M. Cushman.
2678. Albion C., bo. April 7, 1857.

2679. Ida L., bo. Sept. 15, 1859; ma. George W. Hiscock.
2680. Sarah M., bo. Nov. 4, 1861; ma. James B. Greenleaf.
2681. Willie M., bo. July 17, 1867.
2682. Barrett H., bo. Dec. 5, 1871.

(1332) Timothy Ladd, of Vienna, Me., (son of Timothy,[773]) ma. Mary Woodman, Feb. 25, 1828. He died Dec. 23, 1851.

Children.

2683. Mary J., bo. Jan. 31, 1829; ma. Charles Ladd.
2684. Elbridge G. W., bo. June 30, 1831; d. June 1, 1832.
2685. Elbridge G. W., bo. April 8, 1833; ma. Augusta Townsend.
2686. Noah, bo. Feb. 6, 1835; ma. Ellen Newcomb.
2687. Caroline B., bo. March 11, 18—; ma. Warren Walker.
2688. Dexter, bo. ——; ma. Catharine Harrington.
2689. Christianna S., bo June 15, ——; ma. J. C. Wain.

(1336) Ansel Ladd, of Vienna, Me., (son of Timothy,[773]) ma. Mehitable Meader.

Children.

2690. Virginia, bo. Nov. 12, 1839; ma. William Rice.
2691. Laura. bo. Nov. 4, 1840; ma. James Trask.
2692. Abigail, bo. Jan. 31, 1842; ma. James Henry Ladd (2633.)
2693. Thomas Franklin, bo. March 24, 1844; ma. Welthy J. Ford, Jan. 1, 1865.
2694. Jacob, bo. ——; ma. Lucy Whittier; 2d, —— Morse.
2695. Ann, bo. May 27, 1852; ma. Asa Moore, June 20, 1869.
2696. Rosella Amanda, bo. May 27, 1852; ma. George Day.
2697. Isabella, bo. ——; ma. Austin Dary.

(1337) Warren Ladd, of Vienna, Me., (son of Timothy,[773]) ma. Eleanor Meader, Sept. 2, 1837.

Children.

2698. Edwin, bo. June 22, 1838; ma. Adeline Stuart.
2699. Francis Warren, bo. Oct. 30, 1839; ma. Martha A. Thurston, April 20, 1864.
2700. Henrietta, bo. Aug. 8, 1846; ma. Joseph Stuart.
2701. Laura E., bo. Oct. 14, 1847; ma. Watson Winthrop.
2702. Charles H., bo. July 8, 1848; ma. Jennie Cook. No children.
2703. Stateria, bo. June 7, 1852; ma. Robert Gordon.
2704. Marcellus, bo. Aug. 18. 1855.
2705. Drucilla, bo. May 8, 1858; ma. Frost Winthrop.
2706. Amanda, bo. July 10, 1860; ma. Arthur Smith.

(1377) Andrew Ladd, of Deerfield, N. H., (son of Eleazer,[797]) ma. Melinda Ladd,[728] April 9, 1821. She died Aug. 14, 1850, and he ma. 2d, Mrs. Sally (Ladd[1104]) Fuller.

Children.

2707. Albert J., bo. Aug. 30, 1828; ma. Elvira Harris, April 1, 1850.
2708. Freeman P., bo. Sept. 10, 1831; ma. Mary A. Alexander.

(1382) William Perry Ladd, of Deerfield, N. H., (son of Eleazer,[797]) ma. Mary Ann, dau. of Joseph and Rachel (Lock) Brown, of Rye, N. H., May 10, 1843. She died June 23, 1867, and he ma. 2d, Harriet Rebecca, dau. of Abraham and Deborah (Rollins) Chase, Dec. 12, 1872. He was educated at the public schools, and is a carpenter and farmer.

Children.

2709. George P., bo. May 18, 1844; ma. Minnie Stanton, May 12, 1880.
2710. James W., bo. Nov. 28, 1845; d. Feb. 24, 1846.
2711. Emily A., bo. May 1, 1847; ma. Joseph T. Rollins, Oct. 9, 1869.
2712. William H., bo. Dec. 20, 1849.
2713. Mary A., bo. Oct. 6, 1851; ma. James Doe, Nov. 11, 1877.
2714. Caroline, bo. Feb. 18, 1852.
2715. Oliver, bo. ——; d. in infancy.
2716. Eleanor, bo. Sept. 17, 1855; d. Feb. 4, 1873.
2717. Hattie J., bo. Dec. 2, 1856.
2718. Eleazer P., bo. Feb. 21, 1858.
2719. Lewis, bo. Feb. 20, 1860.
2720. Freeman, bo. Dec. 5, 1861.
2721. Charles G., bo. April 4, 1862.

(1383) George W. Ladd, of Deerfield, (son of Eleazer,[797]) ma. Mary A. Elliott, Jan. 27, 1848. She died June 22, 1856, and he ma. 2d, Nov. 20, 1856, Judith B. French.

Children.

2722. Ann M., bo. June 9, 1850; d. Sept. 24, 1851.
2723. Alphonzo, bo. Feb. 2, 1853.
2724. Romanzo L., bo. April 17, 1855; ma. Ella Sargent, Nov. 9, 1881.

Child by second wife.

2725. Alice M., bo. April 9, 1858.

(1389) Reuben Ladd, of Mt. Vernon, Me., (son of Moses,[775]) ma. Christianna Gould.

Children.

2726. Gilbert Taggart, bo. Nov. 17, 1846; ma. Celia F. Jewett.
2727. George, bo. Sept. 23, 1849; ma. Etta Whittier.
2728. James, bo. March 24, 1853.

(1342) Nathaniel Ladd, of Abbott, Me., (son of Nathaniel,[783]) ma. Anne L. Sears.

Children.

2729. Anna May, bo. Dec. 27, 1881.
2730. Nathaniel, bo. Jan. 30, 1883.

(1349) Cyrus Ladd, of Alexandria, N. H., (son of Jonathan,[786]) ma. Rectina Bow, May 21, 1837. He died March 2, 1857.

Children.

2731. Francella, bo. March 29, 1839; ma. Charles W. Rollins, Oct. 14, 1850; 2d, Charles A. Parsons.
2732. Frank Cyrus, bo. July 12, 1857.

(1358) Major Jonathan Ladd, of Lowell, (son of Isaac,[790]) ma. Eunice Stickney, Jan. 8, 1848. The following obituary of Major Ladd is from the Lowell Daily Courier of April 9, 1889 : "The announcement of the death of Major Jonathan Ladd, which occurred at his home, No. 122 East Merrimack street, at 6.30 this morning, of bronchial pneumonia, after an illness of about two weeks, was received with surprise this forenoon, as he was not generally known to have been ill. He had been confined to his bed less than a week. Major Ladd was a native of Alexandria, N. H., and was born Sept. 26, 1819, being therefore nearly seventy years of age. He studied in the old Dracut academy. He came to Lowell when about 14 years old, and has practiced law 45 years in this city. He received his military title by having been a paymaster in the army during the late war. He was commander of Company H., Watson Light Guard, 6th Regiment, before the war, and was chief on the staff of Brig.-Gen. Sutton when the war broke out. Later he was detailed by Gov. Andrew as master of transportation of Massachusetts troops to Washington, with headquarters at the Fifth Avenue Hotel, New York. He was appointed army paymaster in 1861, and served in that capacity during the war. Major Ladd was in the board of aldermen in 1859. He was much interested in agriculture, and was superintendent of the first New England fair held in this city. For several years he was president of the Middlesex North Agricultural Society, and he carried on a large farm in Tewksbury. He leaves a widow and two children,—Frank J. Ladd, a well-known citizen, and Mrs. H. K. Spaulding, of New York city. In his death Lowell loses one of its active professional men. He was a regular attendant at High Street Church. * * * Judge Hadley, at the police court, this morning referred to the death of Major Jonathan Ladd as a happening which impresses all with sadness, but extended allusion was deferred till to-morrow morning, when members of the bar will offer words of testimony."

Children.

2733. Frank J., bo. July 15, 1849; ma. Ella P. Clifford.
2734. Eunice A., bo. March 14, 1853; ma. Henry K. Spaulding, Dec. 27, 1883.

(1369) Artemas Ladd, of Alexandria, N. H., (son of Nathan,[791]) ma. Susan H. Keyser.

Children.

2735. William M., bo. June 30, 1839; ma. Susan M. Abbott, March 26, 1860.
2736. George, bo. ——; not married.

(1628) William Ladd, of Windham, Conn., (son of Erastus,[192]) ma. Malissa Peck, Oct. 13, 1816.

Children.

2737. William Nelson, bo. Feb. 17, 1818; not ma. Lost at sea, Oct. 1842.
2738. Fredus, bo. June 21, 1820; ma. Eliza Maria Frink, June 9, 1844.
2739. Elizabeth Hartshorn, bo. April 13, 1822; ma. Waldo Brigham, Oct. 3, 1854.
2740. Merrill, bo. May 17, 1824; ma. Harriet ——.
2741. James Ellis, bo. Feb. 15, 1827; ma. Jennie ——.
2742. Alfred Peck, bo. May 23, 1829; not ma.; d. in California, Nov. 5, 1869.

(1629) Fredus Ladd, of Waterbury, Conn., (son of Erastus,[192]) ma. Lucy Peck, Nov. 28, 1824.

Children.

2743. Julia Ann, bo. Dec. 25, 1825; ma. Dr. Jeremiah King.
2744. Erastus Perkins, bo. July 1, 1828; d. Dec. 21, 1828.
2745. Myron Ferdinand, bo. Nov. 17, 1829; ma. Mary Champlin.
2746. Jane Ellen, bo. Dec. 3, 1831; ma. Norman Lazell, June 29, 1857. He died June 27, 1868, and she ma. 2d, Edgar N. Bullard, April 17, 1871.
2747. Charles Fredus, bo. June 30, 1837; ma. Frances Elizabeth Ladd.
2748. John Tyler, bo. Sept. 10, 1841; ma. Olive Rebecca Ladd.

(1632) Merrill Ladd, of St. Albans, Vt., (son of Erastus,[192]) ma. Sarah Ladd.[1619]

Children.

2749. Sumner E., bo. Dec. 25, 1831; d. Nov. 18, 1833.
2750. Lucy, bo. March 18, 1835.

2751. Jed. P., bo. Feb. 6, 1840; d. June 1, 1861.
2752. Elizabeth, bo. Jan. 11, 1845; d. Dec. 9, 1847.
2753. William M., bo. Jan. 19, 1849; ma. Diana Booth, Nov. 5, 18—.

(1634) Erastus Perkins Ladd (son of Erastus[192]) ma. Betsey Ladd,[1635] March 31, 1832.

Children.

2754. Cornelia, bo. Feb. 22, 1833; ma. Alpheus Kingley.
2755. Erastus Perkins, bo. Aug. 10, 1834; ma. —— Webster.
2756. Edgar Theodore, bo. May 31, 1836; not married.
2757. Hannah Marie, bo. Jan. 7, 1838; ma. Benjamin Huntington.
2758. Oscar Burton, bo. May 25, 1841; ma. Olive Lake.
2759. William Nelson, bo. March 11, 1843; ma. Mary Hyde.
2760. Charlotte Eliza, bo. May 8, 1845.

(1636) Asa Spaulding Ladd, of Franklin, Conn., (son of Festus,[194]) ma. Harriet Cady, July 4, 1825. He died Dec. 27, 1876.

Children.

2761. Frederick P., bo. March 30, 1827; ma. S. Maria Deane, Feb. 15, 1865.
2762. Henry G., bo. Dec. 6, 1828; not married; d. Oct. 5, 1851.
2763. Austin N., bo. Jan. 4, 1831; not married; d. Sept. 8, 1861.
2764. Allison B., bo. Nov. 10, 1832; ma. Lizzie Raymond, Jan. 23, 1863.
2765. Lysander M., bo. Feb. 16, 1835; not married; d. Jan. 8, 1868.
2766. R. Emily, bo. April 23, 1837; ma. Clark Harrington, Nov. 23, 1856.
2767. Martha A., bo. March 30, 1840; ma. William McNelly, Oct. 15, 1860.
2768. Juliet, bo. Sept. 10, 1842; ma. Clark Harrington, March 21, 1864.
2769. Luther A., bo. April 25, 1845; ma. Lizzie M. Hinman, Aug. 5, 1867.
2770. William, bo. May 30, 1847; d. Dec. 2, 1847.
2771. Arthur, bo. Aug. 4, 1849.
2772. Mary Iva, bo. Dec. 27, 1855; ma. G. Andrew Gardner, Dec. 27, 1871.

(1671) John Ladd, of Sanbornton, N. H., (son of John,[628]) ma. Nancy Badger, 1817. He died July 21, 1820.

Child.

2773. Hannah B., bo. 1818.

(1675) Gould Dimond Ladd, of Sanbornton, N. H., (son of John,[628]) ma. Betsey Colby Chase, April 10, 1832. He d. April 3, 1875. He was a prosperous farmer.

Children.

2774. Ann Hazelton, bo. Feb. 22, 1833; ma. Joseph Brown, June 22, 1853.
2775. John Gould, bo. Dec. 18, 1834; ma. Helen Proctor.
2776. Freeman Weston, bo. April 2, 1839; ma. Marietta Miller.
2777. Elbridge Gerry, bo. April 1, 1844; ma. Henrietta Lamphrey.

(1682)   Barnett H. Ladd, of Belmont, N. H., (son of Edward,[629]) ma. Eliza Ladd,[1677] Nov. 27, 1827. He died Feb. 2, 1877.

Children.

2778. Julia A., bo. Oct. 15, 1828; ma. Stephen A. Hadley, of Laconia, N. H., March 9, 1868.
2779. Eunice L., bo. April 26, 1831.
2780. Emeline S., bo. Oct. 23, 1833; d. Sept. 6, 1861.
2781. Harlon Page, bo. June 22, 1836; ma. Sarah Jane Noble.
2782. Jason J., bo. July 20, 1839; ma. Ann Maria Boynton, Dec. 18, 1865.
2783. Eliza J., bo. April 13, 1843; d. Sept. 18, 1863.

(1683)   Langdon Ladd, of Belmont, N. H., (son of Edward,[629]) ma. Sylvania, dau. of Barnard Colby, Jan. 2, 1837. His father died when he was nine years old. He lived with his mother upon the homestead, and as soon as he was old enough had the management of the farm. He was educated in the public schools, and represented the town in the legislature in 1874. He lived on the farm where his father lived, and in the house built by his grandfather, Col. Samuel Ladd, about 1777, where he died April 26, 1887.

Children.

2784. Arthur Stuart, bo. Jan. 17, 1838; ma. Ellen M. Porter, Feb. 28, 1867.
2785. Martha A., bo. Jan. 10, 1839; ma. Charles C. Gale, March, 1860.
2786. Curtis B., bo. Feb. 13, 1841; d. Sept. 22, 1841.
2787. Grace Colby, bo. May 11, 1842.
2788. Allen Young, bo. Aug. 4, 1853; ma. Kate J. Bennett. Feb. 17, 1876.
2789. Emma J., bo. Aug. 4, 1853; d. April 5, 1870.

(1693)   Lucian Augustus Ladd, of Laconia, N. H., (son of Jonathan,[683]) ma. Mary Jane, dau. of Charles Smith, July 31, 1843.

Children.

2790. Charles S., bo. June 13, 1844; ma. Lilla Good, Jan. 1873.
2791. Francis A., bo. Aug. 5, 1849.
2792. Frederick Y., bo. July 27, 1851; ma. Zoe M. Porter, Sept. 9, 1881.
2793. Clara J., bo. June 2, 1853.

(1697)   David Plummer Ladd, of Shirley, (son of Dudley,[683]) ma. Julia A., dau. of Simeon Hoyt, of Guilford, N. H., Sept. 5, 1839.

Children.

2794. Francis A., bo. Aug. 20, 1844.
2795. Durgan Perry, bo. July 11, 1855; d. Dec. 31, 1867.

(1922)   Randolph E. Ladd (son of Ariel[556] and Mary Ladd) was born at Tolland, Conn., July 6, 1812; ma. Charlotte, dau. of George Pease, of Glastenbury, Conn., in 1832, for his first wife, and Rebekah G. Morse, widow of William G. Morse, of Springfield, Oct. 20, 1857, for his second wife. His first wife died Jan. 19, 1857; his second wife is now (1888) living. Mr. Ladd died Aug. 5, 1874. His youth, up to the age of 16 years, was passed at home, and the ten succeeding years of his early manhood as a clerk in the service of the Hartford Manufacturing Company at Glastenbury, Conn. About 1838 he went into business in a dry goods and grocery store at Chatham, (now Portland,) Conn., as a partner in the firm of Hall & Ladd. There he continued till 1840, when he engaged in the bakery business with his brother, L. E. Ladd, in Cabotville (now Chicopee.) In 1846 he removed to Springfield, where his first position was that of book-keeper for the firm of King & Harding, flour and wool dealers, and on the failure of that firm in 1851 he established what was really the pioneer insurance agency business in Springfield. This was his life-work, and in the direction and management of it he became well and honorably known. Owing to the increase of his business he associated his younger brothers, Charles R. and Ariel, Jr., with him, the former in 1857 and the latter in 1865, constituting the firm of Ladd Brothers, and representing some fifteen to twenty insurance companies. He had only a common school education, but he had a thorough business training, which, with excellent natural abilities, enabled him to grasp and easily to succeed in the practical affairs of life. He was a man of strong physique, intense energy, and a very hard and diligent worker. He was a member of the common council and of the school committee of the city, but he had no taste for public duties, and owing to a slight deafness he declined all other offers of official position. The following from an obituary notice of him in one of the city papers, is a very just and truthful tribute to his worth and character:

"His bearing in affairs was on so high a plane of commercial morality that no man ever impugned his honesty or questioned his integrity of deed or purpose. In truth he was a model of God's noblest work. If we were called upon to say what gave Mr. Ladd his distinctive character in his relations with men, we should say it was his exceeding humanity. Humanity is the broad summation of his qualities. It was well nigh impossible, seemingly, for him to refuse a friend's request when it was in his power to grant it, and his generosity to others exceeded his justice to himself. In his life he lent a helping hand to many not among the very needy, and his return and recompense were frequently only in the satisfaction of the deed. In charities he must have won the love of the Lord, for he was a cheerful giver, and our local institutions for relief have often felt the impetus of his assistance. He joined the Methodist Church when 19 years of age, and continued in that faith till 1842, when he embraced Millerism, and in that faith (somewhat modified and liberalized by his own investigations) remained till his death. So conscientious was he in the discharge of every duty that he often expressed himself in his last illness as ready and willing to die, and what is rarer, as being satisfied with his life. He had tried to do right, and felt that he had succeeded, as much as it is given to man to succeed in that attempt. Of one thing he was at least certain, that he had made no enemy in all his life."

Children.

2796. Wilbur R., bo. Nov. 14, 1839; ma. Augusta M. Allen, of Springfield, May 14, 1862.
2797. Clara, bo. Jan. 27, 1845; ma. Madison Weaver, Nov. 2, 1864.
2798. Orianna C., bo. ——.

(1924) Lucius E. Ladd, of Springfield, (son of Ariel,[556]) was born in Tolland, Conn., Jan. 17, 1817; ma. Delia S., dau. of Reuel Van Horn, of Chicopee, Nov. 24, 1842. At the age of 12 years, in May, 1829, he went to East Hartford, Conn., where he worked on a farm four years; was salesman and book-keeper in a country store at North Manchester, Conn., six years; and was similarly employed in Chatham, Conn., (now Portland) two years. From there he went to Cabotville (now Chicopee) and carried on the bakery business (part of the time with his brother, Randolph E. Ladd) for ten years. In March, 1852, he removed to Springfield, and for thirty years was salesman and a partner in the flour business, in the firms of Hopkins, King & Co., and King, Norton & Ladd. In 1882 he dissolved his connection with the latter firm, and became cashier of the "Mass. Masonic Mutual Relief Association," having an office in Springfield, which position he now (1888) holds. While in Chicopee he held the office of selectman two years, and after his removal to Springfield he was clerk of the common council of the city for fourteen years consecutively. His education was obtained in the common schools and two terms in the East Hartford, Conn., Academy.

Children.

2799. Mary D., bo. July 15, 1844; ma. Charles A. Bly, Nov. 14, 1871, of Springfield. Children: [1]George L., bo. Aug. 1, 1874, d. March 25, 1878; [2]Randolph E., bo. Oct. 9, 1879.

2800. Charles B., bo. Oct. 13, 1849; ma. Ada I. Shattuck, of Springfield, Oct. 1872.

(1926) Charles R. Ladd, of Springfield, (son of Ariel[556] and Mary Ladd,) was born at Tolland, Conn., April 9, 1822; ma. Mrs. Ella Morse Weaver, dau. of William G. and Rebekah G. Morse, of Springfield, April 3, 1886. They have no children. In his boyhood Mr. Ladd attended the public schools, working at intervals on the farm and in his father's saw-mill; also on a farm in East Hartford, Conn., six months in 1837. He spent two years in Westfield Academy, entering it in 1842, and there completed his school education. He taught school five winters between the years 1838 and 1845. In 1844 he began the study of law with Hon. Loren P. Waldo, of Tolland, Conn., afterwards one of the judges of the Superior Court of that State, and was admitted to the bar in 1847. In 1848 he removed to Cabotville, (now Chicopee,) where he practiced his profession till 1857, when he went to Springfield, and giving up the law engaged in the insurance agency business with his brother, R. E. Ladd, and as a member of the firm of Ladd Brothers, which continued till the death of R. E. Ladd in 1874. The firm was then reorganized under the name of Ladd Brothers & Co., the partners being C. R. Ladd, Ariel Ladd, and Thomas R. Weaver. While in Chicopee Mr. Ladd was chairman of the board of selectmen two years, and a member of the school committee. He also represented the town in the Mass. House of Representatives two years, 1853 and 1854. In 1855 he was appointed by the Governor and Council as commissioner for the county of Hampden, under the law passed by the legislature of that year, entitled "An Act to protect the Rights and Liberties of the People of the Commonwealth of Massachusetts." The purpose of the act was to secure to fugitive slaves in the State, arrested under the fugitive slave law of the United States, a fair and impartial trial by jury. No such arrests were made in the county, and he was never called upon to act under his commission. In 1857 and 1858 he was register of probate for Hampden County; was elected treasurer of the county in 1858 for three years, beginning his service in January, 1859. He was reelected in 1861, and again in 1864, and held the office till the end of the year 1867, when he retired from it, having declined to be a candidate for reelection. He represented the First Hampden District in the Senate of the Commonwealth in the years 1869 and 1870, and was a member of the House of Representatives from Springfield in 1873 and again in 1879. At the close of the session of 1879 he was appointed Auditor of Accounts by the Governor and Council, to fill a vacancy occasioned by the resignation of Hon. Julius L. Clarke, and was elected to the same office by the people in November following. He has been reelected each year since, and is holding that office at the present time (1890, it being the last year of his service.) In 1884 his friends desired to send him to Congress to fill the unexpired term of the Hon. George D. Robinson, who had been elected Governor of the Commonwealth, but he declined to be a candidate for the place. Mr. Ladd was four years a member of the city government of Springfield,—two years in the common council and two in the board of aldermen,—between 1868 and 1873. He has also held a commission as justice of the peace since 1850. He is a director in two paper manufacturing companies, and in the Third National Bank of Springfield. His home is in Springfield, and he still retains his interest in the business of his firm, though unable to give personal attention to it, as his official duties require him to spend most of his time in Boston.

(1928) Ariel Ladd, of Springfield, (son of Ariel,[556]) was born in Tolland, Conn., Sept. 27, 1827. He ma. Caroline M., dau. of Israel Gates, of Springfield, Oct. 14, 1868. He was educated at the public schools, and remained with his father until 1847, when he removed to Cabotville (now Chicopee) and was employed for several years in the bakery business with his brothers, R. E. and L. E. Ladd. He was afterwards engaged in the business of a travelling salesman for a large confectionery manufactory in Springfield. In 1865 he became associated with his brothers, R. E. and C. R. Ladd, in the general insurance agency business, in which he is still engaged, as a member of the firm of Ladd Brothers & Co. He has never held any office except that of justice of the peace and ward officer.

Children.

2801. Emma C., bo. Oct. 27, 1869.
2802. Berthia D., bo. Oct. 7, 1872.
2803. Edith H., bo. Aug. 2, 1874.
2804. Mary C., bo. May 5, 1877.
2805. Frank C., bo. Jan. 9, 1879.
2806. Marjorie W., bo. Sept. 10, 1886.

(1058) Rufus Marvin Ladd (son of Asa[501]) ma. Mary E. Morgan, of Norwich, Conn., May 8, 1842. She died, and he ma. 2d, Emily A. Starr, Oct. 3, 1848.

Child.

2807. Rufus Amos, bo. Oct. 24, 1843.

(1939) William Cobb Ladd, of Tolland, Conn., (son of Dr. Ahijah,[563]) was born in Tolland, Conn., and spent most of his life there. For nearly thirty years he taught school in the Winter and looked after the interest of his farm in the Summer months. He was a justice of the peace, and held at different times most of the important town offices; represented the town in the State legislature about 1860; and was always interested in the growth and prosperity of the place, and exerted his influence for its moral and material advancement. He ma. ——, May 4, 1845. She died April 6, 1856, and he ma. 2d, June 1, 1857, Sarah M. Clark, an adopted dau. of Joseph Clark, of Tolland, Conn. He died June 20, 1883.

Children.

2808. William Rodolphus, of St. Paul, Minn., bo. May 12, 1846; ma. Abbie S. Phelps, Dec. 25, 1875. He was born in Tolland, Conn., where his boyhood days were spent, receiving a common school education. At the age of 17 he commenced to learn the dry goods business, and was for three years with E. S. Henry, of Rockville, Conn., after which he went to Hartford, where he remained for five years; then commenced travelling through Illinois, Iowa, and Minnesota, for a New York firm, and spent most of his time in the West until 1881, when he commenced business for himself in St. Paul, Minn., where he now (1888) resides. He has no children.

2809. Henry Johnson, bo. July 29, 1848; ma. Mary E. Chase, Sept. 4, 1877.

2810. Harriet Julia, bo. May 7, 1851; ma. James L. Weeks, Nov. 26, 1872. Child: Mary L., bo. May 21, 1876.
2811. Emily Jane, bo. Jan. 15, 1854; ma. Frank P. Mack, Oct. 23, 1879. Children: [1]Bessie Mabel, bo. Aug. 10, 1881; [2]Hazel Ladd, bo. April 16, 1884.
2812. Charles A., bo. March 12, 1856; d. July 5, 1857.

(1945)   Noah D. Ladd, of Sturbridge, (son of Levi,[564]) ma. Nancy Johnson, March 22, 1843. He was born in Tolland, Conn., Feb. 29, 1820.

Children.

2813. Everett Payne, bo. March 9, 1846; d. Aug. 28, 1848.
2814. Henry Johnson, bo. Feb. 17, 1848; ma. Cynthia Gay, Oct. 2, 1878.
2815. Mary Lucy, bo. Feb. 2, 1850; ma. Samuel O. Ward, Aug. 7, 1872.
2816. John E., bo. June 17, 1852; ma. Sarah E. Hills, Jan. 8, 1874.
2817. Clara Ida, bo. Dec. 25, 1854; ma. Chas. Henry Kayment, Apr. 25, 1877.
2818. George Sumner, bo. March 20, 1857; ma. Eveline S. Plympton, March 20, 1878.

(1948)   Joel Levi Ladd, of Tolland, Conn., (son of Levi,[564]) ma. Achsah Parsons, March 15, 1857. He died Feb. 26, 1877.

Child.

2819. Lucretia, bo. Jan. 20, 1864.

(1951)   George P. Ladd, of Spencer, (son of Levi,[564]) was born in Sturbridge, Aug. 28, 1838, and was educated at the public schools. He entered the army in 1861 as a private, and was soon promoted to first lieutenant. In 1864, at the opening of the great campaign in Virginia, he was commissioned by President Lincoln captain and assistant quartermaster, and assigned to duty as chief quartermaster of 1st Division, 9th Army Corps, Army of the Potomac. He was on duty with the Army of the Potomac until the close of the war, when he was assigned to duty in Washington, D. C. The first of July following he was ordered to Madison Barracks, Sackett's Harbor, N. Y. The first of January following he was ordered to Fort Kearney, Neb., where he was on duty until Aug. 1867, when he left the army and returned to his home and engaged in woolen manufacture. He is now carrying on an extensive business, manufacturing fancy cassimeres for men's wear, producing about one hundred thousand yards monthly. His business requires all of his time and strength, but owing to the political conditions existing in the Third Worcester District he accepted a nomination and was elected senator for 1888. He declined a renomination for 1889. He is a member of the school committee and chairman of the board. He ma. June 24, 1865, Rebecca E., dau. of Edward M. and Deborah (Morgan) Barnes.

Children.

2821. George Upham, bo. Nov. 20, 1866.
2822. Mary Barnes, bo. Jan. 29, 1868.
2823. William Upham, bo. Aug. 1, 1873.

(1698) John Lyford Ladd, of Laconia, N. H., (son of Thomas,[635]) ma. L. Jane Eager, Nov. 15, 1826.

Children.

2824. John C., bo. Sept. 5, 1827; ma. Hannah L. Taylor, April, 1853.
2825. Mary J., bo. April 26, 1829; not married.
2826. Thomas E., bo. March 25, 1831; d. young.
2827. Frances E., bo. July 17, 1833; not married.
2828. Adelia B., bo. Oct. 27, 1839; ma. Oscar Merrill, 1865.
2829. Thomas E., bo. Sept. 17, 1841; ma. Emma Plummer.

(1727) William M. Ladd, of St. Louis, Mo., (son of Dr. William M.,[586]) was born in New London, Ohio, July 7, 1837; settled in Missouri in 1856; served four years in the army and navy of the Confederate States, as captain and adjutant in the army, and as an officer on the iron-clad Fredericksburg in the navy. He is now (1888) living in St. Louis, Mo.; is president of the Ladd Tobacco Co., and is operating gold and silver mines in Colorado. He ma. July 7, 1884, Mrs. Frances (Jones) Stephens, dau. of J. B. Jones, of Washington, D. C.

Children.

2830. Mary, bo. Feb. 24, 1885.
2831. Ann Frances, bo. June 7, 1887.

(1742) William Rice Ladd, of Tolland, Conn., (son of Wareham,[540]) ma. Elizabeth E. Taylor, May 1, 1855.

Children.

2832. Luella Elizabeth, bo. April 21, 1857.
2833. Minnie E., bo. June 11, 1861; ma. Edward W. Pethybridge, Sept. 12, 1878.
2834. Addie Fellows, bo. Sept. 19, 1865.
2835. Willie Norris, bo. June 14, 1868.
2836. George Hill, bo. Oct. 5, 1874.

(1744) Samuel Chapman Ladd, of Pontiac, Ill., (son of Wareham,[540]) ma. Mary E. McDowell, Nov. 28, 1852. He died June 22, 1878.

Children.

2837. Wareham Wallace, bo. May 23, 1854; d. Nov. 4, 1854.
2838. Ellie Amelia, bo. Sept. 10, 1856; d. Sept. 7, 1857.
2839. Samuel C., bo. Sept. 11, 1874; d. March 25, 1875.
2840. William P., bo. June 11, 1858; d. Nov. 1, 1882.
2841. John McDowell, bo. Oct. 15, 1861; not married.
2842. Mary E., bo. July 18, 1864.
2843. Abbie Hortense, bo. Jan. 10, 1868.

(1747) Charles Augustus Ladd, of Vernon, Conn., (son of Wareham,[540]) ma. Almira Fuller, April 23, 1853.

Children.

2844. Frances Adeline, bo. March 26, 1855.
2845. Jennie Adella, bo. Sept. 18, 1856.
2846. Abbie Ann, bo. Jan. 26, 1858.
2847. Hattie Evelyn, bo. April 8, 1866.

(1749) Horace W. Ladd, of Springfield, (son of Jacob,[541]) ma. Charlotte Bates, of Springfield, Nov. 29, 1836. He died March 14, 1868.

Child.

2848. Ellen, bo. April 25, 1838; ma. John C. Wood, Nov. 24, 1857.

(1750) Samuel W. Ladd, of Springfield, (son of Jacob,[541]) ma. Margaret Davis, April 7, 1842. She died Aug. 15, 1845, and he ma. 2d, Lavina Fish, June 2, 1847. He died July 18, 1876.

Children.

2849. Emma M., bo. April 23, 1849; d. Aug. 1854.
2850. Lewis W., bo. July 31, 1850; d. in infancy.
2851. Lawrence W., bo. Nov. 24, 1855.
2852. Everett E., bo. May 20, 1859; d. Nov. 24, 1870.

(1751) Frederick R. Ladd, of Springfield, (son of Jacob,[541]) ma. Roxey Clapp, 1850. She died, and he ma. 2d, Eliza Morrill. He died Feb. 6, 1878.

Child by first wife.

2853. Clarence C., bo. July 10, 1851.

(1754) Hon. Edwin W. Ladd, of Springfield, (son of Jacob,[541]) ma. Mary L. Bailey, dau. of William S. Bailey, of Agawam, Nov. 21, 1855. He died March 29, 1887. We copy the following sketch of Mr. Ladd from the Springfield Republican of March 30, 1887:

"He was a native of Ellington, Conn., where he was born Feb. 18, 1829; but his father, Jacob Ladd, a farmer prominent in the life of that town, came to this city when Edwin was seven years old. The family settled on a farm at the head of the Water-shops pond, which was afterwards bought by the government and overflowed. There young Ladd was trained in those habits of industry and thrift which distinguished him always. His time for schooling was not long, for after he had attended the common schools and enjoyed a brief session at the Connecticut literary institution at Suffield, he began life for himself. Entering Eliphalet Trask's foundry he learned the moulder's trade. After three years in that establishment he went to Westfield and took charge of H. B. Smith's foundry, wherein he secured an interest. He went to Cleveland, O., about 1857, continuing in his trade, and was afterward engaged in the foundry business in Hamilton, Ont., then in Agawam, and finally with the Wason Car Company in this city. * * * He built and rented many houses, especially to people of moderate means, and his kindly qualities made him an indulgent creditor and popular landlord. * * * Edwin W. Ladd was always a Democrat in politics, but he was at the same time a fair-minded man, who never became an aggressive politician or an illiberal partisan. He was elected to the lower branch of the city government of 1877, and was returned the following year. In 1879 he was promoted to the upper board, where his industry, good sense, and practical knowledge, made him a valuable member; and his reelection came about as a matter of course. When the end of 1881 approached, Alderman Ladd rose into unexpected prominence. It was generally expected that Charles Marsh would be put up as the Democratic candidate for mayor against L. J. Powers, the Republican nominee, but at the caucus the workingmen unexpectedly turned the tables and placed Mr. Ladd in nomination. He proved a strong candidate, was handsomely elected, and gave the city a conservative and successful administration. He was a working mayor, and his choice of Col. John L. Rice for city marshal bespoke a vigorous effort to enforce the laws. This early promise was in nowise abated during the year, and violators of the liquor law were followed with vigor, while the houses of ill-fame were broken up. Without making any attempt at parade, and modestly recognizing the limitations which he clearly understood, Mayor Ladd did his duty with credit to himself. He was renominated, but was defeated by Col. H. M. Phillips. Undoubtedly the course of Mr. Ladd while in office served to alienate a portion of his party, but it was characteristic of the man that in all the local factional contests he was steadily allied with the broader and more progressive elements of the Democracy."

Children.

2854. Benjamin W., bo. June 12, 1857; ma. Clara P. Davis, Nov. 28, 1885.
2855. Charles E., bo. May 23, 1861; ma. Hattie L. Morse, April 7, 1886.
2856. Carrie L., bo. Jan. 8, 1867.
2857. Minnie E., bo. Oct. 9, 1871.

(2761) Frederick P. Ladd (son of Asa Spaulding,[1636]) ma. S. Maria Deane, Feb. 15, 1866, in New Haven, Conn.

Child.

2858. Spaulding Wesley, bo. March 3, 1866; d. young.

(2764) Allison B. Ladd, of Newport, R. I., (son of Asa Spaulding,[1636]) ma. Lizzie M. Raymond, Jan. 23, 1865. She died April 14, 1872, and he ma. 2d, Annie M. Breed, Jan. 22, 1873.

Child by second wife.

2859. Allison B., bo. Jan. 17, 1875.

(1794) Jeremiah Ladd, of Garland, Me., (son of Daniel,[617]) ma. Philinda L., dau. of Stephen and Mary (Grant) Reed, of Freeport, Me., June 20, 1829. He was a farmer.

Child.

2860. Mary J., bo. March 22, 1833; ma. James Jackman, Jan. 20, 1859.

(1797) Israel Ladd, of Garland, Me., (son of Daniel,[617]) ma. Isabel Keyes, of Keyesfield, Me., April 10, 1834. His children were all born in Nova Scotia. He removed to Garland, Me., in 1845. He was a farmer. He died Feb. 23, 1888.

Children.

2861. Sarah Kent, bo. Dec. 18, 1835; d. Aug. 10, 1858.
2862. James Daniel, bo. May 30, 1838; d. Feb. 13, 1839.
2863. Pamelia Lusby, bo. May 10, 1840; ma. Hanniel P. Knights, Sept. 16, 1869.

2864. William Rice, bo. Aug. 14, 1842; ma. Francilla E. Ducker, Sept. 15, 1874.
2865. George Edwin, bo. March 1, 1844.

(1292)   Joseph Johnson Ladd, of Manchester, N. H., (son of Joseph,[750]) ma. Lucy A. Dunham, Oct. 1861.

Children.

2866. Halbert, bo. ——.
2867. William T., bo. ——.

(1294)   Charles Hibbard Ladd, of Springfield, (son of Joseph,[750]) ma. Elizabeth Dorsett, May 16, 1866. She died May 3, 1874, and he ma. 2d, Elizabeth Firnin, Dec. 25, 1876. He enlisted in the 3d Reg. H. A., Jan. 17, 1865; was 2d lieutenant.

Children by second wife.

2868. Lawrence Firnin, bo. Nov. 19, 1877.
2869. Leona Elizabeth, bo. June 23, 1879.
2870. Maria' Sophronia, bo. Sept. 13, 1880.

(1174)   Welcome M. Ladd, of Haverhill, (son of John,[706]) ma. Elizabeth Ellis, Sept. 11, 1848.

Children.

2871. Manderville Burrett, bo. July 9, 1850; ma. Mary Quackenbush, June 12, 1871, dau. of Sidney Quackenbush, of Stillwater, N. Y.
2872. Lizzie A., bo. Nov. 1, 1852; ma. Edward A. Marble.
2873. Lindle E., bo. May 13, 1853; ma. Oscar D. Young.
2874. George Ellis, bo. April 18, 1855; not married.
2875. Anna Belle, bo. 1860; d. Sept. 20, 1864.

(1577)   Samuel Bragg Ladd, of Philadelphia, Pa., (son of Eliphalet,[638]) was born at Dover, N. H., Feb. 11, 1793; ma. in 1818, Larissa D., dau. of Amos and Hannah Mattock, who was born in Chester Co., Pa., Feb. 28, 1796. He died June 28, 1827. His widow died Oct. 17, 1887.

Children.

2876. Joseph A., bo. April 25, 1819; ma. Martha Lazarus, Sept. 18, 1841.
2877. Samuel B., bo. Nov. 20, 1821; not married.
2878. Horace, bo. Sept. 14, 1826; ma. Ellen C. Brooks, May 29, 1856. No children.

(1582)   George G. Ladd, of Everett, (son of Charles,[643]) ma. Martha Josephine, dau. of Benjamin and Abigail Nichols, of Everett, Oct. 9, 1860.

Children.

2879. Lillian Hilton, bo. March 22, 1862.
2880. Charles Bradford, bo. June 3, 1866.

(961) Spencer Ladd, of Gardiner, (son of Roger,[429]) was born in Chittenden, Vt., Feb. 11, 1814. He ma. Lucy E., dau. of Eli and Eunice (Chase) Hudson, March 11, 1840. She was born in Pittsfield, Vt., May 28, 1817. He was by trade a chair maker, was employed in several chair factories, and also worked at farming. He was fond of sports, and spent many of his leisure hours in hunting and fishing. They had no children, but adopted, when she was five years old, Mary Ann Allen, and named her Mary A. Ladd. She was born Feb. 18, 1870. Mr. Ladd died Sept. 20, 1884.

(1804) John Ladd, of Sutton, Vt., (son of John,[654]) ma. Abigail Beckwith.

Children.

2881. Gusten, bo. Nov. 30, 1835; ma. Fanny Dexter.
2882. Ellen A., bo. July 21, 1838; ma. Henry F. Baker.
2883. Arzo A., bo. July 21, 1839.
2884. Oscar E., bo. July 16, 1842.
2885. Milan, bo. July 10, 1844.
2886. Amelia M., bo. Jan. 10, 1846; ma. Francis Baker.

(1810) William Ladd, of Holderness, N. H., (son of Elias,[655]) ma. Polly Sturtevant, of Centre Harbor, N. H., Sept. 7, 1821.

Children.

2887. John S., bo. March 22, 1823; ma. Sarah J. Robinson, Nov. 23, 1859.
2888. Hale, bo. Sept. 16, 1825; ma. Betsey M. Wilbur, May 5, 1850.
2889. Ruel W., bo. Oct. 27, 1827; ma. Elizabeth C. Wright, Feb. 3, 1858.
2890. Celitia, bo. Dec. 18, 1831; ma. Samuel Patterson.

(1815) Jesse Ladd, of Holderness, N. H., (son of Elias,[655]) ma. Arthusia Marston, Oct. 31, 1836.

Children.

2891. Herman W., bo. Nov. 6, 1837; ma. Fannie E. Davidson, June 2, 1867.
2892. Maria Eliza, bo. Sept. 26, 1839; not married.
2893. Ann Josephine, bo. Aug. 10, 1841; ma. A. Webster Carter, Aug. 10, 1864.
2894. Dorcas A., bo. June 22, 1843; d..Dec. 19, 1843.
2895. Otis, bo. March 22, 1847; d. March 23, 1847.
2896. Oliver, bo. March 22, 1847; d. April 6, 1847.
2897. James, bo. May 3, 1848; d. May 22, 1848.

2898. Abbie D., bo., June 1, 1849; ma. James D. Spencer, Dec. 18, 1879.
2899. Jessie E., bo. Jan. 17, 1852; ma. Eben W. Lathrop, March 3, 1878.

(1818) Stephen Ladd, of Lawrence, (son of Josiah,[657]) ma. Sally Adams.

Children.

2900. Eliza, bo. Nov. 12, 1820; not married.
2901. John, bo. ——; ma. Hannah Prescott.
2902. Albert, bo. Dec. 8, 1825; ma. Jane Sherwell, 1850.
2903. Stephen, bo. Sept. 10, 1827; ma. Harriet Bryant, 1848.
2904. Sarah, bo. April 24, 1829; ma. William Stevens.
2905. Hannah, bo. Aug. 1831; ma. Edward Foster, Dec. 28, 1857.
2906. Julia, bo. May 5, 1832; ma. Harlow Evans.
2907. Nathaniel, bo. Sept. 2, 1835; ma. Belle Johnson.

(1819) Jonathan Ladd, of Irasburg, Vt., (son of Josiah,[657]) was born in Moultenborough, N. H., Oct. 15, 1802; ma. Mercy Glines, Nov. 29, 1819. He died in Lyndon, Vt., in 1873.

Children.

2908. Eliza, bo. Feb. 15, 1820; ma. Walter Chappel. She d. July 30, 1846.
2909. Ruth, bo. May 29, 1822; ma. Samuel Fisher, July 3, 1844; 2d, William Ruggles, July 8, 1878.
2910. Galen D., bo. May 18, 1824; d. young.
2911. Silas H., bo. March 30, 1826; ma. Addia Hubbard. No children.
2912. Florence W., bo. Jan. 19, 1828; d. May 3, 1850.
2913. John H., bo. Dec. 17, 1830; d. young.
2914. Cynthia A., bo. Jan. 5, 1832; ma. George K. Randall, 1848; 2d, William Cutler.
2915. Marilla E., bo. April 15, 1834; ma. Edmund Chickering.
2916. Ann M., bo. March 17, 1837; ma. Alonzo Gray, 1857.
2917. Abram B., bo. June 17, 1839; d. young.
2918. Caroline D., bo. Aug. 5, 1842; ma. W. K. Roundy, July 1, 1880.

(1820) Asa Ladd, of Lyndon, Vt., (son of Josiah,[657]) ma. Mercy Quimby, Feb. 1824.

Children.

2919. George D., bo. Dec. 25, 1825; ma. Josephine Perham, Feb. 1854.
2920. Sarah, bo. July 17, 1832; ma. Selin Doyle, April, 1832.
2921. Mercy, bo. Oct. 17, 1833; ma. David Wishart, Feb. 22, 1859.
2922. Aaron, bo. July 31, 1837; ma. Emma Roberts, May, 1867.
2923. Helen, bo. Jan. 1, 1839; ma. Halsey Bullock, Feb. 22, 1859.
2924. Charles, bo. May 15, 1844; ma. Isabel Black, March, 1865.

(1824) Elbridge Ladd (son of Josiah[657]) ma. Hannah Kane.

Children.

2925. George, bo. ——.
2926. Harriet, bo. ——.
2927. Josiah, bo. ——.

(1827) Moses Ladd (son of Josiah[657]) ma. Adeline Sawyer.

Children.

2928. Daniel, bo. ——.
2929. Harrison, bo. ——.
2930. Adda, bo. ——.
2931. Emma, bo. ——.
2932. Lilla, bo. ——.

(1828) Charles Ladd, of Lyndon, Vt., (son of Josiah,[657]) ma. Sally Quimby. He died Sept. 28, 1868. His wife d. Jan. 26, 1866.

Children.

2933. Charles, bo. June 4, 1848; d. June 19, 1871.
2934. Mary, bo. July 13, 1850; d. Jan. 4, 1872.
2935. Halsey, bo. Dec. 10, 1853; d. Nov. 13, 1869.

(1829) Dr. Calvin B. Ladd, of Newport, Me., (son of James,[659]) ma. Elizabeth, dau. of Jesse Atwood, Dec. 31, 1834. He died July 3, 1882.

Child.

2936. Henry W., bo. Feb. 10, 1841; ma. Lucy A. Lockling, Oct. 12, 1866.

(1833) Newell H. Ladd, of Clinton, Me., (son of James,[659]) ma. Lorina M., dau. of John Brown, Jan. 11, 1842.

Children.

2937. Ruth Ann, bo. Nov. 21, 1843; d. Oct. 28, 1847.
2938. Abbie B., bo. Nov. 4, 1848; ma. Rev. Edward R. Thorndike, June 13, 1870.
2939. Horace P., bo. Jan. 2, 1851; ma. Mary Ann Brown, June 15, 1875.

(2062) Alvaro Ladd, of London, Canada, (son of Josiah,[665]) ma. Nancy Shotwell. He was a merchant, did business in Ann Arbor and Dearborn, Mich., and in London, Canada, where he died June 11, 1842.

Children.

2940. Sylvania, bo. April 27, 1829; ma. James Cameron.
2941. Samuel, bo. Nov. 23, 1831; not married; d. Oct. 30, 1863.
2942. Oscar, bo. May 23, 1834.

2943. Dennis, bo. Jan. 16, 1837.
2944. Alvaro, Jr., bo. Sept. 1, 1839; not married.
2945. Anna, bo. June 14, 1842.

(2063)   Loram Ladd, of Dearborn, Mich., (son of Josiah,[665]) was born in St. Johnsbury, Vt., March 8, 1803; ma. Nov. 29, 1834, Elizabeth, dau. of William and Elizabeth (Henderson) Ridley, of Northumberland, England. In 1833 he removed from Vermont to Dearborn, Mich., and was engaged for many years in mercantile business, but the latter part of his life he spent on his farm. He died in Dearborn, Nov. 15, 1881.

Children.

2946. Phila, bo. Sept. 6, 1836; not married.
2947. Nancy, bo. Aug. 6, 1838; d. Feb. 4, 1839.
2948. Henry H., bo. March 6, 1841; ma. Annie Edwards, Aug. 18, 1862.

(2065)   Orrin Ladd, of Pontiac, Mich., (son of Josiah,[665]) ma. Lucinda Young, of Shepley, Lower Canada, May 9, 1825.

Children.

2949. Thurman, bo. Feb. 19, 1826; ma. Mary Quellen, 1849.
2950. Daniel Town, bo. April 11, 1827; ma. Margaret James, 1849.
2951. Josiah, bo. Sept. 20, 1829; ma. Sarah Pringle, Feb. 3, 1861.
2952. James, bo. May 13, 1838; d. in the army, Nov. 8, 1864.
2953. Nancy, bo. Nov. 6, 1845; ma. Sheldon Rinehart, Dec. 19, 1865.

(2075)   Alanson Ladd, of Delaware, Upper Canada, (son of Dudley,[670]) ma. Charlotte Decker, of Coburg, Upper Canada, July 15, 1842. He d. at Port Dover, U. Can., April 15, 1857.

Child.

2954. Corrilla, bo. Aug. 19, 1843; d. Dec. 6, 1843.

(2078)   Erastus D. Ladd, of Lawrence, Kan., (son of Samuel,[671]) ma. Julia Shockley, of Honeoy Falls, N. Y., who died without issue. He ma. 2d, ———. He was born in Marshall, Mich., Sept. 10, 1815. About 1848, when the old Morse telegraph line was first being erected between Buffalo and Cleveland by Speed & Cornell, he went East and learned the business, and followed it until about 1853; was manager at Chicago and afterwards at Milwaukee, but in the Spring of 1854 he went West to the Indian Territory (now Kansas) and settled with his brother, John Allen Ladd, on what is now the city of Lawrence, Kan., and took it up as a claim, which they afterwards sold to the Massachusetts Colonization Society. Erastus D. Ladd was the first postmaster of Lawrence, Kan. He built a nice house there, and at the time of the Quantrell raid in 1863 it was burned up, and he and his family barely escaped with their lives, losing everything. Owing to exposure, he was taken sick with fever and died soon after.

(2079) Horace Comstock Ladd, of San Francisco, Cal., (son of Samuel,[671]) ma. at Windsor, Canada, Sept. 26, 1840, Ann Sarah O'Donoghue, born at Quebec, Canada, Aug. 26, 1822, and dau. of Thomas and Mary (Aldrich) O'Donoghue. Mr. O'Donoghue was a retired British officer, who had served in India and fought with Wellington at Waterloo. His wife, Mary Aldrich, was a wealthy English lady of good family and army connections. Mr. Ladd was educated at the public schools. After his marriage in 1840 he settled at Marshall, Mich., and engaged in mercantile business, and was a leading local politician. He went to California in 1849, organized and worked extensive gold mines until 1867, when he retired from business and settled in San Francisco, Cal. He died Oct. 18, 1888.

Children.

2955. George Solon, bo. Aug. 26. 1841; ma. Elizabeth Patterson Miller, Aug. 15, 1872. No children.
2956. Mary Hopey, bo. Aug. 23, 1843; d. in infancy.
2957. Horace James, bo. June 17, 1846; ma. Mary Kirkpatrick, March 29, 1881. No children in 1888.
2958. Frances Caroline, bo. Oct. 22, 1852; ma. Charles Kaeding, March 29, 1876. Children: [1]Henry Barroilhet, bo. Jan. 1, 1877; [2]George Ladd, bo. Nov. 26, 1878; [3]Charles, bo. Aug. 5, 1880.

(2082) John Allen Ladd, of Minneapolis, Minn., (son of Samuel,[671]) was born at a place called No. 9, on the shore of Lake Erie, in Canada West, May 3, 1836; ma. in Chicago, Ill., Nov. 14, 1854, Mary Ellen, dau. of John S. and Mary Mott. He has lived in many parts of the West, but mostly in Illinois, near Chicago. When young he learned telegraphing, which he followed until 1854; was then in railroad business until 1861; then in the government service until the close of the war, and since then in the agricultural implements business. Until the past two years he has been general manager of the Northern Masonic Aid Association. His residence is at Minneapolis, Minn. In Masonic institutions he has held various important offices, including Past Grand High Priest of Masons in Illinois.

Children.

2959. Samuel Morris, bo. Nov. 15, 1857.
2960. Marian Edith, bo. Jan. 3, 1860.
2961. Annie Allen, bo. Sept. 19, 1861; d. Sept. 14, 1862.
2962. Mabel Edwards, bo. April 3, 1868.
2963. John Sydney, bo. March 5, 1871; d. Aug. 23, 1872.
2964. Fanny Kaeding, bo. July 10, 1877.

(2077)　Calvin Ladd, of Delaware, Upper Canada, (son of Dudley,[670]) ma. Lydia Lamson, Sept. 28, 1843.

Children.

2965. Lucius J., bo. Feb. 26, 1848; ma. Anna Morris, Feb. 21, 1871.
2966. Mary K., bo. Nov. 12, 1859.

(1857)　Attilus Alexis Ladd, of St. Louis, Mo., (son of Joseph Park,[1492]) ma. Jane A. Russ, Feb. 2, 1840. She died March, 1890.

Children.

2967. John A., bo. Nov. 1, 1840; ma. Pagie Berthold, Oct. 9, 1867.
2968. Alice E., bo. April 5, 1844; ma. James B. Comstock, July, 1861.
2969. Ralph A., bo. Aug. 15, 1846; ma. Frances Rutherford, Nov. 13, 1875.
2970. Attilus Alexis, Jr., bo. July 16, 1851; ma. Mary Barrett, Nov. 14, 1877.
2971. Jennie E., bo. Jan. 29, 1854; ma. George Townes, March, 1883.

(1861)　Atticus R. Ladd, of Philadelphia, Pa., (son of Joseph Park,[1492]) ma. Susan B. Beck, Oct. 15, 1870.

Children.

2972. Blanche V., bo. Aug. 29, 1871.
2973. Lon B., bo. June 15, 1876.
2974. Oliver G., bo. Oct. 19, 1879.

(1864)　Timothy Boyd Ladd, of Meredith, N. H., (son of Alexander Park,[1495]) ma. Susan Emerson, of Andover, N. H., 1851. He removed to Chateaugay, N. Y., where he kept a hotel and livery stable. He died Jan. 7, 1886.

Children.

2975. Jennie V., bo. Sept. 22, 1854; ma. Guy Clark, June 20, 1877.
2976. George E., bo. Feb. 12, 1862.
2977. Maria A., bo. Dec. 7, 1869.

(1665) George W. Ladd, of Franklin, N. H., (son of Samuel,[627]) ma. Susan Mason, July 16, 1837.

Children.

2978. George W., bo. ——; ma. Irene Flanders.
2979. Abigail, bo. ——; not married.
2980. Eunice, bo. ——; d. in infancy.
2981. Joseph, bo. ——; ma. Luella Sanborn.
2982. Mary Ann, bo. ——; not married.
2983. Frank, bo. ——; not married.
2984. Harrison, bo. ——; ma. Hattie Call, Jan. 29, 1871.
2985. ——, bo. ——.

(1666) Joseph Ladd, of Gilmanton, N. H., (son of Samuel,[627]) ma. Hannah Hill, July 27, 1845.

Children.

2986. Hannah, bo. ——.
2987. Burleigh, bo. ——.

(910) Joseph Ladd, of Everett, (son of Daniel,[378]) was born in Newburyport, April 30, 1815. In early life he went to the West Indies with his father two voyages; then served his time as a ship-carpenter and caulker in Newburyport; was engaged in boat-building under the firm name of Pike & Ladd; removed to East Boston, where he carried on the same business under the firm name of Ladd & Piper. After a while this firm was dissolved, and Mr. Ladd continued the business until Jan. 1886, when his son, William A. Ladd, was admitted a partner, under the firm name of Joseph Ladd & Son. He ma. Louisa Augusta Maria Soldan, Jan. 2, 1844. He died May 26, 1886.

Children.

2988. Charles J., bo. March 26, 1845; not married in 1885.
2989. William A., bo. March 1, 1848; ma. Adelma A. Austin.
2990. Edward O., bo. Sept. 22, 1852; ma. Donna Maria Cass.
2991. Harriet Louisa, bo. Dec. 21, 1856; d. Nov. 23, 1857.
2992. Emily Ward, bo. Feb. 20, 1860.

(1909) Moses Ashley Ladd, of New Albany, Pa., (son of Horatio,[544]) was born on the Scott farm, in Towanda Township, Pa., July 3, 1803. April, 1805, his father removed to New Albany, Pa. Moses was a farmer, and lived in New Albany, Pa., where he cleared land for his large farm of its primeval forest, and resided upon it during the active part of his life. He was an industrious and hard-working man, and knew by experience the hardships incident to life in a new country. He was fond of hunting, and killed his first deer at the age of 14, and the first bear at the age of 15 years. He ma. Oct. 12, 1823, Susannah Lawrence. She died Oct. 25, 1863, and he ma. 2d, Oct. 25, 1865, Margaret J. Strong. He died June 20, 1886.

Children.

2993. Mary J., bo. Oct. 12, 1825; ma. Jacob Brown, May 28, 1843. She d. Nov. 22, 1869.
2994. Catharine, bo. April 20, 1827; ma. John Brown, March 24, 1845.
2995. Margaret O., bo. Oct. 1, 1829; ma. Russell Miller, March 22, 1848.
2996. Maria L., bo. June 26, 1832; ma. William Martin, May 2, 1850.
2997. Horatio J., bo. May 2, 1836, ma. Catharine Harvey, Dec. 25, 1855.
2998. Eliza A., bo. June 13, 1838; ma. Lowell L. Howell, Dec. 25, 1855.
2999. Harriet E., bo. June 14, 1841; ma. Gabriel Davis, 1859. She d. Oct. 23, 1882.

(1916) Arumah Ladd, of Athens, Pa., (son of Horatio,[544]) ma. Laura Ann Bunce, June 4, 1843. She died March 5, 1870.

Children.

3000. Asenath Alinda, bo. Feb. 28, 1844; d. June 26, 1847.
3001. Jane Sophia, bo. Feb. 14, 1846; ma. William Weed.
3002. Addison A., bo. May 17, 1847; d. May 19, 1847.
3003. Marion A., bo. July 19, 1855; ma. Charles S. Kenney.
3004. Alanson B., bo. Aug. 18, 1856.

(1918) Charles Kingsbury Ladd, M. D., (son of Charles Warren,[545]) was born Jan. 21, 1822, at Laddsburg, Bradford Co., Pa., in a stone house which is now (1888) standing. Here he remained until the death of his father in 1832, during the years 1830 and 1831 attending a select school Winters. After his father's death he went to live among his relatives and worked out by the day, attending school whenever he could; some time afterwards he taught school in New Albany and Franklin Townships. About the year 1841 or 1842 he came to Towanda, Pa., and entered the office of Dr. Huston as a student of medicine. After he had read the required time with Dr. Huston he entered the old Pennsylvania Medical College in Philadelphia, Pa., from which college he graduated with honors in 1846. He returned to Towanda the same year and entered upon the practice of medicine, and continued in the same until his death. He was for many years a member of the borough council, and in the Fall of 1869 he was elected treasurer of Bradford County. He ma. Rose Spaulding, Dec. 4, 1852. He died Sept. 11, 1872.

Children.

3005. Mary Ewell, bo. July 23, 1854; d. in infancy.
3006. Charles Kingsbury, bo. Nov. 18, 1855; ma. Fredrika Anna Fox.

(1930) Otis K. Ladd, of North Adams, (son of Stephen,[557]) was born in Tolland, Conn., Oct. 13, 1816; was educated at the public schools, at the academy in Berlin, Conn., and at the Wesleyan Academy in Wilbraham; during this time he taught school Winters; after he was of age he spent three years in teaching in New Jersey and in New York State. He ma. June 1, 1841, Hannah, dau. of Ebenezer R. and Rubie (Herrick) Warner. Since his marriage his occupation has been that of a farmer. He served two years, 1862-63, in the army, and has been a member of the school committee in Springfield and in Windsor. He is now residing in North Adams.

Children.

3007. Rosella Warner, bo. June 8, 1842; ma. Henry Davis, July 4, 1864. She died May 16, 1869.
3008. James Otis, bo. Oct. 25, 1843; ma. Priscilla Thouron, March 17, 1866.
3009. Isabella Hannah, bo. Dec. 11, 1845; ma. Edward ——, May 7, 1873.
3010. Thomas Kingsbury, bo. Oct. 23, 1847; ma. Sadie Killman, May 5, 1881.
3011. Julia Amelia, bo. Sept. 30, 1849; d. July 26, 1866.
3012. Sarah Smith, bo. May 11, 1852; ma. Samuel Harris, Dec. 25, 1872.
3013. Lizzie Maria, bo. April 15, 1854; d. June 24, 1875.
3014. Eva Oranna, bo. July 21, 1856; ma. Eugene Howe, of Chicago, Ill., Sept. 26, 1875.
3015. Abraham Lincoln, bo. Aug. 10, 1861; ma. Rhoda M. Vansicker, of Chicago, Ill., Dec. 23, 1885.

(1934) John Mosely Ladd, of Grinnell, Iowa, (son of Stephen,[557]) ma. Rebecca Kenney. He died Aug. 29, 1886.

Children.

3016. Addilla, bo. Jan. 22, 1850; d. July 24, 1852.
3017. Elizabeth, bo. Feb. 18, 1852; d. Dec. 19, 1861.
3018. Herbert S., bo. Oct. 28, 1853; ma. S. E. Desh, Nov. 27, 1884.
3019. Irwin M., bo. Oct. 28, 1853; ma. L. E. Harris, July 20, 1884.
3020. Mary Ann, bo. Aug. 16, 1858; ma. H. J. Barr, Dec. 24, 1879.
3021. Sarah, bo. Nov. 14, 1861; ma. W. H. Bell, Nov. 19, 1880.

(1935) Samuel Williams Ladd (son of Stephen[557]) ma. Amanda Shaulter.

Children.
3022. Lillie, bo. ——.
3023. Hannah, bo. ——.
3024. Evelyn, bo. ——.
3025. Anna, bo. ——.
3026. Charles, bo. ——.
3027. Lura, bo. ——.

(2753) William M. Ladd, of St. Albans, Vt., (son of Merrill,[1632]) ma. Diana, dau. of A. W. Brooks, Nov. 5, 1875.

Children.
3028. Merrill A., bo. May 28, 1878.
3029. Chloe S., bo. June 15, 1881.

(1447) Henry Ladd, of Enosburg Falls, Vt., (son of Asa,[817]) ma. Celia Leavins, Dec. 20, 1854.

Children.
3030. Albert A., bo. Dec. 9, 1856.
3031. Pascal P., bo. Sept. 7, 1858.
3032. Anna E., bo. March 5, 1861.

(1457) Alphonso Ladd, of East Roxbury, Vt., (son of Avery S.,[820]) ma. Mary, dau. of John and Polly (Gibson) Bailey, of Northfield, Oct. 26, 1846. He is a prosperous farmer, and owns 200 acres ; has held the office of lister and overseer of the poor, and is a member of what is called the Christian Church.

Children.
3033. Andrew J., bo. Aug. 17, 1847; ma. Lucy Wilson, March 4, 1867.
3034. Jennie B., bo. March 29, 1852.

(2404) Oscar B. Ladd, of George, Vt., (son of Ephraim L.,[1013]) ma. Arvesta H. Lawton, Oct. 8, 1876.

Child.
3035. Ralph Lawton, bo. Feb. 27, 1880.

(2426) Samuel Pierpont Ladd, M. D., of Plainfield, Conn., (son of Samuel J. P.,[1064]) ma. Sarah H. Meacham, June 7, 1869.

Child.
3036. Frederick Pierpont, bo. Jan. 1, 1870.

(2430) Sanford H. Ladd, of Beekmantown, N. Y., (son of Henry,[1065]) ma. Elizabeth Parsons, May 14, 1878.

Children.

3037. Ellis Elmore, bo. Sept. 11, 1879.
3038. Walter H., bo. Oct. 1881.

(2796) Wilbur R. Ladd (son of Randolph E.[1922]) ma. Augusta M. Allen, of Springfield, May 14, 1862.

Children.

3039. Albert E., bo. July 17, 1863; d. in infancy.
3040. Alice F., bo. May 7, 1865.
3041. Wilbur A., bo. Feb. 13, 1868.
3042. Charles, bo. July 15, 1870; d. in infancy.
3043. Nellie F., bo. July 15, 1870; d. in infancy.
3044. Clara M., bo. July 6, 1873; d. in infancy.
3045. Mabel A., bo. May 7, 1877.

(2800) Charles B. Ladd, of Springfield, (son of Lucins E.,[1924]) ma. Ada I. Shattuck, of Springfield, Oct. 1872.

Child.

3046. Lucius E., bo. May 23, 1878.

(3008) James Otis Ladd, of Charleston, S. C., (son of Otis K.,[1930]) was born Oct. 25, 1843, at North Adams; ma. Priscilla C. Thouron, March 17, 1866. He enlisted, Oct. 18, 1861, from Windsor, and Oct. 29 entered Capt. M. J. Smith's camp of instructions at Middlefield. He left Middlefield Dec. 4, 1861, passed medical examination at Worcester Dec. 5th, and joined the 15th Mass. Regiment at Poolsville, Md., Dec. 8, 1861, and was assigned to Co. I. He participated in every skirmish and battle in which that regiment was engaged throughout the entire memorable Peninsula campaign, and at the second battle of Bull Run, South Mountain, and Antietam. He was wounded at Antietam, Sept. 17, 1862, by a minnie ball, and on Sept. 19 suffered amputation of the right arm near the shoulder. He was discharged from the service Jan. 13, 1863, at Antietam Hospital, Md. He reentered the service from South Adams, with appointment as 2d lieutenant from the War Department, April 28, 1863; refused to enter the Invalid Corps, and was assigned to the 1st N. C. C. Troops, afterwards designated the 35th U. S. C. Troops, organized at Newbern, N. C., and mustered into service June 30, 1863. He was engaged with the besieging forces at Charleston Harbor, S. C., in 1863, having charge of alternating details of troops in the erection of parallel fortifications facing the enemy's batteries on Morris Island, and in the construction of the famous "Swamp Angel" battery under the fire of the enemy, for the bombardment of the city of Charleston. He was promoted to 1st lieutenant Jan. 12, 1864. In Feb. 1864, his regiment joined the Federal forces at Jacksonville, Fla., and he participated in the battle of Olustee, Fla., Feb. 20, 1864, where his regiment was complimented by Gen. Seymour for gallant conduct, their ranks being depleted by the loss of 15 officers and 250 enlisted men killed or wounded. He was taken prisonor of war from the U. S. naval steamer Columbine, near Horse Landing, on the St. John's river, Florida, May 26, 1864, after a desperate and bloody engagement, the steamer being captured and hastily burned by the enemy, with the dead and many of the wounded on board. He was confined in rebel prisons at Macon and Savannah, Ga., and Charleston and Columbia, S. C., being under fire of Federal forces from the "Swamp Angel" battery from Sept. 13 to Oct. 5, in the jail yard at Charleston. He made his escape from rebel prison at Columbia, S. C., Nov. 4, 1864, and was recaptured on Nov. 9, having been run down by hounds. He was exchanged from the rebel steamer "Fly by Night," off Charleston harbor, Dec. 10, 1864, and taken to Annapolis, Md. After a leave of absence, he was assigned to special duty by the War Department at Annapolis, Md., mustering paroled prisoners of war for commutation of rations. He rejoined his regiment at Branchville, S. C., in June, 1865, and was detailed as acting assistant quartermaster and assistant commissary of subsistence until mustered from the service, June 1, 1866. He was promoted to captain March 1, 1866. After his muster from the service he was employed in the Bureau of Civil Affairs at Headquarters Department of the South at Charleston, S. C., and thereafter assigned as chief clerk in the Adjutant-General's office at those headquarters, Gen. Canby commanding. He was subsequently assigned to duty with the Freedmen's Bureau in South Carolina, under Gen. Scott. In 1868 he entered the State Treasury office in South Carolina as book-keeper, became chief clerk, and served in that capacity until Jan. 1, 1871, when he resigned to assume the duties of superintendent and treasurer of the Chronicle Publishing Co., and business manager of the Washington, D. C., Daily Chronicle, which position he resigned in August, 1872. In 1874 he had charge of the assets of the Bank of the State of South Carolina, under C. C. Puffer, Receiver, at Charleston, and in August of that year assumed the business management of the Union Herald, (Republican,) a paper published at Columbia, S. C., from which position he retired in 1876. He was special deputy collector of internal revenue for South Carolina, from August, 1876, to March, 1882. He was postmaster at Cheraw, S. C., two and a half years, and was removed after President Cleveland's election, to make place for a Democrat. He was appointed commissioner of the U. S. Circuit Courts for South Carolina, Dec. 30, 1876, which position he now holds.

Children.

3047. Joseph Otis, bo. Dec. 18, 1866, at Summerville, S. C.
3048. Emma Julia, bo. Sept. 4, 1868, at Summerville, S. C.
3049. Thomas Nichols, bo. April 9, 1870, at Summerville, S. C.
3050. James T., bo. Sept. 30, 1872, at Wilbraham.

(2809) Henry Johnson Ladd, of South Manchester, Conn., (son of William Cobb,[1839]) ma. Mary E. Chase, Sept. 4, 1877.

Child.

3051. Chester W., bo. March 4, 1881.

(1721) Prof. George T. Ladd, of New Haven, Conn., (son of Silas Trumbull,[584]) was born in Painesville, Ohio, Jan. 19, 1842. He ma. Cornelia Ann Tallman, of Bridgeport, Ohio, Dec. 8, 1869, dau. of John C. Tallman; lived in Hudson, Ohio, from the Fall of 1842 to 1850, then removed to Painesville, Ohio, where he lived until 1860, and then was in Western Reserve College from 1860 to 1864; was in business in Painesville, Ohio, 1864 to 1866; was in Andover Theological Seminary 1866 to 1869; preached in Edinburgh, Ohio, 1869 to 1871; was pastor of the Spring Street Congregational Church, at Milwaukee, Wis., 1871 to 1879; called as Professor of Philosophy to Bowdoin College in 1879, and to Yale University, as Professor of Philosophy, in 1881. We name some of the books he has written: Principles of Church Polity, 1882; Doctrine of Sacred Scripture, 1883; Translation of Loze's Outlines of Philosophy, six vols., 1884–87;

Elements of Physiological Psychology, 1887; What is the Bible? 1888. He was lecturer of Church Polity at Andover Theological Seminary from 1879 to 1881; special lecturer to graduates on Systematic Theology at Andover, 1881-82; lecturer in Yale Theological Seminary, 1881-83. The degree of D. D. was conferred upon him by Western Reserve College in 1880, and the degree of M. A. by Yale College in 1881.

Children.

3052. George Tallman, bo. May 17, 1871, in Edinburgh, Ohio.
3053. Louis Williams, bo. March 15, 1873, in Milwaukee, Wis.
3054. Jesse Brewster, bo. July 28, 1876, in Milwaukee, Wis.
3055. Elizabeth, bo. Feb. 15, 1884.

(2997) Horatio J. Ladd, of New Albany, Pa., (son of Moses Ashley,[1909]) ma. Catherine, dau. of Christian and Martha Haverley, Dec. 25, 1855. He died Dec. 23, 1869.

Children.

3056. Belle C., bo. Sept. 25, 1858; ma. Ahirah Estelle, May 15, 1878.
3057. Lawrence, bo. Aug. 23, 1862; ma. Estilla English, Sept. 28, 1885.

(3006) Charles Kingsbury Ladd, M. D., of Towanda, Pa., (son of Charles Kingsbury,[1818]) was born in Towanda, Pa., Nov. 16, 1855. He attended the Convent of the Sisters of the Holy Child Jesus during the years 1862-63, when he entered the Susquehanna Collegiate Institute of Towanda, Pa., where he remained, with some intervals of absence, till 1872. After the death of his father in 1872 he entered the office of S. M. Woodburn, at Towanda, Pa., as a student of medicine; upon the completion of his reading he went to Philadelphia, Pa., where he was examined for and took a scholarship in the University of Pennsylvania, in Sept. 1874. In 1876 he was graduated as a Doctor of Philosophy, acquiring the highest grade that had ever been taken at that time. (See "History of Class of 1877, Univ. of Penna. *Anders.*") After completing the full three years' course at the University he graduated an M. D. with honor, (unanimous Faculty vote,) and sailed for Europe in May, 1877, where he pursued the study of medicine in the "Allegemeine Kraukenhaus," at Vienna, Austria, for one year, when he returned to Towanda in June, 1878, and began the practice of his profession, and was elected jail physician in 1878. In 1883 he was appointed U. S. pension examiner; was elected trustee of the Susquehanna Collegiate Institute in 1888. He ma. Sept. 8, 1886, Fredrika Anna, dau. of Frederick and Mary (Shumberger) Fox, who was born in Warren, Ohio, Oct. 9, 1865, and was adopted by her uncle, Eleazer T. Fox, who removed to Towanda, Pa., when she was seven years old.

Child.

3058. Lydia Fox, bo. June 28, 1887.

(2371) George Dutton Ladd, M. D., of Milwaukee, Wis., (son of Edwin O.,[976]) was educated in the public schools and academy at Milwaukee; commenced the study of medicine Oct. 1871; graduated at Rush Medical College, Feb. 1875. He is a practicing physician at Milwaukee. He ma. Annette Ashba Dutcher, Nov. 10, 1885.

Child.

3059. Annette Dutcher, bo. Dec. 5, 1887.

(2315) William Ladd, of San Francisco, Cal., (son of Lemuel,[936]) ma. Mrs. Ellen Foley, June, 1867.

Children.

3060. Enoch H., bo. Feb. 1868.
3061. William D., bo. May, 1870.

(2370) Edwin Horace Ladd, of Milwaukee, Wis., (son of Edwin O.,[976]) ma. Jennie M. Atwater, March 26, 1881.

Children.

3062. Milvin H., bo. May 2, 1882.
3063. Mabel Annette, bo. April 1, 1887.

(2356) Nelson G. Ladd, of Benson, Vt., (son of Perry Green,[950]) ma. Mary Ransom, Nov. 20, 1859.

Children.

3064. Charlotte M., bo. Dec. 6, 1860.
3065. Charles A., bo. Aug. 16, 1862.
3066. Henry J., bo. July 14, 1864.
3067. George D., bo. Jan. 1, 1867.
3068. Harriet W., bo. Feb. 23, 1869.
3069. Julia M., bo. Oct. 30, 1871.
3070. William R., bo. July 15, 1873.
3071. Ida B., bo. Jan. 10, 1876.
3072. Jennie J., bo. Nov. 21, 1878.

(2360) Kendall G. Ladd, of Benson, Vt., (son of Perry Green,[950])
ma. Elizabeth Lowry, Nov. 10, 1869. He died June 13, 1884.

Children.
3073. Ned S., bo. Dec. 24, 1870; d. Feb. 19, 1872.
3074. Alice A., bo. May 29, 1873.
3075. Edward W., bo. Nov. 30, 1875.

(2036) James William Ladd, of Oshkosh, Wis., (son of James,[867])
ma. Mary Elizabeth, dau. of Andrew B. and Mary A. (Bassett)
Jackson, May 20, 1874.

Children.
3076. Florence, bo. June 10, 1875; d. May 17, 1877.
3077. Andrew B. Jackson, bo. April 28, 1878.

(2037) George H. Ladd, of Hudson, Dickey Co., Dakota, (son of
James,[867]) ma. Ellen Maria, dau. of Ashel and Harriet Bidwell,
Oct. 19, 1863.

Children.
3078. Mary Ellen, bo. April 10, 1866.
3079. George Franklin, bo. Oct. 19, 1867.
3080. William Henry, bo. Nov. 17, 1869.
3081. Della Edna, bo. Jan. 26, 1874.
3082. Charles Christopher, bo. May 19, 1879.

(2054) Hon. Andrew Robeson Ladd, of Clarion, Iowa, (son of Azel
P.,[892]) was born in Shellsburg, Wis., Sept. 8, 1846. He received a common school education in Wisconsin, and for one
year in Massachusetts. He left school at the age of 17 and
enlisted in the army; served two years before being discharged;
at the close of the war he entered the law office of J. K. Williams, at Shellsburg, Wis., as a student at law, and was admitted to the bar in 1868. He took the gold fever in 1869 and
went to the Territories; spent a season in Montana and returned
to Wisconsin. He removed to Clarion, Iowa, in 1872, and has
remained there since. He is a justice of the peace, and has held
the office of town clerk; is a Free Mason and Knight Templar;
has for some time been commander of the G. A. R. Post at
Clarion, and is now (1888) mayor of the city of Clarion.

Children.
3083. Clara E., bo. May 18, 1879.
3084. Berthia A., bo. Sept. 22, 1881.

(2280) Arthur S. Ladd, of Chicago, Ill., (son of Otis Freeman,[829]) ma. Ruth Ann Nettleton, 1870.

Child.

3085. ——, bo. July 20, 1871.

(2285) William Curtis Ladd, of Centerville, N. Y., (son of Amasa Scott,[833]) removed to Arcada, N. Y., where he has been in the furniture and undertaking business, and has now one of the largest establishments in that line in the country. He has been justice of the peace, police justice, and coroner of Wyoming Co. for three years. He ma. Caroline Matilda Towne, Feb. 5, 1850.

Children.

3086. Mary Louise, bo. Dec. 24, 1851.
3087. Helen Libbie, bo. Dec. 7, 1853; ma. J. H. Howard, of Arcada, N. Y., May 30, 1887.
3088. Berthia M., bo. June 5, 1870; d. Dec. 4, 1874.

(2286) James Madison Ladd, of Memomonie, Wis., (son of Amasa Scott,[833]) was born at Randolph, Aug. 21, 1821; ma. Mary Ann Balcom, May 4, 1845, at Hume, N. Y. She died, and he ma. 2d, Laura L. Hildreth, Dec. 1, 1850. He lived at Hume, N. Y., at Fillmore, N. Y., and at Memomonie, Wis. He learned the trade of harnessmaker, worked at it at Hume, N. Y., and afterwards went into the grocery trade. About 1874 he removed to Memomonie, Wis. He died May 15, 1887.

Child.

3089. Mary J., bo. July 1, 1847; ma. J. M. Hughes, Nov. 4, 1866, of Pittsford, N. Y. She d. Nov. 25, 1875, at Memomonie, Wis.

Children by second wife.

3090. Martha E., bo. Jan. 1, 1852; d. Nov. 8, 1864, at Fillmore, N. Y.
3091. Amasa Samuel, bo. April 5, 1855, at Hume, N. Y.; not married.
3092. Malissa L., bo. Aug. 4, 1857, at Hume, N. Y.; ma. Franklin Booton, Jan. 16, 1880.
3093. Vernon A., bo. Sept. 27, 1860, at Fillmore, N. Y.; d. Oct. 14, 1861, at Fillmore, N. Y.
3094. James H., bo. Sept. 30, 1862, at Fillmore, N. Y.; not married.
3095. William C., bo. March 9, 1867, at Hume, N. Y.
3096. Martha E., bo. Nov. 29, 1869, at Hume, N. Y.
3097. Vernon A., bo. May 17, 1871, at Hume, N. Y.

(2287)   Henry Clay Ladd, of Wheeler, Wis., (son of Amasa S.,[883]) ma. Weltha Amelia Whalley, of Centerville, N. Y., Sept. 21, 1852. He removed from Memomonie, Wis., to Wheeler, Wis.

Children.

3098. Cynthia A., bo. Sept. 1853; ma. Willard H. Willis, of Hume, N. Y.
3099. Charles H., bo. July 26, 1855; ma. Kate A. Wiston.
3100. William B., bo. Dec. 12, 1859; ma. Cory E. Gatley.
3101. Clotilda A., bo. Jan. 25, 1861; ma. Mark R. Hoag.

(2304)   Daniel Ladd, of West Trenton, Me., (son of Daniel,[912]) ma. Martha Southard, of Mt. Desert, Me., Dec. 5, 1852.

Children.

3102. Augustine G., bo. June 22, 1854; d. Nov. 17, 1859.
3103. Flora E., bo. Oct. 30, 1856; ma. Wellington H. Cousins, of Eden, Me., Oct. 20, 1876. Child: Herbert, bo. Oct. 22, 1884.
3104. William Heman, bo. Feb. 22, 1860; ma. Azelle Randolph, of Veazie, Me., Nov. 3, 1887.
3105. Emerson D., bo. Jan. 21, 1871.

(2306)   Rufus Bailey Ladd, of Cranbury Isle, Me., (son of Daniel,[912]) ma. Hannah Caroline Stanley, Nov. 28, 1852. He died at New Orleans, La., Oct. 1864.

Children.

3106. Levi E., bo. Jan. 31, 1854; ma. Clara E. Gilley, Jan. 1, 1875.
3107. Lillian, bo. Jan. 6, 1863; ma. Archie C. Spaulding.

(1446)   Philander Ladd, of West Burke, Vt., (son of Asa,[817]) ma. Susan Thompson, March 17, 1840.

Children.

3108. Julia, bo. ——.
3109. Frank, bo. ——.
3110. Asa, bo. ——.

(1448)   Ebenezer B. Ladd, of Enosburg Falls, Vt., (son of Asa,[817]) ma. Rosetta McAlster, March 1, 1861. She died April 1, 1863, and he ma. 2d, Ann M. Beach, March 25, 1867. He died Nov. 18, 1882.

Children by second wife.

3111. William B., bo. Jan. 1, 1872.
3112. Rosetta Mc., bo. Feb. 17, 1873; d. April, 1876.
3113. Bernard E., bo. July 16, 1876.
3114. Ethel W., bo. Sept. 6, 1877.

(1451)   Jackson Ami Ladd, of East Farnham, P. Q., Canada, (son of Asa,[817]) ma. Esther Hamilton, Jan. 4, 1852. She died in 1853, and he ma. 2d, Anna M. Allen, Dec. 23, 1860.

Child by second wife.

3115. Lucy Luella, bo. Oct. 1867.

(2989)   William A. Ladd, of Everett, (son of Joseph,[910]) ma. Adelma, dau. of Elijah H. Austin, May 5, 1874. She died, and he ma. 2d, Anna A. Darling, March 1, 1880. He carries on the ship carpentry and calking business at Everett, under the firm name of Joseph Ladd & Son.

Children.

3116. Harriet Louisa, bo. March 16, 1875; d. Aug. 30, 1875.
3117. William Joseph, bo. March 17, 1876.

(2990)   Edward O. Ladd, of Everett, (son of Joseph,[910]) ma. Donna Maria Cass.

Children.

3118. Grace Louisa, bo. ——.
3119. Emily Soldan, bo. ——.
3120. Edward Thorndike, bo. Nov. 15, 1882.

(2386)   William D. Ladd, of Weld, Me., (son of Porter,[998]) ma. Hattie M. Chandler, May 13, 1876.

Child.

3121. Pearl F., bo. Oct. 31, 1879.

(2041)   George V. B. Ladd, of Boston, (son of William H.,[872]) ma. Margaret Butler, March 12, 1859.

Child.

3122. George W., bo. Nov. 11, 1859; ma. Alice T. Watson, Jan. 27, 1885.

(2042)   Bela Dow Ladd, of Boston, (son of William H.,[872]) ma. Susan M. Harrison, Dec. 27, 1855. She died Sept. 4, 1859, and he ma. 2d, Susan S. Prince, May 27, 1860. She died May 18, 1880, and he ma. 3d, Mary O'Hara, Sept. 22, 1880.

Child by second wife.

3123. Charles Albert, bo. Jan. 4, 1864.

Children by third wife.

3124. William Bela, bo. 1880.
3125. Edward Harrison, bo. Nov. 14, 1881.
3126. Estella May, bo. April 21, 1883.

(2038)   Richard Fletcher Ladd, of Boston, (son of Bela Orlander,[871]) ma. Esther E. Barney, Dec. 19, 1854. He died, and she ma. 2d, William R. Mann.

Child.

3127. Lizzie B., bo. June 22, 1857; ma. Arthur E. Gile.

(2288)   John Johnson Ladd, of Brookville, Canada, (son of Peabody W.,[836]) ma. Sophia W. Stevens, Dec. 1, 1853. He was born at Haverhill, N. H., May 11, 1828; graduated at Dartmouth College, Hanover, N. H., in 1853; was principal of Warren Academy at Woburn; then engaged in teaching school at Providence, R. I., and at Littleton, N. H., and for ten years was connected with Dr. Barnas Sears, at Stanton, Virginia, with the Peabody educational work. He is now connected with a college at Brookville, Ontario, Canada. His wife died Dec. 30, 1881, and he ma. 2d, Caroline V. Lathrop, July 4, 1883.

Children.

3128. Jennie Stevens, bo. Feb. 9, 1857.
3129. Willie S., bo. May 8, 1862.

(2504)   Ezra Ladd, of Middlesex, Vt., (son of Jacob S.,[1141]) ma. Martha Stevens, March 4, 1858. He was a farmer, and held the office of constable in 1856 and 1857. He removed to Montpelier, Vt., in 1872, where he died in 1873.

Children.

3130. Frank E., bo. April 10, 1857.
3131. Emma H., bo. Oct. 19, 1861.
3132. Gertrude N., bo. Feb. 25, 1864.
3133. Fred S., bo. July 15, 1867.
3134. Hattie, bo. June 6, 1873.

(2709)   George Henry Ladd, of Middlesex, Vt., (son of Jacob S.,[1141]) ma. Emogene L., dau. of Jerry and Louisa Leland, Oct. 25, 1868. He is a farmer where his father and grandfather lived and died. He was one of the selectmen in 1886, and a representative in 1888.

Children.

3135. Ida Elizabeth, bo. Aug. 23, 1871.
3136. Alice Louisa, bo. April 10, 1876.

(2283) Hon. Herbert Warren Ladd, of Providence, R. I., (son of Warren [1505] and Lucy Washburn (Kingman) Ladd,) was born in New Bedford, Oct. 15, 1843. He ma. May 25, 1870, Emma F., dau. of Caleb G. and Elizabeth (Holmes) Burrows, of Providence, R. I. She died April 13, 1889. He was sent when quite young to an excellent private school, taught by Miss Elizabeth Wood; then to the Parker Street public grammar school; entered the High school June 9th, 1856, and graduated May 18, 1860. Soon after he entered the wholesale dry goods house of Tucker & Taber, where he remained until July, 1861, when he entered the employ of Fessenden & Baker, editors and proprietors of the New Bedford Mercury, soon after they took charge of it. This was soon after the breaking out of the civil war, and was a time, particularly in newspaper offices, of intense excitement. "How precisely it came about," writes the senior editor, "I cannot now recall; but young Ladd, though only a boy and expected only to fill a boy's place, soon developed remarkable capacity and tact, and became a valuable assistant, not only in the business department of the paper, but in the editorial room, as a reporter, and then as a correspondent. It is true he came to the office well equipped for work, having been educated in the public schools of New Bedford, than which there were and are none better in the State, and with a home training which had piqued and stimulated his curiosity and kept his mind constantly on the alert. The newspaper office was an admirable school for such a youth, and he easily embraced all its opportunities. As a reporter he was clear, accurate, and graphic; and his letters to the Mercury from various points in the South and West, to which he was sent during the progress of the war, were of exceptional merit and interest. We parted with him with sincere regret, not alone on account of our personal loss, but at his leaving a profession which he was so well fitted to adorn, and in which we felt sure he would achieve a brilliant success." Oct. 22, 1862, the steamers Merrimac and Mississippi sailed from Boston for North Carolina with two regiments, the 3d and 44th, and joined Foster's command. In less than a week after their arrival these regiments were in an engagement with the rebel forces, and young Ladd's account of the same was sent home and published in the Boston Journal, and copied in New York papers, before the New York Herald's correspondent got his account in. The first Sunday paper ever published in New England, outside of Boston, was an extra Mercury which young Ladd got out to announce the battle of Fredericksburg. His attention was early turned to the dry goods business by the fact that he had an uncle who was a member of the firm of George W. Warren, Barry & Co., but who died in 1860, and a cousin, Mr. A. W. Kingman, who was at that time salesman with Jordan, Marsh & Co. Having decided to return to the dry goods business, he on the 7th of January, 1864, accepted a position in the house of White, Brown & Co., Franklin street, Boston. He remained with them until Feb. 9th, when he had a sudden attack of lung fever, from the effects of which he did not recover for several months. Under the advice of his physician, who felt some out-of-door occupation would be of great benefit, he went to look after certain interests of some New Bedford gentlemen in the oil regions of West Virginia and Southeastern Ohio, where he spent some two and a half years. Returning, he again entered the dry goods business with an importing house in Boston, where he remained until the Spring of 1871, when he embarked in the retail dry goods business in Providence, R. I. Never having had any experience in the retail business, he associated with himself a Mr. Davis of Boston, who had been brought up in the business, the firm being Ladd & Davis. Mr. Ladd had remarkable taste in selection of styles and material, and early developed surprising tact in management, and with constant devotion to his business his success was at once assured. "While Mr. Ladd's success has been great," said a New York commission merchant, "his name will always be known as the leader in this country in applying and showing what thorough system in the retail business will do." The firm of H. W. Ladd & Co. is now (1889) one of the best known in the country for nice goods and a nice trade. Occupied as he is and has been with a constant and rapidly growing business, Mr. Ladd yet found time to take an active interest in public matters. He was one of the organizers of the Providence Congregational Club, and the father of the Providence Commercial Club, whose great success and meetings the past Winter have been known all over the country. He is now president of the club. His interest in social clubs is evidenced by his membership in the Hope Club, the Squantum Club, the Press Club, and other clubs. The

Rhode Island Society for the Prevention of Cruelty to Children early elected him for its president, and to him is due the present systematic organization of that most philanthropic society, and its splendid Home, equal to any of the kind in the country. For two years he was vice-president of the Board of Trade, and is a director in the Atlantic National Bank of Providence. He took an active part in the movement for obtaining enlarged and better terminal railway facilities in Providence, and gave his aid and influence to every effort made for the material, intellectual, and moral improvement of the city. He was elected Governor of the State of Rhode Island, on the Republican ticket, May 28, 1889, and held office for one term. His administration was notable for the energy and progressiveness which he infused into it. Thoroughly acquainted as a business man with Rhode Island's status in the commercial world, Governor Ladd appreciated the possibilities for greatly enhancing her importance, and his official efforts were largely directed toward arousing public attention to the natural advantages possessed by the State for inviting commerce, and for securing a large proportion of the transatlantic freight to be landed on her shores in lower Narragansett Bay, and transferred thence by railroad to New York city or distributed over New England. Simultaneously with these propositions for developing the railroad, shipping and business interests of his State, Governor Ladd successfully inaugurated radical movements for the benefit and development of the agricultural interests; secured a commission to revise the State's laws and to devise an improved judicial system; and, urging the necessity of adequate measures for increasing the State's revenues and relieving the people of as much of the burden of direct taxation as possible, urged also the need of public works, and the building of a new State House, on the plans and site for which a commission, of which he was made chairman, is now (1890) at work. During his term of office Governor Ladd had the honor of entertaining, at his Summer residence at Newport, R. I., the president, Benjamin Harrison, (July 5, 1889,) and ex-president Grover Cleveland (August 7, 1889.) He gave to Brown University, an institution in which he has taken a deep interest, an observatory fully equipped with instruments and apparatus for astronomical research and study, the Commencement dinner, June 19th, 1889, at which Governor Ladd was a guest, being made the occasion for this magnificent gift. The observatory bears its donor's name, and will stand as a monument to his liberality, interest in the cause of education, and public spirit.

Children.

3137. Clara S., bo. Aug. 3, 1871; d. Aug. 13, 1872.
3138. Lucy Kingman, bo. Nov. 15, 1872; d. Aug. 26, 1881.
3139. Elizabeth Burrows. bo. Oct. 15, 1875.
3140. Emma Louise, bo. May 16, 1877; d. Aug. 24, 1881.
3141. Herbert Warren, bo. Feb. 25, 1880; d. Aug. 20, 1881.
3142. Hope, bo. Oct. 15, 1882.

(2088) Jeremiah Benjamin Perley Ladd, of Groveland, (son of Gardner P.,[1507]) ma. Anna G., dau. of Levi B. and Johannah W. (Carter) George, March 2, 1859. He was educated in the public schools and at Merrimac Academy. He enlisted, Aug. 13, 1863, as sergeant in the 8th unattached, afterwards Co. D, 3d Reg.; was discharged for promotion, Aug. 30, 1864, and by special order No. 285 was commissioned 2d lieutenant in the 21st unattached Co., afterwards Co. E. 4th Artillery, Aug. 25, 1864. He was mustered into the U. S. service Sept. 9, 1864, and served as post-adjutant at several military posts in Virginia. His term of enlistment expired June 17, 1865, and he was discharged and returned. He is a justice of the peace, a conveyancer, and does probate business.

Child.

3143. Alice M., bo. Jan. 8, 1867; d. April 8, 1887.

(2089) Major Nathaniel Eustis Ladd, of Groveland, (son of Gardner P.,[1507]) ma. Isabella S., dau. of Dean R. and Rebecca Kimball (Foster) Parker, Oct. 15, 1868; was educated at the public schools and at Merrimac Academy, of Groveland. He enlisted as a private in the 33d Mass. Infantry, Col. A. C. Maggie; was mustered into the service of the United States in Co. A, 33d Regt., Aug. 9, 1862; took part in all battles in which the regiment was engaged, until Aug. 26, 1863, when he was discharged, by order of the War Department, for promotion; was commissioned by Gov. Andrew as 2d lieutenant in the 55th Mass. Reg., Aug. 15, 1863, and assigned to Co. G, said regiment being commanded by Col. N. P. Hallowell; was promoted to 1st lieutenant March 24, 1864; was promoted to captain, July 23, 1865; was made a brevet major of volunteers, March 13, 1866. During a portion of 1864 and 1865 he was in command of Fort No. 2, Long Island, and Fort Delafield, Folly Island, Charleston harbor, S. C. From March, 1865, until September of the same year, he was on the staff of Major-General John P. Hatch, as assistant provost marshal, with headquarters at Charleston, S. C. He was in most of the engagements in which the regiment took part, not being present at the battle of Honey Hill, where the regiment met with severe losses, being on detached duty at that time. He was engaged in the manufacture of boots and shoes at Groveland, from Dec. 1865, until 1876. He was appointed a clerk in the railway mail service in 1877, performing duty on the route between Boston and Troy, N. Y., between Boston and New York city, Boston and Waterbury, Conn., Boston and Bangor, Me., and Boston and Portland, Me., until July, 1886, when he was removed as an "offensive partisan." He is a member of the Grand Army, and has been six times elected commander of the Charles Sumner Encampment, Post 101. He was elected to the Massachusetts Legislature, as representative, in the Fall of 1886, and serving the next session, 1887, on the committee on railroads.

Children.

3144. Fred Winthrop, bo. Nov. 28, 1869; d. Dec. 7, 1877.
3145. Arthur Shirley, bo. March 2, 1875.
3146. Stanley Parker, bo. Oct. 29, 1880.

(2096) William B. Ladd, of Groveland, (son of John Ingersoll,[1508]) ma. Gertrude G. Phelps, June 5, 1877.

Children.

3147. Robert Francis, bo. Sept. 12, 1879; d. May 10, 1880.
3148. Freeman Plummer, bo. Sept. 24, 1881.
3149. William Gardner, bo. Nov. 24, 1884.

(1975) Rev. Francis Dudley Ladd, (son of Gen. Samuel G.,[1570]) was born in Hallowell, Me., May 20, 1820; ma. Caroline Rose, June 16, 1846, dau. of Dr. Robert H. Rose. The following sketch of Mr. Ladd was kindly furnished by Prof. A. S. Packard, of Bowdoin College:

"Francis Dudley Ladd was a son of Gen. Samuel G. and Caroline (nee Vinal) Ladd, a niece of the first President Adams. After graduating, he became private tutor for a year or two in the family of Dr. Robert H. Rose, Silver Lake, Susquehanna Co., Pa. He then pursued theological study at the Bangor Seminary, graduating in 1846. Was ordained at Farmington by the Congregational Association, and became pastor of the Presbyterian Church at Silver Lake, ministering at the same time to two other churches a few miles distant, a labor which he performed in unwearied punctuality and earnestness. His services were highly prized, and in demand wherever there was special religious interest. In 1851 he was called to the pastorate of Penn Church, Philadelphia, Pa., then in a state of depression and discouragement, but amid the trials that awaited him he labored faithfully, earnestly, and steadfastly. At one period he thought seriously of devoting himself to foreign mission work, but was hindered by circumstances beyond his control. Having inherited the spirit of genuine love of country and its institutions from those who had been active in establishing them, at the opening of the war of the rebellion, in obedience to what he regarded a call of Christian duty, he visited the army before Richmond soon after the battle of "Fair Oaks." His zeal, however, carried him too far in effort to relieve suffering of the sick and wounded. On his return he began writing an appeal to the public in their behalf, but before it was completed the seeds of disease contracted in camp revealed themselves, and after a short illness he died in his study, July, 1862. His death made a deep impression upon the public, and his funeral was attended not only by his church and the brethren of the Presbytery, but by the clergymen of other denominations, and a large concourse of citizens.

Child.

3150. Ellen Rose, bo. Aug. 28, 1849; d. Sept. 25, 1851.

(1983) Rev. Horatio O. Ladd, of New York city, (son of Gen. Samuel G.,[1570]) was born Aug. 31, 1839; ma. Harriet, dau. of Rev. John S. C. Abbott, at New Haven, Conn., Aug. 6, 1863. His youth was spent in the towns of Farmington, Auburn, and Brunswick, where he attended academies and high schools, and entered Bowdoin College in 1855, graduating in the class of 1859. He studied divinity at Bangor and at Yale Theological Schools, and was graduated at the latter seminary in 1863. After teaching one year in New York he supplied the Crombie

Church at Salem, and was ordained at Cromwell, Conn., where he was pastor till he was called to a position as pastor and teacher in Olivet College, Michigan. He was after this pastor at Romeo, Mich., from 1869 to 1873. He was principal of the New Hampshire State Normal School from that time till 1876, and after another pastorate in Hopkinton he went to Santa Fe, N. M., where he established the University of New Mexico, the Ramona Indian School, and secured in great part the location and establishment by Congress of the Government Indian School at Santa Fe. After remaining ten years in this position as president of the University and in this educational work for the Indians of the Southwest, he was appointed supervisor of the census for New Mexico by President Harrison, and confirmed by the Senate, but resigned his office and located in New York city.

Children.

3151. Lillie V., bo. May 2, 1865; ma. Harry S. Church, Feb. 10, 1886.
3152. Julie E., bo. July 24, 1867.
3153. Harry A., bo. July 20, 1869.
3154. Maynard, bo. Feb. 24, 1872.

(1984) William Ladd, of Hallowell, Me., (son of John,[1573]) ma. Lucretia, dau. of Ezekiel Goodale.

Children.

3155. William Norton, bo. ——.
3156. Mary Elizabeth, bo. ——; ma. Joseph Carter.

(1986) John Ladd, of Hallowell, Me., (son of John,[1573]) ma. Sarah Jane, dau. of Benjamin Nourse, Aug. 31, 1837. He died Oct. 11, 1859.

Children.

3157. William Franklin, bo. Dec. 22, 1838; ma. Anna M. Zabriskie, Dec. 5, 1861.
3158. John Edwards, bo. Oct. 26, 1845; ma. Frances Wilkins, of Sydney, N. S. W., May, 1876.

(1996) William Dudley Ladd, of Concord, N. H., (son of Nathaniel G.,[1575]) was born in New York city, April 24, 1825. He lived with his father in New York until 1834, when he went to live with his uncle, Dudley Ladd, a farmer at Franklin, N. H., where he remained working on the farm until 1840, when he entered as clerk James Colburn's country store at Franklin, and stayed there three years, when he took charge of a store and kept the books for Peabody & Daniels, paper manufacturers, and continued in their employ until the death of Mr. Peabody, in 1854. He then obtained a position with the Franklin Mills Co., who manufactured shirts, drawers, and stockings, and while there performed various duties, and for eight months, while their clerk was sick, he acted as book-keeper. In 1856 he left the Franklin Mills and removed to Concord, N. H., entered the employ of Mr. Gustavus Walker, and had charge of his hardware store for nearly ten years, when he entered into partnership with Mr. Walker, under the firm name of Walker & Co., and opened an iron and steel store in Railroad Square, of which Mr. Ladd had sole charge until 1887, when they sold out the business, and Mr. Ladd retired from active duties, and is now enjoying at leisure the fruits that accrue from an honest and faithful discharge of every duty, and from an active and upright business life. He ma. Nov. 16, 1847, Mary Ann Emerson, dau. of Fenner H. and Clarinda (Baker) Emerson, of Franklin, N. H.

Children.

3159. Georgia M., bo. May 19, 1849; ma. George A. Foster, of Concord, N. H., Jan. 13, 1870. Children: [1]William A., bo. Feb. 3, 1872; [2]Nathaniel L., bo. Feb. 19, 1874; [3]Robert F., bo. March 25, 1876, died March 1, 1883; [4]Lucy C., bo. Sept. 30, 1878; [5]Evelyn Tilton, bo. Oct. 8, 1881; [6]Fred E., bo. Sept. 28, 1883; [7]George Arthur, bo. Nov. 8, 1886; [8]Joseph Dudley, bo. June 13, 1888, d. Oct. 4, 1888.
3160. Fred Norton, bo. Jan. 21, 1859; ma. Carrie T. Sleeper, Dec. 2, 1885.

(1999) Charles George Ladd, of Brooklyn, N. Y., (son of Nathaniel G.,[1575]) ma. Mary Ann Sullivan, June 14, 1866.

Child.

3161. William Dudley, bo. ——.

(2001) Nathaniel Ladd, of Brooklyn, N. Y., (son of Nathaniel G.,[1575]) ma. Mary Jane Irvin, Jan. 4, 1876.

Children.

3162. Nathaniel Morrow, bo. April 17, 1877.
3163. Fred Hutchins, bo. Dec. 10, 1879.
3164. Nellie Marion, bo. 1887.

(841) Hiram Ladd, of Haverhill, N. H., (son of Ezekiel,[355]) ma. Eliza Crouch, Dec. 16, 1830. She was bo. Aug. 1, 1803. He died at Freeport, Ill., May 4, 1875.

Children.

3165. George A., bo. June 18, 1833.
3166. Mary Louisa, bo. Oct. 7, 1836; ma. Oliver J. Hardy, at Haverhill, N. H., Aug. 5, 1857. He died at Haynesville, Ala., Feb. 26, 1858, and she ma. 2d, Loyal L. Munn, at Haverhill, N. H., Sept. 4, 1861. Children, all born at Freeport, Ill.: [1]Ella E., bo. July 25, 1862; [2]George L., bo. Aug. 2, 1864; [3]Loyal L., Jr., bo. Nov. 7, 1869; [4]Florence L., bo. Nov. 25, 1879.
3167. Hiram K., bo. May 1, 1842; d. at Haverhill, N. H., April 7, 1867.

(2161) John Martin Ladd, of Louden, N. H., (son of Daniel,[1757]) ma. Kate Hanrahan, of Boston.

Children.

3168. Frank, bo. April 25, 1860.
3169. Nellie, bo. Nov. 20, 1862.
3170. John Eddie, bo. Sept. 3, 1867.
3171. Fannie, bo. Aug. 10, 1869.

(2174) Austin S. Ladd, of Lowell, (son of Newell Corson,[1766]) ma. Fannie Blake, 1875.

Child.

3172. Paul Austin, bo. Aug. 19, 1879.

(2232) Willard Ladd, of Bradford, Vt., (son of Moses,[1876]) ma. Lucinda S. Ireland, Sept. 6, 1846.

Children.

3173. George W., bo. Feb. 4, 1852; ma. Sarah E. Smith, April 7, 1880.
3174. Lucinda M., bo. Aug. 22, 1854.
3175. Albert H., bo. Aug. 31, 1861.
3176. William B., bo. March 13, 1868.

(2233) John Ladd, of Summerville, Vt., (son of Moses,[1876]) ma. Rebecca Powers, March 2, 1848.

Children.

3177. Mary J., bo. May 24, 1849; ma. Albert Burnham, Jan. 1, 1867.
3178. Lafayette, bo. Sept. 27, 1852; ma. Annella Houghton, Feb. 22, 1881.

(2234) Orange S. Ladd, of Waterford, Vt., (son of Moses,[1876]) ma. Ann Eliza Parker, March 25, 1851. He was educated at the public schools and at St. Johnsbury Academy; is a farmer; has held the office of selectman and other minor offices; has resided in Danville, Vt., and is now living in Waterford, Vt.

Children.

3179. Mary E., bo. Nov. 2, 1858.
3180. Mattie A., bo. Feb. 24, 1863.
3181. Milo E., bo. Nov. 10, 1864.

(2235)　　Alonzo Ladd, of Summerville, Vt., (son of Moses,[1876]) ma. Miriuda Brown, March 25, 1852. She died June 9, 1857, and he ma. 2d, Ellen Wilson, June 9, 1859.

Children.

3182. Luman A., bo. Nov. 9, 1860.
3183. George W., bo. Sept. 25, 1864.
3184. Aldis P., bo. Jan 5, 1871.

(2438)　　William W. Ladd, of Summerville, Vt., (son of Moses,[1876]) ma. Almeda Gilbert, June 1, 1861. She died Sept. 4, 1877, and he ma. 2d, Ellen Blakeslee, March 10, 1880.

Children.

3185. Willie W., bo. Jan. 7, 1864.
3186. Mabel L., bo. March 11, 1866.
3187. Horace F., bo. Dec. 1, 1867.
3188. Sarah A., bo. July 12, 1869; d. Dec. 29, 1879.
3189. Fred M., bo. Nov. 21, 1873.
3190. George W., bo. July 26, 1876.

(1967)　　William Jones Ladd, of Milton, (son of Alexander H.,[1595]) was born in Portsmouth, N. H., Feb. 4, 1844. He entered Harvard College in 1862. He enlisted in the 13th New Hampshire Regt., Sept. 13, 1862; was appointed and mustered as sergeant major, non. com. staff, 13th Regiment N. H. Vols., Sept. 30, 1862; discharged Dec. 30, 1862, and promoted to 2d lieutenant Co. K, same regiment and same date; promoted 1st lieutenant Co. B, same regiment, May 30, 1864; was wounded in the neck, Sept. 29, 1864, in action at Fort Harrison, Va.; was appointed captain U. S. V. by brevet for gallant and meritorious service, to date from March 13, 1865. He was on the staff of Gens. Getty, Brooks, Devens, and some others; was commissary of musters, and was highly respected as a man and as an officer, and I may say, without detracting from the merits of others, that no cooler headed or braver youth went into the army. He was mustered out as 1st lieutenant, June 21, 1865. After the evacuation of Richmond he was one of the three officers who entered the city before the troops, and while riding down by the river he noticed the sloop of war Patrick Henry (nee Jamestown) on fire, with her flag flying, and that the boat that had set the train to her magazine had just landed. He jumped into the boat and boarded the vessel, hauled down the flag, and with it reentered the boat and pulled for the shore, which he reached just as the vessel blew up. The flag thus captured he brought home, and it is now in the possession of his father, and is held as a sacred memento of the event. He ma. June 21, 1869, Annie Russell, dau. of Robert S. and Mary (Hathaway) Watson.

Children.

3191. Adelaide W., bo. Sept. 28, 1870. m. 1900 Alfred Rodman Weld
3192. Robert W., bo. Nov. 26, 1871. died 1893
3193. Alexander, bo. July 28, 1874. Harvard 1897. m. Elinor W. Merriam
3194. Anna W., bo. Nov. 11, 1876. m. Richard C. Storey, Harvard '96
3195. Eleanor H., bo. Oct. 29, 1878. m Elton Clark, Harvard '96
3196. William Edward, bo. Sept. 8, 1880. m.
3196a. Marian W., born   m. John W. Hallowell, Harvard '01

(2948) Henry H. Ladd, of Dearborn, Mich., (son of Loram,[2063]) ma. Annie Edwards, Aug. 18, 1862.

Children.

3197. Nettie King, bo. April 25, 1864.
3198. Dudley Kilne, bo. July 11, 1869.
3199. Edith May, bo. Dec. 20, 1872.
3200. Annie Elizabeth, bo. Nov. 10, 1875.

(2950) Daniel Towne Ladd, of Dearborn, Mich., (son of Orrin,[2065]) ma. Margaret James, Sept. 14, 1849.

Children.

3201. Frederick Otis, bo. Feb. 4, 1850; not married in 1888.
3202. Elizabeth Olivia, bo. April 11, 1852; ma. George Miller, Oct. 4, 1870.
3203. Phila, bo. Oct. 9, 1854; ma. William Hall, Sept. 18, 1872.
3204. Mary Fidelia, bo. April 13, 1858; ma. Chas. A. Schrader, July 4, 1876.
3205. Josiah, bo. Nov. 1, 1860; not married; d. July 29, 1882.
3206. David Orrin, bo. March 12, 1863.
3207. Jennie, bo. Sept. 10, 1865.
3208. Arthur, bo. Sept. 30, 1868.
3209. Annie. bo. Oct. 23, 1869.
3210. Frank, bo. July 7, 1874.

(2184) William Sargent Ladd, of Portland, Oregon, (son of Nathaniel Gould,[1774]) ma. Caroline A. Elliott, of Canterbury, N. H. He was born in Morgan, Vt., Oct. 10, 1826. We make the following extracts from a sketch of Mr. Ladd in "Hodgkin's Pen Pictures of Representative Men of Oregon:"

"The subject of our sketch received the advantages only of a common school education, although he for a short time attended the Northfield Seminary. He was quick to learn, but after all did not particularly relish the routine life of a student, and he soon abandoned it. At the age of 20 he was employed as freight and passenger agent of the Boston, Concord & Montreal Railroad, and won the confidence and respect of his employers. In 1851 he resigned his position, and, in direct opposition to the advice of parents and employers, he started to seek fortune and fame among the undeveloped territories of the Pacific slope, and he reached Portland the same year, where he accepted a position as clerk and book-keeper for the firm of Wakeman, Dimon & Co., who had sent a stock of goods out here in charge of Mr. Gookin, a junior member of the firm. This gentleman shortly afterwards returned East, and Mr. Ladd took charge of their business, and in partnership with C. E. Tilton, Esq., subsequently purchased the interest of the firm, which partnership existed until 1854, when Mr. Tilton withdrew. Mr. Ladd continued the mercantile business until April, 1859, when he sold it to his two brothers and Mr. S. G. Reed. In April, 1859, in partnership with C. E. Tilton, Esq., his former partner, he established the first banking-house on the Northwest coast. He has always taken an active interest in educational matters, having served several times as director in the common schools of Portland. He was one of the founders, and for years a director and liberal supporter of the Portland Academy, and a warm friend of the Willamette University at Salem, of which he is one of the trustees. His liberality is proverbial, and many of our young men have occasion to thank him for substantial aid in securing an education. The Presbyterian Church, of which himself and family are members, has received almost princely contributions from his purse, and scarcely a church or chapel of that denomination in Oregon, Washington, or Idaho Territory, has been started without his aid or assistance. He has also rendered efficient aid to the Methodist denomination, in which his early manhood was spent. He is the senior member of the banking firm of Ladd & Bush, at Salem; was from its early organization a heavy stockholder and director in the O. S. N. Company, as well as director in the Oregon City Woolen Mills and the Salem Flouring Mill Company. He has held the position of mayor of Portland. During the war he was a stanch war Democrat, and has since exercised his right of voting his own ticket, although in national matters he has in late years sided with the Republicans. Such is a brief outline of the history of a man whose active and enterprising spirit, sound business sagacity, open-handed liberality, pronounced Christian character, and love of the beautiful and useful in nature and art, has contributed largely to mold the character of a city of 50,000 souls, and lay deep and broad, in a great measure, the commercial honor, political virtues, enlightened education, and Christian principles of our young and growing Commonwealth."

Children.

3211. William A., bo. Sept. 16, 1855.
3212. Charles E., bo. Aug. 5, 1857; ma. Sarah E. Hall.
3213. Helen Kendall, bo. July 4, 1859.
3214. Caroline Ames, bo. Sept. 3, 1861.
3215. John Wesley, bo. Jan. 3, 1871.

(2193) Hiram E. Ladd, of Palisade. Na., (son of Zoroaster,[1776]) ma. Emma Peck.

Children.

3216. Charles, bo. ——.
3217. Alice, bo. ——.
3218. Nettie, bo. ——.

(2195) Loren Gilbert Ladd, of Pawtucket, R. I., (son of Zoroaster,[1776]) ma. Victor Baldwin, Dec. 18, 1860.

Child.

3219. Albert E., bo. Dec. 17, 1863.

(2196) Charles Wesley Ladd, of Coaticooke, P. Q., Canada, (son of Zoroaster,[1776]) ma. Caroline P. Allard, Sept. 17, 1854, at St. Johnsbury, Vt.

Children.

3220. Eleanor Elizabeth, bo. Feb. 22, 1856, in Iowa.
3221. Charles Ira, bo. Nov. 26, 1858, in Iowa City.
3222. William Edward, bo. Sept. 19, 1860, in Pleasant Valley, Iowa.
3223. A son, bo. Feb. 25, 1863; d. April 5, 1863.
3224. A daughter, bo. April 6, 1868; d. April 7, 1868.
3225. Flora Estella, bo. April 28, 1870, in Coaticooke, P. Q.
3226. Alice Carrie, bo. Oct. 26, 1871, in Coaticooke, P. Q.

(2198) Wesley Johnson Ladd, of Nashua, N. H., (son of Zoroaster,[1776]) removed to Hollis, N. H.; ma. Emeline Whittaker, Oct. 11, 1860.

Children.

3227. George A., bo. Dec. 11, 1863.
3228. Elmer E., bo. March 1, 1869.

(2202) Ira Marshall Ladd, of Coaticooke, P. Q., (son of Zoroaster,[1776]) ma. Mary J. Winslow, April 21, 1881.

Child.

3229. Wilbur H., bo. July 5, 1882.

(2224) Babson S. Ladd, of Boston, (son of John Savilian,[1791]) ma. Ella Cora, dau. of John Wood Brooks, Nov. 16, 1878. He graduated at Harvard College in 1870; studied law at Boston and at Harvard Law School.

Children.

3230. Paul Dean, bo. Feb. 16, 1880; d. Jan. 22, 1885.
3231. Alice, bo. Feb. 5, 1885.
3232. Amelia, bo. Aug. 5, 1886.

(2226) Story Butler Ladd, of Washington, D. C., (son of John Savilian,[1791]) ma. Eliza Brigham Paine, Dec. 18, 1878. He graduated at the Lawrence Scientific School of Harvard University in 1873.

Children.

3233. Halbert Paine, bo. April 2, 1881; d. April 25, 1882.
3234. Mary Butler, bo. Aug. 3, 1884.
3235. Elizabeth Brigham, bo. Dec. 13, 1887.

(2227) Allston Channing Ladd, of Brockton, (son of John Savilian,[1791]) ma. Harriet Amelia Hedenberg, of Medford, June 11, 1883.

Children.

3236. Philip Hedenberg, bo. July 10, 1885, in Medford.
3237. Eleanor, bo. Feb. 9, 1887, in Brockton.

(2864) William Rice Ladd, of Garland, Me., (son of Israel,[1797]) ma. Francilla E. Ducker, Sept. 15, 1874. He is a farmer.

Child.

3238. Rose, bo. May 22, 1881.

(2955) George Solon Ladd, of San Francisco, Cal., (son of Horace Comstock,[2079]) was born at Marshall, Mich., Aug. 26, 1841; ma. Elizabeth Patterson Miller, Aug. 15, 1872, at San Francisco, Cal., dau. of Col. Jeremiah and Mary (Henry) Miller, of Pennsylvania. She was born at St. Louis, Mo., Nov. 30, 1853, and was educated at the convent of Notre Dame, Santa Clara, Cal. Col. Miller was a brother of Gen. Stephen Miller, formerly governor of Minnesota. Mary Henry, the mother of Elizabeth Patterson Miller, was the daughter of Gen. Garven Henry, U. S. A., who was an aid to Gen. Andrew Jackson. Mr. Ladd was educated at the high school at Marshall, Mich.; was engaged in telegraphing in 1856; was prominent in originating and conducting the first overland telegraph between the Atlantic and the Pacific; became general superintendent and manager of all the telegraphs on the Pacific coast in 1865, and retired in 1873, after which he established and successfully developed many other important enterprises, including large land reclamations, electrical manufactures, district telegraphs, and finally the extensive telephone company of the Pacific coast, of which he is now (1888) president. He opened at San Francisco, Feb. 14, 1878, the first regular commercial telephone exchange ever started upon the plan which has since been universally adopted elsewhere. He has no children.

(2205) John Seneca Ladd, of Stockton, Cal., (son of Seneca,[1777]) ma. Mary Caroline Swan, of Methuen, March 12, 1863.

Children.

3239. Mary Alice, bo. Jan. 21, 1864.
3240. Pamelia Estabrooks, bo. Oct. 22, 1868.
3241. John Seneca, bo. Dec. 27, 1873.

(2206) George Seneca Ladd, of Stockton, Cal., (son of Seneca,[1777]) ma. Abby Bourland, May 28, 1852.

Children.

3242. George E., bo. May 11, 1857.
3243. Walter E., bo. May 27, 1859.
3244. J. Marsh, bo. Dec. 31, 1864.
3245. Ira B., bo. May 28, 1868.

(2208) Ira Walter Ladd, of Stockton, Cal., (son of Seneca,[1777]) ma. Emily Jane Sutherland, March 7, 1858.

Children.

3246. Lillie Isabel, bo. June 12, 1859.
3247. Adelaide Amelia, bo. Dec. 13, 1860.
3248. Fred. Grant, bo. April 6, 1862.
3249. Ira Gilbert, bo. Oct. 30, 1863.
3250. Emily Jane, bo. Sept. 28, 1865.

(2775) Dr. John Gould Ladd, of Pittsfield, N. H., (son of Gould D.,[1675]) ma. Helen, dau. of Dr. William Proctor. She died Jan. 10, 1867. He studied medicine with Dr. Prescott, and graduated at Dartmouth College Medical School in 1867.

Children.

3251. John, bo. Jan. 10, 1867.
3252. William, bo. Jan. 10, 1867.

(2776) Freeman Weston Ladd, of Sanbornton, N. H., (son of Gould D.,[1675]) ma. Marietta Miller, of Lowell, Nov. 28, 1870.

Child.

3253. Helen Weston, bo. April 22, 1874.

(2777) Elbridge Gerry Ladd, of Belmont, N. H., (son of Gould D.,[1675]) ma. Henrietta, dau. of Uriah and Abigail (Batchelder) Lamphrey, June 8, 1871. He received a good common school education; is a farmer, and lives on the farm where he was born; was a member of the school committee in 1870-71, and is a director in the Belknap County Agricultural Society.

Children.

3254. Orry Gerry, bo. Jan. 23, 1873.
3255. Edward Gould, bo. Feb. 8, 1876.
3256. Merton Freeman, bo. Jan. 30, 1880.

(2781) Harlan Page Ladd, of Belmont, N. H., (son of Barnett H.,[1682]) ma. Sarah Jane Noble, March 15, 1865.

Children.

3257. Albert Barnett, bo. Nov. 14, 1866.
3258. Anna Eveline, bo. July 8, 1868.
3259. Mattie Zoe, bo. Nov. 26, 1871.
3260. Charlotte Jane, bo. April 4, 1874.
3261. Altie Eunice, bo. March 19, 1876.
3262. Nellie May, bo. May, 1878.

(2784) Arthur Stuart Ladd, of Belmont, N. H., (son of Langdon,[1683]) ma. Ellen M. Porter, of Laconia, N. H., Feb. 28, 1867.

Children.

3263. Edith Sylvina, bo. Nov. 23, 1867.
3264. Florence Emma, bo. Jan. 27, 1872.
3265. Candace Porter, bo. May 23, 1875.

(853) John Quincy Adams Ladd, of Hammonton, N. J., (son of Moody,[358]) ma. Elizabeth Brown, of East Hartford, Conn., 1850.

Children.

3270. Emma C., bo. in East Hartford, Conn., 1851.
3271. Ella, bo. ——; d. 1853.

(2217) Daniel Watson Ladd, of Epping, N. H., (son of Nathaniel,[1787]) was born at Epping, N. H., Feb. 24, 1825. He was educated at the public schools; taught school, studied medicine, was a farmer and phrenologist. He ma. Sept. 7, 1845, Lucy Ann Dustin, dau. of Caleb and Eliza (Kelley) Dustin. He died Feb. 10, 1862.

Children.

3272. Eliza Ann., bo. June 14, 1846; ma. David A. Campbell, Jan. 7, 1866. She died April 8, 1890. She graduated at the Boston University School of Medicine in 1876, and afterwards practiced in Boston and Attleborough. Children: [1]Atwood Watson, bo. Feb. 14, 1869; [2]Mary O. R., bo. June 18, ——.
3273. Nathaniel Watson, bo. Jan. 7, 1848. He commenced to earn his living when he was seven years old, and has earned it ever since. He learned the shoemaker's trade at the age of 11 years and worked at it two years. After the death of his father in 1862 he worked on a farm in Tilton, N. H., about two years, then as clerk in a clothing store for nearly three years, in Kittery, Me. He graduated at Pinkerton Academy, Derry, N. H., in 1869, and at Dartmouth College in 1873. In the meantime he taught school in Maine, Vermont, New Hampshire, and Massachusetts; travelled in the West and South for a year, and graduated at Boston University School of Law in 1875. Travelled in the South and West another year, and since 1876 has practiced law in Boston. He was a member of the Boston common council in 1886 and 1887, and a representative from Boston in 1890.
3274. Francois Joseph Gall, bo. March 24, 1851; ma. Ella M. Byrt, Dec. 23, 1879.
3275. John Savilian, bo. April 7, 1852; ma. Rose Doolittle, May 24, 1881.

(2218) Daniel Watson Ladd, of Epping, N. H., (son of Daniel Watson,[1789]) ma. Dorothy E., dau. of Jonathan and Mercy Thing, Nov. 7, 1846. He died Aug. 22, 1886. His wife died July 9, 1882. "He was educated at South New Market, Hampton Falls, and Hampton Academy, where he is said to have maintained the character of a fine scholar and a lover of books." He was a prosperous farmer.

Children.

3276. Silvina W., bo. Jan. 19, 1847; d. Feb. 20, 1851.
3277. Bina W., bo. July 18, 1850; d. Dec. 24, 1885.
3278. Charles W., bo. April 27, 1852; d. July 31, 1852.
3279. Lizzie W., bo. March 5, 1853; d. in infancy.
3280. Jennie W., bo. Aug. 13, 1854.
3281. Sylvia W., bo. Jan. 8, 1856; ma. Frank R. Hazeltine, July 7, 1880. Child: Roscoe Ladd, bo. Feb. 7, 1885.
3282. Daniel W., bo. March 17, 1859; ma. Grace Alma Furber, July 11, 1888.
3283. Alva W., bo. March 25, 1862. "He became a member of the Congregational Church when but 11 years old. At the age of 13 he entered Phillips Academy, Exeter, N. H.; graduated in class of 1880. He then entered Harvard University, with no conditions and three honors, and had a brilliant career before him, but his health gave out, and he died May 8, 1881."
3284. Linnie W., bo. April 27, 1866; ma. Prof. Warren S. Adams, A. B., June 22, 1886.

(2222) Samuel Plumer Ladd, of Epping, N. H., (son of Daniel W.,[1789]) ma. Sarah J. Dodge, of Raymond, N. H., March 29, 1853. "He was a man of wealth and influence, and of great intellectual powers. He was educated at Phillips, Exeter, and at Hampton Falls Academies. He sustained the character of a good scholar, gifted with rare endowments of mind; he was generous, sympathetic, and persevering, true to his convictions, an able defender of those principles he deemed right; a democrat and an earnest worker in the political field. He is a farmer, and resides on Red Oak Hill, Epping, N. H."—History of Rockingham County, N. H.

Children.

3285. Sarah P., bo. Jan. 13, 1854; ma. Edward M. Smith, June 27, 1872.
3286. Peter, bo. May 27, 1855.
3287. Paul, bo. June 30, 1857.
3288. Rebecca, bo. Dec. 6, 1858; ma. Frank S. Eveans, May 17, 1879.
3289. Silas B., bo. May 3, 1860; d. Sept. 3, 1864.
3290. Lydia W., bo. Aug. 19, 1861.

3291. Elvina L., bo. March 21, 1863; d. June 21, 1863.
3292. Ellen L., bo. March 21, 1863.
3293. Clara M., bo. Sept. 1, 1865.
3294. Louis P., bo. Nov. 10, 1866.
3295. Laura J., bo. Feb. 21, 1868.
3296. Dexter, bo. Jan. 16, 1872.
3297. Harry, bo. Oct. 23, 1874.
3298. Samuel T., bo. Feb. 7, 1877.
3299. Cora B., bo. Feb. 27, 1881.

(2012) Hiram Ladd, of Mt. Vernon, Me., (son of Paul,[1840]) ma. Carrie Wiggin, Dec. 15, 1863.

Children.

3300. George S. W., bo. April 9, 1865.
3301. Carrie Eveline, bo. April 3, 1869.

(2619) David Newell Ladd, of Enfield, N. H., (son of David C.,[1812]) ma. Sarah B. Pool, of Plainfield, N. H., April 1, 1857. He was born in Alexandria, N. H., March 17, 1834, and owing to the reduced circumstances of his parents and the large family dependent upon them for support, was early obliged to leave home and seek his own living, thus being deprived of the meagre advantages of education then available. He learned the sawyer's trade, and has been at different times employed by many of the large lumber concerns of New Hampshire. He enlisted in Co. B, 6th N. H. Vols., Oct. 7, 1861, and served until receipt of discharge for sickness, Dec. 30, 1862. He was wounded at the battle of Shantilla.

Children.

3302. David Marshall, bo. Nov. 5, 1859; not ma. Feb. 1889. We copy the following sketch of him from Moore's History of New Hampshire Newspapers and their Editors: "The subject of this sketch was born in Enfield, N. H., Nov. 5, 1859, and was educated in the common schools of his native town, graduating at Canaan Union Academy, Aug. 22, 1876. At the early age of 19 years he edited and published the Monthly Advertiser, the first and only regular publication printed in Enfield, in connection with the job printing business. In January, 1880, he removed to Boston, Mass., where he was employed by Perry, Cook & Tower, 105 Bedford street. Was afterwards New England travelling agent for Richardson, Howe & Lovejoy, 42 Chauncy street, for nearly two years, during which time he managed their branch business in Lawrence, Mass., under the firm style of D. M. Ladd & Co. During the latter part of 1882 he established the Boston Novelty Advertising Co., (Charles E.

Daniels and William Haywood partners,) and continued the same till May, 1883, when he located in Manchester, N. H., and associated himself with William M. Kendall, under the firm name of Kendall & Ladd, founding and publishing the Manchester Weekly Budget. The success attending the publication of the Budget was phenomenal; from a small beginning it grew to be the leading local weekly publication of the State, a power in politics and the moulding of public opinion. Independent, fearless and outspoken on all matters of public interest, it soon became the recognized organ of the toiling masses, the friend of humanity. The Budget was sold by the founders to Challis & Eastman (employes of the old firm) Jan. 24, 1887. Mr. Ladd, after disposing of the Budget, again located in Boston, where he is at present actively engaged in newspaper work."

3303. Mabel Jennie, bo. Feb. 5, 1867.

(2003) William Henry Ladd, of Boston, (son of William Manley,[1576]) was born Dec. 29, 1824, in Augusta, Me.; ma. May 15, 1852, Jane, dau. of David and Martha J. Pearson, of Boston. She died April 23, 1853, and he ma. 2d, Martha, dau. of Franklin and Martha P. (Edwards) Gregory, of Royalston, Vt., April 2, 1857. He was educated at the academy in Laconia, N. H., and at the Normal School, Bridgewater. While at Bridgewater he accepted a position as an English teacher in a German school in Baltimore, Md., where he was very successful for two years. He afterwards taught in a grammar school in Charlestown, until offered the mastership of the Shepard School at Cambridge, where he remained until Messrs. Thayer & Cushing offered him a position in the Chauncy Hall School in Boston, which he accepted, and remained there until Mr. Thayer retired, when he became associate principal, and when some years later Mr. Cushing retired, he became principal of the school.

Child.

3304. Mary Holmes, bo. ——.

Child by second wife.

3305. Ann Elizabeth, bo. ——.

(2876) Joseph A. Ladd, of West Chester, Pa., (son of Samuel Bragg,[1577]) was born in Philadelphia, Pa., April 25, 1819; ma. Martha, dau. of Nicholas and Rebecca (Hutchins) Lazarus, Sept. 18, 1841. He has lived in Natchez, Miss., Fort Madison, Iowa, Scranton, Pa., and is now (1888) living in West Chester, Pa. Was a carpenter by trade; has been a merchant, school director, member of town council, and is now in the book and stationery business.

Children.

3306. Larissa D., bo. Sept. 22, 1842; ma. William P. Mattock, Dec. 8, 1864.
3307. Alda P., bo. Feb. 6, 1845; d. June 17, 1870.
3308. Martha A., bo. Oct. 9, 1847; ma. G. Coughan, Aug. 1, 1867.
3309. Edith M., bo. June 15, 1850.
3310. Horace, bo. Aug. 6, 1852; d. June 8, 1857.
3311. William A., bo. March 1, 1855; ma. —— Cunningham, Sept. 30, 1877.
3312. Samuel B., bo. Sept. 21, 1858.
3313. Orsemus W., bo. July 5, 1861.

(2630) Dearborn Ladd, of Mercer, Me., (son of Benjamin,[1326]) ma. Laura Hoyt.

Children.

3314. Eliza Jane, bo. Aug. 5, 1845; ma. Alonzo Shepard.
3315. Esther Maria, bo. June 26, 1848; ma. Laforest Morrill.
3316. Emma Frances, bo. Sept. 24, 1851; ma. —— Wyman.
3317. Willie S., bo. Aug. 5, 1862.
3318. Benjamin, bo. Sept. 27, 1864.
3319. Maud E., bo. June 20, 1875.

(2633) Perley M. Ladd, of Natick, (son of Benjamin,[1326]) ma. Caroline McAlvain, 1858. He died Sept. 3, 1879.

Children.

3320. Minnie, bo. Jan. 3, 1860.
3321. Emma, bo. 1864; d. aged 10 months.

(2635) James Henry Ladd, of Mercer, Me., (son of Benjamin,[1326]) ma. Abigail Ladd.[2690]

Children.

3322. ——, bo. 1857; d. 1863.
3323. Benjamin Franklin, bo. Sept. 14, 1861.
3324. Frank, bo. June 1, 1867.
3325. George Henry, bo. March 28, 1869.

(2637) Charles Ladd, of Foxborough, (son of Benjamin,[1326]) ma. Irene Perkins.

Child.

3326. Nellie, bo. ——.

(2638) Albert Ladd, of Worcester, (son of Benjamin,[1326]) ma. Lizzie French.

Child.

3327. Georgianna, bo. 1872.

(2641)　　Frank Ladd, of Mercer, Me., (son of Benjamin,[1326]) ma. Lura Nayson, 1882.

Child.

3328. Winneford Bell, bo. Jan. 7, 1883.

(2643)　　Luther Ladd, of Lawrence, (son of Moses,[1327]) ma. Eliza J. Cheeney, 1842.

Children.

3329. Grace, bo. 1847.
3330. Ellen M., bo. 1853.

(2646)　　William Ladd, of Concord, N. H., (son of Moses,[1327]) ma. Sabra Luce, Jan. 1, 1849.

Children.

3331. Mary E., bo. Nov. 22, 1849; ma. William Lake, June 1, 1868. Children: [1]Franklin O., bo. Dec. 28, 1870, d. Oct. 18, 1871; [2]Julia W., bo. Sept. 30, 1873, d. Sept. 20, 1874; [3]Charles E., bo. April 26, 1875; [4]Flora D., bo. Aug. 28, 1877; [5]George E., bo. Feb. 17, 1880.
3332. Frank P., bo. Jan. 8, 1853; ma. Aura Perham.

(2647)　　Mark Taylor Ladd, of Concord, N. H., (son of Moses,[1327]) ma. Caroline M. Hildrith, 1852.

Child.

3333. Ellen, bo. ——.

(2653)　　Thomas Ladd, of Taunton, (son of Daniel,[1328]) ma. Sarah Pressey, Dec. 7, 1843.

Children.

3334. Sarah, bo. July 12, 1849; ma. Alfred Vibbert, April 9, 1873.
3335. Daniel, bo. Sept. 2, 1851; ma. Josie M. Paine, June 22, 1869.
3336. Flora, bo. May 1, 1855; ma. Edgar F. Talbot, Oct. 9, 1878.
3337. Ella, bo. Aug. 8, 1859; ma. Otis Pierce, Sept. 10, 1876.
3338. Emma, bo. Aug. 28, 1860; ma. Charles Pierce, April 11, 1879.

(2654)　　Guilford S. Ladd, of Charlestown, (son of Daniel,[1328]) ma. Frances M. Gilman, dau. of John and Sarah (Coffin) Gilman, of Deerfield, N. H.

Children.

3339. Frances A., bo. July 11, 1853.
3340. Frederick G., bo. April 17, 1855.
3341. Nellie F., bo. Aug. 12, 1860.
3342. Frank A., bo. Nov. 7, 1862.

(2655) Reuben E. Ladd (son of Daniel[1828]) ma. Anna Eldred, Dec. 28, 1853.

Children.

3343. Clarence H., bo. Oct. 9, 1855; ma. Anna G. Pierce, July 13, 1875.
3344. George W., bo. Dec. 1, 1857; ma. Mary E. Kelley, July 13, 1879.
3345. Emma A., bo. May 19, 1859.
3346. Charles S., bo. Aug. 14, 1860; ma. Sarah Demoranville, July 13, 1879.
3347. Isabel, bo. May 23, 1863.
3348. Willie E., bo. Nov. 29, 1865.
3349. Lorenzo E., bo. July 1, 1868.
3350. Nettie M., bo. Nov. 17, 1870.
3351. Blanche M., bo. Feb. 10, 1873.
3352. Reuben E., bo. Sept. 16, 1875.

(2661) Jonathan P. Ladd, of Meredith, N. H., (son of Asa,[1829]) ma. Anna Harris, of Boston.

Children.

3353. Emma Frances, bo. 1854; ma. Martin Taber.
3354. Clara Bell, bo. 1857; ma. John Flanry.
3355. Horace Parker, bo. June 5, 1860.
3356. John Plumer, bo. April 24, 1874; d. Sept. 27, 1882.

(2686) Noah Ladd (son of Timothy[1832]) ma. Caroline Ellen, dau. of Thomas and Ann Newcomb, Feb. 9, 1861.

Children.

3357. Alice Stuart, bo. July, 1862.
3358. Charles Dexter, bo. Oct. 1864.
3359. Edward Everett, bo. 1867.
3360. Arthur Clifton, bo. 1870.

(2693) Thomas Franklin Ladd, of North Easton, (son of Ansel,[1836]) ma. Wealthy J. Ford, Jan. 1, 1865.

Children.

3361. Nellie, bo. March 6, 1866; d. young.
3362. Charles E., bo. Feb. 19, 1868.
3363. Herbert F., bo. Feb. 1870; d. Oct. 2, 1870.
3364. ——, bo. Feb. 7, 1872; d. before it was named.
3365. Addie May, bo. May 8, 1874; d. Jan. 3, 1876.
3366. Freddie J., bo. Dec. 5, 1877; d. Dec. 5, 1877.
3367. Everett B., bo. June 15, 1879; d. Nov. 3, 1879.
3368. Levi D., bo. Aug. 8, 1881; d. Oct. 16, 1881.

(2699) Francis Warren Ladd, of Brockton, (son of Warren,[1837]) ma. Martha M., dau. of William and Clara (Pike) Thurston, March 19, 1846.

Children.

3369. Lilly May, bo. July 15, 1867.
3370. Freddie Warren, bo. Oct. 9, 1871.
3371. George, bo. Aug. 17, 1877.
3372. Nellie, bo. Aug. 18, 1878.

(2727) George Ladd, of Mt. Vernon, Me., (son of Reuben,[1339]) ma. Etta Whittier.

Children.

3373. Georgianna, bo. ——.
3374. Eva, bo. ——.

(2733) Frank J. Ladd, of Lowell, (son of Jonathan,[1358]) ma. Ella P. Clifford, April 7, 1869.

Child.

3375. Clifford W., bo. June 9, 1871.

(2515) William Oscar Ladd, of Derry, N. H., (son of Horatio H.,[1158]) ma. Ada M. Currier.

Child.

3376. Julia F., bo. ——.

(2888) Hale Ladd, of Boston, (son of William,[1810]) ma. Betsey M. Wilbur.

Child.

3377. Sherman W., bo. Sept. 25, 1857.

(2889) Ruel W. Ladd, of Ashland, N. H., formerly of Holderness, (son of William,[1810]) ma. Feb. 3, 1857, Elizabeth C., dau. of Dr. Samuel and Mary Ann (Webster) Wright. He died Dec. 1849.

Children.

3378. Maria F., bo. Sept. 11, 1859; ma. Dr. S. F. Quimby, April 8, 1883.
3379. Adilla C., bo. March 9, 1866.

(2891) Herman W. Ladd, of Boston, (son of Jesse,[1815]) was born in Holderness, N. H., Nov. 6, 1837. Is a manufacturer of spring beds in Boston. He ma. Fannie E., dau. of Nathan and Aphia Davidson, June 2, 1867.

Children.

3380. Aphia Fannie, bo. Aug. 4, 1868.
3381. Herman Dexter, bo. Sept. 16, 1873.
3382. George Raymond, bo. Nov. 26, 1874.
3383. Franklin Howard, bo. Aug. 3, 1876; d. July, 1877.

3384. Rosa Florence, bo. Nov. 1, 1877.
3385. James Arad, bo. Feb. 1, 1879.
3386. Perley T. D., bo. Feb. 12, 1881.

(2901)   John Ladd (son of Stephen [1818]) ma. Hannah Prescott.

Children.

3387. William, bo. 1858.
3388. John, bo. 1861.

(2902)   Albert Ladd, of Clinton, (son of Stephen,[1818]) ma. Jane Sherwell, 1850. She died March, 1852, and he ma. 2d, Esther Scribner. She died Feb. 20, 1855, and he ma 3d, Eliza Ames, 1857.

Child.

3389. Jane Alberta, bo. March 7, 1851.

Child by second wife.

3390. Ella Alberta, bo. Aug. 31, 1854.

Child by third wife.

3391. George Ellis, bo. Dec. 6, 1859.

(2903)   Stephen H. Ladd, of Plaistow, N. H., (son of Stephen,[1818]) removed to Union City, Randolph Co., Ind.; ma. Harriet Bryant. Was divorced, and ma. 2d, Sarah Howes, July 1, 1856.

Children by second wife.

3392. Ida, bo. March 30, 1858; ma. Heman S. Coates, July 2, 1875.
3393. Verria, bo. March 29, 1861.
3394. Rosa, bo. June 18, 1863.
3395. May, bo. May 9, 1867; d. June 9, 1869.
3396. Henry, bo. July 24, 1870.
3397. Maud, bo. Oct. 20, 1871.
3398. Walter, bo. Aug. 24, 1874.

(2907)   Nathaniel Ladd, of Lawrence, (son of Stephen,[1818]) ma. Bell Johnson.

Children.

3399. Lillie, bo. Aug. 22, 1865.
3400. Gertie, bo. June 24, 1867.
3401. Mabel, bo. May 20, 1870.

(2936)   Dr. Henry W. Ladd, of Newport, Me., (son of Dr. Calvin B.,[1829]) ma. Lucy A. Locking, of Lowell, Oct. 12, 1866. He died Oct. 1, 1873.

Child.

3402. Edith P., bo. Sept. 17, 1870.

(2939)   Horace P. Ladd, of Portland, Me., (son of Newell H.,[1833]) ma. Mary Ann, dau. of Samuel Brown, June 15, 1875.

Children.

3403. Anna Rowena, bo. July 18, 1876.
3404. Florence Dunham, bo. April 7, 1878.
3405. Helen Willard, bo. June 20, 1880.

(2824)   John C. Ladd, of Laconia, N. H., (son of John Lyford,[1698]) ma. Hannah L. Taylor, April, 1854.

Children.

3406. Helen A., bo. Sept. 18, 1855.
3407. Ellen M., bo. Sept. 18, 1855.
3408. Ida N., bo. July 28, 1857.
3409. Emma J., bo. May 25, 1860.
3410. Cora E., bo. May 23, 1864.
3411. Emma F., bo. Feb. 11, 1871.

(2829)   Thomas E. Ladd, of Kansas City, Mo., (son of John Lyford,[1698]) ma. Emma Plummer, 1864.

Children.

3412. Walter L., bo. 1868.
3413. Adelia B., bo. 1872.

(2250)   Leonard Worcester Ladd, of Medina, Ohio, (son of Edward,[1882]) ma. Lewellen Clapp, Jan. 9, 1858.

Children.

3414. Leonard William, bo. March 25, 1859; ma. Ella Gunn, April 13, 1881.
3415. George Wooster, bo. Feb. 2, 1861.

(2260)   Clark H. Ladd, of Berlin Falls, N. H., (son of Joseph,[1884]) ma. Susan C. Mason, Jan. 20, 1846.

Children.

3416. Amelia S., bo. Feb. 26, 1847; ma. William Sheaf, Aug. 20, 1865.
3417. Seth W., bo. Oct. 6, 1848; ma. Lizzie Winslow, June 3, 1873.
3418. Mary J., bo. Sept. 22, 1850.
3419. Eleanor, bo. Nov. 5, 1852; ma. Charles A. Sterling, Jan. 14, 1874.
3420. Martha J., bo. Aug. 20, 1854; ma. Amos Smith, Dec. 1874.
3421. Lizzie C., bo. Aug. 16, 1857; ma. Franklin C. Dunham, July 1, 1878.
3422. Flora B., bo. June 16, 1859; ma. Frank Bigelow, Aug. 18, 1880.
3423. Abbie L., bo. March 23, 1861.
3424. John F., bo. April 3, 1863; ma. Mary McKenly, July 1, 1884.
3425. Nellie G., bo. March 20, 1865.
3426. Luther H., bo. Aug. 25, 1867.

(2262) Luther Ladd, of Island Pond, Vt., (son of Joseph,[1884]) ma. Martha Ewell, Feb. 7, 1855.

Children.

3427. Martin B., bo. Dec. 7, 1855; ma. Lillian Morse, June 7, 1878.
3428. Hattie M., bo. Oct. 27, 1862; ma. A. O. Dechene, Dec. 12, 1882.
3429. Harry J., bo. Oct. 1, 1869.

(2978) George W. Ladd, of Franklin, N. H., (son of George W.,[1685]) ma. Irene Flanders.

Children.

3430. Mary, bo. Nov. 1867.
3431. Joseph, bo. July, 1870.

(2981) Joseph Ladd, of Concord, N. H., (son of George W.,[1685]) ma. Luella Sanborn, Dec. 7, 1865.

Child.

3432. Edgar Joseph, bo. Dec. 14, 1866; d. young.

(2984) Harrison Ladd, of Franklin, N. H., (son of George W.,[1685]) ma. Hattie Call, Jan. 29, 1877.

Children.

3433. Allen Warren, bo. May 25, 1879.
3434. Newell Herbert, bo. Feb. 13, 1883.
3435. Daniel Barnard, bo. Jan. 20, 1885.
3436. Alice Abbie, bo. Jan. 19, 1887.

(2458) Simeon Ladd, of Brewer, Me., (son of Thomas,[1106]) ma. Alice M. Eaton, Oct. 28, 1879.

Children.

3437. Carrie May, bo. April 24, 1881.
3438. Clinton M., bo. Aug. 19, 1884.
3439. ———, bo. Feb. 22, 1888.

(2707) Albert J. Ladd, of Deerfield, N. H., (son of Andrew,[1877]) ma. Elvira Harris, April 11, 1850. He was a carpenter and millwright.

Children.

3440. Alando F., bo. July 17, 1852; ma. Mary Susan Kiniston, Dec. 24, 1877.
3441. Bert S., bo. May 14, 1857.
3442. Paulena, bo. June 28, 1863.
3443. Ernest E., bo. Dec. 8, 1868.

(2708) Freeman P. Ladd, of Lansing, Iowa, (son of Andrew,[1377]) ma. Mary A. Alexander. He is a carpenter and millwright.

Child.

3444. Andrew Grant, bo. 1864.

(2735) William M. Ladd, of Concord, N. H., (son of Artemas,[1389]) ma. Susan M. Abbott, March 26, 1860.

Child.

3445. Susie M., bo. June 26, 1864; ma. Asa J. Stafford, Oct. 27, 1881.

(1478) Timothy Fellows Ladd, of White Hall, Ill., (son of Timothy,[825]) ma. Sallie A. Avery, Dec. 18, 1860. He was elected mayor of White Hall, April 16, 1889.

Child.

3446. Charles Franklin, bo. May 11, 1867.

(1542) Edward N. Ladd, of Brattleboro, Vt., (son of Emery,[1408]) ma. Nellie R. Reynolds, of Brattleboro, Vt., April 2, 1861.

Children.

3447. William R., bo. Oct. 1, 1864.
3448. Isabel Emery, bo. Dec. 11, 1875.

(1543) Constantine F. Volney Ladd (son of Emery[1408]) ma. Abby Jane, dau. of John Henry and Harriet S. Clark, Jan. 15, 1863. She died Feb. 1, 1867, and he ma. 2d, Oct. 9, 1868, Ida M., dau. of Charles D. and Emily A. (Badeau) Loomas, who was born in Maryland, Oswego Co., N. Y., Sept. 4, 1850.

Children.

3449. Jennie H., bo. July 17, 1864.
3450. Frank J., bo. Feb. 1, 1867.

Child by second wife.

3451. Lena Blanche, bo. Nov. 6, 1869.

(3157) William Franklin Ladd, of San Francisco, Cal., (son of John,[1986]) ma. Anna Morris Zabriskie, Dec. 5, 1861. He died Aug. 15, 1877.

Children.

3452. Anna Laura, bo. Sept. 1, 1862; ma. Hume Yesington, of Carson City, Nevada.
3453. Frank Zabriskie, bo. Nov. 24, 1863.
3454. Mary Morris, bo. May 9, 1866.

3455. Louis Dudley, bo. June 1, 1867.
3456. Sarah Frances, bo. Dec. 20, 1868.

(3158) John Edwards Ladd, of Sydney, N. S. W., (son of John,[1966]) ma. Frances Maria Diana Wilkins, May 13, 1876.

Children.

3457. Eva Frances Marian, bo. March 19, 1877.
3458. Leslie Edward William, bo. Oct. 20, 1883.

(3099) Charles H. Ladd, of Menomonee, Wis., (son of Henry Clay,[2284]) ma. Kate H. Winston, April 26, 1880.

Child.

3459. Grace J., bo. Aug. 21, 1881.

(3100) William B. Ladd, of St. Paul, Minn., (son of Henry Clay,[2284]) ma. Cora E. Gatley, Feb. 5, 1882.

Child.

3460. Rolla E., bo. Feb. 14, 1883.

(3122) George W. Ladd, of Roxbury, (son of George B. V.,[2041]) ma. Alice F. Watson, June 27, 1885.

Child.

3461. Lester W., bo. June 4, 1886.

(3033) Andrew J. Ladd, of East Roxbury, Vt., (son of Alphonso,[1457]) ma. Lucy Wilson, March 4, 1867.

Children.

3462. Lucy Adella, bo. Feb. 11, 1871.
3463. Avery Sanders, bo. Nov. 17, 1872.
3464. Mary Alma, bo. Jan. 15, 1874.
3465. Addie, bo. Aug. 8, 1878.
3466. John Parsons, bo. May 17, 1882.
3467. Mabel Viola, bo. May 11, 1884.
3468. Clyde Albert, bo. Aug. 28, 1886.

(3173) George W. Ladd, of Bradford, Vt., (son of Willard,[2232]) ma. Sarah E. Smith, April 7, 1880.

Child.

3469. Willard Elmer, bo. Feb. 12, 1881.

(3178) Lafayette Ladd, of Summerville, Vt., (son of John,²²³³) ma. Annellor Houghton, Dec. 22, 1881.

Child.

3470. Angelina R., bo. April 21, 1882.

(3106) Lewis E. Ladd, of Cranbury Isle, Me., (son of Rufus Bailey,²³⁰⁶) ma. Clara E. Gilley, Jan. 1, 1875.

Children.

3471. Lena E., bo. July 31, 1876; d. Aug. 9, 1876.
3472. A son, bo. Feb. 21, 1879; d. Feb. 23, 1879.
3473. Lena M., bo. Dec. 21, 1882.
3474. Alfred E., bo. Nov. 17, 1887.

(1963) William Fowle Ladd, of Galveston, Texas, (son of Charles Haven,¹⁵⁹²) was born at Portsmouth, N. H., Aug. 31, 1845; ma. in New York, June 12, 1877, Caroline, youngest daughter of Peter James Willis, Esq., deceased, former head of the leading commercial house of P. J. Willis & Brother, of Galveston, Tex. He went first to the private school of R. J. Ambler, Esq., in Fauquier Co., Virginia, and from there, in 1862, to Phillips' Exeter Academy, at Exeter, N. H., and in 1864 to Norwich University, the military school at Norwich, Vt. He went to Europe early in 1865, and continued his education in Dresden and Paris for the next two years. In 1867 he was consular clerk at Zurich, Switzerland, and was for a short time acting consul. He returned home in the Fall of that year, and soon afterwards began his business education in the banking-house of Messrs. Winslow, Lanier & Co., in New York. In 1869 he went to Galveston with his uncle, Alexander H. Ladd, who was purchasing agent for several of the leading New England cotton mills, succeeding him on his retirement in 1874. He is now (1889) head of the house of Wm. F. Ladd & Co., and a member of the exporting firm of Byrne, Ladd & Spencer. He is also president of the Taylor Compress Co., vice-president of the Galveston Cotton Exchange, secretary and treasurer of the Galveston Bagging & Cordage Co., a director in the Texas Land & Loan Co., and prominent in other business enterprises. *Pres. Chamber of Commerce.*

Children.

3475. Charles Haven, bo. Dec. 2, 1879. *Harvard 1900.*
3476. Margaret Sealy, bo. Feb. 3, 1881.
3477. Carolyn Willis, bo. April 19, 1884.
3478. William Fowle, bo. Sept. 15, 1885.

Frederick Chester bo. July 15, 1890
John VanRensaellar bo. July 7, 1894.

525) John Ladd (son of Nathaniel[96]) ma. ——.

Child.

3479. William, bo. ——, at Mt. Vernon, Me.; ma. Sarah Stevens.

(3479) William Ladd, of Mt. Vernon, Me., (son of John,[525]) ma. Sarah Stevens. He settled on Lot 22, then on Lot 21, and removed from Mt. Vernon, Me., to Industry, Me., in 1798.

Children.

3480. Samuel, bo. Aug. 10, 1793; ma. Mary P. Quimby, Dec. 1817.
3481. William, bo. Aug. 9, 1795; ma. Lucy Morrill, Nov. 20, 1817.
3482. John E., bo. Sept. 10, 1800; ma. Mehitable Quimby, Nov. 29, 1821.
3483. Eben, bo. Dec. 19, 1801; ma. Sylvia L. Landers.
3484. Hannah, bo. ——; ma. Jacob Quimby.
3485. Isaac, bo. ——; ma. Sarah Kent. No children.
3486. Stephen, bo. ——; ma. Maria Hapgood.

(3480) Samuel Ladd, of Stark, Me., (son of William,[3479]) ma. Mary P. Quimby, Dec. 1817.

Children.

3487. Sarah E., bo. Nov. 9, 1818; ma. John Batchellor.
3488. John Colby, bo. Aug. 13, 1821; ma. Sophronia W. Atkins, Oct. 17, 1847.
3489. Daniel P., bo. Jan. 26, 1824; ma. Eliza C. Chase.
3490. James T., bo. July 4, 1827; ma. Catherine Orr, Feb. 14, 1851.
3491. Horace B., bo. Nov. 11, 1829; not married.
3492. Manley S., bo. May 16, 1831; d. 1838.
3493. Harriet, bo. May 15, 1833.
3494. Rose C., bo. Sept. 11, 1837.

(3482) John E. Ladd, of Stark, Me., (son of William,[3479]) ma. Mehitable Quimby, Nov. 29, 1821.

Children.

3495. Mary J., bo. Jan. 26, 1826; ma. James W. Hinckley, Jan. 23, 1850.
3496. William, bo. Jan. 16, 1828; ma. Sylvia Ladd (3502,) Jan. 14, 1855.
3497. Sarah K., bo. Sept. 11, 1830; ma. A. Q. Folsom, April 6, 1852.
3498. John, bo. May 31, 1832; ma. Rosella Locke, Feb. 18, 1859.
3499. Amy D., bo. March 29, 1836; ma. Daniel Locke, Jan. 21, 1858.
3500. Lizzie, bo. Aug. 13, 1837; ma. James Taylor, Oct. 1859.

(3483) Eben Ladd, of Stark, Me., (son of William,[3479]) ma. Sylvia L. Landers, Jan. 2, 1825. He died Sept. 29, 1850.

Children.

3501. George T., bo. Nov. 16, 1826; ma. Sarah H. Chandler, Aug. 14, 1856.
3502. Lucy A., bo. Sept. 22, 1829; ma. Nathaniel R. Gilman, April, 1849.

3503. Lizzie, bo. Aug. 8, 1831; ma. Lyman Cheney.
3504. Sylvia, bo. Jan. 14, 1833; ma. William Ladd (3496,) Jan. 14, 1855.
3505. Augusta, bo. Jan. 22, 1835: ma. Daniel Gilman. Children: [1]Alice, bo. Jan. 14, 1854; [2]Alvin, bo. June 13, 1855; [3]Nellie, bo. Oct. 14, 1856; [4]Minnie L., bo. Feb. 21, 1859; [5]Frank, bo. Oct. 6, 1860; [6]Edwin J., bo. Feb. 6, 1864; [7]Fred A., bo. Sept. 2, 1865; [8]Russell A., bo. March 9, 1867; [9]Carrie M., bo. Feb. 4, 1869; [10]Della M., bo. Jan. 1, 1871; [11]Georgie E., bo. Aug. 30, 1874; [12]Lettie S., bo. Aug. 23, 1878.
3506. Ellen D., bo. Feb. 7, 1838; ma. Fayette Vaughn.
3507. Alvan L., bo. May 14, 1840; ma. Helen Bigelow Skinner.
3508. Leonard Murch, bo. Oct. 16, 1842; ma. Theresa Maria Baxter.
3509. Eben S., bo. March 6, 1845; ma. Octavia F. Viles, 1876.
3510. Carrie M., bo. July 25, 1847; ma. George Boswell, 1868.
3511. Mary D., bo. Sept. 9, 1850; ma. Sidney Watson, Dec. 22, 1868.

(3489)　Daniel P. Ladd, of Stark, Me., (son of Samuel,[3480]) ma. Eliza C. Chase, May 2, 1868.

Children.

3512. Frank R., bo. Oct. 6, 1860.
3513. Charles H., bo. Nov. 5, 1867.
3514. Hattie M., bo. Aug. 13, 1875.

(3496)　William Ladd, of Athens, Me., (son of John E.,[3482]) ma. Sylvia Ladd,[3504] Jan. 14, 1855.

Children.

3515. Charles M., bo. Feb. 21, 1857.
3516. Emma B., bo. Nov. 17, 1860, in Athens, Me.
3517. Nellie A., bo. Oct. 8, 1864, in Athens, Me.

(3498)　John Ladd, of Stark, Me., (son of John E.,[3482]) ma. Rosella Locke, Feb. 18, 1859.

Children.

3518. Edwin Fremont, bo. Dec. 3, 1859.
3519. Cora B., bo. July 18, 1861.
3520. Franklin P., bo. Oct. 13, 1865.
3521. Willie S., bo. Aug. 12, 1867; d. April 17, 1868.
3522. Herbert William, bo. Sept. 30, 1870.
3523. Clara M., bo. Dec. 26, 1873.
3524. Forrest D., bo. Nov. 28, 1880; d. Sept. 21, 1883.

(3501)　George T. Ladd, of Stark, Me., (son of Eben,[3483]) ma. Sarah H. Chandler, Aug. 14, 1856.

Children.

3525. Ida May, bo. Feb. 3, 1858; ma. F. O. Nasbe, Dec. 30, 1880.
3526. Lizzie E., bo. April 4, 1860; ma. Robert J. Diffin, Aug. 18, 1878.

3527. Lottie H., bo. Feb. 26, 1862; ma. Charles E. Willis, April, 1880.
3528. Florilla P., bo. July 3, 1865.

(507) Alvan Landers Ladd, of Stark, Me., (son of Eben,[3488]) ma. Helen Bigelow Skinner, of Milwaukee, Wis.

Children.

3529. Leoline Cornelia, bo. March 8, 1869.
3530. Henry Leonard, bo. Oct. 22, 1870.
3531. Howard Moody, bo. May 25, 1873.
3532. Hermone Clark, bo. Jan. 19, 1876.
3533. Belden Louise, bo. July 9, 1877.
3534. Warna Susan, bo. May 26, 1879.
3535. Helen Dyer, bo. May 6, 1881.
3536. Alva Chapman, bo. Sept. 20, 1884.

(508) Leonard Murch Ladd, of Holster, San Beneto Co., Cal., (son of Eben,[3488]) ma. Therzia Maria Baxter.

Children.

3537. Frank Benjamin, bo. Aug. 8, 1872.
3538. Manor Metcalf, bo. Feb. 20, 1874.
3539. Lewellyn Elder, bo. Sept. 6, 1878.
3540. Karl Leonard, bo. May 5, 1881.
3541. Ida May, bo. July 27, 1883.

(509) Eben S. Ladd, of Industry, Me., (son of Eben,[3488]) ma. Octavia F. Viles, 1876.

Child.

3542. Carleton, bo. May 26, 1880.

(3104) William Herman Ladd (son of Daniel[2801]) ma. Azelle Randolph, of Veazie, Me., Nov. 3, 1887.

Child.

3543. Eva Azelle, bo. Jan. 18, 1889.

(518) Luther Manning Ladd, of Bozrah, Conn., (son of Darius,[170]) ma. Wealthy B. Eames.

Children.

3544. Darius, bo. ——.
3545. Lucy Ann, bo. ——.
3546. Freelove, bo. ——.
3547. Miranda, bo. ——.
3548. Eliza, bo. ——.
3549. Mary L., bo. ——; ma. Charles E. Hunt.
3550. Hattie, bo. ——.
3551. Eldridge, bo. ——.
3552. Edwin, bo. ——.

(908)　William Huse Ladd, of Newburyport, (son of Daniel,[378]) ma. Sally Lane in 1843. She died in 1848 without issue, and he ma. 2d, Mrs. Harriet (Colby) Brown, in 1850. He d. in 1876.

Children.

3553. William, bo. 1852; d. 1872.
3554. William, bo. 1873; d. 1875.

(3274)　Francois Joseph Gall Ladd, (son of Daniel Watson,[2217]) ma. Ella M. Byrt, Dec. 23, 1879.

Children.

3555. Arthur Watson, bo. March 2, 1881.
3556. John Savilian, bo. Nov. 29, 1882.
3557. Emma Mabel, bo. Sept. 9, 1886.

(3275)　John Savilian Ladd (son of Daniel Watson,[2217]) ma. Rose Doolittle, May 24, 1881.

Child.

3558. Ralph Simpson, bo. May 3, 1885; d. Nov. 23, 1885.

(1148)　Lorenzo Dow Ladd, of Unity, N. H., (son of Rev. Moses,[698]) ma. Laura Dunnel.

Children.

3559. Elizabeth, bo. ——.
3560. Hannah, bo. ——.

(1149)　Philander Ladd, of Unity, N. H., (son of Rev. Moses,[698]) ma. Ruth W. Adams.

Children.

3561. A son, bo. April 22, 1842; lived nine hours.
3562. A daughter, bo. April 22, 1842; d. May 9, 1842.
3563. Moses, bo. ——.
3564. George, bo. ——. } Twins.
3565. Jennie, bo. ——.

(1134)　James Monroe Ladd, of Unity, N. H., (son of Noah,[690]) ma. Sarah Graves, March 23, 1842. He was born in Unity, N. H., June 1, 1818, where his youth and early manhood was spent. He was engaged in teaching school and working at his trade, shoemaking. In 1856 he moved to Knox Co., Ill., and engaged in farming. In 1881 he removed to Albion, Neb., where his children had preceded him. In 1878 a gradual paralysis of his left side began, growing continually worse until his death, March 11, 1889.

Children.

3566. Monroe Jefferson, bo. June 15, 1850; ma. Mary Elizabeth Carden. April 2, 1874.
3567. Wallace Wingate, bo. Jan. 1, 1854; ma. Mary Margaret Liddell, Nov. 28, 1878.
3568. Arthur Washington, bo. Aug. 24, 1855; d. April 12, 1857.
3569. Arthur Washington, bo. July 29, 1858; ma. Amy Isola Fox, Sept. 29, 1886.

(3566) Monroe Jefferson Ladd, of Albion, Neb., (son of James Monroe,[1134]) was born in Unity, N. H., June 15, 1850. In 1856 he moved with his parents to Oneida, Knox Co., Ill.; attended county and town schools; was of a mechanical turn of mind, and was engaged in saw mills, planing mills, pump factories, &c. In 1882 he removed to Albion, Neb., and engaged in the furniture business. He ma. Mary Elizabeth Carden, at Bushwell, Ill., April 2, 1874.

Children.

3570. James Emery, bo. Dec. 15, 1875.
3571. George Allen, bo. Oct. 5, 1877.
3572. Arthur Monroe, bo. April 23, 1879.

(3567) Wallace Wingate Ladd, of Albion, Neb., (son of James Monroe,[1134]) was born in Unity, N. H., Jan. 1, 1854. In 1856 he removed with his parents to Oneida, Knox Co., Ill.; was educated in the town and county schools; learned telegraphing and followed it a few years; also learned the blacksmith's trade, and was engaged in farming. In 1882 he removed to Albion, Neb., where he was engaged in the book and stationery trade. He ma. Nov. 28, 1878, Mary Margaret Liddell.

Children.

3573. Wallace Ward, bo. April 10, 1880.
3574. Thomas Spencer, bo. Nov. 1, 1881.
3575. James Oscar, bo. Jan. 15, 1887.

(3569) Arthur Washington Ladd, of Albion, Neb., (son of James Monroe,[1134]) was born at Oneida, Knox Co., Ill., July 29, 1858. He was educated in the district and town schools; learned the printer's trade, and in 1876 established the Oneida News, a weekly paper, at Oneida, Knox Co., Ill., which he published three years. In 1879 he removed to Albion, Boom Co., Neb., and commenced the publication of the Albion Weekly News, of which he is now editor and proprietor. Sept. 29, 1886, he ma. Amy Isola Fox. No children in 1889.

(428) Anson Ladd, of Chittenden, Vt., (son of Nathaniel,[139]) ma. Harriet Baird, of Chittenden, Vt. She died Feb. 1813, and he ma. 2d, Betsey Riddell.

Children.

3576. Dexter, bo. Dec. 9. 1810; not married; d. at Avon, N. Y.
3577. Austin, bo. Nov. 9, 1812; ma. Luenda Sowle, Feb. 6, 1839.

Children by second wife.

3578. Harriet, bo. Dec. 9, 1815.
3579. Anson F., bo. June 7, 1817.
3580. Alfred, bo. March 22, 1819; ma. Betsey Fish, 1865.
3581. William Edward, bo. May 17, 1821; ma. Cynthia Sales; 2d, Sophia Vail.
3582. Charles, bo. Aug. 25, 1823; ma. Maggie Birce, Nov. 18. 1866.
3583. Fannie, bo. Aug. 25, 1825; ma. Vernon Tibs.
3584. Melissa J., bo. May 18, 1827.
3585. Angel S., bo. July 6, 1829; ma. Charles Hall.
3586. Wallace E., bo. Aug. 3, 1831; ma. Annis Fish.
3587. Jennie M., bo. July 6, 1833; ma. John Tulard, Sept. 18, 1858.
3588. Sidney V., bo. March 15, 1837.

(3577) Austin Ladd, of North Dorset, Vt., (son of Anson,[428]) ma. Luenda Sowle, of Dorset, Vt., Feb. 6, 1839. She d. Aug. 6, 1881.

Children.

3589. Melissa Jane, bo. June 17, 1841; m. E. N. Streeter, 1857. She d. Oct. 18, 1877.
3590. Sidney Anson, bo. April 2, 1843; ma. Maggie Bovie, July 25, 1869.
3591. Allen Dexter, bo. Nov. 17, 1845; ma. Maggie Frost, Nov. 1, 1880.
3592. Fannie C., bo. Nov. 22, 1847; ma. W. W. Marshall.

(2363) Walter C. Ladd, of Weeping Water, Neb., (son of Charles Green,[966]) ma. Genevra T. Oviatt, dau. of William C. and Pamelia Oviatt.

Children.

3593. Charles O., bo. Dec. 26, 1871.
3594. Williston H., bo. Oct. 6, 1873.
3595. Emma H., bo. June 27, 1878.
3596. Henry M. bo. May 27, 1880; d. Oct. 1, 1880.

(121) Timothy Ladd, of Chesterfield, N. H., (son of Timothy,[37]) ma. Rachel Spencer, May 7, 1761. She died Oct. 25, 1818.

He died Aug. 30, 1834. He purchased land in Chesterfield, Lot No. 3, on Range 11, July 30, 1765. About 1777 he appears to have settled on what has long been known as the Ladd farm, and which was, or at least a part of it, Lot No. 5 in the 12th Range. He was a member of the board of selectmen in 1771-72.

Children.

3597. Esther, bo. Sept. 26, 1762; ma. Jacob Amidon. She d. Mar. 26, 1852.
3598. Abigail, bo. Feb. 19, 1765; ma. Oliver Atherton.
3599. Zebulon, bo. Oct. 10, 1767.
3600. Rachel, bo. May 27, 1770; not married; d. June 21, 1790.
3601. Timothy, bo. Feb. 22, 1773.
3602. Pascal, bo. July 3, 1779; d. Aug. 1, 1792.

(285) Daniel Ladd, of Unity, N. H., (son of Daniel,[89]) ma. Mary, dau. of James Philbrick, of Deerfield, N. H. He removed from Deerfield, N. H., to Unity, N. H., with his brothers James and Nathaniel, and was killed by the fall of a tree he was cutting down.

Child.

3603. Daniel, bo. Aug. 31, 1773; ma. Betsey Dennett, Nov. 12, 1801. After the death of Daniel (285) his widow, Mrs. Mary (Philbrick) Ladd ma. Israel Folsom, of Tamworth, N. H., in 1777. Her children by Mr. Folsom were: [1]John, bo. May 22, 1778, ma. Sally Johnson; [2]Mary, bo. Dec. 15, 1779, ma. David Moulton; [3]David, bo. Dec. 20, 1781, ma. Hannah Philbrick; [4]Sarah, bo. Feb. 7, 1784, d. April 22, 1784; [5]Joseph, bo. March 7, 1785, d. 1804; [6]James, bo. May 6, 1787, ma. James Bryor; [7]Nancy, bo. March 23, 1789, ma. David Moulton; [8]Stephen Philbrick, bo. May 23, 1791, ma. Hannah Mudgett.

(3603) Daniel Ladd, of Levant, Me., (son of Daniel,[285]) ma. Betsey Dennett, Nov. 12, 1801. He died July 30, 1843.

Children.

3604. Mary P., bo. April 11, 1803; ma. David Boyed, 1822. Children: [1]Betsey Jane, [2]Nancy Maria, [3]Daniel L., [4]Elvira M., [5]David, Jr., [6]Simon Harriman, [7]Cynthia Ann, [8]Rachel, [9]Mary Ruth.
3605. Eliza D., bo. Aug. 4, 1805; ma. Simon B. Harriman, Oct. 5, 1834. Children: [1]Simon, [2]George Washington, [3]Abbie H., [4]Simon Alonzo, [5]Charles.
3606. Jacob D., bo. April 18, 1808; ma. Laura Patten, Aug. 6, 1833.
3607. Elvira, bo. July 13, 1810; ma. Sanford C. Fling, Feb. 11, 1834. Children: [1]Ann Elizabeth, [2]Fred. A. H., [3]Frances T., [4]Lucy Pickering, [5]Fred. Warren, [6]Catharine M. G.

3608. Sally, bo. July 4, 1812; ma. George W. Washburn, Dec. 15, 1833. Children: ¹Cyrus A., ²Eliza Ann, ³Horace B., ⁴Adeline M., ⁵M. Estella, ⁶Emma A., ⁷George W.
3609. Daniel T., bo. Oct. 14, 1814; d. May 23, 1815.
3610. Daniel, Jr., bo. April 27, 1816; ma. Betsey M. Cowan. Dec. 18, 1842.
3611. Abigail F., bo. July 17, 1818; d. Aug. 23, 1819.
3612. Cyrus K., bo. May 22, 1820; ma. Mary R. Phillips, Dec. 6, 1843.
3613. Nancy M., bo. March 7, 1824; d. Sept. 16, 1833.

(3606) Jacob D. Ladd, of Kenduskeag, Me., (son of Daniel,[3608]) ma. Laura Patten, Aug. 6, 1833. He died Nov. 1864.

Children.

3614. Charles D., bo. July 5, 1836. Supposed to have been lost at sea.
3615. Frances H., bo. Nov. 13, 1837; ma. William H. Kempton.
3616. Warren Scott, bo. July 3, 1839; d. at Yorktown, Va., June 2, 1862.
3617. Martha J., bo. July 21, 1840; ma. Joseph V. Rocklyft.
3618. Fred. Leroy, bo. April 16, 1842; ma. Cappilia Maud Hayes, March 30, 1871.
3619. Daniel, bo. Nov. 1844; d. in infancy.

(3610) Daniel Ladd, Jr., of Waterbury, Conn., (son of Daniel,[3608]) ma. Betsey S. Cowan, Dec. 18, 1842. He died Dec. 1880.

Children.

3620. James Thomas, bo. Oct. 24, 1843; ma. Margaret J. Leavenworth, Oct. 15, 1866.
3621. Henry Sanford, bo. Nov. 6, 1845; ma. Minnie A. Bierce, Nov. 6, 1871.
3622. Daniel Albert, bo. May 7, 1848; ma. Irene E. Gibbs, Aug. 15, 1871.
3623. Frank Orison, bo. April 20, 1850; ma. Josephine E. Allen, July 6, 1878.
3624. Estella B., bo. June 11, 1852.
3625. Willie F., bo. Oct. 1, 1854; d. April 11, 1855.
3626. Cora J., bo. Dec. 6, 1861.

(3612) Cyrus K. Ladd, of Portland, Me., (son of Daniel,[3608]) ma. Mary R. Phillips, Dec. 6, 1843. She died March 12, 1846, and he ma. 2d, Oct. 31, 1847, Susan, dau. of William and Susan (Mansell) Holt. He was educated at the public schools, and at the age of 14, in 1834, he accepted a position with a cousin, who was a merchant at Bangor, Me., where he remained until 1843, when he removed to Brewer, Me., and was there engaged in mercantile business, and was town clerk for several years. In 1853 he resigned his position of town clerk, and removed to Portland, Me., where he now (1890) resides. For two years he was a member of the common council, for four years a member of the board of assessors, and now holds the office of weigher and gauger. He is a prominent member of the Odd Fellows Association, and has held all the higher offices in that organization in the State of Maine. He died Jan. 23, 1891.

Child.

3627. Cyrus James, bo. Oct. 6, 1844; d. April 11, 1874.

Children by second wife.

3628. Sarah Elizabeth, bo. Aug. 12, 1848.
3629. Alfred Greeley, bo. April 2, 1851; ma. Jessie A. Sweat, Aug. 1, 1882.
3630. Nancy Maria, bo. April 2, 1851.
3631. Julia Ann, bo. Aug. 31, 1859.
3632. Rose Mary, bo. June 8, 1862.

3620) James Thomas Ladd, of Waterbury, Conn., (son of Daniel,[3610]) ma. Margaret J. Leavenworth, Oct. 15, 1866. He died Oct. 29, 1869.

Child.

3633. Fred. Thomas, bo. May 1, 1869.

3621) Henry Sanford Ladd, of Waterbury, Conn., (son of Daniel,[3610]) ma. Minnie A. Bierce, Nov. 6, 1871. He died July 12, 1876, and his widow ma. William A. Sawyer.

Child.

3634. Martha Burton, bo. July 5, 1872.

3622) Daniel Albert Ladd, of Newark, N. J., (son of Daniel,[3610]) ma. Irene E., dau. of Hiram and Elizabeth Gibbs. She died Dec. 8, 1884, and he ma. 2d, ——, but had no children by her. He ma. 3d, Emma S., dau. of Jacob and Elizabeth Barber. He was educated at Waterbury, Conn.; learned the machinist and tool-maker's trade; has been in the employ of Read & Ladd, button manufacturers, and with J. E. Hirsh & Co., and has been engaged in making buttons and jewelry and in manufacturing anodes for coloring and shading, and a new solution for removing green oxide from gold, and does gold plating by a new process.

Children.

3635. Irene Estella, bo. March 16, 1872; d. July 8, 1872, at Waterbury, Conn.
3636. William Albert, bo. Aug. 31, 1877, at Hoboken, N. J.; d. Dec. 1, 1884, at Newark, N. J.
3637. Rena Estella, bo. March 22, 1880, at Brooklyn, N. Y.

Child by third wife.

3638. Hazel Charlestine, bo. July 30, 1889, at Providence, R. I.

(3623)   Frank Orison Ladd, of Brooklyn, N. Y., (son of Daniel,[3610])
ma. Josephine E. Allen, July 6, 1878.

Child.

3639. Arthur Norton, bo. Nov. 29, 1879.

(3629)   Alfred Greeley Ladd, M. D., of Great Falls, Montana, (son of Cyrus K.,[3612]) ma. Jessie A. Sweat, Aug. 1, 1882. He graduated at Bowdoin College with the degree of A. B. in 1873, and from the medical department an M. D. in 1878.

Children.

3640. Margaret, bo. May 21, 1883.
3641. Greeley, bo. Aug. 26, 1885.

(2738)   Fredus Ladd, of Waterbury, Conn., (son of William,[1628]) ma. Eliza Maria Frink, June 9, 1844.

Children.

3642. Agnes, bo. Dec. 19, 1847; d. Oct. 5, 1856.
3643. Gertrude, bo. March 2, 1849; ma. Berclay L. Hinman, Sept. 21, 1871. She died Jan. 20, 1886.
3644. William Nelson, bo. Dec. 24, 1852; ma. Harriet Louisa Lowe, Sept. 5, 1878.
3645. Lizzie, bo. Feb. 12, 1859; d. Dec. 12, 1875.

(2740)   Merrill Ladd, of Chicago, Ill., (son of William,[1628]) ma. Harriet Louise, dau. of Eleazer and Mariana L. (Hovey) Litchfield, Oct. 22, 1849. He died May 10, 1881.

Children.

3646. Helen Louise, bo. Jan. 4, 1851; ma. Joseph C. Humphrey, June 25, 1872. Children: [1]Merrill Lucius, bo. April 8, 1874; [2]Frederick W. L., bo. April 2, 1876; [3]Helen Cleveland, bo. Nov. 9, 1886.
3647. Delia Cleveland, bo. Jan. 23, 1853; ma. Henry M. Banister, M. D., June 14, 1887. Child: Ruth Delia, bo. Jan. 19, 1889.
3648. Helen Cleveland, bo. Nov. 19, 1886.

(2741)   James Ellis Ladd, of Providence, R. I., (son of William,[1628]) ma. Eliza J. Warren, of Providence, R. I., 1851. He died Dec. 13, 1866.

Children.

3649. Alfred Warren, bo. Jan. 1, 1854; d. Sept. 1855.
3650. Julia Elizabeth, bo. April, 1856; d. 1859.
3651. Emma Sophy, bo. Nov. 1858; ma. James B. Brown, Nov. 1884.

486) Stephen Ladd, of Augusta, Me., (son of William,[3479]) ma. Maria Hapgood.

Children.

3652. Augustus A., bo. in Buffalo, N. Y., 1843; not married.
3653. Charles T., bo. Dec. 6, 1847; ma. Sarah F. Kimball, Nov. 29, 1886.

481) William Ladd, of Chelsea, Me., (son of William,[3479]) ma. Lucy Morrill. She died May 16, 1848, and he ma. 2d, Nancy B. Wheeler, Oct. 20, 1850.

Child.

3654. William F., bo. Nov. 27, 1851; ma. Ella F. Moody, Nov. 5, 1876.

282) Daniel Watson Ladd, of Epping, N. H., (son of Daniel W.,[2218]) ma. Grace Alma, dau. of Nicholas P. and Carrie Furber, July 11, 1888, and niece of Mrs. Capt. G. T. Ball, of Greeland, N. H. He was educated at the public schools and at Phillips Academy, Exeter, N. H., where he graduated in 1880. He then read law in the office of Chase & Streeter, Concord. N. H., but business in regard to his father's estate caused him to relinquish the study of law, and he returned home to Epping, where he now resides.

Child.

3655. Sarah Lydia, bo. Nov. 16, 1889.

1165) Leonard E. Ladd, of Philadelphia, Pa., (son of Aaron,[708]) ma. Ida May, dau. of John Q. Brown, Dec. 22, 1882.

Child.

3656. Mary Ethel, bo. June 30, 1887.

3488) John Colby Ladd, of Bangor, Me., (son of Samuel,[3480]) ma. Sophronia W. Atkins, Oct. 17, 1847. He died Dec. 30, 1882.

Children.

3657. John W., bo. Oct. 21, 1848; d. Dec. 30, 1856.
3658. Helen A., bo. Sept. 1, 1850; d. Nov. 28, 1881.
3659. Mary M., bo. Dec. 6, 1856; not ma. in 1890.
3660. Cora A., bo. March 26, 1860; d. Aug. 15, 1863.
3661. George E., bo. Sept. 13, 1862; d. Feb. 16, 1884.

(3582) Charles Ladd (son of Anson[428]) ma. Maggie Brice, Nov. 18, 1866.

Children.

3662. George A., bo. March 30, 1868.
3663. William, bo. Nov. 18, 1869.
3664. Frank R., bo. Sept. 12, 1877.

(3590) Sydney A. Ladd, of North Dorset, Vt., (son of Austin,[3577])
ma. Maggie Bovie, July 25, 1869.

Children.

3665. Frederick W., bo. Sept. 30, 1870.
3666. Clarence S., bo. Oct. 25, 1872.
3667. Morris E., bo. May 25, 1877.
3668. Alfred E., bo. June 16, 1883.

(3591) Allen Dexter Ladd, of North Dorset, Vt., (son of Austin,[3576])
ma. Maggie Frost.

Children.

3669. Clara, bo. ——.
3670. Mary, bo. ——.

(3490) James T. Ladd, of Garland, Me., (son of Samuel,[3480]) ma. Catharine, dau. of Christopher and Sally (Quimby) Orr, Feb. 14, 1851.

Children.

3671. George M., bo. Nov. 23, 1851; ma. Rose M. Folsom, Oct. 29, 1879.
3672. Willis E., bo. March 31, 1854; ma. Mary E. Bohan.
3673. Ella J., bo. Oct. 20, 1860; ma. Fred. G. Mills, March 13, 1885.
3674. Maria A., bo. Oct. 4, 1862.
3675. Fred. W., bo. June 3, 1868.

(2745) Myron Ferdinand Ladd, of Franklin, Conn., (son of Fredus,[1629]) ma. Mary Champlin.

Children.

3676. Ella King, bo. June 18, 1868.
3677. Lucy Martha, bo. Dec. 21, 1874.
3678. Myron Ferdinand, bo. Aug. 8, 1877.
3679. William Merrill, bo. June 22, 1881.

(2748) John Tyler Ladd, of Franklin, Conn., (son of Fredus,[1629]) ma. Olive Rebecca Ladd.[3684]

Child.

3680. Fredus Tyler, bo. Oct. 7, 1872.

(811) Enoch Haskins Ladd, of Franklin, Conn., (son of Enoch,[341]) ma. Mary Elizabeth Griswold, Dec. 26, 1841.

Children.

3681. John Enoch, bo. March 17, 1842.
3682. Frances Elizabeth, bo. 1845; ma. Charles Fredus Ladd (2747.)

(812) Daniel Valson Ladd, of Franklin, Conn., (son of Enoch,[841]) ma. Jane Matilda Griswold.

Children.

3683. Mary Jane, bo. April 20, 1836; ma. Henry B. Lovett.
3684. Olive Rebecca, bo. Sept. 14, 1850; ma. John Tyler Ladd (2748.)
3685. George Courtney, bo. Jan. 13, 1855; ma. Sarah Joyce; 2d, Cornelia S. Gifford.

(1281) Hannibal Enoch Ladd, of Wattsbury, Pa., (son of Hiram,[748]) ma. Martha A. Scammons, Sept. 9, 1856.

Children.

3686. Hiram S., bo. Oct. 29, 1857; d. Oct. 12, 1865.
3687. Harlon, bo. March 22, 1859; d. April 4, 1863.
3688. Benjamin, bo. Oct. 24, 1862; d. Oct. 4, 1865.
3689. Anna A., bo. Feb. 25, 1864; ma. John J. Rouse, Dec. 3, 1885.
3690. Mary A., bo. Sept. 27, 1866.

(1800) Thomas Colby Ladd, of Le Roy, N. Y., (son of John,[654]) ma. Lucy, dau. of Capt. Amasa and Elizabeth Walker, 1827.

Children.

3691. Miles Amasa, bo. April 1, 1828; not married.
3692. Lucy Louise, bo. Nov. 2, 1829; not married.
3693. Ellen Elizabeth, bo. Feb. 3, 1832; not married.
3694. James Smith, bo. May 19, 1834; ma. Abbie Fessenden Bassett, Jan. 4, 1871.
3695. Charles Walker, bo. Sept. 21, 1836; ma. Jennie Schuyler, March, 1872.
3696. Henrietta Colby, bo. Dec. 2, 1839; not married.
3697. Henry Colby, bo. Dec. 2, 1839; d. April 20, 1840.
3698. Harriet Newell, bo. Jan. 3, 1843; not married.
3699. Franklin George, bo. Feb. 12, 1845; not married.
3700. Carlton Thomas, bo. March 9, 1847; ma. Mary Feeney, Feb. 8, 1878.
3701. Grace Agnes, bo. July 17, 1850; ma. Jay G. Wood, Oct. 4, 1876.
    Child: Ralph Thomas, bo. March 1, 1881.
3702. Anna Alice, bo. July 17, 1850; not married.

(3694) James Smith, of Buffalo, N. Y., (son of Thomas Colby,[1800]) ma. Abbie Fessenden, dau. of Gustavus and Susan (Eastman) Bassett, Jan. 4, 1871. He was educated at Le Roy, N. Y., is a member of the Lafayette Street Presbyterian Church, and is extensively engaged in the grocery business.

Children.

3703. Arthur Bassett, bo. Nov. 8, 1871.
3704. Carlton Eastman, bo. April 6, 1873.

3705. Charles Coleman, bo. Nov. 6, 1875.
3706. Walter Manning, bo. Sept. 25, 1884.

(3711) John Ladd (son of Josiah[288]) ma. Lydia Ann Pervier, of Franklin, N. H.

Children.

3713. Charles Knox, bo. Feb. 26, 1839; ma. ——.
3714. Barbara Ann, bo. April 4, 1843; d. Feb. 18, 1890.
3715. Mary Amanda, bo. July 10, 1849; ma. ——.
3716. John Herbert, bo. Sept. 21, 1852.
3717. Frank Zelotus, bo. June 15, 1857; d. Dec. 6, 1862.

(1273) Hiram Ladd, of Fontenelle, Neb., (son of John,[747]) ma. Melinda Mansfield, Sept. 8, 1848.

Children.

3718. Sidney, bo. ——; ma. ——.
3719. Charles H., bo. ——; ma. Loretty Whitney, Sept. 28, 1877.
3720. Frank M., bo. ——.
3721. George E., bo. ——.
3722. Enoch O., bo. ——.
3723. John H., bo. ——.
3724. Anna, bo. ——.

(3718) Sidney Ladd, of Fontenelle, Neb., (son of Hiram,[1273]) ma. ——.

Children.

3725. Louisa Emerson, bo. April 27, 1883.
3726. Lilly Jane, bo. Dec. 6, 1884.
3728. Nellie, bo. March 18, 1886.
3729. George Edward, bo. May 5, 1887.
3730. ——. } Twins.
3731. ——.

(3719) Charles H. Ladd, of Fontenelle, Neb., (son of Hiram,[1273]) ma. Loretty Whitney, Sept. 28, 1877.

Children.

3732. Charles Hurlbert, bo. Aug. 7, 1879.
3733. George Elmer, bo. Aug. 2, 1881.
3734. Myrtle Jane, bo. Dec. 14, 1884.
3735. Arthur, bo. June 14, 1886.
3736. John, bo. July 8, 1889.

(3671) George M. Ladd, of Shrewsbury, (son of James T.,[3490]) ma. Rose M. Folsom, Oct. 29, 1879.

Child.

3737. Myron G., bo. June 17, 1889.

(3672) Willis E. Ladd, of Worcester, (son of James T.,[3490]) ma. Mary E. Bohan, Aug. 15, 1880.

Children.

3738. Annie M., bo. Jan. 16, 1882.
3739. James E., bo. Dec. 24, 1885.
3740. Mary K.. bo. Aug. 30, 1887.
3741. John H., bo. Sept. 23, 1889.

(2967) John A. Ladd, of St. Louis, Mo., (son of Attilus Alexis,[1857]) ma. Palagie Berthold, Oct. 9, 1867.

Child.

3742. Pierre Berthold, bo. June 18, 1869.

(2969) Ralph A. Ladd, of Chicago, Ill., (son of Attilus Alexis,[1857]) ma. Frances Rutherford, Nov. 13, 1835.

Child.

3743. Charles Dickens, bo. Sept. 30, 1876.

(2970) Attilus Alexis Ladd, of St. Louis, Mo., (son of Attilus Alexis,[1857]) ma. Mary Barnett, Nov. 14, 1877.

Child.

3744. John Armstrong, bo. Aug. 11, 1878.

(3745) —— Ladd, of Canaan, Conn., (son of ——,) ma. ——. Removed to Canaan from Coventry, Conn.

Children.

3746. Eliphalet, bo. 1768; ma. Betsey Frank, Jan. 29, 1794.
3747. Phineas, bo. ——.
3748. Elisha, bo. ——.

(3746) Eliphalet Ladd, of Canaan, Conn., (son of ——,) ma. Betsey Frank, Jan. 29, 1794. He d. Jan. 3, 1800, at Casinovia, N. Y.

Children.

3749. Cyrus, bo. Nov. 29, 1795; ma. Prudence Colwell.
3750. Samuel, bo. Sept. 15, 1799; ma. Elizabeth Patterson McNeil.

(3749) Cyrus Ladd, of Quincy, Ill., (son of Eliphalet,[3746]) ma. Prudence Colwell, of Camilus, N. Y. She died March 21, 1843. He died April 29, 1849.

Children.

3751. Chauncy, bo. Feb. 25, 1826; ma. Susan Mayo Pomeroy.
3752. Caroline, bo. Aug. 17, 1828; d. March 4, 1848.

3753. Caldwell, bo. Oct. 12, 1830; ma. Mary Greenman.
3754. Elizabeth, bo. Sept. 1833; d. May 7, 1852.

(3750) Samuel Ladd, of Utica, Mich., (son of Eliphalet,[3746]) ma. Elizabeth Patterson, dau. of Abraham and Mary (Patterson) McNeil, Dec. 26, 1807. He died Dec. 17, 1876.

Children.

3755. William Patterson, bo. Sept. 5, 1830; ma. Emeline Skinner, Feb. 17, 1858. No children.
3756. Cyrus C., bo. June 17, 1832; ma. Olive H. Ferris, March 2, 1859.
3757. George Washington, bo. June 25, 1834; ma. Jane F. Pomeroy, Dec. 23, 1858. No children.
3758. Augustus Frank, bo. April 24, 1836; ma. Annie Taylor, Dec. 6, 1865.
3759. Mary Jane, bo. June 18, 1838; d. June 27, 1841.
3760. Samuel, Jr., bo. Jan. 29, 1841; d. Feb. 24, 1869.
3761. John James, bo. Feb. 21, 1843; d. Jan. 27, 1867.
3762. Isaac Vincent, bo. Feb. 26, 1845; ma. Julia P. Smith, Dec. 4, 1872.
3763. Ira Abraham, bo. July 17, 1847.
3764. Elizabeth Jane, bo. Sept. 9, 1849.

(3756) Cyrus C. Ladd, of Mayville, Mich., (son of Samuel,[3750]) ma. Olive H. Ferris, March 2, 1859.

Children.

3765. Cyrus Eugene, bo. Feb. 14, 1860; ma. Jennie Margaretta McNeill, Sept. 15, 1884.
3766. Jennie Elizabeth, bo. Oct. 5, 1862; ma. William Tell Lewis, March 2, 1887. He is a telegraph operator at Mayville, Mich. Children: [1]Mary Ethel, bo. Jan. 15, 1888; [2]Bessie Louise, bo. Aug. 20, 1889.
3767. George Samuel, bo. Jan. 5, 1864.
3768. William B., bo. Feb. 20, 1866.

(3758) Augustus Frank Ladd, of Avon, Mich., (son of Samuel,[3750]) ma. Annie Taylor, Dec. 6, 1865.

Children.

3769. Mary Jane, bo. June 17, 1867.
3770. John Gilman, bo. Dec. 28, 1871; d. Sept. 1, 1872.
3771. Charles G., bo. Dec. 28, 1873.
3772. Jennie Bell, bo. Dec. 28, 1873.
3773. Adelbert, bo. Aug. 22, 1876.

(3762) Isaac Vincent Ladd, of Moberly, Mo., (son of Samuel,[3750]) ma. Julia P. Smith, Dec. 4, 1872.

Children.

3774. Lizzie Bell, bo. Jan. 1, 1874.
3775. Bessie, bo. March 13, 1879.
3776. Oliver Vincent, bo. Sept. 23, 1881.

3751) Chauncy Ladd, of Quincy, Ill., (son of Cyrus,[3749]) ma. Susan Mayo Pomeroy, Oct. 9, 1852. She was born Aug. 1, 1835.

Children.

3777. Elizabeth, bo. Nov. 14, 1853; d. Feb. 7, 1855.
3778. Chauncy, Jr., bo. Nov. 18, 1855.
3779. Susan Mayo, bo. July 17, 1858.
3780. Harry Caldwell, bo. Feb. 10, 1860.
3781. Jennie Pomeroy, bo. Feb. 27, 1861; ma. Henry W. Alexander, Dec. 9, 1880. Child: Susan Ladd, bo. July 7, 1883; d. Jan. 12, 1886.
3782. Caleb Russell, bo. Feb. 12, 1863; d. Feb. 21, 1863.
3783. Bessie, bo. Dec. 19, 1864; ma. Whitfield Russell, Dec. 2, 1885.
3784. Charles Pomeroy, bo. March 15, 1868.

3753) Caldwell Ladd, of Wichita, Kansas, (son of Cyrus,[3749]) ma. Mary Greenman, of Racine, Wis.

Children.

3785. William F., bo. Dec. 29, 1866.
3786. Mabel E., bo. Oct. 18, 1873.

3788) Ezekiel Ladd, of ——. The Christian name of his father is unknown, but there are circumstances that seem to indicate that he may have been the son of Nathaniel.[30] One of his descendants writes: "I have heard my father and Uncle Lemuel say that William Ladd,[3789] my grandfather, was an only son, and was born in Massachusetts about 1730, either in Haverhill or Cummington, and that my great-grandfather Ezekiel was poisoned by the French or Indians, in the French and Indian war."

3789) William Ladd, of Duanesburg, N. Y., (son of Ezekiel,[3788]) ma. Elizabeth Vining, of Abington, Nov. 4, 1766. He was a pilot on board of DeGrasse's fleet; was a seaman on a vessel engaged in the whale fishery. He lived a short time at Cumington, and in Vermont, near Burlington, and in 1783 he purchased 400 acres of land in Duanesburg, N. Y., where he lived until he died. He was a very successful and prosperous farmer.

Children.

3790. Thomas, bo. Dec. 11, ——; ma. Jennie Cronkite.
3791. William, bo. April 20, ——; ma. Norcha Hannan.

3792. Betsey, bo. ——; ma. Abner Goodspeed. Children: [1]Christopher; [2]Nathaniel, ma. Miss Jones; [3]Elnathan; [4]Ann, ma. Nathan Webber; [5]Abner, ma. Martha Jenkins; [6]Betsey, ma. Peter Markel; [7]Levi; [8]William, enlisted in the U. S. army and was never heard from after.

3793. Sally, bo. ——; ma. Joseph Heatherton. Children: [1]John, ma. Mira Herrick; [2]William, ma. Susan Mayam; [3]Joseph, ma. Miss Herrick; [4]Christopher; [5]Mary, ma. Geo. Conoly; [6]Nancy, ma. —— Williams.

3794. Mehitable, bo. ——; ma. Stephen Curtis. Children: [1]William; the names of the other five not known.

3795. John, bo. Jan. 17, 1774; ma. Alice King.

3796. Hannah, bo. ——; ma. Robert Estus. Children: [1]Abner; and five others.

3797. Lemuel, bo. Jan. 18, 1778; ma. Phebe Herrick.

3798. Polly, bo. ——; ma. Jacob Markel. Children: [1]Lodowich; [2]William; [3]Mehitable, ma. Mr. Spaulding; [4]Finnis M.

3799. Susan, bo. ——; ma. —— Wilts. Children: [1]Elizabeth, ma. Michael Coffin; [2]David; [3]Ann, ma. Mr. Coffin; [4]Otis, ma. Mrs. Coffin; [5]Priscilla; [6]Nancy, ma. Henry Herrick; [7]Sally; [8]John, ma. a Welch girl; [9]Julia, ma. John Hyser; [10]Harriet A., ma. Aaron Brown; [11]Stephen, ma. Silva Sisson; [12]Elijah; [13]Jude.

3800. Levi, bo. ——; ma. Eliza Parlow.

(3790) Thomas Ladd, of Duanesburg, N. Y., (son of William,[3789]) ma. Jennie Cronkite, Dec. 8, 1788. He died at Andes, N. Y., Sept. 22, 1844. She died Jan. 18, 1852.

Children.

3801. John, bo. July 1, 1798; ma. Nancy McDonald, July 8, 1820.
3802. Thomas, bo. Oct. 12, 1800; ma. Caroline Kellogg, March 15, 1826.
3803. Elizabeth, bo. April 3, 1803; ma. Peter Hyser, April 5, 1824.
3804. Margaret, bo. Nov. 21, 1805.

(3791) William Ladd (son of William[3789]) ma. Norcha Hannan.

Children.

3805. William, bo. ——.
3806. John, bo. ——.
3807. Lemuel, bo. ——.
3808. Henry, bo. ——. There were several girls, names unknown.

(3795) John Ladd (son of William[3789]) ma. Alice King.

Children.

3809. Ezekiel, bo. Oct. 10, 1799; ma. Caty Lester.
3810. Hannah, bo. Dec. 18, 1800; ma. Silas Wilber. Children: [1]Samantha, ma. Andrew Conover; [2]John; [3]Lurenda, ma. George Gould; [4]Eliza.
3811. Lydia, bo. June 3, 1802; d. young.
3812. Lydia, bo. June, 1803; d. young.

3813. John, bo. July 23, 1805; ma. Mary Disbrow.
3814. Alice, bo. Nov. 2, 1808; ma. Edward Frisbee. Children: [1]Caleb, ma. Emma Bane; [2]William, ma. Jane Borden; [3]Nancy, ma. Joy Young; [4]John; [5]Charles; [6]Edward.
3815. William K., bo. Nov. 15, 1810; ma. Mary Buchanan.
3816. Elizabeth, bo. June 5, 1813; d. young.
3817. Alonzo, bo. July 23, 1818; ma. Sarah Koons.
3818. Harriet, bo. Sept. 17, 1820; ma. Jacob Koons. Children: [1]John; [2]Alice, ma Daniel Gladwell; [3]William; [4]Brice; [5]Emma, ma. John Gladwell; [6]Hattie; [7]Charles; [8]Jay; [9]Nettie.

(3797)   Lemuel Ladd (son of William[3789]) ma. Phebe Herrick.

Children.

3819. John, bo. Nov. 19, 1800; d. 1819.
3820. Roswell, bo. Nov. 8, 1802; ma. Eliza Schermerhorn.
3821. Ephraim, bo. Sept. 14, 1804; ma. Eliza Norton.
3822. Ann, bo. Nov. 26, 1806; ma. Reuben Norton.
3823. Henry, bo. Nov. 8, 1808; ma. Phebe Ketchum.
3824. William, bo. Jan. 25, 1810; ma. Nancy Koons.
3825. Elijah, bo. Oct. 22, 1811; ma. Harriet Bentley.
3826. Priscilla, bo. Oct. 19, 1814; ma. John Bentley.
3827. Lemuel, bo. March 2, 1816; ma. Amy Pettit.
3828. John, bo. 1818; ma. Jane Merry.
3829. Charles, bo. Nov. 2, 1819; ma. Prudence Victory.
3830. Phebe, bo. June 6, 1822; ma. Lewis Avery.

(3800)   Levi Ladd (son of William[3789]) ma. Eliza Parlow.

Children.

3831. Jane, bo. ——; ma. Charles Scriver.
3832. Susan, bo. ——.
3833. Eliza, bo. ——.
3834. Emma, bo. ——; ma. George Gould.
3835. Marsha, bo. ——; ma. Mr. Brink.
3836. William, bo. ——.

(3801)   John Ladd, of Traer, Tamer Co., Iowa, (son of Thomas,[3790]) ma. Nancy McDonald, July 8, 1820. He died at Buckingham, Iowa. She died Dec. 12, 1876.

Children.

3837. William T. V., bo. April 20, 1821; ma. Catharine Saroyex, July 16, 1846.
3838. James D., bo. Oct. 7, 1822; ma. Rose Ann McMurber, March, 1848.
3839. Margaret A., bo. April 6, 1824; ma. Rev. Walter Stott, Sept. 17, 1845. Children: [1]Nancy J., [2]John E., [3]Rose C., [4]Ellen J., [5]Henry J., [6]Nettie M. S.

3840. Jane Glen, bo. Nov. 20, 1825; ma. Henry E. Davis, March 24, 1853. Children: [1]Henry E., [2]Smith A., [3]Lena M., [4]Homer.
3841. Daniel C., bo. Aug. 21, 1828; ma. Janet George, Dec. 30, 1858.
3842. John A., bo. Oct. 27, 1830; ma. Nancy Rose.
3843. Nancy M., bo. Feb. 14, 1833; ma. Watson H. Brown.
3844. Lemuel, bo. July 21, 1836.
3845. Levi, bo. Jan. 21, 1839; ma. Margaret M. Kerral, Dec. 26, 1867.
3846. Augustus R., bo. Jan. 25, 1843.

(3809) Ezekiel Ladd (son of John[3795]) ma. Caty Lester.

Children.

3847. Eliza M., bo. ——; ma. Elias Perkins.
3848. Delana, bo. ——; ma. Charles Stickney.
3849. Mordica, bo. ——; ma. Miss Rice.
3850. John K., bo. ——; ma. Sarah Tripp.
3851. Olive, bo. ——; ma. Joseph Rice.
3852. Mary, bo. ——; ma. Flecher Joiner.
3853. Mehitable, bo. ——; ma. Rev. George Mills.

(3813) John Ladd (son of John[3795]) ma. Mary Disbrow, Sept. 13, 1823. She died July 6, 1831, and he ma. 2d, Rebecca Disbrow. She died, and he ma. 3d, Catharine Gethen.

Children.

3854. Ira, bo. June 20, 1824; ma. Ann Bigam.
3855. Henrietta, bo. Jan. 8, 1826; ma. James Crawford.
3856. John D., bo. Oct. 13, 1827; ma. Amanda Melvina Jones.
3857. Harriet, bo. Sept. 26, 1829; ma. Asa Carpenter.

Children by second wife.

3858. Louisa, bo. ——; ma. Alfred Kenney.
3859. Mary, bo. ——; ma. Miner Burge.
3860. Martin A., bo. ——; ma. Kate Allen.
3861. Lafayette, bo. ——; ma. Miss Wood.
3862. Sarah, bo. ——; ma. Alexander McMillen.
3863. William K., bo. ——; ma. Harriet Buchanan.

(3815) William K. Ladd, of Duanesburg, N. Y., (son of John,[3795]) ma. Mary Buchanan.

Children.

3864. George W., bo. ——.
3865. Alice, bo. ——.
3866. Edward, bo. ——.
3867. William K., bo. ——.
3868. John, bo. ——.

(3817) Alonzo Ladd, of Duanesburg, N. Y., (son of John,[3795]) ma. Sarah Koons. She died, and he ma. 2d, Sarah E. Morse. He was educated at the common schools; worked on his father's farm until he was twenty years old, when his father gave him a farm, which he cultivated for about twenty-five years, when he sold his farm and worked at the stone mason's trade, and practiced law in the justice court. In 1838 he was one of the twelve men appointed to appraise the land damage on the line of the Troy & Schenectady Railroad. In 1839 he was elected captain of a company in the old State militia. He held the office of commissioner of highways about fifteen years, and was town clerk from 1849 to and including 1852. In 1855 he was elected supervisor of Duanesburg. In November, 1861, he enlisted in Company M, 3d N. Y. Light Artillery, was quartermaster sergeant for the company, and was discharged June 26, 1863. In 1864 he was elected to the office of justice of the peace, and held that office eight years. In 1872 he was appointed a notary public, which office he now (1890) holds.

Children.

3869. John J., bo. Dec. 5, 1838; ma. Augusta Wilber.
3870. William A., bo. Nov. 12, 1840; ma. Parthena Vunek.
3871. Mary Augusta, bo. Feb. 27, 1844; ma. Edgar Fosmire. Children: [1]Willie, [2]Aura, [3]James.

Children by second wife.

3872. Alice K., bo. May 27, 1863; ma. Mark B. Dickenson. Children: [1]Aura, [2]James.
3873. Emery, bo. March 30, 1866.

(3841) Daniel C. Ladd, of Traer, Tamer Co., Iowa, (son of John,[3801]) ma. Janet George, Dec. 30, 1858.

Children.

3874. John T., bo. Feb. 1, 1854.
3875. William J., bo. May 8, 1858.
3876. George D., bo. Nov. 18, 1862.

(3842) John A. Ladd, of Iowa Falls, Iowa, (son of John,[3801]) ma. Nancy Rose, Dec. 31, 1858.

Children.

3877. Ossian, bo. March 7, 1860.
3878. Nettie E., bo. Sept. 19, 1864.
3879. Fred. G., bo. May 23, 1866.

3880. John A., bo. Aug. 28, 1868.
3881. Mabel M., bo. May 18, 1870.
3882. Nancy G., bo. Feb. 10, 1882.

(3845) Levi Ladd, of Oneida, Iowa, (son of John,[3801]) ma. Margaret M. Kerral, Dec. 26, 1867.

Children.

3883. Mary E., bo. Dec. 21, 1870.
3884. J. Romulus, bo. Dec. 5, 1872.
3885. H. Romulus, bo. Dec. 5, 1872.

(3869) John J. Ladd, of Duanesburg, N. Y., (son of Alonzo,[3817]) ma. Augusta Wilber.

Children.

3886. Wilber, bo. ——; ma. Fannie Sterling.
3887. Cora, bo. ——; ma. Daniel Broeffle.
3888. Betsey, bo. ——; not married in 1890.

(3870) William A. Ladd, of Duanesburg, N. Y., (son of Alonzo,[3817]) ma. Parthena Vunek.

Children.

3889. Albert, bo. ——; ma. Mary Sammons.
3890. Minna, bo. ——.
3891. William, bo. ——.
3892. Earl, bo. ——.
3893. Owen, bo. ——.

(3820) Roswell Ladd, of Duanesburg, N. Y., (son of Lemuel,[3797]) ma. Eliza Schermerhorn.

Children.

3894. Phebe Ann, bo. June 23, 1825; ma. John Stillwell.
3895. Isaac P., bo. Aug. 10, 1827; ma. Martha Coughtry, Nov. 28, 1858. No children.
3896. Marcia, bo. July 8, 1831.
3897. Eliza Jane, bo. 1834; ma. John Chism.
3898. Martha M., bo. July 11, 1837.
3899. Lemuel R., bo. June 9, 1839; ma. Lydia P. Wood, Jan. 17, 1865.
3900. Margaret Ursula, bo. June 9, 1841.

(3821) Ephraim Ladd, of Duanesburg, N. Y., (son of Lemuel,[3797]) ma. Eliza Norton.

Children.

3901. Mary Jane, bo. ——; ma. Alonzo Ruff.
3902. Jeannette, bo. ——; ma. Alonzo Quirk.
3903. Ruth, bo. ——; ma. William J. Cary.

3824) William Ladd, of Duanesburg, N. Y., (son of Lemuel,[3797]) ma. Nancy Koons.
Children.
3904. Gilbert, bo. ——.
3905. Eugene, bo. ——.

3825) Elijah Ladd, of Duanesburg, N. Y., (son of Lemuel,[3797]) ma. Harriet Bentley.
Children.
3906. Susan, bo. ——; ma. Danforth Abrams.
3907. Mary Ann, bo. ——; ma. John Slawson.
3908. Eveline, bo. ——; ma. Asael Movy.
3909. Harriet, bo. ——.
3910. George W., bo. ——; ma. Milly Johnson.

(3827) Lemuel Ladd, of Duanesburg, N. Y., (son of Lemuel,[3797]) ma. Amy C. Pettit.
Children.
3911. Elijah, bo. ——.
3912. Calvin, bo. ——.
3913. Lemuel, bo. ——.
3914. Oscar, bo. ——.

(3829) Charles Ladd, of Duanesburg, N. Y., (son of Lemuel,[3797]) ma. Prudence Victory.
Children.
3915. Ursula, bo. Oct. 11, 1842; ma. George A. Falk.
3916. Charles W., bo. Oct. 31, 1844; ma. Sarah Carey.
3917. Anna C., bo. Aug. 7, 1855.
3918. Adele E., bo. Feb. 7, 1860.

(3899) Lemuel R. Ladd, of Schenectady, N. Y., (son of Roswell,[3820]) ma. Lydia P. Wood, Jan. 17, 1865, of Waterford, N. Y.
Children.
3919. Helena P., bo. May 11, 1866, at Burtonville, N. Y.
3920. Harriet Ann, bo. Nov. 22, 1867, at Amsterdam, N. Y.

(3856) John D. Ladd, of Schenectady, N. Y., (son of John,[3818]) ma. Amanda Melvina Jones, Sept. 19, 1860.
Children.
3921. Nettie, bo. Dec. 11, 1862.
3922. Franklin J., bo. May 14, 1872.
3923. Myron B., bo. Feb. 11, 1875.

(3924) Thomas Ladd, of Saco, Me., (son of ——,) ma. Sarah Phillips, of Saco. She died Jan. 28, 1813, and he ma. 2d, Hannah Jose, Oct. 25, 1813. She died in 1842, aged 56 years. He died Nov. 10, 1837, aged 71 years.

Children.

3925. William, bo. April 13, 1793; ma. ——.
3926. Thomas, bo. March 30, 1795; ma. ——. No children.
3927. Isabella, bo. June 3, 1797; not married; d. Jan. 25, 1849.
3928. Eunice, bo. March 12, 1799; ma. Nathaniel Jose, Dec. 26, 1815.
3929. Mary, bo. April 27, 1800; ma. Joseph Bolter, Dec. 25, 1817. He died, and she ma. 2d, Charles D. Bolter, June, 1850.
3930. Edmund, bo. Oct. 4, 1801; ma. Mary Grace, March 3, 1824.
3931. Lucinda, bo. July 7, 1803; ma. Samuel Whitten, 1827.
3932. Andrew, bo. Oct. 28, 1804; ma. Ann Dearborn, Jan. 4, 1844. He died Nov. 24, 1874.
3933. Rufus, bo. Nov. 23, 1806; ma. Susan Boothby, Sept. 9, 1832.

Children by second wife.

3934. Silas, bo. Aug. 2, 1814; ma. Sarah E. D. Sawyer, Oct. 1737.
3935. John, bo. March 8, 1816; ma. Lucinda Bryant, March 20, 1838. He died June 4, 1882.
3936. Samuel, bo. April 28, 1818; ma. Jane C. Peterson, Dec. 17, 1856.
3937. James, bo. Feb. 5, 1822; ma. Caroline Rowe, June 7, 1848. He died Dec. 12, 1883.
3938. Dorcas, bo. Nov. 6, 1824; ma. Luther Taylor, of Hopkinton.
3939. Sarah, bo. 1820; d. Feb. 17, 1826.
3940. Sarah, bo. Dec. 1826; ma. John Dearborn, Feb. 7, 1847.

(3934) Silas Ladd, of Saco, Me., (son of Thomas,[3924]) ma. Sarah E. D. Sawyer, Oct. 1837. She died Oct. 24, 1863.

Child.

3941. Horace, bo. ——; ma. Ann Thompson.

(3942) Jesse Ladd, born in Rutland, Vt., Aug. 15, 1802; died at Glastonbury, Conn., May 2, 1885. (Name of his father unknown.) He ma. Mary Adams, dau. of Benjamin and Jemima (Adams) Blanchard.

Children.

Alonzo Blanchard, bo. Jan. 21, 1834; d. May, 1838, at Vernon, Conn.
3943. Charles Henry, bo. May 21, 1836; d. Feb. 21, 1852.
3944. Mary Calista, bo. May 11, 1839; ma. Woodbridge Kenney, Jan. 20, 1861, of South Manchester, Conn. Children: [1]Lester, [2]Angie M., [3]Clayton, [4]Carrie, [5]Clinton, [6]Arthur Bidwell.
3945. Sarah Almira, bo. July 14, 1841; not married.

3946. Martha Jane, bo. Dec. 1, 1844; not married.
3947. Harriet Elizabeth, bo. July 1, 1848; ma. Edward E. Agard, May 27, 1874.
3948. Frank Henry, bo. March, 16, 1852; ma. Emily L. Bogul, June 22, 1875.
Child: Harry.
3949. George Munroe, bo. Jan. 11, 1857; ma. Abbie May Agard, May 9, 1882.

(3948) Frank Henry Ladd, of South Manchester, Conn., (son of Jesse,[3942]) ma. Emily L. Bogul, June 22, 1875.

Children.

3950. Winifred Blanchard, bo. Sept. 5, 1876.
3951. Flora Madeline, bo. Oct. 9, 1878.
3952. Marian Frances, bo. April 13, 1881.
3953. Ervin Willard, bo. Dec. 28, 1885.
3954. Anna May, bo. Oct. 19, 1883.

(3949) George Munroe Ladd, of Hartford, Conn., (son of Jesse,[3942]) ma. Abbie May Agard, May 9, 1882.

Child.

3955. Florence LeReine, bo. March 6, 1890.

JOSEPH LADD.

We find the following in Austin's Genealogical Dictionary of Rhode Island, page 4: " Oct. 1644, John Anthony sold Richard Tew, of Newport, for good cause, &c., three parcels of land in Newport, east from the Newport mill, within a tract called the great enclosure, amounting to 50 acres ; 40 acres given me by town grant ; ten as a servant, at my first coming ; also two parcels marsh. Witnesses, Susanna Anthony and *Joseph Ladd.*" This is the first record, or mention of the name of this Joseph Ladd.

We next find a record of a deed from William Barker to Joseph Ladd, of Portsmouth, on Rhode Island, of ten acres of land, with a small dwelling-house thereon, situated in said Portsmouth, Jan. 11, 1658.

We find upon the town records of Portsmouth, R. I., the will of this Joseph Ladd. It is as follows :

" April the 12th, 1669. The last Will and Testament of Joseph Ladd, of Portsmouth on Rhode Island, in the Colony of Rhode Island, and Providence Plantation, in New England, in America, being in perfect memory ; do substitute, ordain and appoint Joanna, my wife, my full and sole executrix to see my will performed ; which is as follows :—That all my visible state shall remain in the hands of my wife for the bringing up of my children, so long as she, the said executrix, shall remain a widow ; but in case she shall marry another man, then what my estate shall be shall remain no longer in the hands of my said wife, but in the hands of the Overseers, to be equally disposed of to my children, as followeth, namely : That my son Joseph, at his mother's death or marriage again, shall have my house and land, he paying, or causing to be paid, five pounds sterling apiece to his two brothers, if these surviving. viz. : my son William and Daniel, and what goods or chattels shall remain of my estate, at the time aforesaid, to be equally divided betwixt my two youngest sons, and my two daughters, viz.: Mary and Sara ; and in case either of my youngest sons decease before the time prefixed, then the five pounds above said to be paid betwixt his two sisters, to each an equal share, also in case my eldest son shall depart this life without issue, then the said house and land to fall necessarily to the next son as above said.

Lastly, I do desire and appoint my well beloved Friends, William Wodel and William Hall as Overseers, to see my estate be not imbeseld, and that it be disposed of according to my will above said, and that my children be not wronged by a father-in-law.

That this is my will and Testament, which I desire may be performed. Witness my hand and seal, this day and year first above written.

JOSEPH] LAD. { Seal. }
His mark.

Tests. JOHN X STRANGE.
His mark.
WILLIAM W LANNY.
His mark.

John Strange, of the town of Portsmouth, aged seventy years or thereabouts, being deposed testifieth that the above written was signed and sealed by the above named Joseph Lad, as his Last Will and Testament, and that in presence of this deponent and the above named William Lany. Taken upon oath before us,

JOHN ALBRO, Assistant.
GEORGE LAWTON, Assistant.

The above written is a true copy of the original, entered and recorded the 25th of the 5th month, 1683, by me.

JOHN ANTHONY, Town Clerk."

We think it is evident, though there is no positive proof, that this Joseph Ladd was a younger brother of Daniel Ladd, who came from London in the Mary and John in 1633. The reason for this belief is the fact that John Anthony, whose deed of land to Richard Tew in 1644 Joseph Ladd was a witness, took the oath of Supremacy and Allegiance to pass to New England in the Mary and John, Robert Sayres master, 24th of March, 1633, but "stayed over to oversee the chattle," and came in the Hercules, John Kidder master, which sailed a week later than the Mary and John, in which Daniel Ladd came. [See New England Historical and Genealogical Register, vol. 9, page 267.] John Anthony settled at Portsmouth, R. I. Joseph Ladd lived at Portsmouth, R. I. The inference is that Joseph Ladd, a minor, lived in the family of John Anthony, was a relative of Mr. Anthony or his wife, and went to Portsmouth with him.

We now give his genealogical record.

(3956)   Joseph Ladd, of Portsmouth, R. I., ma. Joanna ———. He died in 1683.

Children.

3957. Joseph, bo. ——; ma. Rachel.
3958. William, bo. ——; ma. Elizabeth Tompkins, Feb. 17, 1695.
3959. Daniel, bo. ——.
3960. Mary, bo. ——.
3961. Sara, bo. ——.

3957) Joseph Ladd, of Little Compton, R. I., (son of Joseph,[3956]) ma Rachel ——, 1685. He sold to Philip Taber, of Dartmouth, July 4, 1714, land in Little Compton, R. I., in that part of the town called Coxet, being the 30th lot in the 31st layout. His wife Rachel signed the deed.

Children.

3962. Rachel, bo. Dec. 17, 1686; ma. to George Kelley, Feb. 15, 1719, by Chester Allen, Justice of the Peace.
3963. Daniel, bo. May 25, 1688; ma. Abigail Hart, May 7, 1712.
3964. William, bo. May 10, 1689.
3965. Joseph, bo. Oct. 16, 1693.
3966. Mary, bo. Dec. 29, 1696.
3967. Benjamin, bo. Jan. 29, 1698: ma. Mary Grinnell, dau. of Jonathan and Abigail (Ford) Grinnell.
3968. Sarah, bo. April 5, 1700; ma. William Enos, Oct. 17, 1737.
3969. Jonathan, bo. Aug. 10, 1701.
3970. Caleb, bo. June 2, 1704.
3971. Rebecca, bo. Sept. 15, 1706.

3958) William Ladd, of Little Compton, R. I., (son of Joseph,[3956]) ma. Elizabeth, dau. of Nathaniel and Elizabeth (Allen) Tompkins, Feb. 17, 1695. His will was dated Aug. 13, 1729; proved Oct. 21, 1729. His wife Elizabeth was named as executrix. He named as legatees each of his children, except John, and "my grandson Nathaniel, son of my son William." After the legacies named are paid, he gives all the residue and remainder to his wife. The witnesses to the will were Josiah Sawyer and Benjamin Seabury. The estate was apprised at £88.14s.0d, by George Peirce, Samuel Tompkins, and William Hunt.

Children.

3972. Sarah, bo. March 22, 1696.
3973. William, bo. Nov. 18, 1697; ma. ——. Had a son Nathaniel. (See will.)
3974. Mary, bo. March 5, 1699: ma. Joseph Seabury. Children: [1]Phebe, bo. May 2, 1723, ma. —— Lawton; [2]Hannah, bo. Feb. 7, 1724, ma. Charles Cadman; [3]Gideon, bo. March 16, 1726, d. young; [4]John;

⁵Elizabeth, bo. Feb. 2, 1730, ma. Daniel Allen; ⁶Sarah, bo. Dec. 4, 1732, ma. Edward Cadman; ⁷Ichabod, bo. Jan. 18, 1734.

3975. Priscilla, bo. June 22, 1700; ma. —— Manchester.
3976. Joseph, bo. Oct. 19, 1701; ma. Lydia, dau. of Samuel and W. (Church) Gray.
3977. Samuel, bo. Oct. 12, 1703.
3978. Elizabeth, bo. Oct. 12, 1704; ma. —— Thurill.
3979. John, bo. Jan. 15, 1706.
3980. Catharine, bo. Sept. 14, 1707.
3981. Lydia, bo. March 1, 1711; ma. Samuel Seabury, March 2, 1732. Children: ¹Barnabas, bo. June 2, 1732; ²Lillis, bo. May 7, 1734, ma. —— Cornel; ³Patience, bo. May 24, 1736, ma. John Devol; ⁴Comfort, bo. July 4, 1738, ma. Samuel Wilcox, Feb. 5, 1761; ⁵Nathaniel, bo. June 27, 1740; ⁶William, bo. May 2, 1742; ⁷Phebe, bo. March 15, 1744, ma. Richard Pearce; ⁸Mary, bo. March 15, ——, ma. William Cory; ⁹Hannah, bo. 1746, ma. James Manchester; ¹⁰Abigail, bo. Feb. 7, 1749, ma. William Watkins; ¹¹Deborah, bo. Aug. 12, 1752; ¹²William, bo. Jan. 24, 1755.
3982. Hannah, bo. Aug. 12, 1712.
3983. Ruth, bo. Jan. 19, 1714.

(3976) Joseph Ladd, of Little Compton, R. I., (son of William,[3958]) ma. Lydia, dau. of Samuel and W. (Church) Gray. He purchased, July 25, 1733, of William Richmond, of Little Compton, R. I., land and house for £200. He sold, Feb. 5, 1744, the land and buildings he purchased of William Richmond to John Bush. Lydia, his wife, signed the deed.

Children.

3984. Deborah, bo. 1732.
3985. Joseph, bo. 1733.
3986. Elizabeth, bo. 1735.
3987. William, bo. Oct. 30, 1737; ma. Sarah Gardner, of Newport, R. I., Dec. 22, 1761.
3988. Lydia, bo. 1740.

(3987) William Ladd, of Newport, R. I., (son of Joseph,[3976]) ma. Dec. 22, 1761, Sarah, dau. of Capt. Benoni and Sarah Gardner, of Newport, R. I. He died at Alexandria, Va., Dec. 4, 1800. His widow died at Alexandria, Va., Oct. 30, 1809. He was a soldier in the war of the Revolution; was a member of the R. I. Legislature; a member from Little Compton, R. I., of the State Convention that ratified the Federal Constitution; and was one of the charter members of the Marine Society, of Newport, R. I., in 1785.

Children.

3989. Lydia, bo. Sept. 17, 1762; d. Dec. 20, 1762.
3990. Joseph Brown, bo. July 7, 1764. Was a poet and a physician at Little Compton, R. I.; removed to Charleston, S. C., in 1784; was appointed Fourth of July orator at the second celebration of the day in Charleston. He died there, Nov. 2, 1786.
3991. Benjamin Gardner, bo. June 10, 1765; d. July 1, 1765.
3992. Sarah, bo. June 2, 1766.
3993. William, bo. Aug. 13, 1767; ma. Mary Haskins, Nov. 7, 1793.
3994. John Gardner, bo. May 16, 1771; ma. Sarah Easton.
3995. Elizabeth, bo. Aug. 23, 1772; ma. John Haskins, 1791.
3996. Samuel Gray, bo. April 7, 1774; d. Sept. 1781.

(3993) William Ladd, of Little Compton, R. I., (son of William,[3987]) ma. Nov. 7, 1793, Mary Haskins, a lineal descendant of Gov. John Carver, who came in the Mayflower in 1620.

Children.

3997. John Haskins, bo. Dec. 24, 1794; ma. Eliza Smith Wyer, Sept. 4, 1819.
3998. William, bo. Aug. 12, 1796; d. Sept. 2, 1796.
3999. Mary, bo. Aug. 9, 1797; ma. Hardy Ropes, June 24, 1824. Children: [1]William Ladd, [2]Sarah, [3]Mary Louise.
4000. William Gardner, bo. Feb. 6, 1799; ma. Margaret Goodale Cushing.
4001. Sarah, bo. Nov. 28, 1800; ma. William Sewall, June 6, 1822. Children: [1]Samuel Green, [2]Mary, [3]William.
4002. Samuel, bo. May 7, 1803; d. July 13, 1804.
4003. Joseph, bo. Jan. 7, 1806; d. Nov. 30, 1809.
4005. Elizabeth, bo. Aug. 7, 1807; not married.
4006. Hannah Haskins, bo. Sept. 1810; ma. James Ingersoll Wyer, Aug. 1839. Children: [1]James J., [2]Sarah, [3]Mary Lizzie. Mrs. Wyer died May 11, 1890, at Red Lake Falls, Minn.

(4000) William Gardner Ladd, of Boston, (son of William,[3993]) ma. Aug. 30, 1821, Margaret Goodale Cushing, dau. of Edward Cushing, and grand-daughter of Hon. Thomas Cushing, one of the foremost patriots of the Revolution, Lieut. Gov. of Massachusetts, Speaker of the House of Representatives, and a member of the first and second Continental Congress. He died at Boston, April 20, 1862. His widow died at Brooklyn, N. Y., May 1, 1883, aged 84 years, 2 months, and 13 days.

Children.

4007. Ann Homer, bo. Aug. 13, 1822, at Fredericksburg, Va.; d. June, 1831.
4008. William Gardner, Jr., bo. Aug. 14, 1824; ma. Adeline Dodge Homer, Sept. 5, 1850.

4009. Edward Homer, bo. March 16, 1827; ma. Julia E. Marvin, Dec. 5, 1855.
4010. Margaret Cushing, bo. June 21, 1829; ma. Thomas C. Green, May 17, 1855, of Providence, R. I. Children: ¹Margaret Ladd, bo. Sept. 28, 1858, ma. Rev. Francis Green, Oct. 6, 1886; ²Samuel Ward, bo. July 10, 1865.
4011. Thomas Cushing, bo. March 18, 1831; ma. Mary E. Raiguel, April 3, 1856.
4012. Ann Homer, bo. March 11, 1833; d. June 19, 1837, in Boston.
4013. George Shattuck, bo. Feb. 5, 1837; d. June 30, 1838, in Boston.
4014. Joseph Brown, bo. March 8, 1838; not married.
4015. Sarah Catharine, bo. Feb. 11, 1841; ma. Robert Baird Torrance, at Singapore, S. E. Asia, Oct. 26, 1865. Children: ¹William Ladd, bo. ——: ²Hope, bo. Sept. 28, 1871; ³Mabel, bo. Oct. 24, 1874; ⁴Alexander Fraser, bo. Feb. 12, 1878. Mr. R. B. Torrance d. Sept. 18, 1889.
4016. John Haskins, bo. Aug. 29, 1843; ma. Ann Kelley French, May 12, 1868.

(4008)   William Gardner Ladd, Jr., of Brooklyn, N. Y., (son of William G.,⁴⁰⁰⁰) ma. Adeline Dodge Homer, Sept. 5, 1850, at Cambridge.

Children.

4017. Edith Homer, bo. in Cambridge, April 16, 1852; d. July 27, 1853.
4018. Charles Homer, bo. in Watertown, Nov. 2, 1854; d. Oct. 3, 1855.
4019. Edward Bromfield, bo. in Watertown, July 29, 1856.
4020. William, bo. in Boston, May 20, 1859.
4021. Francis Parker, bo. in Boston, Feb. 16, 1861.
4022. Homer, bo. in Summit, N. J., Feb. 9, 1867.

(4009)   Edward Homer Ladd, of Westfield, N. J., (son of William G.,⁴⁰⁰⁰) ma. Julia E. Marvin, Dec. 5, 1855, dau. of Thomas R. Marvin, of Boston. She died May, 1885.

Children.

4023. Annie Marvin, bo. in Boston, July 21, 1857; ma. Rev. Chas. J. Ropes, Oct. 4, 1877.
4024. Alice Rogers, bo. in Brooklyn, N. Y., Aug. 5, 1859; d. April 3, 1884.
4025. Edward Homer, Jr., bo. Sept. 30, 1860, in Brooklyn, N. Y.
4026. Ellen Ropes, bo. Sept 19, 1865, in London, England.

(4011)   Thomas Cushing Ladd, of Newark, N. J., (son of William G.,⁴⁰⁰⁰) ma. Mary E. Raiguel, April 3, 1856. In 1866 he was a merchant at Victoria, Hong Kong, China. He d. at Brooklyn, N. Y., May 12, 1887.

Children.

4027. Myra R., bo. Jan. 13, 1857.
4028. William R., bo. July 21, 1858.
4029. Charles C., bo. Feb. 16, 1861.

4030. Westray, bo. Dec. 8, 1863.
4031. Mary E., bo. Nov. 14, 1865.

(4016) John Haskins Ladd, of Wyoman, Balch Hill, Norwood, S. S. London, Eng., (son of William G.,[4000]) ma. Ann Kelley French, May 12, 1868, dau. of William Seabury and Rebecca (Swain) French, of Nantucket.

Children.

4032. Eliza Nevins, bo. Jan. 28, 1869, in San Francisco, Cal.
4033. Waldo Emerson, bo. Oct. 28, 1876, in Bowdon, Cheshire, Eng.

(3994) John Gardner Ladd, of Newport, R. I., (son of William,[3967]) ma. Sarah Easton. He died Jan. 4, 1819.

Children.

4034. Joseph Brown, bo. ——; ma. Harriet Nichols.
4035. Sarah Easton, bo. ——; ma. Rev. Fitch B. Taylor, 1841. Child: Sarienne.

(3997) John Haskins Ladd (son of William[3998]) ma. Eliza Smith Wyer, Sept. 4, 1819. She died 1856.

Child.

4036. John Gardner, bo. ——; ma. Augusta St. John.

(4034) Joseph Brown Ladd, of Cincinnati, O., (son of John G.,[3994]) ma. Mrs. Harriet Nichols. He d. at Cincinnati, O., Dec. 1873.

Children.

4037. Frances, bo. ——.
4038. Harriet, bo. ——.
4039. Ella, bo. ——.
4040. Nicholas Easton, bo. ——.

(4041) Samuel Ladd, of Providence, R. I., was, it is very evident, a descendant of Joseph Ladd.[3956] He was admitted a freeman of the colony, May 4, 1736. He purchased, Jan. 27, 1728, a dwelling-house and land of William Amy Carpenter. He purchased land in Warwick, R. I., July 18, 1750, of Moses Budlong. He sold land in Pawtuxet, R. I., Dec. 1, 1750, to Chas. Rhodes. His wife Bersheba signed the deed. He sold, Sept. 11, 1750, land in Pawtuxet, R. I., to Jeremiah Wescot, being the same land he purchased of Edward Arnold, March 30, 1736. He sold land and dwelling-house in Warwick, R. I., May 22, 1755, to James Green, his wife Bersheba signing the deed. He lived in Providence, Warwick, Johnston, and again in Providence, R. I. He ma. Bersheba ——, but we have failed to find her maiden surname, or the Christian name of the father of this Samuel Ladd.

Children.

4042. John, bo. 1740; ma. Lydia Olney.
4043. Joy, bo. ——; ma. Dorcas Dyer.
4044. William, bo. ——: ma. Martha Gay.

(4042) Rev. John Ladd, of West Schuyler, N. Y., (son of Samuel,[4041]) ma. Lydia, dau. of Gideon Olney. She was bo. 1752.

Children.

4045. Zilphia, bo. ——; ma. John Budlong. Children: [1]Nathan, [2]John, [3]Milton, [4]Celia, [5]a daughter who married a Mr. Brown.
4046. Samuel, bo. ——; ma. Betsey Ford, 1816.
4047. John, bo. 1786; ma. Elizabeth Olney.
4048. Lydia, bo. 1786; not married.
4049. Olney, bo. 1789; ma. Betsey Brown.
4050. Mehitable, bo. ——; ma. Gideon Johnson. Child: Seth.
4051. Hannah, bo. ——; ma. Asa Johnson. Had one daughter.
4052. Anstis, bo. ——; ma. Sarshal Root. Had one daughter.
4053. Bethia, bo. ——; ma. Caleb C. Lammon. Had six children.
4054. Paulina, bo. ——; ma. Perry Buck. Child: Lyman.

(4046) Samuel Ladd, of Schuyler, N. Y., (son of Rev. John,[4042]) ma. Betsey Ford, 1816. He died Sept. 1835. She died April 15, 1875.

Children.

4055. Horace, bo. 1818; d. in infancy.
4056. Maria, bo. April 12, 1820; ma. Levi Burch, Nov. 13, 1861.
4057. Hannah, bo. 1824; ma. Peter Lash, Sept. 30, 1846.
4058. Horace, bo. 1826; d. 1843.
4059. Duane, bo. 1828; d. in infancy.
4060. Harriet, bo. Oct. 4, 1831; ma. W. D. Smith, Jan. 25, 1880.
4061. Elizabeth, bo. Oct. 17, 1834; ma. Isaac A. Brown.

(4047) John Ladd, of Victor, N. Y., (son of Rev. John,[4042]) ma. Elizabeth, dau. of Emor Olney. She died Dec. 11, 1834, and he ma. 2d, Mrs. Betsey Ford, widow of his brother Samuel.[4046]

Children.

4062. Elvira, bo. Oct. 4, 1814; ma. John Hart, Feb. 20, 1834. He died Dec. 1880.
4063. Mahala, bo. Aug. 7, 1818; ma. Alanson Woolsey, Nov. 26, 1837.

4064. Cassandra, bo. May 9, 1820; ma. Henry H. Norman, Oct. 6, 1848. She died Dec. 18, 1889.
4065. William, bo. Oct. 30, 1821; ma. Mary Richardson, Aug. 1862.
4066. Hiram, bo. Jan. 9, 1823; ma. Mary Riddell, Oct. 6, 1845.
4067. Calista, bo. Dec. 24, 1824; ma. Silas Richardson, Nov. 15, 1844.
4068. Adeline, bo. Jan. 1, 1827; ma. Silas Richardson, No. 2, Sept. 20, 1854. Children: [1]Jerry C., bo. Nov. 22, 1860, d. Feb. 3, 1875; [2]Elias Ladd, bo. May 31, 1864; [3]John Murry, bo. Sept. 16, 1867.
4069. Smith, bo. March 20, 1829; ma. Mary Wilson. No children. He died April, 1883.
4070. Jennette, bo. June 6, 1831; ma. Stephen W. Curtis, Sept. 14, 1857. She d. Feb. 18, 1866.

4050) Olney Ladd, of Schuyler, N. Y., (son of Rev. John,[4042]) ma. Betsey Brown. She died Aug. 30, 1825, and he ma. 2d, Mrs. Jane Morris, March 19, 1826.

Children.

4071. Emily, bo. Oct. 3, 1812; ma. George Bullard, June, 1837.
4072. Esther, bo. Dec. 15, 1815; ma. Hawley Gurrills, March 27, 1837.
4073. Luke, bo. Feb. 1821; ma. Sarah Lippet Wilmouth, June, 1845. He died Sept. 1846.
4074. John, bo. ——; ma. Mrs. Luke (Wilmouth) Ladd, May, 1849.

Children by second wife.

4075. James, bo. May, 1827; ma. Elizabeth Burton, 1847.
4076. Samuel, bo. Jan. 1829; ma. Chloe Burton, 1850.

4043) Joy Ladd, of Johnston, R. I., (son of Samuel,[4041]) lived in North Providence and Pawtucket, R. I., and removed to Schuyler, N. Y., in 1804. He ma. Aug. 7, 1774, Dorcas, dau. of Charles and Abigail (Williams) Dyer, grand-daughter of Thomas and Mary (Blackmer) Williams, great-grand-daughter of Joseph Williams, whose father was Roger Williams, the founder of Rhode Island. We copy the following from the town records of Johnston, R. I.: "Joy Ladd, of North Providence, R. I., bought of Phineas Actin, of Johnston, R. I., laborer, land as per deed dated March 30, 1781. Joy Ladd, gentleman, sold land to Solomon Thornton, of Johnston, R. I., yeoman, as per deed dated Dec. 24, 1792." From records of Pawtucket, R. I.: "Joy Ladd, of North Providence, deeded to his son, Elisha Ladd, land and buildings, Sept. 17, 1799. Joy Ladd and Elisha Ladd deeded to Fenner Angell, Dec. 24, 1803. Dorcas, the wife of Joy Ladd, signed the deed." One of his descendants said of him: "He was very temperate, even tempered, and the finest old man I ever knew. The day he was eighty-four years old he walked a half a mile to my father's house, came in, seated himself by the front window, and remarked, 'It is seventy years to-day since I went to learn a trade.'" He was a shoemaker, but never worked at his trade after he purchased his farm. He died July 4, 1826.

Children.

4077. Samuel, bo. Feb. 9, 1775; ma. Susan Smith.
4078. Elisha, bo. Oct. 21, 1776; ma. Rhoda Olney.
4079. Lydia, bo. 1786.
4080. Alfred, bo. Aug. 9, 1791; ma. Sarah Killmer, Oct. 10, 1816.

(4077) Samuel Ladd, of Earlville, N. Y., (son of Joy,[4043]) ma. Susan, dau. of Benjamin Smith. He died in 1838.

Children.

4081. John Brown, bo. ——; ma. Lydia B. Murphy.
4082. Achsah Melvin, bo. Nov. 17, 1797; ma. Henry Dewey, March 20, 1817. Children: [1]Samuel, [2]Benjamin.
4083. Smith E., bo. ——; ma. Clarissa Hall; 2d, Abby Munroe, of New Bedford, 1860. He was for several years landlord of the Parker House at New Bedford, and was at one time a member of Hatch & Co.'s New York and Boston Express Co.
4084. Alfred, bo. ——; not married. He studied medicine with Dr. Alexis Smith.
4085. Lucy Spear, bo. April 6, 1808; ma. John M. Bronson, Oct. 3, 1832. She died Dec. 23, 1877.

(4078) Elisha Ladd, of North Providence, R. I., (son of Joy,[4043]) ma. Rhoda, dau. of Emor Olney, 1804.

Children.

4086. Amy, bo. Sept. 19, 1805; ma. Pardon Angell, June, 1827. She d. July 16, 1832. Child: [1]Louisa M., bo. April 4, 1828, ma. Lomie Chadwick, of Rockfield, Ill.
4087. Otis, bo. March 4, 1807; d. Oct. 15, 1826.
4088. Charles, bo. Aug. 5, 1809; ma. Elizabeth Johnson, Sept. 13, 1831. He died 1847.
4089. Daria, bo. April 20, 1812; ma. David W. Baldwin, Jan. 18, 1831. She died 1840. Children: [1]Eleanor, bo. Nov. 7, 1831; ma. Orson M. Blanchard; children, [1]Arthur M., [2]Laura. [2]William. [3]Marietta, bo. Feb. 15, 1839; ma. Dr. William P. Grannis, Dec. 17, 1863. He studied with Dr. A. M. Holmes, of Morrisville, N. Y., and began practice in Havana, Schuyler Co., N. Y., in 1859. In 1861 he en-

listed in the army and remained in the service a year, when he was discharged and returned to Morrisville until 1869, when he removed to Oswego, N. Y. Child: Lucy S., bo. Jan. 24, 1869; ma. Aug. 31, 1889, William D. Eckstein, of Barbados, W. I. Dr. Grannis died at Morrisville, N. Y., Oct. 19, 1887.

4090. Enior O., bo. July 20, 1814; ma. Huldah Mathew.
4091. Mary Ann, bo. Feb. 28, 1818; ma. George Howard.
4092. James B., bo. Aug. 13, 1821; ma. Harriet Richardson.
4093. Achsah D., bo. Sept. 30, 1824.

(4080) Alfred Ladd, of Old Mission, Mich., (son of Joy,[4043]) ma. Sarah Killmer, Oct. 10, 1816. He was a farmer.

Children.

4094. Adeline M., bo. Sept. 26, 1817; ma. Jacob Gage, Sept. 10, 1837.
4095. Elisha P., bo. May 28, 1819; ma. Mary Wilmarth, Sept. 10, 1850.
4096. Rosella, bo. June 4, 1821; not married; d. Feb. 6, 1839.
4097. Benjamin Franklin, bo. Sept. 6, 1823; d. Oct. 12, 1858.
4098. Dorcas D., bo. July 4, 1826; ma. Owen Hughson. She d. Jan. 10, 1859.
4099. Otis D., bo. Oct. 12, 1828; d. May 21, 1852.
4100. George, bo. May 9, 1831; not married; d. March 4, 1856.

(4081) John Brown Ladd, of Earlville, N. Y., (son of Samuel,[4077]) ma. Lydia B. Murphy. She died 1860.

Children.

4101. Susan M., bo. Oct. 6, 1823; ma. Dr. Harvey G. Beardsley.
4102. Frances, bo. April, 1825; ma. Albert M. Sheldon.
4103. Samuel, bo. ——; not married.
4104. Smith E., bo. ——.
4105. John B., bo. Aug. 18, 1839; ma. Emily Coffin, May 31, 1866. No children.

(4095) Elisha P. Ladd, of Old Mission, Mich., (son of Alfred,[4080]) ma. Mary Wilmarth, Sept. 10, 1850. He was born in West Bloomfield, N. Y., May 28, 1819; moved with his parents to Schuyler, N. Y.; was brought up on a farm; was educated at Whitestown Seminary, in Oneida Co., N. Y.; was engaged for some ten years at school teaching in Herkimer and Oneida Counties, N. Y.; removed to Old Mission, Mich., in May, 1852. He served as supervisor of the township, Grand Traverse Co., Mich., from 1861 to 1869, and was county superintendent of schools from 1872 to 1876.

Children.

4106. Emor O., bo. Jan. 5, 1853; ma. Agnes A. Davis, Nov. 22, 1881.
4107. Rosella M., bo. June 22, 1855; ma. Eugene M. Scofield, Jan. 1, 1880.
   Children: ¹Ray Fremont, bo. Feb. 24, 1882; ²Mabel Laura, bo. June 4, 1884.
4108. C. Fremont, bo. Feb. 5, 1857; not married; d. Oct. 25, 1880.
4109. Jessie, bo. Aug. 29, 1859.
4110. Adoniram Judson, bo. April 28, 1861; ma. Lillian Adelaide Vanvilyer, June 20, 1889.
4111. Scott W., bo. May 17, 1863; d. May 13, 1864.
4112. Cora L., bo. Aug. 12, 1865.

(4106) Emor O. Ladd, of Mapleton, Mich., (son of Elisha P.,[4095]) ma. Agnes A. Davis, Nov. 22, 1881.

Child.

4113. Clarence, bo. Nov. 28, 1882.

(4065) William Ladd, of Clayton, Mich., (son of John,[4047]) ma. Mary Richardson, Aug. 1862.

Children.

4114. Frank A., bo. Sept. 4, 1863.
4115. Edwin H., bo. Jan. 12, 1865.
4116. William C., bo. July 31, 1871.

(4066) Hiram Ladd, of Victor, N. Y., (son of John,[4047]) ma. Mary J. Riddell, Oct. 5, 1845.

Children.

4117. John M., bo. 1854; ma. Mary E. Chapman, 1875.
4118. Smith R., bo. 1857; ma. Lydia Carpenter, 1879. He died Dec. 1881.

(4117) John M. Ladd, of Victor, N. Y., (son of Hiram,[4066]) ma. Mary E. Chapman, 1875.

Children.

4119. Inez, bo. 1876.
4120. Howard, bo. 1879.
4121. Jean, bo. 1884.
4122. Fannie, bo. 1887.

(4118) Smith R. Ladd, of Victor, N. Y., (son of Hiram,[4066]) ma. Lydia Carpenter, 1879.

Children.

4123. Sylvester C., bo. 1880.
4124. Smith R., Jr., bo. 1882; lived 19 days.

(4125)   John Ladd, of Charlestown, R. I., (supposed to have been a descendant of Joseph Ladd,[3986] of Portsmouth, R. I.,) was admitted a Freeman, May 1, 1774. [Records of the Colony of Rhode Island, vol. 5, page 83.] He purchased land of John Wightman, March 11, 1750; purchased land of Waterman Tibbets, May 27, 1765; purchased land of Isaac Stiles, Aug. 21, 1763; purchased land of John Kenyon, Aug. 11, 1763. Sold land to Philip Anthony, March 17, 1756, his wife Mary signing the deed. Sold land to his son James, March 28, 1771. He purchased land of George Briggs, March 16, 1769; purchased land of Elisha Wightman, April 6, 1771. He sold ten acres to Elisha Wightman, April 6, 1771, his wife Ann signing the deed. He ma. Mary Lewis. She died, and he ma. 2d, Mrs. Ann (Arnold) Green, dau. of William and Phebe (Stafford) Arnold, widow of Ebenezer Green, and had by him two children: [1]Ebenezer Green, [2]Peter Green.

Children.

4126. James, bo. April 11, 1746; ma. Sarah Sherman, Jan. 12, 1778.
4127. Daniel, bo. April 7, 1748.
4128. Elizabeth, bo. Dec. 7, 1750; ma. Solomon Lewis, July 18, 1790.
4129. Mary, bo. May 27, 1752; ma. Joseph Crandall, Feb. 16, 1775. Child: Elizabeth, bo. Oct. 5, 1778.
4130. Dorcas, bo. May 27, 1754.
4131. John, bo. May 8, 1756; ma. Sarah Barber.
4132. Lydia, bo. July 8, 1759.

Children by second wife.

4133. Job, bo. ——; ma. Sarah Potter.
4134. Caleb, bo. July 9, 1773; ma. Caty Green, July 30, 1797.
4135. Marianna, bo. ——.
4136. Ann, bo. ——; ma. Alexander Haven, Jan. 1, 1790. He was the son of William and Deliverance (Stafford) Haven, bo. Dec. 22, 1765.

(4126)   James Ladd, of West Greenwich, R. I., (son of John,[4125]) ma. Sarah Sherman, Jan. 12, 1778. He died July 6, 1816. His widow died Sept. 19, 1850.

Children.

4137. Abigail, bo. Oct. 4, 1778; d. Jan. 29, 1807.
4138. Mary, bo. June 17, 1780; ma. Seneca Mahan. She died Dec. 29, 1850. Children: [1]Alexander, [2]Franklin.
4139. Sarah, bo. June 10, 1782; ma. Oliver Wyers. She died Dec. 5, 1814. Children: [1]John C., [2]Eunice, [3]Grant, [4]Hattie.
4140. James K., bo. May 5, 1784.
4141. Sherman, bo. July 6, 1786; ma. Abigail Choate.

(4131) John Ladd, of West Greenwich, R. I., (son of John,[4125]) ma. Sarah, dau. of Agias and Eleanor (Lewis) Barber, of Exeter, R. I. His will was dated Jan. 27, 1817, and proved Dec. 25, 1820. His wife died, and he ma. 2d, Hannah Reynolds, of Coventry, R. I.

Children.

4142. Lydia, bo. Feb. 10, 1779; ma. Stephen Parker, Nov. 11, 1798. Children: [1]James, bo. March 20, 1799. [2]John, bo. Jan. 17, 1801. [3]Rebecca, bo. June 5, 1802. [4]Julia Ann, bo. ——.
[5]Daniel, bo. Jan. 28, 1805; ma. Esther Olin, Nov. 29, 1832. Children: [1]Stephen, bo. Sept. 23, 1833; ma. Julia Griswold. [2]Susan P., bo. Jan. 12, 1835; ma. George B. Medbury, Jan. 22, 1854, and had: [1]Ida, bo. Aug. 13, 1855, d. Sept. 17, 1855; [2]George P., bo. Oct. 9, 1856, d. April 15, 1882; [3]Charles E., bo. Oct. 18, 1859, drowned Dec. 2, 1867; [4]Minnie Susie, bo. Feb. 14, 1864, ma. Charles F. Nugent, July 17, 1889. When a little child Minnie Susie developed rare musical talent. The Norwich Daily Bulletin of Jan. 5, 1869, thus compliments her: " The best concert of its kind ever given in Jersey City, was given last Saturday night by little Susie Medbury. She is four years old, and small at that, but a most beautiful and attractive child, and plays an organ or piano with wonderful skill. She performed some twenty pieces and sung several airs, and among them the touching ballad entitled ' Little Barefoot,' in a most interesting and beautiful manner." [5]Oscar A., bo. Jan. 4, 1868, d. July 20, 1868; [6]Lowell E., bo. Jan. 7, 1872, d. Jan. 7, 1876. [3]Sarah L., bo. Nov. 30, 1836; [4]Emily F., bo. Aug. 12, 1839; [5]Esther, bo. Feb. 13, 1842; [6]John J.. bo. July 10, 1844; [7]Daniel W., bo. March 1, 1847, ma. Josephine Rice, Sept. 1872; [8]George W., bo. Dec. 1854; [9]Jane E., bo. 1858. [6]Esther. [7]Calvin M. [8]Sarah. [9]Noah, bo. Sept. 2, 1814; ma. Lucy Ann James, Sept. 30, 1845. [10]Mary, d. young.

4143. Mary, bo. July 12, 1780; ma. Charles Hawkins, Nov. 21, 1799. Children: [1]Asnel; [2]Eseck, bo. Feb. 2, 1804, ma. Ursula Maples, Oct. 16, 1825; [3]Lydia, ma. Mr. Burdick; [4]George B., ma. Emily Maples.

4144. Daniel, bo. March 9, 1782; ma. Mary Lewis, bo. March 10, 1787.

4145. Eleanor, bo. March 24, 1784; ma. Moses Lewis, Nov. 18, 1804. She died Feb. 18, 1871. Children: [1]Isaac, bo. Sept. 23, 1805, ma. Clarissa Jones, Feb. 7, 1829; [2]Beda, bo. Aug. 13, 1808, ma. Eva Jones, Feb. 1, 1827; [3]John Ladd, bo. May 1, 1811, ma. Lois Squien, June 1, 1839; [4]Sarah, bo. Oct. 13, 1812; [5]Jonathan, bo. Aug. 25, 1814, ma. Orinda Weaver, April 2, 1840; [6]Moses, bo. June 21, 1817, not ma., d. Jan. 1889; [7]Josiah Barber, bo. Jan. 9, 1820, d. Aug. 25, 1823; [8]Asahel Hawkins, bo. Nov. 27, 1821, not ma., d. Aug. 3, 1847; [9]Eleanor Delano, bo. Feb. 13, 1824, d. July 17, 1825; [10]Daniel Ladd, bo. June 18, 1828, d. Oct. 30, 1836.

4146. John, bo. April 8, 1786; d. in infancy.

4147. Sarah, bo. Sept. 10, 1787; ma. Edward Burleson, April 8, 1804. Children: [1]Matilda; [2]Rowena C., not ma.; [3]Olive P.; [4]Clarissa C., ma. William L. Holt; [5]John L., d. aged 11 years; [6]Allen Briggs, ma. Mary L. Fanning; [7]Sarah Ladd, ma. Erastus L. Prior; [8]Lucy A., ma. Dennis Wheelock; [9]William L., ma. Sarah L. Graves, ma. 2d., Martha Day.
4148. John, bo. Dec. 4, 1789.
4149. Esther, bo. Feb. 8, 1792; ma. Jesse Lewis, Nov. 4, 1810. Children: [1]Anna, bo. Dec. 19, 1811, ma. Henry P. Ray, Nov. 18, 1846; [2]Benjamin, bo. April 30, 1815, ma. Lydia M. Jaques, Aug. 16, 1835; [3]Daniel, bo. Aug. 1, 1816, ma. Ann G. Steere, Oct. 12, 1840; [4]Moses, bo. May 12, 1820, ma. Nancy Batcheller, Oct. 6, 1841.
4150. Dorcas, bo. Jan. 27, 1795; ma. Peleg Lewis, 1818. Children: [1]Eolin Porter, bo. May 22, 1819, ma. Alta Merrill, Sept. 10, 1840; [2]Ann Mercy, bo. April 4, 1822, ma. Joseph Squier, Sept. 18, 1843. Dorcas' husband died March 11, 1822, and she ma. 2d, Rufus Peck, Jan. 1828, and had: [3]Marilla, bo. Feb. 25, 1830, ma. Grant Joslid; [4]Rufus Ladd, bo. Jan. 8, 1833, not ma., d. Aug. 11, 1863; [5]John Wesley, bo. May 8, 1837, ma. Margaret E. Wayne, Nov. 11, 1862.
4151. Olive, bo. Oct. 26, 1797.
4152. Anthony, bo. Oct. 26, 1797.
4153. Ann Mercy, bo. 1799.

(4140) James K. Ladd, of White's Corner, Potter Co., N. Y., (son of James,[4126]) ma. ——.

Children.

4154. Sally, bo. ——.
4155. Garret S., bo. ——.
4156. Hannah, bo. ——.
4157. Desdemonia, bo. ——.
4158. William C., bo. ——.
4159. Charles G., bo. ——.

(4141) Sherman Ladd, of Pownal, Vt., (son of James,[4126]) ma. Abigail Choate, 1815. He died May 10, 1854. His widow died Dec. 29, 1873.

Children.

4160. Benjamin, bo. Dec. 20, 1815; ma. Clarinda Haley.
4161. James, bo. Feb. 2, 1817; ma. Emeline Jordan.
4162. John, bo. Dec. 16, 1818; ma. Margaret Flynn, June 26, 1845.
4163. Abigail, bo. Nov. 10, 1820; ma. John Gridley. She d. Jan. 22, 1853.
4164. Joshua, bo. Oct. 4, 1822; ma. Ellen Brown.
4165. Sherman, Jr., bo. Sept. 3, 1824; ma. Lydia Campbell, Jan. 5, 1847.
4166. Moses, bo. Feb. 8, 1826; ma. Delia M. Niles. No children.
4167. Aaron, bo. Feb. 8, 1826; ma. Luduska Niles.
4168. Sarah S., bo. Feb. 9, 1829; ma. John Rearick.

4169. Mary, bo. May 7, 1831; d. Aug. 18, 1847.
4170. Marion, bo. Nov. 8, 1832; d. Jan. 27, 1834.
4171. Eunice M., bo. Dec. 3, 1834; not married.
4172. Elizabeth, bo. Oct. 21, 1836; ma. Hiram Brown.

(4144) Daniel Ladd, of West Greenwich, R. I., (son of John,[4131]) ma. Mary, dau. of Samuel and Elizabeth (James) Lewis. She died Nov. 3, 1839, and he ma. 2d, Lydia Jaques. He died Jan. 8, 1862.

Children.

4173. Alfred D., bo. June 23, 1808; ma. Ruhamah Kenyon, Feb. 13, 1831.
4174. Thirza, bo. March 17, 1810; ma. Joseph Vaughn, Nov. 20, 1838.
4175. Emeline, bo. May 15, 1812; d. Oct. 23, 1812.
4176. Barber, bo. Nov. 7, 1813; d. Sept. 25, 1828.
4177. John, bo. Oct. 22, 1815; ma. Azuba Clark Douglass, July 15, 1839.
4178. James, bo. Nov. 16, 1817; ma. Lavina Kelley, 1846.
4179. Orrin, bo. Jan. 12, 1820; ma. Philenia Tilleston, 1840.
4180. Jonathan M., bo. Dec. 21, 1821; ma. Louisa Prentice, Jan. 1, 1849.
4181. Joseph C., bo. March 6, 1824; ma. Sarah Backus, Nov. 23, 1846.
4182. George R., bo. July 9, 1826; d. June 4, 1847.
4183. Sarah, bo. April 20, 1830; ma. Edwin Grant, 1847; 2d, Israel J. Tafts.

Child by second wife.

4184. Philena, bo. May 4, 1842.

(4160) Benjamin Ladd, of Pownal, Vt., (son of Sherman,[4141]) ma. Clarinda Haley.

Children.

4185. Benjamin, Jr., bo. ——.
4186. Eunice, bo. ——.
4187. Sarah, bo. ——.

(4161) James Ladd, of Pownal, Vt., (son of Sherman,[4141]) ma. Emeline Jordan.

Children.

4188. Emily R. Bell, bo. Sept. 7, 1841.
4189. James A., bo. March 7, 1848.

(4162) John Ladd, of Pownal, Vt., (son of Sherman,[4141]) ma. Margaret Flynn, June 26, 1845.

Children.

4190. Mariana, bo. April 26, 1847; d. July 2, 1847.
4191. Alice M., bo. Jan. 9, 1849; ma. T. A. Trumlan, July 14, 1872.
4192. John V., bo. Feb. 14, 1857; ma. Aggie C. Gibbons, June 30, 1880.
4193. Isabel M., bo. July 22, 1860; ma. Charles H. Noyes, Nov. 10, 1880.
4194. Mary, bo. Aug. 16, 1863; d. Aug. 7, 1864.

(4164) Joshua Ladd, of Pownal, Vt., (son of Sherman,[4141]) ma. Ellen Brown.

Children.

4195. Rufus J., bo. April 2, 1848; d. July 3, 1852.
4196. Abel A., bo. Aug. 21, 1849.
4197. Gates B., bo. Aug. 17, 1851.
4198. Louisa, bo. April 21, 1854.

(4165) Sherman Ladd, Jr., of Pownal, Vt., (son of Sherman,[4141]) ma. Lydia Campbell, Jan. 5, 1847.

Children.

4199. Eunice Adell, bo. Dec. 19, 1848.
4200. A son, bo. March 16, 1852; d. Nov. 18, 1852.
4201. Lee, bo. March 10, 1855.

(4167) Aaron Ladd, of Pownal, Vt., (son of Sherman,[4141]) ma. Luduska Niles, 1850.

Child.

4202. Arthur Gustavus. bo. Oct. 1, 1851; ma. Alice Ford, 1874.

(4173) Alfred D. Ladd, of Clinton, (son of Daniel,[4144]) ma. Ruhamah Kenyon, Feb. 13, 1831.

Children.

4203. George H., bo. April 10, 1832; ma. Elizabeth Worsley, 1855.
4204. Henry C., bo. July 1, 1837; ma. Adrianna Freeman, 1865.
4205. Emily A., bo. Aug. 10, 1839; d. Aug. 8, 1849.
4206. Alfred A., bo. Oct. 11, 1841; d. Dec. 8, 1843.
4207. Julia M., bo. Feb. 12, 1848; ma. Joseph F. Bartlett, 1867. Children: [1]Fred. Edward, bo. Dec. 3, 1868; [2]Dennis K., bo. May 27, 1871; [3]Frank L., bo. Oct. 16, 1872; [4]Rula B., bo. March 27, 1880.

(4177) John Ladd, of Plainfield, Conn., (son of Daniel,[4144]) ma. Azuba Clark Douglass, July 15, 1839. He died Feb. 23, 1873. She died Sept. 24, 1885.

Children.

4208. Azuba Nancy, bo. Dec. 19, 1840; ma. Henry F. Clark, March 18, 1868.
4209. Hattie Jane, bo. June 2, 1853; d. Sept. 16, 1866.

(4178) James Ladd, of Killingly, Conn., (son of Daniel,[4144]) ma. Lavina Kelley, 1844. He died Sept. 1876.

Children.

4210. Merrill A., bo. July 8, 1846; ma. Anna M. Shepard, May 19, 1875.
4211. Andrew J., bo. June 24, 1851; not married.
4212. Daniel Webster, bo. ——.

(4179) Orrin Ladd, of Holyoke, (son of Daniel,[4144]) ma. Philena Tilleston, 1840. She died, and he ma. 2d, Margaret Chapman, 1848.

Children by second wife.

4213. Charles H., bo. April 9, 1849; ma. Mary McBride, Nov. 24, 1877.
4214. Thirza, bo. Dec. 5, 1852.
4215. Louisa, bo. Nov. 15, 1855; ma. Clavis Chapin, 1870.
4216. Emma, bo. March 25, 1861; ma. David Kimball, May 17, 1879.
4217. Edward L., bo. Nov. 15, 1876.

(4180) Jonathan Ladd (son of Daniel[4144]) ma. Louisa S. Prentice, Jan. 1, 1849, dau. of John and Sophia (Brown) Prentice.

Children.

4218. Mary L., bo. May, 1862; d. in early childhood.
4219. Minnie L., bo. Aug. 1864; d. in early childhood.

(4181) Joseph C. Ladd, of Vineland, N. J., (son of Daniel,[4144]) ma. Sarah Backus, Nov. 23, 1846.

Children.

4220. Eldora M., bo. April 20, 1849; d. Oct. 2, 1850.
4221. Emily A., bo. Nov. 24, 1851; ma. Warren O. Collins, June 9, 1880.

(4192) John V. Ladd, of Chicago, Ill., (son of John,[4162]) ma. Aggie C. Gibbons, June 30, 1880.

Child.

4222. John Henry, bo. May 31, 1881.

(4202) Arthur Gustavus Ladd, of Pownal, Vt., (son of Aaron,[4166]) ma. Alice Ford, 1874.

Children.

4223. Lawrence, bo. Dec. 3, 1875.
4224. Bertha, bo. July, 1879.

(4203) George H. Ladd, of Auburn, (son of Alfred D.,[4173]) ma. Elizabeth Worsley, Dec. 31, 1855. She died March 16, 1860, and he ma. 2d, Mary M. Lawrence, Nov. 21, 1861. In the war of the rebellion he was in Co. F, 46th Mass. Infantry, one hundred days.

Child.

4225. Alfred W., bo. Feb. 3, 1860; ma. Ella Louise Fairfield, Aug. 26, 1884.

Child by second wife.

4226. Henry C., bo. Nov. 4, 1864.

(4204)   Henry C. Ladd, of Auburn, (son of Alfred,[4173]) ma. Adrianna Freeman, July 29, 1865. When Governor Andrew issued his call for troops for the protection of Washington, he was one of the first to respond. He left Worcester April 19, 1861, with Co. B, 3d Battalion of Rifles, under the command of Gen. Devens; served three months and returned home. Soon after he went West, and in Sept. 1861, he enlisted for three years in Co. C, 66th Ill. Reg. of Infantry; served his three years and then reenlisted; was with his regiment in all its battles in the West, and was with Gen. Sherman in his grand march to the sea. He was discharged at Washington, D. C., July, 1865. He was on detached duty as clerk at headquarters a part of the time, and at the date of his discharge was clerk in the mail department of Sherman's army.

Children.

4227. Alfred H., bo. Feb. 23, 1867.
4228. Minnie Louise, bo. Oct. 5, 1869.

(4210)   Merrill A. Ladd, of Central Village, Conn., (son of James,[4178]) ma. Anna M. Shepard, May 19, 1875.

Children.

4229. Merrill Augustus, bo. Nov. 9, 1878.
4230. Robert S., bo. Feb. 10, 1884; d. Sept. 1884.
4231. Ellwood S., bo. Jan. 6, 1887.

(4213)   Charles H. Ladd, of Philadelphia, Pa., (son of Orrin,[4179]) ma. Mary McBride, Nov. 24, 1877.

Children.

4232. Maggie, bo. Aug. 4, 1878.
4233. William, bo. June 18, 1880.

(4133)   Job Ladd, of Warwick, R. I., (son of John,[4125]) by 2d wife, ma. Sarah, dau. of Stephen Potter, of Coventry, R. I., Sept. 23, 1792. She died Nov. 21, 1799, and he ma. 2d, Elizabeth Warner. She died Oct. 30, 1865. He died Feb. 23, 1836.

Children.

4234. John Wanton, bo. Aug. 10, 1793; ma. Lydia S. Brown, Sept. 10, 1812.
4235. Caleb, bo. July 12, 1795; ma. Betsey Spink.
4236. Mary Ann, bo. Oct. 11, 1796; ma. Harvey Arnold.

(4134) Caleb Ladd, of Warwick, R. I., (son of John,[4125]) ma. Caty Green, dau. of Christopher and Abigail (Davis) Green, July 30, 1797. She died July 21, 1802, and he ma. 2d, Nancy Burlingame, Feb. 10, 1803. She died, and he ma. 3d, Phebe Kelly.

Children.

4237. Maria, bo. March 19, 1799; d. 1800.
4238. Joseph Warren, bo. May 24, 1801; ma. Almy W. Spencer, Feb. 20, 1826.

Children by second wife.

4239. Alexis, bo. March 10, 1804; ma. Susan A. Wescote, Nov. 15, 1826.
4240. John G., bo. Oct. 6, 1806; ma. Phebe A. Watson, Dec. 30, 1829.
4241. Caleb William, bo. April 6, 1809; d. April 21, 1826.
4242. Cecilia Ann, bo. Feb. 11, 1812; d. Sept. 12, 1813.
4243. Samuel J., bo. June 21, 1815; ma. Lucy A. Rice.
4244. Harriet N., bo. Feb. 12, 1817; ma. William M. Monroe.
4245. Ebenezer Green, bo. Sept. 26, 1820; ma. Minerva Sheldon.
4246. George W., bo. Aug. 1, 1823; d. Sept. 3, 1825.
4247. George W., bo. Sept. 5, 1825; ma. Cynthia Kelly.

(4235) Caleb Ladd, of Warwick, R. I., (son of Job,[4133]) ma. Betsey Spink.

Children.

4248. Bradford S., bo. ——; ma. Miranda Clark.
4249. Mary Elizabeth, bo. ——; not married.
4250. John W., bo. ——; ma. Susan Nichols.
4251. Abbie F., bo. Sept. 17, 1833; ma. John Warner, 1858.
4252. Job, bo. ——; ma. Anna Upham.
4253. Samuel A., bo. ——; ma. Mary E. Madison.

(4238) Joseph Warren Ladd, of Providence, R. I., (son of Caleb,[4134]) ma. Almy Wicks Spencer, Feb. 20, 1826. He died April 29, 1879.

Children.

4254. Catharine Green, bo. Nov. 20, 1826; ma. Herbert M. Carpenter, April 25, 1852.
4255. Almy Spencer, bo. Jan. 25, 1829; d. 1833.
4256. Maria Josephine, bo. Feb. 10, 1831; ma. Dr. Leonard F. Russell, June 25, 1868.
4257. Charles Carroll, bo. March 7, 1834; ma. Mary Ella Lee, 1867.
4258. Almy Spencer, bo. Feb. 16, 1836; ma. James S. Hudson, Mar. 19, 1858.
4259. Abbie Frances, bo. Oct. 14, 1838; ma. Joseph W. Andrews, March 17, 1863. Child: Lillian C., ma. Herbert E. Carpenter, June 7, 1882.
4260. Joseph Warren, bo. March 24, 1841; ma. Emma G. Lovejoy, Sept. 15, 1863.
4261. Susan Loraine, bo. Aug. 24, 1843; ma. Thos. Sawyer, Jr., July 2, 1863.
4262. Clara Louise, bo. Nov. 13, 1845; ma. Ollys A. Jillson, May 17, 1871.

(4239) Alexis Ladd, of Providence, R. I., (son of Caleb,[4184]) ma. Susan A. Wescote, Nov. 15, 1826. She died June 20, 1828, and he ma. 2d, Henrietta Rice, June 30, 1830. She died Dec. 17, 1854, and he ma. 3d, Caroline Brownell, April 30, 1857. He died June 25, 1888. He was a carpenter and builder, and carried on the business at Providence many years; was intelligent, successful, a good citizen, and respected by all who knew him. He passed his boyhood days at Apponaug, on the old homestead known as the " Ladd watering-place," since owned by Amasa Sprague.

Child by second wife.

4263. Mary E., bo. April 23, 1831; ma. Samuel S. White, Dec. 2, 1856. She died Nov. 27, 1887.
Daniel W., bo. July 15, 1834; d. July 28, 1836.
4264. Susan, bo. Sept. 7, 1836; d. July 18, 1838.
4265. Daniel W., bo. Aug. 4, 1838; d. at New Orleans, Dec. 31, 1858.
4266. Henry B., bo. Feb. 16, 1841; not married.
4267. Frances N., bo. March 10, 1843; ma. Alexander Walford, Oct. 2, 1863.
4268. Albert W., bo. Dec. 16, 1845; ma. Amanda Shaw, Oct. 16, 1872.
4269. George Storrs, bo. Dec. 5, 1847; ma. Almy F. Thurber, June 29, 1868.

(4240) John G. Ladd, of Newport, R. I., (son of Caleb,[4184]) ma. Phebe A. Watson, Dec. 30, 1828.

Children.

4270. Sarah Watson, bo. Dec. 10, 1829; not married.
4271. Nancy Burlingame, bo. 1831; ma. Henry E. Webster. Child: Arthur G., bo. April 19, 1857; not married.
4272. John Westgate, bo. Oct. 8, 1833; ma. Carrie Augusta Vaughn.
4273. Isabella, bo. 1839; d. 1840.
4274. Jane Spencer, bo. Feb. 1840; not married.

(4243) Samuel J. Ladd, of Providence, R. I., (son of Caleb,[4184]) ma. Lucy A. Rice, Sept. 1833. He died Oct. 28, 1886.

Children.

4275. Henry Clay, bo. July 4, 1834; d. Nov. 30, 1834.
4276. Harriet Newell, bo. Nov. 9, 1836; d. July 9, 1840.
4277. Charles Frederick, bo. May 2, 1841; ma. Emily J. Martin, May 17, 1865.
4278. Anna Stewart, bo. March 5, 1847; ma. Charles P. Gay, Oct. 12, 1866.
4279. Ella Kane, bo. July 10, 1849; ma. Albert H. Chaffee, Oct. 21, 1868.
Child: Howard Ladd, bo. June 21, 1874.
4280. Sarah Virginia, bo. March 13, 1851; d. Aug. 30, 1852.

(4245) Ebenezer Green Ladd, of Warwick, R. I., (son of Caleb,[4134]) ma. Minerva Sheldon, Nov. 24, 1844. She died May 20, 1853, and he ma. 2d, Catharine W. ——. He died Feb. 10, 1882.

Child.

4281. Theresa Maria, bo. Oct. 15, 1847.

(4246) George W. Ladd, of Providence, R. I., (son of Caleb,[4134]) ma. Cynthia Kelly, Dec. 1847. He ma. 2d, Mary, dau. of Horatio Bennett, of Warwick, R. I., Jan. 29, 1866. He is a manufacturer of watch-cases,—" Ladd's patent watch-case,"—of which he is the patentee.

Children.

4282. Caleb, bo. Dec. 12, 1848; d. May 17, 1858.
4283. George W., bo. Feb. 17, 1851; d. Feb. 22, 1852.

Children by second wife.

4284. Arthur B., bo. July 9, 1869.
4285. Frank Foster, bo. Feb. 1, 1873.

(4260) Joseph Warren Ladd, of Bird Island, Minn., (son of Joseph Warren,[4238]) ma. Emma G. Lovejoy, Sept. 15, 1863, formerly of Calais, Me., dau. of John L. and Mary M. Lovejoy.

Children.

4286. Charles Carroll, bo. May 1, 1865.
4287. Abbie Lovejoy, bo. Jan. 23, 1877.

(4257) Charles Carroll Ladd (son of Joseph Warren[4238]) ma. Mary Ella Lee, 1867. She died, and he ma. 2d, Annie Page Fowle, 1876.

Children.

4288. Arthur Page, bo. April 15, 1877.
4289. Warren Spencer, bo. Sept. 12, 1879.
4290. Annie Lee, bo. Nov. 13, 1881.

(4269) George Storrs Ladd, of Providence, R. I., (son of Alexis,[4239]) ma. Almy F. Thurber, June 29, 1868.

Children.

4291. Cora L., bo. Sept. 8, 1869.
4292. Daniel, bo. Sept. 26, 1874.
4293. Howard C., bo. Dec. 30, 1884.

(4272) Dr. John Westgate Ladd, a specialist, of New York city, (son of John G.,[4240]) ma. Carrie Augusta Vaughn, Sept. 21, 1868.

Children.

4294. Maud Crosby, bo. Aug. 15, 1869.
4295. Harry W., bo. Sept. 21, 1876; d. March 13, 1877.

(4277) Charles Frederick Ladd, of Providence, R. I., (son of Samuel,[4243]) ma. Emily J. Martin, May 17, 1865. He died May 14, 1868.

Children.

4296. Frederick Martin, bo. March 17, 1866; d. Aug. 2, 1866.
4297. Charles F., bo. June 19, 1868.

JOHN LADD,

OF BURLINGTON, N. J.

(4298)   John Ladd arrived at Burlington, N. J., in 1678. He was the son of Nicholas Ladd, of Swingfield, Kent Co., England, who was buried in the Quaker burial-ground at Hythe, in 1699. See page v. In the Reminiscences of Old Gloucester, by Isaac Mickle, Philadelphia, 1845, we find that: "The first court held under the constitution of Arwaumus was in Sept. 1686, and that John Ladd was one of the jurors; that the land on the shore of Deptford township seemed to have been taken up at an early day. In 1688, 500 acres at Cork Cove, above Red Bank, was surveyed to John Ladd and others. Howell's Cove, below Timber Creek, was called Cork Cove by the first English, but afterwards was called Ladd's Cove."

In the "Constitution" of Jan. 25, 1688, a newspaper published at Woodbury, N. J., we find an interesting article on John Ladd and John Ladd, Jr., by Judge John Clement, from which we make the following extracts: "The Plantations in America were the only places towards which the followers of George Fox turned when they found neither their persons or estates were protected by the laws of England as then administered. The boast of her statesmen that civil and religious liberty were assured to all within the realm, was towards this class of professing Christians a deception and a snare, and in view of their removal to this new and unsettled country they proceeded thoughtfully and deliberately to form a code of rights looking to certain security against such infringements thereafter. * * * Nothing seemed impossible to these sturdy men, and they planted a colony which has gone on increasing and expanding until their descendants may be found in every State and Territory within our present form of government. The concessions and arguments were published in London in 1676, and attracted much attention, especially among the members of the Society of Friends. Of these was John Ladd, who arrived at Burlington with many others in 1678. His interest was evidently with the London owners, for his first settlement appears to have been within the territory of Arwaumus, where the London people first proposed to have their town, but were persuaded to go higher up the river to Burlington. * * * John Ladd is mentioned as of Gloucester River, but subsequently called Timber Creek. He was a practical surveyor, and acted as deputy for the surveyor-general of the western division for several years. If tradition goes true, he was employed by William Penn in laying out the city of Philadelphia. When he produced his bill for thirty pounds for services rendered to the Patroon, he offered him a square of land in lieu of money, which was declined, for the young surveyor could see nothing like a city, as described by the sanguine owner, where he had wrestled with briers and tangled undergrowth. There is a tradition in the family that when Mr. Ladd declined the square of land in the city, William Penn remarked, 'John, thou art Ladd by name and Ladd by nature, dost thou not know that this will be a great city?' * * * In 1688, with Jonathan Wood and Samuel Toms, he located a large tract of land in Deptford township, extending from the river on the west to the Salem road and beyond on the east. He soon after purchased Samuel Tom's and Jonathan Wood's interest, and built a dwelling-house for himself on the tract, and where he resided until his death. In 1721 he located an adjoining tract along the river shore, where the fishery was established, and used to the present day. For many years a portion of this tract has been known as the Howell estate, coming into that family by the devise of John Ladd, Jr., to John Ladd Howell, a son of Katharine Ladd, who married John Howell. There is abundant evidence to show that John Ladd was a member of the Society of Friends, and there is little doubt that he was an attendant of the meeting at the mouth of Woodbury Creek, before the erection of the house by the south side of the King's road and west of the before-named stream. * * * He came to New Jersey a young man; about sixty-two years of his life were spent within the province, where he was a prominent and influential citizen. He was a man of considerable estate and of good education, as is shown by his operations in land and the places of responsibility he was called upon to fill. * * * As disclosed in his will dated in 1731, with codicil dated in 1740, John Ladd survived his wife and all his children except John and Katharine. He devised his homestead estate of 560 acres to John, and gave other parts of his property to Katharine and his grand-daughter, Mary Parker, having, as he says in his will, provided for Samuel and Jonathan while they were living. At his death he was one of the largest holders of real estate in the colony, and his selections prove him to have been a man of good judgment in such matters. He established the fishery where his land fronted the river, and which was for many years known as Ladd's Cove. The exact date has been lost, but as he located the flats in 1722, that may be about the beginning of his fishery. Its particular situation on the shore always made it one of the best in those waters. John Ladd was not a negative character, but his opinions were his own and freely expressed. He held a prominent place in the Society of Friends, and although he adhered to the plainness of dress and simplicity of habit, yet about his home could be seen evidence of things generally attendant on wealth and liberality. His slaves, his plentiful board, and his well-appointed household, would convince any one that creature comforts were not neglected."

He ma. Elizabeth ——. She died 1733. He died 1740.

Children.

4299. Samuel, bo. ——; ma. Mary Medcalf, 1713.
4300. Jonathan, bo. ——; ma. Ann Wills, 1723.
4301. Mary, bo. ——; ma. Joseph Parker, of Philadelphia, 1730.
4302. John, Jr., bo. ——; ma. Hannah Mickle, 1732. He died Dec. 20, 1770. No children.
4303. Katharine, bo. ——; ma. John Howell, Jan. 25, 1734.

(4299) Samuel Ladd, of Woodbury, N. J., (son of John,[4298]) ma. Mary Medcalf, 1713.

Children.

4304. Matthew, bo. ——; not married.
4305. Joseph, bo. ——.
4306. Sarah, bo. ——.
4307. Deborah, bo. ——.
4308. Katharine, bo. ——.

(4300) Jonathan Ladd, of Woodbury, N. J., (son of John,[4298]) ma. Ann Wills, 1723. He died 1725.

Children.

4309. Samuel, bo. Sept. 1724; ma. Sarah ——.
4310. Elizabeth, bo. Sept. 1724.

(4309) Samuel Ladd, of Woodbury, N. J., (son of Jonathan,[4300]) ma. Sarah ——.

Children.

4311. Jonathan, bo. Sept. 23, 1755; d. June 6, 1760.
4312. Ann, bo. July 11, 1757; d. June 28, 1782.
4313. Hannah, bo. Nov. 7, 1759; d. Nov. 2, 1789.
4314. Deborah, bo. Sept. 23, 1760; d. March 3, 1771.
4315. Ella, bo. June 2, 1762.
4316. John, bo. Nov. 2, 1764.
4317. Samuel, Jr., bo. Nov. 10, 1771; ma. Ann Wood, July 3, 1815.

(4317) Samuel Ladd, Jr., of Woodbury, N. J., (son of Samuel,[4309]) ma. Ann, dau. of William and Deborah Wood, July 3, 1815. He died July 19, 1833.

Children.

4318. John, bo. May 26, 1816; d. June 9, 1816.
4319. James, bo. Oct. 4, 1817; d. Aug. 8, 1818.
4320. Sarah, bo. March 26, 1820; d. May 15, 1832.
4321. Samuel H., bo. March 6, 1826; ma. Sally Duncomb Johnson, Sept. 22, 1846.

(4321) Samuel H. Ladd, of Woodbury, N. J., (son of Samuel,[4317]) ma. Sally Duncomb Johnson, Sept. 22, 1846.

Children.

4322. William H., bo. July 20, 1847; d. Dec. 12, 1863, in the army.
4323. Samuel H., Jr., bo. Dec. 15, 1849; ma. Kate B. Johnson, Jan. 15, 1879.
4324. Sally Cora, bo. Aug. 19, 1853; d. Aug. 9, 1854.

(4323) Samuel H. Ladd, Jr., of Woodbury, N. J., (son of Samuel H.,[4321]) ma. Kate B., dau. of Thomas L. and Cora B. Johnson, Jan. 15, 1879.

Children.

4326. Cora V., bo. Nov. 2, 1879.
4327. Sallie D., bo. Jan. 1, 1883.

(4303) Katharine Ladd (dau. of John Ladd [4298]) ma. John Howell, Jan. 25, 1734, at the Friends' meeting-house at Haddenfield, N. J. He settled at Woodbury, N. J. Removed in 1739 to Philadelphia, Pa., and from there to Georgia, and from there to Charleston, S. C., where he died. He was the son of Jacob and Sarah (Vernon) Howell, of Chester, Pa., and grandson of John and Sarah Howell, who in 1697 emigrated with their three children, Jacob, Evan, and Sarah, from the ancient city of Aberystwith, Cardigan Co., Wales, and settled in the city of Philadelphia, Pa., where he continued to reside until his death, Jan. 26, 1721. He was a member of the Society of Friends. Sarah Vernon, who ma. Jacob Howell, was the dau. of Randall and Sarah Vernon. He was a man of eminence in those days, and a very active and influential member of the Society of Friends. He had emigrated from Sandway, Cheshire, England, in company with his brothers, Thomas and Robert, and arrived in this country in 1682. Randall Vernon was the son of James Vernon, who was at one time Secretary of State of Great Britain, and brother of Sir Edward Vernon, "Vice Admiral of the Blue" in the British navy, and a descendant from the Staffordshire branch of the Vernon family, one of the oldest and most noble of all England, tracing their descent from Lord William De Vernon, who was sovereign in his own right in Normandy, and accompanied William the Conqueror to England in 1066. Lawrence Washington, an elder brother of George Washington, settled in Fairfax Co., Va., in 1743, and named his estate Mt. Vernon, after Admiral Vernon, under whom he had served in the British navy.

Children of John and Katharine (Ladd) Howell.

4328. Sarah, bo. ——; ma. John Sparks.
4329. John Ladd, bo. March 15, 1738; ma. Frances Paschall.

(4329) John Ladd Howell, of Philadelphia, Pa., (son of John and Katharine [4308] (Ladd) Howell) ma. Frances Paschall, July 23, 1761, at Friends' meeting-house, Darby, Pa.

Child.

4330. Joshua Ladd, bo. Sept. 19, 1762; ma. Anna Blackwood.

(4330) Joshua Ladd Howell, of Woodbury, N. J., (son of John L.,[4329]) ma. Anna Blackwood, Feb. 16, 1786, of Gloucester, N. J. She was born Feb. 2. 1769, and died Jan. 14, 1855. He died Jan. 10, 1818. For several years after his marriage he occupied the old Ladd homestead, known as "Candor Hill." In 1805 he removed to his large new house on the Delaware, called

"Fancy Hill," which was a large estate of six or seven thousand acres, left by his grand-uncle, John Ladd,[4302] to his widow Hannah M. Ladd, and from her by will to Joshua Ladd Howell, where he lived until he died.

Children.

4331. Samuel Ladd, bo. May 11, 1787; ma. Mary Harrison Clayton, Nov. 30, 1809.
4332. Paschall, bo. Nov. 6, 1789; not ma.; d. at "Fancy Hill," Sept. 1, 1811.
4333. Frances, bo. April 2, 1791; ma. Benjamin Butterton Howell, her 2d cousin, March 15, 1810. He was lost on steamer President, with all on board, March, 1841. She d. June 8, 1829. Had ten children.
4334. John Ladd, bo. Jan. 16, 1793; not married; d. Nov. 30, 1828.
4335. Ann Maria, bo. Oct. 1795; ma. Rev. James H. Jones. She d. Jan. 6, 1865. He d. Dec. 22, 1868. Had five children.
4336. Joshua, bo. Nov. 20, 1797; d. Aug. 1800.
4337. Richard Washington, bo. Dec. 15, 1799; ma. Mary Tonkin Carpenter, March 30, 1830.
4338. Abigail Blackwood, bo. Feb. 21, 1802; ma. Rev. Thomas Leiper Janeway, Oct. 28, 1828.
4339. Rebecca, bo. ——; d. in childhood.
4340. Joshua Blackwood, bo. Oct. 1806; ma. Mary Lewis.
4341. Benjamin Paschall, bo. Nov. 26, 1808; ma. Rachel Lewis.

(4331) Samuel Ladd Howell, of Princeton, N. J., (son of Joshua L. Howell,[4330]) ma. Mary Harrison Clayton, Nov. 30, 1809. He died Nov. 1, 1835. His widow died Sept. 9, 1852. He was a professor at Princeton College, and an eminent physician. A chair of medicine was established for him, which lapsed at his death.

Children.

4342. Sarah Clayton, bo. Oct. 31, 1810; not ma.; d. at Georgetown, D. C., May 16, 1878.
4343. Paschall, bo. Aug. 21, 1812; d. Sept. 1, 1813.
4344. Annie, bo. June 24, 1814; ma. A. Hamilton Dodge. She d. April 4, 1871. Had nine children.
4345. Thomas Clayton, bo. Sept. 24, 1815; d. Sept. 14, 1817.
4346. William Meade, bo. Sept. 9, 1817; d. Oct. 3, 1835.
4347. Joshua Paschall, bo. Feb. 13, 1820; d. Aug. 26, 1824.
4348. Samuel Harrison, bo. Dec. 11, 1821; ma. Larned Macomb Williamson, June 15, 1852. Had three children.
4349. Francis Lafayette, bo. July, 1824; d. Sept. 2, 1825.
4350. John Augustus, bo. Aug. 1826; d. Jan. 19, 1829.
4351. Fanny, bo. July 2, 1836; d. Oct. 1836.

(4337) Richard Washington Howell, of Camden, N. J., (son of Joshua L. Howell,[4330]) ma. Mary Tonkin Carpenter, March 30, 1830. He died May 13, 1859. She is now (July, 1890,) living, and will be 85 years old next September. She is a lineal descendant of Samuel Carpenter, the elder, who was the associate of William Penn and Deputy Governor of Pennsylvania.

Children.

4352. John Paschall, bo. 1831; d. 1832.
4353. Edward Carpenter, bo. 1833; d. 1834.
4354. Samuel Bedell, bo. Sept. 20, 1834; ma. Marie Elmer, dau. of Rev. William Neill, D. D., April 13, 1859. Had four children.
4355. Charles Stratton, bo. 1837; not married.
4356. Richard Holmes Offley, bo. 1840; d. 1852.
4357. Joshua Ladd, bo. June 16, 1842; ma. Mary Eyre Savage.
4358. Thomas James, bo. 1844. He was 2d lieutenant in Co. I, 3d Reg. New Jersey Vols., and was killed at the battle of Gains Mills, June 27, 1862, in defense of his country and flag.
4359. Anna, bo. 1848; ma. Malone Lloyd, May 10, 1869, of Philadelphia. Has seven children.
4360. Francis Lee, bo. 1849; not married; d. 1872.
4361. Sarah Carpenter, bo. 1850; d. 1852.

(4340) Joshua Blackwood Howell, of Uniontown, Pa., (son of Joshua L. Howell,[4330]) ma. Mary Lewis, of Philadelphia, Pa., April 7, 1831. She died Sept. 1852, and he ma. 2d, Catharine Whetley, of Newark, Del., Oct. 15, 1854.

Child.

4362. Anna Blackwood, bo. ——; ma. David Shryver Steward, July 30, 1861.

Child by second wife.

4363. Mary Lewis, bo. ——.

(4341) Dr. Benjamin Paschall Howell, of Woodbury, N. J., (son of Joshua L. Howell,[4330]) ma. Rachel Lewis, April 29, 1835. She died Oct. 2, 1882.

Children.

4364. Anna Lewis, bo. Jan. 19, 1836; ma. Dr. Frederick Ridgely Graham, June 14, 1860, of Chester, Pa.
4365. Frances Paschall, bo. June 12, 1839; not married.
4366. Mary Morse, bo. May 14, 1846; ma. John S. Jessup, Nov. 2, 1871. Have seven children.
4367. Benjamin Paschall, bo. Dec. 18, 1847; ma. Catharine A. Veech, of New Haven, Conn., April 21, 1885.

(4357) Joshua Ladd Howell, of Philadelphia, Pa., (son of Richard W. Howell,[4357]) ma. Mary Eyre, dau. of William Littleton and Sarah (Chauncey) Savage, April 15, 1875.

Child.

4368. Evelyn Virginia, bo. July 7, 1877.

(4358) Abigail Blackwood Howell, (dau. of Joshua Ladd Howell,[4330]) ma. Oct. 28, 1828, Rev. Thomas Leiper Janeway, D. D., LL. D., of Philadelphia, Pa. She died April 5, 1885.

Children.

4369. John Howell, M. D., bo. Aug. 12, 1832; ma. Isabella W. Green, June 10, 1855. Had four children.
4370. Martha Gray, bo. Nov. 27, 1833; ma. Charles Hodge, Jr., M. D., son of Rev. Charles and Sarah (Bache) Hodge, D. D., of Princeton Theological Seminary. She was a grand-daughter of Benjamin Franklin. Had seven children.
4371. Anna Howell, bo. Dec. 3, 1835; ma. Rev. Nathaniel Upham, son of Judge N. G. Upham, of Concord, N. H., June 5, 1861.
4372. Rev. Joshua B. Howell, bo. May 16, 1837; ma. June 24, 1863, Margaret E. Berrien.

(4372) Rev. Joshua B. Howell Janeway, Ph. D., of New York City, N. Y., (son of Rev. Thomas L. and Abigail B. (Howell) Janeway,[4338]) ma. Margaret B., dau. of Commodore John M. Berrien, June 24, 1863. She died June 10, 1864, and he ma. 2d, Oct. 25, 1866, Alice P., dau. of Thomas and Sarah (Perry) Beamis, of Randolph.

Child.

4373. Margaret, bo. June 5, 1864; ma. Hugh E. Mitchell, Aug. 19, 1889. Child: Dorothy Berrien, bo. Aug. 2, 1890.

Children by second wife.

4374. Helen Beamis, bo. Aug. 20, 1867.
4375. Anna Howell, bo. Feb. 3, 1869; d. Oct. 10, 1869.
4376. Alice Perry, bo. Aug. 7, 1870.
4377. Thomas, bo. Dec. 13, 1871; d. Oct. 27, 1872.
4378. Robert Bruce, bo. Jan. 16, 1874; d. Aug. 9, 1874.
4379. Edward Carleton, bo. Feb. 15, 1876; d. Nov. 9, 1879.

LADDS OF VIRGINIA.

700 acres of land were granted to John Ladd (4380) in Lynhaven Parish, Lower Norfolk Co., Va., May 25, 1673.

500 acres of land were granted to William Ladd (4381) on the north side of James river, in the fork of Beaver Dam Creek, in Henrico Co., Va., June 16, 1714.

1095 acres of land were granted to Amos Ladd (4382) in Henrico Co., Va., June 16, 1714, in consideration of the transportation of the following persons, (Headrights,) entitling those paying their passage fifty acres each, viz. : John Jones, Andrew King, John Polwin, John Linch, Edward Brooke, William Pinkinton, Thomas Foster, Francis Corley, Richard Franke, Ellen Browze, William Toby, Isaac Sweet, Garret Auburd, John Gedshill, Benjamin French, James Cloyson, M. Masall, Robert Silk, Robert Spardman, William Dobge, and Mark Lifeholly, and the payment of five shillings.

Amos Ladd had other parcels of land granted him, viz. : 343 acres on the north side of James River, Henrico Co., Va., Aug. 17, 1720 ; 300 acres at the same place, Nov. 13, 1721 ; two lots of 400 acres each on the south side of Fluvenna River, in Goochland Co., Va., Sept. 8, 1728 ; 94 acres in same county, June 20, 1733.

We are indebted for the above to R. A. Brock, Esq., corresponding secretary and librarian of the Virginia Historical Society, Richmond, Va.

(4380) John Ladd, of Lynhaven Parish, Lower Norfolk Co., Va. There is a tradition among some of his descendants that he came from New England, but we do not think it is well grounded. He probably came from England, and very likely was a relative of John Ladd,[4296] who settled at Burlington, N. J., in 1678.

Children.

4381. William, bo. —— ; ma. Huldah Binford, June 18, 1701.
4382. Amos, bo. ——.

(4381)   William Ladd, of Charles City Co., Va., (son of John,[4380])
ma. Huldah Binford, June 18, 1701.

Children.

4383. John, bo. ——; ma. Mary Crew, Nov. 21, 1724.
4384. James, bo. Oct. 22, 1703; ma. Judith Ellyson, Dec. 28, 1726.
4385. William, bo. ——; ma. Ursula Ellyson, Feb. 21, 1731.
4386. Huldah, bo. Feb. 17, 1712; ma. Peter Preble, of Prince George Co. She died 1784.

(4383)   John Ladd, of Charles City Co., Va., (son of William,[4381]) ma. Mary, dau. of John and Sarah Crew, Nov. 21, 1724.

Children.

4387. James, bo. ——; ma. Isabella Denson, June, 1767.
4388. Amos, bo. ——; ma. Sarah Binford, Aug. 1763.
4389. John, bo. ——; ma. Unity Harris.
4390. William, bo. ——; ma. Mary Hubbard, May 7, 1773.
4391. A girl, bo. ——.
4392. A girl, bo. ——.

(4387)   James Ladd, of Charles City Co., Va., (son of John,[4383]) ma. Isabella Denson, June, 1767. She died Aug. 3, 1809. He died Oct. 17, 1807. "He was one of the 'F. F. Vs.,' (first families of Virginia.) He owned a farm called Green Meadow, a store, and the Edner Flour Mills. He was considered rich at that time. He was a member of the Society of Friends and a minister of that denomination." We read of him in the Diary of Barnaby Nixon, published in 1814, as follows: "In 1782, with James Ladd as a companion, we visited various meetings of Lower North Carolina. * * * In 1789, in company with James Ladd, we visited the meetings at Rich Square and Jack Swamp." Towards the close of his diary he says: "Cousin James Ladd had been in a consumption, declining way, for several months, and was desirous to see me. His son, James Denson Ladd, came to me in the 9th mo., 1806. After being with him several days, Joseph Ladd took me home. James Ladd lived a little more than two weeks after I left him. A little before his death he said: 'All men must come to this, and I shall make a good end, which will crown all.'"

We make the following extract from the Diary of John Fothergill, a minister of the Society of Friends in England, who visited this country. [See Friends' Library, vol. 13, pp. 379, 380.]

"In 1721, the 23 of the 6 month, we had a meeting at Widow Butler's house, to which came several soberly behaved people. We came back from thence to Robert Honicut's, and had a meeting near his house. The next day we crossed James River to William Ladd's, (4381,) where a small meeting is usually kept. The 27th we had a pretty large meeting at Carles, and lodged at Thomas Pleasants'; on the 28th, with some friends, we rode up the woods to a place called Dover, (Dover Mines, in Goochland Co., Va.,) where a few friends live,—we lodged that night with one John Parsons; on the 1st 7 month we had a meeting at a French settlement called Manikintown,—lodged with Daniel Groom; on the 2d we went to the monthly meeting at Edward Mosby's,—lodged that night with John Johnson, at the swamp. The 4th we went to Black Creek,—lodged with Gerard Ellyson, and had another meeting; 5th had another meeting on the Pamunkey River; came back to Gerard Ellyson's, and had another meeting the 6th at Black Creek; 7th went to a meeting at William Ladd's again,—lodged at John Crew's; and went again at a meeting at Carles,—lodged at J. Pleasants'."

We have introduced the above extract from Fothergill's diary to show where the Ladds, the Ellysons, the Crews, and the Pleasants, who inter-married with the Ladds, lived; and it may enable others to make a more perfect genealogical record of this branch of the Ladd family. He was treasurer of the Yearly Meeting in 1807.

Children.

4393. Clotilda, bo. March 11, 1768; ma. Thomas Harris, March 6, 1787.
4394. Benjamin, bo. Oct. 3, 1769; d. Sept. 10, 1779.
4395. Ann, bo. March 29, 1771; ma. James Bates, 1790.
4396. James Denson, bo. Jan. 23, 1774; ma. Jane Evans.
4397. Joseph, bo. July 18, 1776; not married.
4398. Mary, bo. March 25, 1779; ma. William Henry Pleasants, Sept. 8, 1795.
4399. Benjamin Whitehead, bo. April 21, 1782; ma. Elizabeth Wood, April 20, 1814.
4400. Priscilla, bo. ——; ma. Thomas Stanley, June 5, 1802.
4401. Isaac, bo. Oct. 14, 1787; d. July 1, 1789.
4402. Isabella, bo. June 12, 1792; ma. Thomas Honicut, Nov. 5, 1811.

(4396) James Denson Ladd, of Charles City Co., Va., (son of James,[4387]) ma. Jane Evans. She died Sept. 1814. He died Jan. 14, 1814.

Children.

4403. Oliver, bo. 1801; not married; d. 1832.
4404. Ann Maria, bo. April, 1809; ma. Collier H. Minge, 1828.

(4399) Benjamin Whitehead Ladd, of Smithfield, Ohio, (son of James,[4387]) ma. Elizabeth, dau. of William and Mary (Smith) Wood, April 20, 1814. She died Dec. 4, 1832, and he ma. 2d, Hannah Wood, July 31, 1834. He died March 31, 1851. He came to Smithfield from Virginia in 1814, and purchased from his father-in-law the farm known as the "Prospect Hill," adjoining Smithfield on the west, and erected on it in 1815 a brick dwelling, which is still (1890) standing. In 1817 he built a building for the purpose, and commenced to pack pork and cure bacon. So far as is known, this was the first enterprise of the kind west of the Alleghany Mountains. This business proved successful, and was extended from time to time until he had erected four houses on the farm and one at Martin's Ferry, Belmont Co., Ohio. He was not only remarkably enterprising, but equally disposed to help others. He was the especial friend of the poor and downtrodden colored race, assisting many in their flight from slavery. He was a prominent member of the Orthodox Society of Friends, and faithfully served the church as an elder, as clerk of the Ohio Yearly Meeting, and in various other capacities. Amid all his business calls he found time to attend to his duties as a citizen and a Christian; benevolence and unbounded hospitality being marked traits in his character.

Children.
4405. Isabella, bo. March 22, 1815; ma. Joseph Jones, May, 1837.
4406. Mary Ann, bo. Sept. 17, 1816; ma. Elisha Cook, May, 1837. She died March, 1887. Children: [1]Elizabeth Ladd, bo. March, 1838, d. Oct. 1887, ma. Anderson Cunningham, of Richmond, Ohio, 1857; [2]Mariana L., bo. 1859, ma. Charles G. Robinson, 1880, and had Ada Ladd, bo. 1882.

[2]Benjamin L., bo. Mar. 17, 1840; ma. Ellen Denison Moss, of Stonington, Conn., June 8, 1869. Children: [1]Edith Denison, bo. March 9, 1870; [2]Warren Ladd, bo. Oct. 10, 1872, d. Feb. 5, 1874; [3]Mary Isabella, bo. Aug. 18, 1874; [4]William Moss, bo. July 5, 1876, d. May 10, 1888; [5]Blanch Ellen, bo. Feb. 3, 1878; [6]Benjamin Ladd, Jr., bo. Dec. 7, 1885.

[3]William Mode, bo. May 16, 1842; ma. Cornelia McCue, Sept. 1, 1864. Children: [1]Mary Cornelia, bo. June 9, 1866, ma. J. F. Edwards, Nov. 20, 1886, and had Ralph Earnest, bo. Feb. 5, 1888; [2]Rosamode, bo. Oct. 25, 1877; [3]Wilbur Eugene, bo. Nov. 10, 1880.

⁴George Dillwyn, bo. Feb. 27, 1845; ma. Dora A. Shaw, June 10, 1873, and had Laura Weaver, bo. April 14, 1874. His wife Dora A. died July 14, 1882, and he ma. 2d, Stella Virginia Sturges, of Chicago, Ill., Jan. 1, 1890.

⁵James Denson, bo. June 6, 1847; ma. Stella Shirrill Shaw, Sept. 23, 1868. Children: ¹George Shaw, bo. July 1, 1869; ²Clark Wickersham, bo. July 14, 1887, d. March 2, 1888.

4407. Lydia, bo. Nov. 23, 1818; d. June 5, 1819.
4408. James D., bo. July 16, 1820; ma. Elizabeth Folger, July 29, 1842.
4409. William H., bo. March 12, 1823; ma. Caroline E. Coffin, Aug. 24, 1848.
4410. Rebecca, bo. Feb. 20, 1825; d. March 25, 1825.
4411. Benjamin, bo. Aug. 24, 1830; ma. Maria Judkins, Nov. 25, 1857.
4412. Thomas W., bo. Dec. 4, 1832; ma. Hannah Gifford, Aug. 16, 1854.

Children by second wife.

4413. Elizabeth, bo. Oct. 8, 1835.
4414. Lydia, bo. Aug. 5, 1837; ma. William Gifford, Sept. 30, 1863.
4415. Hannah, bo. Sept. 28, 1840; not married; d. Aug. 9, 1878.

(4408) James D. Ladd, of Ottumwa, Iowa, (son of Benjamin W.,[4399]) ma. Elizabeth Folger, July 29, 1842. She died Dec. 1837, and he ma. 2d, Harriet Holmes, Jan. 19, 1870.

Children.

4416. Ellen Reynolds, bo. April 10, 1844; d. Aug. 16, 1845.
4417. Oliver Mayhew, bo. June 20, 1846; ma. Ada Isabel Upham, Sept. 22, 1881.
4418. Mary Folger, bo. Dec. 15, 1849; ma. Amos Denson Moss, June 1, 1869.
4419. Virginia Isabella, bo. Dec. 5, 1852; d. March 10, 1863.
4420. Caroline Coffin, bo. June 29, 1855; ma. Prof. Lyman Beecher Hall, July 8, 1890, son of Hon. Isaac D. Hall, of New Bedford.
4421. Warren Ransom, bo. Sept. 11, 1861; d. June 17, 1873.

Children by second wife.

4422. James D., bo. June 21, 1871.
4423. Laura L., bo. Aug. 10, 1873.
4424. Harry H., bo. July 15, 1875.

(4409) William H. Ladd, of Brooklyn, N. Y., (son of Benjamin W.,[4399]) ma. Caroline E. Coffin, of Richmond, Ind., Aug. 24, 1848. He spent two years, 1841-2, at Haverford, Pa.; was a teacher at Friend's Boarding School at Mt. Pleasant, Ohio, the Winter of 1842-3. He purchased Ohio's wool for forty-seven years for eastern manufacturers; for twenty years for the Middlesex Co. of Boston, for fifteen years for the Slater Woolen Co. of Webster. In 1844 he purchased a large farm near Richmond, Jefferson Co., Ohio, where for twenty years he successfully dealt in and raised blooded horses and sheep. He imported at one time, from Silesea, three hundred sheep, the first of that breed ever brought into Ohio. He was intimately acquainted with John Brown, of Harper's Ferry fame, at one time having travelled with him three months through New England, selecting sheep. He was elected a member of the Ohio Board of Agriculture in 1850, and its president in 1856. He was a delegate at the convention held at Pittsburgh, Pa., in 1856, at which the Republican party was formed. During the war, in 1861, he was requested by President Lincoln and Secretaries Stanton and Chase (the latter two being special friends) to take charge of the contrabands at Port Royal, Va. On his way South to fulfill his mission he stopped at Cincinnati, Ohio, to assist in the organization of the Contraband Relief Commission, consisting of Levi Clifford, Abraham Taylor, Charles B. Boynton, Robert Carroll, and William H. Ladd. He was a prominent member and minister of the Orthodox Society of Friends. In 1865 he moved to Brooklyn, N. Y., where he lived until 1888, removing in that year to Haverford College, Pa., where he resided until his death, May 30, 1890.

Children.

4425. Ellen C., bo. Aug. 8, 1849; ma. William Conklin, June 3, 1872. Children: [1]Frank Henry, bo. March 30, 1873; [2]Edward Boote, bo. Aug. 10, 1877.
4426. Benjamin W., bo. Sept. 8, 1851; ma. Ida Jordan, May 17, 1881.
4427. Mariana C., bo. Oct. 5, 1858; ma. Prof. Levi Talbot Edwards, June 25, 1890.
4428. William Coffin, bo. Oct. 5, 1863. He spent four years at Friends' Boarding School at Providence, R. I., and entered Brown University, where he graduated in 1881. He is now (1890) a professor of French at Haverford College, Pa.
4429. James Edward, bo. Feb. 14, 1860; d. Sept. 12, 1863.
4430. Isabella J., bo. May 28, 1863; d. May 29, 1863.
4431. Charles F., bo. July 22, 1856; ma. Kate Hedrick, Nov. 11, 1880.

(4411) Benjamin Ladd, of Denver, Col., (son of Benjamin W.,[4399]) ma. Maria Judkins, Nov. 25, 1857. He died Jan. 11, 1890, at Sunset, Boulder Co., Col.

Children.

4432. Linnie Ann, bo. Aug. 18, 1858.
4433. Olla Stanton, bo. Sept. 19, 1860; ma. Robert Billings, Dec. 4, 1884.
4434. Catharine Elizabeth, bo. March 26, 1863; d. Aug. 10, 1863.

(4412) Thomas W. Ladd, of Brooklyn, N. Y., (son of Benjamin W.,[4399]) ma. Hannah P., dau. of Isaac A. Gifford, of Dartmouth, Aug. 16, 1854. He died Dec. 12, 1882.

Children.

4435. Walter J., bo. March 10, 1862.
4436. Isaac G., bo. April 6, 1864.

(4417) Oliver Mayhew Ladd, of Ottumwa, Iowa, (son of James D.,[4408]) ma. Ada Isabel Upham, Sept. 22, 1881.

Children.

4437. Elizabeth Kitridge, bo. Sept. 10, 1883.
4438. Mayhew Tyler, bo. Sept. 4, 1885.

(4426) Benjamin Ladd, of Miles City, Montana, (son of William H.,[4409]) ma. Ida Jordan, May 17, 1881. He received most of his education as a private pupil at Brooklyn, N. Y. He entered Eastham College, Richmond, Ind., but in less than a year his health broke down, and he was obliged to give up his college course. He is now (1890) in the employ of the Hutchinson Salt and Stock Yard Co., at Hutchinson, Kansas.

Children.

4439. Ida Ella. bo. March 13, 1882.
4440. Charles F., bo. Aug. 28, 1883.
4441. Edith J., bo. March 6, 1885.
4442. Stella Maria, bo. March 4, 1887.
4443. William Henry, bo. March 4, 1887.

(4431) Charles F. Ladd, of Ottumwa, Iowa, (son of William H.,[4409]) ma. Kate Hedrick, Nov. 11, 1880.

Children.

4444. Howard William, bo. Feb. 26, 1882.
4445. Caroline F. C., bo. Jan. 29, 1884.

(4388) Amos Ladd, of Charles City Co., Va., (son of John,[4383]) ma. Sarah Binford, Aug. 11, 1763, of North Carolina. She died March 3, 1814. He died May 8, 1790.

Children.

4446. Betsey Kinsley, bo. May 2, 1764; d. July 19, 1764.
4447. Mary, bo. May 14, 1765; ma. Jesse Terrill, Nov. 6, 1787. She d. Nov. 1, 1790.
4448. John Kinsley, bo. Aug. 7, 1767; d. Nov. 14, 1788.
4449. Thomas, bo. Oct. 16, 1769; ma. Ann Bell, Aug. 7, 1799.

4450. Priscilla, bo. Aug. 2, 1772; ma. George Hubbard, March 8, 1791.
4451. Sarah, bo. Aug. 4, 1775; ma. Ebenezer Manle, Sept. 10, 1793.
4452. Amos, bo. Sept. 21, 1778; ma. Mary Bell, Feb. 2, 1811.
4453. Elizabeth, bo. Jan. 20, 1781; ma. Samuel Parsons, Oct. 9, 1804. She died March 23, 1836.
4454. Susannah, bo. Jan. 26, 1783; d. Sept. 13, 1783.
4455. Deborah, bo. Jan. 6, 1785; ma. Mr. Stratton, 1805. She d. Apr. 28, 1832.

(4449) Thomas Ladd, of Charles City Co., Va., (son of Amos,[4388]) ma. Ann Bell, Aug. 7, 1799. He died May 20, 1834.

Children.

4456. Thomas Mifflin, bo. May 5, 1800; ma. Lucy Elizabeth Cawerden.
4457. Rodman, bo. Aug. 26, 1802; d. Aug. 3, 1803.
4458. James Munroe, bo. Oct. 6, 1806; not married; d. 1880.
4459. Nathan Bell, bo. Dec. 9, 1808; ma. Ellen Miller.
4460. William Penn, bo. Nov. 9, 1812; ma. Sarah S. Sherman. No children.
4461. Sebelia Ann, bo. Aug. 4, 1815; ma. Col. R. M. Conn.
4462. Sarah Bell, bo. Aug. 18, 1818; not married; d. Jan. 1849.
4463. Benjamin F., bo. Feb. 15, 1820; ma. Margaret Rigger. No children.

(4452) Amos Ladd, of Charles City Co., Va., (son of Amos,[4388]) ma. Mary Bell, Feb. 2, 1811. He died Nov. 10, 1836.

Child.

4464. Sarah Elizabeth, bo. ——; ma. Edward Garland Sydnor.

(4456) Thomas Mifflin Ladd, of Charles City Co., Va., (son of Thomas,[4449]) ma. Lucy Elizabeth Cawerden, Aug. 7, 1841.

Children.

4465. Aaron Burr, bo. June 14, 1842; d. June 14, 1842.
4466. Thomas W., bo. Nov. 18, 1843; ma. Sarah Mildred King, Jan. 15, 1873.
4467. John Bell, bo. Jan. 30, 1846; ma. Eunice McLellan, July 21, 1886.
4468. Jane McKenzie, bo. Oct. 2, 1828; ma. Samuel B. Quarles, Feb. 5, 1874. Children: [1]William Edward, bo. Dec. 15, 1875; [2]Henry Franklin, bo. May 23, 1876; [3]Lucy Bell, bo. May 18, 1880; [4]James Cawerden, bo. April 8, 1883; [5]Samuel Cleveland, bo. Nov. 1, 1885.
4469. Mary Ann, bo. March 3, 1851; d. Oct. 30, 1864.
4470. Robert Anderson, bo. Oct. 3, 1853; ma. A. M. Lawrence, Dec. 27, 1882.
4471. Benjamin Franklin, bo. Aug. 28, 1858.
4472. Lucy Lavelette, bo. May 31, 1861; ma. H. L. Butler, July 12, 1881. Children: [1]Eunice Norwood, bo. Oct. 10, 1882; [2]Percy Ladd, bo. Feb. 4, 1884.

(4466) Thomas W. Ladd (son of Thomas Mifflin [4456]) ma. Sarah Mildred King, dau. of Nathaniel King, Jan. 15, 1873.

Children.

4473. Barnard Goodale, bo. Nov. 4, 1873.
4474. Lucy Winston, bo. Feb. 6, 1877.
4475. Ella Douglas, bo. May 16, 1878.
4476. Robert Hill, bo. March 22, 1880.
4477. James Russell, bo. May 12, 1881.
4478. Thomas Mifflin, bo. July 16, 1883.
4479. Lemuel Cleveland, bo. Nov. 1, 1885.

(4459) Nathan Bell Ladd, of Charles City Co., Va., (son of Thomas,[4449]) ma. Ellen Miller.

Child.

4480. Malvia, bo. ——.

(4470) Robert Anderson Ladd, of Richmond, Va., (son of Thomas M.,[4456]) ma. Alphia Mildred Lawrence, Dec. 27, 1882, dau. of W. Q. Lawrence.

Children.

4481. Mary Bell, bo. Oct. 20, 1883.
4482. Birdie, bo. March 10, 1885.

(4389) John Ladd, of Charles City Co., Va., (son of John,[4383]) ma. Unity Harris, 1764. He died March 20, 1816.

Children.

4483. Guelielma, bo. March 11, 1769.
4484. Rachel, bo. Jan. 7, 1771; d. Oct. 10, 1795.
4485. Elizabeth, bo. Nov. 29, 1772; ma. Charles Antony, Aug. 8, 1797.
4486. Benjamin Harris, bo. June 18, 1774; ma. Sarah Binford, 1799.
4487. Margaret, bo. Sept. 8, 1776; ma. Benjamin Vaughn, May 6, 1794.
4488. Unity Smith, bo. July 8, 1780; ma. Thomas Harris, Jan. 2, 1805.
4489. Mary, bo. Oct. 29, 1782; ma. James Vaughn, Aug. 6, 1816. He died, and she ma. 2d, John Bell. He died, and she ma. 3d, Mr. Hocking.
4490. Sarah D., bo. April 1, 1785.
4491. John, bo. May 25, 1787; not married.

(4486) Benjamin Harris Ladd, of Charles City Co., Va., (son of John,[4389]) ma. Sarah, dau. of James and Elizabeth Binford, 1799.

Children.

4492. James Harris, bo. May 12, 1800; ma. Isabella Eliza Mills, Dec. 3, 1848.
4493. Samuel, bo. ——; not ma.; d. at Fortress Monroe, 1864 or 1865.
4494. Elizabeth, bo. ——; not married.
4495. Unity, bo. ——; ma. James Hubbard. She died 1860.
4496. Nancy H., bo. ——; ma. Matthew Hargrave, March 6, 1832.
4497. Benjamin Franklin, bo. 1811; not ma.; d. April 7, 1840.

4498. John Milton, bo. Feb. 22, 1815; ma. Martha Lewis, Nov. 22, 1838.
4499. Thomas Elwood, bo. Oct. 19, 1816; not ma.; d. Sept. 1884.
4500. Sally Ann, bo. ——; ma. James Hubbard, Jan. 15, 1855. He was sheriff of Charles City Co., Va., during and after the war of the Rebellion. Children: ¹James, bo. Feb. 13, 1856, d. July 13, 1857; ²James Exum, bo. Nov. 2, 1857, ma. Emma S. Nimmo, Nov. 11, 1884, of Norfolk Co., Va., and had Nimmo, bo. Sept. 30, 1886; ³Eliza Binford, bo. Nov. 2, 1857, ma. R. B. Mountcastle, Oct. 30, 1889; ⁴Thos. Newton, bo. Dec. 7, 1862; ⁵John, bo. Sept. 30, 1866.
4501. Isaac Newton, bo. ——; not ma.; d. 1864 or 1865.

(4492) James Harris Ladd, of Varina Township, Henrico Co., Va., (son of Benjamin Harris,[4486]) was born in Prince George Co., Va., on a farm owned by his grandfather, James Binford, May 12, 1800. He was brought up on a farm in Charles City Co., Va., which his father (4486) Benjamin Harris Ladd inherited from his father, John Ladd (4389.) He ma. Dec. 3, 1848, Isabella Eliza Wills, dau. of George Elkinton and Priscilla (Cobb) Wills, who worked by lease the Black Heath Coal Mines, in Goochland Co., Va. He purchased a farm on Turkey Creek, eighteen miles from Richmond, Va., which formerly belonged to his cousin, James Denson Ladd (4396,) and where he lived at the time of his death, June 24, 1867. His widow died Feb. 11, 1875. There was a grist-mill upon the farm, and one of the old burr-stones is now in a rockery, at the garden-gate of the old mansion, overgrown with stone-crop and ivy.

Children.

4502. Mary Virginia, bo. Jan. 3, 1848; ma. Major William Horner Tantum, who was bo. at New Egypt, N. J., Oct. 19, 1827, and was the son of Thomas and Katharine (Bowker) Tantum. In early life he learned the millwright's trade; then accepted the management of Bottom & Tiffany's Iron Foundry; went to Cuba, W. I., where he erected an iron warehouse. He put up the first "iron fronts" in Philadelphia, Pa., also in Portland, Me. He commenced business for himself a few years before the war, but when Fort Sumter was fired upon by the Confederate States, and war seemed inevitable, he felt a strong desire to perform his part in aiding the national government in crushing the Rebellion, or to state it more mildly, in "bringing back the erring South," with a firm and patriotic purpose he enlisted as 1st Lieut. in Co. B, Capt. Van Sickle, of 1st Reg. of N. J. V., Col. W. R. Montgomery, and was mustered in May 21, 1861. He was promoted to captain Aug. 11, 1862; was mustered out for promotion June 23, 1864, and was commissioned as major of the 38th Reg. N. J. V., Col. William J. Sewell, Sept. 27, 1864. He took part in the following battles: First Bull Run, Benson's Farm, West Point, Gaines Mill, Charles City Co. Cross Roads, Malvern Hill, Manassa, Chantilly, Crompton Gap, Antietam, Wilderness, Spottsylvania Court House, Ann River, Hanover Court House, Cold Harbor, Fredericksburg, Chancellorsville, and Salem Heights. He was on recruiting service at Camp Perrine, Trenton, N. J., Sept. and Oct. 1863; was detached with four companies for service at the military post at Cannon's Landing, James River, Va. He was wounded twice in the battle of Salem Heights, May 4, 1863, first in the left arm and the second time in the calf of his right leg, which compelled him to leave the field for the hospital. Soon after the close of the war and the disbanding of the armies, Gov. Joel Parker offered him promotion by brevet, for brave and meritorious conduct, and urged him to accept, but he replied to all inducements held out that the war was over, the fighting all done, and he had no fancy for empty titles. Not long after the close of the war he bought a large tract of timber land in Virginia, and was engaged for eight years in sawing logs and finding a market for his lumber. He made good investments of his money in real estate and shipping, and has now retired from active business, but holds an interest in a gentlemen's furnishing store, and is the owner of a small pottery, the only one manufacturing Rockingham ware, in Trenton, N. J. He has been often urged to accept civil office, but has always declined, because he prefers the pleasure and comforts of his home to the honors of any office which would call him away from his family circle. They have one child, William Harris, bo. May 18, 1877.

4503. James Milton, bo. Nov. 12, 1849; ma. Nora Johnston, 1876.
4504. Sally Binford, bo. Jan. 22, 1853; d. Dec. 19, 1869.
4505. William Beverly Randolph, bo. Jan. 14, 1855.
4506. Emma, bo. Dec. 27, 1859; ma. Robinson Palmer, Feb. 16, 1884; d. May 8, 1889.
4507. Isabel Eliza, bo. Feb. 27, 1862.
4508. Louise Austin, bo. Feb. 5, 1864; d. April 19, 1864.

(4498) John Milton Ladd, of Mobile, Ala., (son of Benjamin H.,[4486]) ma. Martha Lewis, Nov. 22, 1838.

Children.

4509. Sarah Frances, bo. Sept. 7, 1839; d. Sept. 3, 1843.
4510. Benjamin Horatio, bo. Dec. 23, 1841; d. May 27, 1864.
4511. ——, bo. ——; d. before it was named.
4512. Mary Elizabeth, bo. May 3, 1845; ma. Samuel H. Chambers, Oct. 1, 1868.
4513. Martha Ann, bo. Aug. 5, 1847; d. Sept. 20, 1852.
4514. John Milton, Jr., bo. March 10, 1850; ma. Elodie Hollinger, Dec. 16, 1878.
4515. Unity Virginia, bo. May 17, 1852.

4516. Alice Binford, bo. Oct. 18, 1855; ma. Edward Hollinger, Oct. 21, 1875.
4517. Antoinette, bo. Nov. 1, 1857.
4518. Frank M., bo. May 15, 1860.

(4503) James Milton Ladd (son of James Harris[4492]) ma. Nora Johnston, Sept. 6, 1876. He died March 11, 1885.

Children.

4519. Russell, bo. July 18, 1877.
4520. Louis E., bo. Dec. 13, 1879.

(4390) William Ladd, of Charles City Co., Va., (son of John,[4383]) ma. Mary Hubbard, 1773, dau. of George Hubbard. She died Sept. 30, 1822. He died July 17, 1797.

Children.

4521. Robert, bo. July 14, 1774; ma. Mary T. ——.
4522. Amelia, bo. Dec. 27, 1776.
4523. James, bo. ——.
4524. Ann, bo. Dec. 16, 1779.
4525. Martha, bo. Nov. 19, 1781.
4526. Elizabeth, bo. Aug. 4, 1783; ma. George Hubbard, May 7, 1811.
4527. Mary, bo. Feb. 17, 1790; ma. James S. Binford, June 9, 1812, of Northampton Co., N. C.
4528. Sarah, bo. Oct. 31, 1792; ma. Benjamin Hockaday, April 8, 1817.
4529. Jane, bo. ——.
4530. Millicent, bo. ——.

(4521) Robert Ladd, of Charles City Co., Va., (son of William,[4390]) ma. Mary T. ——. He removed to Short Creek, Harrison Co., Ohio.

Children.

4531. Amos, bo. ——.
4532. Robert P., bo. ——.
4533. Mary, bo. ——.
4534. Lucy, bo. ——; ma. Charles Hargraves, July 13, 1824.
4535. Edna, bo. ——; ma. Micajah J. Johnson, Jan. 5, 1830.

(4384) James Ladd, of Charles City Co., Va., (son of William,[4381]) ma. Judith, dau. of Gerard Robert Ellyson, Dec. 28, 1726. He was a representative at the Virginia Yearly Meeting, from Carles, in 1758.

Children.

4536. Mary, bo. ——; ma. Aquila, son of Peter and Rebecca Binford, July 1, 1758.
4537. Judith, bo. ——; ma. Thomas Binford, 1753.

4538. Agnes, bo. ——; ma. Shadrack Stanley, Dec. 2, 1764.
4539. James, bo. 1736; ma. Sarah ——.
4540. Joseph, bo. ——; ma. Mary Binford, Sept. 1767.

(4539)   James Ladd, of Charles City Co., Va., (son of James,[4384]) ma. Sarah ——. He and his wife attended the marriage of W. Ballard and A. Stanley, in Hanover Co., Va., Nov. 11, 1763, and signed the marriage certificate.

Children.

4541. Peter, bo. Jan. 2, 1763; ma. Sarah ——.
4542. Mary, bo. April 14, 1765; d. Oct. 4, 1818.
4543. Rebecca, bo. Nov. 8, 1767; ma. Waddy Stanley, Nov. 4, 1794.
4544. James Binford, bo. Feb. 11, 1770.

(4540)   Joseph Ladd, of Charles City Co., Va., (son of James,[4384]) ma. Mary Binford, Sept. 1767.

Children.

4545. Sarah, bo. ——; d. Sept. 7, 1771.
4546. Betsey Kingsley, bo. ——; d. Sept. 11, 1771.

(4541)   Peter Ladd, of Charles City Co., Va., (son of James,[4539]) ma. Sarah ——, 1786.

Children.

4547. Deborah, bo. ——; ma. David Crew, June 2, 1820.
4548. Leadbetter, bo. ——.
4549. Peter, Jr., bo. ——; ma. Catharine Crew, July 12, 1824.
4550. Henry, bo. ——.

(4549)   Peter Ladd, Jr., of Short Creek, Hanover Co., Ohio, (son of Peter,[4541]) ma. Catharine Crew, July 12, 1824.

Children.

4551. Lucy Ann, bo. ——.
4552. Mary Emily, bo. ——.
4553. Robert C., bo. ——.
4554. Sarah L., bo. ——.

(4385)   William Ladd, of Charles City Co., Va., (son of William,[4381]) ma. Ursula, dau. of Gerard Robert Ellyson, Feb. 11, 1731.

Children.

4555. Thomas, bo. ——; ma. Ann, dau. of Thomas Ellyson, Dec. 8, 1761.
4556. William, bo. ——; ma. Mary ——.
4557. Gerard, bo. ——; ma. Sarah ——.

(4556) William Ladd, of Kent Co., Va., (son of William,[4555]) ma. Mary ——.

Children.

4558. William, bo. 1759; ma. Mary Crew.
4559. Mary, bo. ——; ma. Mr. Birch.
4560. David, bo. ——; ma. Miss Crew.
4561. Sarah, bo. ——; ma. Mr. McGushee.

(4558) William Ladd (son of William [4556]) ma. Mary Crew.

Children.

4562. John, bo. ——; ma. Martha Mountcastle, 1819.
4563. Elizabeth, bo. ——; ma. Richard Dennett. Children: [1]Mary, bo. March 12, 1816, ma. James A. Oakley, Dec. 26, 1844; [2]Catharine, ma. R. Boars.
4564. James, bo. ——; ma. Fanny Stith.
4565. Martha, bo. ——; ma. John D. Wight.
4566. Mary Jane, bo. ——; ma. William Mountcastle, 1816.
4567. Nelson, bo. ——.
4568. Elvira, bo. ——.
4569. William, bo. ——.
4570. Joseph, bo. Feb. 14, 1802; not married.

(4560) David Ladd (son of William [4556]) ma. —— Crew. She died, and he ma. 2d, Judith Pearsons. She died, and he ma. 3d, Martha Williamson. He died 1823.

Children.

4571. Elvira, bo. ——; ma. Mr. Burch. Child: Lucretia.
4572. Sarah, bo. ——; ma. Mr. Meredith.
4573. Mary, bo. ——; ma. Richard Chandler. Child: William.

Child by third wife.

4574. Mary A., bo. Aug. 24, 1816; ma. David S. M. Crump, Feb. 28, 1833. Children:

[1]Edgar, bo. March 17, 1834; ma. Ellen Green, Aug. 18, 1871. Child: [1]David S. M., bo. Oct. 8, 1872. She d. 1873, and he ma. 2d, Cora Green, 1874, and had: [2]Estella, bo. May 8, 1875; [3]Mary Ann, bo. Feb. 18, 1878, d. 1885.

[2]Lawrence S., bo. Oct. 21, 1836; ma. Lucy Hawkins, Jan. 1863. Children: [1]William, bo. Dec. 1863; [2]Lawrence, bo. April, 1865; [3]Mary, d. in infancy.

[3]Annetta, bo. 1839; ma. Bal. D. Christian, Oct. 29, 1869; d. Dec. 19, 1872. Child: Mary Annetta, bo. Dec. 19, 1872.

[4]Alice Ann, bo. June 17, 1843; ma. George W. Libby, Oct. 29, 1869. Children: [1]Stanhope, bo. May 29, 1870; [2]Luther, bo. Sept. 8, 1871; [3]Mary E., bo. Feb. 1873; [4]George W., bo. Sept. 1876.

⁵David W., bo. April 23, 1844; d. Nov. 2, 1862.
⁶John Seaton, bo. Jan. 29, 1847; d. May 16, 1880.
⁷Elizabeth, bo. Jan. 5, 1850; ma. Robert A. Folkes, Oct. 15, 1869. Children: ¹Mary, bo. Oct. 16, 1870; ²Alice Annetta, bo. Dec. 20, 1872; ³Lawrence Seaton, bo. March 4, 1875; ⁴Edgar Seabrook, bo. March 4, 1875; ⁵Eugia G., bo. Nov. 1877; ⁶Catharine Curry, bo. Dec. 26, 1878; ⁷William Hervey, bo. Dec. 2, 1882; ⁸Robert A., bo. April 7, 1886.
⁸Mary Park, bo. April 9, 1853; d. Aug. 20, 1853.

(4557)   Gerard Ladd, of Mecklinburg Co., Va., (son of William,[4385]) ma. Sarah ——.

Children.

4575. Agath, bo. Jan. 6, 1761.
4576. Elizabeth, bo. July 5, 1762.
4577. Priscilla, bo. March 25, 1764; d. Oct. 26, 1766.
4578. Huldah, bo. Sept. 5, 1765.
4579. Jacob, bo. July 13, 1767; ma. Elizabeth ——.
4580. Sarah, bo. June 1, 1769.
4581. Ursula, bo. June 17, 1771.
4582. Gerard, bo. June 2, 1773.
4583. Priscilla, bo. June 2, 1776.
4584. Lydia, bo. Sept. 8, 1778.
4585. Esther, bo. Jan. 19, 1782.

(4579)   Jacob Ladd, of Mecklinburg Co., Va., (son of Gerard,[4557]) ma. Elizabeth ——.

Children.

4586. Anna, bo. Jan. 28, 1799.
4587. Sarah Gilman, bo. April 8, 1800.

(4382)   Amos Ladd, of Lower Norfolk Co., Va., (son of John,[4380]) ma. ——.

Children.

4588. Amos, bo. ——; ma. Commicila Fraten.
4589. Noble, bo. ——; ma. Miss Davis.

(4588)   Amos Ladd, of Henrico Co., Va., (son of Amos,[4382]) ma. Commicila Fraten. He removed to North Carolina.

Children.

4590. Amos, bo. ——; ma. Anna Stone.
4591. John, bo. ——; ma. —— Sunderland.
4592. William Humphrey, bo. ——; ma. Mary A. Chapman.
4593. Constantine, bo. ——; ma. Mary Boxley.
4594. Milton, bo. ——.

4595. Betsey, bo. ——; ma. Asa Keith.
4596. Patsey, bo. ——; ma. John Sunderland.

(4590) Amos Ladd (son of Amos [4588]) ma. Anna Stone.

Children.

4597. Noble, bo. ——; ma. Milly Holly.
4598. Elkin, bo. ——; ma. Ally Tuggle.
4599. G. G. Terrill, bo. ——; ma. Sally Holly.
4600. Bayles E., bo. Nov. 11, 1810; ma. Rutha Ladd (4641.)
4601. Amos, bo. ——; ma. Nancy Pellitt.
4602. Mary, bo. ——; ma. Nathan Lemmons.
4603. Betsey, bo. ——; ma. Solomon Stone.
4604. Solomon, bo. ——; ma. Feriba Hamba.
4605. Annie, bo. ——; ma. K. Stone.
4606. Constantine, bo. Nov. 20, 1818; ma. Aneoler Ladd (4642.)
4607. Lucinda, bo. ——; ma. Amos Ladd (4640.)

(4599) G. G. Terrill Ladd, of Long Island, Ala., (son of Amos,[4590]) ma. Sally Holly. She died, and he ma. 2d, Louisa Hember.

Children.

4608. Bayles, bo. ——.
4609. James, bo. ——.
4610. Manley, bo. ——.

(4600) Bayles E. Ladd, of Long Island, Ala., (son of Amos,[4590]) ma. Rutha Ladd,[4641] Dec. 27, 1835.

Children.

4611. Louisa, bo. May 27, 1837; ma. W. R. Brown, April 11, 1860. She d. Dec. 9, 1871. Children: [1]Mollie, [2]Katie, [3]John, [4]William.
4612. Washington, bo. Dec. 9, 1839; d. Feb. 14, 1846.
4613. Angelina S., bo. Feb. 7, 1842; ma. D. H. Throupe, June 21, 1865. Child: Elizabeth.
4614. Mary A., bo. Oct. 24, 1844.
4615. Minerva T., bo. March 3, 1846; ma. A. J. Keith, March 30, 1873. Child: Lutha.
4616. Bayles E., Jr., bo. June 26, 1848; ma. Marcella Johnson.
4617. John C., bo. Nov. 23, 1850.
4618. Vincent D., bo. Jan. 30, 1854.
4619. Sarah Isabella, bo. June 20, 1856.
4620. William R., bo. June 26, 1858.

(4601) Amos Ladd, of Fetzerton, Tenn., (son of Amos,[4590]) ma. Nancy Pellitt.

Children.

4621. Martha Ann, bo. ——.
4622. Nannie, bo. ——.

(4606) Constantine Ladd, of Long Island, Ala., (son of Amos,[4590]) ma. Aneoler Ladd.[4642]

Children.

4623. William Humphrey, bo. ——.
4624. Elmira, bo. ——.
4625. Enoch, b. ——.
4626. Amos, bo. ——.
4627. Joseph, bo. ——.
4628. Calvin, bo. ——.
4629. Mat, bo. ——.
4630. Angeline, bo. ——.
4631. George, bo. ——.
4632. Lethy, bo. ——.

(4604) Solomon Ladd, of Tullahama, Tenn., (son of Amos,[4590]) ma. Feriba Hamba.

Children.

4633. Dennis, bo. ——.
4634. William, bo. ——.
4635. Margaret, bo. ——.
4636. Virginia, bo. ——.
4637. Lucinda, bo. ——.
4638. Amos, bo. ——.

(4592) William Humphrey Ladd, of Long Island, Ala., (son of Amos,[4588]) ma. Mary A. Chapman. She d. 1886, aged 100 years.

Children.

4639. Enoch, bo. ——.
4640. Amos, bo. ——; ma. Lucinda Ladd (4607.)
4641. Rutha Ladd, bo. ——; ma. Bayles E. Ladd (4600.)
4642. Aneoler, bo. ——; ma. Constantine Ladd (4606.)

(4640) Amos Ladd (son of William Humphrey[4592]) ma. Lucinda Ladd.[4607]

Children.

4643. Mary Ann, bo. ——.
4644. Enoch, bo. ——.
4645. Aneoler, bo. ——.
4646. William, bo. ——.
4647. Jennie, bo. ——.
4648. Rutha, bo. ——.

(4589) Noble Ladd (son of Amos[4582]) ma. —— Davis.

Children.

4649. Joseph, bo. ——; ma. Catharine Bacey Damon.
4650. Noble, bo. ——.

4651. William, bo. ——.
4652. Constantine, bo. ——.
4653. Amos, bo. ——.
4654. Huldah, bo. ——; ma. Rev. Mr. Majors.
4655. Judith, bo. ——; ma. Mr. Short.

(4649) Joseph Ladd, of Stokes Co., N. C., (son of Noble,[4589]) ma. Catharine Bacey Damon. She died, and he ma. 2d, Mary Angel. He died 1834.

Children.

4656. Anna, bo. Oct. 21, 1785; ma. John Vaughn, of Stark Co., N. C.
4657. Elizabeth Smith, bo. March 1, 1787; ma. Abel Lomax, Dec. 29, 1808.
4658. Constantine, bo. March 11, 1789; ma. Nancy Carr.
4659. Nancy, bo. May 20, 1790; ma. Tristram Starbuck, of Guilford Co., N.C.
4660. Noble, bo. May 8, 1792; ma. Mary Burton.
4661. Judith, bo. Dec. 5, 1794; ma. John Green.
4662. William, bo. Feb. 1, 1797; ma. Isabel Boyd.
4663. Sarah, bo. Nov. 11, 1798; d. in infancy.
4664. Joseph, bo. Sept. 3, 1800; d. in infancy.

Children by second wife.

4665. Mary Davis, bo. Dec. 6, 1802; ma. Paul Frazier. Child: Catharine.
4666. Isaac Newton, bo. Sept. 21, 1804; ma. Elizabeth Hutchins.
4667. Bethanay, bo. Jan. 17, 1807; ma. Samuel K. Boyd. Children: [1]James K., d. Dec. 25, 1853; [2]Isabel, bo. July, 1831, ma. John Fayan; [3]William L., bo. Aug. 6, 1833; [4]Catharine, bo. July 19, 1835, ma. W. M. Goodrich; [5]John C., d. Sept. 19, 1848; [6]Mary J., ma. John Kuver; [7]Joseph L., bo. April 29, 1841; [8]Hannah, d. Feb. 1, 1851; [9]Bethanay J.; [10]Samuel K., bo. Nov. 23, 1848.
4668. Amos, bo. May 6, 1809; ma. Hannah R. Slack.
4669. Catharine, bo. Aug. 13, 1811; ma. Samuel Johnson, Sept. 3, 1830. Children: [1]Mary, bo. June 20, 1832; [2]William, bo. Sept. 4, 1834; [3]Jonas, bo. Dec. 15, 1835, d. 1862; [4]Charles, bo. Aug. 17, 1837, d. 1865; [5]Ruth A., bo. June 6, 1839, d. May 30, 1859; [6]Martha E., bo. July 24, 1841; [7]Sarah, bo. April 23, 1843; [8]Susannah, bo. Feb. 3, 1845; [9]Amos, bo. April 27, 1847; [10]Matilda, bo. April 13, 1849; [11]Amanda J., bo. Feb. 9, 1853.
4670. Charles, bo. Oct. 18, 1813; ma. Charlotte Way; 2d, Sarepta Cummings.
4671. Josephus D., bo. Dec. 3, 1816; ma. Matilda Clement.
4672. Susannah, bo. Dec. 3, 1816; ma. Seth Way.
4673. Benjamin, bo. Aug. 29, 1819.

(4657) Elizabeth Smith Ladd (dau. of Joseph Ladd[4649]) ma. Abel Lomax, Dec. 29, 1808.

Children of Abel and Elizabeth (Ladd) Lomax.

4674. Joseph Lomax, bo. Dec. 19, 1809; ma. Sarah Ann Boyd, Feb. 29, 1844.
4675. Sarah Lomax, bo. July 24, 1811; ma. Henry Study.
4676. William Lomax, bo. March 15, 1813; ma. Sarah Vande Vanter; 2d, Maria Hendrix.
4677. Constantine Lomax, bo. Dec. 31, 1814; ma. Rachel Vande Vanter.
4678. Nancy Lomax, bo. May 10, 1816; ma. Henry Shurgart.
4679. Anna Lomax, bo. April 29, 1818; not ma.; d. Sept. 4, 1849, at Valparaiso, Ind.
4680. Robert Lomax, bo. Feb. 26, 1820; d. Sept. 26, 1821.
4681. Alfred Lomax, bo. Sept. 20, 1822; ma. Almy Ann Anderson; 2d, Mary ——.
4682. Elizabeth Smith Lomax, bo. July 1, 1824; ma. Rev. Alex. McHatten.
4683. Mary Lomax, bo. July 23, 1826; ma. Dr. Silas H. Kusey; 2d, Dillon Baldwin; 3d, Pleasant Foster.
4684. Isabel Lomax, bo. June 26, 1829; ma. Samuel Ross Bryant. She died Feb. 26, 1888.

(4674) Joseph Lomax, of Grand Rapids, Mich., (son of Abel and Elizabeth[4657] (Ladd) Lomax,) ma. Sarah Ann Boyd, Feb. 29, 1844.

Children.

4685. Martha Elizabeth Lomax, bo. Dec. 22, 1844; ma. James Morton.
4686. William King Lomax, bo. Nov. 23, 1846; d. Sept. 1847.
4687. Joanna Lomax, bo. June 10, 1848.
4688. Ann Eliza Lomax, bo. June 10, 1848; d. Sept. 27, 1849.
4689. Mary Eveline Lomax, bo. ——.
4690. Sarah Ann Lomax, bo. Nov. 15, 1852; d. Aug. 3, 1854.
4691. Joseph Abel Lomax, bo. ——.
4692. Luna Belle Lomax, bo. ——.
4693. Jesse Omega Lomax, bo. ——.
4694. Augusta Evens Lomax, bo. ——.

(4660) Noble Ladd, of Weare, Humphrey Co., Tenn., (son of Joseph,[4649]) ma. Mary Burton.

Children.

4695. Peter, bo. ——.
4696. Joseph H., bo. ——.
4697. Constantine, bo. ——.
4698. Ann, bo. ——; ma. John G. Smithson.
4699. William, bo. ——.
4700. Thornton Gwynne, bo. ——.
4701. Rebecca, bo. ——; ma. John D. Wood.
4702. Noble, bo. ——.
4703. Mary, bo. ——; ma. Isaac Massey.
4704. Mackey, bo. ——.

4705. Isaac Newton, bo. ——.
4706. Martha, bo. ——; ma. William Mallard.
4707. Sarah Eveline, bo. ——; ma. Thomas Norman.
4708. Mary Isabel, bo. ——.

(4662) William Ladd, of Wayne Co., Ind., (son of Joseph,[4649]) ma. Isabel Boyd, of North Carolina.

Children.

4709. Katharine, bo. ——; ma. Jonathan Wight.
4710. Samuel, bo. ——; ma. Charity Cook.
4711. Cicero W., bo. March 28, 1830; ma. Hannah L. Bailey, Mar. 13, 1851.
4712. Abel, bo. ——.
4713. Caroline, bo. ——; ma. —— Harris.
4714. Constantine, bo. ——; not married.
4715. Boyd, bo. ——; ma. ——.

(4711) Cicero W. Ladd, of Silver Lake, Ind., (son of William,[4662]) ma. Hannah L. Bailey, March 13, 1851.

Children.

4716. Arline, bo. Oct. 15, 1852; d. April 23, 1854.
4717. Leoudo L., bo. June 25, 1854.
4718. Martha Isabel, bo. Dec. 28, 1856.
4719. William Arlington, bo. Oct. 9, 1858; d. Dec. 13, 1859.
4720. Cicero W., bo. June 24, 1860; ma. Anna Paulus, Sept. 11, 1884.

(4720) Cicero W. Ladd, of Silver Lake, Ind., (son of Cicero W.,[4711]) ma. Anna Paulus, Sept. 11, 1884.

Child.

4721. Roscoe L., bo. March 17, 1887.

(4671) Josephus D. Ladd, of Williamsburg, Ind., (son of Joseph,[4649]) ma. Matilda Clement, Jan. 6, 1839. She died July 9, 1861, and he ma. 2d, Eliza Britton, Dec. 3, 1863.

Children.

4722. Elizabeth, bo. Nov. 24, 1839; ma. Miles Stanford.
4723. Hannah, bo. Sept. 2, 1841; ma. Charles Campbell.
4724. Mary, bo. Dec. 16, 1843; not married.
4725. Susannah, bo. Nov. 17, 1846; ma. Allen Chamness.
4726. Catharine, bo. July 27, 1849; ma. Martin Oler.
4727. William, bo. April 6, 1852; ma. Georgie Lloyd.
4728. Cynthia, bo. April 11, 1854; ma. Allen Oler.
4729. James, bo. Feb. 6, 1858; ma. Mattie Campbell, Sept. 4, 1880.
4730. Matilda, bo. March 23, 1861; ma. Elmer Clark.

Children by second wife.

4731. Lemon, bo. Aug. 6, 1864; ma. Mary Robbins, Feb. 19, 1889.
4732. Charles, bo. Feb. 2, 1867.
4733. Flavius, bo. Feb. 2, 1868.
4734. Edgar, bo. Aug. 20, 1889.
4735. Edwin, bo. Aug. 20, 1889.

(4727) William Ladd, of Portland, Ind., (son of Josephus D.,[4671]) ma. Georgie Lloyd. She died Nov. 9, 1887.

Child.

4736. Opal, bo. Aug. 13, 1884.

(4670) Charles Ladd (son of Joseph[4649]) ma. Charlotte Way. She died, and he ma. 2d, Sarepta Cummings.

Children.

4737. Adelbert, bo. ——.
4738. Charles A., bo. ——.

(4739) William Ladd, of Mecklinburg Co., Va., (son of ——,) ma. —— Pennington. Soon after his marriage he removed to Henry Co., Ky.

Children.

4740. Cynthia, bo. ——.
4741. Pennington, bo. ——.
4742. William W., bo. ——; ma. Mary E. Steele, of Gosport, Ind.
4743. John W., bo. ——.
4744. Harrison, bo. ——.
4745. Robert, bo. ——.

(4742) William W. Ladd (son of William[4739]) ma. Mary E. Steele, 1844.

Children.

4746. Emma, bo. 1846; d. 1848.
4747. Mattie, bo. 1848; ma. James Steele, 1865.
4748. James, bo. 1850; ma. Bell Mason, 1886.
4749. Anna, bo. 1852; ma. Rev. Henry C. Thomson.
4750. Lulie, bo. 1854; ma. A. J. Moore, 1878.
4751. Charles W., bo. 1856; ma. Kittie L. Rearden, Sept. 2, 1882.
4752. Ella, bo. 1858; ma. James Rodes. She died 1881.
4753. John S., bo. 1860.
4754. Frank, bo. 1867.
4755. Robert, bo. 1870.

(4751) Charles W. Ladd, M. D., of Cannelton, Ind., (son of William W.,[4742]) ma. Kittie L. Rearden, Sept. 2, 1882. He graduated in the medical department of the University at Louisville, Ky.

Child.

4756. Anita, bo. Sept. 3, 1883.

(4757) John Ladd (son of ——) ma. Betsey Hardwick.

Children.

4758. James, bo. ——.
4759. William, bo. ——; ma. Henrietta Ladd (his cousin.)
4760. John H., bo. May 10, 1806; ma. Luady Moody.

(4760) John H. Ladd, of Pleasureville, Ky., (son of John,[4757]) ma. Luady Moody. She died, and he ma. 2d, Mrs. Elizabeth (Bohon) Bushun. He died July 4, 1889.

Children.

4761. Mary E., bo. ——; ma. Jacob S. Smith.
4762. James, bo. ——; ma. Mary E. Maddox.
4763. Minerva, bo. ——; ma. Jesse S. Armstrong.
4764. Notan W., bo. ——; ma. Ella J. Taylor.
4765. John M., bo. ——; ma. Mary E. Kelley.
4766. Isham T., bo. ——; ma. Sallie D. Jackson, May 22, 1860.

(4762) James Ladd, of Pleasureville, Ky., (son of John H.,[4760]) ma. Mary E. Maddox.

Child.

4767. Eva M., bo. ——.

(4765) John M. Ladd, of Jericho, Ky., (son of John H.,[4760]) ma. Mary E. Kelley.

Children.

4768. Floris M., ma. William N. Woolfork. 2. Joseph H., ma. Ida Harley. 3. Arthur S. 4. Notan W.

(4764) Notan W. Ladd, of Odessa, Mo., (son of John H.,[4760]) ma. Ella J. Taylor.

Children.

4769. Notan, bo. 1878.
4770. Frank May, bo. 1880.
4771. Robert S., bo. 1883.

(4766) Isham T. Ladd, of Odessa, Mo., (son of John H.,[4760]) ma. Sallie D. Jackson, May 22, 1860.

Children.

4772. John H., bo. Sept. 26, 1868.
4773. George B., bo. Nov. 9, 1872.

Additional Descendants of Daniel Ladd, No. 1.

(1801) Ira Ladd, of Hennepen, Ill., (son of John,[654]) ma. Eliza Gallaher, 1831. He died July 7, 1834.

Child.

4774. Ira, bo. Jan. 10, 1832; d. Aug. 14, 1833.

(1802) Samuel Ladd, of Burke, Vt., (son of John,[654]) ma. Sally Jones, of Burke, Vt., 1826.

Children.

4775. John, bo. 1829.
4776. Silas, bo. 1831; d. 1839.
4777. Virgil, bo. 1837.

(1807) Alonzo Ladd, of Elizabeth, N. J., (son of John,[654]) ma. Juliet C. Nichols, Aug. 27, 1862.

Child.

4778. Willie Nichols, bo. Aug. 18, 1865; d. Sept. 5, 1872.

(3930) Edmund Ladd, of Saco, Me., (son of Thomas,[3924]) ma. Mary Grace, March 3, 1824.

Children.

4779. Hannah, bo. July 25, 1825.
4780. Mary, bo. Sept. 22, 1827.
4781. Thomas, bo. June 29, 1829.
4782. Hiram, bo. March 27, 1831.
4783. Sarah, bo. March 28, 1833.
4784. Emily, bo. June 2, 1841.

(3933) Rufus Ladd, of Saco, Me., (son of Thomas,[3924]) ma. Susan Boothby, Sept. 9, 1832.

Children.

4785. Joseph B., bo. March 28, 1833.
4786. George F., bo. Aug. 4, 1834.
4787. Rufus, bo. May 17, 1836.
4788. James William, bo. Jan. 14, 1842.

(3937) James Ladd, of Saco, Me., (son of Thomas,[3924]) ma. Caroline Rowe, June 7, 1848. He died 1883.

Children.

4790. H. Plummer, bo. April 29, 1849; ma. Loretta Rose, June 30, 1870.
4791. Lorenzo, bo. Sept. 21, 1850; ma. Clara E. Hill, May 2, 1875.
4792. Laura E., bo. Nov. 30, 1852; ma. William Nason, Oct. 20, 1873.
4793. Ella C., bo. Feb. 10, 1855; ma. A. E. Seavy, Sept. 25, 1876.
4794. Clara E., bo. Nov. 29, 1859; ma. Wilmont K. Sanborn, June 30, 1885.
Children: [1]Harold W., bo. May 21, 1886; [2]Florence, bo. July 25, 1888.

(4790) H. Plummer Ladd, of Biddeford, Me., (son of James,[3937]) ma. Loretta Rose, June 30, 1870.

Children.
4795. Boyd, bo. June 21, 1873.
4796. James E., bo. Sept. 8, 1881.
4797. Mirtle F., bo. June 8, 1886.

(4791) Lorenzo Ladd, of Saco, Me., (son of James,[3937]) ma. Clara E. Hill, May 2, 1875.

Children.
4798. Edna E., bo. March 4, 1877.
4799. Eva M., bo. April 6, 1879.
4800. George F., bo. March 17, 1881.
4801. Lorna M., bo. April 9, 1890.

(3935) John Ladd, of Saco, Me., (son of Thomas,[3924]) ma. Lucinda Bryant, March 20, 1838. He died June 14, 1882.

Children.
4802. Jane, bo. March 11, 1839; ma. Isaiah Emmons, Feb. 24, 1882.
4803. Henry, bo. June 3, 1841; ma. Sarah Andrews, Aug. 1, 1867.
4804. Ellen, bo. Nov. 15, 1845; ma. Samuel Blaisdell, June 27, 1868.
4805. Lucinda, bo. Nov. 8, 1849; ma. Frank Winkley, July 8, 1870.

(4803) Henry Ladd, of Andover, Me., (son of John,[3935]) ma. Sarah Andrews, Aug. 1, 1867.

Children.
4806. Warren H., bo. Aug. 20, 1868.
4807. John B., bo. Nov. 28, 1869.
4808. Emma F., bo. Aug. 6, 1872; ma. Orlando Hannaford.
4809. Mary E., bo. March 23, 1874.
4810. Forest W., bo. Dec. 6, 1876.
4811. Willis R., bo. Sept. 26, 1878.
4812. Lucinda, bo. Oct. 23. 1880.
4813. David A., bo. April 25, 1882.
4814. Arthur J., bo. Aug. 7, 1883.
4815. Jesse A., bo. July 28, 1885.

(2510) Jacob P. Ladd, of Plainfield, Vt., (son of Aurin,[1142]) ma. Melissa I. Perkins, Oct. 20, 1863.

Children.
4816. Morton D., bo. Oct. 25, 1865.
4817. —— H., bo. Aug. 26, 1872.

(2380) Alonzo P. Ladd, of Damariscotta, Me., (son of Oliver Hazard Perry,[988]) ma. Ada F. Lunt, Oct. 25, 1877.

Children.

4818. Roydon Perry, bo. March 21, 1878.
4819. Annie Gertrude, bo. June 3, 1880.
4820. William Sumner, bo. Nov. 22, 1882.
4821. Edgar Alonzo, bo. Dec. 22, 1888.

(622) Caleb Ladd, of Tunbridge, Vt., (son of Edward,[258]) ma. Tama Dunham.

Children.

4822. Sally, bo. ——; ma. Samuel Holt, of Chelsea, Vt.
4823. Elijah, bo. ——.
4824. Tama, bo. ——.
4825. Abigail, bo. ——.
4826. Salina, bo. ——.

(1891) John Shaw Ladd, of Waterbury, Vt., (son of John,[620]) ma. Mercy Chamberlain. She died Dec. 21, 1843, and he ma. 2d, Sarah M. Bragg, Sept. 18, 1844. He died Feb. 18, 1873.

Children.

4827. Flora B., bo. Nov. 21, 1841; ma. Dr. James Eaton.
4828. Maria L., bo. Dec. 18, 1842; ma. Albourn Tuttle, June 24, 1872.

Children by second wife.

4829. Melvina, bo. Aug. 17, 1844; ma. William D. Pratt, July 7, 1872.
4830. Chestina, bo. March 25, 1846; ma. James Orier, July 30, 1864.
4831. Emeline C., bo. Oct. 30, 1848; ma. Orris Ayers, Jan. 16, 1882.
4832. John Franklin, bo. Dec. 14, 1850; ma. Eliza Cheney, March 28, 1874.
4833. William Walter, bo. Jan. 1, 1857; ma. Addie Morse, Sept. 6, 1882.
4834. Adda Abigail, bo. Nov. 7, 1859; ma. Fred. Reed, July 16, 1888.
4835. Lafayette R., bo. Feb. 8, 1861; ma. Hattie A. Chester, March 3, 1887.

(1892) Elijah Shaw Ladd, of Waterbury, Vt., (son of John,[620]) ma. Phila West, June 6, 1828. He died at Barre, Vt., June, 1883.

Children.

4836. Jonathan Pierce, bo. 1830; ma. Katharine Town, Jan. 6, 1858.
4837. Eben West, bo. ——.

(1894) Isaac Ladd, of Waterford, Vt., (son of John,[620]) ma. Mary Jennison.

Children.

4838. Lucy, bo. ——.
4839. Martha, bo. ——.
4840. James, bo. ——.

(4836) Jonathan Ladd, of Waterbury, Vt., (son of Elijah,[1892]) ma. Katharine Town, Jan. 6, 1858.

Children.

4841. Fannie E., bo. June 6, 1860; ma. Irwin A. Hill, Sept. 15, 1883.
4842. Frank P., bo. May 14, 1865.
4843. Fred. E., bo. Oct. 16, 1867.
4844. Villa E., bo. Feb. 12, 1870.
4845. Lizzie M., bo. Oct. 14, 1872.

(4832) John Franklin Ladd, of Waterbury, Vt., (son of John Shaw,[1891]) ma. Eliza Cheney, March 28, 1874.

Children.

4846. Lizzie Maria, bo. Oct. 28, 1875.
4847. Cora May, bo. Feb. 15, 1877.
4848. Franklin Smith, bo. Oct. 15, 1878.
4849. Rosie Trafton, bo. April 12, 1880.
4850. Lillian Chestina, bo. March 12, 1883.
4851. Harold Lafayette, bo. Aug. 20, 1885.
4852. Mark Shaw, bo. April 14, 1889.

(625) Nathaniel S. Ladd. The following names of his children were received too late to be inserted in their place. For other children, see page 125.

4853. Anna, bo. June 26, 1820.
4854. Anora, bo. ——; ma. Lucius T. Harris, Jan. 1, 1842.
4855. Sarah B., bo. ——; d. Dec. 19, 1848.
4856. Deborah, bo. ——; ma. Daniel Hinkson. Children: [1]Mark, bo. Jan. 24, 1839; [2]Edward, bo. Jan. 31, 1844; [3]Edwin, bo. Jan. 31, 1844.
4857. Mary, bo. ——; ma. Ransom Spear, Jan. 25, 1836. Children: [1]Marietta, bo. Jan. 9, 1839; [2]Martin, bo. Sept. 9, 1840; [3]Sarah Ann, bo. Dec. 29, 1841.

(1907) Mark P. Ladd, of Worcester, Vt., (son of Nathaniel S.,[625]) ma. Lois Bruce. She died Aug. 18, 1843, and he ma. 2d, Harriet B. Hildreth.

Child.

4858. Sabrina, bo. Oct. 25, 1840; d. Sept. 16, 1842.

Children by second wife.

4859. Stephen, bo. May 14, 1846.
4860. Chester Mark, bo. March 16, 1848.
4861. Henry H., bo. March 31, 1850.
4862. Edward N., bo. Sept. 17, 1851.
4863. Joseph Thing, bo. Oct. 22, 1854.
4864. Adaline D., bo. Jan. 10, 1857.

(802) Robert Ladd, of Tunbridge, Vt., (son of Jonathan[329] and Elizabeth (Patterson) Ladd,) born in 1776, removed from Tunbridge, Vt., to Washington, Vt. He ma. Olive Chapman, June 5, 1800.

Children.

4865. Constantine, bo. 1802; ma. Mary Flint.
4866. Allura, bo. 1803; ma. George Wood.
4867. Samuel, bo. 1804; ma. Sophronia Pepper.
4868. Casadana, bo. 1804; ma. Sanford Carpenter.
4869. Jasper, bo. 1806; ma. Caroline Newton.
4870. Isaac N., bo. 1808; ma. Asenath Flind.
4871. Sarah, bo. 1816; ma. Daniel Lowell.
4872. Hosea, bo. 1818; d. 1848.

(4869) Jasper Ladd, of Chelsea, Vt., (son of Robert,[802]) ma. Caroline Newton, July 22, 1832.

Children.

4873. Aurilla, bo. July 20, 1833; ma. Ethan George.
4874. Lenora H., bo. Jan. 2, 1835; ma. Lewis C. Beckwith.
4875. Louisa, bo. July 9, 1840; not ma. She was at work in the reel room in the fifth story of the Pemberton Mill, at Lawrence, in 1860, when it fell, but she escaped without much injury by sliding down on the *elevator chain* three flights, when she was caught by some men and relieved from her perilous position.

(180) Aphia Ladd, of Franklin, Conn., (dau. of Daniel Ladd,[53]) ma. Levi Crandall, Jan. 27, 1791. He was the son of Edward and Charity (Benson) Crandall.

Children of Levi and Aphia (Ladd) Crandall.

4876. Olivia, bo. Nov. 27, 1791; not ma.; d. Feb. 10, 1838.
4877. Edward, bo. July 4, 1794; drowned June 26, 1821.
4878. Levi, bo. Sept. 23, 1796; d. April 27, 1798.
4879. Simeon, bo. Sept. 23, 1796; d. May 4, 1798.
4880. Levi, bo. June 3, 1799; ma. ——; d. at Steubenville, Ohio, and left a family.
4881. Sarah, bo. May 30, 1801; not married.

The name of the wife of John Ladd (668,) on page 140, should be Electa Ferguson, and the wife of his brother Jonathan Ladd (667,) page 140, should be Alida Olmstead. We enter here a corrected record of the family of Jonathan Ladd (667,) received after his record on page 140 was printed.

(667) Jonathan Ladd, of Danville, Vt., (son of John,[368]) ma. Alida Olmstead, of Lyman, N. H. He removed from St. Johnsbury, Vt., to Danville, Vt., then to Canada, and from there, on account of the war of 1812, to Sandusky, Ohio, where he and his wife both died in 1818.

Children.

4882. Polly, bo. 1806; not ma.; d. in Rochester, N. Y., about 1825.
4883. Relief Electa, bo. 1808; ma. Ralph W. Carver, (son of Aldrich and Asenath (Tarbox) Carver, of Hebron, Conn., who d. at Elkhorn, Wis., 1872,) at West Broomfield, N. Y., 1828. She died in California in 1888. Children, all born in Nunda, Livingston Co., N. Y.:

[1]Albert S., bo. 1828; not ma.; d. in Geneva, Wis., 1888.

[2]Henry Ladd, bo. in 1830; ma. at Richmond, Ontario Co., N. Y., Marietta Ashley, dau. of Hiram and Polly (Gilbert) Ashley, in 1836. Both parents were of New England descent. Child: Helen A., who now resides at St. Paul, Minn. He was educated in the common schools and the Temple Hill Academy at Geneseo, N. Y.; worked upon his father's farm in the Summer, attended and taught school in the Winter. Studied law and graduated from the State and National Law School in 1854. The same year he was admitted to the bar of the State of New York, moved to St. Paul, Minn., and engaged in the practice of his profession; was elected to the Legislature of Minnesota in 1862, and served two sessions. In the same year he enlisted as a private in the 6th Minnesota Infantry; was promoted to 1st lieutenant, and served with his regiment in the campaigns against the Sioux Indians, under Gen. H. H. Sibley, in the years 1862-3; was promoted to captain and a quartermaster U. S. Vols., December, 1863, and from that date served as chief quartermaster of the District of Minnesota until the close of the war. He was breveted major and also lieutenant-colonel, for faithful and meritorious service. He is a member of the Society of the Sons of the Revolution, of the Grand Army of the Republic and the Loyal Legion, a life member and councillor of the Minnesota State Historical Society, and a director of the St. Paul Public Library.

[3]Martha Jane, bo. 1833; ma. at Nunda, N. Y., in 1856, Henry Hubbard. Children: Two sons and two daughters, now residing at Elkhorn, Wis.

[4]Charles P., bo. 1835; ma. Mary J. Taylor. No children. Resides at St. Augustine, Fla.

[5]Edward W., bo. 1838; ma. in 1864, in Walworth Co., Wis., Melissa Field. No children. Now living in New Mexico.

[6]Mary E., bo. 1843; ma. at Nunda. N. Y., Dr. J. M. Baker, in 1866. Now resides at Lake Geneva, N. Y.

[7]Frederick A., bo. 1849; ma. at Troy, N. Y., Emma Alden, in 1879. Child: Arthur, now resides at Troy, N. Y.

(1461) Rev. Alden Ladd, of Berlin, Vt., (son of Avery S.,[820]) ma. Sarah M., dau. of Samuel and Nancy (Edwards) Edwards, of Roxbury, Vt., Nov. 25, 1869. She died July, 1877, and he ma. 2d, Feb. 5, 1879, Mary E., dau. of Joseph C. and Cerenthia (Chandler) Prentice, of Waitsfield, Vt. After finishing the course usually taught in the public schools, he spent some time at the Academy at Groton and at the Academy at Westfield, and studied divinity at the Theological Seminary at Hartford, Conn. Was ordained at Roxbury, Vt., Feb. 14, 1865, where he preached until 1879, when he removed to Berlin, Vt., where he was acting-pastor for two churches, one at Berlin, Vt., and the other at West Berlin, Vt., until 1885, when he was obliged to relinquish his labors on account of failing health. He died at West Randolph, Vt., June 30, 1887.

Children.

4884. Carlos Alphonso, bo. Feb. 14, 1871; d. Nov. 13, 1876.
4885. Grace Edwards, bo. Jan. 7, 1873.

Children by second wife.

4886. Carey Prentice, bo. Dec. 10, 1879.
4887. Percy Chandler, bo. April 21, 1883.

(206) Elisha Ladd, of East Windsor, Conn., (son of Ezekiel,[56]) ma. Tabitha Strong, May 23, 1776.

Children.

4888. Eunice, bo. Feb. 22, 1777.
4889. Clarissa, bo. Oct. 31, 1778.
4890. Elisha, bo. Oct. 24, 1780.

(218) Jonathan Ladd, of Tolland, Conn., (son of Jonathan,[58]) ma. Lydia Johnson, Sept. 26, 1799, of Ashford, Conn.

Children.

4891. Eliab, bo. May 17, 1801; ma. Celia Strong.
4892. Maria, bo. March 25, 1803; ma. Salmon Dart. She died July 1, 1887. Children: [1]Maria, ma. —— Gorham; 2d, —— Willis; 3d, —— Bidwell. [2]Emeline, ma. John Silcox. [3]Mary Ann, ma. Willard Griswold.
4893. Ephraim, bo. 1806; ma. Mary Ann Tucker.
4894. Lydia Minervia, bo. March 14, 1808; ma. Elisha H. Martin. She died Aug. 2, 1885. He died Oct. 13, 1870. Children: [1]Amanda Elmira, d. Oct. 25, 1872; [2]Elisha Johnson; [3]Maria, ma. Henry Eaton; [4]Sarah, ma. Mr. Russell; [5]William Benton, bo. 1854, ma. Emma N. Willis, who died July 24, 1883.

4895. Jonathan Tyler, bo. Feb. 18, 1812; not ma.; d. June 29, 1887.
4896. Amanda, bo. Feb. 27, 1815; ma. Jason Burnham, April 19, 1840. He died May 11, 1885. Children: [1]Emily Olive, bo. March 5, 1841, ma. Oscar W. Sanford, Oct. 25, 1871; [2]Sarah Presenda, bo. May 17, 1843; [3]Amanda Clarissa, bo. May 17, 1849, d. July 20, 1857.

(4891) Eliab Ladd, of Rockville, Conn., (son of Jonathan,[218]) ma. Celia Strong.

Children.

4897. Mariva, bo. ——; not married.
4898. Henry, bo. ——; ma. Lydia Squires.
4899. William Johnson, bo. ——; ma. Harriet L. Abbey. She died Nov. 3, 1852, and he ma. 2d, Mary J. Abbey; 3d, Miss Wolcott.
4900. Sarah Malissa, bo. ——; ma. Harlam Parker.
4901. Theodore, bo. ——; ma. Miss Johnson.
4902. Martha, bo. ——.
4903. Mary, bo. ——.
4904. Charles, bo. ——; ma. Miss Brown.

(4893) Ephraim Ladd, of Tolland, Conn., (son of Jonathan,[218]) ma. Mary Ann Tucker, who died Jan. 7, 1841, and he ma. 2d, Betsey Alexander. She died, and he ma. 3d, Lois Williams.

Children by first wife.

4905. Mary Amelia, bo. ——; ma. Daniel Ely Benton.
4906. George, bo. ——.

(103) John Ladd, of Coventry, Conn., (supposed to be son of Samuel,[33]) ma. Prudence Shepherd, July 26, 1762.

Children.

4907. Hannah, bo. Jan. 13, 1764.
4908. Palmer, bo. March 6, 1765; ma. ——. Child: Rachel, bo. Dec. 23, 1794.
4909. John, bo. Feb. 24, 1767.
4910. Prudence, bo. March 3, 1768.
4911. Susannah, bo. Sept. 11, 1772.

(4912) Samuel Ladd, of Coventry, Conn., (son of ——,) ma. Hannah ——.

Children.

4913. Moses, bo. June 24, 1745; ma. Keziah Killsem.
4914. Mary, bo. Nov. 6, 1746.
4915. Ruth, bo. Jan. 22, 1749.

4913) Moses Ladd, of Coventry, Conn., (son of Samuel,[4912]) ma. Keziah Killsem, June 26, 1768.

Children.

4916. Oliver, bo. July 10, 1769.
4917. Lucy, bo. April 21, 1771, in Windsor, Conn.
4918. Olive, bo. April 13, 1773, in Windsor, Conn.

INDEX.

Page on the right of the number.

LADD FAMILIES.

Aaron, 703, 75. 4167, 303.
Abner, 55, 23. 191, 111. 1616, 169.
Abial Richardson, 949, 164.
Abel, 1206, 183.
Abraham G., 1229, 186.
Ahijah, 213, 43. 563, 129.
Alanson, 2075, 214.
Albert, 177, 40. 2902, 255. 2638, 251.
Albert J., 2707, 257.
Albert W., 1764, 150.
Alden, 1461, 347.
Alexander, 649, 109.
Alexander H., 1595, 132.
Alexander P., 1495, 123. 1504, 147.
Alfred, 455, 68. 4080, 297.
Alfred Greely, 3629, 270.
Alfred D., 4173, 303.
Alfred W., 1182, 181.
Allen Dexter, 3591, 272.
Alliston B., 2764, 209.
Alliston C., 2227, 244.
Alixis, 4239, 307.
Almon A., 1157, 176.
Alonzo, 2235, 240. 3817, 281. 1807, 341.
Alonzo C., 929, 162.
Alonzo P., 2381, 343.
Alpheus, 457, 68. 815, 110.
Alphonzo, 1457, 220.
Alvan Landers, 2507, 263.
Alvaro, 2062, 213.
Alverado, 512, 71.
Amasa Scott, 833, 158.
Ammi S., 1199, 183.
Amos, 4388, 325. 4452, 326. 4382, 333. 4588, 333. 4590, 334. 4601, 334. 4640, 335.
Andrew, 164, 40. 1377, 194.
Andrew J., 3033, 259.
Andrew Robeson, 2054, 226.
Ansel, 1336, 194.
Anson, 428, 266. 444, 66.
Ariel, 1928, 203. 556, 126.
Arthur G., 4202, 304.
Arthur S., 2280, 227.
Arthur Stuart, 2784, 247.
Arthur Washington, 3569, 265.

Artimus, 1369, 197.
Arumah, 1916, 218.
Asa, 108, 32. 346, 58. 501, 70. 817, 95. 1329, 193. 1820, 212.
Asa Spaulding, 1636, 198.
Ashbel, 135, 37.
Atticus Alixis, 1857, 216. 2970, 275.
Atticus R., 1861, 216.
Augustus F., 3758, 276.
Aurin, 1142, 174.
Austin, 536, 72. 839, 137. 3577, 266.
Austin S., 2174, 239.
Avery S., 820, 95.
Azel P., 892, 139.

Babson S., 2224, 244.
Barnett, 1682, 270.
Bayles E., 4600, 334.
Bela Dow, 2042, 229.
Bela Orlanda, 871, 138.
Benijah, 146, 39.
Benjamin, 94, 30. 326, 57. 795, 87. 800, 88. 1326, 192. 4160, 302. 4411, 324. 4426, 325.
Benjamin H., 4486, 327.
Benjamin W., 4399, 322.
Benoni, 424, 65.
Bodwell, 233, 89. 1396, 98. 1424, 105.
Buel, 167, 112.
Byron G., 1517, 146.
Byron P., 1524, 146.

Caldwell, 3754, 277.
Caleb, 239, 93. 1426, 105. 1560, 149. 4134, 306. 4235, 306. 622, 343.
Calvin, 489, 69. 2071, 216.
Calvin B., 1829, 213.
Calvin P., 837, 160.
Chandler, 1025, 168.
Charles, 158, 39. 643, 107. 1828, 213. 2637, 251. 3582, 271. 3829, 283. 4670, 339. 4817, 464.
Charles Augustus, 1747, 207.

Charles B., 2800, 221.
Charles Bodwell, 1562, 149.
Charles Carroll, 4257, 308.
Charles Frederick, 4277, 309.
Charles F., 4431, 325.
Charles George, 1999, 238.
Charles Green, 966, 165.
Charles H., 1047, 169. 3099, 259. 3719, 274. 4213, 305.
Charles Haven, 1592, 131.
Charles Hibbard, 1294, 210.
Charles Ira, 691, 74.
Charles J., 1012, 167.
Charles Joseph, 1771, 152.
Charles K., 1918, 218. 3006, 224.
Charles P., 1239, 186.
Charles R., 1926, 202.
Charles Warren, 545, 126. 2196, 243.
Charles W., 4751, 340.
Chauncy, 3751, 277.
Chester, 1277, 188.
Chester B., 1009, 167.
Cicero W., 4711, 338. 4720, 338.
Clark H., 2260, 256.
Constantine, 4606, 335.
Constantine F. V., 1543, 258.
Crawford, 754, 84.
Cyrus, 144, 38. 1349, 196. 3749, 275.
Cyrus A., 1844, 137.
Cyrus C., 3756, 276.
Cyrus K., 3612, 268.

Daniel, 1, 1. 10, 15. 24, 18. 34, 19. 53, 23. 76, 26. 89, 28. 105, 32. 110, 33. 221, 44. 254, 45. 340, 58. 364, 61. 378, 62. 697, 75. 712, 77. 724, 79. 753, 84. 613, 119. 617, 121. 1757, 149. 912, 161. 1191, 182. 1328, 193. 1178, 178. 2304, 228. 285, 267. 3603, 267. 3610, 268. 4144, 302.
Daniel Albert, 3622, 269.
Daniel B., 1220, 184.
Daniel C., 3841, 281.
Daniel Gorham, 883, 139.
Daniel P., 1163, 176.
Daniel T., 2950, 241.
Daniel Watson, 1789, 154. 2217, 247. 2218, 248. 3282, 271.
Daniel Valson, 812, 273.
Darius, 170, 40. 1496, 124.
David, 15, 16. 49, 21. 114, 35. 159, 39. 1784, 154. 1096, 172. 4560, 332.
David Bean, 1228, 186.
David Chandler, 1312, 191.
David M., Rev., 823, 96.
David M., 1430, 104. 3302, 249.
David Newell, 2619, 249.

David P., 1697, 199.
Dearborn, 2630, 251.
Dudley, 253, 45. 276, 50. 699, 75. 600, 106. 633, 114. 1574, 134. 670, 140.
Dudley F., 686, 74.
Dudley P., 1164, 177.

Eben, 3483, 261.
Eben S., 3509, 263.
Ebenezer, 4245, 308.
Ebenezer B., 1448, 228.
Edward, 77, 26. 258, 46. 629, 113. 623, 125. 1882, 157. 1044, 168.
Edmund, 3930, 341.
Edward A., 1236, 186.
Edward Homer, 4009, 292.
Edward N., 1542, 258.
Edward O., 2990, 229.
Edward Horace, 2370, 225.
Edwin O., 976, 165.
Edwin W., 1754, 207.
Elbridge, 1824, 213.
Elbridge G., 2777, 246.
Eleazer, 797, 88.
Eliab, 212, 42. 1703, 115. 4891, 477.
Elias, 78, 27. 264, 49. 655, 121.
Elijah, 3825, 283.
Elijah Shaw, 1892, 343.
Eliphalet, 272, 47. 231, 77. 638, 106. 1589, 130. 3746, 275.
Elisha, 4078, 296. 206, 477.
Elisha Locke, 411, 64.
Elisha P., 4095, 297.
Emery, 1409, 104.
Emor O., 4106, 298.
Enoch, 341, 58. 749, 83.
Enoch H., 811, 272.
Enoch Place, 1227, 185.
Ephraim, 204, 42. 439, 66. 3821, 282. 4893, 478.
Ephraim Lewis, 1013, 168.
Erastus, 192, 112.
Erastus D., 2078, 214.
Erastus P., 1634, 198.
Ethan Smith, 406, 63.
Ezekiel, 8, 14. 51, 22. 56, 23. 109, 32. 355, 59. 3788, 277. 3809, 280.
Ezekiel Hyde, 519, 71.
Ezra, 2504, 230.

Festus, 194, 112.
Frank, 2641, 252.
Frank H., 3948, 285.
Frank J., 2733, 254.
Frank M., 1554, 161.
Frank O., 3623, 270.

Frank P., 1288, 186.
Francis D., 1975, 235.
Francis W., 2699, 253.
Francois J. G., 3274, 264.
Francois B., 1177, 178.
Frederick, 138, 38. 461, 68.
Frederick P., 1404, 102. 2761, 209.
Frederick R., 1751, 207.
Fredus, 1629, 197. 2738, 270.
Freeman P., 2708, 258.
Freeman W., 2776, 246.

Gardner P., 1507, 144.
George, 2727, 254. 1179, 180.
George A., 1548, 148.
George D., 2371, 225.
George E. M. F. J., 944, 163.
George G., 1582, 210.
George H., 1224, 185. 2037, 226. 4203, 304.
George Henry, 2709, 230.
George M., 1270, 188. 3671, 274.
George Munroe, 3949, 285.
George P., 1951, 205.
George Senaca, 2206, 245.
George Solon, 2955, 245.
George Storrs, 4269, 308.
George T., 1721, 223. 3501, 262.
George Vivian, 1536, 147.
George V. B., 2041, 229.
George W., 1518, 146. 1195, 182. 1383, 195. 1665, 217. 2978, 257. 3122, 259. 3173, 259. 4246, 308.
Gideon, 610, 118.
Gordon, 741, 81.
Gorham, 1839, 136.
Gould D., 1675, 198.
Grant, 478, 69.
Guilford, 2654, 252.
Gerrard, 4557, 333.
G. W. Terrill, 4599, 334.

Hale, 2888, 254.
Hannibal E., 1281, 273.
Harlow, 1705, 115.
Harlow Page, 2781, 246.
Harrison, 2984, 257.
Harvey, 1842, 136.
Hastings A., 897, 139.
Hazen, 155, 39.
Heman, 1905, 103. 1482, 123.
Henry, 40, 20. 128, 36. 418, 64. 647, 107. 941, 163. 1065, 169. 1447, 220. 4803, 342.
Henry C., 2438, 170. 4204, 305.
Henry Clay, 2287, 228.
Henry E., 2050, 129.
Henry H., 2948, 241.
Henry J., 2809, 223.
Henry Martin, 1301, 189.
Henry Sanford, 3621, 269.
Henry W., 2936, 255.
Hiram, 748, 82. 943, 163. 995, 167. 1843, 137. 841, 238. 2012, 249. 1273, 274. 4066, 298.
Hiram E., 2193, 243.
Herman, 419, 65.
Herman W., 2891, 254.
Herbert W., 1074, 169.
Herbert Warren, 2283, 231.
Hollis, 1887, 157.
Horace C., 2079, 215.
Horace H., 377, 62. 1158, 176.
Horace P., 2939, 256.
Horace W., 1749, 207.
Horatio, 544, 126.
Horatio J., 2997, 224.
Horatio O., 1983, 236.
H. Plummer, 4790, 342.

Ira, 1801, 341.
Ira Marshall, 2202, 244.
Ira Walter, 2208, 245.
Isaac, 324, 56. 413, 64. 790, 87. 630, 114. 1894, 343.
Isaac V., 3762, 276.
Isham I., 4766, 340.
Israel, 1797, 209.
Israel S., 491, 69.

Jabez, 511, 71.
Jacob, 541, 118. 4579, 333.
Jacob D., 3006, 268.
Jacob P., 2510, 342.
Jacob S., 1141, 174.
Jackson A., 1451, 229.
James, 116, 35. 183, 41. 286, 52. 359, 60. 612, 119. 659, 122. 867, 137. 935, 162. 4762, 340. 3937, 341. 4161, 302. 4178, 303. 4387, 320. 4384, 330. 4539, 331.
James D., 4396, 321. 4408, 323.
James E., 534, 72.
James Ellis, 2741, 270.
James H., 1242, 187. 4492, 328. 2635, 251.
James K., 4140, 301.
James L. S., 854, 137.
James Madison, 2286, 227.
James Milton, 4503, 330.
James Munroe, 1134, 264.
James Otis, 3008, 221.
James Smith, 3694, 273.
James Thomas, 3620, 269.

James T., 3490, 272.
James William. 2036, 226.
Jasper, 4869, 345.
Jedediah, 293, 54.
Jedediah P., 504, 70. 190, 111. 2436, 170.
Jedediah P. B., 1419, 104.
Jeremiah, 47, 20. 256, 46. 689, 74. 1794, 209. 321, 56.
Jeremiah B. P., 2088, 234.
Jeremiah Q., 1313, 191.
Jeremiah W., 1125, 173.
Jesse, 64, 24. 361, 60. 866, 137. 1815, 211. 220, 44. 3942, 284.
Jesse E., 713, 78.
Jesse T., 593, 117.
Job, 4133, 305.
Joel Levi, 1948, 205.
John, 18, 17. 25, 18. 92, 29. 113, 34. 141, 38. 214, 43. 268, 49. 310, 55. 331, 57. 366, 61. 706, 76. 725, 79. 761, 84. 768, 85. 793, 87. 1402, 101. 1423, 105. 628, 113. 573, 114. 607, 118. 616, 120. 654, 121. 745, 124. 620, 124. 1573, 134. 1880, 156. 1671, 198. 1804, 211. 313, 55. 704, 76. 668, 140. 4042, 294. 4047, 294. 4125, 299. 4131, 300. 4162, 302. 4177, 303. 4298, 311. 4380, 319. 4383, 320. 4389, 327. 3711, 274. 3795, 278. 3801, 279. 3813, 280. 1986, 237. 2233, 239. 325, 261. 2901, 255. 3935, 342. 4757, 340. 103, 348.
John A., 2967, 275. 3842, 281.
John Allen, 2082, 215.
John Brown. 4081, 297.
John C., 2824, 256.
John Colby, 3488, 271.
John D., 3856, 283.
John E., 3482, 261. 3158, 259.
John Folsom. 673, 73.
John F., 1100, 172. 4832, 344.
John G., 4240, 307.
John Gardner. 3994, 293.
John Gould, 2775, 246.
John Haskins, 4116, 293. 3997, 293.
John Hibbard, 747, 82.
John H., 4760. 340.
John Ingersoll, 1508, 144.
John J., 3869, 282. 2288, 230.
John Lyford. 1698, 206.
John Martin, 2161, 239.
John Milton, 4498, 329.
John Mosely, 1934, 219.
John M., 4117, 298. 4765, 340.
John Q. A., 853, 247.
John Redington, 449, 67.
John Savilian, 1791, 155. 3275, 264.

John Senaca, 2205, 245.
John Shaw, 1891, 343.
John Tyler, 2748, 272.
John V., 4192, 304.
John W., 1514, 145. 1122, 173.
John Warren, 1226, 185.
John Westgate, 4272, 309.
Jonathan, 16, 16. 58, 24. 118, 36. 329, 57. 373, 62. 739, 81. 786, 86. 632, 114. 667, 140. 1358, 196. 1819, 212. 4180, 304. 4300, 313. 667, 346. 218, 347.
Jonathan R., 939, 162.
Jonathan P., 2661, 253.
Jonathan Pierce, 4836, 344.
Joseph, 52, 22. 353, 59. 708, 76. 750, 83. 621, 125. 1884, 157. 1902, 157. 1666, 217. 910, 217. 3956, 288. 3976, 290. 3957, 289. 4540, 331. 4649, 336. 2981, 257.
Joseph A., 2876, 250.
Joseph Brown, 4034, 293.
Joseph C., 4181, 304.
Joseph Edwin. 1175, 178.
Joseph E., 1196, 182.
Joseph Hartwell. 1566, 148.
Joseph Hurd, 1588, 130.
Joseph Johnson, 1292, 210.
Joseph Park, 1492, 123.
Joseph W., 1167, 178.
Joseph Warren, 4238, 306. 4260, 308.
Joses, 289, 53.
Joshua, 365, 61. 4164, 303.
Josiah, 79, 27. 283, 52. 318, 55. 759, 84. 657. 122. 665, 140.
Josiah M., 1120, 173.
Josephus D., 4671, 338.
Joy, 4043, 295.

Kendall G., 2360, 226.
Katharine, 4303, 314.

Lafayette, 3178, 260.
Langdon, 1683, 199.
Lathrop, 578, 115.
Leander, 809, 95.
Lemuel, 936, 162. 3797, 279. 3827, 283.
Lemuel E., 1165, 271.
Lemuel R., 3899, 283.
Leonard Murch, 3508, 263.
Leonard Worcester, 2250, 256.
Levi, 1251, 187. 3800, 279. 3845, 282. 564. 129.
Levi D., 740, 81.
Lewis, 510, 71. 831, 158.
Lewis A., 1219, 184.
Lewis E., 3106, 260.

Loram, 2063, 214.
Loren Dudley, 1230, 186.
Loren G., 2195, 243.
Lorenzo, 4791, 342.
Lorenzo Dow, 1148, 264.
Lorenzo S., 1119, 173.
Luther, 2643, 252. 2262, 257.
Luther M., 518, 263.
Lucian A., 1693, 199.
Lucius E., 1924, 201.
—— Ladd, 3745, 275.

Mark P., 1907, 344.
Mark Taylor, 2647, 252.
Marshall C., 971, 165.
Mason, 440, 66.
Mason B., 1503, 147.
Mason W., 982, 166.
Merrill, 1632, 197. 2740, 270.
Merrill A., 4210, 305.
Moody, 358, 60.
Monroe J., 3566, 265.
Moses, 386, 63. 698, 75. 775, 86. 1876, 156. 1327, 192. 1827, 213. 4913, 349.
Moses Ashley, 1909, 217.
Myron F., 2745, 272.

Nathan, 791, 87.
Nathan B., 4459, 327.
Nathaniel, 7, 13. 13, 15. 20, 17. 39, 19. 69, 25. 75, 26. 96, 30. 129, 36. 132, 37. 255, 45. 282, 50. 287, 52. 322, 56. 438, 66. 702, 75. 783, 86. 235, 89. 1400, 98. 614, 119. 1787, 154. 1342, 196. 434, 65. 2001, 238. 252, 35. 2907, 255.
Nathaniel E., 2089, 234.
Nathaniel Gould, 1774, 152.
Nathaniel Green, 1575, 135.
Nathaniel M., 1168, 178.
Nathaniel S., 625, 344. 625, 125.
Nathaniel Watson, 3273, 247.
Nelson G., 2356, 225.
Newell C., 1766, 152.
Newell H., 1833, 213.
Noah, 690, 74. 1070, 169. 1128, 174. 2686, 253.
Noah D., 1945, 205.
Noble, 4589, 335. 4660, 337.
Notan W., 4764, 340.
Noyes, 513, 71.

Oliver, 136, 38.
Oliver Hazzard, 988, 166.
Oliver Mayhew, 4417, 325.
Olney, 4050, 295.

Orange S., 2234, 239.
Orrin, 2065, 214. 4179, 304.
Orson, 589, 117.
Orzo A., 1109, 172.
Oscar B., 2404, 220.
Otis Freeman, 829, 158.
Otis K., 1930, 219.

Parish Badger, 1768, 152.
Paul, 80, 27. 1840, 136.
Peabody Webster, 836, 159.
Perley M., 878, 138. 2633, 251.
Perre Green, 950, 164.
Peter. 288, 53. 762, 85. 4541, 331. 4549, 331.
Philander, 1446, 228. 1149, 264.
Pliny Day, 991, 166.
Plumer B., 1123, 173.
Porter, 993, 166.

Ralph, 454, 68.
Ralph A., 2969, 275.
Randolph E., 1922, 200.
Reuben, 1339, 195.
Reuben E., 2655, 253.
Richard, 347, 59.
Richard Fletcher, 2038, 230.
Robert, 4521, 330. 802, 345.
Robert A., 4470, 327.
Roger, 140, 38. 429, 65.
Roswell, 590, 117. 3820, 282.
Ruel W., 2889, 254.
Rufus Bailey, 2306, 228.
Rufus King, 1408, 103.
Rufus Marvin, 1058, 204.
Rufus, 3933, 341.
Russell, 500, 70.

Sampson, 874, 138.
Samuel, 6, 12. 33, 19. 43, 20. 50, 22. 112, 34. 133, 37. 200, 41. 291, 54. 303, 54. 374, 62. 407, 64. 447, 67. 737, 80. 261, 46. 627, 113. 671, 140. 746, 55. 3480, 261. 3750, 276. 4041, 293. 4046, 294. 4077, 296. 4299, 313. 4309, 314. 4317, 314. 1802, 341. 4912, 348.
Samuel Bragg, 1577, 210.
Samuel C., 163, 40. 188, 41.
Samuel Chapman, 1744, 207.
Samuel G., 685, 73. 1114, 173.
Samuel Greenleaf, 1572, 133.
Samuel H., 4321, 314. 4323, 314.
Samuel J., 4243, 307.
Samuel J. P., 1064, 169.
Samuel P., 2222, 248. 2426, 220.

Samuel S., 1704, 115.
Samuel W., 1750. 207.   1935, 220.
Sanford B., 1553, 161.
Sanford H., 2430, 221.
Septa, 490, 69.
Senaca, 1777, 153.
Senaca A., 1765, 151.
Shaw, 1881, 156.
Sherman, 4141, 301.   4165, 303.
Sidney, 3718, 274.
Sidney A., 3590, 272.
Silas, 3934, 284.
Silas T., 584, 115.
Simeon, 271, 46. 280, 50. 679, 122. 2458, 257.
Smith R., 4118, 298.
Solomon H., 1903, 158.   4604, 335.
Spencer, 961, 211.
Stephen, 301, 54. 716, 78. 729, 79. 735, 80. 1818, 212. 557, 128. 291, 54. 3486, 271. 90, 28.
Story Butler, 2226, 244.
Sullivan, 808, 94.
Sumner, 2440, 171.

Thaddeus, 236, 93.
Thaddeus B., 1549, 148.
Thing, 619, 124.
Thomas, 677, 73. 635, 114. 1106, 172. 2653, 252. 3790, 278. 3924, 284. 4449, 326.
Thomas Colby, 1800, 273.
Thomas Cushing, 4011, 292.
Thomas E., 2829, 256.
Thomas F., 2693, 253.
Thomas H., 1331, 193.
Thomas J., 1041, 168.
Thomas McCleary, 1428, 147.
Thomas M., 4456, 326.   4593, 448.
Thomas S., 1538, 149.
Thomas W., 4412, 325.   4466, 366.
Timothy, 37, 19. 67, 24. 405, 63. 74, 78. 241, 93. 825, 96. 230, 97. 733, 85. 1332, 194. 121, 266.
Timothy Boyd, 1864, 216.
Timothy Fellows, 1478, 258.
Trueworthy, 98, 31.

Ulysses, 508, 70.
Uriah, 242, 58. 813, 95. 1113, 172.

Vernon A., 1160, 176.

Wallace W., 3567, 265.
Walter C., 2363, 266.
Wareham, 540, 118.
Warren, 1506, 141. 945, 163. 1337, 194. 1841, 136.
Welcome D., 1418, 104.
Welcome M., 1174, 210.
Wesley J., 2198, 244.
Wilbur R., 2796, 221.
Willard, 2232, 239.
Willis E., 3672, 275.
William, 74, 25. 646, 48. 367, 61. 787, 87. 807, 94. 1330, 193. 1628, 197. 1810, 211. 2315, 225. 1984, 237. 2646, 252. 3479, 261. 3496, 261. 3481, 271. 3789, 277. 3791, 278. 3824, 283. 3987, 290. 3958, 289. 4065, 298. 3993, 291. 4381, 320. 4390, 330. 4662, 338. 4727, 339. 4385, 331. 4556, 332. 4558, 332.
William A., 2989, 229. 3870, 282.
William B., 2096, 235. 3100, 259.
William C., 1939, 204. 2285, 227.
William D., 1222, 184. 2386, 229. 1996, 237.
William F., 1963, 260. 3157, 258.
William G., 4000, 291. 4008, 292.
William H., 872, 138. 1248, 187. 2003, 250. 3104, 263. 4409, 323. 908, 264. 4592, 335.
William J., 1967, 240.
William K., 3815, 280.
William L., 1627, 112. 1045, 169.
William M., 586, 116. 1150, 175. 1727, 206. 2753, 220. 2735, 258. 1576, 135.
William Oscar, 2515, 254.
William Perry, 1382, 195.
William R., 2808, 204. 1742, 206. 2864, 244.
William S., 1282, 188. 2184, 241.
William W., 2438, 240. 4742, 339.

Zoroaster, 1776, 153.

LADD. CHRISTIAN NAMES.

Aaron, 53, 56, 75, 158, 176, 212, 271, 301, 303, 304.
Aaron B., 326.
Abbie, 149.
Abbie A., 207.
Abbie B., 313.
Abbie C., 181.
Abbie D., 212.
Abbie H., 207.
Abbie J., 153, 157.
Abbie L., 256, 308.
Abby, 22, 107, 193.
Abel, 78, 183, 338.
Abel A., 330.
Abiah, 33, 35.
Abial R., 65, 164.
Abial I. R., 164.
Abigail, 13, 16, 17, 19, 20, 22, 23, 25, 26, 27, 29, 33, 35, 37, 40, 46, 50, 52, 56, 58, 75, 92, 111, 113, 121, 122, 140, 156, 157, 194, 217, 251, 267, 268, 299, 301, 343.
Abigail B., 123.
Abigail M., 61.
Abigail S., 66, 118, 157.
Abner, 16, 23, 40, 70, 111, 112, 169, 170, 171.
Abram, 121.
Abram B., 212.
Abraham G., 79, 186.
Abraham L., 219.
Abzena, 163.
Acelia A. S., 123.
Achsah, 25, 89, 93.
Achsah D., 297.
Achsah M., 123, 296.
Adain, 105.
Adaline D., 344.
Adda, 164, 213.
Adda A., 343.
Addie, 259.
Addie M., 253.
Addie R., 152.
Addison, 70.
Addison A., 218.
Addilla, 219.
Adelaide, 241.
Adelaide A., 154, 246.
Adelbut, 276, 339.
Adele E., 283.
Adelia B., 206, 256.
Adelia J., 165.
Adeline, 39, 64, 74, 111, 138, 295.
Adeline A., 153.
Adeline B., 147.
Adeline H., 110.
Adeline M., 297.

Adilla C., 254.
Agath, 333.
Agnes, 270, 331.
Agnes M., 188.
Ahijah, 24, 43, 129, 204.
Alando F., 257.
Alanson, 140, 214.
Alanson B., 218.
Albert, 22, 40, 192, 212, 251, 255, 282.
Albert A., 220.
Albert B., 246.
Albert E., 221, 243.
Albert H., 161, 239.
Albert J., 195, 259.
Albert W., 119, 139, 150, 151, 307.
Albion C., 193.
Alda P., 251.
Alden, 95, 347.
Aldis P., 240.
Alexander, 49, 108, 109, 133, 241.
Alexander H., 110, 132, 240.
Alexander L., 148.
Alexander P., 98, 123, 147, 216.
Alexis, 306, 307.
Alfred, 37, 38, 68, 71, 78, 79, 163, 167, 168, 266, 296, 297, 305.
Alfred A., 303.
Alfred D., 168, 302, 303, 304.
Alfred E., 25, 115, 272.
Alfred G., 269, 270.
Alfred H., 305.
Alfred P., 197.
Alfred W., 77, 181, 304, 270.
Alice, 45, 46, 97, 115, 170, 243, 244, 279, 280.
Alice A., 226, 257.
Alice B., 330.
Alice C., 243.
Alice E., 216.
Alice F., 221.
Alice Jane, 121.
Alice K., 281.
Alice L., 230.
Alice M., 166, 173, 195, 234, 302.
Alice R., 292.
Alice S., 184, 253.
Alice W., 188.
Allen D., 266, 272.
Allen W., 257.
Allen Y., 199.
Allison B., 198, 209.
Allston C., 156, 244.
Allura, 64, 345.
Almatia M., 123.
Almira, 40, 42, 118, 162.
Almira K., 39.
Almon A., 76, 176.

Almond D., 65.
Almy S., 306.
Alonzo, 41, 121, 166, 240, 279, 281, 282, 341.
Alonzo B., 284.
Alonzo C., 64, 162.
Alonzo P., 166, 343.
Alpheus, 38, 58, 68, 110, 172.
Alphonso, 95, 195, 220, 259.
Alphonso S., 123.
Althea L., 95.
Altie E., 246.
Alva C., 263.
Alva W., 248.
Alvan, 43.
Alvan L., 262, 263.
Alvah J., 184.
Alvaro, 140, 213, 214.
Alverado, 40, 71.
Alvira, 40, 156.
Amanda, 73, 194.
Amanda M., 81, 87.
Amanda R., 136.
Amarantha, 73.
Amarel C., 118.
Amasa, 20, 65.
Amasa S., 59, 158, 227.
Amelia, 244, 330.
Amelia L., 126.
Amelia M., 211.
Amelia S., 256.
Ami S., 78, 183.
Amoretta, 74.
Amos, 319, 320, 325, 326, 330, 333, 334, 336.
Amos B., 87.
Amos M., 147.
Amy, 156, 296.
Amy D., 261.
Andrew, 22, 40, 70, 71, 73, 88, 194, 257, 258, 284.
Andrew B. J., 226.
Andrew G., 258.
Andrew J., 70, 220, 259, 303.
Andrew S., 79.
Andrew Robeson, 139, 226.
Angelina, 68, 101.
Angelina A., 113.
Angelina R., 260.
Angelina S., 87, 192, 334.
Angel S., 266.
Anita, 340.
Ann, 8, 14, 20, 27, 45, 60, 92, 125, 194, 279, 299, 314, 321, 330, 333, 337.
Ann B., 135, 210.
Ann E., 130, 136, 147, 250.
Ann F., 206.
Ann H., 198, 291, 292.
Ann J., 211.

Ann M., 178.
Ann P., 178.
Ann S., 149.
Anna, 18, 19, 20, 23, 24, 30, 34, 37, 39, 111, 214, 220, 274, 333, 336, 339, 344.
Anna A., 273.
Anna Alice, 273.
Anna C., 128, 283.
Anna E., 220, 246.
Anna L., 133, 258, 308.
Anna M., 275, 285.
Anna P., 132.
Anna R., 256.
Anna S., 307.
Anna W., 144, 173, 241.
Annetta D., 225.
Annetta F., 88.
Annie, 241.
Annie A., 216.
Annie E., 241.
Annie G., 341.
Annie M., 275, 292.
Anora, 344.
Ansel, 86, 194, 253.
Anson, 36, 37, 66, 68, 266, 271.
Anson F., 266.
Anson S., 111.
Anstis, 294.
Anthony, 301.
Antoinette, 330.
Aphia, 23, 245.
Aphia F., 254.
Ariel, 43, 126, 128, 201, 202, 203.
Arline, 338.
Arline E., 148.
Arminda C., 157.
Arnaldo W. P., 123.
Arnold D., 94.
Artemas, 87, 197, 258.
Arthur, 178, 198, 241, 274.
Arthur B., 273, 308.
Arthur C., 169, 253.
Arthur D., 184.
Arthur G., 186, 303, 304.
Arthur J., 169, 342.
Arthur M., 265.
Arthur N., 270.
Arthur P., 308.
Arthur S., 158, 199, 235, 247.
Arthur W., 264, 265.
Arzo N., 68, 211.
Asa, 19, 32, 40, 58, 59, 70, 86, 95, 96, 122, 193, 204, 212, 220, 228, 229, 253.
Asa B., 104.
Asa S., 198, 209.
Asael, 123.
Asenath, 53, 86, 88, 98.
Asenath A., 218.
Asenath S., 126.

Asenath T., 122.
Ashbel, 20, 37, 68.
Asher, 22, 34.
Aticus R., 123, 216.
Attilus A., 123, 216, 275.
Austin, 41, 59, 72, 112, 137, 266, 272.
Austin N., 198.
Austin S., 152, 239.
Austing P., 158.
Augusta, 97, 103, 262.
Augustus, 39, 88, 97.
Augustus A., 271.
Augustus C., 147.
Augustus F., 276.
Augustus G., 228.
Augustus R., 280.
Aureanna J., 50, 184.
Aurelia H., 44.
Aurelia F., 123.
Auretta H., 95.
Aurilla, 345.
Aurin, 75, 174, 342.
Avery S., 58, 95, 220.
Avis, 34.
Azel P., 139, 226.
Azuber N., 303.

Babson S., 156, 244.
Barbara A., 274.
Barber, 302.
Barnett H., 113, 199.
Barnard G., 327.
Barrett H., 194.
Barron H., 186.
Bayles E., 334.
Bearfort, 39.
Bela Dow, 138, 229.
Bela O., 61, 138, 230.
Belden L., 263.
Belia E., 172.
Bell C., 224.
Benijah, 20, 39, 69.
Benjamin, 18, 30, 31, 57, 85, 87, 192, 251, 252, 273, 289, 301, 302, 321, 323, 324, 325.
Benjamin F., 58, 94, 119, 164, 251, 297, 326, 327.
Benjamin G., 291.
Benjamin H., 327, 328, 329.
Benjamin W., 209, 321, 322, 323, 324.
Benoni, 36, 64, 65, 164.
Bernard E., 228.
Bertha, 304.
Berthia A., 226.
Berthia D., 204.
Bert S., 257.
Bessie, 272.
Bessie W., 182.

Bethanay, 336.
Bethanay J., 336.
Bethsheba, 16.
Betsey, 32, 35, 37, 49, 53, 56, 60, 75, 86, 87, 92, 112, 113, 121, 124, 163, 198, 278, 282, 334.
Betsey A., 122.
Betsey F., 75.
Betsey G., 39, 119.
Betsey J., 192.
Betsey K., 325, 331.
Betsey S., 85.
Bina W., 248.
Birdie, 327.
Blanch E., 177.
Blanch M., 253.
Blanch V., 216.
Bodwell, 25, 89, 93, 98, 105, 147, 149.
Boyd, 338, 342.
Bradley, 112.
Bradford S., 306.
Bridget B., 86.
Buel, 112.
Burleigh, 217.
Burroughs, 35.
Byron G., 102, 104, 146.
Byron P., 103, 146.

Caldwell, 276, 277.
Caleb, 25, 46, 93, 105, 148, 149, 289, 299, 305, 306, 307, 308, 345.
Caleb B., 106.
Caleb H., 149.
Caleb R., 277.
Caleb W., 306.
Calista, 118, 295.
Calvin, 39, 69, 140, 216, 255, 283.
Calvin B., 122, 213, 255.
Calvin P., 59, 160.
Candace P., 147.
Carey P., 347.
Carleton, 73, 263.
Carlos, 95.
Carlos A., 347.
Carlton E., 273.
Carlton T., 273.
Caroline, 22, 40, 49, 59, 67, 74, 87, 88, 118, 192, 195, 275, 338.
Caroline A., 243.
Caroline B., 194.
Caroline C., 323.
Caroline D., 120.
Caroline E., 178.
Caroline F. C., 325.
Caroline K., 84.
Caroline L., 109.
Caroline M., 61, 158.
Caroline P., 120.

Caroline S., 110.
Carolyn W., 260.
Carrie, 176.
Carrie B., 95, 168.
Carrie E., 178, 249.
Carrie H., 164.
Carrie L., 209.
Carrie M., 257, 262.
Casadana, 345.
Cassanda, 295.
Catharine, 63, 87, 94, 218, 290, 336, 338.
Catharine E., 324.
Catharine G., 306.
Cecelia E., 60.
Cecilea A., 306.
Celenda A., 41.
Celia C., 58.
Celitia, 211.
Chandler, 68, 168.
Charles, 22, 39, 47, 61, 63, 67, 70, 84, 94, 107, 113, 114, 122, 154, 164, 192, 210, 212, 213, 220, 221, 243, 251, 266, 279, 283, 296, 336, 339.
Charles A., 118, 149, 168, 205, 207, 225, 339.
Charles Albert, 133, 151, 229.
Charles B., 105, 149, 202, 211, 221.
Charles C., 226, 274, 292, 306, 308.
Charles D., 134, 157, 253, 268, 275.
Charles E., 60, 107, 209, 243, 253.
Charles F., 88, 152, 197, 258, 272, 307, 309, 324, 325.
Charles G., 65, 135, 165, 169, 195, 238, 276, 301.
Charles H., 69, 83, 110, 131, 139, 149, 163, 169, 194, 210, 228, 259, 262, 274, 284, 292, 304, 305.
Charles I., 52, 74, 243.
Charles J., 68, 119, 152, 167, 217.
Charles K., 126, 218, 219, 224, 274.
Charles L., 62.
Charles M., 76, 262.
Charles N., 66.
Charles O., 266.
Charles P., 80, 152, 167, 178, 186, 277.
Charles R., 128, 202, 304.
Charles S., 199, 253.
Charles T., 211.
Charles U., 172.
Charles W., 42, 85, 126, 130, 153, 165, 185, 218, 243, 248, 273, 283, 339, 340.
Charlotte, 22, 38, 59, 67, 87, 112, 114, 122, 134, 158, 162, 163.
Charlotte A., 41, 156.
Charlotte E., 164, 191, 271.
Charlotte H., 84, 110, 259, 260.
Charlotte J., 246.
Charlotte M., 136, 166, 225.
Charlotte S., 134.

Chauncy, 275, 277.
Chester, 82, 97, 188.
Chester B., 68.
Chester F., 137.
Chester H., 112.
Chester M., 344.
Chester W., 223.
Chestina, 343.
Christianna S., 194.
Christine, 130.
Christopher, 138.
Chloe, 24.
Chloe S., 220.
Clara, 36, 82, 86, 201, 272.
Clara B., 116, 253.
Clara E., 145, 226, 341.
Clara I., 205.
Clara J., 199.
Clara L., 306.
Clara M., 221, 249, 262.
Clara S., 234.
Clarabell, 81, 253.
Clarence, 298.
Clarence C., 207.
Clarence H., 191, 253.
Clarence S., 272.
Clarissa, 32, 38, 39, 58, 68, 126.
Clark H., 157, 256.
Clifford W., 254.
Clinton M., 257.
Clotilda, 321.
Clotilda A., 228.
Clyde A., 259.
Comfort M., 76.
Constantine, 333, 334, 336, 337, 338, 345.
Constantine F. V., 258.
Cora, 282.
Cora A., 185, 271.
Cora B., 182, 249, 262.
Cora E., 256.
Cora J., 268.
Cora L., 298, 308.
Cora M., 344.
Cora V., 314.
Cordelia, 95.
Cordelia W., 68.
Cornelia, 39, 198.
Cornelia E., 164.
Corrilla, 214.
Corrin, 36.
Crawford, 55, 84.
Curtis, 40, 71.
Cynthia, 140, 338, 339.
Cynthia A., 34, 212, 228.
Cynthia H., 61, 62.
Cyrus, 20, 38, 86, 196, 275, 277.
Cyrus A., 123, 136, 137.
Cyrus C., 276.
Cyrus E., 276.

Cyrus F., 71.
Cyrus J., 269.
Cyrus K., 268, 270.

Daisy M., 147.
Daniel, 1, 2, 3, 4, 5, 6, 7, 8, 9, 10, 11, 12, 13, 14, 15, 16, 18, 19, 23, 24, 26, 28, 29, 32, 33, 34, 35, 36, 41, 43, 44, 45, 46, 52, 53, 54, 55, 56, 58, 60, 61, 62, 63, 75, 77, 78, 79, 84, 86, 94, 95, 113, 116, 117, 118, 119, 121, 122, 138, 149, 154, 161, 162, 174, 178, 182, 184, 185, 189, 193, 209, 213, 217, 228, 239, 252, 253, 263, 264, 267, 268, 269, 270, 289, 299, 300, 302, 303, 304, 308, 345.
Daniel A., 268, 269.
Daniel B., 64, 79, 184, 257.
Daniel C., 280, 281.
Daniel G., 61, 139.
Daniel P., 76, 176, 261, 262.
Daniel T., 149, 214, 241, 268.
Daniel V., 58, 275.
Daniel W., 120, 154, 155, 247, 248, 264, 271, 303, 307.
Daria, 296.
Darius, 22, 40, 71, 98, 124, 263.
Darwin, 66.
David, 13, 16, 19, 21, 22, 24, 35, 39, 70, 73, 154, 172, 332.
David A., 342.
David B., 186.
David C., 191, 249.
David D., 66.
David H., 161.
David M., 58, 94, 96, 104, 166, 249.
David N., 191, 249.
David O., 241.
David P., 114, 199.
Dearborn, 192, 251.
Deborah, 57, 88, 124, 125, 293, 313, 314, 326, 331, 344.
Della E., 226.
Delana, 280.
Della C., 270.
Dennis, 214.
Desdemonia, 301.
DeWitt C. L., 113.
Dexter, 194, 249, 266.
Diana W., 78.
Dianna, 73.
Dilley, 32.
Dillie, 24.
Dolly, 57, 64, 120.
Dorcas, 20, 284, 299, 301.
Dorcas A., 211.
Dorcas D., 297.
Dorothy, 18, 27, 56, 60, 61.
Drucilla, 184.

Drusilla, 114.
Duane, 294.
Dudley, 18, 22, 26, 28, 32, 45, 46, 50, 53, 73, 75, 106, 113, 114, 133, 134, 135, 140, 175, 199, 214, 216.
Dudley F., 52, 74, 173.
Dudley K., 241.
Dudley P., 75, 76, 176.
Durant E., 176.
Durgan P., 199.
Dustan, 32.

Earl, 292.
Eben, 261, 262, 263.
Eben S., 262, 263.
Eben W., 343.
Ebenezer B., 95, 228.
Ebenezer G., 306, 308.
Eddie, 167.
Eddie F., 168.
Edgar, 339.
Edgar A., 343.
Edgar J., 257.
Edgar L., 146.
Edgar T., 198.
Edith, 148.
Edith A., 186.
Edith H., 204, 292.
Edith J., 325.
Edith M., 241, 251.
Edith P., 255.
Edith S., 247.
Edna, 58, 330.
Edna E., 342.
Edward, 18, 26, 46, 69, 98, 113, 124, 125, 138, 157, 158, 168, 199, 256, 280, 284, 341, 343.
Edward A., 79, 184, 186.
Edward B., 186.
Edward E., 139, 253.
Edward F., 157.
Edward G., 246.
Edward H., 229, 292.
Edward L., 145, 304.
Edward N., 104, 258, 344.
Edward O., 229.
Edward P., 183.
Edward T., 229.
Edward W., 226.
Edwin, 69, 97, 178, 194, 263, 339.
Edwin C., 174.
Edwin F., 262.
Edwin H., 139, 166, 225, 298.
Edwin O., 66, 165, 225.
Edwin S., 163.
Edwin W., 118, 171, 207, 208.
Effel, 52.
Elbridge, 122, 213.

Elbridge G., 198, 246.
Elbridge G. W., 194.
Eldora M., 304.
Eldridge, 263.
Eleanor, 61, 195, 244, 256, 300.
Eleanor E., 243.
Eleanor H., 241.
Eleanor I., 135.
Eleanor M., 69, 109.
Eleazer, 57, 88, 194, 195.
Eleazer P., 195.
Electa, 42, 158.
Electa E., 113.
Electa J., 41, 158.
Eliab, 24, 42, 44, 114, 115, 128.
Elias, 18, 21, 27, 49, 121, 122, 211.
Elias W., 71.
Elijah, 22, 279, 283, 343, 344.
Elijah S., 125, 343.
Eliphalet, 25, 27, 47, 49, 50, 97, 106, 107, 109, 121, 123, 124, 130, 210, 275, 276.
Elisha, 24, 275, 296.
Elisha A., 39.
Elisha L., 36, 64, 162.
Elisha P., 297, 298.
Elisha S., 36, 64, 162.
Eliza, 59, 70, 87, 88, 95, 107, 112, 126, 192, 199, 212, 263, 279.
Eliza A., 58, 63, 118, 162, 193, 218, 247.
Eliza B., 267.
Eliza E., 81, 145.
Eliza J., 199, 251, 282.
Eliza L., 113.
Eliza M., 280.
Eliza N., 293.
Eliza S., 62.
Elizabeth, 14, 16, 18, 22, 23, 24, 27, 29, 30, 31, 33, 44, 45, 48, 50, 56, 62, 69, 71, 75, 134, 160, 193, 198, 219, 224, 264, 276, 277, 278, 279, 290, 291, 294, 299, 302, 314, 323, 326, 327, 330, 332, 333, 338.
Elizabeth A., 61, 188.
Elizabeth B., 174, 234, 244.
Elizabeth C., 102, 110, 147.
Elizabeth D., 66, 138.
Elizabeth E., 183.
Elizabeth H., 133, 197.
Elizabeth I., 117.
Elizabeth J., 276.
Elizabeth K., 325.
Elizabeth L. H., 41.
Elizabeth M., 165.
Elizabeth O., 241.
Elizabeth R., 68.
Elizabeth S., 236.
Elkin, 334.
Ella, 103, 117, 180, 247, 293, 314, 339.
Ella A., 124, 168, 252, 255.
Ella C., 341.
Ella D., 327.
Ella J., 272.
Ella K., 272, 307.
Ella L., 139.
Ella M., 151, 173.
Ella P., 172.
Ella S., 184.
Ellen 124, 138, 172, 207, 342.
Ellen A., 211.
Ellen B., 99.
Ellen C., 324.
Ellen D., 262.
Ellen E., 148, 273.
Ellen F., 134.
Ellen H., 72.
Ellen L., 249.
Ellen M., 160, 252, 256.
Ellen R., 83, 145, 236, 292, 323.
Ellen S., 133.
Ellie A., 207.
Ellis E., 221.
Ellwood, 305.
Elmar L., 167.
Elmer E., 244.
Elmer F., 168.
Elmer L., 169.
Elsa, 45.
Elvina, 249.
Elvira, 38, 193, 267, 294, 332.
Elvira D., 192.
Elvira M., 61.
Emeline, 63, 136, 157, 193, 302.
Emeline C., 343.
Emeline E., 148.
Emeline H., 87.
Emeline S., 61, 199.
Emily, 39, 60, 69, 105, 295, 341.
Emily A., 102, 106, 110, 195, 303, 304.
Emily E., 136, 153.
Emily J., 85, 124, 205, 246.
Emily R. B., 302.
Emily S., 229.
Emily W., 217.
Emerson D., 228.
Emery, 93, 104, 258, 281.
Emma, 138, 213, 251, 252, 279, 304, 329, 339.
Emma A., 252.
Emma B., 262.
Emma C., 204, 247.
Emma E., 165.
Emma F., 172, 251, 253, 256, 342.
Emma H., 106, 230, 266.
Emma J., 173, 199, 223, 256.
Emma L., 80, 117, 186, 234.
Emma M., 207, 264.
Emma S., 270.
Emma W., 78.

Emor O., 294, 297.
Emory O., 96.
Enoch, 32, 58, 83, 125, 272, 273.
Enoch G., 79.
Enoch H., 55, 58, 83, 225, 272.
Enoch O., 276.
Enoch P., 79, 185.
Ephraim, 17, 23, 37, 42, 66, 68, 126, 279, 282.
Ephraim E., 68, 168, 220.
Erastus, 23, 112, 197.
Erastus D., 141, 214, 215.
Erastus E., 82.
Erastus P., 112, 197, 198.
Ernest E., 257.
Ernest H., 149.
Ernest J., 174.
Ervin W., 285.
Estella B., 268.
Estella M., 229.
Esther, 20, 22, 44, 115, 267, 295, 301, 333.
Esther A., 85.
Esther D., 131.
Esther M., 61, 251.
Ethan Smith, 35, 63.
Ethel, 148.
Ethel W., 228.
Etta, 192.
Eudotia, 119.
Eugene, 283.
Eugene B., 174.
Eugene F., 148.
Eugene H., 123.
Eugene J., 185.
Eunice, 21, 24, 39, 40, 44, 113, 217, 284, 302.
Eunice A., 197, 303.
Eunice L., 199.
Eunice M., 302.
Eunice P., 70.
Eva, 86, 170, 254.
Eva A., 263.
Eva F. M., 259.
Eva M., 115, 173, 340, 342.
Eva O., 219.
Eva P., 147.
Eveline, 283.
Eveline M., 186.
Everett, 186.
Everett B., 253.
Everett E., 207.
Everett P., 205.
Everett S., 168.
Evelyn, 220.
Ezekiel, 11, 13, 14, 16, 22, 23, 24, 33, 40, 41, 42, 59, 60, 112, 137, 238, 277, 278, 280.
Ezekiel H., 40, 71.
Ezra, 43, 159, 174, 230.

Fannie, 239, 266, 298.
Fannie C., 152, 266.
Fannie E., 168, 344.
Fannie H., 174.
Fanny, 65, 70, 97.
Fanny K., 216.
Festus, 22, 112, 198.
Flavia B., 44.
Flavius, 339.
Fletcher, 189.
Flora, 157, 252.
Flora A., 166.
Flora B., 256, 343.
Flora E., 228, 243.
Flora M., 285.
Florence, 158, 170, 226.
Florence D., 256.
Florence E., 177, 247.
Florence F., 186.
Florence K., 144.
Florence Le Reine, 285.
Florence M., 148, 152.
Florence W., 130, 212.
Florilla P., 263.
Forrest D., 262.
Forrest W., 342.
Frances, 293, 297.
Frances A., 145, 207, 252.
Frances C., 215.
Frances E., 41, 197, 206, 272.
Frances H., 268.
Frances M., 60.
Frances N., 307.
Frances R., 109.
Frances S., 103, 147.
Francis A., 199.
Francis D., 133, 235.
Francis P., 292.
Francis W., 194, 293.
Francois J. G., 247, 264.
Francilla, 196.
Frank, 67, 152, 166, 176, 187, 192, 217, 228, 239, 241, 251, 252, 339.
Frank A., 137, 252, 298.
Frank B., 263, 177.
Frank C., 196, 204.
Frank E., 230.
Frank F., 308.
Frank H., 81, 285.
Frank I., 147.
Frank J., 173, 193, 196, 197, 254, 258.
Frank M., 105, 161, 166, 274, 330, 340.
Frank O., 268, 270.
Frank P., 80, 186, 252, 344.
Frank R., 262, 271.
Frank S., 158.
Frank W., 139.
Frank Z., 258, 274.
Franklin, 66.

Franklin B., 77, 178.
Franklin G., 273.
Franklin H., 60, 254.
Franklin J., 283.
Franklin P., 262.
Franklin S., 344.
Freddie E., 162.
Freddie J., 253.
Freddie W., 254.
Fred E., 344.
Fred G., 246, 281.
Fred H., 148, 238.
Fred L., 176, 268.
Fred M., 240.
Fred N., 238.
Fred S., 230.
Fred T., 269.
Fred W., 174, 235, 272.
Frederick, 20, 38, 68, 96, 117, 168.
Frederick A., 147, 186.
Frederick D., 168.
Frederick G., 252.
Frederick H., 172.
Frederick M., 309.
Frederick O., 241.
Frederick P., 92, 102, 146, 198, 209, 220.
Frederick R., 118, 207.
Frederick W., 272.
Frederick Y., 199.
Fredus, 112, 197, 270, 272.
Freelove, 263.
Freeman, 195.
Freeman P., 195, 258.
Freeman W., 198, 246.

Galen D., 212.
Gardner P., 101, 144, 234.
Garret S., 301.
Gates B., 303.
George, 94, 111, 117, 162, 180, 195, 197, 213, 254, 264, 297.
George A., 104, 148, 169, 239, 244, 271, 265.
George B., 88, 130, 174, 340.
George C., 65, 172, 273.
George D., 104, 157, 166, 212, 225, 281.
George E., 146, 166, 210, 216, 245, 255, 271, 274.
George E. M. J. F., 163.
George F., 78, 103, 138, 226, 342.
George G., 107, 210.
George G. T., 334.
George H., 61, 79, 115, 138, 141, 174, 184, 185, 206, 226, 230, 251, 303, 304.
George L., 85, 112.
George M., 81, 144, 172, 188, 272, 274, 285.
George O., 124.
George P., 130, 195, 205.
George R., 139, 254, 302.
George S., 87, 141, 154, 168, 205, 215, 276, 292, 308.
George S. W., 249.
George T., 116, 223, 224, 261, 262.
George U., 206.
George V., 103, 147.
George V. B., 138, 229.
George W., 23, 38, 59, 61, 77, 78, 79, 88, 92, 95, 102, 113, 145, 146, 151, 156, 180, 182, 186, 193, 195, 217, 229, 239, 240, 253, 256, 257, 259, 276, 280, 283, 306, 308.
Georgia D., 174.
Georgia M., 238.
Georgianna, 157, 251, 254.
Georgianna E., 117.
Georgianna Y., 188.
Gerard, 331, 333.
Gertie, 255.
Gertrude, 270.
Gertrude N., 230.
Gideon, 45, 118, 150, 152.
Gilbert, 154, 283.
Gilbert T., 195.
Gilman, 113.
Gordon, 55, 81, 111, 188.
Gordon B., 186.
Gorham, 122, 136.
Gould D., 113, 146, 198.
Grace, 103, 252.
Grace A., 273.
Grace C., 199.
Grace D., 185.
Grace E., 347.
Grace J., 159.
Grace L., 259.
Grace M., 174.
Gracie H., 169.
Grant, 39, 69.
Grata T., 44.
Greely, 147, 270.
Green, 65.
Guelielma, 327.
Guilford S., 193, 252.
Gustavus B., 191.
Gustavus R., 253.
Gusten, 211.

Halbert, 210.
Halbert P., 244.
Hale, 211, 254.
Hallam, 160.
Halsey, 213.
Hamilton, 26.

Hannah, 16, 18, 19, 22, 23, 25, 29, 30, 32, 33, 35, 36, 40, 47, 52, 55, 57, 70, 77, 93, 97, 113, 124, 125, 156, 212, 217, 220, 261, 264, 278, 290, 294, 301, 314, 323, 338, 341.
Hannah B., 86, 138, 198.
Hannah D., 61.
Hannah E., 71.
Hannah H., 109, 291.
Hannah M., 122, 198.
Hannah P., 114.
Hannibal E., 273.
Harlan P., 199, 246.
Harlon, 273.
Harlow, 115.
Harlow T., 168.
Harold L., 344.
Harriet, 39, 49, 59, 73, 74, 89, 112, 113, 114, 119, 137, 213, 261, 266, 273, 279, 280, 309.
Harriet A., 87, 112, 283.
Harriet E., 137, 218, 285.
Harriet F., 66.
Harriet J., 205.
Harriet K., 65.
Harriet L., 134, 158, 160, 217, 229.
Harriet M., 174.
Harriet N., 273, 306, 307.
Harriet S., 115.
Harriet W., 161, 225.
H. H., 162.
H. Plummer, 341, 342.
Harris B., 195.
Harrison, 124, 213, 217, 257, 339.
Harry, 130, 169, 249.
Harry A., 237.
Harry B., 173.
Harry C., 277.
Harry H., 223.
Harry W., 174, 309.
Harvey, 122, 136.
Harvey A., 81.
Harvey B., 167.
Harvey E., 154.
Harvey J., 257.
Harvey W., 60.
Hastings A., 62, 139.
Hattie, 167, 230, 263.
Hattie A., 166.
Hattie E., 207.
Hattie J., 195, 303.
Hattie L., 168, 173.
Hattie M., 162, 165, 257, 262.
Haven, 110.
Hazel C., 269.
Hazen, 22, 39, 52, 69.
Hazen B., 111.
Helen, 115, 157, 212.
Helen A., 256, 271.
Helen C., 103, 147, 270.
Helen D., 65, 263.
Helen F., 192.
Helen K., 243.
Helen L., 106, 137, 227, 270.
Helen M., 153, 163, 164, 170.
Helen W., 246, 256.
Helena P., 283.
Heman, 25, 92, 93, 97, 103, 123.
Henrietta, 38, 163, 194, 280.
Henrietta C., 273.
Henrietta H., 139.
Henrietta I., 72.
Henrietta L., 173.
Henry, 16, 20, 36, 52, 64, 65, 70, 95, 107, 108, 114, 130, 138, 162, 163, 169, 220, 221, 225, 231, 242, 278, 279.
Henry A., 166, 171.
Henry B., 307.
Henry C., 69, 159, 170, 228, 259, 273, 303, 304, 305, 307.
Henry E., 77.
Henry G., 198.
Henry H., 97, 108, 176, 216, 241, 344.
Henry H. M., 163.
Henry J., 204, 205, 223, 225.
Henry L., 263.
Henry M., 69, 84, 189, 191, 266.
Henry O., 130.
Henry P., 165.
Henry R., 64, 84.
Henry S., 268, 269.
Henry T., 158.
Henry W., 39, 134, 156, 213, 255.
Hepzibah, 16.
Herbert B., 80.
Herbert C., 168.
Herbert F., 253.
Herbert I., 73.
Herbert S., 219.
Herbert W., 71, 144, 169, 231, 232, 234, 262.
Herman, 36, 65, 163.
Herman D., 254.
Herman W., 211, 254.
Hermone C., 263.
Hervey W., 88.
H. Romulus, 282.
Hiram, 36, 55, 59, 63, 64, 67, 82, 95, 122, 136, 137, 163, 167, 188, 238, 249, 273, 274, 295, 298, 341.
Hiram C., 193.
Hiram E., 153, 243.
Hiram K., 239.
Hollis, 124, 157.
Homer, 168, 292.
Hope, 234.
Hope S., 66.
Horace, 63, 156, 210, 251, 254, 284, 294.

Horace A., 133, 136.
Horace B., 261.
Horace C., 141, 215, 245.
Horace H., 62.
Horace J., 215.
Horace P., 213, 253, 256.
Horace W., 118, 207.
Horatio, 42, 126, 217, 218.
Horatio H., 76, 176.
Horatio J., 218, 224.
Horatio N., 59.
Horatio O., 134, 236.
Hosea, 345.
Howard, 298.
Howard C., 308.
Howard M., 263.
Howard W., 325.
Huldah, 29, 43, 55, 320, 333, 336.

Ida, 163, 169, 255.
Ida B., 225.
Ida C., 167.
Ida E., 173, 230, 325.
Ida L., 194.
Ida M., 149, 176, 183, 262, 263.
Ida N., 256.
Ida S., 115.
Inez, 298.
Ira, 121, 280.
Ira A., 276.
Ira B., 245.
Ira F., 118.
Ira G., 246.
Ira M., 153, 244.
Ira W., 119, 154, 245.
Irene, 20, 34.
Irene E., 269.
Irene L., 63.
Irene W., 65.
Irwin M., 219.
Isaac, 31, 36, 46, 56, 57, 59, 64, 86, 87, 114, 125, 196, 261, 321, 343.
Isaac G., 325.
Isaac N., 328, 336, 338, 345.
Isaac P., 282.
Isaac V., 276.
Isaac W., 68.
Isabel, 61, 139, 166, 172, 253.
Isabel E., 258, 329.
Isabel H., 219.
Isabel M., 302.
Isabel S., 192.
Isabella, 194, 307, 321, 322.
Isabella J., 324.
Isham T., 340.
Israel, 121, 209, 244.
Israel S., 39, 69, 111.

Jabez, 22, 40, 71.
Jabez B., 112.
Jabez H., 112.
Jabez S., 44.
Jackson A., 95, 229.
Jacob, 22, 41, 70, 118, 194, 207, 333.
Jacob D., 267, 268.
Jacob P., 174, 342.
Jacob S., 75, 174, 209, 230.
James, 19, 23, 29, 33, 35, 36, 41, 45, 46, 49, 52, 60, 63, 64, 74, 78, 97, 119, 122, 123, 124, 137, 152, 153, 162, 195, 211, 213, 214, 226, 284, 295, 299, 301, 302, 303, 305, 314, 320, 322, 330, 331, 332, 334, 338, 339, 340, 341, 342, 343.
James A., 70, 119, 255, 302.
James B., 297, 331.
James D., 209, 279, 321, 323, 325, 328.
James E., 41, 72, 197, 265, 270, 275, 324, 342.
James G., 119.
James H., 80, 187, 192, 194, 227, 251, 327, 328, 330.
James K., 299, 301.
James L. S., 60, 137.
James M., 74, 77, 159, 191, 227, 264, 265, 326, 329, 330.
James O., 219, 221, 265.
James S., 70, 121, 273.
James T., 223, 261, 268, 269, 272, 275.
James W., 138, 195, 226, 341.
Jane, 39, 56, 81, 86, 111, 156, 163, 279, 330, 342.
Jane A., 77, 111, 130, 255.
Jane E., 197.
Jane F., 160.
Jane G., 280.
Jane H., 69, 112.
Jane M., 69, 326.
Jane S., 218, 307.
Jared W., 126.
Jason, 36.
Jason J., 199.
Jasper, 157, 345.
Jean, 298.
Jeanette, 115, 282.
J. Earle, 185.
Jed. P., 170, 198.
Jedediah, 29, 54, 79, 169.
Jedediah P., 23, 40, 70, 111, 169, 170.
Jedediah P. B., 93, 104, 148.
Jennett, 295.
Jennie, 188, 241, 264.
Jennie A., 165, 207.
Jennie B., 146, 152, 220, 276.
Jennie E., 149, 169, 216, 276.
Jennie H., 258.
Jennie J., 225.
Jennie M., 266.

Jennie P., 166, 277.
Jennie S., 82, 230.
Jennie V., 216.
Jennie W., 248.
Jeremiah, 16, 20, 26, 29, 30, 38, 39, 46, 56, 74, 85, 121, 173, 174, 209.
Jeremiah B. P., 144, 234.
Jeremiah F., 178.
Jeremiah Q., 85, 191.
Jeremiah T., 79.
Jeremiah W., 74, 173.
Jerusha, 20, 36, 38.
Jesse, 17, 24, 34, 44, 60, 115, 122, 137, 211, 254, 284, 285.
Jesse A., 342.
Jesse B., 224.
Jesse E., 53, 78, 182, 183.
Jesse M., 174.
Jesse T., 117, 145.
Jessie, 298.
Jessie E., 212.
J. Gertrude, 170.
Job, 299, 305, 306.
Joel, 43.
Joel Levi, 129, 205.
Joannah, 18, 29, 30, 53, 74, 78.
John, 13, 14, 15, 17, 18, 19, 20, 22, 24, 25, 26, 27, 29, 30, 31, 34, 38, 43, 44, 45, 46, 49, 50, 52, 53, 54, 55, 56, 57, 60, 61, 62, 63, 76, 79, 82, 83, 84, 85, 86, 87, 92, 93, 97, 101, 105, 106, 113, 114, 115, 118, 120, 121, 122, 124, 134, 139, 140, 145, 146, 149, 152, 155, 156, 178, 185, 210, 211, 212, 237, 239, 246, 255, 258, 259, 260, 261, 262, 273, 274, 278, 279, 280, 281, 282, 283, 284, 290, 294, 295, 298, 299, 300, 301, 302, 303, 304, 305, 311, 312, 313, 314, 327.
John A., 80, 95, 124, 136, 137, 141, 214, 215, 275, 280, 281, 282.
John B., 296, 297, 326, 342.
John C., 42, 206, 256, 261, 271, 334.
John D., 250, 283.
John E., 145, 205, 237, 239, 259, 261, 262, 272.
John F., 50, 73, 156, 172, 256, 343, 344.
John G., 198, 276, 291, 293, 306, 307, 309.
John H., 55, 82, 95, 188, 212, 274, 275, 291, 292, 293, 304, 340.
John I., 101, 194, 235.
John J., 159, 230, 276, 281, 282.
John K., 280, 325.
John L., 114, 186, 188, 206, 256.
John M., 123, 128, 149, 163, 183, 207, 219, 239, 298, 328, 329, 340.
John O., 123.
John P., 253, 259.
John Q. A., 60, 247.
John R., 37, 67.
John S., 94, 120, 125, 154, 155, 173, 184, 211, 216, 244, 245, 247, 264, 339, 343.
John T., 110, 197, 272, 273, 281.
John V., 302, 304.
John W., 74, 78, 79, 102, 114, 145, 153, 173, 185, 243, 271, 306, 307, 309, 339.
Jonathan, 13, 16, 18, 19, 24, 31, 36, 42, 43, 46, 49, 55, 57, 62, 64, 81, 86, 87, 113, 114, 122, 139, 140, 193, 196, 199, 212, 254, 289, 304, 313, 314, 344, 345, 346.
Jonathan A., 34.
Jonathan M., 302.
Jonathan P., 253, 343.
Jonathan R., 64, 162.
Joseph, 13, 16, 22, 33, 40, 43, 46, 53, 55, 59, 62, 76, 78, 83, 113, 124, 125, 157, 158, 160, 178, 180, 210, 217, 229, 256, 257, 287, 288, 289, 290, 291, 293, 313, 320, 321, 331, 332, 336, 337, 338.
Joseph A., 210, 250.
Joseph C., 302, 304.
Joseph D., 41, 291, 292, 293, 341.
Joseph E., 77, 78, 178, 182.
Joseph H., 106, 107, 130, 148, 149, 337, 340.
Joseph J., 83, 210.
Joseph M., 153, 180.
Joseph O., 223.
Joseph P., 97, 123, 216.
Joseph T., 344.
Joseph W., 76, 119, 178, 306, 308.
Josephine I., 103.
Josephine M., 146.
Joses, 29, 53, 76, 77, 78.
Joshua, 34, 61, 138, 301, 303.
Josiah, 18, 27, 28, 30, 46, 47, 49, 52, 55, 56, 74, 84, 122, 140, 212, 213, 214, 241.
Josiah M., 74, 173.
Josephus D., 336, 338, 339.
Joy, 294, 295, 296, 297.
Joy L., 148.
Judith, 29, 45, 49, 330, 336.
Judson W., 102.
Julia, 60, 192, 212, 228.
Julia A., 134, 184, 192, 197, 199, 219, 269.
Julia B., 79, 178.
Julia E., 106, 113, 237, 270.
Julia F., 254.
Julia H., 135.
Julia M., 133, 225, 303.
Juliet, 198.
J. Marsh, 245.
J. Romulus, 282.

Karl L., 263.
Kate, 83.
Katharine, 130, 312, 313, 314, 338.

Kendall G., 165, 226.
Keziah, 32.

—— Ladd, 275.
Laben, 34, 62.
Lafayette, 65, 239, 260, 280.
Lafayette R., 343.
Langdon, 113, 199, 247.
Laome, 188.
Larry H., 148.
Larrissa D., 251.
Lathrop, 44, 115.
Lathrop W., 45.
Laura, 38, 44, 65, 67, 111, 112, 193, 194.
Laura A., 118.
Laura E., 194, 321.
Laura F., 137.
Laura J., 249.
Laura L., 146, 323.
Laura V., 182.
Laura W., 114, 116.
Lavinia, 57, 59, 88.
Lawrence, 224, 304.
Lawrence F., 210.
Lawrence W., 207.
Leafie, 140.
Leadbetter, 331.
Leander, 58, 95.
Lee, 303.
Lemon, 339.
Lemuel, 64, 140, 162, 225, 278, 279, 280, 282, 283.
Lemuel C., 327.
Lemuel R., 282, 283.
Lena B., 258.
Lena E., 260.
Lena M., 260.
Lenora A., 69.
Lenora H., 345.
Leona, 210.
Leonard E., 76, 262, 263, 271.
Leonard W., 113, 157, 256.
Leoline C., 263.
Leondo L., 338.
Leroy S., 191.
Lester E. W., 259.
Lester W., 259.
Levi, 43, 54, 80, 129, 187, 205, 278, 279, 280, 282.
Levi D., 55, 81, 253.
Levi E., 228.
Levi S., 62.
Levi W., 81.
Levina, 37.
Lewellyn E., 263.
Lewis, 40, 55, 59, 71, 158, 195.
Lewis A., 79, 184.
Lewis E., 260.

Lewis W., 207.
Lilla, 213.
Lillian, 147, 228.
Lillian C., 344.
Lillian H., 211.
Lillian M., 161.
Lillie, 220, 255.
Lillie I., 246.
Lillie V., 237.
Lilly J., 274.
Linda S., 170.
Lindie E., 210.
Linnie, 248.
Lizzie, 96, 261, 262, 270.
Lizzie A., 183, 210.
Lizzie B., 230, 277.
Lizzie C., 256.
Lizzie E., 262.
Lizzie G., 88.
Lizzie H., 139, 165.
Lizzie I., 145.
Lizzie M., 219, 344.
Lizzie W., 248.
Lois, 28, 32, 36, 42, 43, 44, 54, 61, 73, 81.
Lois A. E., 69.
Lois F., 50.
Lon B., 216.
Lora A., 96.
Lora B., 174.
Loram, 140, 214, 241.
Loren, 79, 186.
Loren G., 153, 243.
Lorenzo, 121, 140, 341, 342.
Lorenzo D., 264.
Lorenzo E., 253.
Lorenzo S., 74, 173.
Loretta D., 154.
Lorina, 162, 163.
Lorinda, 74.
Lorinda B., 122.
Lorna M., 342.
Lottie H., 263.
Louis D., 259.
Louis E., 249.
Louis P., 249.
Louis W., 224.
Louisa, 75, 78, 93, 94, 98, 104, 118, 121, 124, 158, 280, 303, 304, 334, 345.
Louisa A., 329.
Louisa B., 59, 193.
Louisa E., 70, 274.
Louisa L. W., 154.
Louisa M., 104, 146.
Louisa R., 192.
Louise A., 329.
Love, 18, 27, 30, 32.
Lovie A., 173.
Lucia A., 67.
Lucia S., 166.

Lucian A., 116, 199.
Lucinda, 37, 53, 126, 284, 334, 342.
Lurenda, 39, 76, 111.
Lurenda M., 239.
Lurenda P., 135.
Lurenda W., 126.
Lucius E., 128, 201, 203, 216, 221.
Lucretia, 53, 76, 93, 205.
Lucretia E., 116.
Lucy, 23, 32, 73, 83, 86, 87, 137, 156, 197, 330, 343.
Lucy A., 60, 67, 79, 163, 259, 261, 263, 331.
Lucy B., 103.
Lucy K., 234.
Lucy L., 229, 273, 326.
Lucy M., 68, 153, 272.
Lucy S., 296.
Lucy W., 327.
Luella E., 206.
Luke, 295.
Lulie, 339.
Luman A., 240.
Lura, 43, 112, 220.
Luther, 43, 44, 75, 157, 192, 252, 257.
Luther A., 198.
Luther C., 85.
Luther H., 256.
Luther M., 40, 263.
Luthera, 96.
Lydia, 13, 14, 15, 17, 23, 24, 25, 28, 32, 35, 42, 50, 73, 81, 85, 97, 111, 137, 278, 290, 291, 294, 296, 299, 300, 323, 333.
Lydia A., 136, 169, 184.
Lydia E., 69, 137.
Lydia F., 225.
Lydia G., 183.
Lydia H., 68.
Lydia S., 112.
Lydia W., 155.
Lyman, 193.
Lyman S., 80.
Lynn B., 146.
Lysander M., 198.

Mabel, 167, 255.
Mabel A., 221, 225.
Mabel E., 216, 277.
Mabel L., 173, 240.
Mabel V., 259.
Mackey, 337.
Maggie C., 80.
Mahala, 175, 224, 294.
Mahala W., 85.
Malinda, 38.
Malissa L., 227.
Malissa J., 266.
Malvia, 327.

Malvin R., 163.
Malvina, 71.
Manderville B., 210.
Mandora, 140.
Manley, 334.
Manley S., 261.
Manora M., 263.
Marcell L., 104.
Marcellus, 194.
Marcia, 44, 67, 282.
Marcia A., 44, 115.
Marcia E., 104.
Marcia M., 78.
Mareanna, 299.
Margaret, 41, 71, 270, 278, 327, 335.
Margaret A., 71, 279.
Margaret C., 292.
Margaret E., 184.
Margaret F., 40.
Margaret L., 174.
Margaret O., 218.
Margaret S., 260.
Margaret U., 282.
Margaretta A., 77.
Margarette, 135.
Maria, 38, 80, 111, 294, 306.
Maria A., 102, 216, 272.
Maria E., 103, 122, 211.
Maria F., 134.
Maria H., 133.
Maria J., 306.
Maria L., 218, 343.
Maria S., 170, 210.
Maria T., 110, 254.
Maria Z., 163.
Marian E., 216.
Marian F., 285.
Mariana, 62, 303.
Mariana C., 324.
Marie, 65.
Marietta, 72, 151, 163.
Marilla, 38, 68.
Marilla E., 212.
Marilla H., 157.
Marion, 302.
Marion A., 218.
Marion A. E., 163.
Marion E., 183.
Marion M., 76.
Marjorie W., 204.
Mark, 125.
Mark P., 125, 344.
Mark S., 344.
Mark T., 192, 252.
Marsha, 279.
Marshall C., 66, 165.
Martha, 17, 24, 28, 34, 57, 58, 60, 62, 64, 65, 73, 98, 103, 124, 164, 330, 332, 338, 343.

Martha A., 79, 81, 133, 158, 184, 192, 198, 199, 251, 329, 334.
Martha B., 116, 269.
Martha C., 95.
Martha E., 69, 94, 188, 227.
Martha F., 163.
Martha G., 144.
Martha I., 338.
Martha J., 95. 136, 167, 256, 268, 285.
Martha L., 48.
Martha M., 165, 282.
Martha P., 61.
Martha W., 147.
Martin A., 280.
Martin B., 257.
Martin L., 163.
Marvin, 39, 40, 70.
Mary, 11. 14, 15, 16, 17, 18, 22, 25, 30, 41, 45, 46, 50, 62, 74, 79, 80, 83, 86, 89, 113, 115, 119, 149, 152, 156, 157, 163, 172, 187, 206, 213, 257, 272, 280, 284, 289, 291, 299, 300, 302, 313, 321, 325, 327, 330, 331. 332, 334, 337, 338, 341, 344.
Mary A., 41, 61, 62, 69, 79, 80, 83, 85, 106, 120, 128, 136, 156, 167, 169, 172, 192, 195, 217, 219, 245, 273, 281, 283, 305, 326, 334.
Mary A. L., 70.
Mary B., 123, 147, 206, 246, 327.
Mary C., 112, 133, 162, 174, 204, 284.
Mary D., 202, 262, 336.
Mary E., 64, 83, 88, 94, 116, 122, 123, 159, 172, 189, 207, 219, 226, 237, 240, 252, 282, 293.
Mary F., 62, 153, 241, 323.
Mary G., 96.
Mary H.; 64, 77, 157, 215, 250.
Mary I., 62, 198, 338.
Mary J., 61, 74, 79, 88, 98, 109, 114, 117, 128, 130, 135, 137, 164, 185, 193, 194, 206, 209, 218, 227, 232, 239, 256, 261, 273, 276, 282.
Mary J. A., 154.
Mary K., 191, 216, 275.
Mary L., 77, 205, 227, 239, 263, 304.
Mary M., 55, 104, 153, 165, 258, 271.
Mary O., 136.
Mary P., 267.
Mary R., 95.
Mary S., 66, 73, 75, 145, 174.
Mary T., 123.
Mary T. H., 110, 132.
Mary V., 328.
Mason, 37, 66, 165, 166.
Mason B., 98, 147.
Mason W., 66, 166.
Mat, 335.
Mathew, 313.

Matilda, 81, 338.
Matilda E., 174.
Mattie, 118, 137, 339.
Mattie A., 240.
Mattie Z., 246.
Maud, 147, 255.
Maud C., 309.
Maud E., 251.
May, 255.
May G., 103.
Maynard, 237.
Mehitable, 18, 19, 25, 29, 30, 31, 35, 46, 50, 52, 54, 55, 57, 113, 278, 280, 294.
Melinda, 54, 88, 194.
Melisse J., 191, 266.
Melvina, 193, 343.
Mercy, 18, 28, 50, 212.
Mercy A., 123.
Merrill, 32, 112, 197, 220, 270.
Merrill A., 220, 303, 305.
Merrimet, 41.
Mertle A., 148.
Merton F., 246.
Milan, 211.
Miles A., 273.
Millicent, 330.
Milo, 67.
Milo E., 156, 240.
Milton, 42, 333.
Milton G., 123.
Milvin H., 225.
Minerva, 40, 340.
Minerva T., 334.
Minna, 282.
Minnie, 251.
Minnie A. L., 175.
Minnie B., 118.
Minnie E., 152, 206, 209.
Minnie L., 305.
Minnie M., 147.
Miranda, 263.
Miriam, 29.
Mirtle, 342.
Mollie A., 148.
Molly, 27, 33, 47.
Monroe J., 265.
Moody, 33, 60, 247.
Mordica, 280.
Morton D., 342.
Moses, 35, 53, 56, 63, 75, 85, 86, 87, 122, 124, 156, 161, 192, 193, 195, 213, 239, 240, 252, 264, 301.
Moses A., 126, 217, 224.
Myra R., 292.
Myron A., 126.
Myron B., 283.
Myron D., 188.
Myron F., 197, 272.
Myron G., 274.

Myrtle J., 274.

Nabby, 49, 64, 93, 97.
Nahum, 97.
Nancy, 22, 29, 35, 37, 42, 49, 54, 56, 61, 74, 81, 85, 86, 93, 111, 113, 124, 140, 193, 214, 336.
Nancy B., 307.
Nancy E., 76, 88.
Nancy G., 282.
Nancy H., 327.
Nancy M., 81, 268, 269, 280.
Nannie, 334.
Naomi, 65.
Nathan, 44, 57, 87, 197.
Nathan B., 226, 327.
Nathan S., 71.
Nathaniel, 10, 11, 12, 13, 14, 15, 16, 17, 18, 19, 20, 25, 26, 27, 28, 29, 30, 36, 37, 45, 46, 47, 50, 52, 53, 56, 57, 65, 66, 73, 75, 76, 85, 86, 89, 91, 92, 93, 94, 98, 101, 102, 103, 104, 113, 119, 120, 135, 141, 144, 154, 165, 196, 212, 238, 247, 255, 261, 266.
Nathaniel E., 144, 334.
Nathaniel G., 106, 119, 135, 152, 237, 238.
Nathaniel M., 76, 178, 238.
Nathaniel S., 125, 344.
Nathaniel W., 192, 247.
Ned S., 226.
Nellie, 86, 239, 251, 253, 254, 274.
Nellie A., 168, 262.
Nellie B., 186.
Nellie F., 221, 252.
Nellie G., 256.
Nellie M., 167, 174, 238, 246.
Nelson, 147, 154, 157, 332.
Nelson G., 165, 225.
Nettie, 167, 243, 283.
Nettie E., 281.
Nettie K., 241.
Nettie M., 253.
Newell, 122.
Newell C., 119, 152, 239.
Newell H., 122, 213, 256, 257.
Nicholas, 311.
Nicholas E., 293.
Noah, 52, 70, 74, 169, 174, 194, 253, 264.
Noah B., 80.
Noah D., 129, 205.
Noah J., 74.
Noble, 333, 334, 336, 337.
Noble A., 72.
Norman N., 76.
Notan, 340.
Notan W., 340.
Noyes, 40, 71.

Olive, 45, 280, 301.
Olive J., 114.
Olive M., 119.
Olive P., 149.
Olive R., 172, 173, 197.
Oliver, 20, 38, 195, 211, 322.
Oliver G., 216.
Oliver H. P., 67, 166, 343.
Oliver M., 323, 325.
Oliver V., 277.
Oliver W., 60.
Olivia, 96, 126.
Olivia E. K., 154.
Olla S., 324.
Olney, 294, 295.
Opal, 339.
Ora A., 136.
Orange S., 156, 239.
Orianna C., 201.
Orrilla A., 118.
Orrin, 38, 140, 214, 241, 302, 304, 305.
Orrin C., 68.
Orrin G., 136.
Orrissa L., 174.
Orry G., 246.
Orsemus W., 251.
Orson, 44, 117.
Orzo A., 73, 172.
Oscar, 75, 213, 283.
Oscar B., 168, 198, 220.
Oscar De W., 163.
Oscar E., 211.
Oscar P., 158.
Ossian, 281.
Otis, 211, 296.
Otis D., 297.
Otis F., 59, 158, 227.
Otis K., 128, 219, 221.
Owen, 282.

Pamelia, 59, 73.
Pamelia A., 167.
Pamelia E., 245.
Pamelia J., 83.
Pamelia L., 209.
Parish B., 119, 152.
Parthena, 37.
Pascal, 267.
Pascal P., 220.
Patsey, 334.
Patta, 39.
Patta A., 69, 111.
Paul, 18, 28, 50, 52, 122, 136, 248, 249.
Paul A., 339.
Paul D., 244.
Paulina, 257, 259.
Pauline, 65.
Peabody W., 59, 159, 230.

Pearl F., 229.
Pelatia. 39.
Pennington, 339.
Percy C., 347.
Perley M., 61, 138, 192, 251.
Perley T. D., 255.
Perre B., 275.
Perry G., 36, 65, 164, 225, 226.
Persis, 59.
Peter, 29, 53, 56, 57, 76, 85, 192, 248, 331, 337.
Phebe, 16, 20, 22, 29, 35, 37, 55, 65, 279.
Phebe A., 282.
Phebe B., 64.
Phila, 140, 214, 241.
Philander, 37, 95, 228, 264.
Philander J., 75.
Philander M., 119.
Philena J., 169.
Philip, 46.
Philip H., 244.
Philip S., 84.
Philura, 66.
Phineas, 19, 275.
Pliny D., 67, 166.
Plummer B., 74, 173.
Polly, 29, 35, 36, 38, 46, 49, 52, 53, 54, 56, 68, 85, 93, 97, 122, 124, 125, 140, 278, 346.
Porlina S., 192.
Porter, 67, 166, 229.
Presinda, 43.
Priscilla, 85, 279, 290, 321, 326, 333.
Pulonia, 73.

Rachel, 19, 32, 36, 77, 97, 267, 289, 327.
Rachel E., 192.
Ralph, 37, 68, 111, 167.
Ralph A., 216, 275.
Ralph L., 220.
Ralph S., 264.
Randolph E., 128, 200, 203, 204, 221.
Ransom S., 114.
Rebecca, 17, 23, 34, 58, 82, 192, 248, 289, 323, 331, 337.
Rebecca A., 95.
Rebecca B., 69.
Rebecca D., 101.
Relief E., 346.
Rena E., 269.
Reuben, 85, 86, 195, 254.
Reuben E., 193, 253.
Rhoda, 52, 53, 82, 122.
Rhoda A., 69.
Rhoda F., 191.
Rhoda J., 83.
Rice R., 121.
Richard, 32, 59, 96.

Richard F., 138, 230.
Richmond, 93.
Roanna R., 65.
Robert, 57, 330, 339, 345.
Robert A., 326, 327.
Robert C., 331.
Robert F., 235.
Robert H., 327.
Robert P., 330.
Robert S., 305, 340.
Rodman, 326.
Roger, 20, 21, 36, 38, 65, 165, 211.
Roger B., 189.
Rolla E., 259.
Rollin, 158.
Rosa, 255.
Rosanna A., 77.
Roscoe L., 338.
Rose, 244.
Rose C., 261.
Rose F., 255.
Rose M., 269.
Rosebell, 172.
Rosella, 297.
Rosella A., 194.
Rosella M., 298.
Rosella W., 219.
Rosetta Mc A., 228.
Rosie T., 344.
Rosina, 119.
Rosina S., 111.
Roswell, 117, 279, 282, 283.
Roswell H., 44.
Rowena, 38.
Roxanna, 36, 38, 42, 64, 125, 156.
Roxy, 43.
Roy B., 177.
Roydon P., 343.
Ruby, 22, 23.
Ruby B., 44.
Ruel W., 211, 254.
Rufus, 40, 47, 284, 341.
Rufus A., 204.
Rufus B., 162, 228, 260.
Rufus G., 101, 144.
Rufus J., 303.
Rufus K., 93, 103, 147.
Rufus M., 70, 204.
Rufus S., 112.
Russell, 40, 70, 330.
Ruth, 15, 19, 22, 23, 24, 34, 35, 36, 41, 45, 54, 58, 66, 85, 118, 212, 282, 290.
Ruth A.. 213.
Ruth B., 55.
Ruth I., 25.
Ruth K., 40, 44.
Ruth M., 60, 81.
Ruth R., 67.
Rutha, 334.

R. Emily, 198.

Sabrina, 344.
Sabrina T., 128.
Salina, 343.
Sally, 38, 57, 59, 68, 73, 75, 92, 93, 97, 111, 112, 124, 128, 268, 278, 301, 343.
Sally A., 38, 328.
Sally B., 329.
Sally C., 314.
Sally D., 314.
Sally P., 145.
Salone, 57, 88.
Samantha, 68, 75, 95, 157.
Samuel, 8, 9, 10, 11, 12, 13, 15, 16, 19, 20, 22, 23, 26, 29, 34, 35, 37, 38, 39, 40, 41, 46, 49, 50, 54, 55, 56, 61, 62, 64, 66, 67, 70, 78, 80, 81, 113, 114, 118, 119, 121, 122, 124, 140, 166, 167, 187, 213, 214, 215, 217, 261, 262, 271, 272, 275, 276, 284, 290, 291, 293, 294, 295, 296, 297, 309, 348, 349.
Samuel A., 188, 306.
Samuel B., 107, 210, 250, 251.
Samuel C., 22, 23, 40, 41, 72, 118, 207.
Samuel E., 81.
Samuel G., 52, 73, 103, 106, 133, 172, 173, 235, 291.
Samuel H., 314.
Samuel J., 64, 306, 307.
Samuel J. P., 70, 167, 220.
Samuel M., 216.
Samuel P., 155, 169, 220, 248.
Samuel S., 115.
Samuel W., 118, 128, 207, 220.
Sampson, 34, 61, 138.
Sampson B., 87.
Sanford B., 105, 161.
Sanford H., 169, 221.
Sara, 289.
Sarah, 8, 11, 16, 19, 20, 24, 27, 30, 31, 32, 45, 48, 55, 56, 58, 63, 66, 68, 73, 81, 86, 87, 106, 111, 140, 156, 212, 219, 252, 280, 284, 289, 291, 299, 301, 302, 313, 314, 326, 330, 331, 332, 336, 341, 345.
Sarah A., 69, 240, 284.
Sarah B., 326, 344.
Sarah C., 292.
Sarah D., 88, 327.
Sarah E., 80, 83, 84, 104, 112, 124, 144, 261, 269, 293, 326, 338.
Sarah F., 259, 329.
Sarah G., 333.
Sarah H., 70.
Sarah I., 334.
Sarah J., 72, 78, 83, 87, 181.
Sarah K., 209, 261.
Sarah L., 135, 271, 331.
Sarah M., 79, 94, 194.
Sarah Mc C., 147.
Sarah N., 136.
Sarah O., 153.
Sarah P., 102, 155, 248.
Sarah R., 77, 114, 161.
Sarah S., 147, 219, 301.
Sarah T., 95.
Sarah V., 307.
Sarah W., 307.
Scott W., 298.
Seba A., 112.
Sebelia A., 326.
Seldon O., 119.
Selina, 140.
Senaca A., 119, 151.
Seneca, 119, 153, 245.
Septa, 39, 69, 111, 168, 169.
Septa G., 69.
Seth W., 256.
Shaw, 124, 156.
Sherman, 299, 301, 302, 303.
Sherman W., 254.
Sidney, 274.
Sidney A., 266, 272.
Sidney V., 266.
Silas, 284, 341.
Silas B., 248.
Silas H., 212.
Silas T., 44, 115.
Silvia, W., 248.
Silvina W., 248.
Simeon, 27, 28, 46, 50, 73, 106, 107, 117, 122, 136, 137, 172, 257.
Simeon H., 69.
Smith, 122, 295.
Smith E., 296, 297.
Smith M., 153.
Smith R., 298.
Solomon, 125, 344.
Solomon H., 158.
Solon, 104.
Sophia, 40, 49, 70, 94, 157.
Sophia A., 60, 70.
Sophia B., 102.
Sophia C., 110.
Sophronia, 40, 65, 93, 97, 126.
Sophronia J. 193.
Sophronia S., 119.
Spaulding W., 209.
Spencer, 65, 211.
Stanley P., 235.
Stateria, 194.
Stella M., 325.
Stephen, 18, 29, 35, 43, 49, 53, 54, 55, 56, 78, 80, 122, 128, 183, 186, 187, 212, 219, 220, 255, 261, 271, 344.
Stephen A., 187.
Stephen B., 64.

Stephen F., 54, 79.
Stephen G., 113.
Stephen H., 255.
Stephen O., 153.
Stephen S., 80.
Story B., 156, 244.
Submit, 36.
Sullivan, 58, 94.
Sumner, 111, 170, 171.
Sumner E., 197.
Sumner M., 171.
Susan, 25, 45, 53, 54, 56, 63, 75, 113, 278, 279, 283, 307.
Susan A., 79, 114.
Susan H., 172.
Susan L., 119, 306.
Susan M., 66, 297.
Susan O., 115.
Susannah, 15, 16, 17, 19, 28, 29, 35, 53, 78, 326, 336, 338.
Susie M., 81.
Sylvania, 213.
Sylvester, 115.
Sylvester C., 298.
Sylvester S., 85.
Sylvia, 262.

Tama, 343.
Temperance, 21.
Thadeus, 25, 93, 104, 148.
Thadeus B., 104.
Thankful S., 66.
Thedocia, 36.
Theodora, 35.
Theodore, 133.
Theodore A., 118.
Theresa M., 308.
Thing, 26, 46, 124, 156, 157.
Thirza, 302, 304.
Thomas, 29, 46, 50, 73, 114, 172, 206, 252, 257, 277, 278, 279, 284, 325, 326, 327, 331, 341, 342.
Thomas C., 121, 273, 293.
Thomas D., 193.
Thomas E., 206, 256, 328.
Thomas F., 194, 253.
Thomas H., 106, 193.
Thomas J., 69, 168.
Thomas K., 219.
Thomas M., 326, 327.
Thomas Mc C., 94, 147.
Thomas N., 223.
Thomas S., 105, 149, 256.
Thomas W., 223, 225, 226.
Thornton G., 337.
Thurman, 214.
Timothy, 16, 17, 19, 24, 25, 35, 54, 56, 59, 63, 78, 85, 86, 93, 96, 97, 104, 123, 147, 192, 193, 194, 253, 258, 266, 267.

Timothy B., 216, 223.
Timothy D., 79.
Timothy F., 258.
Timothy H., 94.
Tirza H., 85.
Trueworthy, 18, 31, 57.
Tryphena, 35, 36.
Tyler, 125.

Ulysses, 40, 70, 169.
Unity, 327.
Unity S., 327.
Unity V., 329.
Uriah, 32, 58, 95.
Uriah G., 73, 172.
Ursula, 283, 333.

Vernon A., 76, 176, 227.
Verria, 255.
Vesta A., 78.
Victoria R., 161.
Victory, 193.
Villa E., 344.
Vincent D., 334.
Virgil, 341.
Virginia, 194.
Virginia B., 152.
Virginia I., 323.
Vivian, 103.

Waldo E., 152, 293.
Wallace, 87.
Wallace E., 266.
Wallace P., 167.
Wallace S., 193.
Wallace W., 74, 265.
Walter, 255.
Walter A., 186.
Walter C., 165, 266.
Walter E., 245.
Walter G., 174.
Walter H., 221.
Walter L., 256.
Walter M., 274.
Walter S., 138.
Wareham, 41, 118, 206, 207.
Wareham W., 207.
Warna S., 263.
Warren, 65, 86, 101, 122, 136, 141, 163, 164, 194, 231, 253.
Warren D., 136.
Warren H., 342.
Warren R., 323.
Warren S., 268, 308.
Washington, 334.
Washington T., 74.

Welcome D., 93, 104, 148.
Welcome M., 76. 210.
Wealthea, 20, 111.
Wealthy. 23, 37.
Wendell P., 152.
Wesley, 87.
Wesley J., 153, 244.
Westray, 293.
Whiting, 22.
Whitney W., 162.
Wilber, 282.
Wilbur A., 76, 221.
Wilbur H., 244.
Wilbur J., 163.
Wilbur R., 201, 221.
Willard, 156, 239, 259.
Willard E., 259.
William, 17, 21, 24, 25, 34, 48, 56, 57, 58, 61, 64, 86, 87, 94, 97, 107, 112, 121, 123, 125, 134, 139, 162, 192, 193, 197, 198, 211, 225, 237, 246, 252, 254, 255, 261, 262, 264, 270, 271, 277, 278, 279, 282, 283, 284, 289, 290, 291, 292, 293, 294, 295, 298, 305, 319, 320, 321, 330, 331, 332, 333, 336, 337, 338, 339, 340.
William A., 103, 217, 229, 243, 251, 269, 281, 282, 338.
William B., 145, 149, 157, 228, 229, 235, 239, 259, 276.
William B. R., 329.
William C., 66, 129, 159, 204, 223, 227, 298, 301, 324.
William D., 79, 135, 166, 172, 184, 225, 229, 237, 238.
William E., 241, 243, 266.
William F., 128, 131, 237, 258, 260, 271, 277.
William G., 235, 291, 292.
William H., 59, 61, 62, 80, 136, 138, 164, 181, 187, 195, 226, 228, 229, 250, 263, 264, 314, 323, 325, 333.
William H. W., 112.
William J., 133, 229, 240, 281.
William K., 279, 280.
William L., 69, 111, 112, 169.

William M., 44, 75, 87, 106, 116, 117, 135, 175, 197, 198, 206, 220, 250, 258, 272.
William N., 197, 198, 237, 270.
William O., 176, 254.
William P., 88, 119, 139, 189, 195, 207, 276, 326.
William R., 67, 104, 118, 128, 204, 206, 210, 225, 244, 258, 292, 334.
William S., 71, 83, 153, 188, 241, 343.
William T., 210.
William T. V., 279.
William U., 206.
William W., 36, 156, 193, 240, 339, 340, 343.
Willie, 94, 152, 187.
Willie C., 165.
Willie E., 253.
Willie F., 268.
Willie M., 194.
Willie N., 206, 341.
Willie P., 148.
Willie S., 230, 251, 262.
Willie W., 174, 240.
Willis, 42, 186.
Willis E., 272, 275.
Willis R., 342.
Williston H., 266.
Winnie, 170.
Winfield S., 182.
Winifred B., 285.
Winneford B., 252.
Woodward N., 65.
Wyllys C., 72.
Wyman, 105.
Wyman H., 172.

Zacheus, 23.
Zama, 105.
Zebulon, 19, 267.
Zenas, 156.
Zilphia, 294.
Zoroaster, 119, 153, 243, 244.
Zurvia, 17.
Zurvia W., 71.

NAMES OTHER THAN LADD.

Abbott, Charles C., 104.
   Della, 129.
   Frank S., 133.
   George N., 83.
   Harriet, 138, 236.
   James, 93.
   John S. C., 236.
   Lavinia, 57.
   Moses S., 119.
   Palatiah T., 68.
   Susan M., 197, 258.
   Walter S., 119.
   William, 57.
Abel, Gideon H., 113.
   Lydia, 58.
Abrams, Danforth, 283.
Actin, Phineas, 295.
Adams, Douglas, 64.
   Edward A., 52.
   Hannah, 162.
   Jonathan, 156.
   Ruth W., 75, 264.
   Sally, 122, 212.
   Warren S., 248.
Agard, Abbie M., 285.
   Edward E., 285.
Ager, Aleazer, 23.
Akerman, Sarah E., 80, 186.
   James, 186.
Aiken, Mary, 66.
Albro, John, 288.
Alden, Arthur, 346.
   Emma, 346.
   Phelinda, 42, 126.
   Timothy, 126.
Aldrich, Jennie M., 166, 225.
   Mary, 215.
   Naoma, 167.
Alger, Amanda A., 79, 185.
Alexander, Henry W., 277.
   Mary A., 195, 258.
   Mirinda, 102, 146.
   Robert, 146.
   Susan, 277.
   Thomas, 161.
Allard, Caroline P., 153, 243.
Allen, Amy, 20.
   Augustus M., 201, 221.
   Chester, 289.
   Daniel, 16, 290.
   Deborah, 31, 57.
   Hope, 50, 140.
   Josephine E., 268, 270.
   Jude, 57.
   Kate, 280.
   Mary, 38, 211.
   Mary A. M., 95, 229.

Allen, Seth, 16.
   Willie, 1.
   Willis, 2.
Allison, John, 97.
Alvord, Elijah, 60.
Ambler, R. J., 260.
Ames, Daniel, 104.
   Eliza, 255.
   Mary, 26, 45.
   Obed, 115.
   Oliver, 115.
   Phebe, 111.
Amidon, Jacob, 267.
Anderson, Albert, 60.
   Alexander, 164.
   Almy A., 337.
   Carrie J., 60.
   Ellen, 60.
   Frank, 60.
   Mary, 60.
   Thomas, 60.
Andrews, Caroline B., 149.
   Hannah, 64.
   Joseph W., 306.
   Levi, 23.
   Lillian C., 306.
   Sarah, 342.
Angel, Fenner, 295.
   Louisa M., 296.
   Mary, 336.
   Pardon, 295.
Anise, Lyman, 58.
Anthony, Henrietta B., 60.
   John, 287, 288.
   Philip, 299.
   Susanna, 287.
Antony, Charles, 327.
Appleton, Elizabeth, 80, 187.
   John, 187.
Armstrong, James, 22, 70.
   Jane, 39.
   Jesse S., 340.
   Rebecca, 23.
   Robert, 95.
   Ruth, 40, 70.
Arnold, Ann, 299.
   Mrs. Cynthia, 34.
   Edward, 293.
   Harvey, 305.
   William, 299.
   ——, 137.
Ashley, Hiram, 346.
   Marietta, 346.
Atchson, ——, 69.
Atherton, Oliver, 267.
Atkins, Sophronia W., 261, 271.
Atwater, Jennie W., 166, 225.

Atwood, Elizabeth, 122, 213.
   Jesse, 49, 213.
   Judith, 85, 191.
   Richard, 115.
Auburd, Garret, 319.
Austin, ——, 23.
   Adelma A., 217, 229.
   Amanda, 54, 80.
   Elijah H., 229.
   Raymond, 58.
Avery, Lewis, 279.
   Miriam, 46, 125.
   Sallie A., 97, 258.
Ayer, Hannah, 17, 25.
   John, 1, 4, 7, 10.
   Orris, 343.
   Peter, 6, 7.
   Ruth, 27, 46.
   Thomas, 3.
   William, 25.

Babcock, Irene, 20, 37.
   Josiah, 20.
   Mary, 20, 38, 68.
Babson, Adelia, 120, 155.
Bache, Sarah, 318.
Backus, Sarah, 302, 304.
   Wallace, 94.
Bacon, ——, 49.
   Phebe, 67.
Badger, Nancy, 113, 198.
Bagley, Belle, 184.
Bailey, Aaron, 22.
   Cora E., 185.
   Daniel, 57.
   Ezra, 40.
   George W., 185.
   Hannah L., 338.
   Jacob, 33.
   John, 33, 220.
   Mary, 220.
   Mary L., 118, 207.
   Paul, 90.
   William S., 207.
   Wina, 139.
Baird, Harriet, 36, 266.
Baker, Alice H., 134.
   Charles D., 134.
   Clarinda, 238.
   Elizabeth R., 39, 69.
   Francis, 211.
   George, 134.
   George W., 82.
   Henry F., 211.
   Horace, 58.
   John L., 134.
   J. M., 346.
   Lillian M., 134.

Baker, N. E., 96.
Balch, ——, 45.
   Daniel S., 92.
Balcom, Mary A., 159, 227.
Baldwin, David W., 296.
   Dillon, 337.
   Elanor, 296.
   Eleazer, 38, 68.
   Eliza, 93, 104.
   Sylvanus, 93.
   Victor, 153, 243.
   William, 37.
Ballard, W., 331.
Ball, Charlotte M., 82, 188.
   Hannah, 57, 86.
Bane, Emma, 279.
Banister, Henry M., 270.
   Ruth D., 270.
Barber, Agias, 300.
   C. Ann, 121.
   Emma S., 269.
   Jacob, 269.
   Robert, 111.
   Sarah, 299, 300.
Barker, Edward, 88.
   William, 287.
Barnes, Charles, 145.
   Edith, 73.
   Edward M., 206.
   Eliza, 73.
   Mary E., 130.
   Oraline, 125.
   Rebecca E., 130, 206.
   Wallace, 73.
   William H., 130.
Barnett, Mary, 275.
Barney, Esther E., 138, 230.
Barr, Dugal H., 85.
   H. J., 219.
Barrett, Carrie M., 134.
   Edward H., 134.
   Frank E., 134.
   George A. P., 134.
   George H., 134.
   Herbert E., 134.
   Mary, 216.
   Rollo F., 134.
   Walter S., 134.
   Willie J., 134.
Barry, George, 64.
Bartlett, Abbie, 79.
   Benjamin, 29.
   Benjamin O., 29, 54.
   Dennis K., 303.
   Eli W., 115.
   Emily, 74.
   Frank L., 303.
   Fred. E., 303.
   Joseph F., 303.

Bartlett, Lucy, 52.
    Lyman. 139.
    Orzo, 73.
    Peter, 29.
    Rula B., 303.
    Sally, 74.
    Wilson, 74.
Barton, Julia, 79.
Bass, Eva, 67, 167.
Bassett, Abbie F., 273.
    Mary A., 226.
Batchelder, Abigail, 246.
    Ambrose J., 174.
    Ann A., 172.
    Asenath, 36, 64.
Batcheller, Nancy, 301.
Batchellor, George H., 144.
    John, 261.
    Lois H., 101, 144.
    Moses, 56.
Bates, Charlotte, 118, 207.
    James. 321.
Baxter, Theresa M., 262.
    Therzia M., 263.
Beamis, Alice P., 318.
    Thomas, 318.
Beane, Arvilla. 54.
    Betsey, 29, 54.
    Deborah, 79, 185.
    James, 185, 186.
    Lezza S., 79.
    Martin, 136.
    Mary, 54. 79.
Beardsley, Harvey G., 297.
Beck, Louisa B., 123.
    Susan B., 216.
Beckwith, Abigail, 121, 211.
    Lewis C., 345.
    Martha, 157.
Bell, Andrew W., 60.
    Ann, 325, 326.
    Elizabeth, 64, 163.
    John, 327.
    Martha, 133.
    Mary, 326.
    W. H., 219.
Bellows, ——, 39.
Benedick, Esther, 157.
Benham, Jacob, 35.
Bennett, George, 77, 115.
    Horatio, 308.
    Kate J., 199.
    Mary, 308.
Benson, Charity, 345.
    Walter S., 68.
Bentley, Harriet, 279, 283.
    John, 279.
Benton, Ada L., 93.
    Alonzo, 193.

Benton, Azariah, 43.
    Daniel, 44.
    George W., 93.
    Helen, 93.
    Henrietta E., 93.
    Jacob, 24, 44.
    Mary C., 93.
    Reuben C., 93.
    Solon L., 93.
Berrien, John M., 318.
    Margaret E., 318.
Berry, Tetratia, 86.
Berthold, Pagie, 216, 275.
Beckford, Juliet, 81, 188.
Bidwell, Ashel, 226.
    Ellen M., 138, 226.
    Harriet, 226.
Bierce, Winnie A., 268, 269.
Bigam, Ann, 280.
Bigelow, Edna E., 184.
    Eliza A., 73, 173.
    Frank, 256.
    Hannah, 16, 23.
    William F., 106.
    William P., 106.
Billings, Robert, 324.
Billington, Rebecca, 50.
Binford, Aquilla, 330.
    Hulda, 319, 320.
    James, 327, 328.
    James S., 330.
    Mary, 331.
    Peter, 330.
    Sarah, 325, 327, 330.
    Thomas, 330.
Bingham, Cary, 37.
Birch, ——, 332.
Bissell, Albert, 69.
    Augustus, 69.
    Eleanor G., 69.
    Harry B., 69.
    Harry P., 69.
Black, Isabel, 212.
Blackman, Elijah, 22.
Blackmer, Mary, 295.
Blackwood, Anna, 315.
    Cora S., 147.
Blake, Agnes, 132.
    Charles C., 132.
    Charles F., 132.
    Edith, 132.
    Eleanor, 132.
    Enoch, 49.
    Fanny, 152, 239.
    Isaac, 37.
    John, 118.
    Mary, 149.
Blakely, Thomas, 122.
Blakeslee, Ellen, 240.

Blaisdell, Betsey, 57, 87.
   Dolly, 31, 56.
   Horace, 76.
   Hosea, 76.
   Samuel, 342.
Blanchard, Arthur M., 296.
   Benjamin, 284.
   Laura, 296.
   Marietta, 296.
   Mary A., 284.
   Orson M., 296.
   Roswell, 73.
   William, 296.
Bliss, Fred W., 168.
   Newell, 174.
Blodgett, ——, 23.
Blossom, Ansel, 50.
Boardman, Frederick, 152.
Boars, R., 332.
Bodwell, Abigail, 13, 15, 17, 25.
   Daniel, 25.
   Samuel, 89.
Bogul, Emily L., 285.
Bohan, Mary E., 272.
Boise, John, 36.
Bolter, Charles D., 284.
   Joseph, 284.
Boody, Aaron, 177.
   Judith C., 78, 177.
Booth, Diana, 198.
Boothby, Susan, 284, 341.
Booton, Franklin, 227.
Borden, James, 279.
Boswell, George, 262.
Bourland, Abby, 154, 245.
Bovie, Maggie, 266, 272.
Bow, Rectina, 86, 196.
Bowker, Katharine, 328.
Bowls, Benjamin, 55.
Bowman, James P., 55, 98.
Boyd, Bethany, 336.
   Catharine, 336.
   Hannah, 336.
   Isabel, 336, 338.
   James, 113.
   James K., 336.
   John C., 336.
   Joseph L., 336.
   Mary J., 336.
   Samuel K., 336.
   Sarah A., 337.
   William L., 336.
Boyed, Betsey J., 267.
   Cynthia A., 267.
   Daniel L., 267.
   David, 267.
   Elvira M., 267.
   Mary B., 267.
   Nancy M., 267.

Boyed, Rachel, 267.
   Simon H., 267.
Boynton, Anna M., 199.
   Charles B., 324.
   Cynthia, 115.
   Hannah, 16, 23.
Boyson, John M., 62.
Boxley, Mary, 333.
Bradley, Ruth, 28.
   Susan, 128.
Bradstreet, Ann, 98.
   Humphry, 98.
   Moses, 98.
Bragg, Elizabeth, 47, 106.
   Samuel, 106.
   Sarah M., 343.
Braley, Mary, 95.
Brastow, L. O., 116.
Breed, Annie M., 209.
Brewster, A. Abraham, 38, 68.
   Benjamin D., 55.
   Elizabeth, 70.
   Emily, 124.
   Jonathan, 124.
   Love, 44.
   Lydia, 69.
   Ruby, 24, 44.
   Wadsworth, 44.
   William, 44.
Brice, Lucius V., 65.
   Maggie, 266, 271.
Bridgman, Abel, 35.
   Eliza A., 35.
   Emeline M., 35.
   George W., 35.
   John L., 35.
Brien, Philip, 61.
Briggs, George, 299.
Brigham, Waldo, 197.
Brink, ——, 279.
Britton, Betsey, 124.
   Eliza, 338.
Brock, R. A., 319.
Brockway, Lyman, 38, 88.
Broeffle, Daniel, 282.
Bronson, John M., 296.
Brooke, Edward, 319.
Brooks, A. W., 220.
   Ella C., 156, 244.
   Ellen C., 210.
   Emily, 76, 178.
   John W., 244.
   Morgan, 44.
Brown, Aaron, 278.
   Abbie E., 162.
   Abel W., 56.
   Abraham, 167.
   Almira B., 99, 186.
   Amasa, 162.

Brown, Augusta E., 162.
  Benjamin F., 120.
  Betsey, 294, 295.
  Charlotte, 68, 167.
  Dolly, 29, 54.
  Elizabeth, 60, 247.
  Ellen, 301, 303.
  Esther, 23, 41.
  F. A., 177.
  Frances A., 120.
  Frank A., 76, 106.
  Frank H., 106.
  George, 3, 6.
  George F., 147.
  Harriet C., 62, 264.
  Harriet H., 68.
  Hattie, 334.
  Hiram, 302.
  Ida M., 76, 271.
  Isaac, 294.
  Jacob, 218.
  James B., 270.
  James H., 77.
  John, 54, 213, 218, 324, 334.
  John Q., 73, 271.
  John W., 186.
  Joseph, 89, 195, 198.
  Lemuel A., 162.
  L. F., 86.
  Lorina M., 213.
  Lorinda W., 122.
  Lucy C., 120.
  Lucy L., 106.
  Lydia S., 305.
  Maggie, 80, 187.
  Mary A., 88, 149, 177, 213, 256.
  Mary F., 58, 95.
  Mirinda, 156, 240.
  Mollie, 334.
  Nancy, 29, 54.
  Orville W., 167.
  Rachel, 73.
  Samuel, 256.
  Samuel H., 61.
  Sawyer, 29.
  Sophia, 304.
  Stephen A., 149.
  Thomas, Jr., 122.
  Watson H., 280.
  William, 334.
  William L., 162.
  W. R., 334.
  ——, 294.
Brownell, Caroline, 307.
Browning, Ida, 169.
Browze, Ellen, 319.
Bruce, Joseph, 79.
  Lois, 125, 344.
  Susan, 54.

Bryant, Harriet, 212, 255.
  Lucinda, 284, 342.
  Samuel R., 337.
Bryor, James, 267.
Buchanan, Harriet, 280.
  Jane, 173.
  Martin H., 173.
  Mary, 279, 280.
Buck, Lyman, 294.
  Nancy, 53, 76.
  Perry, 294.
Budlong, Celia, 294.
  Daughter, 294.
  John, 294.
  Milton, 294.
  Moses, 293.
  Nathan, 294.
Buel, Ward, 35.
Bullard, Edgar N., 197.
  George, 295.
Bullock, Halsey, 212.
Bulwer, Ella, 161.
  Eva F., 161.
  Gertrude M., 161.
  Ida, 161.
  James, 161.
  John, 160.
  John E., 160.
  Mary E., 160.
Bunce, Laura A., 126, 218.
Burbeck, Mary, 34, 62.
Burch, Levi, 294.
  Lucretia, 382.
  ——, 382.
Burdick, Catharine, 58, 95.
  Frank, 69.
  ——, 300.
Burge, Miner, 280.
Burleigh, Judith, 54.
Burleson, Allen B., 301.
  Clarissa C., 301.
  Edward, 301.
  John L., 301.
  Lucy A., 301.
  Matilda, 301.
  Olive P., 301.
  Rowena C., 301.
  Sarah L., 301.
  William L., 301.
Burlingame, Nancy, 306.
Burnham, Albert, 239.
  Samuel B., 74.
Burrill, Louisa M., 61, 139.
Burrows, Caleb G., 231.
  Emma F., 144, 231.
Burton, Chloe, 295.
  Elizabeth, 295.
  Mary, 336, 337.
Bush, William, 61.

Bushum, Elizabeth B., 340.
Butler, Abigail, 17.
   Elijah, 17.
   Eunice N., 17.
   Hannah, 17.
   H. L., 326.
   James, 17.
   Jesse, 17.
   Joseph, 17, 118.
   Margarette, 138, 229.
   Mary, 17, 155.
   Mary A., 155.
   Molly, 25, 97.
   Percy L., 326.
   Phebe, 17.
   Samuel, 155.
   Thadeus, 17.
   William, 17.
Buxton, Charlotte, 59.
   Harriet B., 59.
   Henry M., 59.
   John, 59.
   Lavinia L., 59.
   Mary T., 59.
   Sarah L., 59.
Byram, Martha, 95.
Byington, Jane, 55, 84.
Byrt, Ella M., 247, 264.

Cadman, Charles, 289.
   Edward, 290.
Cady, Elizabeth, 23.
   Harriet, 188.
   Leonard, 34.
Call, Hattie, 217, 257.
Cameron, James, 213.
Camp, Lucy, 109.
Campbell, Atwood, 247.
   Charles, 338.
   David A., 247.
   Hannah, 57.
   Lydia, 301, 303.
   Mary O., 247.
   Mattie, 338.
Candage, Hiram, 63.
Canfield, Gov., 13.
Capron, Ella L., 192.
Carden, Mary E., 265.
Carleton, James D., 41.
   John, 17.
Carpenter, Asa, 280.
   Betsey, 38, 68.
   Henrietta E., 41, 72.
   Herbert E., 306.
   Herbert W., 306.
   Lydia, 298.
   Mary T., 316, 317.
   Samuel, 317.

Carpenter, William A., 293.
   William B., 72.
   William S., 137.
Carr, Albion, 86.
   Daniel, 56.
   Franklin, 86.
   Hannah, 124, 156.
   Helen, 86.
   Henry, 62.
   Hiram, 86.
   Moses, 86.
   Nancy, 336.
   Sarah J., 86.
Carter, A. D., 192.
   A. Webster, 211.
   Betsey, 122.
   Johanna W., 234.
   Joseph, 237.
   Rebecca, 41.
Carroll, Robert, 324.
Carver, Albert S., 346.
   Aldrich, 346.
   Charles P., 346.
   Edward W., 346.
   Frederick M. A., 346.
   Harvey S., 346.
   John, 291.
   Martha J., 346.
   Mary E., 346.
   Ralph W., 346.
Cary, Catharine J., 80, 186.
   Emma C., 95.
   Harriet, 112.
   Jane, 85.
   Sarah, 283.
Case, Alma, 34.
Cass, Donna M., 217, 229.
   Seth, 86.
Caswell, Alonzo, 73.
Cathren, Clara, 139.
Caverly, Joseph G., 158.
   Mary E., 125, 158.
Cawerden, Lucy E., 326.
Chaffee, Albert H., 307.
   Howard L., 307.
Chadwick, Lomie, 296.
Chamberlain, Ella, 172.
   Elzey, 158.
   Mary, 343.
   Rebecca, 44, 117.
Chambers, Samuel H., 329.
Chamness, Allen, 338.
Champlin, Mary, 197, 272.
Chandler, Ann, 68.
   Anna, 38.
   Cerenthia, 347.
   Hattie M., 166, 229.
   Lucy, 168.
   Richard, 332.

Chandler, Sarah H., 261, 262.
   Washington, 119.
   William, 332.
Chapin, Achsah, 129.
   Clavis, 304.
   ———, 39.
Chapman, John, 58, 97.
   Lois, 23, 42.
   Margaret, 22, 41, 303.
   Mary A., 333, 335.
   Mary E., 299.
   Olive, 57, 345.
   Samuel, 41.
   Zurvia, 32, 56.
   ———, 62.
Chappel, Anna, 30, 55.
   Walter, 212.
Charter, Rebecca, 118.
Chase, Amos, 53.
   Abraham, 195.
   Benjamin, 92.
   Betsey, 113.
   Betsey C., 198.
   Daniel, 53.
   Eliza, 92.
   Eliza C., 261, 262.
   Eunice, 211.
   Eustice, 92.
   Hannah, 53.
   Harriet B., 195.
   John, 92.
   Joseph, 53.
   Joseph S., 25.
   Lerin J., 25.
   Martha, 32, 58, 96.
   Mary, 53.
   Mary E., 204, 223.
   Mary J., 92.
   Nathaniel L., 53.
   Phebe G., 53.
   Philander, 25.
   Reginald H., 25.
   Sally, 53.
   Simeon B., 53.
   Thomas, 92.
   Thomas P., 92.
Chauncey, Sarah, 318.
Chauncy, Charles W., 48.
   Samuel, 48.
Chellew, Joseph, 158.
Cheney, Eliza, 343, 344.
   Eliza J., 192, 252.
   Lyman, 262.
Chester, Hattie A., 343.
Checkling Edmund, 212.
Childs, David, 159.
   Mary A., 59, 158.
Chepman, Melissa, 64, 162.
Chism, John, 282.

Choate, Abigail, 299, 301.
Christian, Bal. D., 332.
   Mary A., 332.
Christie, George W., 146.
Church, Harry S., 237.
   W., 290.
Cisco, Flavius, 163.
Clapp, Lewellen, 157, 256.
   Roxey, 118, 207.
Clark, Abby J., 258.
   Annie L., 102.
   Ella, 69.
   Elmer, 338.
   Emily, 102.
   Greenleaf, 102.
   Guy, 216.
   Henry F., 303.
   Irvin K., 102.
   Isabella T., 102.
   James R., 44.
   John H., 258.
   Joseph, 204.
   Judson G., 102.
   Leverett C., 102.
   Lucella, 157.
   Mary A., 80.
   Miranda, 306.
   Sarah M., 204.
   Warren, 102.
Clay, Henry, 180.
Clayton, Mary H., 316.
Clemment, David, 24.
   Hannah, 55.
   Job, 2.
   John, 311.
   Matilda, 336, 338.
   Robert, 2, 3, 4.
   Sarah M., 162.
   Stephen, 32.
Clemmens, Martha, 54, 79.
Cleveland, Grover, 223, 233.
Clifford, Ella P., 197, 254.
   Levi, 324.
   Sarah, 18, 30.
Clone, Ida, 168.
Closson, Amos E., 41.
   Josiah, 63.
Clough, Abial H., 149.
   Hannah, 32.
   Josephine, 125.
   Sally, 124.
   ———, 32.
Cloyson, James, 319.
Coates, Heman S., 255.
Cobb, Almy, 43, 129.
   Jonathan, 97.
   Priscilla, 328.
Cochrane, Betsey, 34.
   James, 33, 34.

Cochrane, John, 33.
  Robert, 33.
  Vashti, 33.
Codding, David C., 126.
Coe, D. Wadsworth, 152.
Coffin, Caroline E., 323.
  Emily, 297.
  Michael, 278.
  Sarah, 252.
  Stephen, 10.
  Miss, 278.
  ———, 278.
Colcord, Samuel, 18.
Colburn, Catharine, 59, 158.
  Caroline, 87.
  James, 237.
Colby, Barnard, 199.
  Dolly, 49, 121.
  Harriet J., 97.
  John L., 97.
  Jonathan, 97.
  Lucy P., 97.
  Luther, 87.
  Martha M., 97.
  Sarah A., 97.
  Sylvania, 113, 119.
  William W., 92.
Cole, Henry, 95.
  Lucy, 58.
  Sally, 95.
Colegate, ———, 49.
Collins, Abigail, 85, 191.
  Betsey, 106, 135.
  Fanny, 56, 85.
  Kate, 149.
  Sarah F., 85.
  Warren O., 304.
  Zacheus, 135.
Colt, George M., 104.
Colwell, Prudence, 275.
Comstock, James B., 216.
Conklin, Edward B., 324.
  Frank H., 324.
  William, 324.
Conn, R. M., 326.
Conoly, George, 278.
Conover, Andrew, 278.
Converse, Horace, 114.
  Perum W., 164.
  R. W., 164.
  Samuel M., 114.
Cook, Benjamin S., 322, 323.
  Blanch E., 322.
  Charity, 338.
  Clark W., 323.
  Edith D., 322.
  Elisha, 322.
  Elizabeth, 322.
  George D., 323.

Cook, George S., 323.
  James D., 323.
  Jennie, 194.
  Laura W., 322.
  Marianna L., 322.
  Mary C., 322.
  Mary I., 322.
  Rosamode, 322.
  Sally, 23, 111.
  Warren L., 322.
  Wilbur E., 322.
  William M., 322.
  ———, 24.
Coombs, Emma, 67.
  Esther, 67.
  Hattie, 67.
  Nancy, 123.
  William, 67.
  William P., 67.
Coope, John, 77.
Cooper, Electa, 163.
Copeland, Charles, 39.
Copp, Sarah E., 192.
Copple, Carrie, 45.
Corey, Daniel, 180.
Corley, Francis, 319.
  George, 3.
Corliss, Eben, 85.
  George, 8, 12.
  John, 10.
  Martha, 11, 12.
Cornel, ———, 290.
Corwin, William L., 135.
Cory, William, 290.
Cotes, Calvin, 157.
  John, 157.
Coughan, G., 251.
Counce, Benjamin F., 81.
Cousin, Herbert, 228.
  Wellington H., 228.
Coverly, ———, 86.
Cowan, Betsey S., 268.
Cowes, Elliot, 110.
  Grace D., 110.
  Hannah L., 110.
  Lewis D., 110.
  Meana T., 110.
  Samuel E., 110, 132.
Cox, Betsey, 20.
Coy, Jane, 56.
Crafts, Warren, 149.
Craig, Charles P., 78.
Cram, Louisa, 137.
Crandall, Edward, 345.
  Elizabeth, 299.
  Joseph, 299.
  Levi, 345.
  Olivia, 345.
  Sarah, 345.

Crandall, Simeon, 345.
　Thomas, 165.
Crandell, Levi, 23.
　Sarah A., 66, 165.
Crane, Louisa, 123.
Crawford, James, 280.
Crew, Catharine, 331.
　David, 331.
　John, 320, 321.
　Mary, 320, 332.
　Miss, 332.
　Sarah, 320.
Cronkite, Jennie, 277, 278.
Cross, Samuel, 19.
Crossman, Abigail, 32, 58.
Crouch, Eliza, 59, 238.
Crump, Alice A., 332.
　Annetta, 332.
　David S. M., 332.
　David W., 333.
　Edgar, 332.
　Elizabeth, 333.
　Estella, 332.
　John S., 333.
　Lawrence, 332.
　Lawrence S., 332.
　Mary, 332.
　Mary A., 332.
　Mary P., 333.
　William, 332.
Cummings, Mary A., 107.
　Pingree, 123.
　Serepta, 336, 339.
Cunningham, Anderson, 322.
　Cushing, 44.
　———, 251.
Currier, Ada M., 176, 254.
　Daniel, 24.
　Humphrey, 83.
　Mary J., 76, 176.
Curry, Samuel, 121.
Curtis, Abigail, 37.
　Byron F., 88.
　Cary, 37.
　Elias, 37.
　Elizabeth, 37.
　Hulda, 19.
　Stephen, 278.
　Stephen W., 295.
　Wealthy, 37.
　William, 278.
Cushing, Edward, 291.
　Margaret G., 291.
　Thomas, 291.
Cushman, Eva M., 193.
Cutler, John N., 112.
Cutter, Anna L., 109.
　Annie J., 109.
　Charles J., 109.

Cutter, Charles W., 109.
　Eliot, 109.
　Francis L., 109.
　Guilford E., 109.
　Henry L., 109.
　Jacob, 109.
　Laura, 109.
　Miriam E., 109.
　Ralph C., 109.
　Ralph E., 109.
　Ralph H., 109.
Cutts, John, 13.

Dadman, Guy L., 106.
　Harry L., 106.
Daggett, Phebe, 66, 165.
Daly, Mehitable, 17.
Damon, Catharine B., 335, 336.
　Lillie, 172.
Dana, Erastus F., 133.
　Mary S., 153.
Daniels, Abigail, 53.
　Almira, 53.
　Betsey, 53.
　Charles E., 250.
　Hiram, 125.
　Ira M., 65.
　Lorena, 53.
　Louisa S., 53.
　Samuel, 53.
　Sylvanus, 53.
　Sylvester, 53.
　Zarend, 53.
Darba, Roxy, 43.
Darby, Samuel, 24.
Darling, Anna A., 229.
　Sarah, 61.
Darwin, Asa, 58.
Dary, Austin, 194.
　Horace, 38.
Dastous, Emily O., 167.
　Lewis, 167.
Davidson, Fannie E., 211, 254.
　Nathan, 254.
Davis, Abigail, 104, 306.
　Agnes A., 298.
　Albert E., 169.
　Calvin, 38.
　Charles H., 184.
　Charles S., 144.
　Clara P., 209.
　Daniel, 83.
　Florence L., 144.
　Gabrial, 218.
　Henry, 219.
　Henry E., 280.
　Homer, 280.
　Hubbard, 146.
　Ira, 123.

Davis, James, 2, 3, 4, 5.
  John, 3.
  Lena M., 280.
  Lizzie, 178.
  Lois, 43, 129.
  Luanda L., 184.
  Margaret, 118, 207.
  Mary E., 103, 146.
  Mattie, 138.
  Miss, 333.
  Noah, 24.
  Polly, 46, 113.
  Roxana, 35, 63.
  Sarah L., 184.
  Smith A., 280.
  Susan E., 144.
  Sylvia, 98.
  Thomas, 3.
  Warren L., 144.
  ———, 335.
Dawkins, George E., 144.
Day, Caroline P., 68, 168.
  George, 194.
  Joannah E., 167.
  Martha, 301.
  Moses, 184.
  Pleny, 38, 167.
  Sarah, 145.
Deane, Amos F., 112.
  Edmund W., 112.
  S. Marie, 198, 209.
Dearborn, Anna, 284.
  John, 284.
  Rebecca E., 79, 184.
Decker, Charlotte, 140, 214.
Delano, Anna, 19.
  Chlorinda, 19.
  Esther, 19.
  Hubbard, 19.
  Jazeb, 19.
  Jonathan, 19.
  Margarette, 19.
  Philip, 19.
  Zubulon, 19.
Delkin, A. L., 162.
Denio, Albert P., 163.
Denman, Harriet C., 163.
  Mary M., 163.
Dennett, Betsey, 267.
  Catharine, 332.
  Mary, 332.
  Richard, 332.
Denson, Isabella, 320.
Desh, S. E., 219.
Devol, John, 290.
Dewey, Benjamin, 296.
  Henry, 296.
  Samuel, 296.
Dexter, Fanny, 211.
  Freeman, 137.

Dexter, Julia A., 122, 137.
Dickenson, Aura, 281.
  James, 281.
  Mark B., 281.
Dickerson, Adeline, 64, 163.
Dickey, Mary, 146.
  Nancy, 146.
Dickson, John, 2.
Diffin, Robert J., 162.
Disbrow, Mary, 279, 280.
  Rebecca, 280.
Dismore, L. Henry, 66.
Doane, Phineas, 64.
Dobge, William, 319.
Dodge, A. Hamilton, 316.
  Edwin, 56.
  Harvey, 69.
  Sarah J., 155, 248.
Doe, James, 195.
Doloff, Thomas, 56.
  ———, 87.
Donaldson, Dwight D., 138.
Doolittle, Rose, 247, 264.
Dorsett, Elizabeth, 83, 210.
Doty, Albert, 111.
  Betsey C., 79.
Douglas, Azuba, 302, 303.
  Edward, 69.
Dow, Comfort, 29, 54.
  Hannah, 25, 93.
  Jeremiah, 85.
  Lydia, 34, 61.
  Susannah, 28.
Doyle, Slim, 212.
Draper, Jacob, 31.
Drown, Charles E., 167.
Drummond, Edith, 144.
  Herbert L., 144.
  Roscoe, 144.
  R. Roscoe, 144.
Drury, Elisha, 36.
  Needham, 36.
Ducker, Francilla, 204, 210.
Dudley, Davidson, 45.
  Jacob, 34.
  James, 28.
  Joannah, 18, 28.
  Moses, 96.
  Samuel, 18.
Dunbar, H. M., 63.
Dunham, Franklin C., 256.
  John, 73.
  Lucy A., 83, 210.
  Tania, 343.
Dunnel, Laura, 75, 264.
Dunsmore, Issaker R., 174.
Durfee, Mrs. Lydia S., 144.
Dustan, Hannah, 24.
Dustin, Caleb, 247.

Dustin, Lucy A., 154, 247.
Dutcher, Annette A., 166, 225.
Dutton, David, 66.
    Susan, 37, 66.
Dwight, Martha B., 158.
Dyer, Anna M., 193.
    Charles, 295.
    Dorcas, 295.
    James, 193.

Eagen, L. Jane, 114, 206.
Eames, Wealthy B., 40, 263.
Easterbrooks, Pamelia, 153.
Eastman, Charlotte, 106, 134.
    Ebenezer, 134.
    Hannah, 19, 34.
    Lyman, 154.
Easton, Sarah, 291, 293.
Eaton, Abiah, 159.
    Alice M., 172, 257.
    Henry A., 173.
    James, 343.
    Jonathan, 32.
    Thomas, 9.
Eccles, W. M., 117.
Eckstein, William D., 297.
Edes, William, 86.
Edgar, John, 89.
Edgerton, Edward, 66.
Edminster, ——, 36.
Edwards, Annie, 214, 241.
    J. F., 322.
    Levi T., 324.
    Molly, 101.
    Nancy, 347.
    Samuel, 347.
    Sarah M., 95, 347.
Eldred, Annie, 193.
Eldridge, Amelia A., 106, 148.
    Henry, 148.
Elethorp, Nathaniel, 8.
Eliot, John, 109.
    Laura, 109.
    Wylls, 109.
Elliott, Calvin A., 153, 241.
    Drusilla, 56, 86.
    Mary A., 88, 195.
    William, 185.
    William F., 185.
Ellis, Elizabeth, 76, 210.
    Hiram, 98.
Ellyson, Ann, 331.
    Gerard, 321.
    Gerard R., 330, 331.
    Judith, 320, 330.
    Thomas, 331.
    Ursula, 320, 331.
Ely, Alfred, 44.

Emerson, Fenner H., 238.
    Mary A., 135, 238.
    Mary J. W., 79.
    Michael, 7.
    Susan, 123, 216.
Emery, Bethia, 15.
    Betsey, 32.
    Eliphalet, 133.
    Ernest, 162.
    Ira, 32.
    James, 32.
    James W., 133.
    Joel, 32.
    John, 32.
    Jonathan, 32.
    Julian, 162.
    Lillian, 162.
    Lydia, 32.
    Malcom C., 162.
    Manning, 133.
    Mary, 32.
    Osmond, 162.
    Ruth, 133.
    Samuel N., 162.
    Seava, 32.
Emmons, Isaiah, 342.
Enos, William, 289.
Estus, Abner, 278.
    Robert, 278.
Evans, Harlow, 212.
    Jane, 321.
    John, 145.
    Rose, 195.
    Sarah B., 102, 145.
Eveans, Frank S., 248.
Ewell, Martha, 157, 257.

Fairbanks, Carrie, 133.
    Ellen L., 133.
    Horatio W., 133.
Fairfield, Ella L., 304.
Falk, George A., 283.
Fanning, Mary L., 301.
Fargo, Mrs. Roxana T., 138.
Farnam, Anne W., 34.
    Cynthia H., 34.
    Eleanor L., 34.
    Jeremiah, 34.
    Mariam E., 34.
    Miriam, 59, 137.
    Samuel, 34.
Farnham, Phebe, 22.
Farnsworth, Ann E., 65.
    Elizabeth, 164.
    Jay H., 163.
Farrington, Theodate, 135.
Farkett, Isaac, 129.
Fassett, Anson, 58.

Faunce, Joseph, 145.
Fay, Lyman, 117.
   Samuel, 85.
Fayan, John, 336.
Feeney, Mary, 273.
Fellows, Abigail, 41, 118.
   Benjamin, 59.
   Peter, 85.
Femsey, Joseph, 138.
Fenner, Gordon S., 41.
Ferguson, Electa, 140, 345.
   Sarah J., 78, 182.
Fernal, ——, 63.
Ferris, Olive H., 276.
Fessenden (Bassett), Abbie, 273.
Field, Cyrus, 30.
   Forbes, 30.
   Johannah, 57, 88.
   Josiah, 30.
   Melissa, 346.
Fifield, Rachel, 29, 53, 75.
Fillebrown, J. S., 133.
Fillmore, Almira, 23, 112.
   Amaziah, 23.
   Daniel, 23, 41.
   Jehiel, 23.
   Mahala, 23.
Fink, Polly, 22, 40.
Firnin, Elizabeth, 83, 210.
Fish, Annis, 266.
   Betsey, 266.
   Lavina, 207.
Fisher, Leonard, 75.
   Samuel, 212.
Fiske, James, 6.
Fitts, Robert, 1.
Flanders, Abigail, 26, 46.
   Irene, 217, 257.
Flemming, Margaret, 40.
   Mary, 71.
Fletcher, Hiram A., 188.
   Jeremiah, 55.
   Mira B., 83, 188.
Flind, Asanath, 345.
Fling, Ann E., 267.
   Catharine G., 267.
   Frances T., 267.
   Fred. A. H., 267.
   Fred. W., 267.
   Lucy P., 267.
   Sanford C., 267.
Flent, Mary, 345.
Flynn, Margaret, 301, 302.
Foley, Mrs. Ellen, 162, 225.
Folger, Elizabeth, 323.
Folkes, Alice A., 333.
   Catharine, 333.
   Edgar S., 333.
   Eugia G., 333.

Folkes, Lawrence S., 333.
   Mary, 333.
   Robert A., 333.
   William H., 333.
Follensbee, Ann, 89.
Follet, Mary, 86.
Folsom, A. Q., 261.
   David M., 267.
   Israel, 267.
   James, 267.
   John, 28, 267.
   John A., 150.
   Jonathan, 14.
   Joseph, 267.
   Martha, 18, 27.
   Mary, 11, 267.
   Mrs. Mary, 120.
   Mrs. Mary G., 154.
   Mercy, 50, 122.
   Nancy, 267.
   Nathaniel, 14, 27, 122.
   Rose M., 272, 274.
   Samuel, 14.
   Sarah, 267.
   Stephen, 267.
Foot, Dorithy, 19, 33.
Ford, Alice, 303, 304.
   Betsey, 294.
   Thomas, 46.
   Wealthy J., 194.
Forrest, Franklin, 52.
Forsyth, Ira, 58.
Fosmire, Edgar, 281.
Foster, Charles H., 161.
   Daniel, 20.
   Edward, 212.
   Evelyn T., 238.
   Fidelia W., 20.
   Franklin, 161.
   Fred. E., 238.
   George A., 238.
   Jemima, 13.
   Joseph D., 238.
   Lafayette S., 20, 21.
   Lucy C., 238.
   Nathaniel L., 238.
   Pleasant, 337.
   Rebecca K., 234.
   Robert F., 238.
   Thomas, 319.
   Victoria H., 161.
   William A., 238.
Fothergill, John, 320.
Fournival, Josephine, 123.
Fowle, Annie P., 308.
   Susan L., 110, 131.
   William, 131.
Fowler, Asa, 58.
   Benjamin, 57.

Fowler, Clarissa, 58.
    David, 58.
    Edward, 130.
    Esther, 57.
    Jerusha, 57.
    John L., 57.
    Mehitable, 57.
    Polly, 57.
    Samuel, 57.
    Simonds, 57.
    Trueworthy, 58.
    Lewis, 88.
Fox, Amy I., 265, 266.
    Eleanor T., 225.
    Frederick, 225.
    Fredrika A., 225.
    George, 311.
    Martha, 52, 73.
    Laura, 172.
    Susan, 73.
Frank, Betsey, 275.
Franke, Richard, 319.
Franklin, Benjamin, 318.
    Fabian, 130.
Fraten, Commicila, 333.
Frazier, Catharine, 336.
    Paul, 336.
    William, 40.
French, Abigail, 86, 193.
    Ann K., 292.
    Benjamin, 319.
    Edward, 53.
    Jacob, 55.
    Jane, 58, 110.
    John, 193.
    Joseph, 53.
    Judith B., 195.
    Levi, 45.
    Lydia, 56.
    Lizzie, 192, 251.
    Mary, 18, 30.
    Melinda, 53, 78.
    William S., 293.
Freeman, Adrianna, 303, 305.
Frink, Anna M., 117.
    Eliza C., 197, 270.
    George W., 70.
Frisbee, Caleb, 279.
    Charles, 279.
    Edward, 279.
    John, 279.
    Nancy, 279.
    William, 279.
Frost, Maggie, 266, 272.
    Silas, 60.
Fuller, Almira, 118, 207.
    Clara M., 105, 161.
    Betsey, 36, 84.
    Huldah, 24, 43.

Fuller, H. W., 77.
    Luther, 73.
    Nabby, 43.
    Mrs. Sally L., 194.
Fullerton, Andrew J., 145.
Fullington, Ebenezer, 92.
Fullom, James, 172.
Fulton, Carlos, 34.
Furber, George A., 248, 271.
    Nicholas P., 271.

Gage, Jacob, 297.
    Josiah, 8, 9, 10, 11, 17.
Gale, Charles C., 199.
    George D., 192.
    Mary, 52.
    Mehitable, 46, 113.
    Polly, 28.
    Sarah, 113.
    ———, 52.
Gallaher, Eliza, 121, 341.
Gardner, Benoni, 290.
    G. Andrew, 198.
    Matilda, 153.
    Mehitable, 119.
    Sarah, 290.
Gates, Caroline M., 128, 203.
    Israel, 203.
Gatley, Cora E., 228, 259.
Gay, Charles P., 307.
    Cynthia, 205.
Gaylord, Alexander, 16.
Gedshill, John, 319.
George, Abbie W., 92.
    Amos E., 92.
    Anna G., 144, 234.
    Eliza H., 92.
    Elizabeth A., 92.
    Ethan, 345.
    Gideon B., 92.
    Janet, 280, 281.
    Jonathan F., 98.
    Levi B., 234.
    Marette, T., 92.
    Mary J. F., 92.
    Moses, 92.
    Nathan C., 92.
    Wallace T., 92.
    William R., 92.
Gethen, Catharine, 280.
Gibbons, Maggie, 302, 304.
Gibbs, Hiram, 269.
    Irene E., 268, 269.
Gibson, Annie, 82.
    Charles, 82.
    Mary, 82.
    Polly, 220.
    Samuel, 82.

Gibson, William, 82.
Gifford, Cornelia S., 273.
   Hannah P., 323, 325.
   Isaac A., 325.
   William, 323.
Gilbert, Almeda, 156, 240.
   Joseph R., 193.
   Polly, 346.
   Sally, 66.
Gile, Arthur E., 230.
   J. C., 60.
   Mary E., 60.
   Paul S., 88.
   Samuel, 2, 3.
   Willie H., 60.
Giller, Edward A., 97.
Gilley, Clara E., 228, 260.
   David H., 182.
   George W., 182.
   Joseph W., 182.
Gilman, Abigail, 14, 26.
   Alice, 262.
   Alvin, 262.
   Ann, 18, 27.
   Benjamin, 27.
   Betty, 27.
   Carrie N., 262.
   Catharine, 14, 17.
   Daniel, 14, 262.
   Deborah, 46.
   Della M., 262.
   Edward M., 17.
   Edwin, 262.
   Elizabeth, 11, 13, 14.
   Francis M., 193, 252.
   Frank, 262.
   Fred. A., 262.
   George E., 262.
   Hannah, 92, 103.
   Jacob, 14.
   James, 86.
   John, 12, 13, 14, 27, 252.
   John Taylor, 47.
   Judith, 27.
   Lettia S., 262.
   Mary, 14.
   Minnie L., 262.
   Moody, 14.
   Nathaniel, 27.
   Nathaniel R., 261.
   Nellie E., 262.
   Peter, 35.
   Russell A., 262.
   Samuel, 103.
   Steven, 14.
   Theophilus, 47.
Gilsey, John, 130.
   Peter, 130.
Gilson, Andrew J., 88.

Gladwell, Daniel, 279.
   John, 279.
Glasford, Samuel, 158.
Glidden, Anna, 14.
   Elizabeth, 14.
   Hannah, 14.
   John, 14, 30.
   Margaret, 29, 52.
   Nathaniel, 14.
   Stephen, 74.
Glines, Mercy, 122, 212.
Golder, Lydia F., 78, 188.
Good, Lelia, 199.
Goodale, Ezekiel, 237.
   Lucretia, 134, 237.
Goodnough, Ephraim, 124.
Goodrich, Hannah B., 61, 138.
   W. M., 132.
   ——, 35.
Goodspeed, Abner, 278.
   Ann, 278.
   Betsey, 278.
   Christopher, 278.
   Elnathan, 278.
   Levi, 278.
   Nathaniel, 278.
   William, 278.
Gookin, Sophia, 124, 157.
Gordon, Eben C., 54.
   Enoch, 24, 29.
   Mary, 120.
   Robert, 194.
   Stephen, 29.
   William, 29.
   Wenan, 71.
   ——, 47.
Goss, Daniel T., 92.
   Philip, 34.
Gott, Deborah, 161.
   Eliza, 161.
   Elizabeth R., 63.
   J. L., 86.
Gould, Christianna, 86, 195.
   Elizabeth, 46, 119.
   George, 278, 279.
Gove, Rhoda, 114.
   ——, 14.
Grace, Mary, 284, 341.
Grady, Mary, 123.
Graham, Eliza, 62.
   Frederick R., 317.
   Jennie R., 69, 169.
   Susan A., 146.
Grannis, Lucy S., 297.
   William P., 296.
Grant, Deborah, 20.
   Edwin, 302.
   Jonathan, 16.
   Mary, 209.

Grant, Mary A., 86, 193.
    Mary E., 112.
    ——, 39.
Graves, Sarah, 74, 264.
    Sarah L., 301.
Gray, Alonzo. 212.
    Lydia, 290.
    Samuel, 290.
Greely, Molly, 17.
Green, Mrs. Ann A., 299.
    Caty, 299, 306.
    Christopher, 306.
    Cora, 332.
    Ebenezer, 299.
    Elijah, 23.
    Ellen, 332.
    Francis, 292.
    Hart, 23.
    Isabella, 318.
    James J., 125.
    John, 336.
    Margaret L., 292.
    Peter, 299.
    Samuel W., 292.
    Thomas C., 292.
    William, 23.
    Mrs., 41.
Greenleaf, James B., 194.
    L. W., 86.
    Mark L., 168.
    Samuel, 45.
Greenman, Mary, 276, 277.
Greenough, Bailey, 144.
    Mary A., 101, 144.
Gridley, John, 301.
Grinnell, Jonathan, 289.
    Mary, 289.
Griswold, James C., 113.
    Jane M., 58, 273.
    Julia, 300.
    Louisa M., 111.
    Mary E., 58, 272.
    Willard, 347.
Grondyke, Asa, 140.
Groom, Daniel, 321.
Guild, Eunice, 21.
Gurrills, Hawley, 295.

Hacket, Charlotte, 98, 123.
    Moses, 32.
Hadley, Stephen A., 199.
Hager, Annie M., 139.
    R. H., 139.
Haines, Daniel P., 172.
    Lydia, 28, 50.
    Mahala, 73.
Hale, Goodman, 3.
    Thomas, 7.

Haley, Clarinda, 301, 302.
Hall, Allen S., 165.
    Alonzo R., 140.
    Austin A., 135.
    Charles, 266.
    Clarissa, 296.
    Isaac D., 323.
    Kinsley, 17, 26.
    Lyman B., 323.
    Mercy, 17.
    Sarah D., 74, 174.
    Sarah E., 243.
    Stephen W., 145.
    William, 241, 288.
    ——, 92.
Halley, Sarah, 67.
Halowell, N. P., 234.
Halstead, Ephraim, 39.
Hamba, Feriba, 334, 335.
Hamel, Mary E., 167.
Hamilton, Esther, 229.
Hamlin, Sarah, 53, 77, 178, 180.
    Theophilus, 77.
Hammond, Hannah, 104.
    John, 93.
    Nabby, 93.
    Oceana, 146.
Hane, Abba, 172.
Hannaford, Orlando, 342.
Hannan, Norcha, 277, 278.
Hanrahan, Kate, 149, 239.
Hapgood, Maria, 261, 271.
Hardsborough, Sarah, 45.
Hardwick, Betsey, 340.
Hardy, A. P., 86.
    Oliver J., 239.
Hargrave, Charles, 330.
    Mathew, 327.
Harlow, Enoch, 67.
    Hollis, 67.
Harman, Daniel W., 160.
    Mary P., 160.
Harmon, Mary P., 59.
Harner, Edward, 129.
Harper, Mina, 162.
Harriman, Abbie H., 267.
    Charles, 267.
    George W. 267.
    Hannah, 49, 122.
    James H., 63, 122.
    Lydia, 18, 31.
    Simon, 267.
    Simon A., 267.
    Simon B., 267.
Harrington, Anna, 30.
    Catharine, 194.
    Clark, 198.
    David A., 30.
    Diantha H., 30.

Harrington, Leonard C., 30.
  Luther, 30.
  Marchia, 30.
  Mary L., 30.
  Warren, 30.
  ——, 30.
Harris, Anna, 193.
  Elisha, 126.
  Elvira, 195, 257.
  L. E., 219.
  Lucius T., 344.
  Samuel, 219.
  Thomas, 321, 327.
  Unity, 320, 327.
  ——, 338.
Harrison, Benjamin, 233.
  Susan M., 138, 229.
Hart, Abigail, 289.
  John, 294.
Hartshorn, Hannah, 13, 15, 19.
  Susannah, 13, 15.
  ——, 60.
Hartwell, John, 63.
  Martha A., 94, 104.
  Samuel, 104.
Hartwick, Helen, 51.
Harvey, Abby E., 52.
  Charles, 157.
  Dudley L., 50.
  Fanny M., 52.
  James, 50.
  James B., 52.
  John M., 52.
  Jonathan, 50.
  Jonathan S., 51.
  Joseph T., 52.
  Mary, 25.
  Mary A., 51.
  Mathew, 52.
  Mathew J., 51.
  Nathaniel, 52.
  Nathaniel G., 51, 154.
  Sadie E., 84.
  Samuel, 50.
  Sarah E., 190.
Haseltine, James, 15.
Haskell, John K., 121.
Haskins, Dorcas, 19.
  John, 291.
  Mary, 291.
  Rachel, 19, 32.
Hassen, Richard, 5.
Hastings, F. A., 138.
Hastins, Robert, 10.
Hatch, John P., 235.
Hathaway, Henrietta B., 137.
  Mary, 94, 241.
  Sarah, 56, 84.
Haven, Alexander, 299.

Haven, Maria T., 49, 109.
  Nathaniel A., 108, 109.
  Rebecca B., 62, 139.
  William, 299.
Haverly, Catharine, 218, 224.
  Christian, 224.
Hawkins, Asael, 300.
  Charles, 300.
  Eseck, 300.
  George B., 300.
  Lavina, 36, 64.
  Lucy, 332.
  Lydia, 300.
Hayden, Nancy, 85.
Hayes, Alexander, 110.
  Cappilia M. H., 268.
  Caroline, 110.
  John L., 110.
  Maria T., 110.
  Susan L., 110.
  William A., 110.
Haynes, Jonathan, 12.
  Joseph, 12.
Hayward, William, 250.
Hazeltine, Frank R., 248.
  Roscoe L., 248.
Hazelton, David, 10.
  John, 10.
  Ladd, 25.
Hazen, Charles E., 40.
  Curtis L., 40.
  Dwight B., 40.
  Electa, 40, 70.
  Eli, 40.
  Hephziba, 13, 16.
  Jabez, 170.
  John, 40.
  Joseph, 111.
  Lois, 39, 69.
  Marcus M., 40.
  Mary, 170.
  Philena B., 70, 169.
  Rebecca, 23, 111.
  Ruth I., 40.
  Sarah, 23, 112.
  Thomas, 70.
Headley, P. C., 189.
Heath, Bert, 6.
  Caroline R., 59, 158.
  David, 35.
  Huldah, 57, 87.
  Nathaniel, 56.
  William B., 61.
Heatherton, Christopher, 278.
  John, 278.
  Joseph, 278.
  Mary, 278.
  Nancy, 278.
  William, 278.

Heaton, Maria, 104.
Headenburg, Harriet A., 156, 244.
Hedrick, Kate, 324, 325.
    William, 103.
Hember, Louisa, 334.
Henderson, Elizabeth, 214.
    Sarah, 36, 65.
Hendrix, Maria, 337.
Henry, E. S., 204.
    Euseba, 34, 61.
    Mary, 245.
Herrick, Henry, 278.
    Mira, 278.
    Phebe, 278, 279.
    Rubie, 219.
    Miss, 278.
Hersey, Love, 67.
Hess, George W., 158.
Hebbard, Chauncy, 128.
    Sarah, 30, 55.
Hewes, William, 88.
Hidden, Charles, 49.
    David, 49.
    Hubbard, 49.
    James, 49.
    John, 49.
    Joy, 49.
    Nancy, 49.
    Otis, 49.
    Otis I.., 49.
    Polly, 49.
Higgins, Addia, 162.
    Charles, 57.
    Charles O., 116.
    Royal, 57.
Hildreth, Harriet B., 344.
    Laura L., 227.
Hildrith, Caroline M., 192, 252.
Hill, Abigail, 27, 47.
    Calvin, 87.
    Clara E., 341, 342.
    Cyrus, 156.
    Hannah, 113, 217.
    Irwin A., 344.
    John M., 172.
    Mary, 155.
Hillery, Adala M., 149.
Hills, Sarah, 205.
Hilton, Abigail, 47, 107.
    Charles, 14.
    Dudley, 17, 18, 26.
    Margaret, 94.
    Mercy, 27.
    William, 14.
    Winthrop, 120.
Himes, Warren N., 125.
Hines, Benjamin, 147.
    Charlotte, 103, 147.
    Lizza, 28, 50.

Hinkley, James W., 261.
Hinkson, Daniel, 344.
    Edward, 344.
    Edwin, 344.
    Mark, 344.
Hinman, Berclay, 270.
    Clark, 96.
    Harriet, 58, 96.
    Henry J., 163.
    Lizzie M., 198.
Hirsh, J. E., 269.
Hiscock, George W., 194.
    Jesse F., 81.
Hitchcock, Albert, 178.
    James, 69.
Hoag, Mark R., 228.
Hobbie, Ebenezer, 116.
    Julia A., 44, 116.
Hockaday, Benjamin, 330.
Hocking, Mr., 327.
Hodge, Charles, 318.
    Charles J., 318.
Hodges, Fanny, 20, 38.
    John A., 105.
    Hannah, 46.
Holcomb, David, 42.
Holden, Rose, 76, 176.
Hollinger, Edward, 330.
    Elodia, 329.
Hollis, William C., 77.
Holly, Milly, 334.
    Sally, 334.
Holman, Chauncy, 121.
    Sylvester, 121.
Holmes, Almira, 39.
    Elizabeth, 231.
    Harriet, 323.
    Rebecca, 137.
    Richard, 39.
Holmstead, Thankful, 34, 60.
Holt, Isabella, 76.
    Samuel, 343.
    Sarah, 121.
    Susan, 268.
    William, 268.
    William L., 301.
Homer, Adeline D., 291, 293.
Honicut, Robert, 321.
    Thomas, 321.
Hoontoon, Elmeda, 78, 182.
    Enoch, 182.
    Josiah, 18.
    Peggy, 52, 74.
    Samuel, 18.
Hopkins, Louisa, 58, 95.
Horton, Jason, 126.
    S. B., 125.
Hotchkiss, Charles A., 68.
Hough, Mary, 112.

Houghton, Annella, 239, 260.
Hovey, Harriet L., 270.
   Mariana L., 270.
Howard, George, 297.
   J. H., 227.
   Sarah, 67.
   Theron, 34.
Howe, Eugene, 219.
   Phebe, 37.
Howell, Abigail B., 316, 318.
   Ann M., 316.
   Anna, 317.
   Anna B., 317.
   Anna L., 317.
   Annie, 316.
   Benjamin B., 316.
   Benjamin P., 316, 317.
   Charles S., 317.
   Edward C., 317.
   Evan, 315.
   Evelyn B., 318.
   Fanny, 316.
   Frances, 316.
   Frances P., 317.
   Francis L., 316, 317.
   Jacob, 314, 315.
   John, 312, 313, 314, 315.
   John A., 316.
   John L., 312, 315, 316.
   John P., 317.
   Joshua, 316.
   Joshua B., 316, 317.
   Joshua L., 315, 316, 317, 318.
   Joshua P., 316.
   Lowell L., 218.
   Mary L., 317.
   Mary M., 317.
   Paschr'l, 316.
   Rebecca, 316.
   Richard, H. O., 317.
   Richard W., 316, 317, 318.
   Samuel B., 317.
   Samuel H., 316.
   Samuel L., 316.
   Sarah, 315.
   Sarah C., 316, 317.
   Thomas C., 316.
   Thomas J., 317.
   William M., 316.
Howes, Sarah, 255.
Howland, Elijah, 53.
Howlet, Margaretta, 76, 178.
Hoyt, Hannah, 46, 113, 172.
   Harriet, 73.
   Julia A., 114, 199.
   Laura, 192, 251.
   Simeon, 199.
Hubbard, Addis, 216.
   Eliza B., 328.

Hubbard, George, 326, 330.
   Henry, 346.
   James, 327, 328.
   James E., 328.
   John, 328.
   Mary, 320, 330.
   Nimmo, 328.
   Thomas N., 328.
Hubbert, Eli, 211.
   Martha, 19, 34.
Hudson, James S., 306.
   Lucy E., 65, 211.
Hughes, J. M., 227.
Hughson, Owen, 297.
Humphrey, Frederick W. L., 270.
   Helen C., 270.
   John, 164.
   Joseph C., 270.
   Merrill L., 270.
   Sarah, 50, 140.
   William, 164.
Hunkins, Persia, 188.
Hunt, Betsey, 124, 157.
   Charles E., 263.
   Justus, 124.
   Patrick, 70.
   Sands, 88.
Hunter, Dexter, 115.
Hunting, George T., 79.
   Mrs. Maranda, 81.
Huntington, Benjamin, 198.
   Lynde, 41.
   Olive, 96.
Hurd, Hannah, 49, 108.
   Joseph, 108.
   Mary L., 49.
Hurley, Alice, 26, 45.
Huse, Elizabeth, 34, 62.
   Mary C., 57, 87.
   Ophelia C., 167.
   Samuel, 62.
Hussey, Christopher, 2, 6.
Hutchins, Bethia, 45, 106.
   Elizabeth, 336.
   Gordon, 106.
   J. M., 103.
   John, 3.
   Rebecca, 250.
   Ruth, 19, 32.
   Samuel, 10.
Hutchinson, Chandler, 57.
   Hovey, 37.
   John, 122, 162.
Huter, Thomas, 73.
Hyde, Augustus, 20.
   Hannah, 16, 22.
   Isabella, 62.
   Jacob, 22.
   James B., 62.

Hyde, Jane, 112.
   Lula M., 62.
   Maria, 40, 71.
   Martha B., 62.
   Mary, 198.
   Ruth, 16, 22.
   Silence, 16, 22.
   William, 62.
Hyser, John, 278.
   Peter, 278.

Ingalls, Betsey, 119, 154.
   Dana G., 95.
   George, 94.
   Josiah, 86.
Ingersoll, David, 98.
   George, 98.
   Medifer, 98.
   Sally, 92.
   Samuel, 98.
   Sarah, 98, 141.
   Zebulon, 98.
Ingerson, Adeline D., 98, 147.
Ingraham, Franklin B., 119.
   J. H., 180.
   Marcia C. P., 77, 180.
Ireland, Lucinda, 156, 239.
   Wilbur W., 74.
Irish, Susan, 42.
Irwin, Mary J., 135, 238.
Ives, Asenath, 42, 126.
   Henrietta, 72.
   Samantha, 37, 68.
   Warren, 59.

Jackman, James, 209.
   Lyman, 93.
   Royal, 93.
Jackson, Andrew B., 226.
   Mary E., 138, 226.
   Sally D., 340.
Jacobs, Jesse, 78.
James, Elizabeth, 302.
   Gleneria M., 184.
   Jeremiah, 184.
   Lewis L., 184.
   Margaret, 214, 241.
   Milton L., 184.
Janeway, Alice P., 318.
   Anna H., 318.
   Edward C., 318.
   Helen B., 318.
   John H., 318.
   Joshua B. H., 318.
   Margaret, 318.
   Martha G., 318.
   Robert B., 318.

Janeway, Thomas, 318.
   Thomas L., 316, 318.
Janvrien, Joseph, 62.
Jaques, Lydia M., 301, 302.
   Jeremiah, 114.
   Richard, 101.
   Sophia, 92, 101.
Jenkins, Martha, 278.
   Morrill, 153.
   Silas, 153.
Jennison, Mary, 343.
Jesseman, Lydia A., 74, 173.
Jessup, John S., 317.
Jewett, Celia, 195.
Jillson, Ollys A., 306.
   William, 74.
Jemson, Elizabeth, 46, 124.
Johnson, Amanda J., 336.
   Amos, 336.
   Asa, 394.
   Belle, 212, 255.
   Charles, 336.
   Eliza, 55, 83.
   Elizabeth, 159, 296.
   Elizabeth L., 59.
   Gideon, 294.
   Hale B., 314.
   Harriet E., 129.
   Hazen, 139.
   John, 7, 9, 10, 159, 321.
   Jonas, 336.
   Lydia, 24.
   Marcella, 334.
   Martha E., 336.
   Mary, 336.
   Matilda, 336.
   Micajah J., 330.
   Milly, 283.
   Nancy, 129, 205.
   Ruth A., 336.
   Sally, 267.
   Sally D., 314.
   Samuel, 91, 336.
   Sarah, 336.
   Seth, 294.
   Susannah, 336.
   Thomas, 159.
   Thomas L., 314.
   Timothy, 10, 91.
   William, 336.
   ———, 24, 164.
Johnston, Nora, 329, 330.
   William W., 131.
Joiner, Flecher, 280.
Jones, Amanda M., 280, 283.
   Ann, 74.
   Annie M., 103.
   Cereno P., 103.
   Clarissa, 300.

Jones, Cyrus, 50.
  Daniel, 111.
  Eliphalet, 97.
  Elizabeth N., 132.
  Elizabeth W., 110.
  Elmira, 61, 138.
  Ernest L., 103.
  Eva, 300.
  Evan, 17.
  Frederick W., 103.
  Grace L., 103.
  Harrison, 103.
  Helen A., 103.
  Herbert L., 103.
  Howard P., 103.
  James H., 316.
  J. B., 206.
  John, 319.
  John R., 61.
  Joseph, 322.
  Josephine M., 103.
  Loa, 95.
  Maria, 67.
  Miriam S., 184.
  Sally, 121, 341.
  St. Clair, 103.
  Susan, 133.
  Susan F., 102.
  Sydney S., 103.
  William, 132.
Jordon, Emeline, 301, 302.
  Ida, 324, 325.
Jose, Hannah, 284.
  Nathaniel, 284.
Joslid, Grant, 301.
Joyce, Sarah, 273.
Judkins, Edwin, 85.
  Maria, 323, 324.
June, Jennie, 163.
Jutua, Amenda, 62.

Kaeding, Charles, 215.
  George S., 215.
  Henry B., 215.
Kane, Hannah, 122, 213.
Katherns, Daniel, 50.
Kayment, Charles H., 205.
Keen, Emily, 67, 166.
  Sophia, 67, 166.
Keith, A. J., 334.
  Asa, 334.
Kelley, Eliza, 247.
  George, 289.
  Lavina, 302, 303.
  Mary E., 340.
Kellogg, Caroline, 278.
  Chauncy, 137.
  Theresa M., 137.

Kelly, Cynthia, 306, 308.
  Phebe, 306.
Kelsey, William, 35.
Kemp, Sally, 57, 87.
Kempton, William H., 268.
Kendall, George C., 153.
  Huldah, 149.
  M. D., 96.
  Percis, 49.
  William M., 250.
Kenedy, Rebecca, 125.
Kenney, Alfred, 280.
  Angie M., 284.
  Arthur B., 284.
  Carrie, 284.
  Charles S., 218.
  Clayton, 284.
  Clinton, 284.
  Lester, 284.
  Rebecca, 219.
  Woodbridge, 284.
Kenniston, J. L., 86.
Kent, Caroline E., 76.
Kenyon, Joel M., 80.
  John, 299.
  Ruhamah, 302, 303.
Kerral, Margaret M., 280, 282.
Ketchum, Phebe, 279.
Keyes, Isabel, 121, 209.
Keyser, Susan H., 87, 197.
Kezer, Joseph, 113.
Kierman, Francis, 81.
Killman, Sadie, 219.
Killmer, Sarah, 296, 297.
Kimball, B. F., 34.
  David, 304.
  Josiah, 27.
  Sarah F., 271.
  ———, 27.
King, Alice, 278.
  Andrew, 319.
  Henry, 37.
  Jeremiah, 197.
  Nathaniel, 326.
  Sarah M., 326.
Kingley, Alpheus, 198.
Kingman, Abel, 143.
  A. W., 232.
  Lucy W., 101, 143, 231.
Kingsbury, Hannah, 43, 125.
  Henry, 1.
  Jabez, 128.
  Sarah, 37, 67.
  Susannah, 13, 16.
Kinison, Sarah F., 92.
Kiniston, Mary S., 257.
Kirkpatrick, Mary, 215.
Ketchell, Charlotte H., 55, 84.
  H. D., 84, 189.

Knights, Augustus, 111.
    Hanniel P., 209.
    William, 34.
Knowles, Henry F., 139.
Knowlton, Louisa C., 93, 104.
    Nathaniel, 104.
Knox, Mary D. C., 58.
Koons, Alice, 279.
    Brice, 279.
    Charles, 279.
    Emma, 279.
    Hattie, 279.
    Jacob, 279.
    Jay, 279.
    John, 279.
    Mary, 279, 283.
    Nattie, 279.
    Sarah, 279, 281.
    William, 279.
Kusey, Silas H., 337.
Kuver, John, 336.

Laird, Marion, 157.
Lake, Charles E., 252.
    Flora D., 252.
    Franklin O., 252.
    George E., 252.
    Julia W., 252.
    Olive, 198.
    William, 252.
Lamb, James, 41.
Lammon, Caleb C., 294.
Lamphrey, Henrietta, 198, 246.
    Uriah, 246.
Lamson, Lydia, 216.
Lanckton, Roger, 2.
Landers, Sylvia L., 261.
Lane, David, 38.
    Gilbert, 118.
    Mary, 54.
    Sally, 62, 264.
Lang, David, 184.
    Eliza, 119, 152.
    Isaiah, 79.
    Lucinda, 79, 184.
    Sarah A., 79, 184.
    Thomas E., 81.
Langdon, Caroline, 49.
    Charlotte, 49.
    Elizabeth, 49.
    Harriet, 49.
    John, 49.
    Mary, 49.
    Sarah, 49.
    Sophia, 49.
Langley, Joseph, 36.
    Melissa, 172.
Lany, William W., 288.

Lash, Peter, 294.
Lather, Eliza, 62.
Lathrop, Benjamin, 128.
    Caroline V., 230.
    Eben W., 212.
    John, 42.
    Oliver, 126.
    Susalla, 24, 42.
Lawrence, Ann, 226, 227.
    Betsey, 114.
    Ebenezer S., 114.
    James, 30.
    John A., 113.
    Mary M., 304.
    Susannah, 126, 218.
    William, 126.
    W. Q., 327.
Lawson, Frank R., 140.
    George D., 140.
    Lydia F., 140.
    Peter, 140.
Lawton, Arvesta H., 168, 220.
    George, 288.
    ———, 289.
Lazarus, Martha, 210, 250.
    Nicholas, 250.
Lazel, Norman, 197.
Leach, Elijah, 113.
    E. P., 111.
    Sarah E., 95.
Leavenworth, Margaret J., 268, 269.
Leavins, Celia, 95, 220.
Leavitt, Stephen, 29.
Lee, Mary E., 306, 308.
Leet, Asa P., 175.
    Bestina A., 175.
    Clarence M., 175.
    Jeffries W., 175.
    Roscoe L., 175.
Leland, Emogene L., 174.
Lemmons, Nathan, 334.
Leonard, Benjamin, 168.
    Fannie A., 68, 168.
Lester, Caty, 278, 280.
Levere, Eugene, 139.
Lewis, Ann M., 301.
    Anna, 301.
    Aschel H., 300.
    Beda, 300.
    Benjamin, 301.
    Bessie L., 276.
    Daniel, 300.
    Daniel L., 301.
    Edwin E., 82.
    Eleanor, 135, 300.
    Eleanor D., 300.
    Eolin P., 301.
    Isaac, 300.
    Jesse, 301.

Lewis, John L., 300.
   Jonathan, 300.
   Josiah B., 300.
   Martha, 25, 89, 328, 329.
   Mary, 299, 300, 302, 316, 317.
   Mary E., 276.
   Moses, 300, 301.
   Peleg, 301.
   Rachel, 316, 317.
   Samuel, 302.
   Sarah, 300.
   Solomon, 299.
   William T., 276.
Libby, George W., 332.
   Lovina A., 95.
   Luther, 332.
   Mary E., 332.
   Stanhope, 332.
Liddell, Mary M., 265.
Lifeholly, Mark, 319.
Liffengwall, Betsey, 22, 40.
Lillibridge, Rhoda, 69, 168.
Lilly, Abigail, 16.
   Emma, 16.
   Hannah, 16.
   Samuel, 16.
Linch, John, 319.
Lincoln, W. A., 62.
Litchfield, Eleazer, 270.
   Harriet L., 270.
Littlehale, Richard, 69, 168.
Lloyd, George, 339.
   Malone, 317.
Locey, Charles, 115.
Lock, Daniel, 89.
   Elisha, 36.
   Hannah, 19, 35.
   Nellie, 79, 186.
   Rachel, 195.
   Sarah, 19, 36.
Locke, Daniel, 261.
   Rosella, 261, 262.
Locking, Lucy A., 213, 255.
Lomax, Abel, 336, 337.
   Alfred, 337.
   Ann E., 337.
   Anna, 337.
   Augusta E., 337.
   Constantine, 337.
   Elizabeth S., 337.
   Isabel, 337.
   Jesse O., 337.
   Joanna, 337.
   Joseph, 337.
   Joseph A., 337.
   Luna B., 337.
   Martha E., 337.
   Mary, 337.
   Mary E., 337.

Lomax, Nancy, 337.
   Robert, 337.
   Sarah, 337.
   Sarah A., 337.
   William, 337.
   William K., 337.
Long, Alvira D., 113.
   Elizabeth M., 108.
Longmaid, Edward, 87.
Loomis, Charles D., 255.
   Elizabeth, 69.
   Sibel, 24.
Lord, Buckminster, 49.
   Caroline, 49.
   Charles, 49.
   Diodate, 39.
   Harriet, 49.
   John, 49.
   John P., 49.
   Mary E., 39.
   Samuel P., 49.
   Susan, 49.
   William, 49.
Loring, Sarah, 153.
Lovejoy, Caleb, 57.
   Emma G., 306, 308.
   Jerusha, 31, 57.
   John, 20.
   John L., 308.
Loveland, Helen, 71, 169.
Lovett, Henry B., 273.
Lowe, Harriet L., 270.
Lowell, Daniel, 345.
   Dean, 73.
   Dorcas, 50, 73.
   Eliza, 73, 172.
   Frederick, 73.
   George, 73.
   George P., 136.
   James R., 159.
   Lois A., 73.
   Richard, 73.
   Thomas, 73.
Lowry, Elizabeth, 165, 226.
Luce, Daniel, 136.
   Lewis, 137.
   Sabra, 192, 252.
Luevey, Sarah, 35, 63.
Luff, Edward, 135.
Lunt, Ada F., 166, 343.
Lyford, Eunice, 46, 114.
   Judith, 26, 45.
Lyman, George, 130.

Mack, Bessie M., 205.
   Frank P., 205.
   Hazel L., 205.
Mackie, Olive, 88.

Macomber, J. E., 104.
Maddox, Mary E., 340.
Maddison, Mary E., 306.
Mahan, Alexander, 299.
   Franklin, 299.
   Seneca, 299.
Majors, Rev. Mr., 336.
Mallard, William, 338.
Manchester, ——, 290.
   James, 290.
Manle, Ebenezer, 326.
Manly, Betsey, 143.
   Thomas, 65.
Mann, Cyrus, 73.
   William R., 230.
Mansell, Susan, 268.
Mansfield, Melinda, 82, 274.
Maples, Emily, 300.
   Ursula, 300.
Marble, Edward A., 210.
   Lydia, 17, 24.
Markel, Finnis M., 278.
   Jacob, 278.
   Lodowick, 278.
   Mehitable, 278.
   Peter, 278.
   William, 278.
Marsh, Onesiphorus, 8, 10, 11.
Marshall, Emily, 98.
   Joseph, 126.
   Sally, 29, 52.
   W. W., 266.
Marston, Arthusa, 122, 211.
   Betsey L., 55, 124.
   J. D., 119.
   Mary A., 157.
   Theodore, 29.
Martin, Abigail, 29, 53, 118, 149.
   Benjamin, 36.
   Emily J., 307, 309.
   James, 126.
   Lydia M., 105, 149.
   Nathaniel, 149.
   William, 149, 218.
Marvin, Julia E., 292.
Masall, M., 319.
Mason, Eleanor, 73, 172.
   John T., 110.
   Polly, 52, 74.
   Susan, 113, 217.
   Susan C., 157, 256.
Massey, Isaac, 337.
Masterman, Clara A., 67.
   Daniel S., 67.
   Eliza E., 67.
   Esther J., 67.
   Phebe M., 67.
Matheny, Joel T., 158.
Mather, Cotton, 89.

Mathew, Huldah, 297.
Mathews, James, 58.
Mattock, Amos, 210.
   Larissa D., 107, 210.
   William P., 251.
McAlster, Rosetta, 95, 228.
McAlvain, Caroline, 192, 251.
McBride, Mary, 304, 305.
McCleary, Martha, 25, 93.
   Thomas, 93.
McClellan, Gen., 181, 182.
McCordia, Alfred E., 130.
McCready, Anna, 55, 82.
McCue, Cornelia, 322.
McDonal, Nancy, 278, 279.
McDowell, Mary E., 118, 207.
McElroy, Sally, 76.
McGreggor, McDonough, 163.
McGushea, Mr., 332.
McHatten, Rev. Alexander, 337.
McKelsey, Maggie, 157.
McKenly, Mary, 256.
McLean, Edwin, 129.
   Obed, 41.
McLellan, Eunice, 326.
McMillen, Alexander, 280.
McMurber, Rose A., 279.
McNeil, Abraham, 276.
   Albert, 165.
   Elizabeth P., 275, 276.
   Jennie M., 276.
McNelly, William, 198.
Meacham, Giles, 128.
   Sarah H., 169, 220.
Mead, Abigail, 153.
   Abigail K., 119.
   George L., 114.
   Perey A., 147.
   Perley A., 94.
   Thomas, 87.
Meader, Eleanor, 86, 194.
   Mehitable, 86, 194.
Medcalf, Mary, 313.
Medbury, Charles E., 300.
   George B., 300.
   George P., 300.
   Ida, 300.
   Lowell E., 300.
   Minnie S., 300.
   Oscar, 300.
Meigs, Renzo, 140.
Melvin, Ethan, 64.
   Mary D., 35.
Meredith, Mr., 332.
Merrie, Joseph, 2.
Merrill, Alta, 301.
   Burke, 65.
   Harriet, 65.
   Henry, 65.

Merrill, Herbert, 65.
    Mary, 13, 17.
    Nathaniel, 7, 17.
    Sally, 61.
    Sarah, 19, 32, 34.
    Wait, 65.
Merrian, Dr. A., 44.
Merry, Jane, 279.
Messer, James, 25.
    Mary, 97, 123.
Mickle, Hannah, 311, 313.
    Isaac, 311, 314.
Miles, Mrs. Maranda, 81.
Miller, Elizabeth P., 215, 245.
    Ellen, 326, 327.
    George, 241.
    Jeremiah, 245.
    Marietta, 198, 246.
    Russell, 218.
    Stephen, 245.
Mills, Fred. G., 272.
    George, 280.
    Isabella E., 327.
Minge, Collier H., 322.
Mitchell, Dorothy B., 318.
    Hugh E., 318.
Moffatt, Mary T., 110.
Moody, Benjamin, 98.
    Ella F., 271.
    Henry C., 103.
    Lewis P., 87.
    Luady, 340.
    Mary, 18, 29.
    Ruth, 98.
Moore, A. J., 339.
    Albion, 63.
    Asa, 194.
    Augustus, 170.
    Daniel, 164.
    Dorcas, 49, 121.
    Edward L., 171.
    Henry, 98.
    Nancy, 170.
    Ransom S., 158.
    Roberta, 170, 171.
    Tryphena, 65.
    Tryphena E., 164.
Moors, Aurilla, 70.
Montgomery, Sarah, 93.
    W. R., 328.
Morey, Charles, 115.
Morgan, David, 32.
    Deborah, 206.
    Ira, 32.
    Jeremiah, 32.
    Jesse, 32.
    Lois, 32.
    Lucinda, 32.
    Mary E., 70, 204.

Morgan, Trueworthy, 32.
Morrill, Dorothy, 54.
    Eliza, 207.
    Laforest, 251.
    Lucy, 261, 271.
    Luther, 140.
Morris, Ann, 216.
    Mrs. Jane, 295.
Morrison, Daniel, 54.
    Eben, 54.
    Gilman, 74.
    Stephen, 119.
Morrow, Ann, 106, 135.
    William, 135.
Morse, Abner, 117.
    Addie, 343.
    A. Frank, 176.
    Darius, 61.
    David, 57.
    Frank B., 102.
    George H., 102.
    Gertrude, 102.
    Harriet M., 45, 117.
    Hattie L., 209.
    Horace, 102.
    Horace H., 102.
    Horace T., 146.
    Ira, 38.
    Leslie, 102.
    Lillian, 257.
    Lyman, 78.
    Mabel, 102.
    Mary, 36, 65.
    Mary E., 202.
    Nellie A., 102.
    Philip, 37.
    Rebecca, 102, 146.
    Rebecca G., 200, 202.
    Sarah, 18, 27, 185.
    Sarah E., 281.
    William G., 200, 202.
Morton, James, 337.
Mosby, Edward, 321.
Moss, Amos D., 323.
    Ellen D., 322.
Mott, John S., 215.
    L. A., 23.
    Mary E., 141, 215.
Moulton, Ann E., 85.
    David, 267.
    Eliza, 81.
    Mary, 80.
    Ruth, 37, 66.
    William, 45.
Mountcastle, Martha, 332.
    R. B., 328.
    William, 332.
Movy, Asael, 283.
Mudgett, Hannah, 267.

Munger, Charles A., 144.
Munn, Ellen E., 239.
   Florence L., 239.
   George L., 239.
   Loyal L., 239.
   Loyal L., Jr., 239.
Munroe, Abby, 296.
   William N., 306.
Murphy, Charles E., 151.
   Daniel F., 134.
   Herman D., 134.
   Lydia B., 296, 297.
Mussey, Rev. Mr., 49.

Nasbe, F. O., 262.
Nash, Abigail, 65.
   Joel, 17.
Nason, Lura, 192, 252.
   William, 341.
Nay, John, 18.
Neil, Frances, 74.
   Marie E., 317.
   William, 317.
Nettleton, Ruth A., 158, 227.
Newcomb, Ellen, 194.
Newton, Caroline, 345.
   Charles, 125.
   Charles I., 125.
   Diana, 125.
   Fanny, 125.
   George, 125.
   Norman, 125.
   Rix, 125.
   Roxanna, 125.
   Truman, 125.
Nickerson, Thomas, 53.
Nichols, Benjamin, 210.
   Harriet, 293.
   Juliet C., 341.
   Martha J., 107, 210.
   Polly, 75, 174.
   Susan, 306.
Niles, Augusta, 109, 130.
   Charles, 145.
   Delia, 301.
   John F., 162.
   Luduska, 301, 303.
Nimmo, Emma S., 328.
Nixon, Barnaby, 320.
Noble Electa, 41, 72.
   Sarah J., 199, 246.
Norcross, Albert, 139.
Norman, Henry H., 295.
   Thomas, 338.
Norris, Dorcas, 124, 156.
   John, 154.
North, Elizabeth, 164.
Norton, Eliza, 279, 282.

Norton, Reuben, 279.
Nourse, Benjamin, 237.
   Sarah J., 134, 237.
Noyes, Aaron, 32.
   H. Charles, 302.
   James, 89.
   Joseph, 89.
   Sarah, 25, 89, 101.
   Thomas, 89.
   William, 89.
Nugent, Charles F., 300.

Oakley, James A., 332.
Obear, Clark H., 98.
O'Donoghue, Ann S., 141, 215.
   Thomas, 215.
O'Hara, Mary, 229.
Oler, Allen, 338.
   Martin, 338.
Olin, Esther, 300.
Olmstead, Alida, 345, 346.
   Simeon, 35.
Olney, Elizabeth, 294.
   Emor, 294, 296.
   Gideon, 294.
   Lydia, 294.
   Rhoda, 296.
O'Neal, George H., 77.
Orien, James, 343.
Orr, Catharine, 26, 272.
   Christopher, 272.
Osgood, Helen A., 183.
   Polly, 45, 118.
   Ulysses, 52.
Ostrander, James, 163.
Otis, Celinda, 23, 41.
   James, 41.
Overstreet, Elizabeth, 77, 178.
Oviatt, Ginevra T., 165, 266.
   William C., 266.
Owen, Huldah, 119, 154.
   Miriam, 34.
   Wesley, 122.

Packard, Prof. A. S., 235.
   Laura A., 122, 136.
   Sarah E., 115.
Page, Charles A., 110.
   George, 87.
   John, 3.
   Widow, 24.
Paine, Amasa, 66.
   Eliza B., 156, 244.
   Josie M., 252.
   ——, 86.
Palmer, Aaron A., 134.
   Abbie L., 134.

Palmer, Amanda, 134.
   Aurelia, 55, 82.
   Charles, 67.
   Charles G., 134.
   Charles W., 67.
   Charlotte E., 134.
   Clara L. H., 134.
   George B., 134.
   Heber C., 134.
   Henry, 2.
   Jane H., 67.
   John W., 79, 134.
   Lucretia J., 134.
   Nancy A., 67.
   Robinson, 329.
   Rose, 67.
   ——, 30.
Park, Joseph, 97.
   Mary, 97.
Parker, Ann C., 156, 239.
   Betsey, 144.
   Calvin M., 300.
   Daniel, 300.
   Daniel W., 300.
   Dean R., 234.
   Emily F., 300.
   Esther, 16, 19, 300.
   George W., 300.
   Henry, 94.
   Isabel S., 144, 234.
   James, 300.
   Jane E., 300.
   Joel, 329.
   John, 300.
   John J., 300.
   Joseph, 38, 68, 313.
   Julia A., 300.
   Mary, 300, 313.
   Noah, 300.
   Rebecca, 300.
   Rev. Robert, 89.
   Sarah, 300.
   Sarah L., 300.
   Stephen, 300.
   Susan P., 300.
Parkhurst, Adelphia C., 75, 175.
Parks, Ann, 37.
   Charles, 37.
   Daniel, 37.
   Eliza, 37.
   Hannah, 37.
   Joseph, 97.
   Mary, 97.
   Susan, 37.
   Wealthy, 37.
Parlow, Eliza, 278, 279.
Parsons, Achsah, 129, 205.
   Ambrose, 157.
   Charles A., 196.

Parsons, Elizabeth, 169, 221.
   Hannah, 44, 115.
   John, 321.
   Samuel, 326.
   Seba, 70, 169.
   William, 56.
Paschall, Frances, 315.
Patten, Laura, 267, 268.
Patterson, Daniel, 135.
   Elizabeth, 345.
   Harriet, 76.
   Mary, 276.
Paull, Margaret, 70.
Paulus, Anna, 338.
Payne, William, 1.
Pearce, Richard, 290.
Pearson, David, 250.
   Henry M., 113.
   Jane, 136, 250.
   Judith, 332.
Pease, Charlotte, 138, 200.
   George, 200.
Peasly, Joseph, 3.
Peck, Barton P., 44.
   Clarissa, 112.
   Ellen A., 44.
   Emma, 153, 243.
   Eugene, 44.
   George W., 61.
   Hannah B., 45.
   Henry C., 45.
   James B., 61.
   James W., 61.
   John W., 301.
   Josiah, 44.
   Lewis J., 45.
   Lucy, 112, 197.
   Malissa, 112, 197.
   Marcus, 66.
   Marilla, 301.
   Mary A., 44.
   Nancy, 40, 70.
   Rufus, 301.
   Rufus L., 301.
   Samuel W., 45.
Pellett, Nancy, 334.
Penn, William, 312, 317.
Pennington, ——, 339.
Pepper, Sophronia, 345.
Percival, Betsey, 24.
Perham, Aura, 252.
   Josephine, 212.
Perkins, Abigail, 16, 23.
   Brimsley, 25.
   Elias, 280.
   Henry, 30.
   Irene, 192, 251.
   Jabez, 30.
   Lizzie, 67, 166.

Perkins, Louisa A. P., 25.
   Melissa, 342.
   Melissa I., 174.
   True, 118.
   Wealthea, 20, 38.
Perley, Martha, 144.
   Stephen, 46.
Perry, Charles, 112, 175.
   Gardner B., 100.
   Louisa, 53, 75.
   Sarah, 318.
   Thomas, 75.
Pervier, Lydia A., 52, 274.
Pervis, Charles, 74.
Peters, Sophronia, 170.
Peterson, Jane E., 284.
Pethybridge, Edward W., 206.
Phelps, Abbie S., 204.
   Gertrude G., 145, 235.
   Martin, 34.
Philbrook, Betsey, 192.
   Hannah, 267.
   James, 267.
   Mary, 267.
   Mehitable, 14, 18.
Phillips, Aphia, 46.
   H. M., 209.
   James, 98.
   Jeremiah, 56.
   Mary R., 268.
   Sarah, 284.
Phippen, G. S., 61.
Pickney, Charles C., 193.
Pierce, Augustus, 42.
   Charles, 252.
   George, 289.
   George W., 104.
   Martha, 89.
   Myrick, 153.
   Otis, 252.
   Sarah, 98.
   Stephen, 40.
   Warren L., 192.
Pierson, William, 65.
Pike, Hannah, 57, 87.
   Hiram, 73.
   Mary, 73.
   Sarah, 73.
   Seymour, 163.
Pillsbury, Esther, 35, 63.
Pingree, John, 88.
Pink, Marian, 66.
Pinkerton, William, 319.
Pixley, William, 38.
Platt, Alfred G., 158.
   Emeline F., 136, 158.
Pleasants, J., 321.
   Thomas, 321.
   William H., 321.

Plumb, Lucy L., 55, 83.
Plumer, Rebecca, 120, 154.
   Samuel, 154.
Plummer, Abigail, 46, 114.
   David, 114.
   Emma, 206, 256.
Plympton, Edward, 44.
   Eveline S., 205.
Pollard, Emily, 93, 103.
   Gardner, 103.
Pollock, John, 82.
   Narcissus, 82.
   Waldron, 82.
Polwin, John, 319.
Pomeroy, Jane F., 276.
   Susan M., 275, 277.
Pool, Sarah B., 191, 249.
Pooler, Anna M., 65.
Poor, Frederick L., 92.
   William, 92.
   William B., 92.
Porter, Ellen M., 199, 247.
   Jonathan, 16.
   Louisa, 104, 148.
   Mary, 49.
   Zoe M., 199.
Post, Nathan, 168.
   Smith, 96.
Potter, Aaron, 124.
   Elias, 40.
   Sarah, 299, 305.
   Sarah E., 77, 178.
   Stephen, 305.
Powers, Rebecca, 156, 239.
Pratt, Charles, 147.
   Mrs. T. W., 178.
   William D., 343.
Pray, John, 85.
Preble, Peter, 320.
Prentice, Joseph C., 347.
   Louisa, 302, 304.
   Mary E., 95.
   Stephen, 23.
Prescott, Abbie M., 88.
   Alvan, 88.
   Benjamin J., 88.
   Celistia, 88.
   Dudley, 114.
   Emily A., 98.
   Greenleaf, 122.
   Hannah, 215, 255.
   Heman, 88.
   Laura, 88.
   Nahum, 88.
   Otis, 88.
   Rachel, 46, 114.
Pressey, Fred., 192.
   Miriam, 92.
   Sarah, 193, 252.

Preston, Albert R., 167.
Priest, Eliza, 146.
   John J., 146.
Prince, James, 30.
Pringle, Sarah, 214.
Prior, Erastus L., 301.
Proctor, Helen, 198, 246.
   William, 246.
   ———, 29.
Prowse, Abigail, 106, 134.
Pryor, Roswell, 20.
   Sally, 20, 38.
Pulsifer, Lewis, 67.
   Mary, 137.
Putnam, Edward F., 25.

Quackenbush, Mary, 210.
   Sidney, 210.
Quarles, Henry F., 326.
   James C., 326.
   Lucy B., 326.
   Samuel B., 326.
   Samuel C., 326.
   William E., 326.
Quellen, Mary, 214.
Quimby, Jacob, 261.
   Mary P., 261.
   Mehitable, 261.
   Mercy, 122, 212.
   Rhoda, 56, 85.
   Sally, 213, 272.
   Sarah, 122.
   S. F., 254.
   ———, 140.

Raiguel, Mary E., 292.
Ralston, John A., 71.
Rand, Alfa, 125.
   Edmund, 185.
   Hannah M., 75, 185.
Randall, Alton, 192.
   George K., 212.
Randlett, John, 124.
Randolph, Azelle, 228, 263.
Ranger, Addie, 88.
Ransom, Mary, 165, 225.
   Roanna, 36, 65.
Rawlins, Rachel, 17.
Ray, Henry P., 301.
Raymond, Lizzie, 198, 209.
Reddington, Elizabeth, 20, 37.
Reardon, Kittie L., 339, 340.
Rearick, John, 301.
Reed, Alvin, 74.
   Fred., 343.
   Maria, 102.
   Milton, 102.

Reed, Philander L., 121, 209.
   S. G., 242.
   Sophia, 102.
   Stephen, 209.
   Waldo, 102.
   William, 102.
Reedhead, Hannah L., 61, 138.
Regan, Mary, 139.
Reynolds, Hannah, 300.
   Mary, 123.
   Nellie R., 104, 258.
Rhodes, Charles, 293.
Rice, Franklin B., 66.
   Henrietta, 307.
   John L., 208.
   Joseph, 280.
   Lucy A., 306, 307.
   Miss, 280.
   William, 194.
Richards, Betsey, 124.
   Lucy, 70, 169.
   Priscilla D., 161.
   Rachel, 53, 77.
Richardson, Abial, 20, 36.
   Bradbury, 27.
   Caleb, 10, 11.
   Eliza, 295.
   Elisha, 25.
   Francis, 156.
   Harriet, 297.
   Jerry C., 295.
   J. H., 136.
   John M., 295.
   Marshall D., 81.
   Mary, 11, 295, 298.
   Martha H., 74.
   Nathaniel P., 88.
   Orson A., 118.
   Ruth, 11.
   Silas, 295.
   W. W., 123.
   Mr., 50.
Riddell, Betsey, 266.
   Mary, 295, 298.
Ridley, Elizabeth, 140, 214.
   Samuel P., 78.
   William, 214.
Rigger, Margaret, 326.
Riggs, Nancy, 36, 64.
Rinehart, Sheldon, 214.
Ring, Daniel, 54.
   Sarah, 33, 59.
Robbins, Eleazer, 29.
   Mary, 158, 339.
Roberts, Daniel, 171.
   Emma, 212.
   F. H., 86.
   Martha, 86.
   Mehitable, 15, 19.

Roberts, Nancy, 56, 86.
   Samuel, 13.
Robertson, Elizabeth, 61, 138.
Robie, Clarie N., 74, 173.
   Jonathan, 93.
Robinson, Abigail, 111, 112.
   Ada L., 322.
   Mrs. Betsey, 88.
   Charles G., 322.
   Daniel, 68.
   Franklin, 54.
   George D., 203.
   Horace, 54.
   John, 2, 3, 7.
   Joseph, 67.
   Lorenda, 53, 75.
   Mary, 50, 184.
   Persis, 37, 68.
   Polly, 111.
   Profinda, 46, 120.
   Sarah J., 211.
   Susan, 54, 176.
   Thomas, 54.
   William, 54.
Rock, Louisa, 74, 173.
Rocklyft, Joseph V., 268.
Rodiman, Amos B., 79.
Rodes, James, 339.
Rogers, Angis, 76.
   Charles E., 76.
   John, 119.
   Thomas J., 192.
Rollins. Aaron, 28, 88.
   Betsey, 57, 88.
   Charles W., 196.
   David, 57.
   Deborah, 195.
   Ebenezer, 172.
   Enoch, 121.
   John, 45.
   John A., 123.
   Joseph T., 195.
   Mary, 192.
   Mary M., 73, 172.
Root, Sarshal, 294.
Ropes, Charles J., 292.
   Hardy, 291.
   Mary L., 291.
   Sarah, 291.
   William L., 291.
Rose, Caroline, 133, 235.
   Loretta, 341, 342.
   Nancy, 280, 281.
   Robert H., 134, 235.
Rounda, Alvin, 74.
   Carrie B., 74.
   Flora G., 74.
Roundy, W. K., 212.
Rouse, John J., 273.

Rowe, Caroline, 284, 341.
   Nancy, 52, 74.
   Robert, 52.
Rowell, Grace, 46, 121.
   Valentine, 2.
Rowen, Jane, 63.
Rowland, Rev. William T., 48.
Ruggles, William, 212.
Rundlet, Anna, 14.
   Catharine, 14.
   Charles, 14.
   Lydia, 14.
   Mary, 14.
   Nathaniel, 14.
Russ, Jane A., 216.
   Jane C., 123.
Russell, Harriet N., 104, 148.
   Leonard F., 306.
   Whitfield, 277.
   William, 7, 87, 106.
   William L., 106.
Rust, Elizabeth, 16, 19.
Rutherford, Frances, 216, 275.

Sabine, Eunice, 22, 39.
   Jerusha, 16, 20.
Sadler, Anthony, 2.
Sales, Cynthia, 266.
Salisbury, Deborah, 89, 98.
Salmond, William, 98.
Saltonstall, Col. Nathaniel, 9.
Sammons, Mary, 282.
Sampson, Joseph, 16.
Sanborn, Benjamin, 18.
   Daniel, 113, 149.
   Elisha, 46.
   Eliza, 46.
   Elizabeth, 14, 18.
   Florence, 341.
   George C., 157.
   Harold W., 341.
   James, 46.
   John, 118.
   John J., 97.
   Joseph, 38, 68.
   Josiah, 57.
   Luella, 217, 257.
   Lydia, 29, 45, 55, 122.
   Nancy, 86, 193.
   Nathaniel, 46.
   Priscilla, 30, 56.
   Ruth J., 149.
   Sally, 184.
   Susan, 55.
   Wilmont K., 341.
   ———, 27.
Sanderson, Nancy, 115.
Sanford, Charles, 82.

Sanford, Hannah, 22, 40.
Sargent, Amos. 125.
   Catharine, 58.
   Ella, 195.
   James F., 61.
   Joshua, 25.
   Thomas, 152.
Saroyex, Catharine, 279.
Savage, Harper I., 66.
   Henry, 2.
   Mary E., 317, 318.
   M. R. Allen, 66.
   William L., 318.
Sawyer, Adeline, 122, 213.
   Hannah, 93, 105.
   Jonathan, 9, 14.
   Moses, 87.
   Sarah E. D., 284.
   Sarah M., 105, 149.
   Thomas, Jr., 306.
   William A., 269.
Sayres, Robert, 1, 288.
Scammons, Martha, 33, 273.
Schermerhorn, Eliza, 279, 282.
Schnägerl, Edward O., 153.
Schrader, Charles A., 241.
Schuyler, Jennie, 273.
Scofield, Eugene M., 298.
   Mabel L., 298.
   Ray F., 298.
Scott, Amasa, 163.
   Elijah, 44.
   Lucius, 40.
   Ruth A., 40, 71.
Scribner, Esther, 255.
Scripture, Abigail, 20, 37.
   Simeon, 37.
Seabury, Abigail, 290.
   Barnabas, 290.
   Comfort, 290.
   Deborah, 290.
   Elizabeth, 290.
   Gideon, 289.
   Hannah, 289, 290.
   Ichabod, 290.
   John, 289.
   Joseph, 289.
   Lillis, 290.
   Mary, 290.
   Nathaniel, 290.
   Patience, 290.
   Phebe, 289, 290.
   Samuel, 290.
   Sarah, 290.
   William, 290.
Sears, Anna L., 86, 196.
Seavey, Benjamin, 57.
Seavy, A. C., 341.
Sellors, Lucy, 23, 60.

Sessions, Susan, 128.
Severence, Charles, 81.
   Luther, 180.
Severns, Benjamin, 125.
   George, 125.
   Hannah E., 125.
   Lizzie, 125.
   Roxanna, 125.
Sewall, Mary, 291.
   Samuel G., 291.
   William, 291.
Sewell, William J., 328.
Sharkey, M. D. L., 135.
Sharpe, Emilus, 118.
Shatwell, Theophilus, 6.
Shattuck, Ada I., 202, 221.
   Mary, 76, 177.
   Norman, 177.
Shaulter, Amanda, 128, 222.
Shaw, Amanda, 307.
   Dora A., 323.
   Stella S., 323.
Sheaf, William, 256.
Sheldon, Albert M., 297.
   Minerva, 306, 308.
Shepard, Alonzo, 251.
   Anna M., 303, 305.
Sherborn, Caleb C., 106.
   Ephel M., 106.
   Eveline M., 106.
   Gertrude A., 106.
   Mabel E. C., 106.
   Nathaniel, 106.
   Nathaniel A., 106.
   William W., 106.
Sherman, H. B., 62.
   Sarah, 299.
   Sarah S., 326.
   Zervia, 64, 163.
Sherratt, Hugh, 6.
Sherwell, Jane, 212, 255.
Shockley, Julia, 141, 214.
Shorey, Sumner B., 166.
Short, Mr., 336.
Shortwell, Nancy, 140, 213.
Shumberger, Mary, 225.
Shurgart, Henry, 337.
Sias, Tamison, 26, 46.
Sibley, H. H., 346.
Siley, Abigail, 20.
Silk, Robert, 319.
Simmous, Patience, 37, 66.
   Thankful, 37, 66.
Simonds, John, 85.
   Walter, 85.
Simons, Meribah, 56.
   Timothy, 30.
   ———, 88.
Singletery, Lydia, 11.

Skews, Mary E., 139.
Skinner, Emeline, 276.
   Helen B., 262, 263.
Slack, Hannah R., 336.
Slafter, Ann, 37.
Slasou, James L., 165.
Slawson, John, 283.
Sleeper, Carrie T., 238.
   Gilbert C., 74.
   Harriet, 74.
   John, 74.
   Melinda S., 74.
Slosson, Horace, 65.
Smiley, James, 53.
Smith, Abigail, 145.
   Alexis, 296.
   Amos, 256.
   Annie E., 136.
   Archia B., 184.
   Arthur, 194.
   Azurba, 93.
   Benjamin, 28, 50, 296.
   Betsey, 39.
   C. K., 117.
   Celeste, 117.
   Charles, 37, 199.
   Charles V., 184.
   D. E., 119.
   D. R., 42.
   Daniel, 26.
   Daniel E., 95.
   Dolly, 46, 119.
   Dorithy, 50, 73.
   Dudley, 50.
   Dyer S., 50, 184.
   Edward A., 184.
   Edward M., 248.
   Elizabeth, 53, 75.
   Ella B., 109.
   Emma, 28.
   Emma L., 117.
   Eva C., 136.
   Ezra T., 184.
   Fanny E., 109.
   Frances, 93.
   Fred. F., 117.
   George, 96, 192.
   Greenleaf, 28.
   Gustavus, 136.
   H. B., 208.
   Harriet A., 56.
   Harry C., 136.
   Henry L., 109.
   Henry, 170.
   J. C., 83.
   Jabez, 39.
   Jacob, 27, 30.
   Jacob S., 340.
   James, 53.

Smith, Jesse, 122.
   John F., 50.
   Jonathan, 28.
   Joseph, 56.
   Josiah, 28.
   Judith, 27, 49.
   Julia P., 276.
   Kate, 136.
   Lorenzo D., 137.
   Lovell R., 169.
   Lydia L., 50.
   Lyman, 93.
   M. J., 221.
   Margaret, 26.
   Mary, 93, 109, 322.
   Mary J., 50, 114, 199.
   Marcia, 50.
   Marcie V., 184.
   Merritt, 172.
   Nathaniel, 11.
   Polly, 28, 50.
   Mrs. Rebecca E., 26.
   Rhoda, 22, 39.
   Richard, 37.
   Robert, 152.
   Samuel, 58, 73.
   Sarah, 44, 114, 119, 152.
   Sarah E., 239, 259.
   Serepta, 165.
   Stephen, 50.
   Steven, 28, 184.
   Susan, 58, 94, 296.
   Susannah, 28.
   Walter G., 136.
   Walter S., 184.
   W. D., 294.
   William B., 83.
   William S., 109.
   ——, 36.
Smitherson, John G., 337.
Snow, Joseph, 122.
Soldan, Louis A. M., 62, 217.
Somers, ——, 57.
Southard, Martha, 162, 228.
Southworth, Alice, 182.
   Benjamin F., 164.
   D. Frank, 164.
   Daniel F., 164.
   Fred. L., 164.
   H. O., 182.
   Ray E., 164.
Sowle, Luenda, 266.
Spardman, Robert, 319.
Sparks, John, 315.
Spaulding, Abigail, 34, 61, 63.
   Archie C., 228.
   Henry K., 197.
   Horace, 61.
   Rose, 126, 219.

Spaulding, ——, 278.
Spear, Marietta, 344.
    Martin, 344.
    Ransom, 344.
    Sarah A., 344.
Spencer, Almy W., 306.
    James D., 212.
    Rachel, 19, 266.
Spink, Betsey, 305, 306.
Sprague, Samuel, 53.
Springer, Marcellus, 78.
Squien, Lois, 300.
Squier, Joseph, 301.
Stacy, Gilbert, 128.
Stafford, Deliverance, 299.
    Phebe, 299.
Stage, Robert F., 65.
Stanford, Miles, 338.
Stanley A., 331.
    Abigail, 63.
    Elizabeth, 63.
    Gilman, 63.
    Hannah, 63.
    Hannah C., 162, 228.
    Hiram, 63.
    John, 63.
    Jonathan, 63.
    Lucinda, 63.
    Margaret, 63.
    Mary E., 63.
    Sarah L., 63.
    Shadrack, 331.
    Thomas, 321.
    Thomas H., 63.
    Waddy, 331.
Stanton, Charles B., 137.
    Minnie, 195.
    Robert, 112.
Stanwood, Frederick W., 25.
    Helen H., 25.
    Henry P., 25.
    Joseph, 25.
    Louisa A. P., 26.
    Susan L., 25.
Staples, Nancy, 28.
Starbuck, Tristram, 336.
Starckweather, Eleanor, 119, 153.
Stead, Owen, 111.
Stearnes, Dorithy, 44.
Stebbens, Samuel, 44.
Steel, James, 153.
Steele, Mary E., 339.
Steer, Rebecca A., 69, 169.
Steere, Ann G., 301.
Stephens, Mrs. Frances, 117, 206.
    Seth, 95.
Sterlin, William, 10.
Sterling, Charles A., 256.
    Fannie, 282.

Steubner, Louisa G., 162.
Stevens, Eben, 97.
    John, 88.
    Martha, 174, 230.
    Samuel H., 183.
    Sarah, 261.
    Sophia, 159, 230.
    William, 212.
    William B., 137.
    William H., 85.
Steward, David S., 317.
Stickney, Charles, 280.
    Eunice, 87, 196.
    Niles T., 92.
Stiles, Isaac, 299.
Stillwell, John, 282.
Stith, Fanny, 332.
Stockwell, Absolem, 129.
Stoddard, Thomas, 111.
Stodorph, Sophia A., 48.
Stowe, Anna, 333, 334.
    Daniel, 42.
    Dolly, 106.
    Henry, 136.
    Herbert, 192.
    K., 334.
    Mary, 162.
    Sarah, 162.
    Solomon, 334.
    ——, 23.
Story, James M., 60.
Stott, Ellen J., 279.
    Fanny, 163.
    Henry J., 279.
    John E., 279.
    Nancy J., 279.
    Nettie E. M. S., 279.
    Rose C., 279.
    Walter, 279.
Stoughtenburg, Charlotte, 36, 65.
Strange, John, 288.
Straton, Sarah, 38.
Stratton, George W., 83.
    M., 326.
Streeter, E. N., 266.
Strong, Alexander, 137.
    Margaret J., 218.
Stuart, Adeline, 194.
Study, Henry, 337.
Sturges, Stella V., 323.
Sturtevant, Polly, 121, 211.
    William, 67.
Sullivan, Anna, 135.
    Mary A., 238.
Summers, Sarah, 156.
Sunderland, John, 334.
Swain, Martha, 114.
    Rebecca, 293.
Swallow, Deidamia, 59, 96.

Swan, Charles, 34, 88.
   Elizabeth, 33, 59.
   Freeman P., 88.
   Henry, 88.
   Josiah, 88.
   Mary C., 154, 245.
   Mary J., 88.
   Robert, 3, 4.
   ——, 88.
Swasey, Alexis, 98.
   Alice J., 98.
   Asenath, 97.
   Benjamin, 97, 98.
   Cassandria, 97.
   Darius, 98.
   Edwin, 98.
   Eliza, 98.
   Emily, 98.
   George B., 97.
   Jane B., 97.
   John B., 97.
   Laura, 97.
   Lydia, 98.
   Mary P., 97, 98.
   Sarah, 56, 84.
Sweat, Bethia, 29.
   Isaac, 319.
   Mary, 69, 168.
Sweetland, Henry P., 103.
Sydnor, Edward G., 326.

Taber, Philip, 289.
Tafts, Edson H., 123.
   Israel J., 302.
Taggart, Gilbert, 86.
Talbot, Edgar F., 225.
Tallman, Cornelia A., 116, 223.
   John C., 223.
Tantrum, Thomas, 328.
   William H., 328.
Taplin, Betsey, 25, 93.
Tarbel, Mary, 98.
Tarleton, Amos, 35.
   William, 35.
Taylor, Abraham, 324.
   Angie, 80, 187.
   Anna, 16, 24.
   Annie, 276.
   Ella J., 240.
   Elvira, 124, 157.
   Fitch B., 293.
   Hannah L., 206.
   James, 261.
   Jonathan, 113.
   Luther, 284.
   Moses, 113.
   Phebe, 85, 192. •
   Rachel, 17, 24.

Taylor, Sarienne, 293.
Terrill, Jesse, 325.
Tew, Richard, 287.
Thatcher, Moses, 37.
Thayer, Maria, 92, 102.
Thing, Alice, 18.
   Catharine, 18, 26.
   Dorothy, 155, 248.
   Jonathan, 248.
   Polly, 46, 125.
   Samuel, 26.
   Zebidee, 29.
Thomas, Archibel, 87.
   Elizabeth, 64, 162.
   Henry, 193.
   ——, 37.
Thompson, Ann, 284.
   Anna L., 79, 156.
   Daniel, 59.
   Ichabod, 89.
   Nancy, 27, 49.
   Peltiah, 52.
   Susan, 95, 228.
   Susan F., 52.
Thomson, Henry C., 339.
Thorndike, Edward R., 213.
Thorne, Samuel G., 49.
Thornton, Solomon, 295.
Thouron, Priscilla, 219, 221.
Throupe, D. H., 334.
   Elizabeth, 334.
Thurber, Almy F., 305, 307.
   John, 55.
Thurill, ——, 290.
Thurston, John, 53.
   Martha A., 194.
   Moses, 53.
Tibbetts, Waterman, 299.
Tibs, Vernon, 266.
Tilden, Rachel, 20, 36.
Tillson, Philena, 302, 304.
Tilton, C. E., 242.
   Hiram, 192.
   Susan, 119, 151.
Titcomb, Lewis H., 133.
Toby, William, 319.
Tolland, George, 17.
Tompkins, Elizabeth, 289.
   Nathaniel, 289.
   Samuel, 289.
Toms, Samuel, 312.
Torrance, Alexander F., 292.
   Hope, 292.
   Mabel, 292.
   Robert B., 292.
   William L., 292.
Torry, Emily, 98.
   Paul, 111.
Towle, Daniel, 53.

Towle, Henrietta, 139.
    James A., 116.
    Jonathan, 149.
    Susan L., 105, 149.
Town, Katharine, 343, 344.
Towne, Caroline M., 159, 227.
    Mehitable, 97, 123.
Townes, George, 216.
Townsend, Augustus, 194.
Tracy, Hiram, 59.
Trask, Eliphalet, 208.
    James, 194.
    Louisa, 85, 192.
    Lyman, 123.
    Phineas, 16.
Treadwell, William, 73.
Tripp, Sarah, 280.
Trowbridge, Mary, 58, 94.
Truax, James N., 192.
Trumball, Betsey J., 61, 139.
Trumlan, T. A., 302.
Tryon, Elizabeth E., 118.
    George, 118.
Tubbs, Benjamin R., 133.
Tucker, Edward P., 63.
    George, 63.
    Horace D., 63.
    Lena S., 63.
    John, 25.
    Nathaniel M., 63.
    Susan, 28.
Tudor, Frederick, 105.
Tuggle, Ally, 334.
Tulard, John, 266.
Turner, Esther H., 37, 67.
    Reuben, 67.
Turpening, Valentine, 89.
Tuttle, Albourn, 343.
    Octavia F., 98, 147.
Tyler, Abraham, 2.
    Larissa C., 145.
    Phineas P., 145.
    ——, 35.

Umphstead, Patty, 50, 140. See p. 345.
Upham, Ada I., 323, 325.
    Anna, 306.
    Nancy, 129.
    Nathaniel, 318.
    N. G., 318.

Vande Vanter, Sarah, 337.
    Rachel, 337.
Van Horne, Delia, 124, 201.
    Reuel, 201.
Van Norden, Sarah A, 77, 178.
Vansicker, Rhoda M., 219.

Van Sickle, Capt., 328.
Vanvilyer, Lillian A., 298.
Varney, Ebenezer, 52.
    Jesse, 107.
Varnum, Mary, 153.
Vaughn, Benjamin, 327.
    Carrie A., 307, 309.
    Fayette, 262.
    James, 327.
    John, 336.
    Joseph, 302.
    Laura, 163.
Veech, Catharine A., 317.
Vernon, Sir Edward, 315.
    James, 315.
    Randall, 315.
    Robert, 315.
    Sarah, 315.
    Thomas, 315.
    William De, 315.
Vibbert, Alfred, 252.
Vickery, Samuel L., 81.
Victory, Prudence, 279, 283.
Vilas, Octavia H., 262, 263.
Vinal, Caroline D., 106, 133.
Vining, Elizabeth, 277.
Virgin, Charlotte, 123.
Vittum, Warren, 81.
Voris, A. C., 165.
Vose, Roger, 118.
Vunek, Parthenia, 281, 282.

Wadleigh, Mark, 73.
Wain, J. C., 194.
Wainwright, Simeon, 14.
Walt, Cora, 192.
    Frank A., 192.
    Fred. H., 192.
    Grace M., 192.
    Mary E., 192.
    Mattie F., 192.
    William, 192.
    William W., 192.
Walbridge, Mary, 16, 21.
Waldo, Loren P., 202.
    Lucretia, 112.
Waldren, George, 55.
Wales, Mary, 109, 130.
    Mrs. Mary, 124.
    Lydia, 22, 39.
    S. R. B., 130.
Walford, Alexander, 307.
Walker, Amasa, 273.
    Caroline, 66.
    Fannie, 77, 181.
    Gustavus, 238.
    Lillian, 139.
    Lucy, 121, 273.

Walker, Rockwell P., 164, 165.
   Seth, 166.
   W. A., 181.
   Warren. 194.
Wallace, Catharine S., 151.
   Mary M., 119, 150.
   William, 150, 151.
Walling, Louisa, 75, 174.
Wallis, Nathaniel, 16.
Ward, Alexander L., 132.
   Eshere, 133.
   John L., 132.
   Mary, 34, 62.
   Miles, 133.
   Samuel O., 205.
Wardell, Eliza D., 145.
   Simeon, 145.
Warner, Ebenezer R., 219.
   Elizabeth, 305.
   Hannah, 128, 219.
   Jerome, 170.
   John, 306.
Warren, Eliza J., 270.
Washburn, Adeline M., 268.
   Cyrus A., 268.
   Eliza A., 268.
   Emma A., 268.
   George W., 268.
   Horace B., 268.
   Lydia, 123.
   M. Estella, 268.
Washington, George, 315.
   Lawrence, 315.
Waterman, Elizabeth, 149.
   William N., 173.
Waters, Mary, 16.
Watkins, Andrew, 114.
   William, 290.
Watson, Alice F., 229, 259.
   Annie R., 133, 241.
   Benjamin, 120.
   Caroline P., 121.
   Clarence B., 121.
   Daniel, 154, 155.
   David, 56.
   Effie C., 121.
   Frances E. A., 121.
   Lydia, 154.
   Mary A., 93, 106.
   Phebe A., 306, 307.
   Robert S., 241.
Way, Charlotte, 336.
   Seth, 336.
Wayne, Margaret E., 301.
Weaver, Mrs. Ella M., 128, 202.
   Madison, 201.
   Thomas R., 202.
Webb, Edward, 78.
   Lizza M., 105.

Webb, Sophia M., 161.
Webber, George N., 84.
   Nathan, 278.
Webster, Abel, 124.
   Abigail, 18, 29.
   Arthur G., 307.
   Edward F., 157.
   Hannah, 44.
   Henry E., 307.
   Mary A., 254.
   Miriam, 49, 122.
   Stephen, 19.
   Verman, 75.
   Dr. W. A., 76.
   William, 75.
   ———, 198.
Weed, Abigail, 53, 75.
   Sally, 53.
   Sally F., 76.
   William, 218.
Weeks, Augustus, 114, 115.
   Calvin, 98.
   James L., 205.
   Joel, 124.
   Mary L., 205.
   Samuel, 88.
Weir, Dr., 45.
Welles, Charlotte, 133.
   Henry H., 133.
   Theodore L., 133.
Wellman, Hiram, 123.
   Lydia, 122, 136.
Wells, Joshua, 56.
Welsh, Charlotte, 160.
Wentworth, Alice, 133.
   Charles E., 133.
   Elizabeth, 133.
   Mark, 133.
   Mark H., 133.
   Strafford, 133.
West, Charles, 125.
   Phila, 125, 343.
Wescot, Jeremiah, 293.
Westcote, Susan A., 306, 307.
Westfal, Augustus, 69.
Weymouth, Frank, 193.
Whally, Weltha A., 159, 228.
Wharton, Thomas R., 124.
Wheeler, Nancy B., 271.
Wheelock, Dennis, 301.
Whetley, Catharine, 317.
Whimple, Alda, 65, 163.
Whitcomb, J. M., 95.
White, Charlotte, 146.
   Emeline, 76, 176.
   Enoch, 192.
   George T., 182.
   Samuel S., 307.
   Sarah, 78.

White, Sarah A., 182.
    Stephen A., 73.
    Timothy, 56.
    William, 2, 6.
Whitefield, Nathaniel, 87.
Whitman, H. Alice, 52.
Whitney, Augustus G., 173.
    A. D., 170.
    Dolly, 36.
    Henry L., 193.
    John, 95.
    Loretty, 274.
    Luella, 73, 173.
    Samuel, 169.
    Susan, 111, 169.
Whittier, Charlotte, 122.
    Elisha, 191.
    Etta, 195, 254.
    Hannah, 122, 136.
    John, 7.
    Lucy, 194.
    Samuel, 79.
    Thomas, 3, 6.
Whittiker, Emeline, 153, 244.
Whitten, Samuel, 284.
Wiggins, Carrie, 136, 249.
Wight, John D., 332.
    Jonathan, 338.
Wightman, Ann, 299.
    Elisha, 299.
    John, 299.
Wilber, Augusta, 281, 282.
Wilbur, Betsey M., 211, 254.
    Eliza, 278.
    John, 278.
    Lurenda, 278.
    Mary, 32, 58.
    Roby, 60, 137.
    Samantha, 278.
    Silas, 278.
Wilcox, David S., 69.
    Henry W., 117.
    Samuel, 290.
Wilkins, Frances, 237, 259.
Willey, Charity, 60, 137.
    Darius, 113.
    Dorithy, 64.
    Lucinda E., 64.
    William, 35.
Williams, Abigail, 295.
    Betsey, 136.
    Elizabeth, 44, 115.
    Ermima, 65, 165.
    Hannah E., 71.
    Harriet E., 40.
    Jacob, 33.
    J. K., 226.
    John, 2, 3, 6.
    Joseph, 295.

Williams, Nabby, 124, 156.
    Olive, 33, 60.
    Paul, 165.
    Roger, 295.
    Ruel, 180.
    Thomas, 295.
    ——. 71, 88, 278.
Williamson, Larned M., 316.
    Martha, 332.
Willis, Caroline, 131, 260.
    Charles E., 263.
    Eben C., 68, 167.
    Peter J., 260.
    Sally, 58, 94.
    Willard H., 228.
Wills, Anna, 313.
    Charles E., 45.
    George E., 328.
    Isabella E., 328.
Wilmarth, Mary, 297.
Wilson, Ella, 240.
    Lucy, 220, 259.
    Mary, 295.
Wilts, Ann, 278.
    David, 278.
    Elijah, 278.
    Elizabeth, 278.
    Harriet, 278.
    John, 278.
    Jude, 278.
    Julia, 278.
    Nancy, 278.
    Otis, 278.
    Priscilla, 278.
    Sally, 278.
    Stephen, 278.
    ——, 278.
Winch, George W., 71.
Winchel, Mary, 43, 126.
    Oliver, 126.
Winkley, Frank, 342.
Winslow, Lizzie, 256.
    Mary J., 153, 244.
    ——, 27.
Winston, Kate A., 228, 259.
Winthrop, Frost, 194.
    Watson, 194.
Wishart, David, 212.
Witham, Parsons, 78.
Wodel, William, 288.
Wood, Ann, 314.
    Mrs. Clarissa H., 39.
    Elizabeth, 231, 321, 322.
    Esther, 24, 43.
    George, 345.
    Hannah, 322.
    Jay G., 273.
    John C., 207.
    John D., 337.

Wood, Jonathan, 312.
    Lydia P., 282, 283.
    R. A., 146.
    Ralph T., 273.
    William, 314, 322.
    Miss, 280.
Woodcock, Nancy, 53, 76.
Woodman, Bettie, 32, 59.
    Greenleaf, 90.
    Lois, 46, 114.
    Mary, 86, 194.
    Sarah, 17.
Woodward, Ann, 16, 20.
    George W., 167.
Woodworth, Arthur W., 111.
    Elisha, 81.
    Hepilonea, 111.
Woolsey, Alanson, 294.
Worsley, Elizabeth, 303, 304.
Worthley, Sophronia, 53, 78, 183.
Wright, David, 34.
    Elizabeth C., 211, 254.
    Lucius W., 65.
    Martha, 40, 71.
    Samuel, 254.
    Wealthy, 34.
Wyer, Eliza S., 291, 293.
    James I., 291.
    James J., 291.
    Mary L., 291.
    Sarah, 291.
Wyers, Eunice, 299.

Wyers, Grant, 299.
    Hattie, 299.
    John C., 299.
    Oliver, 299.
Wyllys, Newell, 41.
Wyman, Esther E., 67.
    George P., 67.
    Hannibal G., 67.
    Hiram, 67.
    Julia F., 67.
    Mary S., 67.
    Pliney L., 67.
    Rodney H., 192.

Yesington, Hume, 258.
Young, Dolly, 55, 81.
    Hannah, 55, 81.
    Hiram, 172.
    John, 80.
    Joshua, 33.
    Joy, 279.
    Lucinda, 140, 214.
    Nancy, 54, 80.
    Oscar D., 210.
    Susan, 55, 81.

Zabriskie, Anna M., 237, 258.

Balch, Daniel, 92.

ADDITIONS.

Ladd, Ambrose E., x, xi.
   Amos, xi.
   Anna H., xi.
   Artless, xii.
   Augusta, xi.
   Byron, xi.
   Caroline, ix.
   Celia A., xii.
   Charles, x, xi.
   Charlotte, ix.
   Cordelia, x.
   David, ix.
   Denison, ix, x, xi.
   Edith, xi.
   Edward, x, xi.
   Effie, x, xi.
   Ella, xi.
   Ellen, x.
   Elizabeth W., xii.
   Estella, xi.
   Eunice, x.
   Frances J., xii.
   Frederick, x.
   George, ix, x.
   Harry, ix, x, xi.
   Hattie, xi.
   Herbert, x.
   Horace, x, xi.
   Ina, x.
   Job, xi.
   Job D., xii.
   John, ix, x, xi.
   John W., x, xi, xii.
   Joseph, x.
   Julia, x.
   Lucy, ix.
   Lucy J., x.
   Lydia B., xii.
   Mary, x, xi.
   Mary A., xii.
   Randolph, x.
   Sarah, x.
   Sarah P., xi.
   Shubael, ix, x.
   Sophronia, ix.
   Sumner, x.
   Warren, xi.
   William, ix, x, xi.

Bard, Mary A., x, xi.
Bailey, Polly, ix, x.
Bleans, Ann, x.
Brown, Lawrence P., xii.
   Lydia S., xi.
Browne, David, ix.
   Henry, ix.
Browne, James, ix.
   Jane, ix.
   John, ix.
   Mary, ix.
Burleigh, Julia, ix.

Campbell, Eliza J., xii.
   Mary S., xii.
Clute, Catharine, x, xi.
Cook, Harriet, x, xi.

Edgerton, Sophia, ix.
Eggleston, Hiram, x.

Giles, Mrs. Eunice, xi.

Hisington, Roxanna, ix, x.

Johnson, Asa, ix.
   Lucy, ix.
   Sophronia, ix.

Lewis, Dolly, x.

Martin, Mary E., xi.
Melvin, Ina, xi.
Moore, Clarinda, x, xi.

Olmstead, Walter, ix.

Provost, Clarinda, xi.

Risley, Jane, ix.

Sperry, Maria, x.
Stevens, Frances, ix, x.

Thompson, Milton S., xii.
Tipple, Alice, ix.
   Elida, ix.
   George, ix.
   Josephine, ix.
   Martin, ix.

Wales, Lucy, ix.
Walker, Joel, xii.
   Mathew B., xii.
Whitehead, Frank H., xii.
Wood, Charles, x.
   Clara, x.
   John D., x.
   Mary, x.
   Nathaniel K., x.